"In addition to essays on Mozart, Schumann,

and Verdi, I have written a few short journal articles

which I have never gathered together."

Edvard Grieg

Edvard Grieg ca. 1900

Edvard Grieg

Diaries, Articles, Speeches

Edvard Grieg

Diaries, Articles, Speeches

EDITED AND
TRANSLATED BY
Finn Benestad &
William H. Halverson

PEER GYNT PRESS / COLUMBUS

Publication of this book was made possible by generous grants
from the following institutions and foundations:
Anders Jahre's Humanitarian Foundation/The Norwegian Academy of Science and Letters, Oslo
Bergen Public Library
Centre for Advanced Study, Oslo
Edvard Grieg Committee/The Norwegian Cultural Council, Oslo
Grieg Forsk/Troldhaugen/Norsk Hydro ASA
Marketing Unit for Norwegian International Non-Fiction (MUNIN)
Library of Congress Catalog Card Number:
00–135386

ISBN 0–9645238–3–3

Designed and typeset by Diane Gleba Hall.
Printed in the United States of America.
The paper in this book meets the guidelines for permanence and durability of the Committee
on Production Guidelines for Book Longevity of the Council on Library Resources.

9   8   7   6   5   4   3   2   1

Preface

The publication of this book marks the culmination of a process that began many years ago, namely the collection and translation into international languages of the most important writings of Edvard Grieg. The gathering of these materials was begun in the early 1960's by the Edvard Grieg Committee, a small group of scholars in Norway and Denmark who undertook the task of preparing a scholarly edition of Grieg's compositions—a task that was completed in 1995 with the publication of Volume 20 of *Edvard Grieg: Complete Works* vols. 1–20 (C. F. Peters, Frankfurt/Leipzig/London/New York, 1977–95). A collection of over 500 of Grieg's letters in English translation was published in 1999 under the title *Edvard Grieg: Letters to Colleagues and Friends*, ed. Finn Benestad (Peer Gynt Press, Columbus, Ohio, 2000). That volume supplements two collections of Grieg letters in German: Finn Benestad & Hella Brock (eds.), *Edvard Grieg: Briefwechsel mit dem Musikverlag C. F. Peters 1863–1907* (Frankfurt am Main, 1997), and Finn Benestad & Hanna de Vries Stavland (eds.), *Edvard Grieg und Julius Röntgen: Briefwechsel 1883–1907* (Amsterdam, 1997).

Edvard Grieg: Diaries, Articles, Speeches contains in English translation the complete text of Grieg's diaries as well as all of the articles, speeches and other miscellaneous writings that the editors have been able to locate. The diaries were published by Bergen Public Library in the original Norwegian (*Edvard Grieg: Dagbøker*, ed. Finn Benestad) in 1993 and are here presented for the first time in English translation with the kind permission of Bergen Public Library. The remaining materials have been gathered from various sources, principally the newspapers and journals in which they first appeared. The sources are identified in the editors' introductions to the respective items. Most of these materials have either not been previously published in English or were published in venues no longer accessible to most readers. Important articles on Mozart and Schumann, for example, appeared in English translation in the American journal *The*

Century Monthly Illustrated Magazine in 1894 and 1897, respectively, but back issues of this defunct periodical are available only in major research libraries. These and the handful of other writings previously published in English have been freshly translated for the present volume.

The editors have attempted to organize this diverse material in such a way as to facilitate the location of any item the reader may be seeking. Part I, "Autobiographical Writings", gathers together all of Grieg's extant writings (other than his letters) about his personal and professional life. The diaries of 1865–66 and 1905–07 constitute the natural book-ends of Part I, the organization of which is roughly chronological. This is followed in Part II by "Articles on Other Composers". Here will be found Grieg's assessments of such luminaries as Dvořák, Mozart, Schumann, Verdi and Wagner as well as of many of his less famous contemporaries. This Part is organized alphabetically by composer; multiple articles about the same composer are ordered chronologically by year of writing. Part III, "Articles on Various Topics", comprises Grieg's writings on a wide array of topics that engaged his interest and his pen at one time or another. It is ordered chronologically except for "Grieg's Reflections on Some of His Own Piano Pieces", with which this Part concludes. Part IV, "Speeches and Impromptu Talks", consists of newspaper transcriptions of Grieg's public comments about various individuals and topics.

Like the letters, the materials assembled in this book provide convincing evidence of their author's considerable skill as a writer. Grieg is undoubtedly at his best in his long articles on Mozart, Schumann, and Wagner and in his delightful and highly informative autobiographical essay, "My First Success", but these are just the highest pinnacles in a mountain range containing many other peaks and an abundance of foothills. Even in his last years, when declining health sapped his strength and depressed his spirits and made his life one of "continuous suffering" (as he wrote in his diary on August 25, 1907), Grieg was capable of turning an occasional memorable phrase. On June 4, 1907, for example—just a few weeks before his own death—he wrote in his diary upon hearing of the demise of Agathe Backer Grøndahl (1847–1907), who remains to this day Norway's most significant female composer: "Agathe died at 4 PM this afternoon. Thus ended this beautiful life. Beautiful in its noble pessimism and in all its suffering. No artist soul has ever walked on purer paths. (. . .) If a mimosa could sing, it would resound with strains like those from Agathe Backer Grøndahl's most beautiful, most deeply felt music." A professional writer could be justly proud of having penned such lines.

This volume was prepared in close conjunction with *Edvard Grieg: Letters to Colleagues and Friends*, and the same editorial conventions have been employed. Titles of Grieg's compositions are given in English, with opus/EG numbers being added only when the precise identity of a composition might be in doubt. For the corresponding original titles, readers are referred to the List of Compositions in *Edvard Grieg: Letters to Colleagues and Friends*, pp. 693–704. Literary quotations are given in English in the main text and in the original language in a footnote. Spellings of place names have been modernized. Grieg's occasional misspellings of proper names have been corrected.

Editorial introductions explain the occasion for each item, the date and venue of its first publication (also of its delivery in the case of a speech), and the source from which the item was taken for use in the present volume. Differences between two or more equally authoritative originals (for example, an article published simultaneously in Norwegian and German) are elucidated in footnotes. Cross-references to passages in Grieg's letters that are especially relevant to a given article or speech are also given in footnotes.

Every effort has been made to identify the numerous individuals mentioned by Grieg in his writings and speeches. When known, dates and brief biographical information are provided in a footnote the first time an individual is mentioned in a given chapter. Since some individuals are mentioned several times, information appearing in a footnote in one chapter is sometimes repeated in another.

Readers desiring a condensed overview of the composer's life are referred to the Chronology of Grieg's Life and Works on pp. 399–422. The Chronology summarizes essential information about Grieg's many concert tours including the dates and locations of his public appearances as a performer or conductor as well as dates of his compositions and writings.

The bibliography on pp. 423–433 begins with a complete list of original sources of the materials presented in this book. It also contains a list of published editions of Grieg's writings and speeches and a comprehensive catalogue of secondary literature including biographies, symposia, and books and articles on various topics related to Grieg and his music. Also included is a delineation of the contents of each of the twenty volumes comprising *Edvard Grieg: Complete Works* as well as information about two other bibliographies that will be of special interest to those doing advanced research in this area.

The General Index catalogs both proper names and topics. Compositions mentioned in the book are entered under the names of the respective composers.

The editors have worked very closely together in the preparation of this volume and are jointly and equally responsible for the final result. In view of their differing backgrounds and expertise, however, Professor Benestad has had primary responsibility for the historical research and editorial introductions, Professor Halverson for the translation of the original materials and the literary form of the whole.

We wish to express our deep appreciation to the infinitely helpful staff at the Centre for Advanced Study of the Norwegian Academy of Science and Letters, Oslo, which provided office and logistical support to the editors during a two-month period in April–May 1998 when the initial planning for this book and its predecessor was carried out. A special word of thanks goes to Karen Falch Johannessen, curator of the Grieg Archives at the Bergen Public Library, and to Øyvind Norheim, senior librarian at the Music Collection of the National Library of Norway, Oslo Division. We also acknowledge with gratitude the assistance of Professor Dag Schjelderup-Ebbe, who read an early version of our manuscript and made many valuable suggestions for improvement.

Lastly, we wish to thank the following institutions and agencies for generous financial support without which this project could not have been completed: Anders Jahre's Humanitarian Foundation / The Norwegian Academy of Science and Letters, Oslo; Bergen Public Library; Centre for Advanced Study, Oslo; The Edvard Grieg Committee / The Norwegian Cultural Council, Oslo; Grieg Forsk / Troldhaugen / Norsk Hydro ASA; Marketing Unit for Norwegian International Non-Fiction (MUNIN).

FINN BENESTAD   WILLIAM H. HALVERSON
Oslo, Norway   Columbus, Ohio

Contents

Part III. Articles on Various Topics

Part IV. Speeches and Impromptu Talks

Chronology, Bibliography, Index

List of Illustrations

Pictures are listed in the order in which they appear in the book. Letters in parentheses indicate the sources of the respective items: (A): Aschehoug, Oslo; (APA): Aftenposten Picture Archives, Oslo; (BPL): Bergen Public Library; (G): Gyldendal, Oslo; (HDS): Hanna de Vries Stavland; (NLN): The National Library of Norway, Oslo Division; (OCM): Oslo City Museum; (OV): Otto Væring, Oslo; (RLC): The Royal Library, Copenhagen; (TR): Troldhaugen, Bergen; (PD): Public Domain; (UBL): University of Bergen Library.

Part I

Autobiographical Writings

Edvard Grieg (1840–1907) did not write an autobiography, but there is scattered evidence in his letters indicating that he occasionally considered doing so. On July 17, 1900, for example, in a letter to his American biographer Henry T. Finck, he declined to supply certain facts requested by Mr. Finck, but he added: "If I should live a long life, perhaps in an autobiography I would include the missing information." Shortly thereafter, German book dealer Albert Langen offered Grieg an honorarium of 10,000 German marks for an autobiographical manuscript of ca. 240 pages, but on August 28, 1902, the composer advised Mr. Langen: "Unfortunately, there will be so many demands on me *during the coming year* that it will be very difficult for me to begin working on the project *at this time* [italics added]." The clear implication was that Grieg thought he might find time to write his memoirs at some later date—but he never did.

He did, however, write ample material that could have been incorporated into such an autobiography. Many of his letters are inherently autobiographical in nature and provide a wealth of detail concerning his thoughts and feelings as well as the outward events of his life during the years 1862–1907. The most important of these have been published in English translation in Finn Benestad (ed.), *Edvard Grieg: Letters to Colleagues and Friends*, Columbus, Ohio 2000.

Grieg's remaining autobiographical writings are presented in the pages that follow. The ordering is chronological except for the grant applications, which were written at various times during the years 1862–78, and "My First Success", which dates from 1903 but deals in large part with the early years of Grieg's career.

Edvard Grieg in the late 1860's

The Diary of 1865–66

Grieg kept diaries during two periods of his life, one at the beginning (1865–66), the other at the end (1905–07) of his illustrious career. In between came all of the compositions that made him famous throughout the world, all of the concert appearances that packed the great music halls of Scandinavia, Great Britain, and continental Europe, all of the trials and triumphs that are related in his diaries and his letters, all of the articles and speeches that fill the pages of the present volume. It was a busy life, and in view of the many pressing duties that occupied him daily during the intervening years we can forgive him for not taking time to also keep a diary during those years. The ones that he *did* keep are for that reason all the more valuable.

It was during the period 1865–66 that Grieg's music suddenly began to sound like that which we now associate with his name. The early compositions in which this characteristically Griegian sound is evident are *Melodies of the Heart*, the *Humoresques* for piano, the *Piano Sonata*, the *Violin Sonata No. 1*, and the *Funeral March for Rikard Nordraak*—all composed in 1865—as well as several other songs and the first *Lyric Pieces* for piano. Here, and in many works to follow, Grieg wrote music that was distinctively his own. By coincidence, it was during this period of the first flowering of his genius as a composer that he began to keep a daily record of his thoughts and activities. Thus his early diary provides an account in Grieg's own words of some of the experiences, impressions and ideas that were beginning to find expression in his music at this critical stage in his development.

On the last day of July, 1865, Grieg set out on a ten-day trip to the northern part of Zealand (Sjælland), the large island on which the city of Copenhagen is situated. Traveling with him were several of his Danish friends, and it was on this trip that he made his first diary entries. By foot, by train and by carriage the young men traversed the pleasant Danish countryside, and as they traveled Grieg recorded detailed accounts of memorable experiences—accounts in which vivid descriptions of nature alternate with witty comments about events on the trip. Now and again the love-stricken Grieg also gives expression to his euphoric infatuation with his cousin Nina Hagerup (1845–1935), who in 1867 would become his wife. The diary also includes a quite detailed account of the young composer's first visit to Italy the following winter.

Grieg's diary of 1865–66 is preserved in Bergen Public Library. It was published in the original Norwegian in Finn Benestad (ed.), *Edvard Grieg: Dagbøker*, Bergen 1993, pp. 17–96.

1865

July 31

From Copenhagen on the steamship "Horatio" to Rungsted, where Feddersen came on board. By steamship to Humlebæk. Then by foot to Kvistgaard railroad station; wrote to Nina. From Kvistgaard to Frederiksborg by train. Met Horneman in the compartment. Lodging at Rasmussen's directly across from Frederiksborg Castle. (Tea, sandwiches, soft-boiled egg, cold chicken.)

August 1

Morning walk in the area of Frederiksborg Castle. Indelukket,[1] the bathhouse,

---

[1] "Indelukket" was a café and service center at Lake Esrum where one could buy food and drink and also rent boats and other equipment.

the fisherman's cottage, The Hunters' Hill [Jægersbakken], with a perfectly glorious view of the whole castle, the surroundings, and the town of Frederiksborg. Here it makes no difference to the viewer whether the castle is old or new: Here is just the pure, genuinely Nordic greatness. Surrounded on all sides by the lake, the castle looks as if it had risen from the waves by magic. The height of the building, the slenderness of the towers and the soaring spires contribute to this impression.

Left at 10:30 AM by mail carriage for Helsinge. Lovely trip through the Grib forest [Gribskov], which contains the most magnificent spruce and larch trees in Denmark. Rain and wind. Shaken up upon our arrival at Helsinge.

Had a miserable noon meal at 1:30 PM. Then walked ten kilometers through long, boring stretches of land to Tisvilde—which should rather be called Tidsspilde,[2] in my opinion—for all that we got out of the trip was a couple of thunder-clouds, on account of which we time and again had to seek shelter. After soon having had our fill of those tedious, monotonous areas, I for my part was bored to the point of despair; for certainly nothing has a greater power to deaden the mind than a vast, desolate plain with here and there a few sand dunes over which the wind howls.

But it must have been written in the book of fate that from this moment on our good Norn[3] would have mercy on us, for from now until evening each sight was more interesting than the preceding one. In Tisvilde we found ourselves almost by accident in front of the home of forest supervisor Hansen, where we decided to stop in to at least quench our burning thirst, which in the sultry air had become quite acute.

We went into the kitchen and asked a maid servant—who in response to all our questions showed herself to be a blockhead—if it would not be possible to get a glass of milk. After having waited for awhile in the courtyard we were given to understand that we were to enter by another door. Naturally we obeyed the order immediately, whereupon we found ourselves in a dark, gloomy hallway from which three doors led in various directions. One of these doors opened, and the owner—the forest supervisor, an old, gray-haired, almost stone deaf man—stood before us. At first he did not seem to be at all interested in us, but as soon as he heard that we were musicians his face suddenly brightened markedly—the very opposite of what usually happens in these areas, where artists are regarded more or less as tramps, defective persons.

As if the news of our profession had transformed him into another person, he led us into a side room in the corner of which stood a piano—with the help of which he hoped to get an opportunity "to profit from our talent". I seated

---

[2] A play on words: "Tidsspilde" means "waste of time".
[3] The Norns, in Old Norse mythology, are the goddesses of fate who spin or weave the fates of men.

*Robert and Clara
Schumann*

myself at the piano, an old Marchals, struck a few chords, and—alas!—it was a
veritable monstrosity of an instrument, a toneless wreck, five octaves, a fourth
or a fifth below standard pitch and—completely untuned.

But what to do? I played a Danish and then a Swedish folk song. The latter
pleased him greatly. He expressed his warm interest in the lovely Madame
Musica and asked who was my favorite composer.

I thought it would have been madness to say the name, so I tried to come up
with a popular name that I thought would please him—for after all, how could
an old forester here in this out-of-the-way hole know anything about my divine
favorite? But Feddersen helped me out of my difficulty by shouting: "Robert
Schumann".

"Aha! Schumann! The one who married Clara Wieck?"

"Right!"

"Oh, I know all about her. As a matter of fact, I am related to her."

"Really?"

And now the conversation really began to flow. "But what do you think about Mendelssohn Bartholdy? He is my favorite!"

So then I had to play the B-minor *Caprice*. It sounded like it does when you pound on old cans, but the forest supervisor was enthused and engaged us in a discussion about all the talented performers of the day. When I sat down at the piano he had shouted excitedly to the maid servant, "Tea and sandwiches, as quickly as possible!" And after the concert was over he invited us to the table with many expressions of thanks, adding that artists were always welcome guests in his home. Tea and sandwiches—and a cognac as well. Everything went down quickly, and we were again invited to stay overnight, but the harnessed horses and carriage waited at the door and we took our leave, sincerely moved by the excellent old man's cordiality and hospitality.

From here we continued through a broad, barren region, filled with windblown sand, to Frederiksværk. This drive was one of the most interesting I have experienced, and I would never have dreamt of encountering natural scenery such as this in Zealand, the rest of which is so lovely. We came upon a number of interesting sights along this road, especially Frederikshøj, which had been opened and dedicated by Frederik VII[4] in 1849. We reached Frederikshøj via a road through the forest. The road was in such miserable condition that we were often very close to tipping over, but the danger only heightened the piquancy of the already rather odd situation.

The view from Frederikshøj is one of the most splendid I have ever seen. Endless stretches of heath on high hills and in deep valleys—much like what one sees in the high mountains in Norway—surrounded by the surging Kattegat, and a sky pregnant with the most terrible storms, and made even more interesting by piercing flashes of lightning—all these elements played a role in evoking this picturesque scene. Wild nature and wild weather belong together; the combination creates a unity. Not so far from here we saw the ruins of Asserbo Castle, which dates from the twelfth century.

Finally, after a journey of two or three hours, we arrived at Frederiksværk, totally windblown from the terrible storm. How welcome a mediocre bed in an attic room was to us I hardly need to say. But the storm made such a racket that, despite our fatigue, it was not possible to close our eyes.

August 2

Early the next morning we contacted a boy who was to show us around the romantic region, and we also viewed it from a magnificent height called The Norwegian Hill [den norske Bakke].

---

4 Frederik VII (1808–63), King of Denmark 1848–63.

Is it not as if, from such a high vantage point—from which one seems almost to observe the whole world—one feels closer to one's God? In truth, in such a moment all that is earthly becomes distant to me, and I feel my soul lifted up toward eternal reconciliation and love.

Oh, my Nina! If you knew with what tenderness my thoughts here dwell on you, with what endless longing I here think of you! Before I fathomed you and all your love, it was as if I did not dare aspire toward the heights, as if all my longing were confined within a boundary beyond which I only peered into an impenetrable fog. It is because of you, my beloved, that with confidence and clarity I dare cast a glance toward the infinite. It is as if you, my good angel, hovered beside me as my thoughts wander through the vastness of space—as if through your intercession I received the power to break the magnetic chain that binds me to the dust! May God shed His peace upon you if you are suffering during these days—you who are my treasure, the light of my life!

During the forenoon we had reserved seats in the mail carriage to Frederiksborg, but quite by chance we learned from our innkeeper—a very obliging man, Mr. Heilman—that an empty first-class coach[5] would be returning in a few hours to Frederiksborg, from whence it had brought some travelers here. We wasted no time canceling the earlier reservation, and after a hearty early dinner we took our seats in the convertible coach—a splendid vehicle that, during the most dreadful downpour, brought us to Frederiksborg traveling the opposite way from that by which we had come.

We had to drive through some uninteresting areas until we reached Lake Arre [Arresøen]—Zealand's biggest fresh-water lake—on our left. This, together with the towers of Frederiksborg Castle gleaming in the distance, contributed greatly to evoking a rather extraordinary landscape.

Upon arriving in Frederiksborg I hurried to the post office to fetch an ominous letter from Nina, but thank God there was no letter for me. It is the first time that I would have given anything in the world not to get a letter from Nina—but how circumstances can change![6]

Since it still looked somewhat rainy, we decided to visit the castle chapel first. Therefore we headed for the castle, where just a few foreigners were waiting for the castle manager, who has the exclusive right to serve as a guide. Entering

---

[5] Wienervogn, literally "Vienna carriage", an elegant coach with a folding top.

[6] What Grieg is alluding to here is not completely clear, but it presumably has to do with the relationship between the Grieg and Hagerup families. In December 1864 Grieg had become engaged to his cousin Nina Hagerup, who lived with her parents in the Copenhagen area. The engagement was kept secret for several months, and neither Edvard's nor Nina's parents were happy when they learned of it. Nina's mother reportedly expressed her opinion of her future son-in-law as follows: "He is nothing and he has nothing and he writes music that nobody wants to hear." Edvard's father called it "this stupid engagement", and it was not until the end of May 1865 that Edvard's brother John could report that "under the existing circumstances" the elder Griegs had given their approval to a public announcement of the engagement.

through the matchless door, artfully carved out of solid oak, one comes immediately into the chapel and is struck dumb with astonishment, so dazzling are all
the gold and silver ornaments with which the chapel seems to be overloaded. It
is not large, nor is it awe-inspiring or conducive to a devotional mood—but for
that reason it is all the more magnificent. The altar and the pulpit are true works
of art and make an unforgettable impression. The materials are: silver, gold,

*Rikard Nordraak, Grieg, Emil Horneman. A friendly triumvirate during Grieg's decisive
Copenhagen period in the 1860's.*

mother-of-pearl, ebony—elements that certainly are capable of making up an impressive whole. (The price to see the church was 24 skillings.)

After fully digesting the imposing impression of the church, we returned on foot to Fredensborg. The road leads through a forest and winds among the handsomest groups of trees. Through the trees on the left one catches glimpses of Lake Esrum [Esrum Sø]. It was a pleasant trip. The evening was clear and mild, nature was fresh after the recent rain, and the moon cast its romantic sheen over the whole.

Arriving at Fredensborg at 9:30 PM, I immediately hurried up to Horneman's in the hope of getting a bed for the night. He was not home, but of course he had left his house unlocked for thieves and criminals. Without, like David, cutting off a swatch of Saul's robe,[7] I stole quietly away and sought lodging at the inn. There, tired and exhausted, I fell asleep.

August 3

The morning brought me to Horneman, who was at the breakfast table with the Schleisner brothers.[8] They soon finished breakfast and we devoted the forenoon to a splendid tour of the park surrounding Fredensborg Castle. The weather was absolutely marvelous, everybody was in good spirits, so the total impression was altogether pleasant.

After a noonday meal at Mad. Hansen's (Bagges Minde[9]) we all agreed to take a trip to Fruebjerg. Thus, together with Feddersen, Horneman and the Schleisner brothers, I headed for the wharfside shed, from where we sailed across Lake Esrum to Holtet. Then we started out on foot through Grib Forest. It was a long, warm, strenuous, but beautiful walk as the Danish forest showed us its handsomest side.

After much running around on the endless forest paths we suddenly found ourselves by Lake Grib [Gribsø], a gorgeous little lake with a mirror-like surface surrounded by dense forest on all sides. Here we did some fishing—that is to say, we threw lines in the water, for that is as far as it went. We thereupon filled our hungry stomachs with raspberries, which grew here in profusion.

After having heard the loveliest echo, which some witty red skirts on the other side of the lake tried to enhance by mimicking our shouts, we hiked over hill, over dale—accompanied by the sweet fragrance of spruce trees—to Fruebjerg. Here one enjoys the most complete view of the wide, beautiful area all the way from Frederiksborg, whose castle towers rise majestically above the tops of the beech trees on the left, to Tisvilde and Frederiksværk and Lake Arre.

---

[7] I Samuel 24.

[8] Danish physician Peter Antoin Schleisner (1818–1900) and his brother Christian Andreas Schleisner (1810–82), a painter.

[9] A well-known inn at that time.

Now it was a matter of finding the shortest, least laborious way to get back, and after much arguing back and forth somebody finally got the unfortunate idea of designating Horneman as the leader—an assignment that he performed with great gusto, albeit anything but satisfactorily; for after having wandered around endlessly in a forest jungle, we finally came out on a country road—which made me extremely happy, for then I did not have to lift up my legs like a rooster each time I took a step. But what did Horneman suggest—no, what did he demand? That we should immediately leave the passable road and head out instead on one that led through a barley field to the devil knows where. Of course it couldn't do any good to resist—particularly because we were all so tired that none of us was inclined to do so. The only thing to do, therefore, was to play the obedient son, which I did until our feet literally got stuck in the muck. But then the anger broke loose, my traveling companions sided with me, and soon there was a sort of fight. In the meantime we took our bearings and discovered that we were near "Indelukket" in Frederiksborg. We rushed to the railway station, arriving just before the train was to leave. After having filled our hands with sandwiches and our bellies with pints of beer, we chugged off for Fredensborg, where tepid potatoes with butter awaited us at Horneman's. We parted at 10 PM, rather exhausted but united in the awareness of having spent an exceedingly pleasant day.

August 4

The forenoon was used for a fishing expedition to Lake Esrum. It was of the same caliber as the recently discussed attempt in Lake Grib, which is to say that the lines were thrown out and that was the end of it. In order nonetheless to be able to boast of having pulled a fish out of the water, I took possession of a minnow (a young Mr. Bournonville[10]) that some gentlemen had left behind in the boat, calmly attached it to my hook and let it sink to the bottom. Then, making an appearance of great effort and with as much commotion as possible, I drew it out of the water—to the great delight of my friends, who had had no idea that it was all a joke.

Noon meal at Hansen's. Afternoon; wrote to Nina and to Colin Archer.[11]

Feddersen left Fredensborg in order to visit a friend for a couple of days. Horneman went to Copenhagen to do some teaching, so only I and the Schleisner brothers remained in Fredensborg. In the evening played three-hand whist with the Schleisner brothers.

August 5

Forenoon: whist with the Schleisner brothers. Noon meal at Hansen's. Afternoon:

---

[10] An attempt at humor on Grieg's part. By "a young Mr. Bournonville" Grieg obviously means "a lively little fellow". The allusion is to French-Danish dancer and choreographer Antoine Auguste Bournonville (1805–79), director of the Royal Danish Ballet, who was in his prime at the time Grieg wrote this entry.

[11] Norwegian designer and boat-builder Colin Archer (1832–1921).

a trip with the Schleisner brothers to Frederiksborg, where, after having a look at the church, we walked about 2.5 kilometers to the "Entrenchment Hills" [Skandsebakker]. The view from there far surpasses the one from Fruebjerg. From here we walked back to Fredensborg.

August 6

Forenoon walk with the Schleisner brothers around the castle park. Inspected the marble garden—a successful copy of the old-French style, an especially striking similarity to the park in Versailles. A few of the marble statues are, from a formal perspective, true works of art, and the marble is some of the most beautiful I have ever seen. Noon meal at Hansen's. Afternoon: whist with the Schleisner brothers. During the evening Feddersen returned from his side trip.

August 7

Left at 9 AM with Horneman, Feddersen and the Schleisner brothers for Marianelund.[12] Walking tour through the Dunstrup and Krogenberg plantings.[13] From Marianelund a side trip to the Gurre Castle ruins. A marvelous outing. Never have ruins aroused in me such a wonderful mood. And why? Because they revived thoughts of Carl Bernhard's chronicles from the time of Christian II. I thought of Claus Daa, who, with his Gundel, sat confined in the corner tower out of fear of the king, who was approaching the castle to call him to task.[14]

And I thought of the splendid tour I took a couple of years ago with an angel of a young girl—and you, my beloved bride, are this angel! Did it ever occur to you at that time that you would come to love me, or did you love me already? I remember reading an inexpressible gentleness in your eyes, but I was altogether

---

[12] A well-known restaurant near Tikøb.

[13] The word Grieg uses here is "hegn", which denotes a hedge or grove planted as protection against wind and weather.

[14] Grieg is referring to Gurre Castle in North Zealand, which was built as a royal hunting lodge by Danish King Valdemar Atterdag (c. 1320–75). The castle was destroyed at the time of the Protestant Reformation. The Danish writer Carl Bernhard—a pseudonym for Andreas Nicolai de Saint-Aubin (1798–1865)—wrote a number of historical tales inspired by Scottish novelist and poet Sir Walter Scott (1771–1832). In one of his books, *Krøniker fra Kristian den andens Tid* (Chronicles from the Time of Christian II, 1865), much of the action is set in Gurre Castle, with the young nobleman Klaus Daa and his fiancee Gundel as two of the principal characters. Klaus Daa had been unjustly accused of attempting to murder King Christian II (1481–1559), and, fearing the king's wrath, he and Gundel had hidden in a tower room in Gurre Castle. While they were there, the king suddenly made an unannounced visit to the castle. Eventually the misunderstanding was cleared up, however, and the story ends happily.

　　The real Daa family has a long history in Denmark. At the time of Christian II a Claus Daa was Canon of the church in Roskilde, and a knight by the same name lived on the Ravnstrup estate in Tybjerg, South Zealand.

　　Memories of Gurre Castle were also revived during the Romantic period by other Danish poets whose works sometimes formed the basis for major compositions. In 1900, for example, Norwegian composer Johan Halvorsen (1864–1935) composed incidental music for the play *Gurre* by Holger Drachmann (1846–1935), and in the same year Arnold Schoenberg (1874–1951) wrote the song cycle *Gurrelieder* for voice and piano using poems by Jens Peter Jacobsen (1847–85) in a German translation by R. F. Arnold. In 1911 this work was expanded into *Gurrelieder,* a cantata for soloists, chorus and orchestra.

too fearful to claim it for myself. But now everything is different. Hope and fear have given way to the most blessed certainty.

I am writing this at Lake Gurre as a fresh gale casts an air of briskness over the entire landscape. Noon meal in Marianelund. Beef, red pudding with cream (4 marks & 5 skillings).

From here, at 2 PM we began a sightseeing trip by carriage—the most beautiful one I have ever taken, not only on this trip but in my entire life. It went through the lovely regions by Lake Esrum, past the Esrum Cloister to Søborg, where we got out of the carriage to inspect the ruins of the old Søborg Castle, which, despite being extremely dilapidated, nonetheless supplied us with complete information. It was especially interesting to observe, in the outline of the foundations, the old style of construction. There is a power and a nobility in the style that our castles and fortresses nowadays generally are lacking. Much of the old Lake Søborg has been drained, so lush grainfields now surround the ruins of the old fortress that once towered majestically above the waves.

On the way back to the coach from the ruins, Horneman—who already in Marianelund had taken the best seat—began hurrying so as to get the same one again. The rest of us noticed this, and the result was a veritable race in the course of which Dr. Schleisner fell and hurt his hands so badly on the stones that we had something quite different from driving on to think about. We had to stop at a little farm to get some water, cloth etc., but although the doctor himself declared the scratches and open cuts to be serious, he did not let himself show any concern but sat down in the carriage with the rest of us without losing a shred of his conviviality.

From Søborg we drove through a rather barren region which, however, provided a wide view toward Nakkehoved, where the horses were [unhitched and] placed in a stall. This indicated, to be sure, that it was going to be a longer stay than seemed reasonable to me, and I was about to inquire as to the reason for it when suddenly I found myself standing in mute astonishment. The whole expanse of the ocean lay before me—at first as gentle and still as a slumbering lion, but ominous clouds on the horizon warned of a change, and it was not long in coming. The waves pounded violently against the shore, and soon the ocean was completely engulfed in turbulence.

At first my interest was focused entirely on Kullen,[15] which towered dark and blue in the distance, but as the ocean sprang to life my thoughts took a different turn. Where does one sense God's greatness more than in the roaring of the sea? In a moment one becomes, as it were, an impotent nothing who in gratitude dares only to call upon the Father whose omnipotence created these wonders! And how

---

[15] Kullen (Kullaberg) is an elevated plateau in the northwestern corner of the Swedish province of Skåne that is visible from Denmark.

beautiful it is that he has endowed his creatures with powers by which they not only can understand and enjoy, but in art can even create works that are echoes of the feelings about God's greatness implanted in the human breast. How aptly Hans Christian Andersen has captured a mood like the one that enveloped nature in that moment when he wrote: "For roar on, seething ocean, your giant breakers raise; the tempest, you and I my God will praise!"[16]

I was filled with the greatness and truth of these words. But I could not neglect also searching in my art for a way to express the wild music in the roar of the sea. Alas, my search was in vain. I sensed the utter impossibility of expressing these mighty sounds in musical form. There was in this rushing and roaring something so boundless that it struck me as presumptuous to consider even for a moment the idea of trying to reproduce it.

But here, too, I found consolation: The artist's task is not to reproduce the physical event itself, but rather to create a reflection of the feelings awakened by that event; if this is done with brilliance, the impression is equally divine despite the absence of those overpowering effects that belong to nature alone.

It was on an escarpment several hundred feet high that I made these observations, and they had a profound impact on my mood for the rest of the day.

Nakkehoved has a lighthouse and handsome boardwalks with greenery that, considering the poor soil and the impact of the sea, is excellent.

After having immortalized our names by recording them in a passenger log, we again climbed into the carriage under the pleasant influence of the magnificent ocean. The last leg of the trip took us to Hellebæk via Hornbæk, and to tell the truth, I have never before witnessed such a beautiful drama in nature. An intense evening glow on the distant horizon gave promise, to be sure, of a lovely sunset, but not to any extraordinary sight. But little by little the surroundings became more and more barren, and the heather-covered moors—which in the beginning were indeed sparsely populated, but did nonetheless have a few buildings—in the end did not contain a single house. Only the old burial mounds, which appeared in increasing numbers as the landscape became more and more bleak, seemed to want to remind us that our forefathers had chosen these barren regions as a stage for their enterprises. The roads became sandier, the evening chillier, the sky continuously more reddish; then a slight turn, and the wide ocean, over which the setting sun cast the most marvelous glow, lay outstretched before us. The endless surface of the water, the distant "Kullen", the barren heaths bordered by dark pine and spruce forests—everything was engulfed in the most ethereal lilac color, and over this fairy world stretched a firmament filled with light as from the mightiest conflagration.

---

[16] "Thi brus kun vilde Hav, opløft din Kjæmpevove; med dig og Stormen jeg min Gud vil love!" Danish author Hans Christian Andersen (1805–75) is best known for his children's stories.

As if struck by a blow, we sat speechless and stared at all this magnificence. Our wise-cracks, of which there had been many as we passed "through Hornbeck",[17] ceased as a matter of course; after the first expressions of astonishment, there could be no thought of anything other than quiet, grateful admiration—no, not even if one were made of stone.

Little by little the sun disappeared: It was as if it went to sleep in the bosom of the sea. Night lowered its veil over nature around us and a marvelously soft, wistful mood came over me.

May it be granted me one day to linger in privacy with you, my beloved, in a time of communion with nature such as this! The awareness of God's great love must in such a moment rise to the highest level!

The trip from Marianelund to Hellebæk cost four Rigsdalers[18] for the coach. After an exquisite supper at Hellebæk Kro [guesthouse] we were accommodated in three separate houses. My companion turned out to be the lieutenant. Evening whist with the Schleisner brothers.

August 8

Terrible downpour. The decision was to go by foot to Kvistgaard, so we trudged off with map and compass through forests, through cultivated and uncultivated fields, through thickets and underbrush. But the rain increasingly got the better of us, and finally, when we no longer knew where we were, we had to stop in at the first building we could find. It was a brick factory which was protected by a she-dog that angrily attacked the weapons—walking sticks and umbrellas—that we had to employ to keep the beast away from us.

The brick factory itself was locked, so we had to seek shelter along the walls, which were protected by a long, overhanging roof. Fortunately there was a very serviceable folding table there, and with the boxes and small barrels that we scrounged up serving as seats we succeeded in passing the time with "Holmblad's Hymnal"[19]—until Horneman, who didn't enjoy playing whist and whom, therefore, we had sent out with umbrellas to reconnoiter the area, finally reported that he had spotted a farmhouse.

But despite this fortunate circumstance, we nonetheless had to flee as a disquieting smoke threatened to take our breath away. So: After having *sneaked our way in* and, in the most literal sense of the word, being *smoked out*, we left this interesting locale.

Shortly thereafter the rain stopped and we set out on the road. But soon it began to pour down again, and since we could not agree on what to do we each chose our own way: The Schleisner brothers walked 7.5 kilometers to Kvistgaard,

---

[17] A play on words: The village through which they passed was Hornbæk, Grieg's friend was named Hornbeck.

[18] A Danish Rigsdaler was equivalent to approximately one American dollar.

[19] "Holmblad's Hymnal" ("Holmblads Psalmebog") is a Danish expression for card-playing. It alludes to Holmblad's factory, which manufactured playing cards of various kinds.

the rest of us 2.5 kilometers to Elsinore [Helsingør], where we arrived dry and enjoyed a fabulously inexpensive noon meal in Hotel du Nord. From here Feddersen headed back to Rungsted, Horneman and I went to Fredensborg by train. Feddersen fussed and fumed about not getting me to go with him, but I could not control my longing for Nina's letter that absolutely had to be awaiting me in Fredensborg. And what joy! I received it, and I was happy again.

After having spent the whole day indoors because of the continuing downpour, following our evening meal we took our farewell tour of the Fredensborg Castle park. It was dark there. The tall lindens, whose crowns touched each other like the columns of a Gothic arch, seemed to be giving me a serious message: Now the pleasure, the fun and laughter, were over.

August 9

I left Fredensborg and my friends at 7:30 AM, traveled by way of Holte and Hirschholm to Rungsted, where lovely letters awaited me which crowned my decision: to work with renewed strength toward the goal—my great, beautiful goal.[20]

Saturday, December 2

Afternoon: with Pettersson[21] from Leipzig to Dresden. Concert by Strauss[22] in Braun's Hotel. (Poor performance of Beethoven's *Symphony No. 7* and Gade's overture *I Højlandene*.[23])

Sunday, December 3

Met Samson. Afternoon and evening with the Ehrhardts.[24] Splendid family, sweet young girls. 1 AM traveled with Prof. Grosse[25] to Vienna.

---

[20] This is the last entry in the diary until December 2. The next page of this part of the diary contains several columns of numbers, probably card-game scores. Some have been crossed out. The very last page contains a drawing of a man's head in profile and a tabletop with a bottle and three shot glasses. Beneath the sketch is an almost illegible list of things that Grieg was to buy, including two pounds of sugar and a quarter pound of tea.

    Grieg stayed at Rungsted until the beginning of October, when he left for Berlin with the intention of joining Nordraak and continuing on to Rome. The travel plans did not work out, however, for when he reached Berlin he discovered that Nordraak was seriously ill and unable to travel. Grieg went alone to Leipzig, where he participated at a concert in mid-November. After a short stay in Leipzig and Dresden he proceeded to Italy—without Nordraak—by way of Vienna. The diary resumes as Grieg is en route to Rome.

[21] At the Leipzig concert, Grieg had played his *Piano Sonata* op. 7 and his *Violin Sonata No. 1* op. 8. His fellow artist in the latter piece was Swedish violinist Anders Pettersson (1841–98).

[22] Austrian composer Joseph Strauss (1827–70).

[23] *In the Highlands* op. 7, 1844.

[24] Samson presumably was a Norwegian acquaintance whom Grieg had met in Leipzig. The Ehrhardts were the in-laws of Grieg's brother John (1840–1901). Marie Ehrhardt (1845–1931) had met and married John during the latter's studies at the Leipzig Conservatory, and the young couple had made their home in Bergen. Her father, Adolph Ehrhardt (1813–99), was a prominent artist who was recognized especially for his portraits.

[25] Probably German professor and painter Julius Grosse (1828–1902), with whom Grieg associated in Rome from time to time.

Monday, December 4

Arrived 3 PM. [Attended] Theater an der Wien: "Wildschütz" by Lortzing.[26] Zahn[27] from Leipzig.

Tuesday, December 5

Gallery Belvedere, The Arsenal by Th. Hansen,[28] St. Stephan's church, Theseus Temple (Theseus with the centaur by Canova[29]), Carltheater: "Die alte Schachtel", music by Suppé.[30]

Wednesday, December 6

In Meisll's Hotel (gigantic fraud). From Vienna 6:45 A.M. Lovely trip. Semmering train magnificent.[31] Arrival in Venice.

Thursday, December 7

Thoroughly disinfected with chlorine at the railway station due to fear of cholera in the city of Munich. St. Mark's Square. Doges' Palace. St. Mark's Church. Piazetta. Many churches. Academia delle belle arti. March from *Tannhäuser*[32] by a military band in St. Mark's Square. Walked to Ponte Rialto, gondola ride through Canal Grande. Bought some photographs of Venice.

Friday, December 8

6 AM in moonlight, through the canals by gondola to the railroad station. Arrival at Padua. By omnibus to Raigo and Pontelagoscuro, from there across the River Po by ferry. Continued by omnibus to Ferrara. Tons of beggars. Table d'hôte. An Italian married couple sat at a remote table. A lovely woman, who knew how to use her eyes. Frightful jealousy, a silent scene, the whole episode an old tragedy.

7:30 PM: From Ferrara by train to Bologna, arrival 8:30. Got a room at Hotel Brun.

Saturday, December 9

7 AM viewed the lovely Church of St. Petrolius, which is very similar to the Roskilde Cathedral except that it is much larger. Two slanting towers.

---

26 German composer Albert Lortzing (1801–51). *Der Wildschütz* is a comic opera (1842).

27 Presumably an acquaintance of Grieg's from his student days in Leipzig.

28 Possibly Danish architect Theophilus Hansen (1837–1901), who designed several large buildings in Vienna.

29 Italian sculptor Antonio Canova (1757–1822).

30 Austrian operetta composer Franz von Suppé (1819–95), who had come to the Carltheater in 1865. *Die alte Schachtel* (*The Old Bag*) was a farce by Austrian writer Oskar Franz Berg (1833–86). The first performance of the work had been given at the Carltheater on December 2, 1865.

31 Semmering is a popular excursion spot in the mountains south of Vienna. The Semmering railroad was built in 1848–54 and is one of Europe's oldest mountain railroads.

32 Romantic opera by German composer Richard Wagner (1813–83), premiered in Dresden 1845.

8:45 by train over the Apennines. Pleasant trip, countless tunnels, over ¾ of the way underground. Magnificent nature, though not half as wild as that of Norway. Numerous green mountain streams. Little vegetation. Highest point Pracchia. Here we entered a huge tunnel of at least 10–12 sections, and when we once again saw the light of day the loveliest Italian landscape abruptly lay before us. It was as if I had suddenly entered a fairytale world—and yet, it was the loveliest reality. As far as I could see, the green meadows with cypresses, stone pines and olive trees interspersed with picturesque groups of houses in genuine Mediterranean style—and in the distance the blue-violet mountains, and over us the dark blue canopy of heaven. It was as if it all came into being by magic.

Down in the valley we saw Pistoia's towers. Once again we went through some short tunnels and then the train stopped at Pistoia. Here we ate our noon meal and the first grapes—sweet as sugar! This is where I got my first real impression of Italy. Everything breathed warmth, spring. Who thought about December!

From here, in burning heat from the sun, we journeyed through delightful landscapes to Pisa, where we arrived as the setting sun was sending its last rays over the reddening nature. Immediately inspected the Leaning Tower, the Cathedral and Campo Santo. From there with Prof. Grosse to a German family named Ritter, where we stayed until 8:30 PM.

8:45 by train to Livorno, arrived 9:30, got a room at Hotel d'Angleterre.

Sunday, December 10

We were supposed to have left by train at 9 AM, but the hotel director insisted that we would be turned back at the city limits if we did not have the passport endorsement of the papal nuncio in Livorno, so there was nothing to do but postpone our trip in order to get in touch with this influential man.

Forenoon: walking tour by the harbor, where one can see the lovely dark-blue sea and the islands of Capraia, Corsica and Elba on the horizon. Thereafter roamed through the streets and observed the teeming crowds of people. After receiving an enormous hotel bill and the papers needed in order to enter the pope's domain, at 2 PM we got into a taxi to drive to the railroad station.

During the trip I began to realize for the first time what it means to be going to Rome. The closer one comes to the world metropolis the greater seems the impossibility of reaching it. Every possible obstacle is put in the way. First, the passport control is almost ridiculous in its severity, especially now when cholera is raging in various places in Italy. Secondly, one cannot walk or drive for ten steps without having to cough up large sums of money for reasons one does not understand. Thus, for example, we first had to pay ten francs for an insignificant piece of paper; to a servant who took care of it, two francs; then no less than ten francs for my suitcase, plus a pile of coins for the examination of the innocuous little thing. Every moment one is stopped and must open one's suitcase. It is as if these people wanted to trick you, and yet everything is done on the basis of orders from higher up.

Finally I was seated in the train compartment, where I had a view of the magnificent blue mountains of Capraia and thus, for a while, could be free of nonsense. From Livorno to Rome I paid 33 francs 55 cents. By train to Nunziatella, by omnibus from 10 PM until 6 in the morning.

Monday, December 11

Arrival at Civitavecchia (where I was again disinfected and examined right down to the innermost parts), then by train from Civitavecchia to Rome, where we arrived at 11:30 AM.

Grosse's friend Preller,[33] a painter, met us at the railroad station and drove us to Grosse's lodgings, where we ate our first Roman meal: ham, soup, eggs and radishes, wine and apples.

Rented a room at Via Sistina 100, first floor. Then visited the Vatican. The first impression was almost too overpowering to even think of enjoyment. The Laocoon group[34] was lovely, so also Raphael's[35] frescoes. Café Greco.[36] Spithöver,[37] 89 scudi. Noon meal. Met scads of German painters and archeologists. Bretschneider.[38] Café Roma. The Spanish Steps. Monte Pincio, evening walk.

December 12[39]

Bohlmann. Consul Bravo. Ravnkilde. Villa Albano with Dr. Münster (Danish) and Bohlmann. Noon meal with Scandinavians. Ibsen. St. Peter's Basilica. Scandinavian Society. Evening with Bohlmann. Read Bjørnson's speech to the University Student Association in Christiania.[40] Nordraak's song mentioned.[41] Rented a piano.

December 13

Morning: I followed Consul Bravo home from Café Greco. Splendid old fellow.

---

[33] German painter Johann Friedrich Preller (1804–78).

[34] According to Greek legend, Laocoon, a priest of the god Apollo, incurred the wrath of the god by breaking his vow of celibacy. As punishment, he and his twin sons were crushed to death by two giant sea serpents sent by Apollo. The Laocoon statue to which Grieg refers is thought to be a first century A.D. Roman copy of a work by the Rhodian sculptors Agesander, Athenodorus and Polydorus.

[35] Italian painter Raphael (1483–1520).

[36] Gathering place for artists in Rome. Norwegian authors Henrik Ibsen (1828–1906) and Bjørnstjerne Bjørnson (1832–1910) often used this restaurant.

[37] Spithöver (first name and dates unknown) was probably a business acquaintance of Grieg in Rome.

[38] Russian archeologist and orientalist Emil Bretschneider (1833–1901).

[39] At this point Grieg stops the practice of writing in the day of the week.

[40] People mentioned in this entry not identified earlier: Danish organist, conductor and arranger Georg Bohlmann (1838–1920), who later orchestrated Grieg's "Bridal Procession" op. 19 no. 2; Danish painter and art agent Johan Bravo (1797–1876), who at various times was both the Danish consul and the Norwegian-Swedish consul in Rome; Danish composer Niels Ravnkilde (1823–90); possibly Danish physician Carl J. N. S. Münster (1831–1903).

[41] The Nordraak song to which Grieg refers may be "Ja, vi elsker" ("Yes, we love this land"), the Norwegian national anthem, text by Bjørnson.

Letters from Father, Nina, Kirchner,[42] Breitkopf & Härtel.[43] Capitolium, Forum Romanum, the triumphal arches of Constantine and Titus, Colosseum (with Bohlmann). Evening: Scandinavian Society (1 scudi), introduced to Danish painters La Cour and Sonne.[44]

December 14

Prior,[45] Evens (sculptor).[46]

December 15

Schou. Fladager. Talked with Munch[47] in the Scandinavian Society.

December 16

Concert in the Scandinavian Society. Quartet by Ravnkilde.

December 17

Terrible music in Chiesa nuova. Bellini, Donizetti, Rossini.[48] Two castratos, unnatural, repugnant.

December 18

Forum Trojanum. Pantheon with Raphael's tomb. Played for Hartmann[49] and Ravnkilde in the Scandinavian Society.

December 19

At Story's[50] with Fladager. Evening with Hartmann at Ravnkilde's.

December 20

Concert by Pinelli.[51] Saw Liszt strutting about for some young ladies. Noon meal and supper at Prior's with Schou, Hartmann, Cand. Nielsen and Nielsen the pharmacist. A nice evening.

---

[42] Hermann Theodor Kirchner was a book dealer in Leipzig who helped Grieg with sheet music and other things.

[43] Breitkopf & Härtel was the Leipzig firm that published some of Grieg's early compositions including *Piano Sonata* op. 7.

[44] Danish painters Janus La Cour (1837–1909), whose name Grieg always spelled "Lacour", and Jørgen Valentin Sonne (1801–90).

[45] Danish wholesaler and shipowner Hans Peter Prior (1813–75), who had come to Rome owing to health problems. Prior lived there all winter together with his family, among whom were two sons, Axel Prior (1843–98) and Oscar F. L. Prior (1847–1903). A third son, whom Grieg never mentions, was the sculptor Lauritz Prior (1840–79), who also lived in Italy 1862–67.

[46] Danish sculptor Otto Evens (1826–95).

[47] Danish painter Ludvig A. Schou (1838–67), Norwegian sculptor Ole Henriksen Fladager (1832–71), Norwegian poet Andreas Munch (1811–84).

[48] Italian composers Vincenzo Bellini (1801–35), Gaëtano Donizetti (1797–1848), Gioacchino Rossini (1792–1868).

[49] Danish sculptor Carl Chr. Hartmann (1837–1901) made a bust of Grieg in Rome.

[50] American sculptor William Wetmore Story (1819–95), who lived in Rome from 1856 until his death.

[51] Italian violinist Ettore Pinelli (1843–1915).

December 21

With Bohlmann at the St. Onofria cloister to watch the sun go down. Wonderful view. Tasso's[52] oak tree.

December 22

Witnessed a funeral. Powerful, gripping impression. The monks bellowed on two notes (interval of a sixth) with a strange effect.

December 24

Christmas party in the Scandinavian Society in the evening. Banquet. After-dinner speeches by Molbech[53] for Scandinavia, for Bravo, for Munch, for Italy; by Bravo for Greece and for the kings [of the Scandinavian countries]; by Sponneck[54] for Scandinavian art and Scandinavian artists; by Munch for the children and for the party planning committee; by Kjellberg[55] for Sponneck and Ibsen; (Materien!)[56] by Cand. Nielsen for Norway and Sweden; by La Cour for the ladies and for loved ones at home; by Ibsen for the inhabitants of Schleswig.[57] Festival march by Bohlmann for piano and children's instruments. Christmas tree with lottery (2 pairs of kid gloves). Dance. Ended 2 AM.

December 25

Forenoon in St. Peter's Basilica with Ravnkilde. Saw Pope Pius IX[58] give the blessing. He was carried under a canopy in the middle of a long, elegant procession. Strange impression to see the assembled crowd kneel as soon as the old, gray-haired and apparently world-weary man passed them. He looked pale and scarcely opened his eyes except when he shakily stretched out his arm, once to each side; then he also allowed his wan glance to scan the kneeling multitude. His facial expression was gentle and intelligent—indescribably attractive, actually, and of a sort to elicit a positive reaction. I can understand how one could learn to like him if one got to know him—even if one did not applaud his biases.

In the evening a party on the leftovers in the Scandinavian Society. Played for Molbech. "Nordic Dance" by [?].[59] Ibsen dead drunk.

December 26

Carriage tour with Prior, Hartmann (lively), Schou, Lorange[60] and Fladager past

---

52 Italian poet Torquato Tasso (1544–95).
53 Danish author Christian Molbech (1821–88).
54 Danish Count Wilhelm Sponneck (1842–1921)
55 Swedish sculptor Johannes Fridtiof Kjellberg (1836–85).
56 Grieg's use of the Norwegian word "Materien", which means "the matter" or "the substance", is inexplicable.
57 Ibsen was irate that neither Norway nor Sweden had come to Denmark's aid in 1864 when the Danish duchies of Schleswig and Holstein were annexed by Prussia.
58 Pius IX (Giovanni Maria Mastai-Ferretti, 1792–1878) was pope 1846–78.
59 The name of the composer is written so unclearly that it cannot be made out.
60 Norwegian curator Anders Lund Lorange (1847–88).

Forum Romanum to the Church of St. Stefano rotundo, the walls of which are decorated with frescoes depicting the sufferings and deaths of the martyrs during the first persecutions of the Christians. These are some of the most awful scenes one can see. The pictures go on and on, each one worse than the preceding one. As a whole they made such a ghastly impression that we all got out of there and into the fresh air again as quickly as possible. Met Count Sponneck on the way home.

December 27

Letter from Nordraak's father.[61] Afternoon with Hartmann and Bohlmann in the Lateran church. Here I heard some church music that had only one thing in common with that which I heard in Chiesa nuova, namely that it was deadly boring. Otherwise it was enormously different, for this was church music by newer Italian masters (?). It was such a monotonous, uninteresting jangle of sounds— nothing but a formless accumulation of tonic, dominant and sub-dominant chords. The only variety consisted of nothing less than some hidden [parallel] fifths and octaves, which were strongly reminiscent of the powerful—yet lovely and effective—passage at the end of the Finale of Gounod's *Faust*.[62] Before the concert was half over I left the church, nervous and exhausted to the extreme.

I saw one priceless sight: A monk in a little cell gave absolution to sinners who knelt before him by giving them a fairly hefty blow on the head with a long stick that he held in his hand. There were a great many sinners in the church, for the stick was in constant motion. (I have read the article in *Morgenbladet*.[63])

December 28

Noon meal and supper at wholesaler Prior's with Hartmann, Schou, Bohlmann. Spent an enjoyable, genuinely cozy evening.

December 30

Morning with Bohlmann at the dome of St. Peter's Basilica. A most strenuous undertaking, but it paid off handsomely, for the view is marvelous! I climbed an iron ladder up to the highest little cupola—which, however, is large enough to hold sixteen people. Here I carved my initials as well as N[ina]'s.

As we descended we looked down into the church from the galleries in the

---

[61] As related earlier, Grieg's and Nordraak's plan to visit Italy together in the autumn of 1865 was frustrated by Nordraak's illness. After arriving in Rome, Grieg received a letter from Nordraak's father, Georg Marcus Nordraach (1811–90), who at the insistent urging of the doctors had gone to Berlin to be at the bedside of his dying son. His letter to Grieg tells of Rikard's despair over Grieg's having left him and of his anger over "the enormous treachery he thought you had committed by leaving him without telling him of your plans." Grieg's reply of May 7, 1866, has been printed in English translation in Finn Benestad (ed.), *Edvard Grieg: Letters to Colleagues and Friends*, Columbus, Ohio 2000, pp. 552–553.

[62] *Faust*, opera by French composer Charles Gounod (1818–93).

[63] A newspaper in Christiania. The article referred to by Grieg was probably one of December 21, 1865, which dealt in some detail with problems in the Philharmonic Society in Christiania.

gigantic dome. What a sight! The enormous tabernacle almost disappeared in the infinite space, and the people down on the floor looked like mice. An oddly indeterminate, soft and yet ethereally beautiful sound could be heard: It was the organ down in the church, the sound of which reaches up to the dome only as a scarcely audible rustling in the distance. One could not discern a distinct harmony, and yet this music—if I dare call it that—was the most beautiful I have heard in my life. At least it put me in a wonderful mood of a sort I had never previously experienced. I enjoyed it not as a composition invented by a human being but rather as the impression of angel voices calling us to the eternal peace. If music—our earthly art—were given the power to depict even vaguely such a situation, I think that everyone who is not made of stone would be compelled to kneel in mute humility at the intimation of eternity.[64]

As I was thinking these thoughts, Bohlmann—who was enthusiastically occupied with estimating the distances and pointing out the function of this or that device—called my attention to the fact that we had to go out on the roof and have a look at one of the apostles' big toes; and as oddly as this change in my train of thought struck me, I was nonetheless willing to admire the enormous contours of the rebuilt big toe. And no less the arrangement on the roof itself, which is such that not only its size but the construction as a whole makes an impression like one of our small towns in Norway. Here there are whole rows of houses inhabited by the scads of workers who, year in and year out, work at repairing the church, which is never completely in shape. Up here there are water tanks, sidewalks, benches, gazebos—in short, everything as comfortable as one is accustomed to seeing in a small town.

By the time we got down to St. Peter's Square, the entire tour had taken us about two hours.

Prior brought me a review of my *Humoresques*[65] in [the Christiania newspaper] *Dagbladet*. Played Gade's *Symphony in G Minor*[66] with Bohlmann in the Scandinavian Society.

December 31

In the evening a wonderful moonlit tour of the Forum Romanum with Bohlmann. This is the right mood in which to view the ruins. The impact of the Colosseum is indescribable. The French watchmen who guard all the entrances were just in process of using lanterns to inspect all the passages and arches. The reddish light reflecting off the old arches and shining in among the ruins created an eerie contrast to the strange half-darkness produced by the blue-green light of the moon and made the whole scene even more ghostly.

---

[64] Grieg here uses the Norwegian words "den Evige", which may imply "the eternal God".
[65] Grieg's *Humoresques* for piano, op. 6 (1865), were dedicated to Rikard Nordraak.
[66] Danish composer Niels W. Gade's sixth symphony, op. 32 (1875).

We walked through the triumphal arches of Constantine and Titus toward the Forum. A profound stillness prevailed everywhere. The moon shone so pale and cold, our imagination began to play tricks on us, and we hurried as fast as we could away from this admittedly poetic but scary world where assaults are anything but rare.

Next we headed for the Scandinavian Society to celebrate New Year's Eve, but it was so formal and uncomfortable in this "homey circle" that after only five minutes or so Bohlmann and I, without telling anybody, just left. We drank our chocolate in the Café Greco and talked about our loved ones at home.

By 11 PM I was sound asleep, so I did not experience that singular hour of transition ushering in the new year.

1866

January 1

At 9:30 in the morning I and a group of other Norwegians gathered in Café Roma to take a hike in the Campagna. We went out through Porta St. Sebastiano on the old Roman highway in the most enormous heat—roughly like a July day at home. The farther we went the more marvelous it became. The sides of the road teemed with ruins of old burial monuments—not like ours, but whole buildings, strange-shaped vaults, stately towers with valuable inscriptions, reliefs and such.

We had breakfast in a little restaurant out there; it consisted of dirty sausage and dirty spare ribs on even dirtier plates, and some almost undrinkable wine, but even so it was a singularly priceless delight. The mere thought that on the first of January—under beautiful green trees, and surrounded by the scent of roses— I was sitting out in the open air and eating my breakfast, made me almost intoxicated.

From here, with our hats and buttonholes adorned with the most beautiful red roses, of which we could pick as many as we could carry, we walked under the dark blue sky and in the sparkling summer air toward the indescribably beautiful Alban Hills in the distance.

Hans Christian Andersen[67] is right: Italy is the land of colors. The light, clear air gives a wonderful harmony to the colors. The mountains look like scent, like ether, like things that are merely hovering in one's thoughts, and yet in such a way that one sees and enjoys all of this with one's outer as well as one's inner eye.

We chose a different return route, across meadows and ditches, passing the

---

[67] On September 14, 1865, shortly before his departure from Copenhagen, Grieg had received the following greeting from Andersen in his autograph album:

Flyv kjernesun til den evige Stad,	Flee haunts of youth for eternal Rome,
kom Dig selv og begeistret tilbage,	Return with excitement abounding,
Lad Norden, med Dig, faae et Tone-Quad	Create then a song for your Nordic home,
For Tusinde Aar og Dage!	A song that for aye will be sounding!

grotto of the nymph Egeria. This grotto is remarkably poetic. Rows of intertwined ground ivy hung down from the ruins of the old wall. I couldn't resist going into the cool vault to taste the ancient spring water.

From here, by way of various side roads, pathways, thickets and bridges, we reached a country road that took us to Porta St. Giovanni, past the Lateran Church and Maria Maggiore to our home, Monte Pincio. It was a demanding tour, an approximately six-hour march. I had dinner at five o'clock with Scandinavians, both women and men, at Lipre's, near Café Greco. Spent the evening in the [Scandinavian] Society. Had a good time, with various Christmas games in which both women and men participated.

Letter from Feddersen.[68]

January 2

Letter from Father, Nina and Kirchner. Barghiglioni 4.[69]

January 3

Concert by Pinelli.[70] String quartet by Ravnkilde,[71] Chaconne by Bach, Violin Sonata (A Minor) by Schumann, Trio in B-flat (op. 97) by Beethoven.

January 4

Went to [the name of the church is omitted] on the Capitoline Hill at 3 PM and heard a piece of church music by Franz Liszt for castrata,[72] natural male voices, and harmonium. Liszt himself led the performance. That is to say: Although someone else was conducting, Liszt led the whole affair with his black-gloved fingers that one moment were waving in the air, the next moment were busy on the organ.

The composition—a *Stabat mater dolorosa*—is a sad proof of the decline of the newer German music. For it would be hard to find a more affected, pale, formless, shallow piece than this. It is unsound and untrue from beginning to end. The beginning did impress me, however; it was brilliant, mystical, and demonic—as Liszt can be in inspired passages here and there. But the whole piece remained in this underworld. All too soon it became evident that he was not capable of mastering his thoughts—indeed, that he was rather the slave of those thoughts, that he is devoid of style, that he soars for one moment only to sink all the deeper in the next. For to employ trite, highly strung, platitudinous

[68] Danish author Benjamin Feddersen (1823–1902), a close friend of Grieg.
[69] Edvard's father was Alexander Grieg (1806–75), proprietor of a seafood exporting firm and British vice-consul in Bergen. His mother, whom he mentions later, was Gesine Hagerup Grieg (1814–75). Hermann Theodor Kirchner was a book dealer in Leipzig who helped Grieg with currency exchanges and other matters. Barghiglioni was a language teacher from whom Grieg took lessons in Italian. The "4" following the name indicates that this was Grieg's fourth lesson, though it is the first mention of the lessons in the diaries.

Wagnerian opera reminiscences in a Stabat mater—that I would call to sink deep. Then comes an utterly banal Italian phrase, after that a completely trivial sequence that is not even deftly placed in the context, then another moment where Liszt is indescribably great—that is to say, one only glimpses his greatness, not more; for one is immediately disabused of the illusion, either by some banality or other or by something boring or baroque.

This much is clear, that if we do not fight with all our might against this genre, the outlook for music in our time is very bad. It is almost as false as the vulgar Italian school—yes, perhaps even more dangerous—because it ventures into an area that is of interest to musicians, namely philosophy. But if true art—consisting in pure immediacy and sparkling poetry—is to progress, then philosophy must be abandoned, and the sooner the better, in my opinion.

The poor Germans present at the concert were very unhappy. Their eloquence vanished; they hung their heads and left the church without saying a word. Liszt looked splendid in his abbot's garb; one could see the visionary written all over him.

Franz Liszt

[70] Italian violinist Ettore Pinelli (1843–1915).

[71] Danish composer Niels Ravnkilde (1823–90).

[72] A castrato is a male singer who has been castrated before puberty in order to preserve the soprano or contralto range of his voice. During the 17th and 18th centuries the Italian term "musico" also referred to a castrato.

January 6

Barghiglioni 5.

January 7

Took a walk in the afternoon via Porta pia with Hartmann,[73] Ravnkilde and Lorange.[74] Lovely natural scenery, Alban Hills enchanting. Wonderful Roman women, models.

January 8

In the Vatican with Bohlmann.[75]

January 9

Barghiglioni 6. Letter from Uncle Herman, his wife and Yelva.[76]

January 11

Visited the Capitoline sculpture collection with Hartmann and Bohlmann. The dying swordsman. Two centaurs. A wonderful collection of busts of famous Greeks and Romans, all from antiquity.

January 12

Hartmann has begun to sculpt my bust.

January 13

A gathering of ladies and gentlemen in the Scandinavian Society. School principal Rovsing[77] proposed a toast in honor of the day[78] (the Nordic holiday, a day of recollection and promise), whereupon Ibsen responded with a speech that created a stir. He reminded his listeners of all the solemn promises that are given on this day by all the Scandinavian student societies—promises about solidarity

---

[73] Danish sculptor Carl Christian Hartmann (1837–1901).

[74] Anders Lund Lorange (1847–88), Norwegian curator.

[75] Danish composer and orchestral arranger Georg C. Bohlmann (1838–1920).

[76] Herman (1816–1900), Adelina (1813–1907) and Yelva (1847–86) Hagerup. They were, respectively, Nina's father, mother and sister.

[77] Danish headmaster Kristen Rovsing (1812–89).

[78] A Memorial Day ("Festival in Memory of our Forefathers") had been established in Norway in 1834 at the suggestion of the great Norwegian poet and patriot Henrik Wergeland (1808–45). Wergeland's theme in his opening address at the Student Association in Christiania on January 13, 1834, was "that the same spirit and the same deeds that made old Norway great are also needed to make present-day Norway happy." The festival evolved, however, from a celebration of Norwegian distinctiveness into a celebration of pan-Scandinavianism, a day on which Norwegians, Swedes and Danes joined in lauding the exploits of the great men whose deeds had brought glory to the Scandinavian countries. As enthusiasm for pan-Scandinavianism waned, however, the January 13 Memorial Day lost its significance and eventually vanished from the scene. (See Anne-Jorunn Kydland Lysdahl, *Sangen har lysning. Studentersang i Norge på 1800-tallet*, Oslo 1995, pp. 95–96.)

Caricature of Henrik Ibsen by Ragnvald Blix

and determination in the time of danger—and how without exception the entire younger generation had failed to come through when distress threatened. It was high time, he said, to end such empty talk as long as it never found expression in deeds, and he wanted most earnestly to advise that we *stop* celebrating a memorial day such as this under the present circumstances.[79]

After a speech like that there naturally was a bit of anxious confusion. You could hear expressions of both approval and displeasure. But the poor school principal felt extremely unwell as a result of the unexpected opposition, and he went over to talk to Ibsen. Of their conversation I heard only a few snatches— that he must not misunderstand him, he had only meant thus and so, etc.—the old rubbish. Count Sponneck[80] also got into the conversation and people began to get hot under the collar. After a few exchanges of opinion and sharp outbursts the party ended at eleven o'clock.

January 14

2:30 PM, armed with a permezzo from Consul Bravo,[81] went to the Collegium Urbanum to hear a whole bunch of talks in all the languages of the world by young people who were to be trained as missionaries. After a long, boring over-ture for orchestra, in which half of the musicians played so badly that in the winds

---

[79] Ibsen was referring to the Prusso-Danish war of 1864 concerning the duchies of Schleswig and Holstein. An ardent Scandinavianist, he had urged his countrymen to take up arms in support of their Danish brothers, but they did not do so. The result was a humiliating military defeat for Denmark and the annexation of Schleswig-Holstein by Prussia.

[80] Danish Count Wilhelm Sponneck (1842–1921).

[81] *permezzo*: permission. Danish painter and art agent Johan Bravo (1797–1876), who at various times was both the Danish consul and the Norwegian-Swedish consul in Rome.

one had to listen to open fourths etc., came a lecture in Latin in which I had so little interest that when it was finished, with great difficulty I fought my way to the exit door. Hartmann did the same.

Went to Sio[82] in the evening. Flirted with a wonderful young Roman woman. Her slight blush as I left the tavern was indescribable.

January 16

Barghiglioni 7. (Failed to show up, without prior notice.)

January 17

Wrote to Father and Nina. Wrote to August Winding.[83]

January 18–19

Read *David Copperfield* by Charles Dickens.[84] Marvelous book.

January 20

Barghiglioni 8. Paid 1 *scudo* 7 *paoli* 5 *baj*. Gathering of ladies and gentlemen at the [Scandinavian] Society in the evening. Music by Italians. Italian folk ballad with variations, for two guitars. The folk song contained much that was peculiar and pretty; the variations were beneath all criticism, but the musicians certainly showed mastery of their instruments. Thereafter a Roman amateur singer, Miss Margaresi, sang an Italian ballad, accompanying herself on the guitar. Her voice was actually excellent, and the song wasn't bad either—a passionate Mediterranean love song. I must admit that she preserved the spirit of the piece, for she interpreted the passion with genuine Italian exaggeration—to the point of sensuality, to say the least, if not to lewdness. The same girl's father later sang Donizetti's "Il furioso"[85]—with verve, to be sure, but also here I had to confirm my old opinion that Donizetti is the worst and most uninspired of them all. (Sarichoro and his wife.)

January 21

Trip to Albano with Bohlmann, Schjøtt, Grev Bonde, Candidate Nielsen, La Cour, Sonne, Kierkegaard and Thiele.[86] In Albano, after our arrival by train, we ate a

---

[82] Sio: presumably the name of a tavern.

[83] Danish composer and pianist August Winding (1835–99), a close friend of Grieg.

[84] Charles Dickens (1812–70) wrote *David Copperfield* in 1849–50.

[85] Grieg is probably referring to an aria from the opera *Il furioso all'isola di San Domingo* by Gaetano Donizetti (1779–1848), the first performance of which took place in Rome in 1833.

[86] Grieg's known companions on this trip: Danish painters Janus La Cour (1837–1909), Jørgen Valentin Sonne (1801–90), and Niels Christian Kierkegaard (1806–82); Danish author and collector of folk sayings Just Mathias Thiele (1795–1874). Possible identifications: Norwegian Professor of Greek Peter Olrog Schjøtt (1833–1926), Swedish author Knut Filip Bonde (1815–71). "Candidate Nielsen" has not been identified.

Roman breakfast consisting of chestnuts, bread and cheese, radishes and fruit. Thereafter we traveled by donkey to Lake Nemi (deep down in a valley, lovely surroundings) and Lake Albano, which is an inactive crater. After an excellent dinner at Hotel de la poste in Albano, we returned by train to Rome.

January 22

Letters from Father and Mother, Nina and Fries.[87]

January 23

After dinner went with Bohlmann to the Jewish quarter. Some of the most revolting, filthy, foul-smelling—but also some of the most original and interesting— phenomena of this type that I have seen. The smell was so bad that it was almost impossible to walk through the area.

January 26

Concert by the Pinelli brothers[88] in the [Scandinavian] Society. *Trio in G Major* by Haydn,[89] *Sonata in G Minor* for violin and piano by Tartini,[90] well played. A marvelous work.

January 27

Went to the Sistine Chapel in the forenoon with Grosse[91] and Preller[92] and a third German painter-"spirit". Here we saw Michelangelo's[93] famous frescoes—"The Prophets", "The Sibyls", "The Creation", "The Fall into Sin", "The Flood", as well as "The Last Judgment" on a wall all by itself. I can certainly see that it is great and brilliant when my attention is called to it, but very little of it was really enjoyable. For one thing, you have to lie on your back and peer up into the vast height through opera glasses, and secondly, the figures are so besmirched with dirt and smoke that have accumulated through the years, that it is hardly to be expected that an amateur should be able to ignore all of this and just concentrate on the main idea. I can well understand that a creative artist, on the other hand—one who understands the means whereby the effects are achieved—does not require brilliance of color in order to appreciate such works. Eve as depicted in "The Fall into Sin" is the loveliest female figure I have seen, enchantingly graceful.

---

[87] German-Norwegian violinist and conductor August Fries (1821–1913), whom Grieg knew from Bergen.

[88] Italian violinist Ettore Pinelli (1843–1915), pianist Oreste Pinelli (1844–1924), and the lesser known cellist Decio Pinelli. Ettore made significant contributions to Rome's musical life for almost half a century. In 1876 he collaborated with Italian pianist Giovanni Sgambati (1843–1914) in founding the Liceo Musicale of the Accademia di S. Cecilia.

[89] Austrian composer Joseph Haydn (1732–1809).

[90] Italian composer and violinist Giuseppe Tartini (1692–1770).

[91] German professor and painter Julius Grosse (1828–1902).

[92] German painter Johann Friedrich Preller (1804–78).

[93] Italian sculptor, painter and architect Michelangelo Buonarroti (1475–1564).

January 28

Dinner and the evening at the Priors.[94] Started taking cod-liver oil and iron drops.

January 30

Sent letters to Feddersen, to Uncle and Auntie, to Yelva Hagerup. Visited the Priors.

January 31

Completed a sketch of the *Overture in D Major*.[95] Went to Pinelli's concert in the afternoon. One of the most interesting concerts I have attended. A concerto for piano by Liszt[96] played by Sgambati was well suited to show the composer as well as the performer in the most favorable light. This piece is the best thing I have ever heard by Liszt. Brilliant from beginning to end. He slings out colossal masses with a demonic power. But it is a pity that the modulations are confused and too frequent; if they were used more sparingly the effect would be doubled. Judging from this performance, Sgambati is one of the world's top piano *virtuosos*. Not a piano player in the generic sense, for the manner in which he performed Beethoven's *Trio in D Major* op. 70 revealed, unfortunately, an incessant striving for an outward show of virtuosity, and in a work like this it is of course necessary above all to subordinate oneself.

February 1

Sent letters to Father, John[97] and Nina.

February 2

Festival in St. Peter's Basilica. Kyndelmesse (*candele missa*).[98] A grand procession in which even the diplomats participated. The Pope was carried as on Christmas Day.

---

[94] Danish wholesaler and shipowner Hans Peter Prior (1813–75), who had come to Rome owing to health problems. Prior lived there all winter together with his family, among whom were two sons, Axel Prior (1843–98) and Oscar F. L. Prior (1847–1903). A third son, whom Grieg never mentions, was the sculptor Lauritz Prior (1840–79), who also lived in Italy 1862–67.

[95] Grieg here alludes to the overture *In Autumn* op. 11, which was finished on March 14 of the same year. See the diary entry of that date. In May Grieg showed it to Danish composer Niels W. Gade (1817–90), who gave it a decidedly negative judgment. Then Grieg made a reduction for piano four hands that he sent to Stockholm as an entry in a prize competition announced by the Swedish Academy. The overture won the prize—Gade being on the judging committee! It was printed in 1867 by Abraham Hirsch, Stockholm, as "I Höst / En Fantasi for Pianoforte til 4 Händer" (In Autumn. A Phantasy for Piano Four Hands). The overture was re-orchestrated twenty years later and premiered at the Birmingham Music Festival on August 29, 1888.

[96] Franz Liszt wrote two piano concertos: No. 1 in E-flat Major (1849, revised 1853 and 1856) and No. 2 in A Major (1839, revised 1849–61). Grieg does not specify which concerto he had heard.

[97] Edvard's brother John Grieg (1840–1901).

[98] Candlemas, also called "Presentation of Christ in the Temple," is a Christian festival celebrated on February 2 to commemorate the visit to the temple by the Virgin Mary to present the infant Jesus to God as recorded in Luke 2:22–38. The name derives from the prominent use of lighted candles in the ceremony marking the day.

February 3

The Carnival got under way. Went with Schou[99] through the Via del Corso, where we got completely covered with confetti, flour, and God knows what else. The whole business seems like childish nonsense to me. The only part that was interesting was the horse races as darkness was falling.

February 4

Wrote to Nordraak, to Biese,[100] to Kirchner.

February 5

Made a copy of Nordraak's choral work.[101] Evening with Ravnkilde at the Wrangels.[102] Prominent people—he's a cabinet minister and admiral—but also splendid human beings. Three sweet young girls.

February 6

Afternoon with Hartmann at the Carnival. Enjoyed myself immensely. In order to get in the mood we went first to *Sio* to down half a bottle of Fogliette,[103] and this helped surprisingly much and emboldened me to take part in the merriment.

February 7

With Hartmann and Bohlmann at the Carnival. Made a valiant try at bouquet-throwing to (among others) Wrangel's three young daughters, who lowered a trumpet to which was attached a package of bon-bons. What was remarkable about the latter was that the wrapping, which consisted of a musical score, upon closer inspection proved to be not only a complete piece of music but in fact one composed by me, namely "Jägerlied", text by Uhland.[104]

February 8

Afternoon at the Carnival with Fladager[105] and Hartmann. Streets teeming with wagons with burlesque decorations, which were really funny. Still, it inconvenienced me in that it was not possible for me to find any space at all to engage in my favorite pastime, namely throwing bouquets. Read about Euterpe's third concert.[106]

---

[99] Danish painter Ludvig A. Schou (1838–67).

[100] Possibly German piano builder Wilhelm Biese (1822–1902).

[101] Grieg is referring to "Kaare's Song" from Nordraak's incidental music (for baritone solo, chorus and orchestra) to "Sigurd Slembe", a play by Bjørnstjerne Bjørnson. See the entry of February 17.

[102] Possibly the Russian naval officer and polar explorer Ferdinand Wrangel (1796–1870).

[103] An Italian wine.

[104] "Hunting Song", op. 4 no. 4, to a text by German poet Ludwig Uhland (1787–1862).

[105] Norwegian sculptor Ole Henriksen Fladager (1832–71).

[106] "Euterpe" was a music society in Copenhagen which Grieg, Nordraak, Danish composer Chr. F. Emil Horneman (1840–1906) and others had established in 1865. Its aim was to give public performances of new music, especially music written by Nordic composers. It was modeled after a music society by the same name in Leipzig.

February 13

The Carnival is over. At Mockoli restaurant in the evening. Lovely, most unique illumination in the Via del Corso. The ladies on the balconies, each of whom had a candle in her hand, looked wonderful. I saw beauty in each of them.

What were most enjoyable and stimulating, though, were the processions after we left Mockoli. People were covered with big white cowls that came right up over their heads, with the result that not only did one become unrecognizable but it even became absolutely impossible to distinguish the men from the women. Thus garbed, they chatted with passers-by. In order to be absolutely sure that they would not be recognized, everyone—men and women alike—talked in their highest, most squeaky register, and this circumstance undoubtedly helped to make the situation extremely titillating. That is how it came about that all of a sudden, for example, I found one of these white-hooded apparitions under each arm (absolutely without any encouragement on my part), and only the soft outlines of the female body that pressed itself tightly against me enabled me to distinguish between the sexes.

Moreover, I admit that I found myself in a rather desperate situation by getting into the middle of this comedy, because I couldn't answer a single word to all their Italian gibberish. I therefore resorted to yelling—at the top of my lungs and in the same shrill register—Holberg's[107] inimitable "Rinkolaveski spekave" and the like.

Another time I got into trouble by patting a white figure quite gently on the shoulder, whereupon another white figure—evidently a companion who was following us—got so angry that all of a sudden I felt a clenched fist strike me from behind so hard that it rattled my spine. When I turned around I saw the same fist raised toward me, accompanied by some words that sounded like a frightful howl, which I, of course, did not understand. Hartman told me what it was all about. The words meant, "Don't touch the women!" I had no idea it was a woman that I had touched, and if only I had been able to speak Italian I would of course have said so; under the circumstances, I had to swallow my pride and remain silent.

Hartmann, with whom I for the most part went arm in arm down the Via del Corso, showed that he was an expert in his field. He acted as if he were born for the Carnival. He was constantly in demand, surrounded by great and small, old and young, and with all of them he engaged in the most elaborate conversation. He established acquaintances, expressed regret at his hasty departure and God knows what else.

February 14

In the evening, at my place, the first general rehearsal of Nordraak's choral work

---

[107] Norwegian author Ludvig Holberg (1684–1754).

by Messrs. Nielsen, Candidate Nielsen, Axel Prior, Bohlmann, Falkman, Stramboe, Renton, La Cour and Hartmann.[108] Later at the Priors.

February 15

Letters from Father, John and Nina. (Letter to Ibsen.[109]) Evening with Bohlmann and Hartmann at Ravnkildes.

February 17

At 8:15 PM I saw the Colosseum illumined with Bengal light. Marvelously efficient, although somewhat verging on the sensational. From 9:30 in the Scandinavian Society. Performance of Nordraak's "Sigurd Slembe Chorus". The solo was sung first by Hartmann, and the second time—when the piece had to be repeated—by Axel Prior.

February 18

At 11 AM the Danish Pastor Hansen gave a sermon in the Scandinavian Society. Naturally there were a lot of women, fewer men. Bohlmann performed the organist duties at the piano. In short, everything went as it was supposed to. To what extent those in attendance could just as well or to their advantage have taken a walk on Monte Pincio I cannot rightly say. What is certain is that I for my part left with the same indignation that I always feel after a sermon in which the preacher appears with medals on his chest, trying through play-acting and an affected delivery to appropriate the dignity that he thinks he needs in order to impress his flock. And yet, I wouldn't have missed this forenoon for anything. It shook me out of my lethargy and provided food for thought.

At 2:30 in the afternoon a number (14) of Scandinavians gathered at Piazza Barberini. After having distributed ourselves in five taxis, we drove in a procession through the streets out to Porta St. Carlo and on out to the Protestant cemetery. How beautiful it is! I could almost wish to be buried there. Situated on a hill right beside Rome's old mural walls, this home of peace commands the most glorious view of the surrounding landscape. It is nicely maintained; there is hardly a grave that is not adorned with a marble headstone. At the foot of most of the graves grow the loveliest cypresses, tall and slender, as if they were pointing toward heaven. The snow-white marble in contrast to the evergreen trees creates a marvelous effect; in the whole cemetery one sees no colors other than these

---

[108] The people in this list not previously identified in footnotes are: a Danish pharmacist named Nielsen; Swedish painter Severin Gabriel Falkman (1831–89); Danish ballet dancer Edvard J. L. Stramboe (1825–95); English physician Dr. Renton.

[109] This letter has not been found. The extant correspondence between Grieg and Ibsen is published in English translation in Finn Benestad (ed.), *Edvard Grieg: Letters to Colleagues and Friends*, Columbus, Ohio 2000, pp. 438–450.

two—the colors of innocence and hope—and both in their most pristine originality.

A magnificent monument in the upper corner attracts attention; it is simple and unassuming, a lone marble colossus, but one's expectation is aroused and it increases steadily as we approach the site. Midway up the stone one sees a marble plaque with the inscription: "Peter Andreas Munch,[110] historiarum professore norvegias". It is our great countryman who is buried here. The whole situation gave me a strange sense of melancholy; I had a feeling as if I did not at all want to leave the place.

Near this monument were the graves of deceased Scandinavian artists: those of the Norwegian Bruun, the Danish sculptor Schierbeck, and also Consul Hage's daughter, the young Mrs. Bissen,[111] whose resting place is marked by a barely visible wooden cross!

We walked from the cemetery out to St. Paul's Church, this elegant building that in some respects even surpasses St. Peter's Basilica. At first sight, in any case, it is more striking. One sees almost nothing other than white marble that shines and reflects in all directions.

When one hears that this enormous church exists only for show, one cannot help asking the question: Where in the world does all the money come from? For as everyone knows, the country is anything but rich! Ah yes, the people are coerced into paying this enormous church tax because that is pleasing to God! The terrible illusion that the worship of God consists in building majestic temples that can, indeed, be admired—but for the sake of which the people sigh in bondage and misery.

An enjoyable trip home by omnibus. Evening at the Priors.

February 20

Letter from Uncle Herman, Auntie and Yelva Hagerup.

February 21

At 10 AM I met the following Scandinavians at Piazza Barberini: Munch and his wife, Sverdrup[112] and his wife, Rovsing and his wife and their son and daughter, Mrs. Rørdam, Hartmann and Bohlmann—to take a trip to Tivoli. We mounted two coaches that had been ordered for that purpose and headed off toward the Campagna.

It was cloudy, so the hills could not be seen in their best light. Nonetheless, it turned into an extremely interesting drive, especially because I ended up sitting

---

[110] Norwegian historian, geographer and linguist Peter Andreas Munch (1810–63).

[111] Possibly the 18th-century Norwegian painter Hans Bruun; Danish sculptor Peter Christian Schierbeck (1835–65); Johanne Vilhelmine Bissen (1836–62), wife of Danish sculptor Wilhelm Bissen (1836–1913).

[112] The Sverdrups were a prominent family in Norway, but the members of the family to whom Grieg is referring here have not been identified.

next to A. Munch on the front seat. He was extraordinarily cordial and led the conversation in this way and that. Finally we ended up talking about his poem, "Bridal Procession of the King's Daughter",[113] concerning which we agreed that it was well suited to a dramatic treatment—i.e., as an opera text—and Munch was not unreceptive to the idea of getting to work on it if I wanted to compose the music.[114]

Then the conversation turned to Asbjørnsen's legends and fairytales about nymphs,[115] then to his life work, then to ballet and its significance, then to Hartmann[116] and his music. During all of this we got farther and farther away from Rome, and Tivoli came into view in the hills off in the distance.

After getting a bite to eat in a tavern, we were sufficiently strengthened to begin the steep climb leading up to the town of Tivoli itself. We drove step by step upward through an infinitely beautiful and large olive grove, over the top of which we saw the cupola of St. Peter's Basilica on the horizon. Finally we reached the city gate. Then, followed by a clutch of the most ragged and down-and-out beggars, we proceeded at a gallop through the littered, stinking, narrow streets to "Hotel della Sibylla", where we went in.

After our noon meal we engaged a guide, who showed us around the lovely, magnificent and yet gentle (typically Mediterranean) surroundings. It was a strenuous hike that took us up steep hills, down into deep valleys and into subterranean caves, but it was all worthwhile. What I had to admire most of all was the big, wild waterfalls, which seem so remarkable to us Northerners in that they are surrounded not by dark, gloomy mountains, like the ones at home, but by lush, fragrant foliage that winds in arabesques and garlands around the foaming cascade. Pushing its dark leaves right up against the surging water, it looks as if it were playing a most amusing and boisterous game with the plunging torrent that mercilessly grabs every tiny particle that comes too close to its domain.

I had been looking forward to taking a shower by standing close to the waterfall, as we do in Norway, but I had to give up on this as it was not possible to get to the proper distance for this. When we got home an evening meal awaited us, and the merriest and happiest mood ensued. Rovsing offered a toast to the two Danish poets Andersen and Holst,[117] who exactly 22 years ago today had stood in the same room and looked out over those roaring waterfalls.

---

[113] Kongedatterens Brudefærd.

[114] The idea of a collaboration between Grieg and Munch based on "Bridal Procession of the King's Daughter" never came to fruition.

[115] Peter Christen Asbjørnsen (1812–85) was a well-known collector of Norwegian folk tales. Grieg refers to the fairytales as "Huldre-Eventyr". A Norwegian "Hulder" (nymph) is a supernatural female creature (with a beautiful face, but sway-backed and with a cow's tail) who has her own livestock, lives inside mountains and hills, and tries to entice young men, particularly by playing and singing to them.

[116] Danish composer Johan Peter Emilius Hartmann (1805–1900).

[117] Danish authors Hans Christian Andersen and Hans Peter Holst (1811–93).

February 22

At 10 AM the guide was waiting for us with donkeys. We first visited the other side of the landscape facing Tivoli, then rode to Hadrian's villa, which contains the most comprehensive ruins of ancient splendor to be found.[118] The Medicean Venus, the Capitoline doves and many other treasures were dug up here. Upon returning to the hotel at 1:30 PM we had our farewell dinner, which also was very convivial (I offered a toast to Gade, whose birthday it happened to be), then mounted our coaches.

The trip homeward was less interesting. I sat between Rovsing junior and Bohlmann, and there was a lot of silliness of all kinds. Two ladies—Mrs. Rørdam and Miss Rovsing—occupied the other seat in the carriage. Hartmann recommended some games to amuse the ladies, and as a result there was no end of trivial courtesies. We almost didn't make it through the city gates, as our coach was new and was about to be assessed duty (!), but we finally got past this snag and arrived at Piazza Barberino in the twilight at around 6 PM. The trip cost me 2 scudi and 88 baj.

February 24–28

Sent letters to Father and Nina. Confined to bed with fever and stomach ache. Dr. Renton visited me twice a day. Very weak and exhausted after the illness despite its brevity.

March 1–2

Feeling miserable after the illness. Hartmann left.

March 5

Afternoon. Trip by coach via Ponte Mallo with Reinau, Mag. Edman and architect Dahl.

March 6

Letter from Feddersen. News of Stybe's death.

March 7

Forenoon with Prior family at Hadrian's mausoleum (Castel Sant'Angelo), viewed the dark underground cells in which Beatrice Cenci and Benvenuto Cellini were imprisoned.[119] They have a remarkable similarity to those in Valkendorf's Tower in Bergen, the racks of which correspond to other torture equipment

---

[118] Hadrian (76–138) was Roman emperor during the years 117–138. His "villa" was actually a complex of many buildings encompassing a land area of nearly twenty square kilometers.

[119] Roman noblewoman Beatrice Cenci (1577–99); Italian sculptor Benvenuto Cellini (1500–71).

here—such as the big, concrete vats that were to be filled with boiling oil in which the unfortunate prisoner would be forced to confess.

The view from above is quite remarkable. Later in St. Peter's Basilica. Viewed a new tasteless monument by Tenerani.[120]

March 8

Wrote to Father, Nina and Elisabeth.[121] Wrote to Kirchner, to Nordraak, to Feddersen, to Uncle Herman.

March 12

Letters from Father, Mother and Nina. Borrowed 10 scudi from Prior in order to repay Bohlmann the money I had borrowed from him. Received from John "Slaattevisen" ["Harvest Song"] for the overture.[122]

March 13

Borrowed 30 scudi from Consul Bravo.

March 14

Finished the autumn overture.

March 15

Letter from Kirchner. Draft on Spithöver for 150 *thaler*. With Priors at Villa Ludarsi. Viewed a fine sculpture collection (Head of Juno, "Pluto and Proserpina" by Bernini,[123] which struck me as a most charming and brilliant group despite the exaggerated sensuality and materialism and despite the fact that experts regard it extremely negatively). The garden, with its straight rows of cypresses and holly oaks, is stiff in its layout, but it is shady and has a nice Mediterranean smell. Later to the ruins of the imperial palace. An interesting trip.

In the evening Consul Bravo gave a party for all the Scandinavians at the Piccolo Colosseum, a Roman café. An exceptionally lively evening, with fine toasts—by Molbech for Consul Bravo; by the Consul for the Nordic kingdoms, then for the ladies; by Councillor[124] Tang for the kings in Scandinavia; by Ibsen

---

[120] Italian sculptor Pietro Tenerani (1789–1869).

[121] Edvard's sister Elisabeth Grieg (1845–1927), often referred to as Bet or Betten.

[122] Edvard's brother John Grieg. The overture to which Grieg refers is *In Autumn* (*I Høst*) op. 11. Grieg was under the mistaken impression that "Slaattevisen" ("Harvest Song") was a kind of mowing song, but in fact it is a Norwegian peasant dance (*springdans*) in 3/4 time. Called "Nordfjordingen", it was published by Carl Schart (d. 1883) in Bergen in 1865 in *VIII Norske Slaatter for Hardangerfele* (Eight Norwegian Peasant Dances for Hardanger fiddle). Grieg's confusion about the character of the piece is owing to the fact that the Norwegian word "slått" has two unrelated meanings: It can mean either "instrumental peasant dance" or "harvest".

[123] Giovanni Lorenzo Bernini (1598–1680), Italian architect. Sculptor and painter.

[124] Grieg uses the Danish word "Etatsraad", which was an honorary title of high rank given by the King to citizens having done much for the country.

for Holbech and for Molbeck; by Pastor Hansen for Wolfhagen; by Wolfhagen for all who continued to be the same, continued to do good work in their respective callings, with unflagging belief and hope in Scandinavia's cause; by Kjellberg for Jerichau;[125] by La Cour for Sonne, for Renton as a representative of the English nation, for . . .[126] The party ended at 12:30 AM in an exceptionally jovial mood.

March 16

Received from Kirchner one copy of *Humoresques* [op. 6] and one of the *Violin Sonata in F Major* [op. 8]. Visited Villa Doria-Pamfili with the Nielsen brothers. Magnificent, Mediterranean, opulent—especially the grounds, which stretched out boundlessly. The villa itself, on the other hand, cannot be compared to Villa Albano, no matter how beautiful its setting may be.

March 18

Spent the forenoon with Axel Prior at an exhibit of paintings by Roman artists at the Piazza del Popolo. Once again I was convinced in a sad way that Rome is the ruins of a vanished greatness, nothing more. One would think that here in the home of art, the cradle of the art of painting, something bearing a hint of greatness might be presented, but this was so pitiful, so wretched from beginning to end, that I don't remember having seen the likes of it in any backwater village. It is dangerous for a people to have a great past, whether it be in the political sphere or in art, for it leads either to what the Germans are currently sinking into—striving with all their might to hold themselves up, and with this striving producing nothing but artificial, grotesque, unnatural things—or, as here in Rome, to quite phlegmatically sitting back and resting on their laurels. One searches in vain here for the slightest effort to create something good, something solemn. The subjects are insignificant, petty, titillating, and the execution is slovenly, ragged, clumsy and unpolished. The same painstaking care that is lacking in the contemporary Italian musicians is totally lacking here as well, and where art is treated with such a total lack of respect, it seems to me that the longing of the people for freedom must also be wanting. Where people do not respect the laws of art they also do not respect the laws of the state, and political freedom must then lead to complete degeneration and downfall.

Spent the evening with Kjellberg at the Priors.

March 19

Wrote to Dr. Abraham[127] and to Kirchner. With Axel Prior in a church outside

---

[125] The individuals in this list who have not been previously identified are: Danish author Christian Molbech (1821–88); Danish landowner and politician Andreas E. M. Tang (1803–68); possibly Danish painter/sculptor Niels Holbech (1804–49); possibly Danish minister for Slesvig (until 1864) Friedrich Hermann Wolfhagen (1818–94); Swedish sculptor Johannes Fritiof Kjellberg (1836–85); Danish sculptor Jens Adolf Jerichau (1816–83).

[126] The elliptical dots are Grieg's.

[127] Max Abraham (1831–1900), director of C. F. Peters Musikverlag in Leipzig.

the city, San Lorenzo, which I did not find very interesting except for a row of beautiful Corinthian marble columns. The unique cemetery was all the more interesting in contrast, however. Here, in the first section, are 365 graves, one for each day of the year. Each day one body (not in a casket) is thrown into the appropriate grave and is covered with lime to accelerate decomposition. The grave is then carefully covered. The result is that the next year, when the grave is opened again, there is no trace of the person last buried there except for a few bones, which are placed in an urn and preserved in the family's burial plot. The cemetery itself is ugly: it is paved, so one does not see so much as a blade of grass, much less a flower.

Beyond this section of the cemetery stretches one of another kind that can be compared to some extent with what we are accustomed to seeing in Scandinavia. Here, at least, there is just one person in each grave, and each resting place is also marked by a little cross decorated with wilted flowers or a small lantern in which a candle is kept burning. But if one calls to mind the peaceful beauty of a Protestant Cemetery, the difference is striking, and one feels ill at ease among these barren, monotonous, unending rows.

On the return trip we stopped in at one of these typically Roman taverns where pigeons and chickens scamper between your legs—and where you are glad if you can escape before you get a sick stomach and a soiled coat.

March 20

Received an invitation from Munch to visit him on the 19th. The good man must be totally confused from sheer sadness and passion. When I called on him to beg his pardon for not turning up, he continued to insist with the greatest intrepidity that he had written the correct date on the invitation, and when I then showed it to him, he refused to be budged and steadfastly maintained his position despite almanacs and calendar.

Evening at the Priors. Met two Tang girls from Jutland, daughters of Councillor Tang. What was unique about them was that their eyes made one fear that they might be overcome by sleep at any moment, also that their voices were of such a character that despite their skirts etc. I didn't know for sure whether to regard them as boys or girls. In other respects they were as charming as all young girls.

Presented Dr. Renton with a paperweight as a token of gratitude for his many visits during my illness.

In the afternoon I heard a knock on my door, and in strode Dr. Hadler[128] from Hamburg, who very generously had left his wife in the carriage. That they are paying me a visit only out of a sense of duty or as a matter of form is perfectly clear from the fact that they have been in Rome for eight days (if not more)

---

[128] Dr. Hadler was married to Norwegian soprano Wibecke Meyer, who had sung four of Grieg's songs (op. 2) at his first public concert in Norway on May 31, 1862. Op. 2 was dedicated to her.

without letting me hear from them. That they didn't know my address is a flimsy excuse since the Scandinavian Society is here. Therefore, once I have made my return visit I will let them go their merry way, much as I would like to have spent some time with Wibecke M., the sweet girl, who was every bit as amiable and pretty as when I last saw her. There is no doubt that she would have looked me up right away if the decision had been up to her, just as she displayed as much pleasure upon seeing me as could be imagined in the presence of a jealous husband—but it wouldn't take much to convince me that the fellow is a jackass of a martinet. I got into their carriage and rode with them through the Via del Corso out to the Colosseum—a tour that under other circumstances certainly would have been indescribably interesting but which, despite all my efforts to enliven it, was utterly stiff and boring.

March 21

Afternoon: Concert by [Ettore] Pinelli at his home. The program was outstanding and the performance, for the most part, was successful. It started with a string quartet by Beethoven. It was long and unpopular, but it contained some wonderful passages. On the whole I don't like it. It lacks the architectonic perfection that distinguishes Beethoven's works from his best period. This quartet undoubtedly is one of the last ones. It was in five movements, and everything about it indicates that it dates from his stone-deaf period.[129]

Next came Schumann's piano quartet, in which Sgambati played the piano— and he performed his parts quite wretchedly. The same incessant striving for effect and outward show of the virtuoso that I have had occasion to criticize in his performance of a Beethoven Trio. Several times during the first and second movements I was ready to walk out on the whole thing, and it was nearly always due entirely to Sgambati. The violist was bad, the cellist superb.

Then came Chopin's *Fantasie in F Minor* performed by Sgambati. But such a performance I have never heard before. In the presence of this feat the world's foremost pianists can just as well call it quits, for both technically and with respect to interpretation it left absolutely nothing to be desired. The nobility in Chopin's work came into its own in the most beautiful way. Never before have I heard anyone bring Chopin's hidden Romanticism into the light of day as Sgambati did. The audience was also enthused and clapped him back for several curtain calls.

The program concluded with a Bach violin concerto with quintet accompaniment. It is a marvelous piece, one of the most inspired of the many brilliant works Bach has given us. It was excellently performed by Pinelli, who was also rewarded with a curtain call.

After the concert I talked with Countess Moltke[130] and her foster daughter,

---

129 The Beethoven quartet referred to must have been either op. 130 in B-flat Major or op. 132 in A Minor.
130 Possibly Danish Countess Caroline Moltke (1827–86).

Miss Brase, a sweet, lovable girl. Was also introduced to an Englishman by the name of Kennedy—one of these perfectly remarkable youths whom Heine[131] made the subject of a poem. He is wild about music—arranges for 8-hand performances of Liszt's Dante Symphony in his home, to which he invites a small group of selected guests. Since the man on one occasion had been impressed with my *Humoresques*, which were played by some lady at a party, I was also included among the lucky few chosen to share this pleasure. Unfortunately, the event occurred at the very time when I had to stay home due to illness, so I missed out on this comedy.

Had dinner and spent the evening at the Priors. Enjoyed playing whist with the wholesaler,[132] Axel P[rior], and Dr. Renton. As I walked home around 10:30 in the evening, a man came walking quickly toward me just as I was approaching my door. I had raised my umbrella in order to give a mortal blow to what I assumed was a bandit when the man spoke a few words to me in Danish, and it turned out that it was Ravnkilde. So we went down to the Propaganda Tavern together and sat talking about old times until midnight.

March 22

Received Ibsen's letter to John.[133]

March 23

Forenoon with Priors in the underground vaults of St. Peter's Basilica. They didn't really have anything interesting to offer: Pope after pope lay in sarcophaguses, each one looking just like the other. Some bas reliefs (biblical subjects) were equally lacking in real artistic importance. Thereafter to Palazzo Corsini, where we saw an attractive collection of paintings. Queen Christina of Sweden once lived in this palace. After breakfast we went to Palazzo Doria, where we looked casually through a large and important collection of paintings in which masters of the most varied art schools were represented.

March 24

In the evening I gave a concert at the Scandinavian Society. The program included the following pieces: 1) Sonata for piano and violin [in F Major] by me, which I played with [Ettore] Pinelli. 2) a) Aria by Bellini[134]; b) Aria from "Elisa" by Kuhlau,[135] sung by the sculptor Holbech. The latter was an absolute farce, for

---

[131] German poet Heinrich Heine (1797–1856).

[132] Grieg is obviously referring to wholesaler and shipowner Hans Peter Prior and his son Axel.

[133] Edvard's brother John Grieg. Edvard had put them in contact with each other regarding a possible translation into German of Ibsen's play *The Pretenders*. John later undertook the task with the help of his German-born wife Marie Ehrhardt (1845–1931).

[134] Italian composer Vinzenzo Bellini (1801–35).

[135] Opera *Elisa* (1820) by German-Danish composer Friedrich Kuhlau (1786–1832).

in spite of his fine voice the man is so thoroughly unmusical that it was a hopeless task for me to keep him in time. Suddenly he would be half a measure ahead of me, then half a measure behind—with me trying to follow him—so the whole affair took on more the character of playing tag than of performing art. We finally got through it, however, and the audience was delighted—and that, of course, is what counts! 3) Axel Prior and I then played some pieces in march form for piano four-hands, op. 18, by Niels W. Gade.[136] It went fine despite a bit of faking by Prior.

At this point the planned program was at an end, but the audience (ca. 60 people) was so much in the mood for more that they wouldn't leave me alone. They demanded that I play my *Humoresques*, which I haven't looked at for a long time. Naturally I winced at first, but that didn't help, so I decided that I might as well get it over with at once. I can't remember ever playing them so spontaneously and freshly. I loved them and felt happy with them. As I played, old memories were awakened, the whole situation gripped me. The thought that I was sitting here in Rome and making Scandinavian music for Scandinavians excited me, and that no doubt affected the performance.

Everyone present responded to both the *Sonata* and the *Humoresques* far more generously than I dared to hope. One after another came to me to express thanks and appreciation. I held the daintiest, silky-soft hands of lovable, young girls in mine; I felt so thankful. The truth is, this evening was one of the happiest of many happy evenings I have spent in Rome.

Introduced to Sgambati; that, unfortunately, had to be the end of it, as we have no common language. Said goodbye to the Priors. Conversation with Mrs. Ibsen.[137]

March 25

The Prior family left at 5 AM this morning. As I was going out in the morning I met La Cour, who gave me the terrible news that young David, son of the Danish finance minister, with whom we had been together at the concert last evening, had jumped out of a window in a fit of madness during the night. They found him lying in the street by the Via del Corso at 5 AM, dead. He was quite naked. He had fallen on his chest, from which blood was spattered all over the street. He also had a broken arm and his whole body was terribly mangled. It was an appalling experience. Such is life: In the evening cheerful and full of hope, in the morning—dead, and in the most frightening manner.

March 26

My silver tea-spoon has been stolen from my room as a result of the carelessness

---

[136] The Gade pieces referred to by Grieg are *Tre Karakterstykker* (Three Character Pieces) op. 18 (1848).

[137] Suzannah Ibsen (1836–1914), wife of playwright Henrik Ibsen.

of my fairy-like landlady, who always leaves the door open when she goes out with my breakfast dishes.

March 27

David was buried.

March 28

Sent letters to Father, Mother and Nina.

Afternoon with Mag. Edman in the Sistine Chapel, where one of the most heralded sacred festivals was to take place. So I took all my piety—or rather my mood—with me, but also all my expectation and curiosity. But it went with this as it has gone with everything else in Rome: Every time an event's great renown has led me to expect something excellent, I have been disappointed—and when I expected nothing at all, there I found the beautiful, the poetic.

To be sure, the enormous crowd of people made me doubtful right from the beginning, for rarely does one see an audience voluntarily come streaming in where true art in its greatness and beauty has its home. (NB, unless it is something fashionable.)

First, huffing and puffing, I and a crowd of other creatures stood at the entrance to the chapel like sardines in a barrel waiting endlessly as the excitement grew and grew. Finally I heard some four-part singing—quite pretty, albeit in the same genre as what I had heard previously in St. Peter's Basilica. This didn't last long, however, for it was supplanted by a plethora of lamentations and cantus firmus, i.e., alternating choir and solo singing *unisono*. No, one can't really call it choral singing. It was more like cockcrow. It went on like this for hours:

The droning on *G* was like the sound of a swarm of bees. People spoke all at once at least a score of syllables to each other on this one note, and *A* was forced out with an unnatural and ugly accent, just like it is with poultry—although there's a bit of humor among the poultry, whereas this was deadly boring.

Finally, after having been irritated by this "solemn ceremony" for over two hours, there was a momentary pause, and it is almost impossible to describe what a salutary effect this had on the nervous system and how I suddenly felt myself elevated from the world of hens to the realm of the sacred when, as if from on high, I heard the sound of a choir singing *pianissimo*. It was a "Miserere" by Baj[138] composed in 1714, and even if the composition had been ten times more boring

---

[138] Italian composer Tommasso Baj (1650–1714).

than it really was, it would have been refreshing after all the torture that preceded it. I heard some remarkably interesting things, though, especially when the two choirs came together with the one continuing to sing *pianissimo* above the other's *fortissimo*. Then the music was remarkably gripping, with an effect similar to that of an organ when one draws a flute stop or a fifth stop out in such a way that the highest note can be heard only as a faint echo of the lower principal tone. Such things are effective the first time, but with incessant repetition it, too, finally gets boring.

By the time I left I was numb and sluggish, utterly limp. The famous extinguishing of the candles seems to me much like when one sticks one's tongue out the window to see if it is raining: One conjures up such a mystical picture in imagination that one would have to be disappointed, even if it were far more gripping than it really is. For not only did it not grow dark in the chapel, but the sun, which to this point had held back, even played an amusing trick by sending its brightest beams through the windows at the very moment when the paraffin candles (13 of them) were extinguished. The effect was hilarious. The rays of the sun, in a single moment, destroyed the intended effect of the entire meaningless comedy.[139]

I bumped into the Wrangel family in the crowd as I was leaving, and I so completely forgot that it was a church festival that I had attended that I asked Mrs. Wrangel very innocently, "Wie haben Sie sich amüsiert?"[140]—whereupon her gentle countenance suddenly turned into that of the most disapproving prudish lady. Then I realized, of course, that I had committed a *faux pas*, but unfortunately it was too late.

The best part of the whole experience was seeing the fresh, warm, dark blue sky and drinking in big gulps of the intoxicating, lovely Mediterranean evening. An indescribable calm hovered over the Tiber; everything around me looked so handsome, the whole scene was so light, so transparent, so romantic.

March 29

Forenoon: went alone to St. Peter's Basilica. Inside the church I heard some sacred music by Palestrina. Outside, on the other hand, at 12 noon I saw the Pope, who stood on the balcony and held out his arms blessing the multitude, who with heads bared knelt in the dust before their deity. I, too, had to howl with the wolves. He sang something in Latin up there, and I heard him talk about

---

[139] Grieg's account is something of a caricature of the *Tenebrae*, a service in the Roman Catholic Church (sung only on Wednesday, Thursday and Friday of Holy Week) in which the crucifixion of Christ is commemorated with the progressive extinguishing of a series of candles. The service contains no songs of praise. The congregation sings a series of penitential hymns, and after each hymn one of the candles is extinguished. The intended result is increasing darkness, hence the name "tenebrae" ("darkness"). The concluding hymn, "Miserere", takes its name from the first word in the Latin text of Psalm 51. Many composers have set this text, one of the most famous settings being that of Gregorio Allegri (1584–1652) for 9 voices. See Grieg's diary entry for March 29.

[140] "How did you enjoy yourself?"

"omnibusser", "Domino", "stoler" or "apostoler"[141] and more of the same. The situation was not totally without effect, especially when all the bells started chiming and the canons roared.

At 4:30 in the afternoon went with Ravnkilde to the Sistine Chapel to hear the famous "Miserere" by Allegri, which was supposed to replace the boring lamentations at about this time. I knew the composition from the score, so I listened excitedly to the opening chord: Yes, it was in G Minor, so I felt sure that must be it. But who can describe my embarrassment when what followed was something else, and it became apparent that we had been cheated out of Allegri.

So, then, nothing came of it, but that evening I heard that the Allegri "Miserere" was sung later, after I in my vexation had run away. That's what I call a dirty trick, and the worst part is that it happened to me here, for one of the things that would have had the greatest significance for me would have been to hear this "Miserere", which I had thoroughly studied ahead of time so that I would be better able to note its effects.

March 30

After dinner, I took a walk with Mag. Edman to Villa Borghese, where we enjoyed the lovely fountain for which Raphael[142] had drawn the model. On the way home we wanted to shorten the trip by taking a side road, but we came to regret bitterly having done so, for it led outside the city wall. Thus, we had to go half way around Rome on this road, which has high, steep masonry walls on both sides, before we reached a gate through which we could at least get into the city.

Ibsen has written in my autograph album,[143] and also suggested that he write to Bjørnson and Dunker about not filling the music director position at the Christiania Theater.[144]

---

[141] Grieg is here playing with Norwegian words: "stoler" and "apostoler" mean "chairs" and "apostles" respectively.

[142] Italian painter Raphael (1483–1520).

[143] The little poem written in Grieg's autograph album was later included in Ibsen's *Collected Works* under the title, "I en komponists stambok" ("In a Composer's Album"). It reads as follows:

Til Edvard Grieg!	To Edvard Grieg!
Orpheus slog med Toner rene	Orpheus with his golden lyre
Sjæl i Vilddyr, Ild af Stene.	Soothed the beasts, set stones on fire.
Stene har vort Norden nok af;	Stones our homeland has no lack of;
Vilddyr har det og en Flok af.	Beasts it also has a pack of.
Spil saa Stenen sprucer Gnister;	Play so stones with sparks redound!
Spil saa Dyrehammen brister!	Play so meadows peal with sound!

[144] Bjørnstjerne Bjørnson was artistic director of the Christiania Theater at this time, Norwegian attorney and politician Bernhard Dunker (1809–70) was chairman of the board. Grieg had sought Ibsen's support of his candidacy for the position of musical director at the Theater. In the back of the diary Grieg also wrote a list of the conditions that he intended to stipulate if he were offered the position. See also Grieg's 1866 correspondence with Ibsen in Finn Benestad (ed.), *Edvard Grieg: Letters to Colleagues and Friends*, Columbus, Ohio 2000, pp. 438–441. Ibsen's support came too late to be of help to Grieg, however, as the position had already been given to Norwegian cellist and conductor Johan Hennum (1836–94).

March 31

Afternoon: Went home with Ravnkilde, who showed me his composition for solo voice, chorus and orchestra entitled "Skriftemaalet" ("The Confession"). It may well be that a completely different sound—and, as a consequence, a greater effect—would be present when the piece is heard in its entirety for the intended instruments and voices, but nonetheless the whole work strikes me as rather weak and ineffective. Certain it is that this genre is his weak point, whereas in chamber music he does his best work.

April 1

At 9 AM went with Thiele, La Cour, Sonne and Evens[145] to St. Peter's Basilica. I didn't get much out of Palestrina's "Tu es Petrus".[146] The large sanctuary swallowed up half of the sound and the crowd of people the other half. The church was almost completely filled.

At 12 noon the Pope, to the sound of bells and cannons, appeared on the balcony to give the blessing. The crowd was much larger, even, than on Maundy Thursday, and as a result the effect of the whole situation was more spectacular. At the moment when he stood up, stretched out his arms and in a loud voice pronounced the blessing upon the silent, enormous, kneeling multitude, I was gripped by a strange mood. A feeling came over me as if he had the authority from God, as if it really was a holy, reverent moment. But this thought soon disappeared, for he had barely finished before the crowd began enthusiastically to clap their hands and shout "viva!" as for a performing artist. And the Pope stood up and bowed in thanks for the ovation. It was an utterly unpleasant and annoying scene.

I do not remember ever having seen before such a crowded throng of people as I encountered on the return trip over the Ponte Sant'Angelo, not even at the illumination—the fireworks—on the Field of Mars[147] in Paris on August 15. For half an hour nobody could move. It was impossible to make any progress at all, and yet—this must be said to the credit of the Romans—everything went comparatively calmly.

We spent the evening at Ravnkilde's, and from his windows we viewed the marvelous illumination of St. Peter's Basilica. Such a thing I had never dreamt of. My imagination could never venture to create such a poetic, unreal, and

---

[145] Danish sculptor Otto Evens (1826–95).

[146] "Tu es Petrus" (Thou art Peter), motet for six voices by Italian composer Giovanni Peirluigi da Palestrina (1526–94).

[147] Grieg's mention of Paris probably refers to his visit there in the summer of 1862 with his father and his brother John. He witnessed the illumination on Champ de Mars, which in 1867 was to become the venue for the World Exhibition. In 1889 the Eiffel Tower was built on the Champ de Mars. The most famous Field of Mars—Campus Martius—is in Rome. It is a place outside the walls of the old city—between the Tiber, Monte Pincio, the Quirinal and the Capitoline Hill—that is dedicated to the ancient Roman god of war.

colossal picture. The whole church was a sea of fire; all the contours, right down to the tiniest details, could be seen with surprising clarity, even the cross above the dome. Therefore, it is no wonder that the man who is assigned to place the lamps up in this dizzying height always takes the sacrament of communion before he climbs up. But the thing about this that must not only astonish but outrage every thinking person is that people think they can please God by such audacious enterprises.

April 2

Letters from Father and Nina.

Afternoon with La Cour, Thiele, Kjellberg, Edman, Budal and Reinau in the Capitoline Art Museum, which I did not find especially uplifting. Later in the sculpture collection, where I again admired the singular authenticity with which "The Dying Swordsman" has been captured. "The Capitoline Doves", a handsome mosaic found in Hadrian's villa.

April 3

Big fireworks on Monte Pincio. The weather was not good: It blew and started to rain a little, but still the whole event went well. It was brilliant, at times absolutely magnificent, albeit far from equal to the Paris fireworks on August 15. La Cour made a drawing in my album.

April 4

Composed a song entitled "The Harp" to a text from Munch's "Sorg og Trøst" ("Sorrow and Consolation").

April 5

Composed "Cradle Song" [op. 9 no. 2] to a text from Munch's "Sorg og Trøst" ("Sorrow and Consolation").

April 6

Letter from Uncle Herman and his wife. Letter from Feddersen!

✝ The saddest news that could strike me—Nordraak is dead! He, my only friend, my only great hope for our Norwegian art! And I do not have a single person here who can truly understand my sorrow. Let me, then, flee to the tones that never fail in time of sorrow! Composed a Funeral March in honor of Nordraak!

April 7

With Dahl and Edman in Palazzo Sciarra, where I saw an outstanding collection of paintings. Bought photographs of the two most handsome ones: Raphael's "Violinist" and Titian's "Bella". Wrote a Trio for the Funeral March.

April 8

With Edman in Palazzo Farnesina. "Galatea" by Raphael: wonderfully beautiful, it is the complete Mozart in poetic fragrance, charm, and purity of style. It is a fresco, and the colors stand out as freshly as if they had been painted yesterday. Fresco landscapes by Poussin,[148] Psyche's story. Raphael's composition, completed by his successors, adorns the upper parts of the walls. Palazzo Braschi, handsome marble staircase.

Read in the Swedish *Aftonbladet* about Nordraak's death on March 20.

April 9

Had a visit from Munch. In the evening a concert by some Italians at the Scandinavian Society. Schumann's Quartet for piano and strings[149] played extremely roughly by Sgambati, [Ettore] Pinelli, Fiorino and [name omitted]. Still, Fiorino was an exception: He was the master on his cello, as always.

Thereafter came Chopin's "Fantasie" in F Minor,[150] which Sgambati performed just as marvelously as he had in the concert at Pinelli's. Then Tartini's *Violin Sonata*, excellently played by Pinelli (and Sgambati). Lastly the same duo played the wonderful "Rondo" in B Minor by Schubert.[151]

After all this, Ibsen—who had drunk a few Fogliettes that had gone to his head—got the idea that we ought to dance. He then proceeded to get the table and chairs cleared out of the way and urged Ravnkilde (!) to strike up a tune. When Ravnkilde, naturally enough, declined to do as he was asked, Ibsen got so angry that he took his hat and cane and stalked off. He is accustomed, when we are alone, to having us obey his command, "Strike up a tune, you fellows!" By this "strike up a tune" he means music of any kind whatsoever, and he cannot understand how an artist can care about what kind of music it is. It is remarkable that such a great man can be so tactless and, in one specific area, so limited. Just as if we were to ask Ibsen to recite some verses by Erik Bøgh,[152] we would hear an indignant outcry. No, it is a fact: First of all an artist must maintain his own dignity, for only then does the public learn to do so. If he relinquishes that, no matter how splendidly he performs, the crowd will not recognize him for what he is.

(Nordraak obituary in *Morgenbladet*.[153])

April 10

Morning: trip with Edman to Monte Cavallo, where we saw the lovely Greek horses, also took a peek at the Quirinal gardens. Afternoon in the Vatican art collection. Raphael's "Ascension" and Madonna Foligni.

---

[148] French painter Nicolas Poussin (1593–1665).
[149] *Quartet* for piano, violin, viola and cello op. 47 in E-flat Major (1842) by Robert Schumann (1810–56).
[150] *Fantasie in F Minor* op. 49 (1841) by Frédéric Chopin (1810–49).
[151] *Rondo in B Minor* ("Rondo brillant") D 895 (1826) by Franz Schubert (1797–1828).
[152] Danish writer of light verse Erik Bøgh (1822–99).
[153] A Christiania newspaper.

April 11

10 AM departure with Edman for Naples, where we arrived at about 5:30. Strolled in the Toledo. A marvelous city, with bustling activity—the greatest possible contrast to Rome.

April 12

In "Museo nazionale" we viewed a collection of marble sculpture the likes of which I have never seen. As far as I am concerned, if you will give me this you can have the whole Vatican. Saw a moving scene from Pompeii, namely solidified ashes containing the imprinted form of a beautiful female breast.

Afternoon: took a trip by carriage through Via "Victor Emanuele", the most beautiful street I have seen. It is beautifully situated along the shore.

April 13

Took an incomparably enjoyable and interesting trip by coach with Munchs and Sverdrups to Pompeii. The weather was exceedingly beautiful. We had our dinner out there among the ruins under a clear sky. Blistering hot, naturally. When I began to think about where I really was, an utterly strange mood came over me. After returning home we had our evening meal in Café Suisse. Sverdrup toasted Nina in "Lacryma christi", a wine that I drink enough of each day to make me happy and in a good mood.

April 14

Trip with Edman to Capri. After we were safely on board I got a pleasant surprise when I heard that we were on wholesaler Prior's former ship "Falken" ("The Falcon"), now named "Giovanni da Procida".[154] It was outfitted comfortably enough, but it rolled so wildly that despite the most splendid weather I was a bit out of sorts on the whole trip—although my condition never reached the stage of what one would call seasickness.

The steamer stopped outside the famous Blue Grotto. Here, in the genuinely Italian impractical style, we had to first climb down into one boat, and then, in the middle of the sea, step over into a rather small one. This was especially difficult for the poor ladies, among whom there was a wonderfully captivating little Russian. I wished I had been a sculptor, though the fact is that I drank in the beautiful female forms in all their voluptuousness as if I were a sculptor. She came into our boat, and when we were to go through the small opening leading into the grotto, and the command "a terra" ["heads down"] was given, the sweet little Russian lady, so as not to be crushed, had to obey the order and clung tightly— half afraid, half bashful—to me.

---

[154] Hans Peter Prior had taken the little steamer from Denmark to Italy to sell it. Before it was sold, Prior's sons Axel and Oscar and three of their friends had used it for a cruise on the Mediterranean.

One stroke of the oars and, with the help of a wave, we were in the grotto. It is pretty and unique, but it certainly does not deserve its great renown. After having read [Hans Christian] Andersen's "Improvisatoren" ["The Improviser"] one would inevitably have formed such a supernatural, ethereal picture of it that one would have to be disappointed upon seeing it.

The color of the water is remarkable—transparent blue, and brilliant. If you put your hand down, it looks as if it is covered with silver. This color is, of course, a reflection of the rocks that arch over the cave, but it is not so pronounced but that one can see very well that what one has overhead is ordinary rocks.

I might have gotten a more favorable impression if the mood inside the cave had been more appropriate to the situation—if, for example, in addition to me there had been at most two people, silent and devout. In fact, however, the cave was full of boats, and the boats were full of people who were yelling, screaming, hollering, and clapping their hands, so any thought of a solemn moment had to be abandoned.

So out we went, repeated the boat-switching nonsense to get back on board, then endured the swindling of the Italian rascals who had transported us to and from, and with that we had seen the Blue Grotto. No, I certainly never imagined that the trip would be as utterly prosaic as it proved to be—so much so that I can hardly claim to have seen the grotto, for something of which I have gotten no impression I have not really seen. The entrance was mystical, allowing one to imagine all sorts of things. The dark sea lay so calm, the cliffs jutted up so abruptly, and the opening was so strangely silent and eerie. But with the young girls giggling in the boats as we passed it, every trace of eeriness quickly vanished.

Thereafter the steamer continued to the town of Capri, where we went ashore and had our noon meal. The hotel where we ate was high up between the peaks, from which vantage point we enjoyed the most enchanting view out over the Mediterranean to Naples in the distance. What a strange similarity there was between this view and the one I enjoyed in long stretches each day last summer at Rungsted.[155] The sea is the same everywhere, and the island "Hveen" on which one rested one's eyes up there is replaced here by Vesuvius, which thrust its light blue top skyward in the distance.

At 3 PM it was already time to leave again. The ship blew its whistle and off we steamed to Sorrento. We didn't get to enjoy this pretty little speck of a town nearly long enough, but we did see the setting, which is paradisiacally beautiful and fully worthy of its great renown. Barren cliffs thrust straight up from the sea, and high above lies the town, beyond which an endless forest of orange, fig and olive trees stretches all the way to the top of the hill. Home at 7:30.

---

[155] Rungsted is a coastal village a few miles north of Copenhagen, Denmark.

April 15

When I awoke the rain was splashing down. Outside the door beneath the open sky stood my boots, which it had pleased the caretaker to forget to take care of. Thus I picked them up in a "beautiful" condition, and all day long I had to tramp around in the filthy city in these heavy beasts. It was a sad story.

The only place where I really felt good was in "Museum nazionale", where I admired the enormous collection of beautiful and valuable things. Everything found at Pompeii and Herculaneum is preserved here: statues and groups in marble and bronze, the most marvelous things—kitchen utensils, weapons, artifacts—in short, everything that had belonged to the people of long ago. One can never tire of walking among these treasures. What I had to admire most of all was their handwritten documents in rolls, which time has carbonized and quite simply petrified. Thus one sees these rolls lying there like fixed masses of matter, like stones. An Italian has now discovered a chemical process to soften the crust so that the whole document can be unwound. Thus the whole work can be spread out before you. In truth, it takes more than cleverness to figure out something like that: it takes enormous brilliance.

April 16

Forenoon: drove around to the estimable consuls to get my passport stamped. Consul Dankertsen[156] seemed to be a splendid fellow. After dinner a carriage tour over Vomero and Belvedere to the Posillipo Grotto and Virgil's grave. Marvelous views over the Mediterranean and the blue islands in the distance.

April 17

10 AM departure for Rome. Arrived at 6 PM.

April 18

Letters from Father, Nina and Kirchner (150 *Thalers*). Farewell visit with Ravnkilde at Wrangels.

April 19

Made a fair copy of the *Funeral March*. Wrote to Kirchner. To Ravnkilde. 6:30 in the evening: Departed from Rome with Thiele and Evens for Civitavecchia, where we spent the night in Hotel de l'Europe.

April 20

Morning departure for Nunziatella by stagecoach, from there by train to Florence, arriving at midnight. Took lodging at Hotel de la Ville.

---

[156] Swedish-Norwegian consul in Sorrento.

April 21

Forenoon in Palazzo Uffizi and Pitti. Lovely art collections. Cathedral in Renaissance style, wonderfully beautiful. Departed at 10 PM for Milan.

April 22

Arrived Milan at 8 AM. Took lodging at Hotel Tre Svizzeri. Sent a letter to Father and Mother. Took a trip to the cathedral tower, from where one gets a marvelous view of Switzerland. The Alps lay so white and shining in the sun. Ate a marvelous dinner at the hotel.

April 23

Departure by train to Cameslata, then by carriage to Como, then by steamship across the lovely Lago di Como to Colico, arriving at 6 PM. Since the stagecoach was not to leave until 10, we had an opportunity to look around a bit in the beautiful surroundings. Departed by stagecoach over Splügen to Chur. Definitely the most extraordinary trip I have taken thus far.

After we had driven a few miles up into the Alps, we were at such an altitude that we were in snow. Thus we had to leave the omnibus and take a sled over the Alps. This was the most memorable part of the trip. We went higher and higher through almost impassable roads and dark tunnels. The drifts became ever deeper until at last we could see nothing but an enormous carpet of snow. It was a remarkable sight.

It was a dangerous business, however, especially when we started down the frightfully steep slopes after passing the Splügenpass. Despite field boots and blankets, it had been so cold up there that one got as stiff as a stone from the frost. We began to warm up as we went downward, and that in a quite peculiar way: The sled whipped from side to side as it sped down, bouncing here and there, so you sat in constant fear of being smashed to pieces. One moment the sled was balancing on one side, the next moment on the other side, and it rumbled over the chunks of ice and snow, so one had plenty to do other than sit there and freeze. On the contrary, one sat in such terror that the sweat gushed out from every pore. Still, the situation was interesting. The memory of it is wonderful, and I would not have missed it for anything.

April 24

Arrived at Chur at 5 PM. Left at 6 by train for Rorschach, where we spent the night.

April 25

11 AM went by steamship across the lovely Bodensee to Lindau. From there by train to Augsburg, then to Nuremberg (arriving at night at 1 am), where I parted from Evens. Without stopping here I continued on

April 26

to Hof, then took a trip to Leipzig, where I arrived at 5:30 PM and took lodging at Stadt Wien. Then I dashed over to the Conservatory to see and talk at once with my old acquaintances. The first one I met was Wenzel,[157] who came running down from the upper floor.

"Wo kommen Sie her?"

"Aus Rom."

"Ach! Sie haben gut reden, ich komme oben aus No. 5!"[158]

I tried to convince him that he shouldn't fret over it, that the time would certainly come when I would be coming from a Room No. 5, that he had also been young once and traveled around, and this seemed to make him quite content. I took a walk down the street with him; he was the same splendid fellow as before. Evening at the Kirchners.

April 27–30

In Leipzig. Visited Schleinitz.[159]

May 1

Visited Reinecke.[160] Attended a *Prüfung* at the Gewandhaus. Good performances.

May 2

Sent a letter to Uncle Herman Hagerup. Ditto to Bjørnson.

May 3

1 PM left for Berlin with the pianist Leipholz. Took lodging at Hotel Americain.

May 4

Afternoon: Visited Nordraak's grave. Jerusalem Kirchhof (entrance from Bergmannstrasse No. 5), ninth circuit.[161]

---

[157] German pianist and teacher Ernst Ferdinand Wenzel (1808–80) had been one of Grieg's instructors at the Leipzig Conservatory.

[158] "Where are you coming from?"

"From Rome."

"Oh! That's fine for you. I came down from Room No. 5!"

[159] Conrad Schleinitz (1802–81), Director of the Conservatory.

[160] German composer and conductor Carl Reinecke (1824–1910) had been Grieg's composition teacher in Leipzig. The "Prüfungen" (public examination concerts) at the Conservatory were open to the public and usually were held in the large auditorium of the Gewandhaus. Grieg had had the pleasure of playing some of his piano compositions at such a concert as he was about to graduate from the Conservatory in 1862.

[161] Rikard Nordraak had been buried just a month earlier. On May 7, Grieg sent a long, beautiful letter to the grieving father in which he tried to explain why, contrary to his explicit promise, he had left his dying friend alone in Berlin and proceeded on to Italy without him. See Finn Benestad (ed.), *Edvard Grieg: Letters to Colleagues and Friends*, Columbus, Ohio 2000, pp. 552–553.

May 5

Evening at the opera house. Saw "A Midsummer Night's Dream" by Shakespeare with Mendelssohn's lovely music.[162]

May 6

At Wallner's Theater, saw a boring farce called *Die Liebhabereien*.

May 7

Wrote to old Nordraach[163] in Christiania.

May 8

Bought Berlioz's book on instrumentation.[164] In the same store I asked about my *Humoresques* and was told that it was completely sold out. The man said that the composer had so many friends in Berlin who were interested in him! An amusing situation, for I didn't tell him who I was.

May 9

7 AM visited by the Polish Mr. Herz. 7:30 departed Berlin for Lübeck, arriving at 4 PM. 6 PM departed by steamship for Korsør.[165] After a so-so voyage, stepped on Danish ground at 5 AM the following morning.

May 10

7 AM train to Copenhagen. Arrived at 10 AM in the same miserable weather as when I left last autumn.

May 12

Rented lodging at No. 11 Gasveien, first floor.

May 13

Nina's arrival from Bergen. Wrote to Kirchner.

May 15

Rented a piano. Organ lesson 1.[166]

---

[162] Felix Mendelssohn (1809–47) completed his incidental music for *A Midsummer Night's Dream* op. 61 in 1842 to the play by William Shakespeare (1564–1616). The overture was already written in 1826 as op. 21.

[163] Georg Marcus Nordraach (1811–90), father of Rikard Nordraak. Rikard had changed the spelling of his name in order to "Norwegianize" it.

[164] *Grand traité d'instrumentation et d'orchestration modernes* by French composer Hector Berlioz (1803–69) was first published in 1843.

[165] Korsør is a seaport on the west coast of Zealand, Denmark.

[166] Grieg was concerned about how he was going to make a living, so he decided to take organ lessons from his Danish friend Gottfred Matthison-Hansen. If he failed in his attempt to get the position of Music Director at the Christiania Theater, he reasoned, perhaps he could at least get a job as a church organist!

May 16

Sent a letter home.

May 18

Organ lesson 2. Visited the Priors.

May 21

With Nina at the Priors.

May 22

Took the Overture ["In Autumn" op. 11] to Gade. Gave him copies of opp. 6 [*Humoresques*], 7 [*Piano Sonata*] and 8 [*Violin Sonata No. 1* in F Major].

May 23

Evening with old Horneman[167] in the beer hall on Østergade.

May 24

Letter from Father.

May 25

Organ Lesson 3.

May 29

Organ Lesson 4.

June 1

Organ Lesson 5.

June 3

With Nina at the Hornemans in Fredensborg.

June 4

Sick.

June 5

Ditto.

He took a total of 15 lessons. His biggest challenge came when he played Bach's Fugue in G Minor for his friend's father, the famous cathedral organist in Roskilde, Hans Matthison-Hansen. He met the challenge with flying colors.

[167] Danish music publisher Johan Ole Emil Horneman (1809–70), father of Grieg's friend Chr. F. Emil Horneman.

June 8

Organ Lesson 6.

June 9

Letter from Father. (100 *spesidalers*)

June 10

Sent a letter to Ibsen.[168]

June 11

Visited [Andreas] Munch, No. 13 Overgaden by the water, second floor, also land-scape painter Læssøe.[169] Paid Gehrke the tailor 12 *riksdalers* for pants and vest.

June 12

Organ Lesson 7.

June 15

Organ Lesson 8.

June 16

Telegram from Father on the occasion of my birthday.[170]

June 19

Organ Lesson 9.

June 20

Wrote to Tonny. Wrote to Father and Yelva.[171]

June 22

Organ Lesson 10.

June 26

Organ Lesson 11. (Paid 10 *riksdalers*)

June 29

Organ Lesson 12.

---

[168] Grieg's correspondence with Henrik Ibsen is printed in English translation in Finn Benestad (ed.), *Edvard Grieg: Letters to Colleagues and Friends*, Columbus, Ohio 2000, pp. 438–450. The June 10 letter (pp. 438–440) deals with Grieg's attempt to secure the position of Music Director at the Christiania Theater.

[169] Danish painter Torald Læssøe (1816–78).

[170] Grieg was born on June 15, 1843.

[171] Tonny Hagerup (1844–1939) and Yelva Hagerup (1847–86) were Nina's sisters.

July 1

With Nina in Rungsted, Hirschholm and Holte.

July 3

Organ Lesson 13.

July 10

Organ Lesson 14.

July 13

Organ Lesson 15.

July 16

Letter from Father.

July 18

Sent a letter home.

July 25

Concert in Tivoli at 1 PM to raise money for the survivors of the fire in Drammen. Net income 242 *riksdalers.*[172]

August 6

Letter from Father.

August 14

Sent a letter home! Ditto to Fries, to Feddersen, to Nina!, to Uncle Herman Hagerup.

August 28

Sent letters to Ravnkilde, Svendsen,[173] Bürgel.[174]

---

[172] Grieg wrote to Ravnkilde that at this concert he had played the piano part of his *Violin Sonata No. 1 in F Major* to the great delight of the audience, but he confessed that he "couldn't really understand how farmers suddenly acquired the ability to comprehend cucumber salad."

[173] Norwegian composer and conductor Johan Svendsen (1840–1911).

[174] German composer and piano teacher Constantin Bürgel (1837–1909), presumably a friend from Grieg's Leipzig period 1858–62.

The Diary of 1865–66 ends abruptly at this point. In the back of the book are many miscellaneous entries: prices of goods and trips, columns of figures showing how money was spent, a long list of names and addresses. Grieg also used these pages to write rough drafts of material entered later under the appropriate dates in the diary.

Grant Applications and Related Documents (1862–78)

During the early years of his career, Grieg sent a number of letters to the Ministry of Church and Education in connection with applications for grants of various kinds. Three of them were addressed to the King (nos. 1, 2 and 7), two to the Royal Ministry of Church and Education (nos. 3 and 5), one to the Norwegian Parliament, *Stortinget* (no. 4). After being passed over for a grant in 1877, despite the unanimous support of the committee considering the matter, Grieg wrote directly to the Minister of Church and Education (no. 6), requesting an explanation of the reason for the denial of his application.

Grieg's applications are preserved in the National Archive of Norway, Oslo.

1

Bergen, July 12, 1862

To His Majesty the King:

Edvard Hagerup Grieg humbly requests that he be graciously awarded a grant in order, through travels abroad, to further prepare himself as a composer.

As may be graciously observed in the accompanying testimonials,[1] I have lived in Leipzig for three and a half years[2] and, as a student at the Conservatory there, have sought to prepare myself to become a composer.

I trust that I will not be considered immodest if I humbly venture the hope that these testimonials will verify that I possess such an aptitude for composition and piano playing—and at the conservatory made such progress and received such training—that I should perhaps yield to the hope that with further study I might achieve results that could be of importance, not only for me but also for music in my native land, where it is my intention to remain.

It would be highly desirable for me if, while I am still young, I could have an opportunity to visit some of the larger cities abroad where the cultivation and practice of music are most advanced. But I do not have the means for this, and

---

[1] In addition to the official testimonial from the Leipzig Conservatory, Grieg could also enclose special letters of recommendation from two of his teachers, Moritz Hauptmann (1792–1862) and Carl Reinecke (1824–1910). Both letters are preserved in Bergen Public Library.

    Hauptmann's letter of recommendation, dated February 2, 1862, reads as follows in English translation: "Mr. Grieg from Bergen, a student at the Conservatory in this city, who has distinguished himself as an excellent pianist, also is among the best students of composition, both theoretically and practically. His happy talent has always found backing in an exemplary diligence and love of study. He has therefore acquired a respectable degree of learning, and his prospects of making the greatest of successes are evident."

    Reinecke's letter of recommendation, dated April 20, 1862, reads as follows in English translation: "It is my pleasure to testify hereby that Mr. Edvard Grieg has a remarkable musical talent, particularly for composition, and that it would be highly desirable that he be given an opportunity to develop his talent as fully as possible in all directions."

[2] Grieg entered the Leipzig Music Conservatory on October 6, 1858, and the final examination concert took place at the Gewandhaus on April 12, 1862. In the spring of 1860, he contracted pneumonia and had to return to Bergen, where he stayed until autumn. Then he returned to Leipzig to continue his studies.

my father—Alexander Grieg,[3] the British Vice-consul here in Bergen—also does not consider himself able to offer me the assistance necessary for this purpose.

I can also tell Your Majesty that I am nineteen years of age. I take the liberty, therefore, for the reason stated above, humbly to petition Your Majesty graciously to grant me a stipend out of public funds so that I may go abroad to further prepare myself in that art to which I have devoted myself, and to which my soul's entire interest is bound.[4]

> Humbly,
> EDVARD HAGERUP GRIEG

2

Christiania, January 10, 1869

To the King:

Edvard Hagerup Grieg humbly requests that he be awarded a grant in order, by means of an extended stay abroad, to continue his studies as a composer. As may be graciously observed in the enclosed testimonials[5] written in the German language, in my childhood I spent three and a half years in Leipzig and began my musical studies at the Conservatory there. When my health broke down because of the climate, I was obliged to come home to try to regain my strength, after which I continued my studies in Copenhagen. At that time (1863) my father, who is British Vice- consul in Bergen, announced that he could no longer contribute the support needed for my studies, but he nonetheless gave me a loan in the confident hope that the royal grant which I humbly sought at that time would not be denied to me. After thus having embarked on a trip primarily for the sake of my health, I shortly thereafter received the disheartening news that my application for the royal grant had been turned down.

After returning to Norway, I spent a short time in my home city, Bergen, and thereafter settled in Christiania, where since the autumn of 1866 I have worked continuously in the service of our national music, partly as a composer and conductor, partly as a music teacher. This latter activity unfortunately has impaired my spirit to a considerable extent, but I have had to resort to it in order to support myself and my family (I have been married since June, 1867).[6] It is, therefore, my highest desire, by means of a stay abroad, to win time and quiet for creative work as well as an opportunity, through association with art and artists, to rejuvenate

---

[3] Grieg's parents were Alexander Grieg (1806–75) and Gesine Grieg, nee Hagerup (1814–75).

[4] Grieg did not receive the grant he was seeking on this occasion.

[5] The testimonials referred to by Grieg are most likely the two letters of recommendation from Moritz Hauptmann and Carl Reinecke. See footnote 1.

[6] Grieg was married to his cousin Nina Hagerup (1845–1935) on June 11, 1867, in Copenhagen. Their only child, Alexandra, born in 1868, was still living at the time this letter was written. She died from meningitis on May 21, 1869.

my mind and broaden my view of the ideal, which, under the circumstances in which I am living, can only become narrower.

In addition to the aforementioned testimonials from the Leipzig conservatory, I enclose four recent letters: from Abbé Dr. Franz Liszt[7] and professors N. W. Gade,[8] J. P. E. Hartmann[9] and I. Moscheles,[10] to which I humbly request that attention be principally directed since these will more clearly indicate my present standpoint.

Since I unfortunately do not have the means to enable my wife to remain in Norway, in the event of a trip abroad she will accompany me. I mention this so that the motivation for the size of the amount for which I am humbly applying will not be misunderstood.

My activity here in the city will be well known. Thus, in addition to noting

---

[7] The letter of recommendation from Franz Liszt (1811–86), written in French and dated Rome, December 29, 1868, is preserved in Bergen Public Library. It reads as follows in English translation:

> Monsieur:
> It is with the greatest pleasure that I express to you the sincere joy that I felt upon reading through your sonata, opus 8.
> The sonata bears witness to a great talent for composition and shows a well-conceived, inventive and excellent treatment of the material; it demonstrates a talent that needs only to follow its natural bent in order to attain to a high level. I hope and trust that in your homeland you will receive the success and the encouragement that you deserve; surely that is not asking too much. If you should come to Germany this winter, I cordially invite you to make a visit to Weimar so that we could meet.
> Receive, monsieur, the assurance of my deepest regard.
> FRANZ LISZT

[8] The letter of recommendation from Danish composer Niels W. Gade (1817–90), dated Copenhagen in December, 1868, is preserved in Bergen Public Library. It reads as follows in English translation:

> During Mr. Grieg's stay in Copenhagen I have had an opportunity to see some of his compositions, which interested me in a high degree because they bear witness to a rare gift and an important talent for composition.
> He is still in process of learning as a composer, and I would wish for him that he might be put in a position to continue his work in peace and finish his studies with an extensive stay at a place where there are opportunities to hear much music, for instance in Berlin or Vienna.
> It is a special pleasure for me to give Mr. Grieg this recommendation, and I would be pleased if it could contribute to the fulfillment of his wish.

[9] The letter of recommendation from Danish composer Johan Peter Emilius Hartmann (1805–1900), dated Copenhagen, November 23, 1868, is preserved in Bergen Public Library. It reads as follows in English translation:

> The undersigned is familiar with compositions by Mr. Edvard Grieg in various genres. All of them bear witness to an exceptional and sharply individualized musical gift of invention and also to a deep feeling and desire to compose. Even though Mr. Grieg's musical knowledge is already far advanced, there is no doubt that a stay abroad at his present stage of development would be extremely useful to him, both as a means to expand his knowledge and to reinforce and refresh his spirit and his gift of invention.
> Mr. Grieg's compositions have won for him many friends among us. If his talent is protected and encouraged, he will no doubt assert for himself a prominent place in Norway among the most gifted composers in the country. It is, therefore, a great pleasure for me to recommend him for any public support and encouragement by which this goal can be reached.

[10] The letter of recommendation from Grieg's piano teacher in Leipzig, Austrian pianist and composer Ignaz Moscheles (1794–1870), has not been located.

Grieg ca. 1870

that I am twenty-five years of age, I shall take the liberty in accordance with the above-mentioned information of humbly requesting of Your Majesty that out of public funds the sum of 500 *spesidalers*[11] be graciously granted to me so that, through an extended stay abroad, I can devote myself entirely to the art to which I have dedicated my life.[12]

Humbly,
Edvard Grieg

---

[11] One *spesidaler* was equivalent to approximately one American dollar.
[12] This time Grieg received the scholarship for which he was applying.

3

Christiania, September, 1870

To the Royal Ministry of Church and Education:

In accordance with the directive given to me by the Office of the Ministry of Church and Education, I shall take the liberty of reporting the following concerning my stay abroad from autumn, 1869, to summer, 1870, which stay was made possible by the royal grant.

When I left home in September, 1869, my first destination was Copenhagen, where it was important to me to get my more recent compositions performed. I succeeded in doing so, thanks to the singular kindness and consideration of Danish and Norwegian performing artists as well as the Danish Student Association. With the support of these people, as well as a large orchestra, I gave a matinee concert for an invited audience in the Casino auditorium, and later a public concert in the same place. The artistic results of these performances have given me a foothold in Denmark that will be productive for my creative work and for my artistic career in general.[13]

After these concerts, I remained in Copenhagen for a while, partly to secure the quiet to complete compositions already under way, partly to make preparations for the publication of my art songs and folk songs that came out at Christmas time.[14]

In November, I went to Italy by way of Germany. Since it was my intention to be in Rome for Christmas Eve, I was not able to spend much time in Germany —which seemed unnecessary to me as well, since from previous extended stays in this country I have had sufficient opportunities to get acquainted with German music life. Nonetheless, en route through Germany I was fortunate enough to gain many wonderful impressions. Thus, for example, I heard several outstanding operas in Berlin and Vienna, and in Leipzig some concerts of the highest quality.

On December 22, after short visits in Florence and Venice, I came to Rome, where I spent the winter months. Life here filled me with an endless series of impressions that it would be impossible for me to try to describe. In Rome I discovered what I needed: not a distinctive music life, for I would not have had either the physical or the mental strength to participate in such, but the opportunity to concentrate on myself and the greatness around me, the daily influences of a world of beauty.

---

[13] Grieg gave two concerts in Copenhagen during this visit: a chamber-music concert on October 3 and an orchestral concert on October 9, 1869. At the latter concert, the Norwegian pianist Edmund Neupert played the *Piano Concerto in A Minor*, op. 16, which he had premiered in the Danish capital on April 3 of the same year.

[14] The "compositions already under way" presumably were *Pictures from Folk Life* op. 19, first published in 1872. The compositions published in 1869 were *Twenty-five Norwegian Folk Songs and Dances* op. 17 and *Nine Songs* op. 18.

It is of the greatest importance for a Scandinavian musician who has received his elementary training in Germany to later spend some time in Italy, for in so doing he can clarify his ideas and purge them of that one-sidedness that only results in further concentration on German things. The national character of a Northerner contains so much that is heavy and introspective, which in all truth cannot be counterbalanced by an exclusive study of German art. In order to serve national interests, we need mental balance, a spiritual vitality that can be acquired only by discovering what can be learned in southern Europe. A freer and more comprehensive view of the world, and of the arts in their fullness, develops down here. Thus, I consider it my duty to recommend most warmly to younger artists who have mastered the technical side of their art that they spend some time in Italy. In addition to the influence of the natural surroundings, the life of the people and the pictorial arts, I must emphasize the benefit of association with Nordic artists whom one encounters at the Scandinavian Society in Rome.

But what for me personally has been of the greatest importance is my acquaintance and association with Franz Liszt, who was staying in Rome at that time. In him I have gotten to know not only the most brilliant of piano players but, what is more, a phenomenon—intellectually and in stature—unmatched in the sphere of art. I brought him several of my compositions, which he played; and it was of supreme interest for me to observe how the national element in my work at first made him hesitant, but then enthusiastic. A triumph of this kind for my efforts and my views on the national element is itself worth the journey.[15]

In May, 1870, after having observed southern Europe's spring in the Naples region, I returned to Denmark in search of peace and quiet in which to work, for on the trip itself, and during the stay in Italy, the impressions were so numerous and overpowering that the one, so to speak, destroyed the other the moment it occurred. The result is that while I indeed made a number of sketches and wrote several small lyric pieces,[16] I have not had the tranquility required to immerse myself in the larger forms. I have a wealth of material in my memory, however, and this must presumably be the most important point. If, in addition, I succeed in implanting at home a little of the confidence and belief in the future of our art which the trip has reawakened in me, then I am sure that the esteemed Ministry will, like me, see the significance of the trip for me and, through me, for the art of our homeland.

EDVARD GRIEG

---

[15] Regarding Grieg's meetings with Franz Liszt (1811–86), see Grieg's letters to his parents Alexander (1806–75) and Gesine (1814–75) Grieg in Finn Benestad (ed.), *Edvard Grieg: Letters to Colleagues and Friends*, Columbus, Ohio 2000, pp. 271–278.

[16] Grieg wrote ten volumes of *Lyric Pieces*, the first of which, op. 12, was published in 1867, the second, op. 38, in 1884. Any specific lyric piece dating from 1869–70 is not known.

4

To the Norwegian Parliament:
The undersigned hereby apply for an annual public grant of 400 *spesidalers* each in order thereby to be enabled to dedicate themselves to their work as composers.

Since our economic circumstances compel us to spend nearly all our time in routine teaching, which totally destroys the creative power that we feel is necessary to proceed successfully on the path that we have chosen, we venture to submit the above request.

We would not fail to call your attention to the stature of musicians in foreign countries. In the biggest countries artistic activities abound: There are sinecures, positions for artistic consultants under a wide variety of forms and titles, all of which exist exclusively to give creative talents an opportunity to develop and thereby enrich their country. But in the smaller countries, with which the comparison in our case perhaps is most appropriate—and restricting ourselves to Scandinavia, and especially Denmark—all the outstanding creative musicians have public annual grants. We would especially stress that such an arrangement must appear even more necessary here in our developing artistic environment, where we still have none of the institutions that in foreign countries have a stimulating effect on the creative artist's imagination; for we lack the fundamental support that is to be found in a national opera with an orchestra and a chorus corresponding to the requirements of art and of our time.

Lastly, we venture to call attention to the fact that we, so far as we have been able, have worked for the advancement of our art here in Norway, and with respect to the actual circumstances of our lives we refer to the enclosed biographical summaries.[17]

JOHAN SVENDSEN
EDVARD GRIEG[18]

5

To the Office of the Royal Norwegian Ministry of Church and Education:
I humbly take the liberty of applying for a grant of 500 *spesidalers* to enable me to dedicate myself to the study of dramatic music during a stay abroad.

Since the [annual] state grant of 400 *spesidalers* which I receive from the

---

[17] Thanks not least to the energetic support of Norwegian author Bjørnstjerne Bjørnson (1832–1910) and the President of the Norwegian Parliament, Johan Sverdrup (1816–92), Grieg and Johan Svendsen (1840–1911) both received grants of 400 *spesidalers* (about $400) per year—a substantial sum in those days.

[18] The letter is signed by both Grieg and Svendsen, but the body of the letter is in Grieg's hand and certainly was composed by him.

Norwegian Parliament will be totally insufficient to enable me to realize the afore-mentioned plan, and if, at the same time, I am to devote myself to creative work in the dramatic field, and since I am aware that several of the scientists who receive state grants have taken journeys abroad with the assistance of public funds, I do not hesitate to ask that I be considered when the above-mentioned grants are awarded.[19]

> Humbly,
> EDVARD GRIEG

6

Børve, Hardanger, September 6, 1877

Mr. Cabinet Minister Nissen,[20] Christiania:

I take the liberty respectfully to turn to you concerning a matter that is of impor-tance to me and that supposedly can be most competently decided by you. At the most recent distribution of governmental travel grants for artists, as you perhaps will remember, I was passed over despite the unanimous favorable recommen-dation of the committee. In this connection I take the liberty of asking: Was the fact that I as a composer have been awarded an annual grant of 400 *spesidalers* by the Norwegian Parliament the reason for my being passed over, and does such a grant eliminate for the artists receiving it any possibility of being considered when the funds set aside for travel abroad by artists are distributed?[21]

Since it is vitally important for me to know how to plan for the future with respect to this matter, I would be especially grateful to you, Mr. Cabinet Minister, for a kind reply to these lines.

> Most respectfully,
> EDVARD GRIEG

P.S. My address is: Mr. Consul John Grieg Jr.,[22] Bergen.

7

Lofthus, Hardanger, March 17, 1878

To the King:

In humbly applying for a grant of 500 *spesidalers*—from the funds set aside for travel abroad by artists—to defray the cost of an extended stay abroad for the purpose of devoting myself entirely to my art, especially to studying dramatic

---

[19] Grieg did not receive the grant.
[20] Norwegian theologian and politician Rasmus Tønder Nissen (1822–82), Cabinet minister 1875–82.
[21] Regarding the answer from the government, see Grieg's next letter.
[22] Edvard's brother John Grieg (1840–1901), who was a businessman as well as British consul in Bergen.

music and hearing performances of the works of contemporary masters, I venture to remind the Ministry that last year, notwithstanding the committee's unanimous favorable recommendation, I was passed over. Pursuant thereto, I wrote to Mr. Cabinet Minister Nissen respectfully asking whether the fact that I as a composer receive from the Norwegian Parliament an annual grant of 400 *spesidalers* was the reason for my being passed over and whether such a grant eliminates, for the artists receiving it, any possibility of being considered when the funds set aside for travel abroad by artists are distributed. Through Mr. Cabinet Minister Holmboe[23] I was given the answer that, while the fact that I receive an annual artist's grant was the cause of my being passed over during the fierce competition that prevailed at that time, the possibility that I might indeed be considered at another time is not absolutely excluded.

It is this interpretation of the matter by the Ministry that has made it a duty for me to resubmit my application, for at the current stage of my artistic development I am very aware of the necessity of immersing myself at the present time in developed musical environments if my art is to be of benefit to our homeland.[24]

> Humbly,
> EDVARD GRIEG

---

[23] Norwegian lawyer and politician Jens Holmboe (1821–91), Cabinet Minister 1874–84.
[24] Grieg received a travel grant of 400 *spesidalers,* and in the autumn of 1878 he and Nina began a vagabond life that was to last for nearly two years.

My First Success (1903)

In spring 1903, German book dealer and author Albert Langen (1869–1910)—son-in-law of Norwegian author Bjørnstjerne Bjørnson (1832–1910)—transmitted to Grieg an invitation from the American *McClure's Magazine* to write an autobiographical article of ca. 8,000 words. On October 20 Grieg wrote to Langen saying that he would write an article of 7,000 words on the condition that he would receive an honorarium of 500 dollars. He added: "If that [7,000 words] is still not enough, I will write the three articles of the Apostolic Creed at the end. That certainly will suffice to fill up the space."[1]

Grieg wrote "My First Success" in November–December, 1903. But then something totally unexpected occurred: After receiving the manuscript, the editor of *McClure's Magazine* decided not to print it. Grieg was very angry and demanded that his article be returned to him immediately. At the same time he asked Langen to do his best to get it placed in another American journal, possibly in *The Century Illustrated Monthly Magazine*, where he had previously published articles on Schumann and Mozart.[2] Nothing came of this idea, however, and on March 9, 1905, Grieg wrote to Langen: "It is almost fifteen months since you received the article 'My First Success', which I wrote at your request. From this fact I can probably conclude that you—after the shameful behavior by the American [journal editor]—have not succeeded in getting the article placed anywhere else. But you can also easily understand that there comes a time when my patience is exhausted. This time has now been reached."[3]

"My First Success" was first published in the distinguished American journal *The Independent* in June 1905. One month later it was reprinted in the English *Contemporary Review*, London, and in a German translation in Velhagen & Klasing's *Monatshefte*. Later it was published in Danish in *Det ny Aarhundrede*, and to Grieg's annoyance excerpts appeared in unauthorized versions in various Norwegian and Danish newspapers. The article was first published in its original Norwegian form in Øystein Gaukstad (ed.), *Edvard Grieg. Artikler og taler* (*Edvard Grieg: Articles and Speeches*), Oslo 1957, pp. 10–30. A new German translation by Hella Brock appeared in her book *Edvard Grieg als Musikschriftsteller*, Altenmedingen 1999, pp. 15–48.

The present version has been translated directly from the Norwegian original, the manuscript of which is preserved in Bergen Public Library.

I have been strongly urged to write about my first success! The task appears so complicated that I am almost tempted to say that it would be my first success if I got through this enterprise unscathed! The subject puts forth its antennae in many directions. For which success is the first one? Is there any success at all? Is it not true that when we have achieved something that for the moment seems to be of value, we are confronted by the heavy, dark glower of life's disillusion that says: "It is nothing, nothing"? Our entry into the world undoubtedly is a success, but chiefly for that great artist whom we call Nature. Whether it is a success for

---

[1] The letter is published in Norwegian translation in Finn Benestad (ed.), *Edvard Grieg: Brev i utvalg 1862–1907*, Oslo 1998, vol. II, p. 510.

[2] See pp. 255–274 and 225–239, respectively.

[3] See Finn Benestad (ed.), *Edvard Grieg: Letters to Colleagues and Friends*, p. 469.

ourselves, on the other hand, might certainly be disputed. And the very concept of success! Does it not vary greatly in the minds of different people? What others would call a success is not so for me, and *vice versa*. What constitutes a success—if there is such a thing? This is the interesting part of the question. Is what is called winning the applause of a random group of people—is that the real, the decisive success for the artist himself? Or is it a matter of satisfying the few whose judgment he highly respects? Or rather, isn't the essence of success that which takes place in the artist's workshop, where he, hammer in hand, like Ibsen's Miner,[4] makes his way to the very heart of the hidden secrets? Is it not the striving spirit that digs and digs, goes deeper and deeper in order to reach the most intimate, most hidden secrets that hover before his mind, the seeking and seeking in the hope of one day finding even one tiny little patch of new land—is it not precisely that which, for the artist, constitutes the supreme joy? Or is it, perhaps, the yearnings and longings, the dreams and hopes of childhood and early youth that embody life's highest poetry and create the noblest and most ideal *joie de vivre* and thus the greatest inner success?

It would be of little use, in responding to these questions, to select one's first and best concert and report the number of rounds of applause it may have evoked. That, in my opinion, would not even touch the question. I choose, therefore, to proceed in quite another way. I shall relate a few experiences from my early youth—its joys and sorrows—leaving it to the reader himself to find within these accounts the kernel that constitutes what he, in accordance with his own disposition, would call a success.

When I rummage through my brain among the memories from days long vanished—in order to find something resembling a success—I am suddenly in the midst of childhood, when life and its many possibilities for the future lay before me as a single, great success. And then it swarms as if from a veritable labyrinth of young shoots seeking the light. Half-forgotten childhood memories stretch out their arms to me. Youthful dreams that never were fulfilled, thoughts that I should have thought through to the end, accuse me like the "threadballs" in *Peer Gynt*.[5]

But I also recall dim presentiments of happiness that I did not dare to trust but that were completely fulfilled. A miscellaneous assortment of figures, longings and hopes presses forward, each one whispering, "Here am I—and I—and I." All insist on being included. All claim to have contributed to my early successes.

---

[4] The allusion is to the poem "Miner" ("Bjergmanden") by Henrik Ibsen (1828–1906), written in 1850 and revised in 1863 and 1871. Grieg sketched a setting of the first stanza and the first two lines of the second from the 1863 version. The sketch is printed as EG 132 in *Edvard Grieg: Complete Works*, vol. 15, pp. 327–328.

[5] Henrik Ibsen's *Peer Gynt*, Act 5, Scene 6—a night scene in the forest. Peer Gynt hears voices from threadballs on the ground: "We are thoughts; you should have thought us . . ."; from withered leaves flying before the wind: "Watchwords of action; you should have cried us . . ."; from sighing in the air: "We are songs; you should have sung us . . ." etc. Translation by John Northam, Oslo / Oxford 1993, pp. 147–148.

Not the noisy outward successes—there were not many of those in any case—but the quiet, inward ones that wrought confidence in myself. And if I try to emphasize one success at the expense of another, I hear a sound like the distant sobbing of a child: "And will you disown me—and me—and me? You cannot be so heartless!"

What am I to do? Draw a thick line over all of them as unworthy of consideration? No, that is the very thing I neither want to do nor can do. For all these little recognitions and happy feelings during childhood have done their job by playing a role in the development of my personality. Today I would certainly not have regarded them as successes, but at the time, from the child's point of view, they were events of the greatest significance. Let me, therefore, set down at random what I remember from those distant days. Perhaps some, like me, will find among these recollections, if not a success, at least materials for a success.

I could go very far back—to the earliest years of my childhood. For who is so keenly aware of recognition as the child? It may well be this awareness that the preachers refer to as "the old Adam". I would call it the urge to sunshine and gentleness in life rather than to gloom and severity. How this urge in the child is satisfied determines the character of the child's future artistic life.

I could mention many small triumphs of those years that had a decisive influence on my imagination. As, for example, when as a little boy I was allowed to watch funeral processions, to attend auctions and so on—so that afterwards,

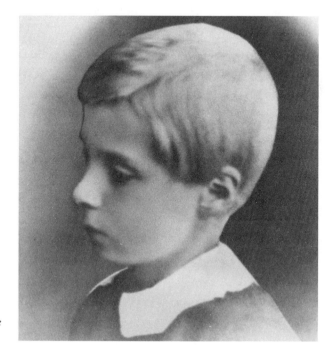

Grieg at age eleven. This detail from a daguerreotype is the earliest known picture of Grieg.

mind you, I might report all my impressions to my family. If I had been forbidden to do this, to follow my childish instincts, who knows whether my imagination might not have been shackled or turned in a direction different from its true nature.

What peace of mind it brings to trace such reminiscences back to the dawning of the first morning. Yes, why not go all the way back? Why not begin by remembering the strangely mystical satisfaction of stretching my arms over the piano keyboard and bringing forth—not a melody. Far from it! No, it had to be a harmony. First a third, then a triad, then a seventh chord. And finally, both hands helping—O joy!—a ninth chord, with five tones. When I had discovered this, my rapture knew no bounds. That was a success! No later success has been able to enrapture me like this. At that time I was about five years old.

One year later my mother began giving me piano lessons. Little did I suspect that already here disappointments were lurking. Only too soon I realized that I didn't enjoy practicing what I was supposed to practice. And mother was strict, unrelentingly strict. Although it may indeed have gladdened her mother-heart that I sat there experimenting with this and that, because it provided evidence of a musical nature, she certainly gave no outward sign of this. Quite the opposite. She was not to be trifled with when I idled the time away in piano reveries instead of concentrating on my assignment. And then, when I had to work on my scales and exercises and all that other technical deviltry that gave my childish yearning stones for bread, it sometimes happened that she still guided me, even when she was not in the same room. One day she shouted menacingly from the kitchen, where at that moment she was busy preparing dinner: "But shame on you, Edvard: F sharp, F sharp, not F!"[6] I was deeply impressed with her superiority. If in those years I had been more diligent, and had followed more willingly her loving but strict guidance, I would have escaped many unpleasantries later in life. But my unpardonable tendency to dreaming was already beginning at that time to create for me the same difficulties that were to follow me far into the future. Had I not inherited my mother's irrepressible energy in addition to her musical talent, I would certainly never have progressed from dream to deed in any sphere of my life.

My school days began at the same time as did my piano lessons, and I may as well admit it right away: I was at least as lazy in school as I was at the piano. The successes I can report from this period are not of a sort to set me in a favorable light. But there they are, and they are part of the picture. So here they are!

At first I went to a school attended by both boys and girls. How vividly I can

---

[6] In the original manuscript Grieg has crossed out the following lines: "And if I did not quickly correct the mistake, I could not be sure to avoid in the next moment a box on the ear. I therefore sat trembling like an aspen leaf as soon as I heard my mother's voice."

recall an arithmetic lesson from that period! We all had to do the same multiplication assignment, and whoever finished it first—thus proving himself or herself to be the cleverest—was to receive special recognition. My ambition was immediately aroused. "Aha!" I thought. "Now I must be smart." And I hit upon a brilliant idea in order to get finished as quickly as possible: to omit from the calculation all the zeros, which to my childish understanding were of no value! I note: This was a success with a question mark—or, more correctly, it was a total fiasco. But it taught me a lesson. Since then I have learned to include the zeros in the calculation—whether it concerns numbers or—people! And what I learned, when all is said and done, proved to be a personal success. There is no use denying it. Thus I can go boldly on with the story of my fiascoes.

From the time that I was ten years old my parents lived during the summers at the lovely country home "Landås" just a mile or so from Bergen. Each morning my elder brother and I had to trudge off to school in the pouring rain for which Bergen is famous. But I used this pouring rain in what I thought was a very clever boyish prank. The rule at school was that a pupil who came late would not be admitted to class, but as a punishment had to stand outside until the end of the period. One rainy day when it happened—and it happened very often—that I came to school entirely unprepared, I arranged so that I not only came a little late, but I stayed down on the street, where I placed myself under the downspout of a house until I became absolutely soaked to the skin. When I was finally admitted to the room, such rivulets of water streamed from my clothes down to the floor that the teacher, for the sake of both my classmates and myself, couldn't think of letting me stay, but immediately sent me home to change clothes. Because of the long distance to "Landås", this was tantamount to excusing me from forenoon instruction. That I repeated this experiment rather often was already risky, but when I finally went so far as to come to school soaking wet one day when it was hardly raining, they became suspicious and sent someone out to spy on me. One fine day I got caught, and then I received a memorable introduction to "the percussion instruments". Another fiasco! But it enriched my experience of life, so in other words, it was another success, albeit a negative one—indeed, almost a criminal one! For what is this growing foolhardiness that in the end runs right into the arms of the law but the criminal nature in men! I will say in my defense that school life was so profoundly unpleasant for me—its materialism, its coarseness, its coldness, were so abhorrent to my nature—that I devised the most incredible ways of escaping from it, even if only for a short while. And that this was not only the fault of the child, but at least equally the fault of the school—that I now see. Then, I could see nothing in school life but a boundless calamity, and I could not understand the need for all these childhood miseries. I do not doubt that the school developed in me that which was bad and left the good untouched.

But back to my fiascoes! I remember that in history and geography I was not very exact about names and that my teacher, a good-natured man, when he called on me, would shout, "Now it's your turn, name-botcher!" That title I did not like. One day I had answered the questions even worse than usual and got what I deserved: "Ah, poor Edvard, how much you have to contend with in the rain now when you go home to 'Landås': first your heavy raincoat, secondly all your books, thirdly a big 4 (a very bad mark), and lastly all the steep hills leading up to 'Landås'!" The teacher painted it so vividly that it seemed to me as if I had the weight of the whole world on my shoulders. It was no enviable success to be ridiculed in that way in front of my classmates.

I will go on—to one negative success after another, each worse than the preceding one. One day in German class, to the delight of my classmates, I translated *der gemeine Holunder* (the common elder bush) as *den gemene Hollender* (the vile Dutchman).[7] In English class I boldly asserted that "veal roast" meant "beef of veal". The teacher burst out laughing and said, "Go home and tell your father (he was the English consul in Bergen) that 'veal roast' means 'beef of veal'." I turned beet-red with embarrassment. It was a terrible defeat that for a long time reduced my respect for my abilities both in school and at home, where my stupidities were promptly reported by friendly souls.

But then, as luck would have it, I experienced a brilliant restoration of my dignity—indeed, in the very class where I had been humiliated. The word "Requiem" occurred in the text, and the teacher asked if any of us could say what great composer had written a piece of church music with that title. No one answered until I, quite softly, ventured to say: "Mozart". The whole class stared at me as if at an incomprehensible, strange creature. That felt like a success, but I sensed immediately that it might carry something sinister in its bosom. And all too soon I learned that I was right. For, as so often happens, the class didn't like having such a creature in its midst. From this time on, my classmates pursued me in the streets whenever they had the chance and taunted me with the words, "Hey, look, there comes Mosak!" In the distance I could hear the words "Mosak! Mosak!" after I had escaped from my pursuers down a side street. I felt this mistreatment to be an injustice and considered myself a martyr. I came very close to absolutely hating my classmates. As a matter of fact, I withdrew from virtually all of them.

Obviously my school successes were not, as a rule, particularly flattering to me. But there were also exceptions that brightened my life like a ray of sunshine. In music class, for example, all went well. One day we were tested on our knowledge of the scales. Not one of the other thirty boys in the class knew them, but

---

[7] The German word "gemein" can mean either "common" or "base, mean, vile" depending on the context. The corresponding Norwegian word "gemen" normally has only the latter connotation.

I had them at my fingertips. Finally the teacher, a lovable old Czech by the name of Schediwy,[8] said: "Well, I won't give any marks, but Grieg was the best." I was the lion of the moment and savored the situation.

But let me not forget to report a success in one of my exams. In history we had at that time a very intelligent teacher who did not insist that we repeat the lessons word for word but required us to tell in our own words the substance of what we had learned. Fate decreed that because of an eye ailment I was obliged to be away from school for some time. I, who never learned my lessons, did not think I was missing much. My father, however, had different ideas. I had to continue at home where I left off at school. But that was not enough. Father required me to memorize the history of Louis XIV[9] and insisted that I repeat it to him word for word. It was a bitter task, but I was in a tough spot and couldn't get out of it. I daresay that my knowledge of Louis XIV became very exhaustive, but that was the only period of world history in which I was at home. Then came the examination day. Before the test began, one of the boys amused himself by "predicting" the part of the history book on which each of us would be questioned. His method was very simple: He opened the book at random, and wherever it happened to be—that was where he predicted we would be examined. For me he opened it up—to the chapter on Louis XIV! "Well," I said, "then it will be a simple matter," and I told the class how I had been obliged to memorize that material for my father. The boy was about to try another prediction when suddenly the teacher came in. I was one of the first to be called upon. The teacher, as usual, sat balancing himself on one leg of his chair as he paged back and forth in the book, uncertain as to where he had the greatest likelihood of catching me. A long and uncomfortable silence ensued. At last he came out with, "Tell me something about Louis XIV." I heard suppressed giggling from all over the room. God knows what I looked like myself. I was at least a head taller than usual. You bet I told him everything I knew. It was as if someone had opened the tap of a barrel. My speech gushed forth in a steady stream. Not a word was left out. Everything was there as if nailed to my memory. The teacher was struck dumb with astonishment. He could not believe his own ears—but the facts had spoken. He found nothing to criticize. Once again a paging through the book. Once again a balancing on the leg of the chair. Hot and flushed, I stood there, sweating from anxiety. For I could not possibly have such dumb luck a second time. But my lucky star did not forsake me. "Can you tell me which generals were on the Black

---

[8] Ferdinand Giovanni Schediwy (1804–77) was born in Bohemia but spent most of his adult life in Bergen. He served as an organist and music teacher and was for some time also conductor of the Bergen orchestra "Harmonien". Schediwy later gave Grieg the great biography *W. A. Mozart* (Leipzig 1856) by Otto Jahn (1813–69) with the following dedication: "Til min kjære Ven Edvard Grieg fra Ferd. Gio. Schediwy" ("To my dear friend Edvard Grieg from Ferd. Gio. Schediwy").

[9] French King Louis XIV (1638–1715).

Sea under Catherine II?"[10] With a loud voice I answered, "Generals Greig and Elphinston".[11] For those names had been chiseled into my brain ever since my father had told me that our family shield, which bore a ship, indicated that our original ancestor was in all probability the Scottish Admiral Greig. The teacher slammed the book shut. "Right. You should have had a 1 with a star (the best mark possible), but in view of your performance throughout the year you will have to be content with a 1.5." I was more than happy. I was as proud as a general after winning a battle. I almost think it was the greatest success of my school days. All the greater shame for me that the actual reward was so small! This success confirmed my conviction in the truth of what the great Norwegian politician Johan Sverdrup[12] once said in the Norwegian Parliament: "One must be lucky. There is nothing unluckier than to be an unlucky politician."

Finally, one day—I was perhaps twelve or thirteen years old—I brought to school a folder of my own music, and on the title page I had written in the most ornate handwriting of which I was capable, "Variations on a German Melody for Piano by Edvard Grieg, Opus 1". I had fun showing it to a classmate who seemed to be interested. But what happened? In the middle of the German class the same classmate was heard mumbling some unintelligible words that caused the teacher to shout somewhat crossly, "What are you saying over there?" Once again the indistinct mumbling, once again a shout from the teacher, and then my classmate said in a near whisper, "Grieg has something." – "What do you mean, 'Grieg has something?' "—"Grieg has composed something!"

The teacher, with whom I did not exactly enjoy any popularity—which is easy to understand after what I have related—stood up, came over to me, inspected the music booklet, and said in a singularly ironic tone: "Well, well, so the fellow is musical. The fellow composes. Look at that!" Thereupon, he opened the door to the adjacent classroom, brought the teacher from that room into ours, and continued: "How about that! The little fellow over there writes music." Both teachers paged through the manuscript with apparent interest. There was general commotion in both classes. Already I felt confident of a great success. But one should not do this too soon, for the visitor was scarcely out of the room before the teacher suddenly changed his tactics. He pulled my hair so violently that I almost fainted, and he growled sternly, "Next time he will take the German dictionary along as he is supposed to, and leave such trash at home." Alas! So near fortune's peak, and then in a moment thrown down into the depths! How often in life something like this has happened to me. And always I have had to think back to that first time.

---

[10] Russian Empress Catherine II (1729–96).

[11] Sir Samuel Greig (1735–88) and John Elphinston (1722–85) were British officers serving as admirals in the Russian fleet. (Grieg spells the names: Greigh and Elphinstone.)

[12] Norwegian politician Johan Sverdrup (1816–92).

Opposite the school house there lived a young lieutenant who was a passionate lover of music and a skillful pianist. I fled to him with my fledgling attempts at composition, and he showed such interest in them that I always had to make copies for him. That was a success of which I was not a little proud. Fortunately, I was later able to get the copies back from him in order to consign them to the wastebasket, where they belonged. I have often thought with gratitude of my friend, the lieutenant, who later advanced to the rank of general, and of the encouraging recognition that he accorded to my first artistic efforts. That, to my boyish temperament, was a pleasant contrast to all the jabs and scoldings that I constantly experienced at school.

At this time it never occurred to me for a moment that I might want to become an artist, and if the thought ever struck me, I immediately put it aside as something unattainable, something altogether too inconceivably high. If someone asked me what I wanted to become, I answered without hesitation: a clergyman. My imagination furnished such a black-garbed shepherd of souls with the most alluring characteristics I could imagine. To be permitted to preach or speak to a listening crowd seemed to me to be something great. Prophet, preacher—that was the thing for me. And how I recited over and over again for my parents, sisters, and brother! I knew all the poems in my Norwegian reader by heart. Every day after dinner, when father wanted to take a little nap in his easy chair, I would not leave him alone. Using a chair as a lectern, I started reciting, in total disregard of his wishes. I kept an eye on father, who appeared to be dozing. But once in a while, between his cat-naps, he smiled. Then I was happy. That was indeed recognition. And how I could keep on pestering father. "O, just one more piece!"—"No, that's enough."—"O, just one more!" What childish ambition! It knows exactly the tingling feeling of scoring a success.

The end of my school days—and with it my departure from home—came more quickly than I had expected. I was almost fifteen years old but was still far from achieving senior class standing. Then one summer day at "Landås" a rider on a galloping horse approached from the road below. He drew near, reined in his magnificent Arab, and leaped off. It was that fairytale idol of whom I had dreamt but had never before seen: It was Ole Bull.[13] There was something in me that didn't like the fact that this god, without further ado, dismounted and acted as if he were a mere mortal, came into the living room, and smilingly greeted us all. I remember distinctly that when his right hand touched mine, something like an electric shock went through me. But at last the god began to tell jokes, and then I realized—with quiet sorrow, to tell the truth—that he was only a human being after all.

---

[13] World-famous Norwegian violinist Ole Bull (1810–80). Ole Bull and Edvard Grieg were distantly related through the marriage of Grieg's aunt, Johanne Margrethe Hagerup (1817–88), to Ole Bull's brother, Jens Munthe Bull (1815–1905).

Unfortunately, he didn't have his violin with him. But he could talk, and that he did in full measure. We listened speechlessly to his hair-raising accounts of his travels in America. That was something for my childish imagination. When he heard that I liked to compose and improvise, there was no getting away from it: I had to go to the piano. I don't understand what Ole Bull could have found at that time in my naive, childish pieces, but he grew very serious and talked quietly to my parents. What they discussed was not disadvantageous to me; for suddenly Ole Bull came over to me, shook me in his peculiar way and said: "You are to go to Leipzig to become an artist!" Everyone looked tenderly at me, and I understood only this one thing, that a gentle fairy was stroking my cheek and that I was happy. And my parents! Not a moment's objection or even hesitation. Everything was settled, and it seemed to me the most natural thing in the world.

Only much later did I realize what an enormous debt of gratitude I owed to my parents—and to Ole Bull. I was under a magic spell, and I had no room for other powers. But stop: Ambition was also there. I cannot deny it. Ambition obviously must be one of the main ingredients among the many with which one prepares that very mixed salad called an "artist". For unconsciously a voice was whispering within me, "A success!" Well, what does my reader say to that? Am I not permitted to claim a success? I do so in any case, with or without permission. And here I conclude the list of the more or less honorable successes from the days in my childhood home.

Still, since I have undertaken the task of finding my first real success, an inner voice tells me that I must continue searching a while longer. And now my path leads me to the Leipzig Conservatory, to which I was sent a few months after Ole Bull's visit to "Landås". It is not by chance that the phrase "was sent" comes naturally to mind in this connection. I felt like a package stuffed with dreams. I was sent under the care of one of my father's old friends. We crossed the North Sea to Hamburg, and after a one-day stay there we continued by train to medieval Leipzig, whose tall, dark, and gloomy houses and narrow streets almost took my breath away. I was delivered to a boarding house, my father's old friend said good-bye—the last Norwegian words I was to hear for a long time—and there I stood, a fifteen-year-old boy, alone in that foreign land among only foreign people. I was overcome by homesickness. I went into my room, and I sat crying continuously until I was called to dinner by my hosts. The husband, a genuine Saxon post-office official, tried to console me: "Look here, my dear Herr Grieg, it is the same sun, the same moon, the same loving God you have at home!"[14] Very well intended. But neither sun nor moon nor loving God could compensate for my father's vanished friend, the last link that had bound me to my home.

---

[14] Grieg's quotation is in German: "Sehen Sie, mein lieber Herr Grieg, das ist ja dieselbe Sonne, derselbe Mond, derselbe liebe Gott wie bei Ihnen zu Hause!"

Children's moods change quickly, however. I soon got over the homesickness, and although I didn't have the foggiest idea of what it really meant to study music, I was nonetheless cocksure that the miracle would happen—that in three years[15] after completing my studies there, I would return home as a wizard in the kingdom of music! This is the clearest proof of my great naiveté and of the fact that it was purely and simply the child in me that was in control. It is not my intention to convey anything other than that I was a child-student at the Conservatory, for that is what I was, even in the way I dressed. I went around in a short blouse with a belt around the waist, just like the boys back in Norway customarily wore. At first my fellow students looked down their noses at me. There was even one violinist who amused himself by taking me on his lap, which drove me to despair. All such things soon stopped, however.

To be admitted into the sanctuary of the Leipzig Conservatory,[16] thereby confirming the presupposition of the statutes—that those being accepted must possess musical talent—that, for the young beginner who feared nothing less than that he might be rejected, was a colossal triumph. Then, to win the first artist-heart among my fellow students! What a conquest! And next, the favorable opinion of the teachers! To receive a word of praise from a teacher during a lesson —that was a joy that excited my youthful spirits quite differently than did the applause of thousands later in life. At first, however, none of this kind of thrill came my way. I was anything but a prize conservatory student. Quite the opposite. At the beginning, I was lazy to the core. I still remember an incident with my first piano instructor, Louis Plaidy,[17] whom I very much disliked. One day, as I sat pounding away at what I considered an abominable Clementi[18] sonata that he had forced me to study, he suddenly grabbed the music off the piano and pitched it in such a way that it flew through the air in a great arc and came to rest in the farthest corner of the large classroom. Since he couldn't very well do the same thing with me personally, he contented himself with thundering, "Go home and practice!"[19] I must admit that he had a right to be furious, but the punishment was especially disgraceful for me because so many other students were in the room. I must describe this episode as—to use a mild understatement—a doubtful success. It proved useful, however, for my pride was greatly provoked

---

[15] Grieg entered the Conservatory on October 6, 1858, and the final examination concert took place at the Gewandhaus on April 12, 1862. In the spring of 1860, he contracted pneumonia and had to return to Bergen, where he stayed until autumn. Then he went back to Leipzig to continue his studies. Perhaps this interruption in the Leipzig studies explains why Grieg talks about three years at the Conservatory.

[16] The Leipzig Conservatory of Music, which had been founded by Felix Mendelssohn (1809–47) in 1843— the very year of Grieg's birth—was considered one of Europe's leading musical institutions.

[17] German piano instructor Louis Plaidy (1810–74) had been selected for the position by Mendelssohn when the Conservatory was started. Plaidy remained at the Conservatory until 1865.

[18] Italian composer, pianist and pedagogue Muzio Clementi (1752–1832) wrote more than a hundred piano sonatas and sonatinas.

[19] Grieg's quotation is in German: "Gehen Sie nach Hause und üben Sie!"

by Plaidy's brutal treatment. Moreover, since he never let me play anything but Czerny,[20] Kuhlau[21] and Clementi, all of whom I hated like the plague, I made my decision. I went to the Director of the Conservatory[22] and demanded that I be released from Plaidy's lessons. My request was granted. I was proud of this result. It took away some of my excessive timidity, and I became more courageous.

It has been said that Plaidy was a good technician and that he knew how to cultivate his students' technique. Whether the reason is to be sought in my stupidity, my idleness or my antipathy to Plaidy, it is certain that he taught me no technique at all. His method of teaching was one of the most uninspired imaginable. How he sat there during the lesson—that fat, bald little man, huddled close to the piano, his left forefinger behind his ear as the student played—intoning to the point of the deadliest weariness the incessantly repeated words: "Always slow, firm, lift your fingers; slow, firm, lift your fingers!"[23] It was enough to drive you crazy.

By the way, it sometimes happened that when the student got up from the piano, Plaidy took his place; but this was only in quite specific circumstances which I shall mention shortly. When this happened, we students had a private joke of our own. We knew beforehand exactly *when* Plaidy was going to demonstrate his playing: It was when the student brought with him Mendelssohn's *Scherzo capriccioso in E Major* or his *Capriccio in B Minor*.[24] In either case Plaidy adopted a very pompous posture during the slow introduction. It is said that Bülow[25] displayed too much of the pedagogue in his performances. But what, then, shall one say of Plaidy? His playing was a living illustration of his theories: "Slow; firm; lift your fingers!" And besides, there was his everlasting "punctuation", if I may so express it. His constant separating of the smallest phrases: endless commas, semicolons, exclamation marks, dashes—and between these, absolutely nothing. Not a trace of content! It was an unpalatable, run-of-the-mill performance. But then came the priceless moment. The slow introduction was over. The allegro was to follow, and we knew exactly what would happen. Just as surely as two and two make four, Plaidy would get up from the piano and, with an assumed calmness, would remark, as if casually, "And so on". Imagine: to be a professor at the Leipzig Conservatory on the basis of the outstanding ability[26] to play only the slow introductions of two Mendelssohn capriccios! And still the poor man seriously believed that we did not see through him! It was most comical.

---

[20] Austrian pianist and pedagogue Karl Czerny (1791–1857), whose piano etudes are still in use.

[21] German-born Danish composer Friedrich Kuhlau (1786–1832).

[22] After Mendelssohn's death in 1847, German lawyer Conrad Schleinitz (1802–81) became Director of the Conservatory.

[23] Grieg's quotation is in German: "Immer langsam, stark, hochheben, langsam, stark, hochheben!"

[24] Grieg seems to mix up the titles a bit. Most likely he is referring to Mendelssohn's piano composition *Rondo Capriccioso in E Major*, op. 14 (1824), and *Capriccio brillant* for piano and orchestra in B Minor, op. 22 (1825–26), both of which have slow introductions.

[25] German conductor and pianist Hans von Bülow (1830–94), who had studied with Franz Liszt (1811–86).

[26] Grieg here uses the German word *Leistungsfähigkeit.*

However, I do not want to be unjust. I have already indicated that I may have lacked the conditions necessary for appreciating Plaidy. There really were students who, by blindly following Plaidy's principles, were able to achieve surprisingly brilliant technical results. The finest technique among all the students was that displayed by the Englishman J. F. Barnett,[27] who was a sworn follower of Plaidy. Hard-working and energetic, he employed this technique in a performance of Beethoven that, in his simple way of delineating the great contours of the work, commanded our highest respect. I cannot refrain from relating the following episode. It was a dark winter evening, and Barnett, playing for the first time at the Gewandhaus—a rare honor for a Conservatory student—was to perform Beethoven's *Piano Concerto No. 5 in E-flat Major*. It was 6 P.M. (the concert was to begin at 7), and I had gone to the Conservatory—which was usually empty at that time—to retrieve a music book that I had forgotten. To my astonishment, I heard tones coming from a staff room, sounds like those of a rank beginner— one note following slowly after another. The next moment, it struck me that these notes were passages in the *allegro* movement of the Beethoven concerto, played, not *adagio*, but much, much slower! I opened the door slightly. It was Barnett. He had the courage to carry out the Plaidy method with utmost consistency, even immediately preceding his public appearance. And I did not begrudge that amiable and modest artist the results of his tenacity. A couple of hours later, the *allegro* passages cascaded like a shower of pearls with the loveliest clarity. He had a brilliant success. Here again, as so often, Goethe's words apply: "Nothing suits everybody."[28]

As I have said, Plaidy was not the right teacher for me. I needed a different kind of authority. Better days dawned for me when I became a piano student of Ernst Ferdinand Wenzel,[29] Schumann's highly intellectual friend, who soon became my favorite. As a matter of fact, he did not play the introductions to Mendelssohn's capriccios. Indeed, he did not play at all. It was rumored that in his youth he had suddenly lost his memory in the course of a public perform-ance, that he had never gotten over it and could no longer be induced to play in public. But he was a master at imparting to me his understanding of the music. He could give a detailed description of a measure in a way quite different from that of Plaidy—and above all, there was music behind his words.

Later I advanced to taking lessons from the famous Ignaz Moscheles.[30] Under the influence of these two professors it was as if all my idleness blew away. Many hard things have been said about old Moscheles as a teacher. I stand up for him

---

[27] English composer and conductor John Francis Barnett (1837–1916).

[28] Grieg quotes from the poem *Beherzigung*: "Eines schickt' sich nicht für Alle" by German author Johann Wolfgang von Goethe (1749–1832). Grieg often quoted German poetry, notably that of Goethe and Friedrich von Schiller (1759–1805).

[29] German pianist and piano teacher Ernst Ferdinand Wenzel (1808–80).

[30] German pianist and composer Ignaz Moscheles (1794–1870), who was in charge of the piano department at the Leipzig Conservatory.

Ignaz Moscheles. "His interpretation of Beethoven was especially outstanding."

with the greatest warmth. It is true that he was naive enough to believe that he could impress us during his lessons by seizing every opportunity to run down Chopin[31] and Schumann, whom I secretly loved. But he could play beautifully, and he did, sometimes taking up almost the whole lesson. His interpretation of Beethoven, whom he worshiped, was especially outstanding. It was sincere, full of character, and noble, and there was no straining after effect. I studied Beethoven's sonatas with him by the dozen. Often I could not play four measures without his laying his hands over mine, pushing me gently from my seat, and saying, "Now listen to how *I* do that."[32] In this way I learned many a little technical secret and came to value his sensitive interpretations to the utmost. The story was told of him at the Conservatory—though, fortunately, I cannot verify it from my own experience—that he gave his piano students this piece of advice: "Play diligently the old masters: Mozart, Beethoven, Haydn—and me."[33] I dare not vouch for this anecdote but mention it because I myself, at his strong urging, took in hand his *24 Etudes* op. 70, which I do not regret having indefatigably studied with him from beginning to end. I liked them, so I did my best to satisfy both him

---

[31] Polish pianist and composer Frédéric Chopin (1810–49).
[32] Grieg's quotation is in German: "Nun hören Sie, wie *ich* das mache."
[33] Grieg's quotation is in German: "Spielen Sie fleissig die alten Meister; Mozart, Beethoven, Haydn und—mich."

and myself. He must have noticed this, for he became more and more kindly disposed toward me. And it was, to be sure, a simple yet very significant success for me when one day, after I had played one of his etudes without his interrupting me, he turned to the other students and said, "Look here, gentlemen, that is what I call musical piano-playing."[34] How glad I was! That day the whole world lay before me bathed in light.

My successes in harmony, on the other hand, were nothing to brag about. In E. F. Richter's[35] class, where we were given a bass line, at first I always wrote harmonies that I myself liked instead of those prescribed by the rules of the thoroughbass. Later I could certainly invent many a theme suitable for use in a fugue, but to make this theme conform to the conventional rules—that, for the time being, was not for me. I started from the faulty premise that if my works just sounded good, that was the main thing. For Richter, on the other hand, the main thing was that the problem should be solved correctly. And when solving problems rather than creating music was the matter of greatest importance, then from his point of view he was certainly right. But this is what I could not comprehend at that time. I defied him obstinately and stuck to my own opinion. I did not yet understand that what I was supposed to learn was: to limit myself, to do as I was told, and—as it says in the preface to his harmony textbook—not to ask why. Fortunately, we never became enemies. He only smiled indulgently at my stupidities, and with a "No! wrong!" he corrected them with a thick pencil-mark, which did not in fact teach me much. But there were many of us in the class, and Richter could not spend time with each of us individually.

Dr. Robert Papperitz,[36] from whom I took harmony lessons at the same time, gave me a freer rein. The result was that I went so far out of the beaten path that in my chorale arrangements I made use of chromatic voice-leading wherever I possibly could. One day Papperitz exclaimed, "But all this chromaticism! You are becoming a second Spohr!"[37] And since I regarded Spohr as an academic pedant of the first rank, I did not at all appreciate this verdict.

Finally, I had lessons from Moritz Hauptmann;[38] and I am still grateful to that amiable old man for all that he taught me through his sensitive and insightful comments. Despite his erudition, he represented to me the essence of non-scholastic learning. For him, rules were important only because they embodied

---

[34] Grieg's quotation is in German: "Sehen Sie, meine Herren, das ist musikalisches Klavierspiel."

[35] German theorist, teacher and composer Ernst Friedrich Richter (1807–79).

[36] German theorist and teacher Robert Papperitz (1826–1903).

[37] Grieg's quotation is in German: "Aber diese Chromatik! Sie werden ja der zweite Spohr!" The reference is to German violinist and composer Louis Spohr (1784–1859).

[38] German theorist, teacher and composer Moritz Hauptmann (1792–1868). In 1842 he had been appointed Thomaskantor, i.e. cantor and music director of the Thomas Church—Thomaskirche—in Leipzig, a position that Johann Sebastian Bach (1685–1750) had previously occupied. The Thomas Church was affiliated with the Thomas School (Thomasschule).

essential laws of nature. I will mention here an episode that in a weak moment I might call a success. Even before I knew Hauptmann—I was not yet sixteen years old, and I still wore a boy's blouse—I had received the honor, in a *Privat-Prüfung* (a kind of annual private examination in which all the students without exception were obliged to take part), of being allowed to play a piece that I myself had composed. When I had finished, and was leaving the piano, to my surprise I saw an old gentleman rise from the professors' table and come towards me. He laid his hand on my shoulder and said, "Good day, young man! We must become good friends."[39] That was Hauptmann, and naturally I loved him from that moment on. Sickly as he was in the last years of his life, he gave lessons in his own home—the Thomasschule, Johann Sebastian Bach's old residence. Here I had the pleasure of getting to know him better. I well remember him sitting on his sofa, wearing a bathrobe and skullcap, his spectacles buried deep in my exercise book, which still contains more than one drop of the yellowish-brown liquid that dripped continuously from his snuff-filled nose. He sat with a big silken handkerchief in one hand with which to catch the drips—but it didn't work. So it was used as a washcloth to clean the exercise book, which still clearly shows evidence of such wiping.

There was at that time a questionable practice at the Conservatory—and it

Moritz Hauptmann. "I am still grateful to that amiable old man for all that he taught me . . ."

---

[39] Grieg's quotation is in German: "Guten Tag, mein Junge! Wir müssen gute Freunde werden."

may well be that it is still in use—of having students take lessons from two different teachers in the same subject. In piano playing this was downright bad, for we
had to follow two often contradictory methods at the same time. I remember only
too well how Plaidy not only boasted of the results of his teaching method compared with that of Moscheles, but also allowed himself in class to make abusive
remarks about Moscheles whenever he found an opportunity. It was not pleasant
for the students to listen to, and I think also that on most of us Plaidy made an
impression exactly the opposite of what he intended. He underestimated his
students' powers of observation, which often happens to those who do not have
too much of it themselves. In harmony, this system of studying simultaneously
with two teachers only had the disadvantage that we had more work to do than
we could manage, especially when we got so advanced that we were supposed to
write for each of them complicated fugues with two or three subjects. I assume
that more than one student did as I did and presented the same exercise to both
teachers. This practice, however, brought me an additional success. A fugue on
the name "Gade",[40] which had not found favor with Richter, won Hauptmann's
approval to such a degree that, contrary to usual practice, after reading it
through, lingering over some passages in my work, he exclaimed, "That must
sound very nice. Let me hear it!"[41] When I had finished he said, with a gentle,
amiable smile, "Very nice, very musical!"[42]

In my last year at the Conservatory I had lessons in composition from Carl
Reinecke,[43] who at that time had just begun his work as musical director of the
Gewandhaus concerts and professor at the Conservatory, succeeding Julius
Rietz,[44] who had moved to Dresden. As an illustration of how things went on in
these lessons, I will mention just the following: I, who had presented myself as
one who did not have the slightest understanding of either musical form or of
string technique, was immediately required to write a string quartet. It struck me
as so absurd that I had the feeling that a delivery boy could have made the same
proposal. It seemed utterly preposterous to me. I was reminded of my old nurse.
She wanted me to do something that I thought I couldn't do, and when I objected,
"I can't do it," she used to say, "Forget about the *can't* and just do it!" This witticism, which many a time has given me courage, did so once more. What Reinecke
failed to teach me I tried to pick up from Mozart and Beethoven, whose quartets
I diligently studied on my own initiative. So I somehow finished my assignment,
wrote out the parts, and heard the work played in an ensemble class by some

---

[40] Danish composer Niels W. Gade (1817–90), whom Grieg greatly admired.

[41] Grieg's quotation is in German: "Das muss sehr hübsch klingen. Lassen Sie mal hören." Some of the fugues
Grieg wrote for Hauptmann have recently been published by C. F. Peters in *Grieg: Klavierwerke (Piano
Works) IV*, Frankfort 2000, pp. 101–114.

[42] Grieg's quotation is in German: "Sehr schön, sehr musikalisch!"

[43] German composer and conductor Carl Reinecke (1824–1910).

[44] German composer, cellist and conductor Julius Rietz (1812–77).

fellow students. The Director of the Conservatory wanted to have the quartet played at a *Haupt-Prüfung* (public performance of the best student compositions), but Ferdinand David,[45] the celebrated violinist and teacher, who attended the rehearsal, was of a different opinion. He took me aside and gave me the advice, certainly as well-intended as correct, not to let the work be performed: It was his opinion that "people would say it is music of the future."[46] In characterizing it as "music of the future", however, he was wrong. There was not a trace of "future" in it. It went along the lines of Schumann, Gade and Mendelssohn. But I soon realized that it was an utterly mediocre piece of work, and I have been very grateful to David for preventing its performance. I only wish that it, like so many other works from that period, had been consigned to the flames. Unfortunately, I did not succeed in getting it destroyed. It exists somewhere in the world, but I just don't know where. One day a fellow student who admired my creative efforts led me into temptation. He had a complete score of Schumann's piano concerto, which he had written out himself, and which at that time had not yet been published except for a piano reduction and the separate orchestral parts. "If you will give me your quartet," he said one day, "I will give you the score of Schumann's concerto." I could not resist the offer. I still think with secret dread about the fact that my abortive early work very likely still exists somewhere in one of the countries of southern Europe.[47]

After the negative success that proved to be the lot of my first string quartet, Reinecke said: "Now write an overture!"[48] I, who had no knowledge of orchestral instruments or of orchestration, was supposed to write an overture! Again I thought of the delivery boy—and of my nurse. I went at it hammer and tongs, but this time I fell short. I literally got stuck in the middle of the overture and could go no further. It seems incredible, but there was no class at the Conservatory in which one could get a grounding in these things. It is no wonder that nothing resembling even a modest success is associated with these lessons. It was fortunate for me, however, that in Leipzig I got to hear so much good music, especially orchestral and chamber music. This made up for the knowledge of compositional technique which the Conservatory failed to give me. It developed my mind and my musical judgment in the highest degree, but at the same time it created confusion in the relationship between what I wanted and what I was able to do. Unfortunately, the result of my stay in Leipzig was this confusion.

---

[45] German violinist Ferdinand David (1810–73).

[46] Grieg's quotation is in German: "Die Leute werden sagen, es ist Zukunftsmusik."

[47] Grieg's statements about his first string quartet are difficult to understand in relation to some other known facts. When returning to Bergen in 1862 after his studies in Leipzig, Grieg rented the large Labor Union hall for a concert given on May 21—his first public appearance in Norway. The program included, among other things, Beethoven's *"Pathétique" Sonata*, some etudes of Moscheles, Schumann's *Piano Quartet*, and his own *String Quartet in D Minor*. Thus, if he conveyed the score to his fellow student in Leipzig, it must have occurred after the years of study. Unfortunately, nothing is known of the fate of the quartet after 1862.

[48] Grieg's quotation is in German: "Jetzt schreiben Sie mal eine Ouverture!"

Carl Reinecke. "What Reinecke failed to teach me I tried to pick up from Mozart and Beethoven."

It may seem difficult to find the stuff of success in what I have related here, but to me it appears otherwise. I noted that things were out of balance. I withdrew into myself because I wanted something different from what they taught and what they failed to teach me in the classes. But this very feeling of wanting something different had a stimulating effect on me, for it pointed to the future and gave me courage to work further on my own. Above all, however, this feeling brought me many disappointments. It cannot be denied that it hurt me to see how I was outdistanced by my fellow students, who made rapid strides forward and got assignments that they were able to handle.

I especially remember some young Englishmen who—partly by unflagging diligence, partly by facility in acquiring knowledge—accomplished things in the presence of which I had a crushing feeling of my own impotence. Among these were Arthur Sullivan,[49] afterwards so celebrated as the composer of *The Mikado*; the pianists Franklin Taylor[50] and Walter Bache,[51] also Edward Dannreuther,[52] who died too young. Dannreuther was the gifted and tireless champion of Liszt in England and one of the first in that country to stand up for the music of Wagner. He was an exceedingly intelligent and skillful pianist. Lastly there was

---

[49] English composer and conductor Arthur S. Sullivan (1842–1900). Sullivan's comic opera *The Mikado or The Town of Titipu* (1885) is one of his most popular works; libretto by Sir William Schwenck Gilbert (1836–1911), who collaborated with Sullivan on 14 comic operas.

[50] English pianist and teacher Franklin Taylor (1843–1919).

[51] English pianist Walter Bache (1842–88), who also studied with Franz Liszt.

[52] English pianist and musicologist Edward Dannreuther (1844–1905). See Grieg's letters to him in Benestad (ed.), *op. cit.*, pp. 207–209.

the excellent John Francis Barnett, whom I mentioned earlier, who is working as a teacher in London. Sullivan immediately distinguished himself by his talent for composition and by his advanced command of orchestration, which he had acquired before he entered the Conservatory. While still a student he wrote the music to Shakespeare's *The Tempest*, a few measures of which he once wrote in my autograph album.[53] This entry shows a hand as skilled as that of an old master. Although I did not associate much with him, I did have the pleasure of being with him on one occasion which I shall not forget. It was during the dress rehearsal for a performance of Mendelssohn's oratorio *St. Paul*. We followed the music in the score. But which score? It was Mendelssohn's own manuscript, which Sullivan had borrowed for the occasion from the Director of the Conservatory, Conrad Schleinitz, who, as is well known, had been an intimate friend of Mendelssohn. With what reverence we turned page after page! How we admired the clear, firm musical notation that was so in keeping with the concept of the composition.

The name Schleinitz revives memories of some experiences which contributed to making me what I am. When I came to Leipzig, he was already an elderly man who was held in great esteem. It soon became clear to me, however, that he was not well-liked. But I, on the whole, have no reason to complain about him. At first, to be sure, I had the impression that he did not like me, and it seemed to me that he was avoiding me. I suspected that Plaidy had spoken ill of me to him. But I had been at the Conservatory for less than half a year when an apparently unimportant incident occurred that immediately sent my stock soaring in Schleinitz's eyes. Thereafter, he was kind and gracious to me at every opportunity. The event was this: One evening I and some of my fellow students had the misfortune of arriving late for one of the evening programs held weekly at the Conservatory. Good manners required us to remain outside until the first piece of music was finished, after which we entered the hall as a group. Schleinitz had a weakness for intervening with a fatherly admonition at every opportunity. When the last note of the program was over, Schleinitz rose and urged everyone to remain, for he had a few words to say. Great suspense, and also amazement. The purpose of his speech was nothing less than to reprimand all the students who had come in late. He concluded with the startling assertion that it was by and large the least skillful students who were guilty of such unpunctuality. This "success" was *too* negative for me. Such an affront was more than a young hothead like me could stand. The next morning at nine o'clock I knocked at the

---

[53] *The Tempest*, a philosophical comedy (1611) by William Shakespeare (1564–1616). Sullivan's incidental music for the play was produced at the Gewandhaus in Leipzig in 1861, a new version following in Crystal Palace, London, in 1862. The entry in Grieg's autograph album consists of five measures from the beginning of *Entr'acte*. Below the music, Sullivan has written: "In remembrance of your friend & fellow-pupil Arthur S. Sullivan. Leipzig. Easter, 1861."

Director's door and was admitted. Without beating around the bush, I told the Director exactly what I thought. I told him how inconsiderate and hurtful his conduct had been in tarring all of us with the same brush and that I was of no mind to tolerate such treatment. He got absolutely furious, abruptly stood up and showed me the door. But I was in a fighting mood. "Certainly, Mr. Director, I will go; but not until I have said what I have to say." At that moment, something astonishing occurred: Schleinitz completely changed his tune. He came over to me, patted me on the shoulder, and said as sweetly as a lark: "It really is very nice

The conservatory graduate, 1862

that you defend your honor."[54] That "success" is one that no one can ever take away from me.

After this episode, Schleinitz completely altered his behavior toward me. I had the feeling that I had won him forever. We became the best of friends, and he didn't know how to do enough for me. An example: One winter day when the letter bringing my regular remittance from home failed to arrive, I was compelled for the first—and fortunately for me, also the last—time to pawn my watch. In some incomprehensible way, Schleinitz learned of it, sent for me, and encouraged me most urgently never again to resort to such a solution, but always to come to him if I needed an advance. A success? Well, yes, a moral success, which I immediately credited to my account! That was a beautiful trait in Schleinitz, one that deserves to be mentioned alongside the sharp criticism of his supposed moral weaknesses about which I have so often heard.

I would have found it quite understandable if neither the Director of the Conservatory nor the professors had taken any interest in me, for during those three years I never succeeded in producing anything suggesting a promising future for me. If, therefore, in the course of these glimpses of the Conservatory I have had to criticize various things both in individuals and in the institution, I hasten to add that I take it for granted that it was primarily owing to my own nature that I left the Conservatory more or less as stupid as I was when I entered. I was a dreamer with absolutely no talent for competition. I was unfocused, not very communicative, and anything but teachable. Moreover, we Norwegians usually develop too slowly to show fully by the age of eighteen what we are good for. Be that as it may, I did not understand myself at all. The atmosphere of Leipzig had thrown a veil over my eyes.[55]

But a year later, when I came to Denmark, the veil fell off, and suddenly my wondering eyes beheld the world of beauty which the Leipzig fog had hidden from me. I found myself, and with the greatest ease I now overcame all the obstacles that in Leipzig had seemed insurmountable. Out of my imagination, finally liberated, within a short time I composed one large work after another. That the critics at first characterized my music as contrived and odd could not lead me astray. I knew what I wanted and, ready for battle, pressed toward the new goals that enticingly drew me forward.

---

54 Grieg's quotation is in German: "Nun, das ist ja sehr hübsch, dass Sie auf Ihre Ehre halten."

55 Here and elsewhere, Grieg's assessment of his experience at Leipzig is more negative than is warranted by the facts. His exercise books from the Leipzig years, for example, demonstrate that he had acquired a high level of technical competence in theory and composition. So also do various early works published by C. F. Peters Musikverlag: several short piano pieces written in 1858–62 (EG 101, 104, 105, 179, and 184 a–g, first published in 2000 in *Grieg: Piano Works IV*) and the piano pieces and songs in opp. 1 & 2, published in 1863. Grieg's only symphony (EG 119) was composed in 1863–64, just one year after he left the Conservatory. It was first published in 1984. Grieg's negativity regarding the Conservatory may be related to the fact that his individuality as a Norwegian composer was not awakened until the mid-1860's.

Before I close, however, let me return once more to my Leipzig days. It must be admitted that I have not depicted myself in a flattering light. But I do not want to make myself appear worse than I was, and for that reason I do not want to omit what might tend to rehabilitate me in the eyes of the many readers who certainly will have found that most of my successes have been dragged in by their hair. So I hasten to give one example of what people call a *real* success. It was Easter time, 1862, just before I left the Conservatory, when I enjoyed the singular honor of being among the chosen few selected to appear at the public examination concert in the large auditorium of the Gewandhaus. I played some of my own piano compositions. God knows they were the fumbling products of a green Conservatory student, and I still blush to think that they were printed and figure as my Opus 1.[56] But it is a fact that I scored a formidable triumph with them, and I had to make several curtain calls—so I did finally have an undisputed success in the usual sense of the word, no doubt about that. Yet, to me it meant nothing at all. Moreover, the audience consisted of invited people—friends and relatives of professors and students. Under these circumstances, it was the easiest thing in the world for a fair-haired young man from the far north to score a triumph.

Now I ask: Where, in all that has here been related, is the first success to be found? Everyone will certainly have been able to read between the lines that for me and my development no one event constitutes an answer to that question. I cannot point to the first success and say, "Here it is." And why? Because it is something abstract. If, however, one surveys the totality of what I have written here, the attentive observer will soon see what I was aiming at. As I indicated at the beginning of this article, it was my intention to compel the reader to answer the question himself. But perhaps I have overestimated my powers. Let me, therefore, by briefly summarizing, provide the key. In the husk of these experiences is concealed the essence of the answer to the question: That I had within myself the power to later shake off the yoke—all the superfluous ballast that had distorted my nature through the education that I received both at home and abroad, an education that was as deficient as it was leaden and one-sided—that was my salvation, my good fortune. When I became conscious of this power, when I understood myself, then I experienced something that I will call my first, my greatest, my only success, for that success became decisive for my whole life. All the joys and sorrows, the triumphs and disappointments, of my childhood and early student years have contributed to this single great success. Indeed, without them it would never have become a reality.

---

[56] *Four Piano Pieces*, op. 1 (1861)—*Vier Stücke für das Pianoforte.*

The Composer's Hut in Hardanger (1886)

In 1877 Grieg's long-suppressed irritation over the constricting circumstances in Christiania reached a critical point. He felt that now he had to sever all of his connections with city life and renew his strength in a different and healthier milieu, one that would allow him to give himself wholly to creative work. Toward the end of June he took lodging on a farm called Børve in Ullensvang, Hardanger. It was a uniquely beautiful place with the fjord—Sørfjorden, an arm of the Hardangerfjord—immediately below and the sparkling glaciers of Folgefonnen high up on the other side of the fjord: pastoral charm and majestic grandeur in perfect harmony. Before winter came he moved to Lofthus, a small village on the fjord about five miles north of Børve. Here he and his wife secured more comfortable quarters, and a warm friendship developed between the Griegs and the innkeepers, Hans Utne (1827–95) and his wife Brita (1847–1941).

In a letter of February 10, 1878, to his Danish friend Gottfred Matthison-Hansen (1832–1909), Grieg wrote about the "handsome, noble and enlightened farmers,"[1] although he seldom managed to win the confidence of the locals to any great extent. The residents had a long-standing mistrust of visiting tourists from the city. They just turned away with a sly smile when the diminutive Griegs, all bundled up in warm clothing, took their walks in the area—Nina Grieg with short-clipped hair, her husband with an artist's mane; she with tiny little steps, he with longer strides—and with rubbers over his boots.

On one occasion, however, the farmers came to Grieg's rescue. Grieg could not tolerate having anyone nearby when he was composing, and for that reason he arranged to have a little work hut built for him at some distance from the inn. The hut was jokingly called "Komposten"—a play on words suggesting both "the composer's hut" and "the compost heap". Grieg gave a highly amusing account of the moving of his hut in an 1886 issue of *Norden, Illustreret Skandinavisk Revue*. The article, entitled "Komposten," is given below.

The Compost—truly a bad-sounding name for an artist's abode! But that is how the country folks in Hardanger humorously christened the little cottage I arranged to have built during my hibernation there. Small, and still only a few years old, it nonetheless has its own history that the editor of this publication has asked me to relate, thinking that, if I told it myself, it might be of interest to friends of my art.

It was in the year 1877 that, in order to find the peace and quiet needed for work, I made my way to Sørfjorden in Hardanger. I spent the summer at a farm called "Børve" and became so enraptured with the majesty of the natural surroundings that I decided to spend the following winter there as well. But since Børve lacked most of the amenities required even by a "native", I chose to move to nearby Lofthus in Ullensvang, whose natural splendor has been immortalized in a poem by Wergeland.[2]

---

[1] The letter is printed in English translation in Finn Benestad (ed.), *Edvard Grieg: Letters to Colleagues and Friends*, Columbus, Ohio 2000, pp. 501–502.

[2] Norwegian patriot and national poet Henrik Wergeland (1808–45). Grieg is most likely alluding to the poem entitled "Hardanger", which occurs as the penultimate poem in Wergeland's novel *Den engelske Lods* (*The English Pilot*), 1844.

The composer's hut in Hardanger. The String Quartet *op. 27 and* The Mountain Thrall *op. 32 are among the works written here.*

I had to find a place for my composer's hut here, and unfamiliar with the area as I was at that time I chose a remote hill, to which no visible path led, in the hope of getting away from people. However, it was just my bad luck that a time-honored old footpath—about whose existence I was ignorant—led right up to the place. And the farmers—let me tell you, they found that path in no time at all! They wanted to "listen in". All winter, when the weather was not too bad, I had the dubious pleasure of hearing stealthy footsteps outside the house while I sat working. Many a time when I got up from my writing desk to try out a new-born musical idea on the piano, more than one embryo got strangled by the critical comments of the farmers who stood behind the house listening in the hope of becoming the child's godfathers.

The path across the meadow through the knee-deep snow often was hard enough for me, and moreover, it turned out that the hut was so exposed to the fierce weather that during powerful winter storms I often thought that I and the whole building were going to blow away. One day the situation became intolerable. I decided, like a new Aladdin,[3] to move my whole castle, and I was lucky enough to find a sheltered and quiet place—one with a view toward Folgefonnen's glaciers—far down by the fjord, between cliffs and copsewood.

It was already nearing Easter when I proceeded to carry out my plan. I got

---

[3] Aladdin (Arabian: *Ala ad-din*), the hero in one of the fairytales in *A Thousand and One Nights*.

about fifty farmers—at least that many were needed—who most willingly promised to help. N.B.: not as workers—I couldn't get them to do that—but as friends and acquaintances. Our farm folk have the custom, as old as it is nice, of helping each other with jobs that require a lot of manpower and expecting no remuneration other than food and drink. Their word for this sort of thing is *dugnad.* I have heard several explanations of the origin of the word. Some think it corresponds to the Danish word *davre,* others that it comes from the verb *duge* (Danish *due*).[4] Thus one shall demonstrate that one is "capable". It is likely that the latter interpretation is better.

One lovely morning at the stroke of nine the whole crowd of brawny men gathered in an obviously festive mood, which was in no way diminished by the sight of the abundant preparations in the way of food and drink—for which I had wisely made provision. A barrel of Hardanger beer, famous for its strength, stood ready for serving beside adequate stocks of genuine Norwegian aquavit and appropriate delicacies such as flat-bread, lefse,[5] pastries and the like. All these wonderful national edibles were sent to the new building lot, where, after the work was finished, the real serving of refreshments was to take place under the guidance of my amiable landlady, who is known throughout Hardanger for her beauty and intelligence.

Together with my fellow Bergensian, the painter Vilhelm Peters,[6] who was also spending the winter there, and who on this occasion functioned with conspicuous success as a kind of general in charge, I marched at the head of my army to the appointed place. The tasks were now assigned. Everyone was ordered to his place, and I will not soon forget that glorious moment in "The Compost's" history when, with a tremendous heave, it was torn from its foundation—see sketch: "Dugnaden I"—to the thunderous applause of the assembled spectators. Meanwhile, the pupils from a nearby girls' school, who had lined up outside the site to watch, waved their handkerchiefs and filled the air with an enthusiastic "hurrah" that was full of youth and springtime. It was as if all of us were electrified by these light and cheerful female voices, and with much shouting the house was moved—see sketch: "Dugnaden II"—sometimes dragged, sometimes rolled on heavy logs, to its new home.

A delightful situation developed during a rest break when Messrs. Grieg and Peters went from man to man pouring aquavit left and right, and all the while juicy wisecracks whirled around like hail bearing witness to the general sense of well-being—see "Dugnaden III".

---

[4] The Danish word *davre* means "morning meal" or "breakfast", the old Norwegian word *duge* means "to be capable".

[5] Lefse: a thin Norwegian bread resembling a soft tortilla.

[6] Norwegian painter Vilhelm Peters (1851–1931) made the series of hastily-drawn sketches of the events described in Grieg's report.

Sketches made by Norwegian painter Vilhelm Peters

Then we continued forward, and with renewed cries of "hurrah" we reached our goal. When the house was finally lifted up on its new foundation, it looked quite splendid, nestled between the birch and the mountain ash beside the crystal clear fjord. Then the ale bowls were passed around, and they were needed, too; for many a husky fellow was seen wiping the sweat from his brow after the exertion. People gathered in small groups here and there on the grass, yielding to their need for rest. The Sørfjordingers demonstrated at this stage of the party just how amiable and cordial they can be. Bantering talk laced with wit and humor flew from mouth to mouth, and legends and stories flowed from eloquent lips with a primitive power and terseness worthy of the sagas in the wonderful, sonorous dialect of the area,[7] so that for me it was like listening to the most beautiful music.

But the work was still not completely finished, for now the piano had to be moved to its place. A detachment of troops was sent off, and a few minutes later in a mood of excessive gaiety they came galloping with the heavy box as if it were a ball of feathers. Meanwhile, the guests who had stayed behind had been guzzling the beer to such an extent that the atmosphere was becoming more animated than one might have wished. A couple of drunken fellows could already be seen lying like dead bodies on the grass. The rest of the crowd now insisted that I play—which I obviously neither could nor would refuse to do—and in a moment the little hut was so jammed full of listeners that I could scarcely move my arms. Those who couldn't find standing room inside stood in the open door or sat in the window, while the rest of the listening crowd stood outside and craned their necks to see the performance.

To the accompaniment of a listener to my left, who constantly staggered against me so that I almost fell off the stool, and another to my right, who recited with such fervor that the saliva sprayed out onto the keys, I struck up the Norwegian folk dance called "Stabbelåten".[8] I must admit that now there was a moment in which it was perfectly quiet—but it was only for a brief moment.[9] Suddenly a husky voice in the corner of the room pronounced, "Thanks. Now, damn it all, that's enough for today!" A most encouraging response! I didn't let that scare me away, though, even if the laughter made it hard to keep on playing; but I kept on until the dance was finished, fired up by the fact that the fellow who so rudely interrupted me got what he deserved by being—to speak literally—kicked out of the "concert hall". When the last note had faded away, one of the group who was still sober congratulated me on my new house, to which I replied by expressing thanks to everyone who had participated in the "dugnad" and proposing a toast to the people of Sørfjorden.

Meanwhile, outside the house things began to get even wilder. People began throwing stones and clumps of turf. First they tried to hit each other, but they soon got tired of this sort of thing. Then the ale bowls, which were being passed from one man to another, became the chosen targets. The aiming was remarkably accurate. Beer and turf showered down upon the bystanders in such quantities that the air itself seemed to be darkened; and when one person or

---

[7] Grieg's stay in Hardanger proved to be extremely important, not only for his art but also for the opportunity it provided for him to become acquainted first-hand with one of the rural dialects on which *nynorsk*—a form of the Norwegian language that sought explicitly to eliminate all evidence of Danish influence—was based.

[8] "Stabbelåten" ("Peasant Dance") is no. 18 in Grieg's *Twenty-five Norwegian Folk Songs and Dances*, op. 17.

[9] Grieg evidently is alluding to a brief pause between two sections of the piece he was playing.

another got himself a regular "beer bath" there was a deafening shout of laughter. It was a grotesque sight!

While this was going on up by the cabin, some tipsy fellows for whom the beer keg had a magical power of attraction were lying down by the fjord. The sketch—"Dugnaden IV"—shows one of these who had selected a place directly under the spout so the beer could run right down into his open mouth. At last the insensibility took over completely. One poor fellow, who had collapsed dead drunk on the grass, was almost buried alive under clumps of sod while the onlookers laughed demoniacally.

At this point in the festivities, I found it wisest to slip away unnoticed. The next morning, when I returned to the place, it presented a sorry sight. The beautiful lawn had totally disappeared, and clumps of torn-up turf, tree-stumps, branches, and stones—here and there even stained with dried blood—covered the battlefield.

This was the consecration of my hut—and I dare say that if *that* cost blood, my stay there did so every bit as much. For nowhere has my heart's blood flowed as in the music that came into being here.[10] It was a glorious time. Here there was peace and quiet right up to the time of the summer holidays, when tourists began to gather in boats right outside my window. Then that pleasure passed away, too.

I later sold The Compost, which now has been moved to the Ullensvang rectory, where it is used as a—doll's house.[11]

---

[10] One of Grieg's most significant compositions, *String Quartet in G Minor*, op. 27, was written in Ullensvang.

[11] "Komposten" was later moved to Bokn, where it served as a wash house for the employees of a steamship company. In 1949, on the initiative of the Ullensvang Youth Society, it was purchased and brought back to Ullensvang. Here it was placed in a beautiful setting close to the fjord, and the Ullensvang Hotel—now an enlarged and modernized five-star tourist hotel still in the possession of the Utne family—has outfitted it as a miniature Grieg museum.

A Cosmopolitan Credo (1889)

As Grieg's career progressed he became increasingly sensitive about being identified as a purely national composer, one who merely took materials from Norway's folk tradition and passed them off as original compositions. Grieg was adamant about the fact that his music, except for compositions explicitly identified as arrangements, was entirely original. Moreover, his works were intended for an international audience, and he in fact enjoyed a worldwide popularity equaled by few of his contemporaries.

Grieg's frustration came out clearly in 1889, when he issued what he himself, in a letter of November 21, 1889, to Danish musicologist Angul Hammerich (1848–1931), called a "cosmopolitan credo".[1] It was written in response to an article by German music critic Alexander Moszkowski (1851–1934) in the Copenhagen *Musikbladet*, edited by music publisher Alfred Wilhelm Hansen (1854–1923). Grieg's response was printed in the same journal on October 8.

Troldhaugen, Bergen, September 14, 1889

Dear Mr. Wilhelm Hansen!

In an article entitled "About National Compositions", which appeared in your music periodical, you have quoted the views of a Berlin critic on this topic—views that are patently open to contradiction. However, I shall not take the trouble to act as the defender of national art in general, for the history of art has taken care of that defense so thoroughly that any further attempt is superfluous. The author of the aforementioned article has, however, tracked down a statement that I made many years ago, a remark that belongs so completely to my very "green" period that I consider it my duty to publicly disavow it here. The remark to which I refer was this: "We (Nordraak[2] and I) conspired against the Mendelssohn-inspired, effeminate Scandinavianism of Gade,[3] and we set out with enthusiasm on the new road on which the Nordic school now finds itself."

You will understand that from my present standpoint I cannot acknowledge a statement that to a greater degree than one might wish expresses mere youthful arrogance. I hardly need to assure you that I am neither so one-sided as not to have deep respect and admiration for a master such as Gade, nor so superficial as to—as the author of the article puts it—actually claim to be "the most national among the national composers, the true Messiah of Norwegian music." Faced with such an assertion, I dare say that the author lacks the most essential qualifications for judging me. If the author had been familiar with my work in its entirety, it would hardly have escaped him that in my more recent compositions I have striven increasingly toward a broader and more universal view of my own

---

[1] Norwegian: "kosmopolitisk trosbekjennelse".
[2] Norwegian composer Rikard Nordraak (1842–66). See Grieg's reviews of Nordraak's songs on pp. 246–249.
[3] Danish composer Niels W. Gade (1817–90).

individuality, a view influenced by the great currents of our time—that is, by the cosmopolitan movement. But this I willingly admit: Never could I bring myself to violently tear up the roots that tie me to my native land.

As I regret that such misleading statements about my art have found their way to the Danish reading public, I venture to request a place for these few lines in your esteemed periodical.

Respectfully,
EDVARD GRIEG

Bequest to Bergen Public Library (1906)

Grieg did not receive royalties for his compositions. Like other composers of his day, he received a one-time honorarium from his publisher when one of his compositions was published—though C. F. Peters, in a very unusual arrangement, in 1889 began paying him in addition an annual honorarium. Nonetheless, it was his publishers who made the big profits under these arrangements, for Grieg's compositions sold exceptionally well.

It was not until the establishment of the Norwegian Performing Rights Society (TONO) in 1928 that composers and their heirs began to receive royalties for performances of their works. International copyright law now provides that such royalties shall be paid for 50 years after the death of the composer. Partly because of the interruption of World War II (1939–45), the period of copyright protection for prewar works was further extended by six years. Thus Grieg's works were protected until 1963. Hundreds of thousands of Norwegian crowns therefore flowed into the "Edvard Grieg Fund", thereby fulfilling Grieg's hope that this fund might grow to such an extent that it would provide "steady support for Bergen's higher music life".

Ten months before Grieg's death in 1907, he and his wife willed his collection of manuscripts, music, books and letters to Bergen Public Library. Parts of this legacy were conveyed to the library in 1919, and the most valuable items—including 150 manuscripts, about 700 letters from Grieg and some 5,000 letters to Grieg—were received as late as 1930, by which time Nina Grieg (1845–1935) was living in Denmark.

Edvard and Nina Grieg in 1906

The Grieg Archives of Bergen Public Library became a reality in 1930. Through the years the Collection has grown and today consists of approximately 25,000 pages of handwritten material: manuscripts of compositions, sketches, letters, articles, diaries, and account books. The Collection also contains first editions of Grieg's works, concert programs, Grieg's own collection of the music of other composers and some of his books and sound recordings. By virtue of its unique store of source material, it has become an international center of Grieg research.

Grieg's letter of bequest is preserved in Bergen Public Library.

Christiania, November 12, 1906

Governing Board of Bergen Public Library
Bergen.
In our testamentary decisions, my wife and I have expressed the wish that our remaining sheet music, books, manuscripts, autographs and letters from artists shall, after our deaths, become the property of Bergen Public Library on the assumption that it will preserve them and make them accessible to the Bergen citizenry.

I take the liberty in that connection to ask whether the Governing Board of Bergen Public Library is willing to accept such a gift.[1]

Respectfully,
EDVARD GRIEG

---

[1] On the same date, Grieg wrote an addendum that was published in the Bergen press. It had the heading "Edvard Grieg's Fund" and reads as follows: "Since the committee for the 'Edvard Grieg's Fund' established in 1903 in honor of my 60th birthday has, in a letter of October 27 of this year, placed this fund at my disposal, I wish to express my heartfelt thanks to everyone far and near who has been willing to honor me by contributing to its growth, and among these not least to the Committee for its initiative and work in bringing it into existence. It is my wish that, when the fund has grown to 100,000 Norwegian crowns, the interest therefrom shall be used for the furtherance of music in Bergen, the city of my birth. I have thought that this fund could become the basis for a larger collection of capital which, with the addition of legacies, gifts etc. from the city's women and men who have an interest in music, could grow to such a size that it might become the so long desired steady support for Bergen's higher music life. With this great goal in view, I myself have made testamentary decisions in the hope that other citizens of Bergen may feel encouraged to do likewise in support of this cause that is so important for the cultural future of our city."

The Diary of 1905–07

By 1905, nearly forty years had passed since Grieg had last kept a diary—years in which he had experienced both success and failure. Mostly the former, however, for his music had become known and loved all over the world. His *Piano Concerto* and the two *Peer Gynt* suites continued to attract throngs of music-lovers to the great concert halls, and his *Lyric Pieces* were favorites in virtually every home where piano music was played.

Grieg was also highly sought after as a conductor, often accepting invitations to conduct abroad. The result was a series of long, demanding, exhausting concert tours that took an inevitable toll on his energy—with the unfortunate result that in his later years he had neither time nor strength to do much composing.

Increasing illness also marked Grieg's old age. Both his letters and his diary during the years preceding his death in 1907 contain heart-rending accounts of the pain he had to endure as a result of his multiple ailments.

Notwithstanding his busy professional life and the increasingly debilitating state of his health, Grieg remained vitally interested in current events both at home and abroad. 1905 was a particularly critical year for Norway as negotiations with Sweden regarding the political relationship between the two countries reached an impasse and both sides prepared for the possibility of armed conflict. The Swedish-Norwegian union was eventually dissolved without bloodshed, however, and on November 25, 1905, independent Norway welcomed its new royal couple, King Haakon VII (1872–1957) and Queen Maud (1869–1938). The event was celebrated in Christiania with a three-day festival culminating in a gala theatrical performance at the National Theater in the course of which Grieg met the new king and queen for the first time. It was shortly after this meeting that Grieg made his first diary entry for the year 1905.

The Diary of 1905–07, like that of 1865–66, is preserved in Bergen Public Library. It was published in the original Norwegian in Finn Benestad (ed.), *Edvard Grieg: Dagbøker*, Bergen 1993, pp. 97–215.

1905

November 28

Gala performance in the National Theater in honor of the king and queen. *Sigurd Jorsalfar*,[1] preceded by a pompous and melodic "Festival March" composed for the occasion by Johan Halvorsen[2] and a "Prologue" by Theodor Caspari masterfully presented by Halfdan Christensen.[3] A festive atmosphere accompanied the performance of the play, but the actors and actresses didn't get the applause they deserved because, unlike the Bernadottes,[4] the king didn't give the signal for the audience to clap. This will certainly be different when the king is informed about the custom regarding this matter.

---

[1] *Sigurd Jorsalfar (Sigurd the Crusader)* by Norwegian author Bjørnstjerne Bjørnson (1832–1910), for which Grieg had composed incidental music in 1872.
[2] Johan Halvorsen (1864–1935), musical director of the National Theater in Christiania, was one of Norway's most prominent composers. See Grieg's tribute to him on pp. 389–390. Halvorsen's festival march was entitled "Greeting to Norway's Royal Couple".
[3] Norwegian author Theodor Caspari (1853–1948) and Norwegian actor Halfdan Christensen (1873–1950).
[4] Grieg here means the Swedish royal family.

Bjørnstjerne Bjørnson and Grieg

After the conclusion of the second act, Bjørnson and I were fetched from our first-row orchestra seats by the lord chamberlain, Rustad,[5] who escorted us to the royal box. The king and queen stepped forward to greet us with the greatest kindness. If they are as unpretentious and straightforward as they here appeared to be, then we may dare to hope for a democratic monarchy.[6]

The queen reminded me of the time in 1887 when Nina and I visited her mother[7] in London, when she and her teenage sisters came with their albums to get our autographs. She, like the king, spoke positively about my music and said they were looking forward to the Music Association concert, where I have been asked to conduct. So also did Prince Heinrich of Prussia, the brother of Keiser Wilhelm. [8] He even maintained that he knew my music by heart. Fortunately, I myself do not.

---

[5] Fredrik F. M. W. Rustad (1852–1930) was lord chamberlain (*hoffsjef*) in 1905.

[6] As a matter of principle, Grieg personally preferred a republican form of government. He felt, however, that in the situation in which Norway found itself in 1905 a monarchy was the only reasonable choice. On October 26 of that fateful year he wrote to his colleague Gerhard Schjelderup, "As much as I love the idea of a republic, I do not doubt for a moment that what is needed now is a monarchy."

[7] Queen Maud was the daughter of Prince Albert Edward (1841–1910), King Edward VII of England from 1901 to 1910, and his wife Alexandra (1844–1925), eldest daughter of Prince Christian (1818–1906), King Christian IX of Denmark from 1863 to 1906. Grieg's first visit to England occurred in April/May 1888, but the visit to the Princess of Wales at Marlborough House in London took place on March 27, 1889, during his third concert tour in England.

[8] Wilhelm II (1859–1941).

This first meeting with free Norway's first king and queen struck me as something beautiful and meaningful, and for that reason I choose this day to start my long-intended diary.

November 29

With Bjørnson and Karoline for dinner (without Nina, who was tired) as guests of Sigurd and Bergliot Ibsen[9] at Slemdal. Wonderful weather, a nice time.

[Sigurd] Ibsen explained his position to me. He had wanted to have—and already during the time of the Hagerup[10] cabinet had recommended—the nullification of the Union Treaty[11] and, therewith, of the Union [between Norway and Sweden]. He had even informed King Oscar of his standpoint, and the King had agreed that in this event one of his sons could become king of Norway. Michelsen supposedly had been ready to go along with this plan until Schøning[12] persuaded him to join him in resigning from the Hagerup ministry. For Michelsen the only thing of importance originally was just the resolution of the consular issue,[13] whereas Ibsen was primarily concerned about the nullification of the Union Treaty and the transformation of the union into a [so-called] personal union [between the two countries]. Michelsen did not follow Ibsen but chose the path that led to the 7th of June.[14]

It is Ibsen's opinion that Sweden was completely ready to implement his proposal, whereas Michelsen's has created so much violent anger in Sweden that it will take a long time to get over it. The future will show who was right. I for my part think that nothing would have freed us from the union except Michelsen's deft handling—that and the Swedes' many stupidities and mistakes.

Ibsen is writing a book in which he will clearly spell it all out, and this book

---

[9] Bjørnstjerne Bjørnson's wife, Karoline Bjørnson (1835–1934); Edvard's wife, Nina Grieg (1845–1935); Sigurd Ibsen (1859–1930), son of Henrik Ibsen (1828–1906) and Suzannah Ibsen, nee Thoresen (1838–1914); Bergliot Ibsen (1869–1953), daughter of Bjørnstjerne and Karoline Bjørnson and wife of Sigurd Ibsen.

[10] Sigurd Ibsen was the Norwegian foreign minister in the coalition cabinet of Francis Hagerup (1853–1921), which was in power from October 1903 to March 1905. His office was in Stockholm, where he played an active role in the final negotiations regarding the union issue. On February 8, 1905, the Norwegian Parliament (*Stortinget*) was informed that the result of these negotiations was negative, whereupon the Hagerup cabinet resigned and Christian Michelsen became prime minister on March 11.

[11] In 1814, after having been subordinate to Denmark for over 400 years—a period that Grieg once called "the four-hundred-year night" in Norwegian history—Norway was separated from Denmark, adopting its own constitution on May 17 of that year. At the end of the Napoleonic Wars, however, Denmark had already promised Norway to Sweden. A short war between Norway and Sweden ended in a peace treaty, and in November 1814 Carl XIII (1748–1818), who had been King of Sweden since 1809, also became King of Norway. The Union Treaty—"Riksakten"—which was signed on August 6, 1815, was an agreement outlining mutual rights and obligations between the two countries. This is the document to which Grieg is referring. It became null and void with the action of the Norwegian Parliament (*Stortinget*) on June 7, 1905.

[12] Jacob Marius Schøning (1856–1934), Norwegian politician, one of the prominent figures in 1905.

[13] In 1892 the Norwegian Parliament (*Stortinget*) had passed a resolution establishing an independent consular service, but the king had refused to sign it. The resulting impasse precipitated a major program of rearmament in Norway and nearly led to war between Norway and Sweden.

[14] On June 7, 1905, the Norwegian Parliament unanimously passed a resolution declaring that the union between Norway and Sweden had ceased to exist and authorized the cabinet to continue in office and rule the country.

may become one of the most remarkable of all the strange documents from this significant period.[15]

At 9:00 in the evening a rehearsal of "Land-sighting" with the choir in the Businessmen's Hall. A splendid choir of 130. We are living in the time of ovations. There were speeches, shouts of "hurrah" and clapping—so much that I had to urge them to save their strength so they would have a little left for the big *fortissimos*. They sing with enthusiasm, and if we had a suitable hall in this city there would be a magnificent sound when everything comes together. But there's not a single auditorium here where a choir and an orchestra can perform together successfully.

November 30

2:30–6:00 P.M. Dinner at "Engebret"[16] for Bjørnson and Karoline, Bjørn, Einar, Jacobsens (only Mrs. Jacobsen came, and she left early as she was going to perform in *Alexander the Great*[17] at 7:00), Frits Thaulow and his wife, Eilif Peterssen and his wife, Hildur Andersen, cabinet minister Fr. Stang Lund and his wife, Stang Lund Jr. and his wife (Nina, the blue lady!), Joachim Grieg, Frida Grieg, Johan Halvorsen and his wife, Benedicte and Bet.[18] I sat between Karoline and Mrs. Thaulow. Nina sat by Bjørnson, who gave a beautiful, fine talk in our honor. The mood was wonderful.

December 1

First orchestra rehearsal of the *Lyric Suite*.[19] I think it is going to sound good. Attended a big dinner party at Einar Bjørnson's celebrating Karoline Bjørnson's 70th birthday. Bjørnson was hoarse, so he spoke only briefly to Karoline—beautifully, of course—but Bjørn spoke many heart-warming words as he patted and hugged her. It was special and moving. I thanked her from her friends.

---

[15] Sigurd Ibsen's account of the events preceding the dissolution of the union in 1905 did not come out in book form as Grieg suggested, but in 1906 was published as an article in the journal *Samtiden*. It aroused considerable interest.

[16] The restaurant "Engebret"—which Grieg always spelled "Engebregt"—exists to this day on Bankplassen ("The bank square") in Oslo, close to the old Freemasons' Lodge where Grieg had so many artistic triumphs. Nina and Edvard often used this restaurant for festive gatherings.

[17] *Alexander the Great*, a light comedy by Danish author Gustav Esmann (1860–1904). The performance took place at the Tivoli Theater in Christiania, as part of a series of plays given by the Danish guest ensemble "The Eights" ("De Ottes").

[18] The guests mentioned here are Bjørnstjerne and Karoline Bjørnson's sons Bjørn (1859–1942) and Einar (1864–1942); Danish actors Jacob Jacobsen (1865–1955) and his wife Olivia Jacobsen (1869–1945); Norwegian painter Frits Thaulow (1847–1906) and his wife; Norwegian painter Eilif Peterssen (1852–1928) and his wife; Norwegian pianist Hildur Andersen (1864–1956); Norwegian attorney and politician Fredrik Stang Lund (1859–1922) and his wife; Fredrik Stang Lund's son and his wife; Bergen ship broker and politician (Edvard's second cousin) Joachim Grieg (1849–1932) and his daughter Frida Grieg Shetelig (1880–1955); Johan Halvorsen and his wife (Edvard's niece) Annie Grieg Halvorsen (1873–1957); Edvard's sisters Benedicte (1838–1918) and Elisabeth ("Bet", "Betten") Grieg (1845–1927).

[19] *Lyric Suite* consists of four numbers from the fifth volume of *Lyric Pieces* op. 54: "Shepherd's Boy", "Gangar", "March of the Dwarfs", and "Nocturne". They were written for piano in 1891 and arranged for orchestra by Grieg in 1905.

December 2

Big supper at Michelsen's with the king, the queen, the diplomatic corps, local authorities, the press, a few scientists, Bjørnson and Karoline. Karoline was my table companion, Bjørnson was Nina's.

The royal couple again deported themselves with discretion and forthrightness. Parties like that are so deadly boring and superficial and utterly inane, however, that for me they are an abomination. And the stiffness! These people should take a lesson from the royal couple.

I had to laugh when Nina told me, after we got home, that the king had said that the whole experience of becoming king seemed like such a fairytale to him that in the morning he had to pinch his arm to make sure that it really was happening to him. Besides, he added, I intend to continue being the same person I was before. And when Nina then related concerning Copenhagen Professor Rovsing[20]—whom the king knew—that, upon being named professor, he had expressed the hope that he wouldn't "get possessed by professorhood", the king said: "No, I promise you that I will never allow myself to get possessed by majesty!" Natural and unspoiled, in a way that one does not expect in a sovereign—perhaps with the sole exception of Christian IX and his descendants.[21]

December 4

Had the second orchestra rehearsal of the *Lyric Suite*, and I wish we were having twice as many rehearsals of it. It ought to be much freer and more delicate. But one must howl etc. [with the wolves one is with]. Unfortunately, the second flute had become sick, and in his place was a boy who will drive me to despair if he doesn't count better tomorrow than he did today. No, I'm too old for that sort of thing. I simply am not good at standing there and drilling people on their ABC's any more.

December 5

Final dress rehearsal in the Music Association. Svendsen's[22] *Symphony in B-flat Major* sounded marvelous, as Svendsen's orchestral pieces always do. Moreover, the orchestra handles the technical difficulties and tricks flawlessly. The main shortcoming, however, consists in the fact that whereas Svendsen conducts sensitively and in an even tempo, Holter conducts everything with big, mechanical motions, then suddenly for no reason at all he slows down a bit at a place where

---

[20] Danish physician and professor Niels Ivar Asmund Rovsing (1850–1909). For another account of this amusing story see Grieg's letter to Frants Beyer (1851–1918) of December 12, 1905, in Finn Benestad (ed.), *Edvard Grieg: Letters to Colleagues and Friends*, Columbus, Ohio 2000, p. 99. Frants and Marie Beyer (1852–1929) were the Griegs' closest friends in Bergen.

[21] Danish King Christian IX (1818–1906), grandfather of Norway's new king Haakon VII.

[22] Norwegian composer and conductor Johan Svendsen (1840–1911). See Grieg's review of an 1867 concert by Svendsen on pp. 280–283.

Svendsen continues in the same tempo. When the tradition is as fresh in people's minds as it is here, any arbitrariness should be off limits.

The *Lyric Suite* went well for the most part when I make allowances for the small number of strings and the altogether too timid harpist (open though she indeed was to suggestions). Mrs. Gulbranson[23] no longer has the charm that she once had in "Solveig's Cradle Song", "From Monte Pincio" and "A Swan", but she sang confidently and for the most part with good intonation. "Land-sighting", as sung by the 130 singers from the Businessmen's Chorus, sounded wonderful. Lammers[24] was at his heroic best. Yes, there is manliness in his performance of these verses, I tell you, and that is something I value highly in this particular piece.

Hopefully all the performers will do their duty tomorrow and not allow themselves to be distracted by looking at the royal couple.

December 6

Shortly before I was going to go to bed last evening, my head began—for the first time—to spin. Everything was moving, and my legs almost went out from under me. The condition continued until I fell asleep. As I was getting dressed this morning I still felt a little shaky. Could it be the beginning of the end? Perhaps the slight exertion of the rehearsals has been too much for me. For the sake of all the others I hope that I will be able to manage things this evening. I myself no longer have any ambition. Just the artistic satisfaction of turning in a good performance.

December 7

Artistically, the concert last evening was successful—but the audience was inconsolable because the queen did not come! She had a cold, but the king was there.

Yes, there we see: What is music in comparison with an absent queen and a present king! If a royal couple—or even a single royal person—is able to produce a stimulating effect on a street, the very opposite is true in a concert hall. Here, people like that tend to subdue enthusiasm. [That people react that way reflects] an unbelievably low and snobbish attitude—and such a country is supposed to be ready to become a republic!

Mrs. Gulbranson sang splendidly. She was at her very best. *Lyric Suite* also went magnificently, and "Land-sighting" went so well that at the end I myself was completely enchanted. It was wonderful to work with Norwegian musicians again.

---

[23] Swedish-Norwegian soprano Ellen Nordgren Gulbranson (1863–1947).

[24] Norwegian baritone and choral conductor Thorvald Lammers (1841–1922). See Grieg's tribute to him on pp. 391–392.

December 31

Just got home from an 8-day stay at Our Lady's Hospital [Vor Frues Hospital], where I was obliged to flee because of my poorly functioning digestive system and my shattered nerves. A daily stomach-pumping has perhaps helped a little, but no doctor can tell me how to keep this illness at a respectable distance.

Perhaps I overexerted myself at the concert on the 6th. Have been ailing ever since, hence no diary entries.

I have done a lot of reading in Peter Tchaikovsky's *Life and Letters* by Modeste Tchaikovsky. English edition.[25] What a noble and true person! And what a melancholy joy to continue in this way the personal acquaintance established in Leipzig in 1888![26] It is as if a friend were speaking to me.

Now the year 1905—the great year—goes to rest, and I part from it with deep gratitude because I experienced it! And yet, without the youthful dreams that this year has made real, my art would not have had its proper background. The longings have transformed my personal experiences into tones. Had the 7th of June come in my youth, what would have happened?

No, it is good that things happened as they did. The lifelong struggle has been the greatest good fortune both for the individual and for the nation. Freedom is: the *struggle* for freedom!

1906

January 7

People who attended last evening's benefit concert for the unemployed have told about how absurdly Mrs. Cally Monrad[27] interpreted several songs including "The First Meeting". Oh, these prima donnas! Here, for example, is a highly talented one who can't think of any better way to amuse herself than to deliberately

---

[25] Grieg is referring to Modeste Tchaikovsky (1850–1916), *The Life & Letters of Peter Ilich Tchaikovsky*, edited from the Russian with an introduction by Rosa Newmarch, London, 1905. Modeste Tchaikovsky was the composer's brother.

[26] Grieg met Peter Tchaikovsky (1840–93) for the first time on January 1, 1888, at a party in Leipzig at the home of Russian violinist Adolf Brodsky (1851–1929). Four weeks later he was with Tchaikovsky again at Brodsky's, and after this meeting he wrote enthusiastically to his Bergen friend Frants Beyer, "We made music all the time. First, at Tchaikovsky's request, Brodsky and I played my new sonata. Then Sinding's quintet was tried out, with Sapelnikov at the piano, and lastly my *String Quartet*. Those fellows can really play! My God, what a sound! (. . .) In Tchaikovsky I have gained a warm friend for my music. He is as favorably disposed toward me as I am toward him, both as an artist and as a human being. You will learn to know him because he undoubtedly will be coming to Troldhaugen."

   Tchaikovsky wrote warmly of Grieg's music in his autobiographical account of his journey abroad in 1888: "What enchantment, what spontaneity and richness in the musical inventiveness! What warmth and passion in his singing phrases, what a fountain of pulsating life in his harmonies, what originality and entrancing distinctiveness in his clever and piquant modulations, and in the rhythm as in everything else— how unfailingly interesting, new, original!" (From Tchaikovsky's *Autobiographical Descriptions of a Journey Abroad in 1888* via translation into Norwegian of the Russian original by Jon-Roar Bjørkvold.)

[27] Norwegian soprano Cally Monrad (1879–1950).

do the very opposite of realizing the composer's intentions. Why? In order to be original, in order to be sensational. Virtually all prima donnas forget that in so doing they fail to achieve what they intend. The desired effect escapes them because the performance is based on a false perception. They destroy the work of art by chopping it up into little pieces, singing *forte* where the composer has indicated *piano* and *piano* where he has indicated *forte*. Then they go on to take the slow parts fast and the fast ones slow. In short: They allow themselves everything except the slightest degree of reverence or respect for the work of art or for the artist. And as I have said, when they destroy the work of art in this way they must necessarily achieve the very opposite of what they want. They lose the good will of their audience, especially of the sophisticated members of the audience. That is something the prima donnas here in Norway should start to take into account.

What are prima donnas? They are the epitome of vanity, stupidity, ignorance and dilettantism. I hate them one and all! "Also your wife?" someone may interject. I reply: "Excuse me, but she, fortunately, is not a prima donna."

I saw Moser's[28] cheap, riotous farce *Ultimo*, in which Klausen[29] still performs as brilliantly as ever in his old starring role as the Professor. Løvaas,[30] buoyed by a wealth of natural talent, is masterful as the Consul. Mrs. Mette Bull[31] was a sweet ingenue.

January 9

Today was a truly enjoyable day. First, I got a good laugh as I was sitting in the barbershop reading *Dagbladet*.[32] An article by Mr. Haarklou about new music discusses some organ preludes by O. Winter-Hjelm and "Improvisata and Legend for Organ" by Chr. Cappelen.[33] Regarding these two gentlemen, Haarklou writes that "both of them once made serious attempts at composition, but they stagnated as a result of their boundless admiration for two of their contemporaries whose works attracted attention abroad.[34] (!) Now that these springs have run dry—and had to run dry—because of their one-sided nationalism, Winter-Hjelm and Cappelen have begun to consider whether they, too, might perhaps have made more worthwhile contributions to Norwegian music if they had cultivated others a little less and themselves a little more." And later: "As composers, both [Winter-]Hjelm and Cappelen tend in a more universal direction,

[28] German playwright Gustav von Moser (1825–1903).
[29] Norwegian actor Henrik Klausen (1844–1907). Klausen had played the title role in the premiere production of *Peer Gynt* in 1876.
[30] Norwegian actor Johan Løvaas (1870–1916).
[31] Norwegian actress Mette Marie Bull (1876–1946).
[32] Liberal newspaper in Christiania.
[33] Norwegian composers Johannes Haarklou (1847–1925), Otto Winter-Hjelm 1837–1931), and Christian Cappelen (1845–1919).
[34] Haarklou is alluding to Grieg and Johan Svendsen.

and that is most remarkable since one could expect that in this field also they would have presented themselves as apostles of sorts for the contemporary ideals by imitating their jargon. They don't do that, though, and it should not be held against them."

Well, that's what it says. But it is incredible that the "contemporary ideals" still cannot escape the poison arrows with which Mr. Haarklou—for nearly a generation, on every imaginable and unimaginable occasion—has tried to strike them in the press. This article is supposed to be just a review of a few short organ pieces. But see how inventive he is: One, two, three—and there he stands aiming at the unsuspecting "contemporary ideals". He uses up all his imaginative ammunition shooting at others, and nothing is left over for his own compositions—where it is so sorely needed.

It occurred to me that Mr. H. is like Cicero[35] at this point. Just as Cicero concluded all his talks with the statement, "It is my opinion that Carthage must be destroyed," so Mr. H. is careful in ending his talks to insert the words, "Svendsen and Grieg must be destroyed!" There is a small difference, however. Cicero's words were fulfilled: Carthage was destroyed, whereas Mr. H. still has not succeeded in dispatching the "contemporary ideals" of Winter-Hjelm and Cappelen.[36]

Later in the forenoon I had the great joy of seeing at the piano once again the most musical pupil I had as a young piano teacher: Betty Egeberg, now Mrs. Rev. Tandberg.[37] What a sensitive, brilliant person she is! How she awakened old memories! Both of us dreamt at that time of the life that lay before us. Now we both sat there and dreamt back to the life that has vanished. But there was no room for melancholy in my heart. Just as the lessons in those days were sheer beauty, so also was this time together.

Now it is evening and I am going to read aloud to Nina from Tchaikovsky's *Life and Letters*. That, too, is one of the high points of my present existence. All in all: a nice day!

January 13

I just came from the dress rehearsal for the concert to be given at the Christiania Theater and was moved to tears by *Death and Transfiguration*. Why, why did Strauss[38] not continue to go further in this direction, which is filled with poetry,

---

[35] Roman statesman Marcus Tullius Cicero (106–43 BC).

[36] A strained relationship had existed between Grieg and Haarklou for many years, especially after the Norwegian music festival in Bergen in 1898 when Grieg, to the great displeasure of many Norwegian musicians, had engaged the Concertgebouw Orchestra of Amsterdam instead of a Norwegian orchestra. See pp. 337–344, "The Norwegian Music Festival in Bergen (1898)". See also numerous contemptuous references to Haarklou in Finn Benestad (ed.), *Edvard Grieg: Letters to Colleagues and Friends*, Columbus, Ohio 2000.

[37] Norwegian pianist Betty Egeberg Tandberg (1853–1930).

[38] German composer Richard Strauss (1864–1949). His symphonic poem *Death and Transfiguration (Tod und Verklärung)* is op. 24 (1888–89).

instead of striking off down the road of sensation and empty virtuosity! No conjuring with the orchestra can compensate for the lack of inspiration and imagination. The orchestra's rendition was absolutely meritorious, at times excellent.

Alnæs' *Variations*[39] is a promising work. He is perhaps the cleverest of the younger composers. If only he could outgrow the almost too great heaviness, solidity, that characterizes his music.

Saint-Saëns'[40] spiritual masterwork *Suite Algérienne* seemed doubly fresh and jocular in contrast to the *Variations*. [Johan] Halvorsen's "Østerdal March" is a winner. It couldn't be better and it will speak for itself. Lammers must sing more freely. I cannot with the best will in the world get anything out of Selmer's[41] [song] "Wunsch" ("Wish"). It *tries* to be something, but it always misses the mark. "Åsmund Frægdegjæver"[42] does not succeed with the orchestral accompaniment Halvorsen has written for it. Since the melody is in the violins at all times, there is no need for a voice part. Not only that, but the song itself is ineffective because it is labored.

Notwithstanding this bit of criticism, the whole program is excellently put together, and Halvorsen deserves the greatest praise for both the program and the performance.

January 14

Have received a request by telegram from *Neue freie Presse* in Vienna to write a Mozart article for the master's 150th birthday on January 26. I have two days in which to write it. The article must be sent Wednesday forenoon at the latest, as they request that they receive it on Friday the 19th. I thought of Falstaff's question: 'What is honor?'[43] For this is indeed a huge honor—that someone from Mozart's city asks me, the foreigner from far-off Scandinavia, to do what 100 others could have done. But I forgot Falstaff's philosophy of life. I cabled: *Yes!* Well, we shall see. It means two days in the office. I'll lock my door and do my best. Good Lord, life is so short. What a joy to have an opportunity to honor my immortal master, the love of my childhood, Mozart in his own glorious Vienna![44]

---

[39] *Symphonic Variations for Orchestra* by Norwegian composer Eyvind Alnæs (1873–1932).

[40] French composer Camille Saint-Saëns (1835–1921).

[41] Norwegian composer Johan Selmer (1844–1910).

[42] A Norwegian folksong.

[43] In his letters Grieg often makes use of these words from the first act of the opera *Falstaff* by Giuseppe Verdi (1813–1901). The libretto, written by Arrigo Boito (1842–1918), was based on the comedy *The Merry Wives of Windsor* by William Shakespeare (1564–1616). In the scene in question, Falstaff is cursing his followers Bardolph and Pistol because they refuse to take some love letters to two ladies, whom he wants to try to fool. They insist that their honor will not allow them to take part in such a transaction. Falstaff then sings the aria "L'onore! Ladri!"

[44] The Mozart article of 1906 is printed in English translation on pp. 240–245.

January 18

The Mozart article is finished and mailed off. *Politiken* and *Verdens Gang* will carry it as well. I have also offered it to *The Times* and *Le Figaro* and am anxious to find out if they will take it.[45] After all, I am just as well known in London and Paris as in Vienna, so it is not altogether improbable. It would be fun to air my enthusiasm for Mozart in Vienna, Paris, London, Copenhagen and Christiania on the same day. (My article is a revision and summary of the article on Mozart that I wrote ten years ago for *The Century Magazine*. There was not time for a completely new article.)[46]

January 29

I know it in advance: Give the press an inch and it will take a mile. Or much more: Have anything at all to do with it and it becomes a source of aggravation. It is the lack of integrity reduced to a system.

Such irritation I have had because of that poor little Mozart article! The telegram from *Neue freie Presse* exhorted me to send the article for use "nächsten Sonntag" (next Sunday), by which, in accordance with common usage in the German language, I understood "Sonntag über 8 Tage" ("eight days from now"). Thus, in the belief that it would be run on the 28th, I made contact with *Verdens Gang*, *Politiken* and *The Times*, all three of which indicated that they would be glad to print the article. Then I got a telegram informing me that it was printed in *Neue freie Presse* already on the 21st (a week earlier), and there I stand [looking like a fool] in relation to the other three newspapers. Naturally neither *Politiken* nor *The Times* would print it after it had already appeared in *Neue freie Presse*; thus, they could not use it. *Verdens Gang* was the only newspaper that in all haste had time to print the article in almost the same moment that it was written.

That I have not received the honorarium previously agreed on from *Neue freie Presse* is consistent with the above account. I am almost amused by it, for it proves the incredible moral laxity of the press. Fortunately I have nonetheless received the reward that matters—much artistic pleasure from the little article in the form of expressions of thanks, both verbal and written, from home and from abroad. Even *Neue freie Presse* butters me up with milk and honey. That is cheapest for them!

It is said that "injury makes one wise". But I will never get wise. Each time I have something to do with the press, I bump into one form or another of meanness and shabbiness.

---

[45] The newspapers to which Grieg refers are *Politiken* in Copenhagen, *Verdens Gang* in Christiania, *The Times* in London, and *Le Figaro* in Paris.

[46] The earlier Mozart article written for *The Century Illustrated Monthly Magazine* is given in a new English translation on pp. 225–239.

February 15

Attended Mrs. Clara Hultgren's[47] concert. She has talent, but she still has a lot to learn. I was in agony when she sang "Solveig's Cradle Song", "From Monte Pincio", and "Say What You Will". The first two, especially, contained a series of mistakes. Good Lord! In a city where the composer lives, at least the tempi should not be completely off the wall. And there sits a talented musician—Alnæs—at the piano and lets a thing like that happen! I don't understand it.

This forenoon I took a trip to Gulleråsen,[48] where I was met by Chr. Collin,[49] who very cordially showed me around up there. Ah, lucky the man who could acquire a nice place to live in that area! I feel like a somewhat better person in that air.

February 17

Last evening Gerhart Hauptmann's[50] "The Weavers". Remarkably interesting. The fact that there are absolutely no leading characters is a real discovery. For such is life. What is interesting is *life*, not individual people. When you look at them more closely you see that they all are altogether too much alike to be interesting. This is what we constantly forget when we bow the knee to the individual.

There was something else that aroused my philosophical passion: We learn from this play that an intense, idealistic uprising is always short and is followed by a reaction. That is what we must expect. I expressed this thought to Prime Minister [Christian] Michelsen, who sat right behind me, and he replied: "It's true. You are right."

And yesterday as I was having breakfast I finally received a letter from Richard Strauss in reply to the telegram that I, in a moment of exhilaration, had sent him after the most recent performance of *Death and Transfiguration*. The letter is very typical. Just as one can speak of hidden [parallel] fifths, so also can one speak of hidden enemies. In this case they are hidden under the guise of amiability. But it is certain that if Strauss had an ounce of positive feeling toward me, this would have been the time to express it. Still, far be it from me to infer or expect such positive feeling. My music is so infinitely far removed from his that I do not dare to count on his understanding it. Obviously, I cannot compare myself with a master in the realm of technique such as Strauss, but since there is more to music than virtuosity, one would think that Richard Strauss might be aware of this except for the fact that the representatives of the small countries have an inestimable advantage vis-a-vis those of the large countries in that we, the former, who have to know everything, acquire a wider horizon than those who get stuck in the

---

47 Norwegian soprano Clara Falck Hultgren (1877–1956).
48 Gulleråsen is now a station on the subway line to Holmenkollen.
49 Norwegian literary historian Christen Collin (1857–1926).
50 German playwright Gerhart Hauptmann (1862–1946).

middle of their own one-sided culture. For that reason, I have greater chances to understand what is significant in Strauss than he has to see what may possibly be good in me.

February 23

Last evening in the University's large auditorium Georg Brandes[51] gave a lecture on the mutual relationship between Voltaire and Frederick the Great.[52] He is an intellectual giant and a master of wit and clear discourse. And the satanic sneer with which he relishes the passionate quarreling of these two great men is priceless. I am inclined to think that he exaggerates their weaknesses in order to display his own virtuosity. That is one of his weaknesses. And then there is his use of anecdotes, which *he* ought not to have to resort to as often as he does. Unfortunately, for reasons of health I had to miss the banquet that followed.

February 24

Last evening Sven Scholander[53] again demonstrated that he knows how to enchant [an audience] with his ballads. He is a genuine talent, equally significant in the tragic and the comic genres.

February 25

I am about to go mad because of a Danish woman, a real she-elephant, who lives directly above me. It is impossible to take a nap in the afternoon: She shuffles around incessantly, banging and thumping. I wanted to go to the Student Association and hear Brandes talk about [Henrik] Ibsen, but my nerves have gotten so distraught that I had to give up the idea. These hotels! When will it come to an end!

March 19

Have just come home after a 14-day stay at the Holmenkollen Sanitarium. The stay did not come up to expectations. I had some bad nights, with difficulty in breathing and hallucinations. One thing this stay has taught me: I should not live at a high altitude. And that lesson will come in handy when I am about to settle down in Christiania next fall, which I firmly intend to do.

But I can say with Kierkegaard:[54] What are all human decisions? The big mountain in the form of a concert tour to Prague, Amsterdam, and London lies before me and obstructs my view of the glorious, quiet time of which I am

---

[51] Danish literary historian and critic Georg Brandes (1842–1929).
[52] French philosopher and dramatist François Marie Arouet de Voltaire (1694–1778) and German King Frederick II (1712–86).
[53] Swedish composer and singer of ballads Sven Scholander (1860–1936).
[54] Danish philosopher Søren Kierkegaard (1813–55).

Edvard and Nina Grieg en route to Holmenkollen, 1906

dreaming. Will this trip be my last? And shall my life come to an end somewhere out there? Dark premonitions enshroud my outlook. But I shall not complain. I shall depart this world with thanks, wherever it may occur—though God knows I would prefer to go to my rest here in Norway!

March 21

Tried to act like Rubinstein[55] this evening by playing, for the first time, a complete concert program. Nothing but small pieces, to be sure, but for me it was a test of what I could manage in the way of public piano-playing now that my breathing problem has improved so much. Thank God! I myself was surprised at how well I managed it. It has given me more courage for the concert tour. The program consisted of 1) From *Moods* op. 73: "Resignation", "Folk Melody", "Hommage à Chopin", "Students' Serenade", and "The Mountaineer's Song"; 2) *Holberg Suite;* 3) *Album Leaves* op. 28; 4) Songs, sung by Miss Borghild Bryhn;[56] 5) From *Norwegian Peasant Dances* op. 72: "Gangar", "Bridal March from Telemark", "Halling from the Fairy Hill", "The Maidens from Kivledal", "The Prillar from Os Parish", and "The Goblins' Bridal Procession at Vossevangen"; 6) a. "Humoresque" (G-sharp minor), b. "Cradle Song" (from op. 38), c. "Wedding Day at Troldhaugen".

---

[55] Russian pianist Anton Rubinstein (1829–94).
[56] Norwegian soprano Borghild Bryhn Langaard (1883–1939).

Miss Bryhn will have a beautiful future if she is capable of development. She has a nice voice and she is willing to learn—yes, perhaps more willing than able. What I admire most of all, however, is how much Nina has imparted to her recently. Her ability to mesmerize her students is incredible. How much individuality Miss Bryhn has—if she has any at all—I cannot say after this brief exposure. Surrogates are dangerous. Individuality must come to the fore in one's youth—the deviltry, everything. If one sees no sign of it then, I fear there isn't any. Miss Bryhn sang "Outward Bound", "Ragnhild", "The Princess", "Hope", and (as an encore) "Two Brown Eyes". I played as well as I could and felt that I was in top form. Nina thought I had *never* played better.

If the concert went well, the credit is due in large measure to an excellent new piano from Hals Brothers.[57] It is a great joy to see that Karl Hals' descendants can produce such a fine instrument, which in my opinion surpasses anything else of the kind that the firm has produced previously. When, upon being called back on stage again and again, I saw the many women waving their handkerchiefs, a new mood came over me, and each time I played more: first "Dance from Jølster", then "Solfager and the Snake King", and finally the "Minuet" from the *Piano Sonata*. But then—the tank was empty.

Everything has one negative point. What hurt me was that the *Norwegian Peasant Dances* didn't strike home as they should have. I played them with all the affection and magic that I could muster. But—where my development as a composer has now led me, I don't have my own people with me, and that is hard to bear. Here they always draw heavily on works from my youth, which on suitable occasions are praised at the expense of my recent ones. But—I must not let that hinder me. I hope that I can continue to develop as long as I live. That is my fondest wish. The understanding of the general public will come in due course.

March 27

Second performance of the concert—at reduced prices—in the Mission House on Calmeyer Street. Audience of nearly 3,000 people, who cheered the *Norwegian Peasant Dances* that had achieved only a *succes d'estime* the previous time. In general: The attentiveness and understanding of this audience was much greater and more genuine. I am grateful to have been able to manage these two evenings.

March 30

As feared, the reaction set in. Asthma, insomnia with difficulty in breathing and the terrible hallucinations left just one wish: away, away from all of it. No one

---

[57] The Hals Brothers piano manufacturing company was founded by Karl Hals (1822–98) and Peter Hals (1823–71). At the time this entry was written, the firm was operated by Karl's son Sigurd Hals (1859–1931).

understands how little life is worth when one is subjected to such agonies. No one understands that then there is only one friend: death.

April 1

But—I recuperated. Took a lot of bromine sodium, and last evening I was even able to visit the students, who were giving a party for me in the Association building. They were kind enough not to smoke as long as I was there, and since I had almost nothing to drink until I left at midnight, I have been feeling fine today. How wonderful it is to be with young people! Not least to see all the pretty and intelligent eyes of young women among them!

I had not touched a piano since the concert because of a sore finger, but they importuned me so fervently that I sat down at the piano—a beautiful Bechstein—and played some dance tunes ("Myllarguten's Gangar"), "Cradle Song", "Minuet" from the *Piano Sonata*, and "Wedding Day at Troldhaugen". Then the students sang, whereupon Messrs. Arvesen, Halvorsen Jr., Svendsen and Buschmann[58] played my *String Quartet* op. 27 (it was agonizing to hear such poor ensemble playing and so many misunderstandings). After that the president of the student union made a nice speech and gave me a laurel wreath, in response to all of which I delivered a short talk. I tried to be funny, but when that didn't work I changed my tune. In my opinion I botched it, but when I sat down the man next to me—old Professor Dietrichson[59]—said "You handled that just fine!" I found that very comforting. The meeting became very jovial at this point, but it was getting on toward 12 o'clock when, in deference to my health, I would have to leave. There was one more speech, this one by Frits Thaulow for Bergen and for Nina (whom the student president had also called to mind earlier), whereupon I rose and said, "After this enthusiastic speech for Bergen (it was, to say the least, incoherent) I think it is time for me to bow out." (Laughter)

Anyway, who can give a good speech after an introduction like this: The student president taps his glass and says, "I have asked Mr. Frits Thaulow to say something about Bergen." Thaulow: "I beg your pardon! You expect me to make a speech on such terms?" (Laughter) It's no wonder, then, that the speech achieved neither form nor focus. Otherwise, Thaulow is charming. I love both him and his colorful art, which is pervaded by an urge to light and joy. It strives to include everything, having tried to leave behind every trace of national distinctiveness. However, we always carry the national element with us, be it as joys or sorrows: One never departs from it! Therefore, Thaulow is "national against his own will". And that is not a bad way in which to be national. At any rate it runs no risk of becoming hypernational.

---

[58] Norwegian violinists Arve Arvesen (1869–1951) and Leif Halvorsen (1887–1959), violist Severin Svendsen (1871–1940), and cellist Otto Buschmann (dates unknown).

[59] Norwegian art historian Lorentz Dietrichson (1834–1917).

April 5

Left Christiania for Gothenburg.

April 6

During the night in Gothenburg I suffered such a serious attack of asthma, difficulty in breathing and hallucinations that I considered returning home. Went on to Copenhagen, though, where, thank God, I got a good night's sleep at Hotel Bristol.

April 7

Departure for Berlin. Hotel Continental.

April 8

Rehearsal with Karl Nissen. Dinner at the Kempinski Restaurant. Evening with Halfdan Cleve.[60]

April 9

Rehearsal at 11 with Cally Monrad, at 12 with Fridtjof Grøndahl.[61] Dinner at the Cleves.

April 10

Departure for Leipzig. Hotel Hauffe. Evening with the Hinrichsens.[62]

April 11

Played six of my piano pieces at Hupfeld's on his "Phonotist" electric piano.[63] What this instrument does is incredible. The Pianola, which impressed me last year, is nothing in comparison. There is no *metrostyle*, nothing that is dependent on a person leading the performance, for there is no such person.[64] I heard a Liszt "Rhapsody" played by Reisenauer,[65] and it was really like listening to Reisenauer himself. I am very excited at the prospect of hearing my things replayed by this instrument.

Dinner at the Hinrichsens. Ollendorffs, Straube (organist at Thomas Church) and his wife.[66] Evening at Krause's[67] with the Hinrichsens.

---

[60] Norwegian pianists Karl Nissen (1879–1920) and Halfdan Cleve (1879–1951).

[61] Norwegian pianist Fridtjof Backer-Grøndahl (1885–1959).

[62] Henri Hinrichsen (1868–1942), from 1900 the Director of the C. F. Peters Music Publishing Company in Leipzig, publisher of most of Grieg's compositions.

[63] The "electric piano" was a piano recording device—similar to the Pianola and Welte-Mignon systems—that used perforated paper rolls for recording and playback. See also the entry for April 17.

[64] The *metrostyle* was a mechanical device used in the *Pianola* system, which required an operator to regulate articulation, for example *forte* and *piano*. Such assistance was not necessary in the *Phonotist* or *Welte-Mignon* systems.

[65] Hungarian composer Franz Liszt (1811–86), German pianist Alfred Reisenauer (1863–1907).

[66] Paul Ollendorff (1868–1931), an employee of the C. F. Peters Music Publishing Company; German organist and choral conductor Karl Straube (1873–1950), cantor at Thomas Church in Leipzig.

[67] Grieg is most likely alluding to "Mutter Krause", a restaurant on Katharinenstrasse in Leipzig.

April 12

Departure for Prague.

April 13

First rehearsal with the Bohemian Philharmonic Orchestra. Magnificent. *Autumn Overture*[68] was played splendidly, the *Lyric Suite* must be still better tomorrow. "The First Meeting" and "Solveig's Song" first-rate. I was greeted with timpani and trumpets: "More I received than I ever had deserved."[69]

In the afternoon a glorious drive in the warmest summer weather with Nina, Cally Monrad and Mojmir Urbánek,[70] who does everything imaginable to make things nice for me.

April 14

Last orchestra rehearsal in Rudolphinum. Magnificent sound. In the *Lyric Suite* the harpist, unfortunately, doesn't understand what is going on—has a dry and sharp tone that at times detracts from the overall effect. Karl Nissen played well— sincerely and earnestly.

April 15

Last evening had a party in the hotel restaurant with Urbáneks, Cally Monrad and Karl Nissen. At least 68° F., crowded, poor air (gray with tobacco smoke), plus beer! Owing to that I had a bad night, awaking this morning with a pounding headache.

Urbánek just walked in and reported that his wife also did not tolerate the evening well and today is staying in bed.

At 11 AM, upon invitation, I went to the Choral Society "Hlahol" with Urbánek, Nina, Cally Monrad and Karl Nissen. This choral society has built its own building, dedicated just recently. We were welcomed at the entrance by the president, who led me into the main hall where the whole chorus—at least 300 ladies and men—stood in formation and sang a welcome greeting by Smetana[71] that was as short as it was impressive. Then came a speech by the president in Czech, to which I responded in German. Thereupon we heard a beautiful choral piece by Smetana performed absolutely magnificently under the conductor, Prof. Adolf Piskacék.

Departure accompanied by ovations and autograph-writing. Then went by carriage to Rudolphinum, where I first had a rehearsal with Cally Monrad, then a rehearsal alone on the piano, after which Urbánek picked me up and drove me home. Thereafter resumed rehearsal at the hotel with Cally Monrad on "To

---

[68] *In Autumn* op. 11.

[69] Grieg often quoted this line from "Last Spring", the poem by Norwegian poet Aasmund Olavsson Vinje (1818–70) set by Grieg in op. 33, no. 2.

[70] Czech music publisher Mojmir Urbánek (1873–1919), Grieg's impresario in Prague.

[71] Czech composer Bedrich Smetana (1824–84).

Springtime My Song I'm Singing" and "Good Morning", both of which took on a very different character than previously.

April 16

11 AM concert in Rudolphinum. Everything went marvelously well. Greeted with timpani and trumpets accompanied by laurel wreath etc. Wonderful, receptive audience, which at the end continued to demand curtain calls until I finally had to come on stage in my winter overcoat in order to get them to leave. The Suite went well (the *Lyric Suite*), each movement being warmly applauded. There was not time for anything to be repeated, as everything had to stay right on schedule because of the train's departure at 3 PM.

Karl Nissen played excellently, though perhaps a bit too objectively in the *A-minor Concerto* for my taste. But much went *better* than in rehearsal, and that is a good artistic sign. Cally Monrad's singing was ravishingly beautiful, albeit far removed from my intentions much too often. Both soloists scored great successes, and I am very proud and relieved about that inasmuch as I was responsible for their having been invited.

3 PM departure for Leipzig with Urbánek. A frightfully warm trip. I was wiped out when I got there.

April 17

Had a bad night, finally got to sleep at 3 and slept until 6:30. At 10 Ollendorff picked me up to take me to Popper & Co.[72] to try "Mignon." It was not first-rate piano playing that I produced, for I felt pretty battered after all the exertions [of the concert in Prague and the trip to Leipzig], but fortunately I performed only 3 short pieces: "Butterfly", "Bridal Procession" and "Little Bird".[73]

Dinner at the hotel with Urbánek. Took the afternoon train to Berlin.

April 18

Wonderful sleep and wonderful air. Dinner at the Kempinski Restaurant with the Cleves, Cally Monrad, Karl Nissen, Fridtjof Grøndahl and P. Vogt Fischer.[74] In the evening attended *The Marriage of Figaro* with Lola Artôt Padilla[75] as a charming countess. She really showed understanding, art of high rank. What wonderful things one stumbles upon all of a sudden! Mozart, Mozart!

---

[72] Piano manufacturing firm in Leipzig.

[73] Grieg is referring here to some recordings he made using the so-called Welte-Mignon system. During the recording phase, holes are punched in a long column of paper that passes through the apparatus as the piano is played. During playback, air rushing through the holes as the paper again passes through the apparatus causes the piano keys to strike. Grieg's recordings are still in existence and can now be heard in modern CD transcriptions.

[74] Norwegian impresario Peter Vogt Fischer (1863–1938).

[75] Lola Artôt da Padilla (1876–1933), Belgian-Spanish singer.

April 19

Did some shopping. Dinner with Nina at the Kempinski Restaurant. Visited by Blessing Dahle.[76] (Nordraak's monument.)[77]

April 20

Forenoon with Grøndahl and Fischer. Departure for Amsterdam. Arrived 9:50 in the evening. Welcomed at the railway station by Engelbert Röntgen. Warm reception by our dear friends Julius and Mien.[78]

April 21

Wonderful sleep from 1 to 6 AM. Unheard of. Here there is healthy, fresh, cool air. I have not felt better since leaving home—or, more correctly, I feel better than I felt at home. If only I am able to sleep, I have no anxiety for anything. The city is marvelous, absolutely bursting with originality. I made a quick visit to the Concertgebouw to try the Bechstein, which unfortunately is not first-rate. In the evening Norwegian chamber music which Julius Röntgen had touchingly arranged for in my honor. First my G-major *Violin Sonata* (Röntgen and concertmaster Flesch[79])—superbly, sensitively performed. Then the Romance for two pianos,[80] also performed excellently. Last came Sinding's[81] *Piano Quintet* [op. 5] with Röntgen at the piano. Everything was met with warm applause—least, strangely enough, after the quintet, which I thought would beat my pieces hands down because of its grandiose breadth.

At the Tiefenthals[82] after the concert. Splendid people.

April 22

Breakfast at the Tiefenthals. Oysters, Mosel wine. Good for the soul. Dinner at Röntgens with Tiefenthals, Brucken-Fock and his wife, and Harold Bauer.[83] Thereafter an unforgettable evening of music. Brucken-Fock, who is an excellent, outstanding pianist as well, played a few of his own Preludes. Some are of great originality, full of depth and poetry. It is a long time since any modern music has charmed me as much as this.

---

[76] Norwegian clergyman Peder Blessing Dahle (1877–1946).
[77] The reference is to Grieg's late friend, Norwegian composer Rikard Nordraak (1842–66), who was buried in Berlin. A monument marking his grave was to be unveiled on May 17, 1906.
[78] Dutch cellist Engelbert Röntgen (1886–1958), his parents Julius (1855–1932) and Abrahamine (Mien) Röntgen (1870–1940). Julius was Grieg's best friend outside of Norway.
[79] Hungarian violinist Carl Flesch (1873–1944).
[80] *Old Norwegian Melody with Variations* op. 51.
[81] Norwegian composer Christian Sinding (1856–1941).
[82] German-Dutch banker Benjamin (Benno) Tiefenthal (1851–1905).
[83] Dutch composer and pianist Gerard von Brucken-Fock (1859–1935), sometimes called "the Dutch Chopin"; English-American pianist Harold Bauer (1873–1951).

The Concertgebouw in Amsterdam was dedicated on April 11, 1888. The opening concert featured a performance of Beethoven's Ninth Symphony *conducted by Grieg's good friend Julius Röntgen.*

Next, Harold Bauer gave a masterful rendition of César Franck's[84] *Prelude, Chorale and Fugue.* Then people insisted that Nina sing. It is strange that she can do it when she never practices or uses her voice in any way. She certainly wishes that she could do it 100 times better than she did—but everyone was enchanted. It felt like sunshine in autumn.

Lastly, Röntgen played his new *Cello Sonata* with [his son] Engelbert. It was composed by a master, but I must say that I am fearful of using just one theme through four movements. Engelbert is an excellent cellist, young though he is. In the evening Lulla[85] also came from Düsseldorf.

April 23

First orchestra rehearsal at the Concertgebouw. The same splendid orchestra as before. I was moved upon being welcomed as a dear friend. It was the first time we had seen each other since the music festival in Bergen in 1898.[86]

Rehearsed the *Lyric Suite, Bergliot,* and *Land-sighting.* It sounds as smooth as velvet. A capacity to understand what is required that is impressive.

---

[84] Belgian-French composer César Franck (1822–90).
[85] Dutch violinist Julius (Lulla) Röntgen Jr. (1881–1951), a son of Julius Röntgen.
[86] See pp. 337–344, "The Norwegian Music Festival in Bergen".

April 24

Spent the day quietly. Evening: arrival of Tonny, Bet and Neergaards.[87] Seeing them here is like a fairytale. And what an affectionate reception!

April 25

Morning: Rehearsal of the *Lyric Suite*, "Evening in the Mountains", "Last Spring", and the *Piano Concerto*.

[Fridtjof Backer-] Grøndahl played splendidly despite the fact that he was suffering from the same gastrointestinal disease that is going around in the whole family. Nina is now better, but today Julius Röntgen is feeling very sick and Engelbert is in bed with a fever of 103–104° F. Everyone thinks it is from the oysters we enjoyed together at Tiefenthals on Sunday. If so, I have been incredibly lucky, for I ate many oysters there too.

I am so happy about being able to manage my duties as I am. The orchestra is favorably disposed toward me. That contributes enormously to a good result. Now, at 5 PM, with the help of rest and beefsteak I have prepared myself for the big evening rehearsal from 6:30 to 9:30. But I have a feeling that I will be able to manage it. Good will has such a marvelously calming effect on one's nerves.

What wonderful people are Röntgen, Mien, and their whole family! Love, hospitality, self-sacrifice, plus broad-mindedness and respect for those who think differently. What a standard they set! Here one breathes clear, bracing air. It is good to be here. Dear, dear friends! Lucky is he who has friends like these. And their home is filled with music, whether or not anyone is singing or playing. Here music has become the good power that ennobles the minds and the mores.

The dress rehearsal at 7–10 in the evening was exhausting. First a piano rehearsal of *Bergliot* with Marie Brema.[88] She turns things inside out, and yet there is plenty of talent. But of course, as with all prima donnas: no regard for either composer or poet. Considerable alteration of the text's relation to the music. No reverence, no—distinction. If I could just have had two rehearsals, everything could have been improved, but now it will have to go as well as it can. We'll probably get stuck in the middle of it.

Lyric Suite went splendidly, as also did "Evening in the Mountains", "Last Spring", and *Land-sighting*—the last-named with the 120-man "Apollo" men's chorus (of whom 40 were missing!). Had this happened ten years ago, I would have put down the baton, both because of the singers' absence from—note well—the *only* rehearsal and because of the Brema-ish impossibilities. But I have grown older, more resigned, and—I think—nicer! And more liberal. That consoles me. For otherwise life would not be bearable.

---

[87] Nina Grieg's sister Antonie (Tonny) Hagerup (1844–1939), Edvard's sister Elisabeth ("Bet", "Betten") Grieg, Danish business proprietor Rolf Viggo Neergaard (1837–1915) and his wife Bodil (1867–1959).

[88] Marie Brema was the stage name of English mezzo-soprano Minny Fehrman (1856–1925). In *Bergliot* she performed as a narrator.

April 26

Röntgen and Engelbert are sick in bed! Forenoon rehearsal at the piano with Marie Brema. She is a cantankerous woman and no Bergliot, but still she now and then gets through to me. As a whole, however, the interpretation is too hollow and artificial.

April 27

Like Vinje, I must say again and again: "More I received than I ever had deserved!" A lucky star shone over the whole concert last evening. It is true: Julius Röntgen and Engelbert were sick in bed. It was a great disappointment and a great loss that they were not present. But—"man kann nicht Alles haben".[89] As I came on stage I was met by prolonged applause, which, as the evening progressed, grew and grew into thundering ovations. The audience had completely filled the large auditorium, and in so doing had sufficiently demonstrated that they had kept me in fond remembrance and wanted to receive me as an old friend. This feeling made my task an easy one. And the orchestra! How sensitive, how perceptive— and how happy about playing under my baton! What Mengelberg[90] said is true: "The performances were of the absolutely highest quality."[91]

The *Lyric Suite* sounded magnificent. So also did the *Piano Concerto*, which Grøndahl played proudly and in an elevated manner, and with which he achieved a powerful effect. It was a great success for him.

Bergliot went well, fortunately, but—as Welhaven[92] said—I will never come to terms with "fart and gut painter L."

And then the string pieces! I myself was completely taken with "Evening in the Mountains", where the oboe was concealed behind the stage. What playing! It *couldn't* have been better. It sounded as if it were improvised.

And "Last Spring"! It was perfect. And *Land-sighting* resounded through the auditorium with great intensity, despite the fact that the poetically good translation by Cläre Mjøen[93] seems a little effeminate in comparison with the powerful original.

I was given four laurel wreaths. It embarrasses me to get such things when I am going to conduct, but at the same time it of course pleases me as well. I am filled with a deep sense of gratitude, not least at the opportunity to introduce Fridtjof Grøndahl, who deserves to move ahead as soon as possible.

---

[89] "One cannot have everything". Grieg often used this German saying in his correspondence. In a letter of September 3, 1902 to his friend Sigurd Hals, he explained the background: "Man kann nicht Alles haben," said the German sweetheart of [Bergen] bookdealer [Fredrik] Beyer [1827–1903], when he wanted to kiss her after having eaten *gammelost* [a highly pungent, old Norwegian cheese]."

[90] Dutch conductor Willem Mengelberg (1871–1951), musical director of the Concertgebouw Orchestra.

[91] "Es waren Leistungen allererster Ranges".

[92] Norwegian poet Johan Sebastian Welhaven (1807–73). The source of the crude saying attributed by Grieg to Welhaven has not been identified.

[93] German-Norwegian author and translator Cläre Behrendt Mjøen (1874–1963).

Today, after a good night's sleep, I feel as if I had been in a fight and came out of it without a scratch. The critics are effusive in their praise. Yes, when things go right, they go right!

Dinner with Sillem.[94] Genuine Dutch congeniality. The meal itself was a cornucopia of food and wine. Grøndahl and Fischer came after dinner. Here I met all the old acquaintances from before. All of them have kept us in cordial remembrance. Mrs. Pollones,[95] who was my table companion, is still a beauty.

Lots of music in the evening. First I played, then Bodil [Neergaard] sang, then Nina sang, then Grøndahl played. It was a complete concert program. Grøndahl took everyone by storm with his excellent performance and his noble and modest personality. Mrs. Pollones confided to me: He will be *very* dangerous for the young girls—precisely because he does not seem to realize it himself.

April 28

Julius is on his feet again, but not quite sure of himself. Breakfast in "De Port van Cleve", where the famous beefsteak with Holland gin and red wine was consumed with great jubilation. Thereafter, cheese, coffee and cigarettes. Stayed quietly at home the rest of the day.

April 29

Afternoon concert in the Concertgebouw under Mengelberg. In my honor he played *In Autumn* and *Peer Gynt Suite No. 1*, both masterfully. After both works I had to stand up at my place in the middle of the auditorium and bow to right and left. Also played were Sinding's *Rondo Infinito* and Svendsen's *Carnival in Paris*, but I didn't get to hear them as I had to leave owing to an unbearable draft that would have destroyed me if I had stayed.

Dinner at 6 at Mrs. Hartogh's.[96] A wonderful, genuine Dutch home. Music by Julius, Nina and me.

April 30

Fine forenoon rehearsal with Julia Culp,[97] who has a marvelous alto voice and a very temperamental nature. But although she is just becoming known, she is already in process of letting vocal display become her main concern. She seems very intelligent (I think she is Jewish), but the composer's intentions are not respected if they are a hindrance to her own self. And yet she is one of the best. What I miss is a sense of contrast and feeling for rhythm. But I will grant her this

---

94 Jerôme Alexander Sillem (1840–1912), member of the executive council of the Concertgebouw Orchestra in Amsterdam.
95 Cläre Pollones (dates unknown), wife of The Hague notary J. Pollones.
96 Catharina (Kitty) Hartogh (1853–1907). Her husband, Abraham Hartogh (1844–1901), was a Dutch attorney and politician.
97 Dutch alto Julia Culp (1880–1970).

Edvard and Nina Grieg with their Dutch friend Julius Röntgen

much: I am confident that if I had had more time to work with her I could have gotten her to agree with my concept. Tomorrow we have another rehearsal. We'll see what happens.

Dinner with the Röntgens at Mengelbergs. Host and hostess very amiable, almost ingratiating. But I feel unsure of myself [in their company]. That Röntgen does the same is easy to understand for anyone who knows the situation in Amsterdam. He [Mengelberg] promised me that he would invite Grøndahl next season. (Promises are cheap.)[98]

May 1

Forenoon rehearsal with Julia Culp. She produces some beautiful things; if only I didn't have to transpose most of the songs down into the cellar. I don't understand Brahms, who had nothing against doing that; for *me* it is a plague. It's worst when I myself am going to accompany. She is singing 12 songs in German: 1) "Frühling" ["Last Spring"], 2) "Mit einer Primulaveris" ["The First Primrose"], 3) "Verborgene Liebe" ["Hidden Love"], 4) "Im Kahne" ["On the Water"], 5) "Ausfahrt" ["Outward Bound"], 6) "Solveigs Wiegenlied" ["Solveig's Cradle Song"], 7) "Was ich sah" ["A Vision"], 8) "Ein Schwan" ["A Swan"], 9) "Eros" ["Eros"], 10) "Mit einer Wasserlilie" ["With a Water Lily"], 11) "Das alte Lied"

---

[98] Grieg here uses a Norwegian dialect expression: "Me kunne nok løva det", meaning: "We could promise that all right [but keeping the promise is another matter]."

["The Old Song"], 12) "Ich liebe Dich" ["I Love But Thee"]. The songs are divided into three sets. She sings everything with great talent, but for my ear her overall style is too dark and unvaried. And there is one other abomination that I see more and more: self-complacency! Naturally: She is, after all, a prima donna. Therefore: first herself, then art. After hearing about her I had hoped ever so slightly that she might be an exception—but no, the rule holds. I have said it many times and I repeat it: I hate the whole lot of them, be they famous or unheralded—perhaps the famous ones most of all!

May 2

A day of despair! In countless small ways a regular Tycho Brahe's[99] day, one that made me nervous. First, the cellist—the so highly regarded Casals[100]—has still not arrived in the city. Owing to misunderstandings and to the demonstrations in Paris on May 1 he had not received a telegram. But he arrived at 2 PM, and I, poor fellow, was to rehearse the demanding *Cello Sonata* with him for the concert the same evening. For a moment I considered playing without a rehearsal, but I abandoned that idea as it would have resulted in even greater nervousness. And it is good that I did, for as a result I got a great pleasure. Casals is incomparable, a *great*, great artist for whom the work of art is No. 1 and the artist No. 2.

After the rehearsal, off to the theater to make sure that the piano was properly set up. Then all the streetcars were full, so we had to stand and wait for a long time until finally a taxi took us home. I had a beefsteak, and then I made the colossal blunder of drinking a *big* cup of coffee. Consequently, I didn't get a single wink of the after-dinner nap that I so desperately needed, with the result that I shook from nervousness during the entire concert. I was ill at ease and displeased with myself throughout the evening. In addition to playing the *Cello Sonata*, I played *Lyric Pieces* op. 43 and accompanied all the songs, so I was at the piano the whole time.

Fortunately, my displeasure was not shared by the audience that filled the auditorium. There was demonstrative warmth in the applause, and there were many curtain calls. Except for "The Old Song" and partly also "With a Water Lily", and "I Love But Thee", which was sung splendidly, Mrs. Culp was steadily far too slow, and often she didn't come in on time, so I had to sit and wait for her. She certainly had "einen schönen Vortrag" (!), but I would rather have seen it in the music than in her batteries![101]

---

[99] The allusion is to Danish astronomer Tycho Brahe (1546–1601). A "Tycho Brahe Day" was a general designation for a day when one was predicted to have bad luck. For example, Tycho Brahe had calculated 32 ominous days a year for Rudolf II (1552–1612), who was German emperor 1576–1612.

[100] Renowned Spanish cellist Pablo Casals (1876–1973).

[101] Grieg is alluding jokingly to Mrs. Culp's appearance. He uses the German words "einen schönen Vortrag" (literally: "a beautiful interpretation") within the Norwegian text, but the word "batteries" is obviously a reference to her prominent bust.

After the *Lyric Pieces* people continued to shout "Hurrah" and to call me out, but I was so nervous that I *couldn't* play any more. Röntgen absolutely wanted me to play "Wedding Day at Troldhaugen", but I wasn't up to it.

Then we came home, where the best thing of all awaited us: a wonderful pineapple bowl with delicious sandwiches. Thereafter followed a flurry of "hurrahs" and then—incredibly!—a whole concert. First Röntgen at the piano with "Wedding Day at Troldhaugen" (in honor of Viggo and Bodil Neergaard's wedding anniversary). Next they got Nina to sing, and she—with the help of the sandwiches (and, I think, Casals' presence)—was in high spirits, and her singing resounded in a way that it rarely has done of late. Then Casals gave a brilliant rendition of a solo sonata of Bach. He is astonishing. He is a dramatist on his instrument. Thereafter Fridtjof Grøndahl played Schumann's *Toccata*, but now it was well past midnight, and the happy party broke up in the most buoyant of moods.

I can't find words to describe Röntgen and Mien. They rejoice with us and they suffer with us. How they helped me get through this nervous day. He even sat faithfully beside me in the theater and turned pages for me during the *Cello Sonata*.

May 3

The critics were inordinately positive. Breakfast at home with Casals. Concert: Beethoven's 8th Symphony, Richard Strauss' *Till Eulenspiegel* and Sinding's symphony[102]—all excellently conducted by Mengelberg.

May 4

Trip to Sandford with Mien, Neergaards, Tiefenthals, Fischer, Grøndahl, Bet and Tonny. Splendid view by the sea. Dinner at 7 at the Tiefenthals with the whole band.

May 5

With Nina in Kalverstraat. Bet left this morning with Engelbert. Grøndahl and Fischer left in the evening. Fridtjof was moving when he said goodbye to me. Completely un-Norwegian, but beautiful nonetheless: He kissed me on the cheek and said with great sincerity, "Thank you for everything that you have done for me!" Is it possible? Gratitude? And in a *Norwegian* artist? All the others have used me in every way they could and then—given me a kick. But I still have this much optimism: I confidently believe that Fridtjof Grøndahl will never do that.

May 6

Trip to Voolendam with Röntgens, Neergaards and Tonny. A most interesting fishing village with an original way of folk life and equally original inhabitants.

---

[102] *Symphony No. 1* in D minor (1893).

May 7

Breakfast in Port van Cleve[103] with Röntgens, Neergaards and Tonny. Dinner at Pollones'.[104]

May 8

Party at home. Miss Scheffer,[105] Sillem, Mrs. Seelig,[106] Hartoghs, also Flesch and his fiancée. Julius and Mien played *Variations and Fugue on a Theme by Beethoven* for 2 pianos (theme from the *Bagatelles*) by Max Reger.[107] That this music is hailed in Germany as brilliant is a lamentable sign of decadence. It is nothing but leaden constipation. It is outrageous to charge ahead at the expense of the healthy nature. I am liberal—yes, liberal to the extreme—and I normally don't make a judgment after a first hearing, but I am making an exception here, for this arrogant creature made me furious. What is technique except a means to an end? And what kind of technique do we find here? A superfluity of polyphony, a dearth of light and air. And to what good can a solitary ray in this desert contribute?

After the others had left, we sat with the Neergaards until midnight and then drank a toast to Julius in honor of his dawning birthday. (Tonny left at 7 PM.)

May 9

At 3 PM left on a trip with Röntgen, Neergaards and Tiefenthals to Brökkeln, partly by train, partly by carriage along canals with old villas. Dinner in a roofed veranda, or more correctly, outside the house under the trees. Lively, festive mood. Unforgettable. Said goodbye to the Neergaards.

May 10

7 AM departure for London. Mien and Julius accompanied us to the station, and the dear Tiefenthals met us there. In Vlissingen we were met by Johannes Wolff,[108] who had arranged everything for us in the best possible way—rented a cabin on the deck and ordered beefsteak and champagne.

At first the sea's whitecaps were unpleasant, but conditions soon improved and we had a marvelous, fine crossing.

We were met at Victoria Station by our host, Mr. Edward Speyer,[109] who took us to the elegant Claridges Hotel, where we had everything we wanted and even

---

[103] A restaurant in Amsterdam.

[104] J. Pollones, Dutch notary public from The Hague.

[105] Dutch pianist Johanna Scheffer.

[106] Grieg's entry is somewhat unclear. He writes "Seely" but is probably alluding to Eva Emmelina Seelig, wife of Grieg's and Röntgen's mutual Dutch friend Moritz Ferdinand Seelig.

[107] German composer Max Reger (1873–1916). The work referred to was Reger's op. 86 (1904).

[108] Dutch violinist Johannes Wolff (1863–?).

[109] German-English businessman and impresario Edward Speyer (1839–1934). Grieg mistakenly calls him "Edgar".

more. A stack of letters containing requests of all kinds made me nervous, but the night, fortunately, was entirely satisfactory.

May 11

Lunch at Speyers with Sir Charles.[110] Ben Jones. Wolff was our dinner guest at Café Royal.

May 12

Lunch with Wolff. Visited Nansen.[111] Evening at home.

May 13

Matinée concert in Queen's Hall with Mrs. Speyer.[112] Here I got to hear Mendelssohn's *A-minor Symphony* under the leadership of the excellent conductor Henry Wood.[113] He is at one and the same time both lively and infinitely sensitive. Rare for an Englishman. Later in the evening, at the Speyers, I got to know him personally as a gracious and natural human being. We moved to the Speyer residence from the hotel this forenoon. In the afternoon, when we were quite alone with our host and hostess, we were fortunate enough to get to know them better. First I played various things, then they persuaded Nina to sing, and she did so in such a way as to move Mr. Speyer to tears. (!) *That* was something none of us had imagined. Then I played the G-major Sonata[114] with Mrs. Speyer, after which she performed Bach's *Chaconne*. To be sure, one notes now and then evidences of amateurism, but otherwise I have deep respect for her musicianship. Fresh, rhythmic, energetic and musical. We discovered that we had been together nine years ago with Nikisch[115] in Leipzig, where we had played the same sonata. Sometimes the world is small!

I think we live even more elegantly than kings and emperors. We wade in the masterworks of old art.

May 14

Lunch at the home of Felix Moscheles, who looks very much like his father, my dear old teacher.[116] I think his portraits are excellent, despite the fact that he is not recognized as an important painter. He and his wife showed us and Wolff the greatest kindness.

---

[110] Irish-English organist and composer Sir Charles Villiers Stanford (1852–1924).

[111] Norwegian polar explorer Fridtjof Nansen (1861–1930), who at this time was Norway's ambassador to England.

[112] English singer and amateur violinist Antonia Speyer (1857–?), wife of Edward Speyer.

[113] English orchestral conductor Henry Wood (1869–1949).

[114] *Violin Sonata No. 2 in G Major* op. 13.

[115] Austro-Hungarian conductor Arthur Nikisch (1855–1922) was conductor of both the Leipzig Gewandhaus Orchestra and the Berlin Philharmonic Orchestra from 1895 until the end of his life.

[116] Austrian-born English painter Felix Moscheles (1833–1917), son of Austrian pianist Ignaz Moscheles (1794–1870), who was in charge of piano instruction at the Leipzig Conservatory when Grieg studied there.

May 15

First orchestra rehearsal in Queen's Hall. Warm welcome by the orchestra. It was so excellent and so receptive that it made my task easier. Miss Stockmarr[117] surprised me with her energy.

Evening at home with von Zur Mühlen,[118] who sang Schumann *magnificently*, and with Henry Wood and his wife. Mrs. Wood gave a good and intelligent rendition of some songs by [Richard] Strauss. (I did not enjoy them, much as I wanted to.) Madame Raunay from Paris, who was pretty to look at and has a nice voice, sang an old Giordano[119] and—"A Dream" [Grieg's composition]. The latter was in French. Nina also sang and was well received.

Mr. Wood is the first English artist (musician) who has treated me with warmth and understanding. How strange human beings are: They *immediately* have a gut feeling as to whether or not they like each other. I was captivated by Wood from the moment we met, and I noted immediately that the feeling was mutual. How touchingly helpful he was—like a friend—during the orchestra rehearsals.

May 16

Last orchestra rehearsal. Miss Tita Brand[120] recited "Bergliot" in very much the same manner as her mother, [Marie] Brema, but the rendition, like that of her mother, was talented and energetic. Miss Dolores[121] (Trebelli's daughter) was impossible in "Solveig's Cradle Song", "From Monte Pincio" and "A Swan"—all with orchestra. Completely wrongheaded. No concept of the whole.

May 17

Concert in Queen's Hall at 3 PM. Thunderous reception, increasing warmth as the concert progressed, enormous enthusiasm at the end. The *Lyric Suite* and *Peer Gynt Suite No. 1* went exceptionally well. So did the whole concert, as a matter of fact. I am happy about having gotten through it so well.

In the evening I was at the Norwegian Club. Close to 200 people. Nansen is president. His speech in honor of the day[122] was moving to the point of tears. A speech in my honor by Mr. Hagelund[123] was *so* awful that Nansen gave a new speech for me—and that was indeed quite different. Nansen is amazing. He always knows how to strike the right tone—or more correctly, the right *tones*, for

---

[117] Danish pianist Johanne Stockmarr (1869–1944).
[118] German singer Raimund von Zur Mühlen (1854–1931).
[119] Italian composer Umberto Giordano (1867–1948).
[120] English actress. For her mother, see footnote to April 25.
[121] Dolores Antonio, stage name of French soprano Antoinette Trebelli, daughter of French singer Zelia Trebelli-Bettini (1832–1925).
[122] May 17 is Norway's Constitution Day. The observance of this day in 1906 had special significance in that it was the first such observance since the dissolution of the union with Sweden on June 7, 1905, when the Norwegian Parliament (*Stortinget*) declared Norway's independence.
[123] A Norwegian manufacturer living in London at that time.

he was versatile that evening. I responded with a speech for those who had worked for independence for more than a generation, and of these, first and foremost for [Bjørnstjerne] Bjørnson, whom I toasted at the end of my speech.

The evening was very successful. How strange and how beautiful to be greeted as a friend with a warm handshake from young Norway. Young girls came over to me and looked me in the eye with a warmth that thrilled me. I can feel like Andersen:[124] "You love me. You dare to tell me. People know that you just mean my poetry!"

May 18

Some of the reviews were surly. Easily understandable, unfortunately, as I have not been willing to talk with any interviewers. Lunch at Brodskys[125] with Johannes Wolff.

May 19

Lunch at Nansens with several Norwegians and the Speyers. Pleasant and relaxed. In the evening attended *Tristan and Isolde* with the Brodskys. Richter[126] conducted brilliantly. Ternina's[127] Isolde was consistently excellent, as was also Van Rooy[128] as Kurvenal. But Tristan was impossible both in appearance and in his singing, although he at least sang in tune.

May 20

In St. Lennards (Hastings) at the Augeners.[129] A rainy day. Returned for dinner at 8 PM. Then from 10–11:30 I played the *Cello Sonata* with Becker[130] and the G-major *Violin Sonata* with Mrs. Speyer. It's remarkable what I can manage here.

May 21

Happy about having had a good night after the exertion. Lunch at the home of Mr. Henry Wood, who, together with his wife, is singularly kind to us. In the forenoon: rehearsal at Bechstein with Wolff on the C-minor *Sonata*,[131] which he played brilliantly. What a joy!

In the afternoon: big reception at the home of Mr. and Mrs. Speyer in honor of Mr. and Mrs. Grieg! Close to 200 people. Printed music program. Started at almost 11 PM! The whole program was by Dr. Grieg,[132] who had to play the G-

---

[124] Danish author Hans Christian Andersen (1805–75).
[125] Russian violinist Adolf Brodsky and his wife Anna had lived in England since 1895.
[126] German conductor Hans Richter (1843–1916).
[127] Croation-Austrian soprano Milka Ternina (1863–1941).
[128] Dutch baritone Anton Van Rooy (1870–1932).
[129] German-English music publisher George Augener (1830–1915).
[130] German cellist Hugo Becker (1863–1941).
[131] *Violin Sonata No. 3*.
[132] Grieg had been awarded an Honorary Doctorate of Fine Arts at the University of Cambridge on May 10, 1894.

major *Violin Sonata* with the hostess. She has a lot of talent and life, but she is too shallow. Nina sang two sets of songs, and her voice took the listeners by storm. If only the prima donnas could understand [as Nina does] that *the interpretation of the poem* is everything! But—that requires a certain fluid[133] that is allotted only to the chosen few.

Lastly, Percy Grainger[134] played two of the *Norwegian Peasant Dances* in a dazzling manner. Yes, he is brilliant, that's for sure. I am happy about having gained a young friend such as he.

We got to bed at 2 AM. I say: Once and never again. This was for our kind host and hostess as thanks for their hospitality. But polite society! To hell with it. Fortunately, there were a few artists. The cellist Sandby,[135] also Becker and Miss Stockmarr, who played the *Cello Sonata* superbly. Stanford and his wife, and Zur Mühlen.

May 22

Very tired. In the evening we dined at Café Royal with Johannes Wolff, who overdosed us with champagne, which I bitterly regretted having drunk, for

May 23

the night was not good. Still very tired and overly nervous. Afternoon sleep impossible.

† Received word of Ibsen's death. Although I was prepared for it, the news came as a blow. How much I owe him! Poor, great Ibsen! He was not a happy man, for it is as if he carried within him a chunk of ice that would not melt. But under this chunk of ice lay a fervent love of mankind.

May 24

After a very bad night—I slept from 3 to 6 with the help of bromine sodium— I was completely dejected. At noon I took 3 drops of opium (Rovsing[136] once recommended 5 as a stimulant), and at 3 PM as I was driving to the concert I already had a feeling of reduced nervousness. To my inexpressible joy, I noted increasing relaxation during the demanding concert.

The *Cello Sonata*, with Hugo Becker, went well. Thereafter Miss Emma Holmstrand[137] sang a) "The Enticement" b) "The Tryst", c) "Ragna", d) "Ragnhild". It was a nice voice in the upper register, but otherwise absolutely nothing. For the little bit that she did get out of the songs she can mainly thank Nina, who, with

---

[133] Grieg obviously means temperament.
[134] Australian-born pianist and composer Percy Grainger (1882–1961), whom Grieg met for the first time on this trip to London.
[135] Danish cellist Herman Sandby (1881–1965).
[136] Danish physician Niels Ivar Asmund Rovsing.
[137] Swedish mezzo-soprano Emma Holmstrand (1866–?).

Portrait of Henrik Ibsen by Norwegian painter Nils Gude. The original hangs in the Ibsen Museum in Skien, Norway.

her great ability to communicate her own and my intentions to others, had rehearsed the songs with her the first time she sang. *Schwamm darüber.*[138]

Then I played a) "Myllarguten's Gangar" from *Norwegian Peasant Dances*, b) "Folk Melody", c) "The Mountaineer's Song" (which especially caught on), and d) "Wedding Day at Troldhaugen", which elicited a regular storm. After three curtain calls I had to do an encore, and I chose "Cradle Song" [Op. 38, No. 1], and after innumerable additional curtain calls I played the "Minuet" from the *Piano Sonata.*

Thereafter Miss Holmstrand sang a) "The First Meeting", b) "Hope" (not hopeful!), c) "The First Primrose", and d) "Say What You Will", which she sang twice. She scored a success of sorts despite a total lack of personality.

Then, finally, came the last number: The C-minor *Violin Sonata* with Johannes Wolff. He played it with a more beautiful tone at the rehearsal, but he retained the characteristic old flight and passion that so endear his playing to me. A storm of applause. After several curtain calls I was really forced to sit down at the piano. Incredibly, I was still able to function and I played "To Spring" [Op. 43, No. 6]. Then came so many curtain calls that I lost count. I myself have the feeling that my piano playing was successful, although with a Steinway I would have achieved much finer results. In general it seems to me that Bechstein has seen its best days. None of the pianos I have played abroad on this trip have appealed to me. In any case I can say that they do not suit *me*. For a piano virtuoso perhaps it would be a different story.

When we were about to get into the carriage, I was nearly smothered by young folks, mainly females, who held out programs and pencils in order to get my autograph. I hurriedly did what I could, but I had to leave most of them in the lurch.

A change of clothes (I was drenched to the skin), then rest (sleep was out of the question), then dinner at 7:30 with Speyers and Beckers. Very nice, but I missed Johannes Wolff and the marvelous Percy Grainger, who turned pages for me at the concert and whom I love as if it were a young woman. It is a dangerous thing to be strongly admired, but when one admires in return, as I do in this case, that evens it out. I have not met anyone who *understands* me as he does. And he is from Australia. So what is there to this reproach by the honorable critics to the effect that my music is too Norwegian? It is stupidity and ignorance and that is all.

---

[138] *Schwamm darüber:* literally, "Sponge over it". The meaning is "No more of this! Forget it!" Quotation from the operetta *The Beggar Student* (*Der Bettelstudent*, 1882) by Austrian composer Carl Millöcker (1842-99); libretto by German conductor, librettist and composer Richard Genée (1823-95) and German-Austrian author Friedrich Zell (Camillo Walzel, 1829-95) after *Les noces de Fernande* by French dramatist Victorien Sardou (1831-1908).

May 25

A trace of bronchitis. Now I must remember: Take care. Spent the whole forenoon answering hundreds of autograph letters.

May 26

More of the same. Terrible work. Wrote a long letter to Agathe Grøndahl.[139] The bronchitis is not worse, but it is insidious and dangerous. Received Mr. Kittelsen, Aftenposten's correspondent. Evening visit from Johannes Wolff, Percy Grainger and Miss Stockmarr.

Grainger is remarkable. He played and sang English folk songs with [his own] brilliant harmonizations. Here are the beginnings of a new English national style.

Unfortunately the bronchitis feeling will not go away despite taking cod liver oil and putting oil on my chest at night. I have to take it easy in order to be up to traveling on the 31st.

May 27

Bronchitis unchanged.

May 28

Forenoon: Visited court photographer Thomsen. Nansen came at 1:30 and lunched with us. At 2:30 the three of us drove together to Buckingham Palace, whence we had been summoned to meet the King and the Queen.[140] They were both very kind. I was so fortunate as to have an opportunity right away to tell the King that the telegram I had sent him last summer on the day when Norway was within a hair's breadth of going to war, and in which I had asked him to intervene for the sake of peace with the help of arbitration—that this telegram was a manifestation of the nervousness that pervaded the whole of Norway at that time, and I expressed the hope that he had not misunderstood it, but had perceived it for what it was. And he stated that he had done so. With that, he immediately asked if the Norwegian royal couple were popular in Norway, to which I could only say yes. Then he (who is said to be the most unmusical Englishman) said he was very fond of my music, which he often heard when it was played outside the palace by the military band. (!)

And then something happened that I had not imagined possible: Both the King and the Queen wanted to have some music. What could I do? Into the music room where I attacked a Bechstein, and remembering the Queen's deafness I pounded away at the "Minuet" from the *Piano Sonata*. So what happened? The king, who sat beside Nansen, began quite calmly to converse aloud with him. This

---

139 This letter is given in English translation in Finn Benestad (ed.), *Edvard Grieg: Letters to Colleagues and Friends*, Columbus, Ohio 2000, pp. 298–300.

140 Edward VII (1841–1910), English king 1901–1910, and Alexandra (1844–1925), queen 1901–1910.

happened just before the Trio, so I paused at this point and looked questioningly over toward the King, who answered my questioning look with a broad smile. Then I continued—but God help me, the same thing occurred all over again. Now I got angry and made an even longer pause that, according to what Nansen said later, he understood and took to heart. It's pretty rude to request music and then act like that! Then the Queen wanted to have a song. Which song? Of course: "I Love But Thee", which sounded good in that large room.

Next we talked for awhile with the Queen, who is by no means as deaf as she is said to be. She had been led to believe that we were not in Bergen when she was there two years ago, but next time she had to see us. She asked for our auto-graphed portraits, then we said goodbye and left. One thing one can say about the King and the Queen: They were exactly the same as they used to be when they were Prince and Princess of Wales—natural and easygoing, with none of the Germanic *von oben herab* such as one sees in the petty nobility in *das grosse Vaterland*.[141]

After I had had a rest at home, Speyer's physician, Dr. Fürth, came and examined my lungs. There was just a little whistling on one side, he said, and in general he said there was nothing to worry about. But I could also assure both him and myself that since this forenoon there had been some improvement. This improvement is obviously a result of the fact that I have been out in the open air a lot today and have let the warm sun shine upon me.

May 29

10 AM: Went with Speyers and Miss Stockmarr to Oxford, where I was created a Dr. Honoris Causa with all due ceremony. With Falstaff I must ask: What is honor?[142] I preferred the ceremony at Cambridge; somehow it was more festive, although here [in Oxford] there were also speeches in Latin and gold-embroidered gowns and tasseled mortar-boards. In Cambridge the audience consisted of students; that made it more lively. Here the audience consisted almost entirely of women. Still, the loud applause at the entrance, and especially when we left, showed that people liked my music, and that could not but warm my heart.

Lunch before the ceremony was at the home of Mr. Strong, Dean of Christ Church College. The speech in Latin was given by the composer Hubert Parry,[143] and that raises misgivings, for English composers as a rule have the least possible regard for their foreign colleagues. We'll find out if I am right about this when the speech, a copy of which I took with me, is translated.

---

[141] Grieg is here alluding to the condescending behavior he had encountered in Germany among the nobility.

[142] See footnote to entry of January 14, 1906.

[143] English composer Hubert Parry (1848–1918).

May 30

Lunch at the Margrave of Hessen (Nina stayed home). We had to split up, because the author Mrs. Humphry Ward[144] was coming to lunch with our hosts. I regret not meeting the author of "Robert Elsmere", whom I hold in very high regard. The Margrave is the same as before: amiable, lively—suddenly displaying a slight evidence of royal birth, but immediately becoming again like the rest of us.

We ate at a well-decked table d'hote—a nice little table just for us. He had three pleasant companions: two military men and a musician who is his companion and copyist. The unavoidable table music is unbearable, but it was worst today, because they wanted to honor me. First came the whole *Peer Gynt Suite [No. 1]* for a minimum of instruments. "The Death of Åse" was awful. But then came the first movement of the *Cello Sonata!* Very sensibly played. That was followed by the second movement of the C-minor *Violin Sonata!* Most original table music.

The food was not exactly to my liking, but as Peer Gynt says, "It's written: Thy nature must be subdued." Soon I had the occasion well in hand, having given my better self the required kick!!

Grieg at Oxford, 1906

---

[144] English author Mary Augusta Ward (1851–1920).

I spent my last evening in London at home with Miss Stockmarr, Percy Grainger and Herman Sandby. Our host and hostess were out, and we acted as if it were our house. First we had a fine dinner with 3–4 servants, then coffee and music in the library.

Fate decreed that on this day I would hear the *Cello Sonata* for the second time, as Grainger and Sandby wanted to hear my opinion of their interpretation of it. Their performance was excellent from beginning to end. There were things that Grainger got much more out of than I myself did, and on the whole I got a good lesson. It isn't often that I have an opportunity for that kind of learning.

My joy over having found and won the affection of these two young artists is great, for Sandby, too, is an important talent. To be sure, the string quartet by him that I heard recently was confused and unstructured, but it had what is most important: ideas and a feeling for sound. I see a promising future in his talent, and since he is highly regarded as a cellist it is to be hoped that he will achieve that for which he is destined. He played the first of the *Norwegian Peasant Dances* on his cello, and it was an excellent performance.

And how Percy Grainger played several of them as arranged for piano! There is no Norwegian pianist at the moment who can match him, and that is significant in more ways than one. It shows that we still do not have a Norwegian pianist who has enough understanding to tackle such challenges. It also shows that if this understanding does not exist where it ought to, namely in Norway, then it can be found elsewhere—yes, even in Australia, where the marvelous Percy Grainger was born. In general, this harangue about having to be a Norwegian in order to understand Norwegian music, and especially to perform it, is sheer nonsense. Music that has staying power, in any case, be it ever so national, rises high above the merely national level. It is cosmopolitan.

After the *Cello Sonata*, Miss Stockmarr played some of my "Moods" and a couple of absolutely brilliant Preludes and Fugues by Franz Neruda.[145] The performance demonstrated that she is more than a dexterous pianist who knows how to let her fingers run.

May 31

Departure (with Speyers, who were going to Paris) from Victoria Station at 9 AM. Breakfast and goodbyes in Calais. Evening arrival in Cologne, Domhotel.

June 1

Morning: Continued on to Hamburg, Hotel de l'Europe.

---

[145] Czech-Danish composer and conductor Franz Neruda (1843–1915).

June 2

Bad night with difficulty in breathing, presumably as a result of the strenuous two-day trip. Spent the day in Hamburg. In the evening took a First Class sleeping compartment across the islands to Copenhagen.

June 3

The night began well but later turned bad. Same story as the previous night. Got to Copenhagen feeling like a rag. Bad weather and cold all the way. An hour-long forenoon nap helped a lot. In the evening we visited with Gottfred Matthison-Hansen and Helga,[146] with whom we had supper in Hotel Bristol's café.

June 4

Had a better night in Hotel Bristol. Dinner at the home of the Melchior sisters in "Villa Melchior" near Springforbi. Here we met old Henriques and Anna, Otto Benzon and his wife, Admiral Jøhnke and two of his daughters, Herman Trier and his wife[147]—with all of whom we spent a pleasant, Danish evening, with the glorious juxtaposition of the blue Øresund[148] and the green beech forest, which awakens memories of my youth and its passionate enthusiasm for Denmark. Now that enthusiasm is mixed with melancholy, for so many of those who constituted the picture framed by this nature are gone—no one knows where?

June 5

Another bad night with difficulty in breathing. This time apparently for no particular reason, for we *walked* from Østerbro to Vesterbro, and I had had almost nothing to eat or drink. The doctors—they are either ignorant or unconcerned. And if the doctors really think that this is going to end in death, then they can just tell me that. But here I go around thinking that it is just my bad luck that I can't find the right man to help me, and this depresses me, angers me, and makes me sicker than necessary. Dinner at the home of Mrs. Ruben[149] at "Bella vista".

June 6

Dinner at the home of old Henriques at "Petershøj". Renewed my impressions of the glorious Danish nature as seen in forest and sound. The evening, with a full moon, was wonderful.

---

[146] Danish organist Gottfred Matthison-Hansen (1832–1909), one of Grieg's closest friends in Denmark, and his wife Helga (1841–1919).

[147] The members of this group (all Danish) who have been identified are: Martin R. Henriques (1825–1912), a banker; Otto Benzon (1856–1927), a poet whose verses Grieg used in opp. 69 and 70; Admiral Ferdinand Henrik Jøhnke (1837–1908); Herman Trier (1845–1925), a teacher and politician.

[148] Øresund is the sound that lies between Denmark and Sweden.

[149] Ida Ruben (1845–1913).

June 7

The great day dawns for the first time since the liberation.[150] Would that I could be in Norway on this day! But it was not to be. Nina spent the forenoon at the dentist's and I with an internist and eye doctor. Met Rosenfeld, Andreas Hallén and his wife, and Anton Svendsen[151] in Café King of Denmark. Lamentable news: Emil Horneman, the best friend from my youth, is on his deathbed! How sad, how sad that we became estranged from one another—that you *wanted* it thus. You have been mentally ill, that is the only solution to the riddle.[152] How I have cared for you! How I bless your memory! No one else has taught me what you taught me! All trifles and misunderstandings disappear into nothingness, and all that remains is what is great and beautiful. Thank you again and again for the good time, the time of youth, when you did more than anyone to help my development. I shall remember you as a benefactor to my final hour!

Dinner at 6:30 at Alfred Hansen's with Johan Svendsen and his wife, Holger Drachmann (without his wife), Tofft, and Børresen and his wife.[153] Highly enjoyable. Drachmann talked a lot and said some excellent things—but also a lot that was strangely unreliable. Happily he has acquired a calmness that is good to see. Svendsen—fat, amiable and gentle. How he has retained what is most important: that which is noble in the train of thought. He has reconciled himself to life as it—unfortunately—has turned out for him. How many are able to do that? Only a deep, true nature. Or let me say: a *beautiful* nature.

Drachmann could not stand the word "true" (*sand*) yesterday. It was too indeterminate. He wanted to replace it with the word "beautiful" (*skjøn*). (!) I understand his meaning, but "beautiful" can never take the place of "true".

After dinner, Nina had to sing. She sang a few songs under the most frightening acoustic conditions. The sound didn't carry at all. Not even the piano. But she plucked up her courage and made everyone happy, not least Drachmann, who took turns with Svendsen "smothering" her.

---

[150] The Norwegian Parliament (*Stortinget*) had declared Norway's independence from Sweden on June 7, 1905.

[151] Danish composer Leopold Rosenfeld (1849–1909); Swedish composer and conductor Andreas Hallén (1846–1925); Danish violinist Anton Svendsen (1846–1930), concertmaster of the Royal Opera House Orchestra.

[152] In summer of 1895 the Griegs had invited their Danish friends Emil Horneman, Gottfred Matthison-Hansen and August Winding and their wives to visit Troldhaugen as their guests. Unfortunately, for reasons that Grieg was never able to understand, a feeling of ill will developed between him and Horneman in the course of the visit that permanently poisoned their friendship. See also Grieg's article on Horneman on pp. 211–216 and his letters to Horneman in Finn Benestad (ed.), *Edvard Grieg: Letters to Colleagues and Friends*, Columbus, Ohio 2000, pp. 431–437.

[153] Music publisher Alfred Wilhelm Hansen (1854–1923); Norwegian composer and conductor Johan Svendsen (1840–1911), musical director of the Royal Opera House Orchestra; Juliette Haase Svendsen (1866–1952), ballet dancer and wife of Johan Svendsen; Holger Drachmann (1846–1908), whose poems served as texts in several of Grieg's songs; Danish composers Alfred Tofft (1865–1931) and Hakon Børresen (1876–1954).

June 8

† Emil [Horneman] died this forenoon, quietly and without regaining consciousness. I wrote to Louise.[154] Fortunately I got to spend the day with the Steenbergs, who perhaps understood Emil best. We had dinner at Tivoli and had a very pleasant time together, though it was tinged with sadness.

June 9

Breakfast at Johan Svendsen's in Hellerup with [Hakon] Børresen and Alfred Hansen. Took a drive in the zoo.

June 10

Breakfast at Hotel d'Angleterre with Alfred Hansen, Bjørn, Oselio and Dagny. Visited old Bjørnson and Karoline at the hotel.[155] Bjørnson was in bed with a cold. 9:30 PM departure for Christiania. Wrote to Enevold Sørensen, the Danish Minister of Culture, regarding the possibility of public support for Emil Horneman's widow.[156]

June 11

Arrived in Christiania at 3 PM.

June 12

Had the unpleasant task of conveying greetings from King Edward and Queen Alexandra to the Norwegian royal couple. We were received at 2 PM by both the King and the Queen. Both were very amiable and easygoing, as before, but when the conversation turned to art, to music, all hell broke loose. When the King insisted that King Edward loved music, I could not resist saying that it must be an original kind of love, for I had almost created a scandal in Buckingham Palace because the King sat and talked out loud to Nansen while I played, so that twice I had to stop. Then King Haakon spoke the divine and characteristic words: "Yes, but King Edward is the kind of person who can very well listen to music and carry on a conversation at the same time!" That was more than I could take, and I exclaimed, "Well, whether he is King of England or an ordinary man, it's crazy and I will not accept it. There are some things I absolutely cannot do out of regard for my art." Then the King made a motion like a jumping jack and with a smile took the conversation off on a different track. It's all well and good to want to defend his father-in-law, but there is a limit to everything.

---

[154] Louise Horneman (1844–1919), wife of Chr. F. Emil Horneman.

[155] Norwegian actor and theater director Bjørn Bjørnson (1859–1942); Gina Oselio, stage name of Norwegian soprano Ingeborg Aas (1858–1937), wife of Bjørn Bjørnson; Dagny Bjørnson (1876–1974), Bjørn Bjørnson's sister. Norwegian author Bjørnstjerne and Karoline Bjørnson, parents of Bjørn and Dagny.

[156] Danish editor Enevold Sørensen (1850–1920), Minister of Culture in 1906. The relevant portion of Grieg's letter to Sørensen is given in English translation in Finn Benestad (ed.), *Edvard Grieg: Letters to Colleagues and Friends*, Columbus, Ohio 2000, p. 431.

The conversation about the coronation in Trondheim was interesting. I thought that our police did not have enough experience to handle the situation, to which the King observed: "Precisely. For that reason I have sought to engage police from abroad. I have done everything I could, but—it costs money." Once again came the jack-in-the-box motion. Poor King! Everything is almost too hard. It really won't do to resort to Norwegian indifference here. Once we've gotten ourselves a king we have to protect him as well as we can. And that terrorists will be out on the prowl—not for King Haakon, but against Russian noblemen and their consorts—that is more than likely.

It is, of course, the prerogative of royalty to bring an audience to an end, but I violated the rules of etiquette. For several reasons I thought enough was enough, so I rose, Nina and I said goodbye and disappeared with Eilif Peterssen[157] into a room where he showed us his new portrait of the King. The pose is noble and handsome, perhaps a bit stiff.

June 13

Dinner with my sisters and Christen Smith in the Tostrup Cellar.[158]

June 14

The same with Vogt Fischer and Annie.[159]

June 15

Tooth extraction and excruciating rinsing. Dinner at Vogt Fischers. Heard Agathe Grøndahl's voice in the telephone. Singularly melancholy!

June 16

Departure from Christiania to Bergen via Valdres. A terribly hot 8-hour train ride to Aurdal. Stayed overnight at Løken.

June 17

Stifling hot. Stayed overnight at Maristuen.

June 18

Spent a beautiful forenoon up there. Left for Lærdal at 2:30 PM. The mountain was more beautiful this year than ever. I say it with thanks, for as long as the

---

[157] Norwegian portrait painter Eilif Peterssen, whose works include two well-known portraits of Grieg.

[158] Edvard's sisters Benedicte Grieg and Elisabeth Grieg Kimbell; Christen Smith (1864–1934), brother-in-law of Grieg's close friend Frants Beyer. Tostrup Cellar was an elegant restaurant situated across the street from the Parliament Building.

[159] Annie Grieg Halvorsen, daughter of Edvard's brother John Grieg (1840–1901) and wife of Norwegian composer and conductor Johan Halvorsen.

mountain seems new and beautiful to me it is because I have something to *read into it.*[160] May that be true until my final hour!

June 19

2 PM boarded the "Alden" for Bergen. Still the most wonderful weather. A voyage like this is life for me—or more correctly, a life-renewer. My nerves are repaired, my sleeping improves, a feeling of peace steals over me—a calm, joyful *joie de vivre.* I am again able to *want* to do something in my art. I become aware that my creative imagination is still alive. Now all that is lacking is the main thing: health. I am writing this on the boat on

June 20

in Alverstrømmen, a couple of hours from dear old Bergen.

June 21

Arrival at Troldhaugen. Newly painted, with a new veranda, new steps, and sundry repairs—all of which put me in such a blissfully happy mood and filled me with gratitude to Frants and Marie [Beyer], who have worked out all the details, and to Gabriel Smith,[161] who designed the veranda.

July 6

Breakfast at Conrad Mohr's with the German Kaiser, his guests, and the Michelsens.[162] The Kaiser was as before: the incarnation of amiability and openness. His political statements were especially interesting. Something to the effect that last year, when he went to the Baltic Sea with his fleet and King Oscar[163] came aboard, he [Kaiser Wilhelm] had found him "completely disoriented" regarding the Norwegian question. For regarding the 7th of June, he [King Oscar] had said, "It is just some radical republicans that are fomenting a revolution. But I know my Norwegian people. They love me, and I can count on that. Let them go ahead and establish their republic. Then Sweden will step in and establish a new union the way it ought to be." It sounds absolutely incredible, but that is what he said. How marvelous, then, that our government acted the way it did.

At coffee I spoke for a long time with the Kaiser—partly about music, partly

---

[160] Grieg expressed the same thought more fully in a letter to Gottfred Matthison-Hansen dated December 19, 1906: "We made everything beautiful because we ourselves read all our striving for beauty into the landscape and the folk life, into the saga and the history. The fact that we ourselves were so full of beauty—that was the secret!" See Finn Benestad (ed.), *Edvard Grieg: Letters to Colleagues and Friends,* Columbus, Ohio 2000, p. 521.

[161] Norwegian engineer Gabriel Smith (1853–1934), a brother of Marie Beyer.

[162] Norwegian businessman Conrad Mohr (1849–1926); German Kaiser Wilhelm II (1859–1941); Norwegian statesman Christian Michelsen (1857–1925).

[163] Swedish King Oscar II (1829–1907), who was also King of Norway until Norway declared its independence on June 7, 1905.

about our King and Queen, partly also about *Sigurd the Crusader,* which he now is absolutely determined to have performed in Berlin next season because his brother Heinrich[164] was so enthused about the performance he heard in Christiania. Very tactfully, the Kaiser did not request music this time as it was the first time he had visited Conrad Mohr since Mrs. Mohr's death.

It was great to talk with Michelsen again. I am in sympathy not only with his politics but also in the highest degree with his way of talking about politics. He does not consider himself too good [for the rest of us], that man, as did the megalomaniacs of the old school. Politics got closer to us, more intelligible, healthier.

July 10 and 11

Trip via the Voss train line to Myrdal with Frants [Beyer] and Christen Smith. Marvelous mountain scenery and above all a marvelous ascent. But—complete insomnia up there. Life in the mountains from now on is but a memory—but a beautiful one, which I shall return to with thanks. For without sleep, life is agony.

July 12

Glorious, refreshing sleep! Renewed. I love my dear Troldhaugen as never before.

July 31

Ever since [my last entry] I have been very dejected. Constant difficulty in breathing (though fortunately without hallucinations) plus a nasty attack of rheumatism—this despite a week of marvelous weather, with temperatures as high as 22° Réaumur[165] in the shade. Ah, Troldhaugen! Yes, Western Norway is a costly love for me, for it is taking my life. But Western Norway gave me life, the seminal enthusiasm for life, my life goal—to recreate it in tones. The gift has been only a loan; I must repay it when it is required of me. If only I could take the step, tear myself away from Troldhaugen and live the rest of my days in the drier air that I need. But I don't have the heart to do that. I reproach myself for my sentimentality. Still, there must be something to it, since it will not allow itself to be swayed; it is there, and it demands its due.

August 6

I had the great joy of welcoming to Hotel Norge [in Bergen] my dear friends Adolf and Anna Brodsky, who came from England by steamship just to visit us. They had two boys with them—Toni Maaskoff and Alfred Barker,[166] one 13 and the

---

[164] Prince Heinrich of Prussia (1862–1929).

[165] Réaumur denotes a temperature scale in which 0° represents the freezing point and 80° the boiling point of water. Thus 22° Réaumur equals ca. 28° Celsius and 82° Fahrenheit.

[166] American violinist Anton (Toni) Maaskoff (1893–?); English violinist Alfred Barker (1895–?). Grieg's estimate of their respective ages was slightly in error.

Troldhaugen, Grieg's villa south of Bergen, was built in 1884–85.

other 15, both of whom are pupils of Brodsky and also are boarding with him—
as well as his niece, Miss Antonnia Schadowski. In clearing weather we drove in
landau and gig to Troldhaugen, where a good dinner awaited us. What wonderful people! They seem to me to be standing at the culmination of the heart's finest
development.

In the afternoon Brodsky absolutely wanted to have the C-minor *Violin
Sonata,* which he played as beautifully as ever. Nina sang, we walked around a bit,
then we went up to the tower for a moment, and the cozy time together was over.
I accompanied them with Tonny and Nina to the station.

August 7

A glorious, refreshing sleep after what for me was a somewhat strenuous day.
Picked up the Brodskys at 1 PM and drove in two landaus across Mt. Fløjen and

on to the end of the road. From there we climbed Mt. Blåmand, where beer, port wine and cakes really hit the spot and elevated the mood, which was already high, to an even higher level. Great enthusiasm about the view. Back to the Fløjen Restaurant, where we had dinner. From there we went to Hotel Norge, where the Brodskys improvised a lovely evening. Everything went as well as could be. They accompanied us to the station, and we got home late at night in a state of blissful weariness.

August 8

Met the Brodskys at Hop Station at 2 PM. Weather still wonderful. Magnificent dinner at Troldhaugen. We took a nap, and then it was once again Brodsky who created a music program. Both of my earlier *Violin Sonatas* (G-major and F-major) had to be performed; it awakened many old memories. Then both of his pupils played. It was very interesting. Both are gifted, and both show what a great teacher Brodsky is. The 15-year-old (formerly a circus clown!) played two movements of Mendelssohn's *Violin Concerto* very energetically, but then came the 13-year-old—a mixture of Hungarian and American blood—who played a solo sonata by Bach. It was such an outstanding performance that one dares to expect the greatest from this boy. How moving it was to see the respect and love that these two boys have for their teacher! And how they enjoyed the situation!

We ate a light supper. Then Nina sang, concluding with an absolutely stunning performance of "Ragna" and "Hope", which she sang more beautifully than ever. There were not many dry eyes when she finished. Then we all went to the station, and soon the train chugged off. We sauntered slowly homeward in the beautiful night—this time, in my case, more tired than is permissible.

August 9

I had a very hard time getting to sleep. Today I need peace and quiet—but I'm not going to get it yet, for I must go into the city to celebrate the Brodskys' departure with them.

August 10

It was a cheerful and thoroughly delightful occasion. A nice dinner in the Grand [Hotel] Café, after which we accompanied them to the railway station and with a wistful twinkle in our eyes watched them depart. Ten minutes later we ourselves left, and with that I treasure yet another beautiful memory. This meeting has strengthened me as only true understanding is capable of doing.

August 11

Today I feel the emptiness. The strained nerves must relax again. It is the darndest process.

September 15

Completed three psalms for mixed chorus and soli, a free arrangement of Lindeman's[167] Norwegian folk songs. They are so beautiful, these melodies, that they deserve to be preserved in artistic garb. These little works are the only things my miserable health has allowed me in the course of the summer months. This feeling: "I could, but I can't"—it drives one to despair. I wrestle in vain against heavy odds and soon, no doubt, must give up altogether.

September 16

Last evening I was at Marta Sandal-Bramsen's[168] concert and was again most impressed and often even enchanted by her substantial and noble art. Happily for her and for the rest of us, she has abandoned the affected stylization that in the past has marred her healthy nature. It was a joy to hear freshness and confidence win out over artificiality.

October 1

Det ny System at the National Theater.[169] Magnificent, real national art.

October 2

The Merchant of Venice[170] at the National Theater. Superb performance.

October 3

Karl Nissen's concert. I take my hat off to him for the seriousness with which he takes hold. But something is certainly missing—if it is not still lying latent [within him]—namely, what I will call "by God's grace". It seems to me that Brahms suits

---

[167] Norwegian organist and composer Ludvig Mathias Lindeman (1812–87). Lindeman had collected a large number of Norwegian folk tunes which he published in simple piano arrangements in *Ældre og Nyere Norske Fjeldmelodier* (*Older and Newer Norwegian Mountain Melodies*), vols. 1–10, 1847–67. The "three psalms for mixed chorus and soli" to which Grieg refers are nos. 2–4 of *Four Psalms* op. 74.

[168] Norwegian mezzo soprano Marta Sandal (1878–1931) was married to Danish cellist Henry Bramsen (1875–1919).

[169] *Det ny System* ("The New System") was a play by Norwegian playwright Bjørnstjerne Bjørnson written and printed in 1878. When Bjørnson saw a copy of the printed version of the play, however, he was so displeased with it that he destroyed the whole printing. A year or so later he returned to it, reworked it, and had it printed anew.

Bjørnson had by this time broken with Christianity, and in a series of polemical articles published in 1878–79 had also taken unpopular stands on a number of current issues. Not least, he had affirmed his opposition to *landsmål* (later called *nynorsk*), an indigenous form of the Norwegian language that explicitly avoided Danish influences. The harsh criticism to which he was subjected as a result of his bold public statements helped him understand how difficult it can be to speak the truth in a small, homogenous society such as that of Norway, and "The New System" was an attempt to deal with this issue in a dramatic context.

Grieg sympathized by and large with Bjørnson's way of thinking, though he did not agree with his views regarding *landsmål*. Indeed, many of Grieg's most beautiful songs are *landsmål* texts, notably the songs of opp. 33 (Vinje) and 67 (Garborg).

[170] Comedy (1596) by William Shakespeare.

him best. When he played *Norwegian Peasant Dances*—"Halling from the Fairy Hill" and "The Goblins' Procession at Vossevangen"—a voice within me cried: "Why in all the world does the Australian Percy Grainger play these things perfectly with respect to rhythm and modulation, whereas the Norwegian Karl Nissen can't get the hang of either? That is certainly backwards."

October 4

An Ideal Husband by Oscar Wilde[171] at the National Theater. Interesting, witty, decadent. The playwright's talent for paradoxes was enough to make you laugh yourself silly. One could say much about the acting. We are not able to depict that kind of refined people of the world, but Mrs. Dybwad[172] had some first-rate, enchanting things "mezzo voce" and Oddvar[173] also had some outstanding lines. The one who succeeded completely in creating an illusion was Selmer[174] as the father. That was convincing.

October 5

Music Association Orchestra rehearsal. [Halfdan] Cleve played his concerto with a string orchestra. It's a work that was written as a quintet for piano and strings. In its present form, I have an impression of something nondescript, and that is a misfortune for the piece, which has many beautiful features. One unfortunate thing about Cleve is the fact that his music, which is so full of seriousness, energy and uplift, is an example of "Berlineri".[175] As a pianist he is without peer in Norway. In that department he beats all the others hands down. He is a new Neupert,[176] with whom on the whole he has much in common. Especially the splendid way of bringing out the main contours.

October 8

This evening a veritable piano orgy. It was the marvelous Ernst K. Dohnányi,[177] who is the greatest living pianist known to me. How he lifted me up into better worlds when he performed Schubert's A-minor *Sonata*, Brahms' fine *Sonata*,

---

[171] English playwright Oscar Wilde (1854–1900).

[172] Norwegian actress Johanne Dybwad (1867–1950), who had played Solveig in the 1892 production of "Peer Gynt" in Christiania.

[173] Norwegian actor August Oddvar (1877–1964).

[174] Norwegian actor Jens Selmer (1845–1928).

[175] Halfdan Cleve, who was studying in Berlin at this time, had already—at age 27—written three piano concertos. Grieg is expressing concern that Cleve may be trying to compose at such a pace that his music will be lacking in depth.

[176] Norwegian pianist Edmund Neupert (1842–88), who had premiered Grieg's *Piano Concert in A Minor* in Copenhagen in 1869.

[177] Hungarian pianist, conductor and composer Ernst (Ernö) von Dohnányi (1877–1960). Grieg had written to Dohnányi on January 8, 1906: "You write that you will be playing in Copenhagen sometime—and maybe in Christiania? I hereby request that you change this 'maybe' to 'quite certainly'!" See Finn Benestad (ed.), *Edvard Grieg: Letters to Colleagues and Friends*, Columbus, Ohio 2000, p. 214.

Liszt's Bach fugue, and Chopin Mazurkas.[178] With him, technique is only a means, not—as with virtually all the so-called great pianists—an end in itself.

October 9

Dinner at Fischer's with Dohnányi. In the evening the National Theater performed *Gurre* in honor of Drachmann's sixtieth birthday.[179] Mrs. Dybwad recited a beautiful "Prologue " by Vilhelm Krag[180] in her own enchanting way. After the first two acts, however, I ducked out. I was tired and—bored. All praise to beautiful lyricism, but—.

October 18

Last evening I accompanied Mrs. Marta Sandal-Bramsen in the whole song cycle *The Mountain Maid* in a benefit concert for Queen Maud's Fund for the Mentally Retarded.[181] I had no choice but to do it. Marta Sandal has lost her girlish innocence,[182] and as Mrs. Bramsen she has become more worldly-wise, more self-confident—but not any more accurate in her note-reading or in her intonation. And worst of all, her singing has become somewhat trite. The same old mistakes over and over again! Oh, these prima donnas! [Henry] Bramsen gave an excellent rendition of Tchaikovsky's *Rococo Variations*. Fridtjof Grøndahl also played Brahms, Schumann, Field's[183] E- major *Nocturne* (excellent) and [Anton] Rubinstein's C-major *Etude*. It, too, was a most talented performance. Fridtjof is developing handsomely and naturally under Dohnányi, who, as luck would have it, was in the audience. We later left with Dohnányi. He is as simple and unassuming as a person as he is great as an artist.

November 1

The day before yesterday we had dinner with [Bjørnstjerne] Bjørnson at the home of attorney Helliesen.[184] At coffee Bjørnson began to talk about the idea of immortality, and a long conversation developed in which he naturally played the main role and defended his position, but in which others—especially our hostess—also chimed in. As a Unitarian[185] I am close to Bjørnson's position, but I do

---

[178] Dohnányi's concert program on October 8 consisted of the following compositions: Liszt, *Prelude and Fugue on the name BACH* (1855/1870); Schubert, *Sonata in A Minor*, op. 42; Brahms, *Sonata in F Minor*, op. 5; Chopin, *Nocturne in E Major*, op. 62; *Mazurka in C Major*, op. 56 no. 2; *Mazurka in A Minor*, op. 59 no. 1; *Waltz in C-sharp Minor*, op. 64 no. 2; *Scherzo in C-sharp Minor*, op. 39. Dohnányi gave two more concerts in Christiania, on October 11 and 16, each with completely new programs.

[179] Danish author Holger Drachmann (1846–1908). *Gurre* is a melodrama much of which Drachmann wrote during a trip to America in 1898. It includes some of his profoundest nature poetry.

[180] Norwegian poet Vilhelm Krag (1871–1933). Grieg's op. 60 comprises settings of texts by Krag.

[181] [Grieg's footnote]: The King and Queen attended the concert.

[182] Grieg here uses a manufactured word: "Sommerfuglstøvet", literally "the butterfly dust".

[183] Irish pianist and composer John Field (1782–1837).

[184] Norwegian attorney Henrik Michael Helliesen (1856–1933).

[185] Grieg had become acquainted with the Unitarian movement in 1888 during a visit in Birmingham, England, and he had immediately felt drawn to its teachings.

not quite understand his concept of God. [God as] a primal power is all well and good, but to be able to see a great love behind its inexorable manifestations (cause and effect), which look a bit like the work of an evil demon—that is the big trick, the big question, and the big dividing line between many freeborn, truth-seeking people. What is beautiful about Bjørnson is the great tolerance that permeates everything he says. This is something we should all try to emulate, for what we don't know, we don't know.

November 2

The day before yesterday I hosted dinner at "Engebret" for Bjørnson and Karo-line, Bergliot,[186] Einar and his wife and Bjørn and his wife. Extremely pleasant. A remarkable family that *can be* charming. But they can also be the opposite. You have to know them in order to take them in the right way. And on that day I was lucky enough to find the key to understanding them. Despite the marked family feeling that they share, and despite the fact that this time only family members were present, the members of this family just can't get along with each other. Bjørnson is irritated by Bjørn because he talks too much (instead of letting *him* talk?!), and Bergliot is irritated no less by Bjørn, presumably because as the wife of Sigurd Ibsen she can't stand to hear Bjørn's incessant explanations of the stands of Michelsen, concerning whom he appears to have a great weakness for wanting to play the role of best friend.[187] Consequently, I had the greatest difficulty when I phoned trying to gather this heterogeneous group. I told them this in a light-hearted speech that I yelled out so loudly that even Karoline (with the help of Bjørn as prompter) could understand it. I compared the Bjørnson family with the crew on the "Fram",[188] the members of which could not stand to see each other and avoided each other as much as possible. On the whole, all of them had it coming to them. My speech evoked a storm of laughter, and with that the whole Bjørnsonian—or more correctly, the *young* Bjørnsonian—temper sprang *fortissimo* out of the bag. The old man is subdued nowadays because he can no longer hear anyone except those who are the very closest to him. He was amiable and spoke some inexpressibly beautiful words to me.

---

[186] Bergliot Ibsen (1869–1953) was the daughter of Bjørnstjerne and Karoline Bjørnson.
[187] Norwegian diplomat Sigurd Ibsen, son of the famous playwright, had played an important role in nego-tiations with Sweden concerning the so-called "consular question", which revolved around Norway's demand that it be allowed to establish an independent consular service. The failure of these negotiations had been a deep disappointment to Ibsen, who had feared that a more aggressive stance by Norway would lead to war. The "more aggressive stance" that Ibsen feared had been championed by Christian Michelsen, and it was this view that had prevailed and had led to Norway's independence in 1905. See Grieg's diary entry for November 29, 1905.
[188] "Fram" was the name of the ship that Norwegian scientist and diplomat Fridtjof Nansen designed for use in the polar explorations that made him famous.

November 3

Yesterday the Music Association Orchestra had its dress rehearsal. Svendsen's D-major *Symphony*.[189] It is eternally young—but the tempi were too fast except for the introduction to the Finale, which was too slow. It is irritating and incredible. A *Valse Triste* by Sibelius[190] was beautiful and noble. An Italian violinist named Antomotti played the B-minor *Concerto* by Saint-Saëns.[191] He played with a thin but fine and noble tone, with good intonation and clarity, but altogether too impersonally.

The concluding number on the program was *The Death of Magnus the Good* for male chorus, baritone and orchestra. It was written by Per Reidarson,[192] a native of Bergen, who has been in the National Theater Orchestra for several years. He is a young status-seeker, and he himself conducted—so consistently bad that the Music Association should not have permitted it. Their concerts are not practice sessions for future conductors.

I hear that the newspapers are warmly praising Mr. Reidarson's piece. Well, I don't doubt it. Although awarded a prize by Mr. Schibsted,[193] it was rather amateurish, formless, and pompous, and for the most part meaningless trash. A couple of short attempts at a Norse lay[194] vanished as quickly as they appeared. No, this is nothing, and unfortunately it won't become anything either unless the composer gets over the smugness that takes the breath and the motion out of all his phrases. I expect of a young talent something that at least resembles a flight of imagination, but I did not see it. I will not say anything about the fact that the work contained nothing new, nothing requiring a deeper analysis.

After the rehearsal [yesterday] I gave a dinner at "Engebret" for Marie (I cannot attend her birthday today) with my sisters, Halvorsens, Ingo, Signe and Asbjørn.[195] I was terribly bored, but everyone enjoyed the gathering by stuffing themselves, especially with champagne and liqueur. Thus the mood was maintained with surrogates and, according to what Nina says, something else.[196] But the air is heavy, the horizon is covered; in short. . . ! It could be my fault. But, as Wergeland[197] says: That's the way I am.

---

[189] See Grieg's review of the first performance of Svendsen's symphony on pp. 280–283.

[190] Finnish composer Jean Sibelius (1865–1957). "Valse triste" (originally called "Tempo di valse lente") is part of the incidental music for the play *Kuolema* (*The Death*, 1903), by Arvid Järnefelt (1861–1932). It has become one of Sibelius's best-known shorter works.

[191] *Violin Concerto No. 3* op. 61 by French composer Camille Saint-Saëns.

[192] Norwegian composer Per Reidarson (1879–1954), referred to by Grieg as Petter Reidarson.

[193] Amandus Theodor Schibsted (1849–1913), owner and editor of the Christiania newspaper *Aftenposten*.

[194] *Drapatone*. Grieg means "attempts at creating a touch of Norwegian folk tune".

[195] Marie Halvorsen Nedberg, older sister of Johan Halvorsen; Johan Halvorsen and his wife Annie; Ingo Grieg (1886–1917), son of Edvard's brother John Grieg and Marie Ehrhardt Grieg (1845–1931); Signe Grieg Müller (1868–1960), daughter of John and Marie Grieg; Asbjørn Bjerke, son-in-law of John and Marie Grieg (husband of their daughter Alexandra).

[196] Grieg probably is referring to "hjemmebrent," i.e., home-brewed hard liquor.

[197] Norwegian poet Henrik Wergeland (1808–45).

November 4

Last evening a pleasant game of boston at Halvorsens. Came home after midnight. I am beginning to relax the reins. There you see: *Alter schützt* etc.[198] I have to be more careful. "It's time for thralls to take up their tasks"[199] so long as one's health does not require one to bid "pass". By the way, during these days I have rejoiced with many over Michelsen's splendid clarity, strength and eloquence with which he overcame and triumphed over the rumor-mongers. But of course it can't last long. The effort required of him last year was too great. Not even a man such as Michelsen can endure that for more than a couple of years at the very most.

The Norwegian people are a strange people, a barbarian people. Their greatest joy is to shoot each other down—from behind. What the so-called Liberal Party has done in recent days is a living illustration of such banditry. Speaking and acting against their conviction, as they have recently done in the Parliament—it's a sin, perhaps the only real sin, the sin against the Holy Spirit. And to openly admit that they do so—that also manifests an impudence and a meanness that should be repaid by kicking them out of the ranks of the nation's political representatives. But unfortunately, our laws don't allow such a thing— a fact that *Verdens Gang*[200] today justly characterizes as a great lack.

November 16

5 PM: The students' memorial service for Frits Thaulow. High up on a pedestal stood the urn containing the ashes of the dear, great artist, and lower down hung his palette—with the fresh colors. A stark contrast to all the floral wreaths roundabout. It was a short, gripping moment. When they departed with him in the hazy evening, escorted by torches and a big, silent crowd of his friends and admirers, it was a sight that I shall never forget. Here at last the tones of Chopin's *Funeral March* were appropriate.

What a beautiful death Thaulow had! Lucky is he who can end his days so easily! I loved him both as an artist and as a human being. It was easy enough to see his faults, but no one among us could match his great, warm gentleness. That is what we should learn from him, and that is what is in such terribly short supply in our homeland. Yet another piece of irreplaceable Norway is lost! What will be next?

---

[198] Grieg is alluding to an old German saying, *Alter schützt vor Torheit nicht*, i.e., "Old age does not protect one from folly".

[199] This line comes from "Bjarkemål", an Old Norse poem that appears in the *Saint Olaf Saga* of Icelandic historian and poet Snorre Sturluson (1179–1241). Grieg was familiar with the poem through its use by Bjørnstjerne Bjørnson in his epic poem *Arnljot Gelline* (1870).

[200] A liberal Christiania newspaper.

November 17

A symphony concert in the Theater—without a symphony. But how I enjoyed the wonderful *Hebrides Overture* by the "unmodern" Mendelssohn. What originality—and what masterliness! The new school that condemns such a work has passed judgment on itself. As it is written: "The ax is laid to the root of the trees."[201] Then came Saint-Saëns' brilliant frenzy, the "Bacchanale" from [his opera] *Samson et Dalila*. He is a counterpart to Mendelssohn insofar as it is his masterliness that impresses us first and foremost. But, to be sure, there is more to it than that. What eastern Mediterranean opulence! It went exceptionally well. So did the "Hebrides Overture", though I would have preferred that the tempo be a bit slower here and there. I have grown up with the Gewandhaus tradition,[202] which certainly is the right one since it stems from Mendelssohn himself.

The young virtuoso Mr. Brandt Rantzau[203] played X. Scharwenka's[204] *Piano Concerto in C-sharp Minor*. It was technically successful, but disjointed and unpolished. For that man, the music is not the main thing but "the man himself". To hell with all this great technique that rests on a soulless dilettantism. My words sound cruel, but such was my impression. If this conceited and spoiled nature could come under the influence of a deep, serious personality, then I think it could achieve more. I had not heard him play solo for three years, and to tell the truth, I was able to detect progress since then.

Scharwenka's concerto surprised me with its broad style and aspiring character. I would place it above his well-known *Concerto in B-flat Minor*.

November 18

Some of the critics do not mention Saint-Saëns or Mendelssohn, others make derogatory remarks about the former! Fantastic! The whole concert, naturally, was just a frame around the pianist, who is showered with praise in mile-long reviews. Yes, here is understanding! We are barbarians, with a sense only for barbaric pursuits. Our political sense, too, is a legacy from the barbarians. So also our juridical sense. It is Njål's Saga[205] that we are living on. And that would be good enough, as far as it goes, if we also adopted the saga's great vision—but for that we are too fresh, too self-indulgent, too shallow.

---

[201] Matthew 3:10 (RSV).

[202] As a student at the Music Conservatory in Leipzig 1858–62, Grieg was able to attend dress rehearsals and concerts given by the Leipzig Gewandhaus Orchestra as often as he wished.

[203] Norwegian pianist Rolf Brandt-Rantzau (1883–1935).

[204] German pianist and composer Xaver Scharwenka (1850–1924).

[205] Njål's Saga is a long Icelandic poem depicting the perils of life in a society in which ties of blood and memories of past insults are considered more important than ethical standards or the rule of law. Njål and his family are burned to death in their home by a man who feels that only through this act of vengeance can his honor be restored.

*Edvard and Nina Grieg
ca. 1903*

November 19
Nina and I signed the bequest codicil at Joachim Grieg's.[206]

November 20
Received *Bergens Aftenblad* with a warm editorial in connection with my bequest and my testamentary arrangements regarding the "Edvard Grieg Fund".

November 30
Music Association Orchestra dress rehearsal. A wonderful, poetic piece by Sibelius: "Spring Song" for orchestra. It reveals the longings of a suppressed people for springtime, the springtime of freedom. When all the strings (except the double basses) join together to sing out the melancholy, half-wild melody to the accompaniment of the trombones, I cannot but be strongly moved.

Mendelssohn's *Symphony* in A minor[207] sounded good. What a masterwork, this scherzo!

---

[206] Grieg is referring to an addendum to the legal document whereby he and Nina willed their "sheet music, books, manuscripts, autographs and letters from artists" to the Bergen Public Library. The text of the letter of bequest and the codicil are given in English translation on p. 99. Joachim Grieg was Edvard's second cousin.

[207] *Symphony No. 3*, the so-called "Scottish" symphony.

The female singer this time was Lola Rally, who sang awfully in a concert aria by Mozart. She did notably better in "Er ist's", a splendid song with orchestra by Hugo Wolf,[208] "Wiegenlied" by d'Albert,[209] and later with piano accompaniment in songs by Richard Strauss, Bizet[210] and Brahms, whose inevitable "Feldein-samkeit" she took slower by half than it ought to be. At that tempo it becomes utterly absurd, however poetic it is otherwise.

After the rehearsal, dinner at "Engebret" with Kajanus[211] and his daughter and son.

December 2

Visited Kajanus at Voksenkollen.[212] He gave a splendid breakfast with oysters, champagne, goose liver, caviar etc. etc. on the occasion of his fiftieth birthday. I sat next to his wife—an amiable, fine person. How wonderful it is to get some fresh air up there once in awhile. It is revivifying.

December 4

Hjalmar Borgstrøm,[213] concert at Hals.[214] The person giving the concert had not sent me a ticket, so I went into Hals's box, where I have a standing invitation. Of Borgstrøm's compositions we heard two piano pieces excellently played by his wife (Amalie nee Müller[215]): "Vårbrud" ["Spring Bride"] and "Drikkevise" ["Drinking Song"]—interesting things—also a violin sonata that she played with Gustav Lange.[216] It is a remarkable work. The first movement possesses great depth and demonstrates a considerable talent for combining diverse elements. The Andante is weaker; the last movement, on the other hand, again takes a mighty upswing. Sonatas such as this are not being written in Norway nowadays.

I was so completely taken with this that I had to go into the green room after the concert to express my enthusiasm, but I was received with such an icily negative coldness that I said only a few words. It is indeed incredible how uppity people (or more correctly, the composers) have become here in Norway. I make no objection to the fact that I feel Sinding's influence now and then in the sonata, but I do object when Sinding is being copied as a superman. Much good may it do to both of them! I for my part will continue to look up to the composers whom I consider to have value, even if these composers look down on me. It is

---

[208] Austrian composer Hugo Wolf (1860–1903).
[209] German pianist and composer Eugene d'Albert (1864–1932).
[210] French composer Georges Bizet (1838–75).
[211] Finnish composer and conductor Robert Kajanus (1856–1933).
[212] Voksenkollen Sanitarium. See Grieg's article "The Soria Moria Castle" on pp. 354–357.
[213] Norwegian composer Hjalmar Borgstrøm (1864–1925).
[214] The piano factory owned by the Hals Brothers also included a renowned concert hall.
[215] Norwegian pianist Harriet Amalie Müller Borgstrøm (1868–1913).
[216] Norwegian violinist, composer and music theorist Gustav Fredrik Lange (1861–1939).

only here at home that I am singled out for treatment such as I received this evening. It is not for nothing that we are Europe's rudest people.

December 7

A very nice dinner at Peter Vogt Fischer's with old Bjørnson, Karoline, Thorvald and Mally Lammers,[217] and Fridtjof Grøndahl. The beautiful calmness that has come over Bjørnson is impressive. Lucky is he who can advance so far!

December 8

Orchestra rehearsal in the National Theater rehearsal room on tomorrow's French concert. Godard,[218] *Scènes poétiques*; Debussy,[219] *L'après midi d'un faune*; Saint-Saëns, *Tarantelle* for flute and clarinet with orchestra; Berlioz,[220] "Tristia" march from *Hamlet* with unison chorus, and *Roman Carnival*. Thanks to Halvorsen, we now live to some extent in a musical Europe in Christiania. To get acquainted with Debussy—for a gourmet[221] that certainly was a real treat. It is a brilliant orchestral web that he weaves. A strange harmony, freed from all traditions, but genuine and felt—although exaggerated. As experiments by a personality suited thereto I find these things highly worthy of note, but a school must not be established along these lines. Unfortunately, that certainly is going to happen anyway, for this is precisely the sort of thing that copycat composers will try to counterfeit.

December 16

Premiere at the National Theater: *East of the Sun and West of the Moon*, dramatized after Asbjørnsen's[222] fairy tale by Miss Fredrikke Bergh (a schoolteacher) and with music by Olga Bjelke Andersen (wife of the chief of police in Drammen). This, then, is the substitute for Schjelderup's[223] musical drama by the same name, which the National Theater has so obstinately refused to stage. A great blunder, in my opinion. If the National Theater incurs a deficit by presenting a national work of art—I mean a work by an artist—it thereby demonstrates most clearly the necessity for public financial support. Even if an amateur work such as the one by these ladies draws a crowd, this helps the Theater's status only at the moment and leads the Parliament [*Stortinget*]—which has no understanding of art—to say, "There you see, public financial support is not necessary if only you have enough sense to produce things that will draw a crowd!" What a wonderful

---

[217] Mally Sars Lammers (1860–1929), wife of Thorvald Lammers, was a singer.
[218] Benjamin Godard (1849–95).
[219] Claude Debussy (1862–1918).
[220] Hector Berlioz (1803–69).
[221] Grieg uses the German word "Feinschmecker".
[222] Norwegian folklorist Peter Christen Asbjørnsen (1812–95).
[223] Norwegian composer Gerhard Schjelderup (1859–1933).

attitude toward art! The Parliament's view, however restricted it may be, is nonetheless forgivable. The National Theater's, on the other hand, is an artistic declaration of bankruptcy, a sheer scandal.

But I hasten to add that both of these amateurs have talent. The fairytale is well adapted, although more was done to create cheap effects than is desirable, and the music, albeit highly unoriginal, is sincere and fresh, and it really does have a mood reminiscent of the Norwegian fairytale. But this does not outweigh my main thesis: A society does not advance its cultural standing by regarding its artists like air and replacing them with amateurs—because this is cheaper!!

December 18

Request from "Nationalzeitung" in Berlin, apropos a survey, to express my opinion regarding the significance of the press! A pleasant task! If I say what I think, I will be bitterly excoriated at the first opportunity—for example, next spring when I conduct a concert in Berlin—and if I don't reply, I will be regarded as a rude barbarian.

I have just made the following draft: "I do not think my opinion regarding the question you have asked should be made public, and I therefore take the liberty of requesting that I kindly be excused from giving an answer."[224] I admit that it is a trick, but—at the same time, it is my view. (Opted later not to answer at all.)

In honor of Benedicte's 68th birthday I invited her, Bet, Marie and Ingo to dinner at the Tostrup Cellar Restaurant at 4 PM. Ingo came but had to leave immediately because he could not *get permission* from his boss to frequent the Tostrup Cellar! He had made a special request and had told him whom he was going to be with, but the answer was: No! It's absurd.

December 23

At Sigurd and Bergliot Ibsen's for dinner at 6 PM in honor of Sigurd's 47th birthday. Wonderful up there at Ris[225] with such people. Ibsen had just returned from a several-month stay in Rome. Present at the party in addition to us were Bjørn and Einar and their wives, also Oscar Nissen and his wife.[226] Oysters, champagne, old Bordeaux and Rhine wine; light, top quality food with mountain air and free discussion. Got home at 11.

---

[224] Grieg's draft was written in German: "Ich finde nicht, dass meine Ansicht über die hier von Ihnen vorgelegte Frage der Öffentlichkeit gehört und gestate mir deshalb die Bitte, von einer Beantwortung meinerseits mich gütigst dispensieren zu wollen."

[225] Ris is an area a couple of miles north of downtown Christiania/Oslo.

[226] Norwegian physician and politician Oscar Egede Nissen (1843–1911) and his wife, Norwegian pianist Erika Lie Nissen (1845–1903).

December 24

A marvelous letter from Julius Röntgen, a true manifestation of his noble character as an artist and as a person—a character marked by its wide horizon. His view of the correspondence between Brahms and the Herzogenbergs[227] should not surprise me, but I am glad nonetheless to hear it expressed so openly and honestly by him. The dyed-in-the-wool Brahmsians are no better than the dyed-in-the-wool Wagnerites. It is typical that Mrs. Herzogenberg would not even allow Fritzsch,[228] in his [music journal] *Musikalisches Wochenblatt,* to accord both Brahms and Wagner the place of honor, that she wanted Brahms to keep his distance from Fritzsch, and that Brahms could not be persuaded to go along with this narrow view. Yes, my dear, dear friends Herzogenbergs, how lovable you were, how deeply gifted and how highly developed! *But*: how biased!

This is where Julius Röntgen stands far above them. Therefore he is not as Brahmsian in his compositions as he used to be either, whereas Herzogenberg little by little became so much like Brahms that in the end Brahms was almost ashamed to say anything about Herzogenberg's works (when urged to do so by Mrs. Herzogenberg) because they were—as if he had written them himself! But— I love the Herzogenbergs nonetheless and bless the memory of both of them.

Christmas eve at Halvorsens with Rolf H.[229] Very nice. I can overlook Halvorsen's peculiarities, for he is so unfailingly genuine.

December 25

Dinner at Marie John's[230] with all the members of the family who were in this area. Did not feel completely well.

December 26

Forenoon walk with Nina in lovely winter conditions to Bygdøy and on toward Lysaker. Visited Axel Heiberg[231] and Lammers.

In the afternoon I destroyed myself eating old Mrs. Bolette Krohn's plum-filled cookies! Yes, this sweet Christmas time with its temptations that even an experienced old patient can't resist!

In the evening, a premiere at the National Theater: *The Merry Widow,* operetta in 3 acts by Lehár,[232] a new sensationalist who very skillfully helps

---

[227] German composer Heinrich von Herzogenberg (1843–1900) and his wife, German pianist Elisabeth von Herzogenberg (1847–92). They belonged to Grieg's circle of friends in Leipzig.

[228] German music publisher E. W. Fritzsch (1840–1902).

[229] Norwegian businessman Rolf Halvorsen (1862–1926), brother of Johan Halvorsen.

[230] Edvard's brother John Grieg had committed suicide in October 1901, and when writing of John's widow, Marie, Grieg often used the name "Marie John" to distinguish her from Marie Halvorsen Nedberg, sister of Johan Halvorsen. Marie Beyer, wife of his close friend Frants Beyer, he usually called "Majs" or "Majsen". Marie Grieg had moved to Christiania some years after her husband's death.

[231] Norwegian businessman and patron of the arts Axel Heiberg (1848–1932).

[232] Hungarian operetta composer Franz Lehár (1870–1948).

himself to Offenbach, Strauss and all their successors. Plot, lines and music balance on the edge of banality—as people want them nowadays—but everything is so well perfumed that for that very reason it tickles our demoralized race. Here everything—even nobility—is made a subject of flirtation. That is evident from a gentle waltz that stands out strangely from the surroundings, and just for that reason—deliberate as it is—sounds all the more intriguing.[233] Technique and instrumentation (trumpet from time to time together with the melody) are excellently suited for their purpose: to tickle an idle audience. That is what has to be done to create a success at the National Theater in the year 1906! What a miserable world!

December 28

Dinner at Mrs. Sänger's in her new villa at Slemdal.[234] She, Hanchen[235] and her old mother are all equally lovable. How pleasant it was there! Yes, it was just the kind of house a person ought to have! NB: Plus a study!

December 29

The days are going by quickly and nothing gets done except answering letters from all sorts of tormentors at home and abroad, albeit mainly the latter. And still I reply only to the most necessary ones. I don't understand how other people manage such things. I can't seem to finish the copying of my *Four Psalms* op. 74, which I should have had off my back before this year is over. And as if that were not enough, such work is also starting to affect my eyes. Yes, old age, old age! Why?

Dinner with Halvorsens in the Tostrup Cellar Restaurant. Nice. Evening: played boston at Halvorsens, with pig's feet, Norwegian cheese,[236] and a lot of good cheer.

1907

January 7

"Oh, how each step is as heavy as lead, when we have to walk it backwards!" Yes, yes, my dear Drachmann,[237] that's how it is. But—cheer up!

This forenoon I had an orchestra rehearsal for the Music Association

---

[233] [Grieg's footnote]: I learned later that this waltz is a Serbian folk tune in duple time that has been adapted to fit the triple waltz rhythm!

[234] Slemdal is a residential area half a mile north of Ris. Both Ris and Slemdal are today stations on the railway line to Holmenkollen, Voksenkollen and Frognerseteren.

[235] The sisters Helga Waagaard Sänger (1854–1931) and Hanchen Waagaard Alme (1846–1936) were friends of Nina Grieg from early youth. Helga Sänger had been married to German Dr. Max Sänger (1853–1903), Leipzig, and had moved back to Norway after her husband's death. Dr. Sänger had from time to time been Nina Grieg's physician in Leipzig.

[236] *Gammelost*, a highly pungent Norwegian cheese made from sour milk.

[237] Danish poet Holger Drachmann (1846–1908).

concert, at which I have promised to conduct my *Piano Concerto in A Minor* with Karl Nissen.[238] He was outstanding today. He has improved enormously since I heard him in Prague in spring of last year.

I also wanted to conduct *Old Norwegian Melody with Variations* op. 51, but a sudden return of the old bad mucus problem compels me to avoid all exertion. In this depressed mood I am also today taking the big step of declining the invitation to conduct the Lamoureux Orchestra (Chevillard)[239] in Paris on March 24. An instinct tells me that for several reasons it is the best thing to do. And I take my hat off to the first instinct. It is nature's voice in us.

January 10

Forenoon trip to Frognersæteren with Halvorsen.[240] Wonderful weather. We walked from the Holmenkollen Tourist hotel to Frognersæteren and back to the terminus of the train line,[241] and I was happy that my hips could tolerate it. But the kind and jovial Halvorsen is a great fellow to walk with. Despite much that is different in our approach to music: How I love him, both as an artist and as a person. Not conservatory-spoiled, but with the happiest result of being self-taught. To use one's ears and eyes, and by so doing to acquire knowledge— that is and always will be the true way of learning for every talented, artistic temperament.

Came home from the trip as a new and better person.

January 11

Morning rehearsal in the auditorium of the Freemasons' Lodge, where I rehearsed the *tuttis* in the *Piano Concerto* that needed some polishing. With Holter[242] conducting I heard the remarkable "Bacchanal" from *Tannhäuser*, full of chords reminiscent of *Tristan and Isolde*. It went really well. "Forest Weaving" ("Waldweben"), on the other hand, sounded stiff and dry. And "Magic Fire" ("Feuerzauber") was absolutely taken too fast. It is too bad that Holter lacks the sensitive feeling for tempo nuances. A minuscule difference can completely destroy the whole piece, and that is exactly what happens in "Feuerzauber".[243]

---

[238] Norwegian pianist Karl Nissen (1879–1920).

[239] French conductor and violinist Charles Lamoureux (1834–99) had established the highly successful "Concerts Lamoureux" in Paris in 1881. In 1897 he had relinquished the post of permanent conductor of the orchestra and was succeeded by his son-in-law, Camille Chevillard (1859–1923). Some of Grieg's works were in the repertoire of the Lamoureux Orchestra, but Grieg never conducted the ensemble.

[240] Norwegian composer, conductor and violinist Johan Halvorsen.

[241] Holmenkollbanen—the Holmenkollen train line—that runs from downtown Oslo to Holmenkollen (Besserud) was opened in 1898. It was 6.5 km long. In 1916 it was extended an additional 5 km up to Frognersæteren.

[242] Norwegian composer and conductor Iver Holter (1850–1941), musical director of the Music Association at this time.

[243] Grieg is referring to four operas by Richard Wagner (1813–87): *Tannhäuser, Tristan and Isolde, The Valkyrie,* and *Siegfried*. The latter two are from *The Ring of the Nibelung*. See Grieg's Wagner articles pp. 290–318.

But what a thrill it was to sit beside my old friend Christian Cappelen and listen to this *Tannhäuser* music. It brought us back to our Leipzig days.[244] We sat up in the balcony abjuring any thoughts of critical evaluation and drinking in all this Romanticism like children. And more: at each beautiful passage to look [knowingly] at each other because we were feeling exactly the same thing! Such moments I have not experienced since Neupert's[245] time. For no one—no, not one—of the younger generation of musicians has a power of being entranced such that being with them during a performance of a great work of art can yield the same joy as my contemporaries and I had when we were young. We had a good time together. Cappelen and I were equally happy—as long as it lasted. No, a little longer, for we were in such a good mood that I went with him to Jensen in Market Street,[246] where he bought a flopping codfish fresh from the tank. There were movement and life in the contents of this tank that were worth more than that of certain conductors!

January 13

Last evening the Music Association concert (to benefit its pension fund). Fortunately an almost full house in the main auditorium. Since the *Piano Concerto*, which I was to conduct, was the last piece on the program, I heard the whole rest of the concert from my seat in the first row of the auditorium. One could note a certain festive mood, but great was the disappointment when the King came without the Queen.[247] He headed straight for me, "stuck out his hand" as he does to everyone, and expressed deep regret that "his wife" could not come along because she had a cold.

Then the concert began, and the *Tannhäuser* "Bacchanal" roared in my ears so loudly that my eardrums had all they could do to stand it. Then came "Forest Weaving" and "Magic Fire". They went satisfactorily but without feeling, it seemed to me. Still, I can't make any judgment from my [front-row] seat, where everything sounds bad.

Between the last pieces, Mrs. Hildur Fjord-Thue[248] sang "Elsa's Dream" from *Lohengrin*. It was one of the worst performances I have heard. A dry, brittle voice—and the voice was nonetheless the best of the whole thing. But what unmusicality, what lack of understanding, what dullness, emptiness, and plain-

---

[244] Grieg went to study at the Leipzig Conservatory in 1858 at the age of 15, and had been in the city for only a couple of months when Wagner's music drama *Tannhäuser* was performed there. Grieg later reported that he had been so enthralled that he went to see it 14 times. He and Cappelen (1845–1919) overlapped at Leipzig in 1860–62.

[245] Norwegian pianist Edmund Neupert (1842–88), who had premiered Grieg's *Piano Concerto* in Copenhagen in 1869.

[246] Norwegian: *Torvegade,* now spelled *Torggate.* Jensen's fish market was the best-known shop of its kind in Christiania/Oslo for over a century.

[247] King Haakon VII (1872–1957), king of Norway 1905–57; Queen Maud (1869–1938).

[248] Norwegian soprano Hildur Fjord-Thue (1870–1936).

ness! Damn it all! And they *have* to put such stuff on the program because, it is said, the lady in question is insistent and would stop at nothing to get her way. However, it is a very wrong thing [for the program committee] to do. It is cowardice. Strange as it may seem, the audience had the right instinct: Mrs. Fjord-Thue did not get even one curtain call. She did better with a couple of songs with piano, although Brahms[249] would have said "No, thanks" to this kind of "Liebestreu"! Elling[250] could not have been pleased with her in his beautiful "Fuglenes Sang" ["Song of the Birds"], although it was her best achievement. This lady, whom Colonne[251] compelled me to use in my concert in Salle Pleyel a few years ago, and who was already impossible at that time, has, in my opinion, gotten even worse.

Then, at the end came the *Piano Concerto*, which [Karl] Nissen performed in a technically excellent manner and with growing life and motion and which elicited a storm of enthusiasm. There really was also a lot of enchantment in the ensemble. The orchestra was in its best humor, and for me it is of course a piece of cake to conduct this work, which I have lived with, so to speak, ever since my youth. I was grateful in the depth of my soul, and that makes one nice.

Although I would have preferred to be driven right home, I invited Karl Nissen, Doctor Oscar Nissen[252] and Holter to "Engebret" for oysters etc. We spent a couple of pleasant hours, thanks mainly to Oscar Nissen, who certainly is an unusual and interesting man.

January 18

4 PM: Went by train to Bækkelaget[253] and walked to Grøndahls, where we had a most lovely dinner with the family, Harriet Backer, and Professor Julius Nico-laysen.[254] I had taken with me a small notebook and pencil, and when I got an opportunity to sit beside our dear Agathe Grøndahl, there was good use for it. Poor thing, she is—or at least seems to be, in any case—stone deaf and was glad that I conversed with her through the pencil. "It is a long time since anyone has talked with me this much," she said sadly. What must she not have suffered before she won the peace that now characterizes her! But I sense that she is suffering still.

---

[249] German composer Johannes Brahms (1833–96). "Liebestreu" is op. 3 no. 1. The German title means "Fidelity of Love".

[250] Norwegian composer Catharinus Elling (1858–1942). See Grieg's homage to Elling on pp. 203–204. The Norwegian title "Fuglenes Sang" means "The Song of the Birds".

[251] French conductor Edouard Colonne (1838–1910), founder of the Colonne Orchestra in Paris. The concert to which Grieg refers took place on April 27, 1903.

[252] Norwegian physician Oscar Egede Nissen, father of Karl Nissen.

[253] Bekkelaget (Bækkelaget) is a residential area some five miles south of Christiania/Oslo.

[254] The Grøndahls were Norwegian choral conductor Olaus A. Grøndahl (1847–1923) and his wife, pianist and composer Agathe Backer Grøndahl (1847–1907). Harriet Backer (1845–1932), an artist, was Agathe's sister. Julius Nicolaysen (1831–1909), a physician, was a prominent member of the Music Association in Christiania.

Agathe Backer Grøndahl. "If a mimosa could sing, it would resound with strains like those from Agathe Backer Grøndahl's most beautiful music."

Prof. Julius [Nicolaysen] had gotten very old and quiet since I last saw him, and not a little hard of hearing as well. All of us are slipping downward, downward! And we are egoists enough to console ourselves with the thought that in time the young people who are now so spry will do the same!

January 20

Concert with orchestra featuring Birger Hammer[255] in the Freemasons' Lodge. Yet another pianist! And one from Bergen! With all the determination and initiative of a Bergensian. Here, undoubtedly, are great possibilities—but, but! One could write Jeremiads about the artistic conditions in Norway that force the young people to go to Germany *at too young an age*—or more correctly, at too early a point in their development. We have all been messed up by German sentimentality, which is so far removed from our Norwegian temperament.

The Norwegian artists still have the capacity to deliver naive, healthy, straightforward art if only it is formed out of the national temperament and not out of the foreign one. And now even the music of the Germans has strayed so far afield from the healthy nature that their modern interpreters deliver an utter caricature of their own masters. The Wagnerites' art (including that of Bülow[256]) has had

---

255 Norwegian pianist Birger Hammer (1883–1958).
256 German pianist and conductor Hans von Bülow (1830–94).

such a bad influence on contemporary musicians that they feel *all* music as Wagneritish (I deliberately do not say "Wagnerian"[257]) in the sense that they cannot create or perform [so much as] four measures in the same tempo.

Such was not Schumann's[258] opinion, however. He wanted his music to be performed at the indicated tempo, without "improvements".[259] Why can a *tranquillo* passage not be played in such a way that the *character* is calm but the tempo is essentially the same? Now, so far as piano music is concerned, everything has to be exaggerated, thanks to the above-mentioned school—with Bülow leading the way. When the first, and to some extent the second, movement of Schumann's *A-minor Concerto* is performed like it was yesterday, the noble master must turn over in his grave. It was like a rubber mask that was distorted beyond recognition by being pulled in all directions; it was like the music of a drunken man. The music staggered, it lurched, it did not walk naturally. *Allegro* became *Presto*, a passage that was supposed to be calm in character became *Adagio*, the wonderful harmonies in the ensemble could scarcely be heard as the orchestra rushed through them. This is a crime. The tradition here is not in doubt. Schumann died in 1857.[260] I came to Leipzig in 1858, and a few months after my arrival I heard the bewitching Clara Schumann[261] play the *Concerto*, and each tempo remains indelibly impressed on my soul. Youthful impressions such as that do not lie. The brain is as soft as wax to receive impressions, and the imprint remains for life. That even talented musicians here in Norway cannot get hold of Schumann when this [Wagneritish] jargon is the prevailing one is only too easy to understand. Fortunately, the *Finale* of the *Concerto* was better. Here the rhythms do not tempt the performer to make such big mistakes.

Mr. Hammer's performance of the *C-minor Concerto* by Saint-Saëns' was, on the whole, more mature. It was a pleasure to note the clarity, energy and seriousness that he displayed. He also played Brahms' *Intermezzi and Ballade* op. 118[262] with vigor, but I was not familiar with these pieces and was not able to accord them the interest and admiration that they perhaps deserve.

Miss Kaja Hansen[263] sang—nicely and naturally—songs by Schumann, Schubert, Sjögren and Lange-Müller[264]

---

[257] Grieg distinguished between the "Wagnerians"—composers who admired and sought to emulate some features of the music of Richard Wagner (1813–87)—and the "Wagnerites", i.e., slavish imitators of Wagner. The corresponding adjectives are "Wagnerian" (*Wagnersk*) and "Wagneritish" (*Wagneriansk*).

[258] German composer Robert Schumann (1810–56). See Grieg's article on Schumann on pp. 255–274.

[259] Grieg uses the German term *Bessermachen*.

[260] Grieg is mistaken; Schumann died in 1856.

[261] German pianist Clara Wieck Schumann (1819–96), wife/widow of Robert Schumann. The concert to which Grieg refers took place in Leipzig on November 29, 1860.

[262] *Six Piano Pieces* op. 118 (1892).

[263] Norwegian singer Kaja Eide "Norena", nee Hansen (1884–1968).

[264] Austrian composer Franz Schubert (1797–1828), Swedish composer Emil Sjögren, (1853–1918), Danish composer Peter Erasmus Lange-Müller (1850–1926).

January 22

At 8 PM last evening I had dinner with the King at the royal estate on Bygdøy.[265] I wanted to decline on grounds of health, but Cabinet Secretary Grønvold,[266] with whom I conferred by telephone, didn't think this was a good idea. I then put on two pair of underwear, ordered a heated cab, and, bundled up in fur, drove out to Bygdøy. Sure enough, the guests consisted primarily of supreme court judges and generals, but even among these I knew two (Reimers and Edvard Bull[267]), and since I was placed between Bull and Emil Stang,[268] who were very cordial toward me, I had a pleasant time. And the dinner was one of the most polished and elegant events I have ever participated in. Why? I find it absurd.

I spoke for a long time with the King after dinner, also a bit with the Queen, and both—each in his/her own way—were charming. I told the King that it was "a Fatherlander" (a joke from *The Merry Widow*) that I had gone out there this evening, as I probably would go home with an attack of bronchitis. This amused him, and he assured me in that connection that I could leave quietly whenever I wished. That would have been difficult to do, however, as the cab had been ordered for 10:30 PM.

The time passed, however. I talked with several people—Admiral Børresen, Archdeacon Jensen, Grønvold, District Governor Furu (unpleasant, fat and snobbish), and I also shook hands with Captain Roald Amundsen.[269] We were both "graciously requested" to write in the Queen's album! Today I am happy about the fact that the whole affair has done me good.

January 23

Last evening Oselio Bjørnson[270] gave her long-heralded art-song recital in the Freemasons' Lodge. She has not been on stage for six years, and during these six years she has undergone the most incredible surgeries. It surely is a wonder, and an indication of an indomitable constitution, that her voice has lasted as much as it really has. But what I could not hear in the flattering room of her home, that I heard here in the concert hall: that a lot of the resonance is gone and that the former lushness and drive have been replaced by cautious calculation. But what does all of this imply in relation to the fulfillment of the task that lay before her: to sing art songs?

---

[265] The King of Norway owns an estate on Bygdøy, about three miles west of Christiania/Oslo, where the royal family used to spend several weeks each year.

[266] Norwegian attorney Hans A. M. Grønvold (1846–1926).

[267] Norwegian Supreme Court Judge Herman Reimers (1843–1928); Norwegian attorney and politician Edvard Bull (1855–1938).

[268] Norwegian attorney and politician Emil Stang (1834–1912).

[269] The guests to whom Grieg refers (all Norwegians) are: Rear Admiral Urban Jacob Rasmus Børresen (1857–1943); Rev. Gustav Jensen (1845–1922); Hans A. M. Grønvold; Ole Andreas Furu (1841–1925); polar explorer Roald Amundsen (1872–1928).

[270] Gina Oselio was the stage name of Norwegian soprano Ingeborg Aas (1858–1937). She was married to Bjørn Bjørnson (1859–1942), who for many years was Director of the National Theater in Christiania.

Unfortunately, singing art songs has never been her strength, and it never could be despite all her determination. To see a face that always expresses something totally different from the content of what she is singing is enough to drive you out of your mind. Here one learns that singing art songs requires a special talent. Yes, it is fine if it can also include "bel canto", but this "bel canto" alone, isolated as it is here, is of no use. And then this endless monotony, these wrong rhythms, and this—clear, yes, but simple—articulation of the text! Everything was a real trial. In *one* sense I can commend her rendition of "Say What You Will", because it calls for a lot of volume and she certainly has the voice for that. *But*: Instead of the rhythm ♩♪♪♩ one consistently hears ♪♪♩ !

The *musician* Backer Lunde[271] did the same thing in the piano part!!! That I call dilettantism—and that is the right designation even if the soloist regards herself as the world's leading artist! (That is not far from being the case, either—unfortunately!) In one respect she has a true mastery, namely, in the ability to claim success on the flimsiest evidence. The faintest applause evoked an encore or a *da capo*.

Oh, you prima donnas! I say of them as Ole Bull[272] said of the theater management in Bergen: "May the devil really salt them down!"[273]

January 26

Fridtjof Grøndahl's[274] concert with orchestra in the Freemasons' Lodge. He began with Tchaikovsky's *Piano Concerto in B-flat Minor*, which he completely mastered. His technique, power, bravura and rhythm are superb, as was also the understanding of the piece manifested in his performance. A feeling for the gentler element was lacking, however—but that can still come in one who is so gifted. His use of the pedal is also overdone and sometimes lacks harmonic clarity. This lack was even more evident in the old Italian pieces by Scarlatti[275] that he played later. And in Chopin's[276] marvelous *Fantasie* in F minor there are also more opportunities for "the eternal feminine"[277] than Grøndahl lets his hearers believe. He is still like a young animal that cavorts about in an excess of youthful energy. It is a transitional period that must be gotten through, but with talents and performances like these when he is in his early twenties, I anticipate absolute greatness [in due course].

Grøndahl had outstanding assistance by Miss Ellen Beck,[278] whose artistic

---

[271] Norwegian pianist Johan Backer Lunde (1874–1958).
[272] Norwegian virtuoso violinist Ole Bull (1810–80).
[273] Norwegian: "Fanden han inderlig 'grønsalte' dem!"
[274] Norwegian pianist Fridtjof Backer-Grøndahl (1885–1959) was the son of Olaus Grøndahl and Agathe Backer Grøndahl.
[275] Italian composer Domenico Scarlatti (1685–1757).
[276] Polish composer Frédéric Chopin (1810–49).
[277] Grieg uses the German "das ewig weibliche [zieht uns hinan]"—a famous phrase borrowed from *Faust*, by German author Johann Wolfgang von Goethe (1749–1832).
[278] Danish mezzo soprano Ellen Beck (1873–1953).

approach is refreshingly wholesome. Clear, deliberate art, outstanding resources —which, however, I will not maintain are correctly employed. There were a lot of forced tones here—but no diva-like whims. Therefore, it was good to hear her, and the audience was highly pleased. Fides' aria from *The Prophet*,[279] with its beautiful beginning and the banal ending, was an achievement, as were also two old Italian songs. Lastly she gave us as a bonus two songs by Agathe Grøndahl, who sat there as an *observer*, not a listener. It is tragic! The songs were full of poetry. It was a beautiful idea of Miss Beck that after the songs she turned toward her and greeted her with profound respect. It was a well chosen and deeply felt tribute.

I had to admire Halvorsen, who got up from his sickbed (influenza) to conduct.

January 27

Dinner (alone, unfortunately, as Nina has a light case of influenza) at the home of Mrs. Andrea Butenschøn at Gulleråsen. An ideal home. A charming hostess. I spent a couple of unusually pleasant and interesting hours with her, attorney J. Ramm,[280] and Christen Collin and his wife.

February 7

Symphony concert at the National Theater with Johannes Wolff, who gave an outstanding performance of Sinding's[281] *Violin Concerto* and Halvorsen's *Airs Norvégiens* and, with Halvorsen, of Bach's splendid *Concerto for Two Violins and Strings*. What music! The Andante was enough to bring one to tears. It went outstandingly; Halvorsen excelled this evening equally as conductor, composer and violinist. To be sure, his *Airs Norvégiens* is almost a collage of folk tunes, but it is so well done that it has become a work of art. Debussy's *L'après midi d'un faune* also went excellently.

Svendsen's[282] Prelude to *Sigurd Slembe*, on the other hand, was not handled well. An excessively fast tempo and all the uncertainty that goes along with it. The beautiful passages go by unnoticed because they get drowned in the rush. This is a weak point to which Halvorsen, unfortunately, appears to be blind. When I called his attention to it, he merely replied, "I have kept to the metronome indication." It is quite true that I have not studied this metronome indication. I only know that Svendsen performed his work at a different fundamental tempo and in such a way as to bring out the nuances. It would be regrettable if Halvorsen's choice of tempos should become the norm in the performance of this piece.

---

[279] Opera (1849) by French composer Giacomo Meyerbeer (1791–1864).
[280] Norwegian attorney Johnny Theodore Ramm (1854–1928).
[281] Norwegian composer Christian Sinding (1856–1941).
[282] Norwegian composer and conductor Johan Svendsen (1840–1911).

February 10

Said goodbye to Wolff, who left for Russia. We spent four pleasant days with him except for the fact that I had altogether too much champagne.

February 16

Lady Hallé's[283] concert in the Hals auditorium. She played beautifully, as always —but how she has aged! And despite the beauty of her tone it was as if the roundness in her structuring of the music had become more jagged. Still, if I closed my eyes and listened, she was still the eternally young Neruda. Brahms' *G-major Sonata* (performed with her sister Olga[284]) and the old Italian pieces suit her remarkably well, even if I wish that Brahms might be brought from the aristocratic world up there among the clouds, where Lady Hallé keeps him, down to our sinful world, with its struggle and its triumph.

In front of me sat the royal couple. That the King was bored with the music was obvious, even though he tried to conceal it. That made a sad impression on me. Suddenly he turned to me and said, "Tell me, when is the Dutchman coming—the one who is to be decorated?" "Is to? I assure your majesty, the honor will go to exactly the right man." I was glad that he had been informed, and for that I can thank Michelsen,[285] to whom I had expressed the wish that Röntgen might be decorated during his visit here in March.

February 17

Have written an article for the papers that will appear on March 2, when Röntgen performs at the Music Association.[286]

February 18

Sleepless night. Difficulty in breathing. Good Lord, what is going to come of it? I certainly can't give concerts abroad feeling like this. I hope a change of climate will help.

February 19

Last evening Madame Cahier.[287] Finally! A magnificent singer. Great art, all technique [treated only as] means. Everything imbued with soul. She was able

---

[283] Czech violinist Wilhelmina Neruda Hallé (1838–1911), who had played Grieg's *Violin Sonata No. 1* at his first concert in Christiania in 1866. She had also performed with him in later years at concerts in Manchester, London and Copenhagen. See Grieg's letter to her in Finn Benestad (ed.), *Edvard Grieg: Letters to Colleagues and Friends*, Columbus, Ohio 2000, p. 546.

[284] Czech pianist Olga Neruda (1858–1945), who had been a pupil of Clara Schumann.

[285] Norwegian statesman Christian Michelsen (1857–1925), who negotiated Norway's separation from Sweden in 1905.

[286] The article is given on pp. 252–254.

[287] American alto Sara Cahier, nee Sara-Jane Layton-Walker (1875–1951), was married to Swedish businessman Charles Cahier. Her stage name was Madame Cahier.

to express everything. No, there is no boundary between the lyrical and the dramatic. The art song and the dramatic production require both. But woe is me! I forgot that I hate all prima donnas! My hate turned into admiration and approval! Of course: not a trace of the diva! She sang in a completely unaffected manner. She was *gifted enough for that.*

February 23

Heard Madame Cahier at three concerts and am thrilled anew by her deep musical-lyrical-dramatic gift. Among other things she gave a superb rendition of "Mandoline", a brilliant song by Debussy. Then at a private event I heard her sing [my compositions] "A Dream" (excellently, but a *third* too low—B-flat Major), "A Swan" (in Norwegian!) absolutely beautifully, and "Farmyard Song" (that too in Norwegian)—everything with spirit and wit. She would like to give evening programs consisting entirely of my songs. Ah, if only I were ten years younger!

February 28

Julius Röntgen arrived at 7 AM. Orchestra rehearsal in the Music Association at 10. Julius played Beethoven's[288] G-major *Piano Concerto* beautifully and conducted his *Ballade on a Norwegian Melody.* He immediately won the goodwill of the orchestra.

March 1

Dress rehearsal, where Julius scored a great success as pianist, composer and conductor.

March 2

Evening: Music Association concert. We had dinner at the Frognersæteren Restaurant, so I was afraid that Julius would get too tired, but everything went splendidly in the evening and Julius was a smashing success—played his own arrangement of Dutch folk songs as an encore, and after the *Ballade* he received an orchestral fanfare and many curtain calls. I am happy that he was such a hit, as I am basically responsible for his appearance here. Luckily, my article in the newspapers has contributed to the fact that the audience had the feeling of being in the presence of someone they already knew.

I must not forget one of the main pieces of the concert: Bach's *Brandenburg Concerto*[289] in F Major for string orchestra, flute, oboe, trumpet and violin solo. Marvelous, jovial Kirmes atmosphere.[290]

---

[288] German composer Ludvig van Beethoven (1770–1827).

[289] *Brandenburg Concerto no. 2.*

[290] Kermes, Kirms (Kirchenmesse) was a carnival-like folk festival held annually in Köthen, where Bach lived and worked at the time he wrote the *Brandenburg Concertos.* We know that Grieg's good friend Johan

The four soloists were outstanding, but the string orchestra, which stumbled along as best it could, seemed to me to not be well led. After a curtain call, which presumably was for the soloists, Holter[291] came out and claimed the applause for himself. Then he went out, and when the applause continued, showed his face once more and again accepted the applause without so much as a gesture toward the soloists, who were sitting right beside him. What can you say about such behavior? It is, to say the least, unfortunate, and it—creates bad blood. Poor Holter! He is so afraid of losing some of the crumbs that are thrown to the orchestral musicians from the audience. [What a pity] that he still does not know that it doesn't pay to go chasing after applause!

After the concert I was with Julius, Holter and the Music Association's Board in the Theater Restaurant, having an utterly boring time. Yes, those Norwegians! They invite the man who has honored their Association—and they don't have *a single word* to say to him. At the end, as we were about to leave, *Julius thanked them* for the good will and hospitality they had extended to him! That could be called "heaping coals of fire"![292] Again I must wonder at Holter, who could not say a word in honor of his colleague.[293] As a guest myself, *I* couldn't do it. So we parted in silent embarrassment.

March 3

At Hals Concert Hall in the forenoon. Rehearsal of Brahms' divine G-minor *Piano Quartet.* I think a stone would resound in ecstasy the way Röntgen handles it. But stones such as, for example, the violist Severin Svendsen[294] cannot be smashed. He doesn't budge for a moment from his dry note-reading. Buschmann[295] is also too weak. Not up to the task. Halvorsen is of course completely in tune [with Röntgen]. Dear Halvorsen! Dinner with Julius at the home of my sisters.[296]

March 4

Dinner with Julius at "Engebret" Restaurant. Kragerø Ø.[297]

March 5

Dinner with Julius at the home of Mrs. Sänger.[298] Evening concert at Hals Concert

---

Svendsen was once present at this festival, and there is no doubt that Grieg was also familiar with it. In using the expression "Kirmes atmosphere", therefore, he obviously means "festive music".

[291] Iver Holter (1850–1941), conductor of the Music Association Orchestra in Christiania.

[292] An allusion to Proverbs 25:21–22.

[293] Grieg means that at an occasion such as this it would have been appropriate for Holter to stand up and say a few words of welcome and thanks to their guest from Holland.

[294] Norwegian violinist and violist Severin Svendsen (1871–1940).

[295] Norwegian cellist Otto Buschmann.

[296] Benedicte and Elisabeth Grieg.

[297] Kragerø is a coastal village in southern Norway and "Ø" denotes island, but the allusion is cryptic.

[298] Helga Waagaard Sänger (1854–1931) was a friend of Nina Grieg from early youth. She had been married to German Dr. Max Sänger (1853–1903), Leipzig, and had moved back to Norway after her husband's death.

Hall: Thibaud and Wurmser.[299] The former is a master of the first rank, with a flexible tone the likes of which I have rarely heard. The latter is an outstanding virtuoso, but his pedal work is imperfect.

In the forenoon I went with Julius to see the King, who awarded him the Order of St. Olaf and was so very kind as to ask me if I wanted him to come to Julius' concert tomorrow, for if so he would gladly be at my service. Truly a people's king! I of course grabbed the opportunity with both hands.

March 6

Röntgen's concert at Hals. 1) Bach: *Toccata*, Brahms: *Intermezzo* and *Rhapsody*; 2) Beethoven: *Sonata* op. 111, in C Minor; 3) Grieg: *Norwegian Dances* op. 35, which I played with Julius; 4) Schumann: *Papillons*; 5) Grieg: Songs: a) "The Ocean" b) "With a Water Lily", c) "To My Son", d) "Hope", sung by Nina; 6) Röntgen, *Variations on a Czardas Theme*.

The whole concert proceeded in a mood of excitement that intensified as the evening progressed, and there was a good-sized audience if not a full house. Julius played so splendidly that even the King, the Queen, and Princess Victoria[300] clapped enthusiastically. The *Norwegian Dances* went very well and were a smashing success, and after Nina's singing there was wild applause. Thank God, I had no cause to regret my daring deed. Of course, we wanted to do everything, everything for Julius. As an encore she sang "Kidlings' Dance"! And, when the wild applause continued, she concluded with "Moonlit Forest". It was—old youth! But the listeners amply demonstrated that it was youth that triumphed!!

March 7

A big farewell dinner for Julius at "Engebret". 42 people. Wonderful atmosphere. Unfortunately, Michelsen couldn't come because of a deputation, but I had his charming and sweet wife beside me at the table. In the evening there was a concert in the Quartet Society. 1) Beethoven, *Les Adieux, l'absence et le retour* (Julius), 2) Grieg, *Norwegian Dances* for piano four hands as an improvisation number while we waited for the strings from the Theater, 3) Röntgen, *Violin Sonata* (Halvorsen and Röntgen), 4) Brahms, *Piano Quartet in G Minor* (Röntgen with Halvorsen, Severin Svendsen and Buschmann).

Julius carried everybody along. When the last tone had died away, the listeners and the board stood up and shouted a "hurrah" for the guest of honor, then took

---

[299] French violinist Jacques Thibaud (1880–1953) and French pianist and composer Lucien Wurmser (1877–? after 1957) were on a concert tour in Scandinavia, starting in Christiania. Their first program consisted of Grieg's *Violin Sonata in C Minor*, Chopin's *Piano Sonata in B Minor*, and Mendelssohn's *Violin Concerto in E Minor*, plus some minor works by Schumann, Mendelssohn, Saint-Saëns, Hungarian composer Karl Goldmark (1830–1915) and Polish composer Henri Wieniawski (1835–80). Their concerts in Christiania (March 5 and 7) were tremendously successful.

[300] English Princess Victoria, sister of Queen Maud.

their coats and hats and went their ways. In general, this Society seems to be totally lacking in understanding. They clap dutifully, but this president—the same martinet as the one in the Music Association—brings no joy and no life with him. The Association used to be totally different in the old days. Julius felt this, unfortunately, and it discouraged him.

Halvorsen was so dazed by "Widow mood"[301] when he arrived that he didn't enter fully into the *Violin Sonata* (what a scandal for the Theater to exploit him in that way, and what a curiosity to *let* himself be thus exploited), but in Brahms he was right on a par with Julius. The other two were not up to the task, but they did their best.

It is characteristic of this Society that Julius, sweating and thirsty after the exertion, had to *pay* for a pint of beer—and that I had to *pay* for tickets for four women despite the fact that I am an honorary member. I even asked the president if I couldn't take along some ladies—enthusiastic music-lovers—who had no possibility of being admitted except by invitation. "Oh, sure," he said, "You can buy tickets from Mr. Bye[302] for one and a half crowns since you are a member!" He wisely avoided saying "honorary member"! "What is Honor?" said Falstaff. Mere words! True, true.

March 8

Julius left at 2:30. He was melancholy, but happy. He had won the hearts of everyone as an artist and as a person. In the morning I went with him to see Michelsen, whom we met and who was the epitome of amiability. Now Julius feels that he has received the new Norway in its entirety! In the evening I saw Bernard Shaw's[303] interesting play "The Devil's Disciple".

March 12

(Tuesday) Left with Tonny[304] for Copenhagen. Stayed overnight in Gothenburg.

March 13

Evening arrival in Copenhagen. Took lodging at Hotel Bristol.

March 15

Dinner at the hotel with Steenbergs.[305]

---

[301] Halvorsen had just come from a performance of "The Merry Widow" at the National Theater.
[302] Probably Christiania music dealer Oluf Bye (1854–1932).
[303] Irish dramatist, critic and novelist George Bernard Shaw (1856–1950).
[304] Tonny (Antonie) Hagerup (1844–1934), Nina Grieg's sister.
[305] Danish singer Julius Steenberg (1830–1911), a close friend from Grieg's youth, and his wife Cathrine.

March 16

First orchestra rehearsal on *In Autumn*, *Lyric Suite* and *Bergliot*. Unfortunately: There is a lot to work on here—and too little time.

March 17

Dinner at Melchiors.[306] In the evening, saw *Lohengrin*. It was sad to see Svendsen on the conductor's podium again. His beat is still concise and elastic, and the orchestra sounds wonderful, but the production as a whole is what Rubinstein called *nicht gut*. Everything on stage is a mess: Lohengrin's arrival is appalling, his plea is torn to bits by falsity and wretched staging. Herold[307] is strained and off key in the first act, excellent in the second. Mrs. Ulrich[308] as Elsa is fine, almost *too* fine. Miss Krarup-Hansen[309] as Ortrud is often excellent; she has made great strides. Telramund (Høeberg[310]) is so-so, the king (Müller[311]) exceedingly poor. The production as a whole is not worthy of Svendsen's spirit, not to mention Wagner's.

March 18

Second orchestra rehearsal. Great progress. I still have faith that it will go well. If only Mrs. Blad[312] were up to the task. Dinner at Henriques'[313] with Irmingers and Melchiors.

March 19

Third orchestra rehearsal. Significant progress. Mrs. Blad gives me good hope for *Bergliot*. Tried the *Piano Concerto* with Miss Stockmarr on a Hornung & Møller piano that didn't have a penny's worth of vim and vigor. It was an absolute "Bølle-mose"![314] For these instruments somebody will have to write piano concertos that take their limitations into account!

Dinner with Carl Nielsen[315] at Bodil and Rolf Viggo Neergaards.[316] Thereafter went to the Royal Theater, where we saw Carl Nielsen conduct—and very expertly—his witty and no less expertly written opera *Masquerade*. The first act is excellent, the second lags, the third is better again. It seems to me to reflect the

---

306 The Melchiors, a Danish family of Jewish origin, were friends of Nina and Edvard Grieg.

307 Danish tenor Vilhelm Herold (1865–1937).

308 Danish soprano Emilie Ulrich (1872–1952).

309 Danish mezzo-soprano Johanne Krarup-Hansen (1870–1958).

310 Danish baritone Alberg Høeberg (1879–1949).

311 Danish bass Max Müller (1866–?).

312 Danish actress Augusta Blad (1871–1953).

313 Danish banker Martin R. Henriques (1825–1912), a close friend of Grieg in Copenhagen.

314 *Bøllemosen* was a favorite resort area north of Copenhagen with which Grieg was well acquainted (see his diary entry for June 8, 1907). The Danish word "mose" means "moss bog" or "marsh". In using this name (followed by an exclamation mark) to characterize the Danish-built Hornung & Møller piano, Grieg was saying that it produced a weak sound—as if one were playing in a moss bog.

315 Danish composer Carl Nielsen (1865–1931).

316 Danish business proprietor Rolf Viggo Neergaard (1837–1915) and his wife Bodil (1867–1959).

influence of Berlioz, but Nielsen doesn't think so as he knew so little about him. Often I find, as it were, surrogates for music, things that are the products of pure intellect. But just as often there are great lines with music that is truly felt. And a mastery, a singular technique that is surprising. If Nielsen would follow what is good in his talent, he would produce great things. But it is not for nothing that he belongs to a generation that insists first and foremost on being original, even if it be at the cost of beauty.

March 20

1 PM dress rehearsal. Every seat sold. It went as well as a dress rehearsal, strictly speaking, ought not to go. But I think the performances now rest on a secure basis. The listeners' approval was absolutely effusive. Mrs. Blad, whose recitation of *Bergliot* has gotten better and better, received three curtain calls, which says something in view of the kind of work being performed.[317] The *Piano Sonata* was too feminine for *me* on that kind of piano. The short pieces, on the other hand, made a good impression. Miss Beck was not at her best. I hope it will go better tomorrow. After the *Lyric Suite* I was called out again and again. It also went excellently.

March 21

Unfortunately I caught a cold at the dress rehearsal. Today I am staying in and taking medicine. My only hope is to drive the germs of illness out by sweating as I conduct this evening. But weakness in the body is not good. Received a heartfelt, discerning letter from Elisabeth Rosenberg that moved me in the depths of my soul. It was balm in the old sore![318]

---

[317] *Bergliot* is a melodrama.

[318] Elisabeth Rosenberg was the daughter of Danish composer Christian Frederik Emil Horneman (1840–1906), who had died on June 8, 1906. Grieg and Horneman had met as students at the Leipzig Conservatory in 1858 and had been close friends for many years thereafter. Their friendship suffered a permanent rupture in 1895, however, following a visit to Troldhaugen by Horneman and his wife and the Griegs' and Hornemans' mutual Danish friends Gottfred Matthison-Hansen (1832–1909) and August Winding (1835–99) and their wives. Unfortunately, to Grieg's despair and for reasons that he never understood, in the course of the visit a feeling of ill will developed between him and Horneman that lasted for the rest of their lives. That is why Mrs. Rosenberg's letter was, for Grieg, "balm in the old sore". She wrote: "It is like living my life over again when I hear something by you. I feel as if I had my father beside me all the time, and that is both painful and joyful! Your music brought me the fragrance of the time when both of you were young, and full of courage and joy and enthusiasm, and with your pockets bursting with talents that you dipped into with both hands. (. . .) I don't know what came between you and father during the last years of his life. He never mentioned the matter to me, but I shall always regard you as father's old friend, which I think you are to this very day—and to those who loved my father I am bound with strong bonds! Thank you for all the beautiful and rich memories that are tied to you and Nina—memories reaching all the way back to my childhood. Thank you for the concert yesterday. It awakened such vivid memories."

Grieg replied immediately to Mrs. Rosenberg's letter: "Thank you, thank you for your letter! If only you knew how it has gladdened—no, more than gladdened me! It is so filled with the pure and genuine feeling that also was your father's most endearing characteristic. No, dear Beth, you do not know what came between him and me during the last years of his life, and I dare say that I do not know either! But this I know: The fact that your father could not understand who were his best friends proves that the seriousness of

March 22

The concert took place last evening, and everything went well. I sweated the disease-producing substances out of my system, and today I am decidedly better. The warmth in the hall yesterday was enormous, but the audience was somewhat smaller than at the dress rehearsal. Miss Beck cooled off, for she was not consistently at her peak, and her eight songs were absolutely too many. They caused the concert to last for two and a half hours. What made me happy was that *Bergliot* again gripped people and that the *Lyric Suite* elicited applause that finally grew into ovations with fanfare and laurel wreath. The orchestra played excellently throughout.

After the concert, the three amiable ladies who had participated—Miss Beck, Mrs. Augusta Blad and Miss Stockmarr—had arranged a nice room at Hotel Bristol with oysters and champagne, which we couldn't resist. We didn't get to bed until 1:30!

March 25

Dinner in the hotel as guests of Hennings and his wife.[319] There were too many heterogenous elements for the situation to get altogether comfortable. The table groaned under the weight of oysters and champagne, but that didn't help. I had Mrs. Hennings as my dinner partner, whereas Nina ended up in a corner between two gentlemen—the only ones at the whole party whom she didn't know—and this blunder brought its own punishment. We broke up at 10 PM. Carl Nielsen, Børresen, and Tofft[320] were there as well as several musicians and men of letters, also [Vilhelm] Herold and his wife.

March 26

Evening: *Anna Bryde*[321] in the Dagmar Theater with the Hansen brothers.[322] Matinee repeat at 1:30 of the March 21 concert. An almost full house and grow-

---

his illness was not limited to its physical aspects. It is certain that he can never have had a warmer or more faithful friend than me. No matter how different we may have been from one another, he was from my youth onward the very epitome of friendship. He was The Friend. For that reason, I cannot begin to describe my pain upon seeing him little by little coming to regard me as his enemy. At the end it was as if I more or less did everything I could to get him out of my mind. The effort to do that failed completely, however, and now—after his death—I remember only the good things that he did for me both as an artist and as a human being."

Mrs. Rosenberg's letter, dated March 20, 1907, is preserved in Bergen Public Library. Grieg's response, dated March 21, 1907, is in the possession of Horneman's great-grandson, Danish pianist Niels Bondesen, and his wife Jytte Bondesen. Grieg's most important letters to Horneman are printed in English translation in Finn Benestad (ed.), *Edvard Grieg: Letters to Colleagues and Friends*, Columbus, Ohio 2000, pp. 431–437. Grieg also wrote an article about Horneman, given in the present volume on pp. 211–216.

319 Danish music publisher Henrik Hennings (1848–1913) and his wife, Betty Hennings (1850–1939), a singer.
320 Danish composers Hakon Børresen (1876–1954) and Alfred Tofft (1865–1931).
321 *Anna Bryde*: a play by Danish poet and playwright Otto Benzon (1856–1927). Grieg had set several of his poems in opp. 69 and 70.
322 Danish music publishers Alfred Wilhelm Hansen (1854–1923) and Carl E. J. Hansen (1850–1919).

ing warmth in every respect. The income will go to a fund for the building of a lepers' hospital in Danish West Indies. The ideal connecting link for me was my distinguished friend Armauer Hansen. His great cause is one that I would gladly serve.[323]

March 28

Departure for Berlin. Hotel Continental.

March 29

Forenoon rehearsal of *Bergliot* with Mrs. Rosa Bertens-Block.[324] Rather discouraged about the prospects. Dinner at the Cleves.[325]

March 30

Breakfast at Hotel Kaiserhof as guests of Mr. Charles Cahier and Madame Cahier. Forenoon rehearsals with Cleve and Rosa Bertens.

March 31

Forenoon rehearsals again with Cleve and Rosa Bertens and dinner at Kempinski Restaurant with the Cleves.

April 1

Departure for Munich. Hotel Vier Jahreszeiten. Arrived overtired and got a room with a terrible racket from streetcars and automobiles. The consequences did not fail to materialize.

April 2

An almost sleepless night, with difficulty breathing. Today impossible. My nerves are absolutely sick. Oh, what if I have to leave without giving the concert! My will to live is at low ebb—and no one can console me! Nina is loving and sweet and helpful, but I lack a powerful, will-strengthening, nerve-bracing element. I still have a lot of hope for improvement, however!

April 3

One gram of antipyrine plus a cold compress on my abdomen helped me get a

---

[323] Gerhard Armauer Hansen (1841–1912), a physician and scholar from Bergen, made the important discovery that leprosy was not hereditary but bacterial in origin. His contribution to the eradication of the disease in Norway made him world-famous, and the laws developed in Norway at his urging have served as a model for other countries desiring to institute preventive measures to control the disease. See Grieg's letter to him in Finn Benestad (ed.), *Edvard Grieg: Letters to Colleagues and Friends*, Columbus, Ohio 2000, pp. 359–360.

[324] German actress Rosa Bertens-Block (1869–1934).

[325] Norwegian pianist and composer Halfdan Cleve (1879–1951) and his wife Berit Vinderen Cleve (1878–1964).

good night's sleep! But my condition is: shortness of breath and a feeling of weakness. Forenoon: Called on Weingartner and Mottl,[326] but didn't see either of them. Pleasant dinner at Markus Grønvold's.[327] After dinner we sat with him and his wife and their three charming daughters on a wonderful balcony overlooking the yard and soaked in the sunshine for hours. That did me good. Upon arriving home I found both Weingartner's and Mottl's cards. Too bad. So I probably won't get to see them at all. In the evening had a visit from Paul Schlesinger, editor of *Allgemeine Zeitung*. He wanted to know my opinion about the *modern* German music. But I am no longer stupid, and I simply kept my ammunition to myself as I, like a diplomatic eel, twisted myself through the most incredible coils. I think I managed the task: to get him to leave just as ignorant as when he came! Anyway, he was an amiable Jew.

April 4

Yet another almost totally sleepless night! I am utterly depressed. And then a three-hour rehearsal with the Kaim Orchestra.[328] The beginning of the rehearsal was difficult to get through, but after a while I got the hang of things and straightened a whole lot out with this good but undisciplined orchestra. Strangely enough, *In Autumn* seemed to be the number that interested them most of all. Today I cautiously revealed my amiable side, but if the discipline is not better tomorrow I will exercise a little authority. I *will* maintain discipline in all matters. Still no female singer has arrived with whom I can go through the orchestra songs on the piano before the dress rehearsal tomorrow at 8 PM, and de Greef[329] won't even come to the dress rehearsal. These soloists! They should be eradicated. One should use them to put each other to death. They are egoists one and all. First themselves, then art!

The Jewish editor from yesterday really published an excellent interview in *Allgemeine Zeitung* today.[330] This evening, in our room (at 9 PM!), a song rehearsal with Mrs. Hilgermann.[331] Passable, not exceptional in any respect.

---

[326] German conductor Felix Weingartner (1863–1942); Austro-German conductor Felix Mottl (1856–1911).

[327] Norwegian painter Markus Grønvold (1845–1929).

[328] The Kaim Orchestra was founded in 1893. In the 1920's it was merged into the Munich Philharmonic.

[329] Belgian pianist Arthur de Greef (1862–1940).

[330] The interview was also published on the same day in the evening edition of the Berlin newspaper *Berliner Lokal-Anzeiger*. It is interesting in several respects, not least in its picturesque description of Grieg: "Atop the dwarf-like little figure sits a head that radiates determination, high-mindedness and goodness. The short moustache conceals the pursed lips. The round, childlike eyes have a sharp and penetrating look."

Grieg makes some incisive comments about the music of Richard Strauss: "I have an extraordinarily high opinion of Richard Strauss' *Death and Transfiguration*, and I have listened to his *Till Eugenspiegel* with great interest. I have studied the scores of his later works. This of course gives a certain impression of the works, but not the right one in any case. One must hear the music. I don't think I can follow Strauss all the way, however. I recently read an article by Weingartner that expressed a very simple but great truth roughly as follows: 'The employment of the resources of the orchestra is raised to an unheard-of level, but on stage there is still the singing voice—and the voice is quite simply incapable of being enlarged.' That's how it is. I think that now—after Richard Wagner's appearance—German music must have a rest, just as a field must lie fallow for a time [after the harvest] before it is plowed and tilled anew."

April 5

Thank God, five hours of sleep without antipyrine. Awoke at 4 AM and lay awake until I got up at 7, but fortunately without difficulty in breathing or hallucinations. At 10 AM I had the second and last orchestra rehearsal. I am *not* enthusiastic about the Kaim Orchestra. It is highly undisciplined and has some poor players. The first oboe is terrible. He totally destroys "Evening in the Mountains". At first Mrs. Hilgermann was incomprehensibly frightened; she sang both too low and too high, and her vibrato was too strong. Later she improved. But ugh! "It was just Tambak!"[332]

Rehearsed the *Piano Concerto* without the soloist. A boring exercise. Dinner in the Hoftheater Restaurant with Thyra, Neovius and Saima[333] as guests. In the evening in our room: rehearsal with de Greef, who played more beautifully than ever. He is a significant artist, one whose playing is filled with poetry. He is an artist from head to toe. We must get him to Christiania.

April 6

A poor night of sleep. Now I have to pull myself together.

April 7

Finally the concert was launched, and it was successful. Since then I have slept the sleep of the just. There was a full house. The whole court was present—unfortunately, for in general it is the case that these crowned types[334] have a paralyzing effect on the listeners. However: The overture sounded hale and hearty, eliciting warm applause and a curtain call.

Grieg also comments on his own relation to German music: "I was educated in the German school. I studied in Leipzig, and musically speaking I am completely German. But then I went to Copenhagen and got acquainted with Gade and Hartmann. It then struck me that I could develop myself further only on a national foundation. It was our Norwegian folk tunes that showed me the way. In Germany the critics treated me badly because I didn't fit into the categories into which composers are commonly placed. In Germany it is often said: "He Norwegianizes!" [*Er norwegert!*] It is true that I I draw on the Norwegian folk tune, but even Mozart and Beethoven would not have become what they did had they not had the old masters as models. The proud German folk song was a foundation for the old masters, and without folk music no art music is possible. I realized this clearly. And then they [the German critics] say: 'He Norwegianizes!' The treasures of our folk song are not at all brought to light. I knew what I wanted to do when I was twenty years old. However, since these treasures have not been collected, there is no one who knows them. That is why it is so careless to say: 'He Norwegianizes!' I know very well why my music sounds altogether too national to German ears, but I surely must also take into consideration the fact that a good deal of my individuality is due to my Germanization, for it is not to be found in the Nordic national character. I believe nonetheless that there is a capability in the Norwegian people to grasp this harmony—indeed, that it perhaps lies there hidden in an enigmatic way. As our poets again and again create works based on material from the sagas, so also the composer can and must search out the musical sources for his art."

[331] Austrian soprano Laura Hilgermann (1857–1945).

[332] *Tambak* was what today would be called "gaudy finery; rubbish". Grieg is suggesting that Mrs. Hilgermann is less of a singer than she claims to be.

[333] Finnish mathematician Edvard Rudolf Neovius (1851–1917); his wife, Thyra Hammerich Neovius; their daughter, Saima Neovius.

[334] Grieg uses the term *krondyr*—a play on words, as *krondyr* is also the ordinary word for a species of red deer.

Mrs. Hilgermann's rendition of the songs with orchestra also came off better than she deserved. When we came into the green room she said, as she pressed close to me, "Sind Sie zufrieden, Meister?" ["Are you pleased, maestro?"]—and she kissed me close to the mouth. Her solo songs—"The Princess", "Ragna", and "The First Primrose"—were just so-so, and they brought her only one curtain call instead of the four that a diva expects.

De Greef created an enormous sensation, and he deserved it. Not only in the concerto, but in his solo pieces also he showed himself to be a great artist. His rendition of the little "Puck" (Norwegian: "Småtrold") was a masterpiece of interpretation, and it brought him a storm of applause.

Finally—after "Evening in the Mountains", which was almost caviar for the people, and "Last Spring", which elicited a lot of curtain calls—came *Peer Gynt Suite No. 1*, which this time, as always, took everyone by storm.

Then, after the royal family had left the hall, there were endless curtain calls; handkerchiefs by the hundreds waving in the air; "Wiederkommen, Wiederkommen!" ["Come back, come back!"]; four or five laurel wreaths, and jubilant applause. All well and good as far as it went. But what made me even happier was that Weingartner came in to see me and was warm and friendly. Max Schillings[335] also came, as did several other less well-known musicians, the Norwegian consul Offerheim, Mrs. Elisabet Lindemann and two children, whose gratitude was deeply moving. Also Grønvolds, Neovius's and others.

Went straight home—declining all invitations—and went to bed, because by 9 AM the next morning we were already chugging off for Berlin, where I am writing this in the Kaiserhof Hotel.

April 8

Wonderful day of rest. Corrected orchestral parts in the evening.[336]

April 9

First orchestra rehearsal with the Berlin Philharmonic. It was quite different from the Kaim Orchestra. The slightest hint, and there is a response. I accomplished in one and a half hours what I used three hours to do in Munich. Dinner at the Kempinski Restaurant with the Cleves.

April 10

Second orchestra rehearsal. The performances are so good that *one* rehearsal is enough. That I have never experienced before. And my demands truly have not

---

[335] German composer and conductor Max Schillings (1868–1933).

[336] Before orchestra rehearsals it was Grieg's practice to check the orchestral parts in order to unify bowing, articulation, dynamics etc.

decreased through the years. Quite the opposite. Cleve played the *Piano Concerto* like a true musician—but he didn't let himself go, and unfortunately he probably won't do so either. Too bad! Mostly for himself, for a cold reception could make him discouraged and unsure of himself. Dinner at 3 PM at the home of von Ditten,[337] our new Norwegian ambassador, together with Mrs. Schrader, Backer-Lunde, and Michael Lie[338] and his wife. Very pleasant.

April 11

Last orchestra rehearsal. Mrs. Bertens bellowed—also where it is not necessary—and I do not expect anything of her. It is *possible* that the Germans like it that way, but it is untrue and dull—be it ever so correct literarily and academically. If only I had had the lovely Mrs. Blad, with her beautiful organ voice! Cleve was freer today. He let himself go more—but still he seemed to insist on keeping everything under control. It was good to hear Mrs. Gulbranson's lovely voice again. She certainly sang beautifully in her old three songs with orchestra: "Solveig's Cradle Song", "From Monte Pincio" and "A Swan".[339]

Dinner with Mrs. Gulbranson at the Kempinski Restaurant. Upon arriving home at Hotel Keiserhof I found an invitation from the Kaiser[340] to have breakfast with him tomorrow at 1 PM. How unfortunate that it is on the very day of the concert, but I presumably will go in the hope that I can get away after an hour. Drove out to see Bernt Grønvold,[341] but unfortunately we missed him.

April 12

A difficult day. Thank God it is over. At 12:15 I was picked up in von Ditten's carriage and accompanied by the ambassador himself to the palace. Since the Kaiser was attending a dress rehearsal of a play by Wildenbruch,[342] the party, contrary to usual practice—it allegedly had not happened for many years—was delayed for almost one and a half hours. Immediately upon my arrival I had asked the Lord Chamberlain—or more correctly, the aide-de-camp—if I might leave at 3 PM in view of my concert. Now this became an impossibility, and I found myself in an annoyingly nervous condition.

After I had been sitting for awhile, in strode first Saint-Saëns, then Massenet, then Leroux[343] (the composer of *Dorothea*, which is being performed at the

---

[337] Norwegian diplomat Thor von Ditten (1860–1936), ambassador in Berlin from 1906.

[338] The Norwegian counselor of legation, Captain Michael S. Lie (1862–1934).

[339] These three (from opp. 23, 39 and 25, respectively) were among the songs that Grieg arranged for voice and orchestra in 1894–95 and published in 1895–96 as *Six Songs with Orchestra*. He did not include them on his opus list, however, and in *Edvard Grieg: Complete Works* the collection has been designated EG 177.

[340] German Kaiser Wilhelm II (1859–1941).

[341] Norwegian painter Bernt Grønvold (1859–1923).

[342] German author Ernst von Wildenbruch (1845–1909).

[343] French composers Camille Saint-Saëns (1835–1921), Jules Massenet (1842–1912) and Xavier Leroux (1863–1919).

Opera House by a troupe from Monte Carlo). Then came the old rubbish: "Ah! Je suis heureux de vous voir!" ["Ah! I am happy to see you!"]—and with that I had exhausted my vocabulary. These great men speak no language except their own, and that being the case no further conversation was possible. Saint-Saëns was rather reserved (he still had not forgotten Dreyfus![344]). Massenet was more cordial and tried to carry on a conversation—among other things, about our new king and Norway's joy over the new situation. With the Prince of Monaco[345] I could speak English, and I got the impression of a noble personality.

Finally the Kaiser showed up. The first person he headed for was me, and after a few cordial words he went on to the rest of the row. Then we sat down at the table. It was a most sumptuous dinner. I sat between the master of ceremonies Count so-and-so and Gunzberger, the impresario for the Monte Carlo Opera Company.

When we got up from the table at around 3:30, and when the Kaiser—who at that time was talking with the French composers—realized that I had to leave, he came quickly over to me and was as friendly and charming as he can be, or more correctly, as he really is. I regret that I had to leave before coffee, for I am certain that if I could have stayed I would have been able to engage him in a real conversation. I drove home in von Ditten's carriage and got a wonderful one-hour nap.

Then I got dressed and went off to the Philharmonic concert, which became a triumph that grew steadily in intensity toward a colossal climax, with endless curtain calls.

The orchestra was at its best. Mrs. Gulbranson only part of the time. She sang best in "Kind Greetings, Fair Ladies", which also received stormy applause. Otherwise she didn't have the audience with her. No, it doesn't work to do as she does—to undervalue the study of the details, least of all when one does not even master the overall structure.

Cleve played like a real artist, but he did not let himself go. He should be able to do it much better with his great talents.

---

[344] In 1894 Captain Alfred Dreyfus (1859–1935), a French army officer of Jewish descent, had been convicted of high treason and condemned to life imprisonment on Devil's Island. In due course it became clear to many that the conviction had been based on falsified evidence, but a series of scandalous legal proceedings resulted in the acquittal of the person actually guilty of the crime. On June 3, 1899, Dreyfus's conviction was overturned and the case was referred to a new court martial in Rennes which, despite overwhelming evidence that Dreyfus was innocent, had reaffirmed the verdict of 1894. The day after hearing the news from Rennes, Grieg received an invitation from French conductor Édouard Colonne (1838–1910) to give a concert with the Colonne Orchestra in Paris. On September 12, 1899, he wrote to Colonne pointedly declining the invitation. With Grieg's permission, the letter was published in *Frankfurter Zeitung* and soon thereafter was reprinted in newspapers all over Europe. See Grieg's letter to Colonne in Finn Benestad (ed.), *Edvard Grieg: Letters to Colleagues and Friends*, Columbus, Ohio 2000, p. 199. See also Grieg's reply of June 22, 1899, to a series of questions posed by French musicologist Jules Cambarieux (1859–1916), in the current volume p. 351.

[345] Prince Albert of Monaco (1848–1922).

Mrs. Rosa Bertens got a lot of applause for *Bergliot*—but she was terrible by my standard and that of any Scandinavian. What a sea of falseness in the interpretation! I was relieved when we were finished, for she is such a perfect example of unmusicality that she can easily destroy everything. If only it goes tolerably well on Sunday. Went quietly home, drank a glass of beer and went to bed.

April 13

The critics were not exactly sour-sweet, but they were misleading and did not hit the target. Dinner in the hotel restaurant with Hinrichsen,[346] his wife and mother-in-law, Mrs. Gulbranson and the Cleves. In the afternoon I went with Blessing Dahle[347] to visit Nordraak's grave.[348] I laid a laurel wreath beside his magnificent monument, and in so doing was filled with memories. Forty-one years have passed since I stood beside this grave—that is to say: my life. It was as if for a moment I stood face to face with everything I have experienced—and first and foremost the Nordraak period, the wonderful period!

April 14

Repeat of the concert as a matinee at 12 noon. Everything went excellently and the jubilant response was the same as before. There were many more handkerchiefs and shouts of "Wiederkommen". And the curtain calls were so interminable that I finally had to don my winter coat and go on stage wearing it. That helped. At 4:30 I hosted a dinner at the Kempinski Restaurant with Mrs. Gulbranson, the Cleves, Christian Sinding and his wife, Børresen, and the young Fredrik Gade.[349] Very pleasant.

Thereafter, incredible as it may sound, we went to the "Wintergarten", where we saw Cléo de Mérode[350] and drank Munich Beer—and acquitted ourselves well.

April 15

Dinner at Bernt Grønvold's. Thereafter we went to the Opera House: *Salome*, by Richard Strauss. What shall I say? As music this work is an impossibility, and decadence is in full swing. It is the triumph of technique over spirit. I grant that the technique is often brilliant, but what has become of imagination, the very foundation of music? The piece lasted nearly two hours—but it felt like seven because of the overabundance of cacophony.

---

[346] Henri Hinrichsen (1868–1942), Director of the C. F. Peters Music Publishing Company in Leipzig.

[347] Rev. Peder Blessing Dahle (1877–1946), a Norwegian clergyman.

[348] Grieg's close friend, Norwegian composer Rikard Nordraak (1842–66). See Grieg's diary entry of April 6, 1866.

[349] Norwegian physician Fredrik Georg Gade (1855–1933).

[350] French ballet dancer Dianne-Cléopâtre de Mérode (1881–?).

April 16

Dinner with the Cleves, Børresen and Mrs. Magnus (nee Crowe) at the home of the counselor of legation, Captain Michael Lie.

April 17

Forenoon: Børresen and I called on Richard Strauss. He impressed me as a genuine person and was very cordial. Lunch in the hotel restaurant as guests of Hotel Director Trulsson and his wife. Exceedingly pleasant. Afternoon departure for Leipzig with Børresen.

April 18

Dinner at the home of Dr. Paul Klengel with Johanna Röntgen, Julius Klengel and his wife, Susanna Klengel.[351]

April 19

Dinner at Hinrichsens with Max Reger and his wife. In the evening, *Salome* in Neues Theater with Børresen and Mrs. Hinrichsen. The part of Salome was performed quite excellently by Aino Ackté.[352] To be sure, the orchestra under musical director Hagel[353] was inferior to the Berlin Orchestra under Strauss, just as the staging in Berlin was better.

April 20

In the forenoon I went to the Peters Music Library, where I spent some time studying the score of *Salome*. It reveals the hand of a master, no doubt about that, but there is no future for all this artificiality. Dinner at Hinrichsens. I wanted to be at the Thomas Church to hear the Thomas Boys' Choir at 1:30, but the program was so boring that I gave up the idea.

Last evening—on Hinrichsen's advice, and accompanied by him—we went to call on Professor Gustav Schreck,[354] conductor of the Thomas Boys' Choir, to ask him to schedule a Bach piece instead, but he wasn't home. Later in the evening, when I returned to the hotel, there was a cordial letter from him with an invitation to come up to the Thomas Boys' Choir's rehearsal room at 5:30 today; there they would sing some works by Bach and by some Italian composers for me. That was a surprise.

I arrived at 5:30 on the dot with Nina, Børresen and Hinrichsen. It was an unforgettable hour. What greatness, nobility, elevated purity! *Three* complete

---

[351] German violinist, pianist and composer Paul Klengel (1854–1935); Dutch drawing teacher Johanna Röntgen (1857–1926); German cellist, conductor and composer Julius Klengel (1859–1933).

[352] Finnish soprano Aino Ackté (1876–1944).

[353] German conductor Karl Hagel (1847–1931).

[354] German choral conductor Gustav Schreck (1849–1918).

motets by Bach, a piece by an unknown wonderful old Italian composer from the thirteenth century, and lastly—unfortunately!—a boring one from the 1860's or 70's by Georg Vierling,[355] a German philistine. At the end, when Gustav Schreck told me that the Thomas Boys' Choir now had shown me the same honor as Mozart, inasmuch as they one time had invited him so that they could sing for him—and that they had felt happy to be allowed to sing for me, whose name and works they knew because many of them played piano—I felt that I was obliged to thank them, and I did so in the fewest possible words: "Ich danke Ihnen herzlich, Sie haben mir eine kolossale Freude bereitet!" ("I thank you from the depths of my heart. You have given me an enormously great joy!")

How young boys of ten can sing so enthusiastically and with such seriousness is a mystery to me. We Norwegians do not know or understand the German discipline and dedication to a great task. As [Bjørnstjerne] Bjørnson has said, we lack "the long goals".

April 21
Departure for Kiel.

April 22
Orchestra rehearsal.

April 23
Orchestra rehearsal.

April 24
Orchestra rehearsal.

April 25
Public dress rehearsal in the evening at 8 PM.

April 26
Conducted in Kiel upon invitation by the Music Association. 1) *Three Orchestral Pieces from "Sigurd the Crusader"*; 2) "Solveig's Cradle Song", "From Monte Pincio" and "A Swan" with orchestra, sung very well by Ellen Beck; 3) *Piano Concerto* played by Grøndahl;[356] well played, but I think his performance in Amsterdam a year ago was better; 4) *Before a Southern Convent* with Miss Ellen Beck as soprano and Frau Weinbaum as alto. Women's chorus of 80; 5) *Two Elegiac Melodies* op. 34; 6) "Eros", "At Rondane" and "A Dream" sung by Miss Beck.

---

[355] German composer Georg Vierling (1820–1901).
[356] Norwegian pianist Fridtjof Backer-Grøndahl (1885–1959).

Grieg in Kiel, 1907

Exceptionally good; 7) *Land-sighting* with a 100-voice men's chorus and a pip-
pip solo (although musical) by an amateur singer (a chemist). The orchestra was
the Hohenzollern ensemble augmented with additional musicians. It was a bit
robust and coarse, to be sure, but in the end it performed things on a par with
any good orchestra. One trumpeter, though, was unbelievable: I was literally never
sure of him.

The audience welcomed me very warmly. The applause during the concert
was not especially enthusiastic—one or two curtain calls after each set. At the end,
however, it took on enormous dimensions and grew into ovations with fanfare,
handkerchiefs, "Wiederkommen!", wreaths bigger than myself, baskets of flowers,
etc.

It was almost 11 PM when we got home. Nonetheless, we went to a la-di-da
affair in a room that had been reserved in the hotel, where I got my six oysters
and where Music Director Richard Schmidt, who really was extremely cordial,
toasted me in champagne with a few "well-chosen" words. At 1 AM we slipped
away from the party, but by that time I was indeed—finished.

April 27

Fischer[357] and Grøndahl left for Berlin, we and Miss Beck for Copenhagen via
Korsør, in the most glorious weather. Evening in Hotel Bristol Café with Miss
Beck.

April 28

Forenoon: Visit by Birger Hammer[358] and Christian Danning.[359]

May 2

Last evening Christian Danning gave a concert. He conducted Tchaikovsky's *Symphony Pathétique* with verve and swing, albeit in a very showy manner and with
exaggerated tempi, also two movements of an original "Dante" Symphony in
which I was unable to develop much interest. When one is dealing with such a
grand theme it's not enough to write pretty dance music. The young Bergensian
Birger Hammer performed Saint-Saëns' *Piano Concerto in C Minor* and acquitted himself exceptionally well. The audience thought so too, giving him several
curtain calls. I regard this as a promising debut. He plays with seriousness and
energy. I feel something of a personal joy in seeing signs of life in old Bergen.[360]

I can't find any peace and quiet here: friends, acquaintances, letters,

---

[357] Norwegian impresario Peter Vogt Fischer (1863–1938).

[358] See also Grieg's diary entry of January 20, 1907.

[359] Norwegian pianist Birger Hammer (1883–1958); Danish composer and conductor Christian Danning
(1867–1925).

[360] See also Grieg's opinion of Hammer's playing on pp. 162 and 163.

autographs, portraits—I certainly must move. It seems to me as if the *big* move is not so far away. Well, so it may be!

I had my first electric bath at Rosenvanget, Finsen's electric-light bath institute.[361] Dinner at 6:30 with Børresen and Miss Beck at Johanne Stockmarr's. Pleasant. After dinner, whist, then singing by Miss Beck. Accompanied by Miss Stockmarr, she sang three songs by Børresen—which sounded fine, but impersonal—and [my song] "At the Grave of a Young Wife". The singing and the playing were equally superb. Rarely or never have I been able to listen to my songs and enjoy the experience instead of, as usual, suffering all the agonies of hell. I will remember this experience.

May 3

Second electric-light bath.

May 4

Dinner at 5 PM at Børresen's with Alfred Hansen, Otto Benzon and his wife, Krøyer[362] and Miss Brodersen, his lady friend from Skagen.[363] Pleasant. Krøyer is very talkative and amiable—but, as has been said, already declining toward the dark sea of melancholia. Poor fellow! He would like so much to paint us again—at Skagen—because now he is better than he was the last time! Nina concluded the evening by singing a few songs to the delight of everyone.

May 7

Third electric-light bath. No improvement.

May 10

Fourth electric-light bath. No improvement. Just the opposite. Increasing difficulty in breathing, weakness and insomnia.

May 13

Dinner at Alfred Hansen's with Børresens, Miss Beck, Miss Stockmarr, old Andersen, his son-in-law Vink, Wolff and his wife, and old Mrs. Hansen.[364] Unusually pleasant. Playing and singing and unconstrained joy. I made the acquaintance of an excellent and amiable architect Tvede.[365]

---

[361] Danish physician Niels R. Finsen (1860–1904), who won the Nobel prize for medicine in 1903, offered "electric-light baths" to patients at "Finsen's Medical Light Institute" in Copenhagen. Grieg was hopeful that this experimental therapy would improve his steadily worsening health, but it did not.

[362] Danish artist Peter Severin Krøyer (1851–1909), whose works include a famous painting of Edvard and Nina at the piano. The painting is in the possession of the National Museum in Stockholm.

[363] Skagen is a tiny coastal village at the northernmost tip of Denmark that is often portrayed by Scandinavian painters.

[364] Johanna Cathrine Hansen (1826–1914), widow of Copenhagen music publisher Wilhelm Hansen (1821–1904). Andersen, his son-in-law, and Wolff have not been identified.

[365] Danish architect Gottfred Tvede (1863–1947).

May 14

Fifth electric-light bath.

May 15

Letter from Fischer, who went home from Berlin with Fridtjof [Backer-Grøndahl] after receiving a telegram.[366] Wrote to Agathe Grøndahl. Dinner and evening at Tivoli with Neovius's, Mrs. Ruben, Carl Ruben, Angul Hammerich.[367]

May 17

Sixth electric-light bath. Had to stop with that. All the maladies are getting worse.

May 26

I have wanted to leave for Norway each day, but was too miserable. Went out to Skodsborg Sanitarium. We got rooms and good service, but since the building is undergoing repairs we have been moved from bad to worse. Steadily increasing insomnia and shattered nerves. And then a vegetarian diet, which stirred up my stomach worse than ever, plus weakness. Neovius and Thyra,[368] with whom we played whist in the evening, were my consolation.

May 29

Børresen came with his carriage to pick me up. He drove us through the forest and out to his home in Vedbæk, where we got a fine meal—good food and red wine—that brought me back to life for a few hours. Still, I decided to leave the next day.

May 30

Nothing came of the planned departure. I was too lacking in energy, too low. And Neovius's insisted that I stay, so I did. But without courage. It is unpleasant here in this endless wind and cold.

May 31

Afternoon: visit by Børresen and Neovius's. Went to Copenhagen to see the ailing Saima [Neovius] at the clinic.

June 1

A deeply felt but sad letter from Fridtjof Grøndahl. Agathe Grøndahl is on her deathbed. And suffering, suffering. To what end? *One* thing those two opposites,

---

366　The telegram came from Fridtjof's mother, Agathe Backer Grøndahl, who was on her deathbed. She died on June 4. See Grieg's diary entry on that date. Grieg's letter to her is printed in English translation in Finn Benestad (ed.), *Edvard Grieg: Letters to Colleagues and Friends*, Columbus, Ohio 2000, pp.301–302.

367　Mrs. Ida Ruben (1845–1913); her son, Danish textile manufacturer Carl Ruben (1876–1967); Danish music historian Angul Hammerich (1848–1931).

368　Thyra Hammerich Neovius, wife of Edvard Rudolf Neovius.

Erika[369] and Agathe, had in common: They suffered—more than most. Nerves! What a blessing, what a curse! And this dubious gift of infancy is something we artists have received to excess.

June 3

Picked up in a carriage by the Melchior sisters, who took us on a wonderful trip through the forest and across the Eremitagesletten [the "Hermitage Plain"] to Villa Melchior, where we had dinner at 5 PM, played a game of boston as we had our coffee, and from where we walked home at 9 PM.

The poetry of the Danish forest is unique, and the first strong impression from youth remains. As I felt it then, so it was now. Just as overwhelming—yes, perhaps even more so. I noticed late in the evening how much good it had done my nerves to be out in the open air almost all day. Bed-rest therapy is excellent.

June 4

Sleep, sleep! How much good it did! Feeling better today. Børresen came on his bicycle to pay me a visit. So did Neovius. In the evening I got a telegram from Grøndahl.[370]

† Agathe died at 4 PM this afternoon. Thus ended this beautiful life. Beautiful in its noble pessimism and in all its suffering. No artist soul has ever walked on purer paths. There are few of young Norway's musicians of whom that can be said. I loved this serious idealism. It had its unique charm. If a mimosa could sing, it would resound with strains like those from Agathe Backer-Grøndahl's most beautiful, most deeply felt music.

June 5

Received a request from the editor of *Morgenbladet*[371] to write an obituary for Agathe. It was hard to say no, but I am not up to it.

June 6

Telegram to old King Oscar[372] and his wife on the occasion of their golden wedding anniversary. Everyone in Norway should have sent him a telegram as a gesture of thanks because in 1905 he didn't want war—and didn't want to come to Norway!

June 7

Forenoon in Copenhagen. I managed it. I will now stay an additional week to

---

[369] Norwegian pianist Erika Lie Nissen.
[370] Norwegian choral conductor Olaus Grøndahl (1847–1923), husband of Agathe Backer Grøndahl.
[371] Conservative Christiania newspaper.
[372] Oscar II (1829–1907), King of Sweden and Norway 1872–1905 and of Sweden thereafter until his death.

make secure the tiny bit of progress I have achieved and to increase my chances of avoiding a relapse.

June 8

Cabled Grøndahls. Agathe's funeral. Cabled Karl Nissen, who according to *Verdens Gang*[373] is being married to Miss Aagot Kavli.[374] Forenoon walk with Nina in Bøllemose.

June 10

Visited Johan Svendsen in Hellerup with Børresen. He was well enough that we took him with us up Karoline Road and over to Tuborg's Restaurant by "Flasken", where we sat in the baking forenoon sun enjoying our shrimp with bread and Ålborger G Major.[375] He was pleasant and amiable, but he has been marked— not so much with illness as with having lived beyond his time. I thought: Will we ever meet again? We agreed to turn up at Alfred Hansen's in Marienlyst on June 15.

June 11

In the morning all indications were that people knew about our 40th wedding anniversary. The rooms were flooded with tons of beautiful flowers. Norwegian, Swedish and Danish flags adorned the front of our dining room, and at dinner the table had been set for I don't know how many people. When I asked about it the answer was, "Well, we didn't know how many guests the doctor[376] wanted at dinner!" Then, suddenly, Bernt Grønvold tramped in, then Neovius and Thyra. Then we sent a message to Doctor Ottosen and his wife,[377] and we had a very lively time together at a dinner of plaice, asparagus bits, chicken, strawberries (not exactly what my doctor would have ordered), toasts, speeches, hurrahs, and everything else that goes along with such an affair. Mrs. Ottosen—the remarkable, highly gifted Norwegian-American "valley girl" (as she called herself)—spoke especially beautifully. There must be some old royal blood from Gudbrandsdalen in her veins. What nobility![378]

---

[373] Liberal Christiania newspaper.

[374] Norwegian actress Aagot Kavli (1882–?).

[375] Hellerup is a community north of Copenhagen. Tuborg is one of denmark's biggest breweries. "Ved flasken" ["at the bottle"] was a popular restaurant. "Ålborger G-dur" [Ålborger G Major"] was a brand of Danish aquavit.

[376] Grieg had been awarded honorary doctorates by the universities in Cambridge and Oxford in 1894 and 1906, respectively. See the diary entry of May 29, 1906.

[377] Danish physician Carl Jacob Ottosen (1864–1942); his Norwegian-born wife, Johanne Pauline Norderhuus Ottosen (1864–1921).

[378] Mrs. Ottosen was from Lesja in Gudbrandsdalen. As a child she had emigrated with her family to the United States, and it was there that she had met and married Dr. Ottosen. Although she spent her adult life in Denmark, she retained her Lesja dialect.

June 13

I suddenly got the idea of leaving in order to avoid the many invitations on the 15th.[379] Went to Copenhagen in the forenoon, and at midday, accompanied by Neovius, took the America steamship "St. Olav" in the most glorious weather to Christiania, where we arrived the next morning. It was a marvelous trip. The mighty ship glided through the glassy sea without our being able to hear the sound of the propeller. It was a trip that gave healing to body and soul.

June 15

Dinner at my sisters' with Signe, Ludvig Mowinckel, Mrs. Sänger, and Neovius.[380] In Christiania, no one took any notice of the day. It's not in fashion! Sad!!

June 16

At Voksenkollen with Neovius and Skredsvig.[381] Rainy weather, unfortunately, but it was pleasant—and we had a no less pleasant dinner with them and my sisters in the Grand Hotel Restaurant afterwards.

June 17

Departure for Fagernes,[382] arriving at 4:30 in the evening. Got a chill in my stomach at the bridge over the river, where I stood for a long time watching the logs that came dancing downstream. It was a splendid sight. But the next morning all hell broke loose. I lived for four days on opium and sago paste. Had a day's rest at Grindaheim.

June 22

Got to Lærdal after a nice—albeit strenuous and somewhat subdued—trip through rainy and cold weather. Neovius has been incredible.[383] Cheerful, fresh, communicative, interesting, plus full of kindheartedness—a first-class nurse, who on the whole does everything that might cast sunshine into the shadows. We stopped at Lindstrøm Hotel, Room 45, which I will make a note of as being the best room in the hotel. For the first time in five days I had proper food: small whiting with red wine and roast pork. I'm beginning to perk up. During the night, left for Bergen on the fjord steamer "Sogn".

---

[379] June 15 was Grieg's birthday.
[380] Edvard's sisters Benedicte and Elisabeth Grieg; Signe Grieg Müller; Norwegian shipowner and politician Ludvig Mowinckel (1870–1943).
[381] Norwegian painter Christian Skredsvig (1854–1924).
[382] Fagernes is a village in Valdres—a natural stopover for Grieg en route from Christiania to Bergen.
[383] Neovius accompanied Edvard and Nina Grieg all the way from Copenhagen to Troldhaugen.

June 23

Arrival in Bergen at 12 midnight—in rainy weather, of course. Took lodging at Hotel Norge.

June 24

First dinner at Troldhaugen with Neovius.

June 28

After three pleasant days with Neovius despite bad weather, he left for Copenhagen this evening on the "Melchior". We went with him in the carriage from Troldhaugen to the steamship pier, and it was very sad to see him leave. He is an unusual, highly gifted man with a broad horizon and a warm heart. Both my minimum of political understanding and my instinct tell me that his perception of the Finnish question is the right one and that he has been dealt a great injustice.[384] But of course: With chauvinistic loudmouths and windbags against you, you don't stand a chance—but only for a time, fortunately. For in the end, right will prevail. My life experience has also taught me that, not least the Bergen Music Festival. How happy I am today that at that time I dared to scorn both the chauvinistic narrowness and all the hateful acts of meanness as well.[385]

July 3

In the afternoon the soon 86-year-old Fries[386] and Oscar Riis[387] came to see me. It was the first time I ever saw Fries at Troldhaugen. Neither of us mentioned the event that came between us, but I think that he, like me, was glad about the reconciliation. Even if neither of us can admit that the other was right.

---

[384] Neovius, a mathematician by training, was also active in Finnish politics. In 1905 he had held a high position in the Finnish department of the treasury, but after a general strike in that year he had been forced to resign, whereupon he left Finland and thereafter made his home in Copenhagen. See Grieg's letters to him in Finn Benestad (ed.), *Edvard Grieg: Letters to Colleagues and Friends,* Columbus, Ohio 2000, pp. 342–345. The letter of July 17, 1907, is especially poignant.

[385] Grieg is alluding here to a music festival held in Bergen in 1898, when he incurred the wrath of several important figures in Norwegian music life by insisting that the Concertgebouw Orchestra of Amsterdam be invited to the festival rather than a Norwegian orchestra. The festival was a huge artistic success, and the concerts were received with enthusiasm by the public. See Grieg's articles pertaining to the festival on pp. 337–344.

[386] The German-born August Fries (1821–1913) was highly regarded both as a violinist and as a conductor in Bergen, where he lived and worked for many years. As conductor in 1864–73 of the Music Society "Harmonien", the predecessor of the modern Bergen Philharmonic Orchestra, Fries conducted a number of Grieg's early works including his only symphony. Grieg dedicated his *Violin Sonata No. 1* in F Major, op. 8, to Fries, who played portions of it in 1869 at a concert in Bergen with Grieg's mother, Gesine Grieg (1814–75), at the piano. In 1880–82, when Grieg was conductor of "Harmonien", he relaxed by playing chamber music with Fries and his brother John Grieg, a cellist. The breach with Fries to which Grieg alludes presumably occurred at the time of the Bergen Music Festival controversy.

[387] Oscar Riis (1848–1913), an old Bergen friend of Grieg.

July 13

Ten sad days that have convinced me that I am going downhill faster than I had thought. The difficulty in breathing is increasing despite fourteen days of massage; my brain and my digestion together are putting me in a state that could drive me crazy. Anything, but not that. Would that I had the means to just quietly sleep away into that eternal sleep when the time comes that I just can't stand this any longer.

Although—I would probably lack the courage. I am not one of those who consider suicide an instance of cowardice. To the contrary. I have the greatest admiration for the courage that I feel I do not have myself. Well, it will have to go as it does. I only hope there will not be a tremendous amount of physical pain, for I could not endure that. What a bad position society takes [on the issue of euthanasia]: with its prohibition against administering to the ill that which gives peace, they inflict pain and suffering upon people instead of alleviating their agonies. The future will be wiser and more humane!

This morning my dear Bet[388] came from Christiania on the steamship "King Sverre" after having concluded 29 years of work at the elementary school. Few deserve the rest as she does, conscientious and indefatigable worker that she is. She brought the sunshine with her, both inwardly and outwardly. May summer finally come after perpetual rain and cold for a long, long time.

July 22

Summer really did come. First with a cold north wind, to be sure, but sunshine and clear sky give vigor and the will to live, and our dear Bet gives supreme calm and security. And yesterday afternoon my splendid friend Julius Röntgen finally came, full of Jotunheim, warmth and enthusiasm. Add to that the ideal summer, with 18° Réaumur[389] and the authentic, light fairytale mood, with beautiful *huldra*[390] and bell sounds in the air. Although I have never before felt as left in the dust as I do now, in the midst of the melancholy there is so much joy that I am grateful for it nonetheless.

July 27

Thus the beautiful Röntgen days came to an end! Last evening all of us accompanied him to the steamer that took him to Copenhagen. One could learn equally much from him as an artist and as a human being. And in his new cello sonata there is again evidence of development.[391]

---

[388] Grieg's sister Elisabeth Kimbell Grieg.
[389] See footnote to entry of July 31, 1906. 18° Réaumur equals approximately 23° Celsius and 73° Fahrenheit.
[390] A *hulder* (definite form: *huldra*), a figure that appears frequently in Norwegian fairy tales, is a supernatural female being (beautiful, but with a cow's tail) who lives in the mountains, where she raises and tends cattle.
[391] Grieg is referring to Röntgen's *Cello Sonata No. 4 in C Minor* (1906).

L to R: Grieg, Percy Grainger, Nina, Julius Röntgen at Troldhaugen on July 26, 1907. "I had the great joy of introducing these two splendid people who I knew would understand each other."

On the morning of the 25th, Percy Grainger arrived. Thus I had the great joy of introducing these two splendid people who I knew would understand each other. A horizon such as Julius has is rare. He immediately discovered the significant element in Grainger's talent, despite all that is strange, and he listened enthusiastically to his music, his eminent piano-playing, and to his masterly and so deeply original arrangements of English folk tunes. For myself I can say that I had to be 64 years old in order to hear Norwegian piano music interpreted so perceptively and brilliantly. The way he plays the *Norwegian Peasant Dances* and the folk-song arrangements, he is breaking new ground for himself, for me and for Norway.[392]

And this enchanting, natural, deep, serious and childlike nature! To gain a young friend such as this—what a joy! I could forget the physical ailments if the contrast did not so forcefully announce, like writing on the wall: He is ——— , you are ——— . And to look objectively at this truth is difficult.

---

[392] Grieg is alluding to his *Norwegian Peasant Dances* (*Slåtter*) op. 72 and *Nineteen Norwegian Folk Songs* op. 66.

August 5

Last evening we accompanied the dear Percy Grainger to the steamship that was to carry him to his mother in Denmark. What an artist, what a human being! What a high idealist, what a child—and at the same time, what a great and highly developed view of life! A socialist of the future of the first rank. Of him it can be said: "Aus mitleid wissend, der reine Thor."[393]

His work with the folk songs is of the greatest significance, as it unites musical superiority, expertise in comparative linguistics, historical and poetic vision, and a colossal enthusiasm for the task of collecting the material. And not just enthusiasm, but, it appears, also the practical grasp of things. It looks as if he wants to devote all of his best efforts to the folk song—which I very much regret, for it presupposes an underestimate of his qualifications as a pianist, which he demonstrates only all too clearly. It's the old story: "Willst du immer weiter schweifen?"[394]

I do not know whom among the *very best* pianists I could compare him to. But all comparisons are irrelevant when one has to do with greatness. He is himself. Perhaps I am partial to him because he has in fact realized my ideals regarding piano-playing. If I had possessed his technical prowess, my perception of the essence of piano-playing would have been exactly the same as his. He hovers like a god over all suffering, all struggle. But one feels that they have been there, but have been overcome. It is a human being—a great, distinguished human being—who is playing. May he have a good life!

August 25

The 6th–25th has been continuous suffering. Difficulty in breathing and insomnia increasing. We spent the 20th, 21st, and 22nd with Beyers[395] and [my sister] Elisabeth at Voss. I hoped that the inland climate would allow me to sleep. But no, I can only say that my general condition has improved somewhat. We had one calm, warm, sunny day—the *only* such day in the whole summer, I think—and I felt that that was what I needed. But the next day it poured down again, and so it has continued.

Last evening (the 24th) Klaus Hanssen[396] and his wife came to see us, and oddly enough they arrived at exactly the same time as my new masseur, Mr.

---

[393] Grieg is quoting (slightly in error, substituting *Aus* for *Durch*) from Wagner's opera *Parsifal:* "Knowing through compassion, the innocent fool." According to Wagner—and Grieg as well—it is only through compassion, shared suffering, empathy that one can achieve true insight and understanding. Grieg perceived Percy Grainger as an innocent young man (*der reine Thor*), a quality that he also saw reflected in his straightforward piano-playing. Presumably Grieg's thought was that just as Parsifal was led by good powers, so perhaps he could guide his Australian friend forward toward high artistic goals.

[394] "Will you always roam yet farther?" A paraphrase from *Parsifal*, which in the original reads, *Hör mich und sag': wo schweiftest damals du umher, als unser Herr den Speer verlor?*

[395] Grieg's close friend Frants Beyer and his wife, Marie Smith Beyer.

[396] Grieg's physician, Dr. Klaus Hanssen (1844–1914).

Olsen, who was going to give me massage and compresses à la Skodsborg. Klaus examined me with the greatest care and stayed with me for the entire treatment. The upshot is that the massage therapy is to be discontinued, since it is hard on the nerves. The compresses are to be continued, however, as they did me some good and made it possible for me to get a little sleep, at least in the first part of the night.

Today, the 25th, I am miserable after breakfast, I just don't know why, it must be the strain of the massage last evening.

August 27–30

Spent at the hospital in Bergen under Klaus Hanssen's observation. Also under a steady worsening of the illness, unfortunately. The first night was without sleep, the second and third I slept on [the drug] Kloral.

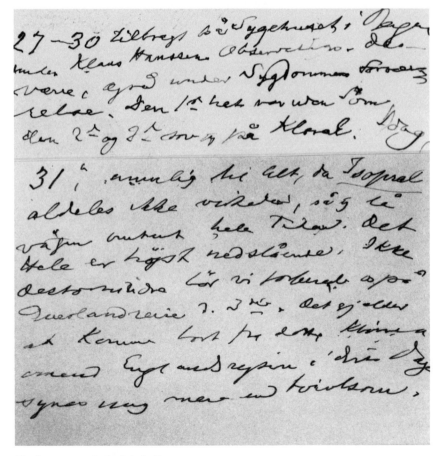

The last two entries in Grieg's diary

Upon Nina's death in 1935, her ashes were placed beside those of her husband in this unpretentious crypt at Troldhaugen.

August 31

Today, the 31st, I am not good for anything, as Isopral didn't help at all, so I lay awake virtually the entire time. The whole situation is most depressing. Nonetheless, we ought to prepare for the trip overland [to Christiania] on the 3rd. I've got to get away from this climate, though the trip to England at this time appears to me more than doubtful.[397]

---

[397] The entry of August 31 was Grieg's last. He was hospitalized on September 3 and died the night of September 4. A few months later the urn containing Grieg's ashes was placed in a small crypt at Troldhaugen. Frants Beyer, Grieg's closest friend, wrote to Nina on April 7, 1908: "Now Edvard's ashes have come to their final resting place. I set the urn in the crypt, and then the stone was placed in front of it. A blackbird was singing in the spruce trees overhead. The sun was just setting behind gold-rimmed clouds, casting its last beams across the water and upon Edvard's name."

Part II

Articles on Other Composers

Grieg's acquaintance with art music was surprisingly broad and deep, especially in view of the fact that he lived before the time when sound recordings have made it possible to listen to professional performances of virtually any music one might wish to hear. He used every opportunity available to him to attend concerts, and he often studied the scores of works that piqued his interest. He also formed definite opinions about the music that he heard, and he did not hesitate to express those opinions. His letters and diaries abound with comments about works that he had heard performed, and his comments—both positive and negative—are nearly always pithy and to the point.

On a few occasions, Grieg had opportunities to write at greater length about the music of other composers. The earliest such writing of which we have knowledge is an August 1865 review of a song opus by his compatriot Rikard Nordraak. The deaths of composers whom he admired prompted him to write a number of eulogies (Halfdan Kjerulf 1868, Giuseppe Verdi 1901, Antonín Dvořák 1904, Louis Hornbeck 1906), and these invariably provided venues for Grieg to give his assessment of the music of the deceased. His long articles on Mozart (1897), Schumann (1894) and Wagner (1876) are particularly impressive examples of his ability to write knowledgeably and convincingly about the music of others.

The articles that follow comprise all of Grieg's known writings dealing explicitly with other composers and their music.

Grieg in 1888. Reproduction of a photograph, by Elliot & Fry of London.

Antonín Dvořák (1904)

Grieg met the Czech composer Antonín Dvořák (1841–1904) for the first time in Vienna in 1896, but his impression of him at that time was somewhat mixed. In a letter of March 28, 1896 to his Norwegian colleague Iver Holter he wrote as follows: "I was with Brahms a lot. He was cheerful and gracious. I cannot say the same of Dvořák, with whom, however, I developed only a superficial acquaintance."[1]

On a visit to Prague in March 1903, however, Grieg got quite a different impression of his Czech colleague. On April 1, 1903, he wrote to his countryman Frants Beyer: "It was fun to spend a little time with Dvořák. He is, to say the least, one of a kind. But he was amiable."[2]

Upon hearing of Dvořák's death on May 1, 1904, Grieg sent his condolences to the composer's daughter Magda Dvořák, who had been one of the vocal soloists at Grieg's concert in Prague the preceding year. She responded: "The hours of your presence in Prague are among the most wonderful moments of my life, and it pleases me doubly that you have remembered me. My father always spoke of you with the greatest love, and the sound of your name is very dear to us. I can assure you that your appearance [in Prague] was appreciated not only by our family but by our whole musical world, and I pray to God that he will take care of you, dear maestro, for a long, long time."[3]

Grieg expanded on his impressions of Dvořák in his eulogy. It is clear that he greatly admired him as a composer, fully understanding that Dvořák's music had the same significance for the Czech people as did his own works for the people of Norway.

Grieg's eulogy, dated Christiania May 11, was published in Norwegian in the Christiania newspaper *Verdens Gang* on May 13, 1904.

I have received from Prague a letter with black borders: Antonín Dvořák is dead. The brilliant Bohemian composer whose name is known all over the world is no more. With his death, one of the few original and truly national composers has passed from the scene.

Obituaries of the deceased appeared in Danish newspapers more than a week ago, but I have sought in vain for any such item in the Christiania papers I have read. Is it really the case that the news of Dvořák's death is a matter of indifference to us? To be sure: We live north of the civilized world. And silence is eloquent, for that matter. But I am not so pessimistic as to suppose that we live as *far* north as the Christiania press would have us believe. I think, therefore, that a few words about the deceased by way of orientation will be appropriate.

---

[1] Grieg's letter to Norwegian composer and conductor Iver Holter (1850–1941) is preserved in The National Library of Norway, Oslo Division, and printed in English translation in Finn Benestad (ed.), *Edvard Grieg. Letters to Colleagues and Friends*, Columbus, Ohio 2000, pp. 412–413. Grieg had given a concert in Vienna on March 24, 1896, which Johannes Brahms (1833–97) had attended. After the concert Grieg and Brahms and a number of others who had participated celebrated the event until the early hours of the morning.

[2] The letter to Frants Beyer (1851–1918) is preserved in the Royal Archives, Oslo, and printed in Norwegian in Finn Benestad & Bjarne Kortsen (eds.), *Edvard Grieg: Brev til Frants Beyer 1872–1907*, Oslo 1993, pp. 287–288.

[3] The letter from Magda Dvořák (1881–1952) is preserved in Bergen Public Library and is printed in the original German in Hella Brock, *Edvard Grieg als Musikschriftsteller*, Altenmedingen 1999, p. 257.

*Antonín Dvořák.
Reproduction of a
photograph, by Collier
of Birmingham,
England.*

Antonín Dvořák passed away suddenly on May 1 at the age of 63 years. He was very productive and had written the most varied works before Europe's attention was directed toward him. It was Johannes Brahms who discovered him, so to speak, and became his advocate.[4]

At the beginning of the 1870's I read his name on the title of some vocal duets with piano accompaniment. These most remarkable poems set in the style of Czech folk tunes were well suited to making his name famous, which in short order it also became. The songs were soon disseminated throughout the civilized world.[5]

But Dvořák aimed higher. He incorporated this folk-tune character in his

---

[4] A firm friendship was established at an early date between Brahms and Dvořák. In 1874 Brahms tried to secure an Austrian state scholarship for him, and he recommended him to the Berlin music publishing company Simrock, which became Dvořák's main publisher.

[5] Grieg is obviously referring to Dvořák's *Moravian Duets (Klänge aus Mähren)*, op. 32, which consists of 13 songs for soprano, alto and piano. They were all composed in 1876 and published in Prague in the same year. The first Simrock publication in Berlin took place in 1878, so Grieg's reference to "the beginning of the 1870's" is a mistake. The Grieg Archives of Bergen Public Library contain a copy of the Simrock publication with Grieg's handwritten signature, the title page of which is printed in facsimile in Brock, *op. cit.*, p. 250.

larger compositions, and it had such a stimulating effect on his imagination that in these works he created his very best. He tried his hand in all musical genres, from the smallest to the largest. He wrote operas, symphonies, symphonic poems, overtures, major sacred works—and much more. It was his chamber music, however, that elicited the greatest admiration from his contemporaries. In addition to the Vienna classicists, he learned much from Brahms, later from Liszt and Wagner; yet, he is himself from start to finish. His string quartets and quintets are masterworks that undoubtedly will long outlive him.[6]

His music is not often performed in Norway. A string quartet was played a few years ago in Bergen and was given a very capable performance by Mr. Arve Arvesen[7] and his fellow artists. It made a deep impression. In Christiania, Johan Halvorsen recently performed a symphony—the so-called American, "From the New World."[8] Beyond these two performances I do not know if anyone has given attention to his music here in Norway. In Copenhagen his works are part of the standard concert repertoire, thanks above all to Franz Neruda, his outstanding countryman.[9] In Germany and England he is performed regularly. The Germans cannot really stomach his nationalism—but they play him anyway.

It is in England, however, that he has garnered his largest and most faithful crowd of admirers. I shall never forget the excellent performance at the Birmingham Music Festival in 1888 of one of Dvořák's most beautiful works for chorus, soloists and orchestra: his *Stabat mater*.[10] Hans Richter conducted and his enthusiasm was transmitted to all, performers as well as listeners.[11]

In the 1890's Dvořák accepted an appointment in New York as Director of the Conservatory there, but he was not able to adapt to the American environment.[12] He was overcome by longing for home, and he steered his course once again to his beloved Prague, where he continued to live and work thereafter. There, last year, I heard his opera *Rusalka*, which contains the most splendid things. The

---

[6] Dvořák composed a large number of chamber works for various instruments, the most well-known being the *"Dumky" Piano Trio* op. 90 (1890–91), the *String Quartet no. 12 in F Major* (the "American"), op. 96 (1894), and the *Violin Sonatina in G Major*, op. 100 (1893). Grieg's statement about Dvořák having learned from Franz Liszt (1811–86) and Richard Wagner (1813–83) in this connection is somewhat puzzling.

[7] Arve Arvesen (1869–1951) was one of the leading Norwegian violinists of his day.

[8] Dvořák's *Symphony no. 9 in E Minor*, op. 95 (1893, also referred to as no. 5), "From the New World", was performed in Christiania on March 15, 1902, at a concert given by the National Theater Orchestra under Johan Halvorsen (1864–1935).

[9] Franz Neruda (1843–1915), brother of the Czech violin virtuoso Wilhelmina Neruda (1838–1911), was a renowned cellist, composer and conductor. After concert successes in Copenhagen in 1862–63, he settled in the Danish capital in 1864. He had an illustrious career there, particularly as leader of a string quartet bearing his name and as conductor of the Music Association Orchestra from 1891 until his death.

[10] *Stabat mater* op. 58 (1876–77) is even today regarded as one of Dvořák's most important compositions.

[11] The Austro-Hungarian conductor Hans Richter (1843–1916) was one of the most celebrated orchestral leaders of his time. In 1876 he conducted the first performance of Wagner's entire *Ring* cycle in Bayreuth (see Grieg's articles about this event on pp. 290–318). From 1885 to 1909 Richter was music director of the triennial Birmingham Music Festival.

[12] Dvořák was Director of the National Conservatory of Music, New York, 1892–95.

subject is Hans Christian Andersen's fairytale "The Little Mermaid". On Dvořák's desk at that time lay *Armida,* an opera that he had just completed, which, according to what I heard recently, does not appear to have been well received at its premier performance.[13]

Antonín Dvořák as a human being? Well, about that I can hardly make a judgment. I met him for the first time in Vienna some 6–8 years ago. I was going to conduct there one evening, and he came through the room where I, just before the concert, was pacing nervously back and forth. It was a big anteroom where many musicians were passing by. When I was told that one of these was Dvořák, I hurried toward him, happy to see him. But my enthusiasm was immediately damped. He was terse, abrupt and unaccommodating. I was completely at a loss to understand his behavior, and the next day I reported this to his friend Brahms. "Don't worry about it," said Brahms. "That's the way he is. He is a strange fellow. But in his heart of hearts he is a good person." Fortunately, last year I had an opportunity to experience this. Through his daughter, who sang my songs beautifully at a concert that I conducted in Prague, I got to know him better. Both at the concert and later in his home I came to know him as an amiable, absolutely charming original. There was something outspoken and impetuous in his personality that, for those who did not know him, could seem forbidding. This quickly vanished, however, and I am happy that my last impression of him is that he aimed just as high as a human being as he did in the artistic sphere.

He was strongly Czech in his political views. He was idolized by his nation. Not long ago the Austrian emperor even made him a member of the *Herrenhaus,* an honor that theretofore had never been accorded an artist.[14]

Antonín Dvořák will be remembered as one of the few completely genuine personalities of our time. The message of his sudden death at the prime of his productive life will be received everywhere—I dare to believe: even here, north of the civilized world—with profound sadness.

---

[13] Dvořák composed thirteen works for the stage, of which the lyric fairytale *Rusalka* op. 114 (1900) has been a lasting success. The libretto was written by the Czech poet Jaroslav Kvapil (1868–1950), based on the fairytale *Undine* (1811) by German author Friedrich Fouqué de la Motte (1777–1843), the fairytale *The Little Mermaid* (1837) by Danish author Hans Christian Andersen (1805–75), and the fairytale drama *Die versunkene Glocke* (1896) by German author Gerhart Hauptmann (1862–1946). *Armida* op. 115 (1902–03), Dvořák's last opera, to a libretto by Czech author Jaroslav Vrchlický—pseudonym for Emil Frida (1855–1912)—was based on *La Gierusalemme liberata ovvero Il Goffredo* (1575) by Italian author Torquato Tasso (1544–95). *Armida* never achieved real success either in Dvořák's homeland or abroad.

[14] "Herrenhaus" was at that time the name of the so-called "First Chamber" of the public administration in Austria. It consisted of royal princes, heads of certain families that had been given hereditary membership by the monarch, and a number of high-ranking officials. In 1901 Dvořák was appointed a member of the Herrenhaus by Emperor Franz Joseph I (1848–1916).

Catharinus Elling (1885)

Norwegian composer and folk-music specialist Catharinus Elling (1858–1942) earned great respect in the artistic milieu of his homeland. After Grieg's article had been published, and thanks in no small measure to Grieg's strong support, Elling received a large travel grant that enabled him to go to Berlin for advanced study in composition. He remained in the German capital for a decade and while there composed a number of large works. In a letter of May 25, 1885, to Norwegian composer Johan Selmer (1844–1910), Grieg wrote: "As an artist, Elling has my warmest appreciation."[1]

In 1900 Grieg again wrote very positively about Elling in connection with a recommendation regarding the latter's work in gathering and transcribing Norwegian folk melodies: "That a talented musician such as Elling will devote his energies to this cause is as happy a circumstance as can be imagined. It should be explicitly emphasized that this task requires not only an intelligent and interested person but also a real artist, and perhaps a creative artist at that. These are the qualities that, by a lucky coincidence, are united in Elling."[2]

Grieg's article, entitled "A Promising Young Norwegian Composer", was printed in the Bergen newspaper *Bergens Tidende* on March 14, 1885.

Catharinus Elling is a young Norwegian musician who has recently sent to me from Christiania, where he lives, a huge stack of manuscripts for my perusal. Such packages are not rarities in my experience, but since the quantity usually smothers the quality, I honestly confess that I, made wise by experience, did not open the package with great anticipation. How great was my surprise and joy, therefore, when a few measures made it clear to me that I was in the presence of a lyric talent of a high order. Reading, playing, humming, I could not get my fill of all this buoyant *joie de vivre*, this nature-freshness and soulful fervency that in broad musical flight resounded from the rich, overflowing heart of a singer. When one knows how rare it is to encounter genuine spirit instead of witticisms, when one knows how rarely one finds a feeling that is deep, a pathos that is true, then I can do nothing but predict a promising future for the young artist possessing these great advantages—despite the fact that his technique does not yet seem to be commensurate with his intentions. Of all the beautiful erotic moods that he has expressed in songs, I have chosen some which I shall use the welcome opportunity to introduce to the public at my concert tomorrow.[3] I ask the listeners not to be frightened by an individuality that it does not know and to which many must first become accustomed. It requires that one listen with an open mind and not approach unfamiliar chords and progressions with prejudice and mistrust.

---

[1] The letter is printed in English translation in Finn Benestad (ed.), *Edvard Grieg: Letters to Colleagues and Friends*, Columbus, Ohio 2000, p. 624.

[2] See *Stortingsforhandlinger* (*Proceedings of the Norwegian Parliament*) 1900–01, Part 5, Document no. 45.

[3] Grieg gave two concerts in Bergen in the spring of 1885: March 12 and 15. In the latter he introduced some songs by Elling.

Catharinus Elling

Then the understanding will follow. To be sure, in these songs the composer is up to his ears in German Romanticism, but—and this is the main point—he is at the same time both original and healthy to the core. All in all: If his great talent gets the opportunity to unfold freely, the day will not be far off when we will be proud to have him in our midst. Catharinus Elling will then prove once and for all that the day of lyricism is not over. He will become Scandinavia's Holger Drachmann[4] of music.

I take the liberty of asking the Christiania newspapers to reprint these lines. Every effort to direct attention to the impoverished young artist will hopefully contribute to his finally getting the state grant that for four years he has applied for in vain.

---

[4] Danish author Holger Drachmann (1846–1908).

Johan Peter Emilius Hartmann (1885)

In his youth, Grieg regarded Danish composer Johan Peter Emilius Hartmann (1805–1900) as one of the foremost composers in Scandinavia, on a par with his countryman Niels W. Gade (1817–90). Although he eventually rejected pan-Scandinavianism in favor of the national Norwegian idiom for which he is known, Grieg always acknowledged his debt to Hartmann and admired him greatly. On the day of Hartmann's death—March 10, 1900—Grieg, who was in Copenhagen at that time, wrote some beautiful words regarding Hartmann to his Bergen friend Frants Beyer (1851–1918): "As we drove to the concert hall we saw the flags on the Royal Theater and many other buildings at half mast. It was for old Hartmann, who had just died. (. . .) We went to a floral shop and from there, with roses in hand, down to the old man's home, where all the children and grandchildren had gathered. It was solemn. There he lay, the 95-year-old, not yet cold but with the peace of death upon him. So it is: to be or not to be. Now Gade-Hartmann is a saga! But a beautiful one. And how it is interwoven into the mysteries of my own existence. It is as if this beautiful old word *saga* acquires new and deeper meaning for me as my own life belongs more and more to the past. Soon everything will be saga, saga!"[1]

Grieg's tribute to Hartmann in connection with his 80th birthday was published in *Musikbladet*, Copenhagen, on May 14, 1885.

Few of the heroes of music have been able to look back on their oeuvre with a clearer conscience than the old master whose 80th birthday we celebrate today. Many of them have shone more brightly and have made their names more famous far and near—but none have deserved more than he the honor of being crowned in the evening of his life as one of the chosen high priests of music. For he never catered to the tastes of the moment. Only the demands of the ideal mattered to him. What composer in Scandinavia with a genuine feeling for the spirit of Scandinavia does not remember today what he owes to Hartmann! The best, the most profound thoughts that a whole posterity of more or less important spirits have lived on have been first expressed by *him,* have been made to resound in us by *him.* Let us today remember that the rich formal development of Danish art through his successors would never have occurred without him.

There are two kinds of great men. In the world of music I would call the one kind "tone artists", the other "tone poets".[2] Hartmann certainly belongs to the latter group, just as Gade—the other eminent leader in Danish music—represents his exact opposite in this respect. That two stars in art's heaven complementing each other in this way should stand face to face as contemporaries is undoubtedly more than a coincidence. It appears as if, through inscrutable laws of nature, they influence each other in a double way: first positively, in that they attract each other

---

[1] Grieg's letter to Beyer is published in English translation in Finn Benestad (ed.), *Edvard Grieg: Letters to Colleagues and Friends,* Columbus, Ohio, 2000, pp. 89–90.
[2] Norwegian: *Tonekunstnere* and *Tonediktere.*

by their light; but no less negatively, in that each is repelled by the darker side of the other. Thus, despite the similarities owing to the circumstance of growing up under the same national and social influences, each has developed his unique qualities and has been prevented by the aforementioned hidden processes in the secret workshops of nature from fusing their musical styles or even coming close to doing so.

Danish music history provides another example of the same phenomenon in Kuhlau and Weyse.[3] And no one with the gift of understanding doubts for a moment that in this case Kuhlau, with his great ability to shape the music, is the *tone artist* and Weyse, despite all his canonic artifices, is the *tone poet*. Hartmann stands on Weyse's shoulders. He is the poet, the seer who looks into the future. He has visualized for many, many years the dreams that now inspire our young Nordic composers. It is also for this reason that our young people look with more than admiration to this man, who even at an advanced age can express their thoughts. We love him because there is this special gripping power in his lyre when he loudly plucks his strings—this power that brings all the young people who have ears to hear to gather around him and listen. Notwithstanding his white hair, he still speaks—indeed, better than ever—the exuberant language of

Johan Peter Emilius
Hartmann

---

[3] German-born composers Friedrich [Frederik] Kuhlau (1786–1832) and Christoph Ernst Friedrich Weyse (1774–1842), both of whom spent most of their professional careers in Denmark.

youth, this language to which one might apply the telling words that Beethoven wrote regarding his *Missa solemnis*: "From the heart it has come, to the heart it shall make its way."[4] No wonder, therefore, that the young people love him, for he has had music to express all the shifting moods of their longings and hopes.

Still another indication that he is at the forefront is the fact that he is a representative of the struggle to find expressions for his ideals that in general are peculiar to the Nordic artist. And he has never stood still in this struggle, never let us younger ones get the impression that now he was content with the results, that now he could be permitted to relax and rest on the gilded laurels of victory. No, "Onward, forward!" has been his watchword, and if he occasionally lost a battle, he thought, like the great Napoleon: "There is time to win a new one!" And he won it! This is what is distinctive of Hartmann, that his creative work right into old age has been a continuous progress, a continuous development. Except for Haydn,[5] we know of scarcely any other old man of whom we can say that his last works are the most beautiful. I shall mention one of the most outstanding: *The Vølve's Prophecy*.[6] We tremble in holy awe before a spirit to whom such visions were revealed.

Since I intend to leave the objective details of Hartmann's life to the biographer, I will here limit myself to mentioning the most distinguished of his many works, some of which will secure his reputation far into the future. Among these we see nearly all genres represented in his production. Operas (*The Raven, The Corsairs, Little Christine*), dramatic music (*Hakon Jarl, Axel and Valborg, Seven Sleepers' Day*), ballets (*A Folk Tale, The Valkyrie, The Legend of Thrym, Arcona*), cantatas upon the deaths of all the Danish rulers of his day—all bear the distinctive mark of their composer. Perhaps the cantatas and ballets most of all. Among his concert pieces, *The Dryads' Wedding, Gypsy Song* and *The Vølve's Prophecy*[7] carry the stamp of brilliance as do none other. The big classical symphonic forms, which Gade has cultivated with such great mastery, have evidently

---

[4] "Vom Herzen ist's gekommen, zum Herzen soll es dringen." The words by Ludwig van Beethoven (1770–1827) were quoted in German by Grieg.

[5] Austrian composer Joseph Haydn (1732–1809).

[6] *Vølvens Spaadom* op. 71 (1872) was a cantata in which Hartmann tried to create an "Old Norse" style. In Old Norse mythology the "vølve" was a woman who practiced witchcraft and had the ability to foresee the future.

[7] Danish titles of the works mentioned by Grieg:

    OPERAS: *Ravnen* op. 12 (1832, revised 1885; libretto: Hans Christian Andersen); *Korsarerne* op. 16 (1835; libretto: Danish poet Henrik Hertz (1798–1870)); *Liden Kirsten* op. 44 (1846, revised 1858; libretto: Hans Christian Andersen).

    DRAMATIC MUSIC: Incidental music for the drama *Hakon Jarl* op. 40 (1844–57), by Danish poet Adam Oehlenschläger (1779–1850); incidental music for Oehlenschläger's play *Axel og Valborg* op. 57 (1856); incidental music for *Syvsoverdag* op. 30 (1840, revised 1872), a play by Danish author Johan Ludvig Heiberg (1854–1928).

    BALLET MUSIC: *Et Folkesagn* (1854, collaboration with Niels W. Gade); *Valkyrien* op. 62 (1861); *Thrymskviden* op. 67 (1868); *Arcona* op. 72 (1875).

    VOCAL: *Dryadens Bryllup* op. 60 (1858); *Zigeunersang; Vølvens Spaadom*.

not suited Hartmann's personality inasmuch as he has almost totally avoided them. Still, a work from his youth—his prize sonata for piano—is convincing proof of his ability to create in the larger forms. But like everyone, he has been subjected to the inexorable power of circumstances. Daily association with a circle of friends that included Hans Christian Andersen and Auguste Bournonville[8] has perhaps been too tempting and has enticed him into other fields. A unique significance must be accorded his melodramatic treatment of Oehlenschläger's poem *The Golden Horns,*[9] because here for the first time he strikes the Nordic tone that for himself and his successors in Denmark has become such a rich gold mine. And when I mention his song cycle *Sulamit and Solomon*[10]—how many of us recall the most beautiful moments of our youth in connection with this music, which is so full of nobility, grace and originality. Nor can I forget his short sacred songs, which possess a true depth of genuine childlikeness and simple religious spirit.

It is not my intention here to write a critical evaluation of Hartmann and his works. For such a task I lack the required data, and the available space is too limited—and moreover, this is not the proper time for it. The final judgment, which underscores both the bright and the dark sides in an artist's work, is a task for the historian.

When Denmark and the Nordic countries gather around the old man who is being honored today, it is to pay tribute to him—and only for that reason. Yes, there are three generations that he has managed to enchant and fill with the treasures of his spirit. In the breasts of three generations he has caused the noblest and best strings to vibrate. Over the great men of three generations he himself, from the organ of Our Lady's Church,[11] has played the mighty sounds of his proud *Funeral March for Thorvaldsen's*[12] *Burial.* He has moved three generations to tears with these strains, which eventually—a long time from now, we hope— will also, from the same place, bring him our farewell. Is not a person who manages all that a giant? Or when did we hear anything like it? Let us, therefore, not be stingy with our praise. With full hearts let us include all the flowers of spring in our embrace of the noble singer as an expression of our awe, our admiration, our gratitude—and of the best of all: our love!

---

[8] Danish poet and children's writer Hans Christian Andersen (1805–75) and ballet dancer and choreographer Antoine Auguste Bournonville (1805–79).

[9] Danish title: *Guldhornene.* Hartmann's composition is a melodrama (1832).

[10] *Sulamith og Salomon* op. 52 (1850 and 1866), song cycle to texts by Danish poet Bernhard Severin Ingemann (1789–1862), based on *Song of Songs* from The Old Testament.

[11] Vor Frue Kirke in Copenhagen.

[12] Danish sculptor Bertel Thorvaldsen (1770–1844).

Louis Hornbeck (1906)

Danish composer, violinist and organist Louis Hornbeck (1840–1906) was one of Grieg's Copenhagen friends who joined Grieg and others in founding the musical association "Euterpe" in the winter of 1864–65. In a letter of September 9, 1895, Grieg wrote to him: "Although our paths do not often cross, you may be sure that I am not one of those who forget memories of the kind that you and I share. I don't own a safe—I leave such things to the merchants—but I have an invisible *mental* safe that is fastened more securely than one in which a banker keeps his dough. Memories are—with all due respect—like flounder: They live on the bottom and stay there until someone brings them up to the surface. But they ought not to come up, because then their eyes explode and it's all over for them. So let us hide our treasures like misers and count them every day. That is what I do, anyway, and I am often inspired by this exercise."[1]

Grieg's eulogy was written aboard the steamer "Alden" on the Sognefjord in Western Norway on September 22, 1906, and published in the Copenhagen newspaper *Politiken* on September 28, 1906.

I read in *Politiken* the cold and dry announcement that Hornbeck, the precentor at Trinity Church, has passed away. The brevity of the announcement is telling. It shows that people in Denmark were remarkably ignorant of who Louis Hornbeck was. In fact, he was no less than a highly gifted lyrical composer who wrote songs that are among the best in Danish song literature. It is now more than thirty years since these songs first saw the light of day. It is strange, therefore, that they could remain unnoticed in an environment as highly cultivated and musical as that of Denmark. I think the composer's great modesty may have been an obstacle for him. His self-criticism no less. For he was the very opposite of a modern status seeker. To win the understanding of a few friends meant everything to him.

He created his best works during a happy period in the 1860's and 1870's when the air in Denmark was full of musical lyricism. Among the poets of his day he easily found those who appealed to his natural bent. Ludvig Bødtcher, Christian Richardt and Carl Ploug[2] were his favorites and the ones whose verses he set most successfully.

The Denmark of today can no longer provide Hornbeck with the joy of recognition that he deserved. But it can nonetheless right the wrong to some extent by admitting his name and his songs into the ranks of those that the Danes should be obliged to hold in high esteem. I urgently ask everyone who not only has a voice but also makes claim to a modicum of music sense: Go down to

---

[1] See Finn Benestad (ed.), *Edvard Grieg: Letters to Colleagues and Friends*, Columbus, Ohio 2000, p. 430.

[2] Danish poets Ludvig Bødtcher (1793–1874), Christian Richardt (1831–92) and Carl Ploug (1813–94). Grieg himself set four of Richardt's poems to music: "A Mother's Grief" ("Modersorg"), op. 15 no. 4, and "Autumn Storm" ("Høststormen"), op. 18 no. 4 for voice and piano, and for male chorus "Fredriksborg", EG 160 no. 2, and "Student Life" ("Studereliv"), EG 160 no. 3.

Wilhelm Hansen's Music Store and get a copy of Hornbeck's music to Ploug's "I Believe in You in Life's Bright Morning" ("Jeg tror paa Dig i Livets lyse Morgen") as well as Richardt's "Now You Lie Prostrate, O Mighty Beech Tree" ("Nu ligger Du ramt, Du stolte Bøg"), and you will ask yourself in amazement: How can it be that songs of such great beauty have been available in printed form for over a generation without becoming known to those whose emotional life they touch most closely? To concert singers both male and female I say: Put these songs on your program, sing them and sing them well, and you will win great applause both for the composer and for yourself.

Through his first wife, whose maiden name was Sanne, Hornbeck was related to Bjørnstjerne Bjørnson and his cousin Rikard Nordraak.[3] It was through the latter that, in 1864, I became acquainted with Hornbeck. We were often together and, along with C. F. E. Horneman and Gottfred Matthison-Hansen, belonged to the youthful clique that gathered around *Euterpe*, the association that had just been organized—under Horneman's leadership—for the advancement of new Nordic music. Hornbeck was a man with a clear and critical mind. He also had a priceless, dry sense of humor with which he, to our delight, spiced up our meetings and basically calmed down Horneman's brilliant but vehement passion in debate.[4]

In Hornbeck's home I saw an oil portrait of his father in full uniform as a member of the Royal Theater Orchestra. It was Hornbeck's dream that he, too, would one day hold such a position, which is a much-sought-after goal for every Danish violinist. But he did not succeed. No doubt his nature did not favor him in this respect. Like his personality, his violin playing sometimes seemed a little stiff. Moreover, he was not especially energetic. Quite the opposite. He sometimes displayed, often to the point of absurdity, an apparent indifference, which now and then drove his friends to despair. That, however, was only a shell, within which lay hidden all the warmth and moving beauty of the man and the artist that found such beautiful expression in his songs. May these lines contribute to rescuing them from oblivion.

---

[3] Norwegian author Bjørnstjerne Bjørnson (1832–1910) and his cousin Rikard Nordraak (1842–66). Bjørnson wrote the text and Nordraak the music for Norway's national anthem "Yes, we love this land, our country" ("Ja, vi elsker dette landet").

[4] Danish composers Christian Frederik Emil Horneman (1840–1906) and Gottfred Matthison-Hansen (1832–1909). Grieg had extensive correspondence with both of them. A large number of Grieg's letters to them are published in English translation in Finn Benestad (ed.), *Edvard Grieg: Letters to Colleagues and Friends*, Columbus, Ohio, 2000. Grieg also wrote an essay on Horneman which is printed in English in the present volume, pp. 211–216.

  In the public announcements in Copenhagen newspapers on March 1, 1865, for the first *Euterpe* concert, the goal of the joint Danish and Norwegian association was stated: "*Euterpe* will eagerly endeavor to become a voice for the musical youth of the Nordic countries whose compositions hitherto have lacked the opportunity for general dissemination."

Christian Frederik Emil Horneman (1881)

The Danish composer Christian Frederik Emil Horneman (1840–1906) was one of Grieg's best friends during his student days at the Leipzig Conservatory and a close ally in the mid-1860's in Copenhagen. Grieg wrote of him in glowing terms on a number of occasions. His statement in a letter of September 3, 1886, to their mutual friend August Winding is typical: "I think especially of you and Emil Horneman, (. . .) whose noble heart and deep musical feeling I have to thank for several of the most significant influences of my youth."[1]

Grieg's article was written in April 1881 in response to a request from the editor of the Danish *Ugeskrift for Theater og Musik (Weekly Journal for Theater and Music)*. It was not published at that time, however, because the journal went bankrupt and ceased publication. The first printing (in Norwegian) is found in Øystein Gaukstad (ed.), *Edvard Grieg: Artikler og Taler (Edvard Grieg: Articles and Speeches)*, Oslo 1957. Grieg's manuscript is preserved in Bergen Public Library.

It is not very desirable to be one of the composers in the prime of life in Denmark these days. The musical conditions in this country have long been unhealthy. During the 1830's and 1840's the musical scene brightened as a result of the work of the brilliant masters Hartmann and Gade,[2] but then a period of stagnation set in. Ever since that time Danish music has lacked an infusion of new ideas. The conservative, disgruntled, all-knowing spirit that has dominated the scene for more than a generation and has, *inter alia*, found an only too true expression in the public critical reviews—this spirit, that preaches contempt for the young prospects for the future and idolizes formalism as a dogma of infallibility, has unfortunately had an extremely damaging effect on the vast majority of younger talents. I refer especially to the talents that began to emerge during the 1850's. For the youngest generation is far better off. One senses much more now than before a serious effort to take one's place under the banner of progress. One senses it among the older ones with a melancholy feeling that the influence comes too late, among the younger ones with a confident hope for that which is to come. By "the older ones" I mean just the talents from the 1850's, who were limited by an upbringing that was altogether too one-sided. To be sure, they received healthful fare as they were growing up—but it was always the same. And above all, they never got to feel the fresh breeze of opposition, for there was no opposition. Everyone knelt before the established order.

Obviously one cannot complain about the fact that the classical masters lead the way in the halls where the scepter of music holds sway. But youth requires more. Young people want to know their own time. Indeed, even more: They want

---

[1] Danish composer August Winding (1835–99). See Finn Benestad (ed.), *Edvard Grieg: Letters to Colleagues and Friends*, Columbus, Ohio 2000, pp. 680–681.

[2] Danish composers Johan Peter Emilius Hartmann (1805–1900) and Niels W. Gade (1817–90). See Grieg's article on Hartmann on pp. 205–208.

to be led up to the heights from which they can see the great vista that stretches out toward the future. I don't know if it is officially expressed, but I do know this: Among the more forward-looking musicians of that day there is only one opinion regarding the fact that the systematic exclusion from the ideals of our time—the endless rehashing of the classical and post-classical masters at the expense of more recent composers that has long held sway in Denmark—has had disastrous results. The young talents had to choose between two alternatives: to adopt the artistic views of the ruling authorities or waste away from lack of development, perhaps also from lack of recognition. Energetic natures who were unwilling to submit to "the school", and who through lack of knowledge of their own time have been unable to find themselves during their youth, have, because of this dilemma, waged many a hard battle.

I have been obliged to dwell on these facts because they constitute an absolutely indispensable context for the judgment of the talents from the 1850's. Among these, no one has struggled against stagnation with greater enthusiasm, persistence and dedication than Christian Frederik Emil Horneman—and he has done it in the face of an incredible lack of appreciation.

He was born in Copenhagen on December 17, 1840, into a family in which art has long ruled the roost. His father was Emil Horneman,[3] the great natural talent, whose first piano compositions even won him Robert Schumann's[4] admiration and whose patriotic songs have found a response wherever Danish folk music is heard. His mother Agnes, nee Scheuermann,[5] also comes from an artistically gifted family and possesses a richly endowed musical temperament. When the parents saw that their son had the makings of a composer, they arranged even during his childhood for him to receive instruction in composition.

In 1857 his highest wish was fulfilled: He was sent to Leipzig, the city of music. Horneman once related a sadly typical incident from those days that sheds considerable light on his artistic nature. Upon taking leave of his [Danish] teacher he naturally received much good advice. He was urged, among other things, to watch out for the newer, modern composers, who represented apostasy from the true ideals. There was one in particular for whom he was warned to be careful— a man by the name of Schumann. (That was then!) The boy did not know this name, which was still not popular outside of Germany, but he had great respect for his teacher and solemnly promised to be an obedient pupil. The very first day that he was in Leipzig he got a ticket to the dress rehearsal for one of the Gewandhaus concerts. As he came into the auditorium somebody was singing an old concert aria to which he listened with the dispassionate respect for authority

---

[3] Music publisher Johan Ole Emil Horneman (1809–70).

[4] See Grieg's article on German composer Robert Schumann (1810–56) on pp. 255–274.

[5] Agnes Scheuermann Horneman (1808–91).

befitting a student. Then a lady sat down at the grand piano and began to play a piece with orchestral accompaniment. Not many measures had been played before young Horneman became as if electrified. A new world opened up for him, a world full of that for which he yearned with all the longing of his heart— without realizing it himself. He listened and listened; it became more and more beautiful. Finally he could no longer stand not knowing what he was listening to. He turned to the fellow sitting next to him and whispered, "Who is this by?" "By Schumann!" "Schu – – – mann? Well, but then . . ." He made a face that caused

Grieg with his Danish friends Emil Horneman and Louis Hornbeck

his companion to fear lest he might have a madman at his side. (It was Schumann's *Piano Concerto in A Minor* that he heard, and the lady at the grand piano was Clara Schumann.[6])

With that, Horneman's fate was sealed. He swore that he would love this music no matter what a whole legion of teachers might say about it. And that he has done. Not, however, in the sense that he has become a typical "Schumannian". His individuality was too strong for that. But he has preserved the young man's first love and has charged forward under the young banner of Romanticism—a banner which at that time was raised by Schumann, Chopin[7] and others.

At the Leipzig Conservatory he studied under Moscheles, Hauptmann, Richter and Rietz.[8] He was especially attracted to Rietz, who in turn had great affection for his Danish student.

In spring 1860 Horneman had to return home, thus bringing this joyful chapter of his life to an end. But he had learned much, as evidenced by the works from this period. During his years in Leipzig, in addition to many songs and piano pieces he wrote a string quartet and two overtures—none of which have been published.

Upon his return home another kind of life began. Various practical activities required his attention. Nonetheless, he continued to compose assiduously in his spare time. At the beginning of the 1860's he conceived the idea and wrote the first outline of an opera, *Aladdin*, which at various times he has alternately let lie and renewed work on. It is still unfinished, which is a great pity, for the finished fragments—and there are many—reveal his great dramatic gift. As everyone knows, the overture to the opera not only has been published but is played to great applause in many of Europe's finest concert halls. In addition to reflecting the influence of the post-classicists, this overture reveals a creative spirit that is outstanding for its uniqueness as well as for its mastery in the treatment of the material. The instrumentation is superb. It is to be hoped that Horneman may still find the inclination and encouragement to put the final touches on his work, for everything indicates that it would be a credit to the Danish stage.[9]

Among his compositions published in recent years—in addition to an *Ouverture héroique* (1867) and the previously cited *Aladdin Overture*—should be mentioned especially many songs with piano accompaniment. These songs are his autobiography. He has shut himself and his struggle inside those songs—with his privation as well as his rich, warm temperament. Often—and this, I think, is

---

[6] German pianist Clara Schumann (1919–96), widow of Robert Schumann.

[7] Polish composer and pianist Frédéric Chopin (1810–49).

[8] The professors mentioned by Grieg are: Austrian pianist Ignaz Moscheles (1794–1870), German music theorist and composer Moritz Hauptmann (1792–1868), German music theorist Ernst Friedrich Richter (1808–79), German composer and conductor Julius Rietz (1812–77).

[9] *Aladdin* had its first performance at the Royal Theater in Copenhagen on November 18, 1886, but was not well received. It was staged anew on April 4, 1902, this time to great acclaim.

owing to the circumstances touched on earlier—there is something unresolved in them. But on the other hand: What a world of true music, of glowing enthusiasm and of deep feeling is contained in many of them. To be sure, they are not "popular" in a vulgar sense, but—so much the better for them! "It's good that some things hang so high that everybody can't reach them!" says Bjørnson.[10] If you consider just one song such as Horneman's setting of Heine's[11] poem "Der Asra" ("The Asra"), you must admire the originality, the richness of imagination, the ability to portray, all of which manifest a noble spirit. Manuscripts of great significance lie on his desk, among which I shall mention "Valfarten" ("The Pilgrimage")[12] and "Ein fremder Kavalier" ("A Foreign Cavalier") for voice and orchestra, also "Die drei Lieder" ("The Three Songs") to texts by Uhland[13] for solo voice, men's chorus and orchestra—all works capable of creating interest.

In addition to being a richly gifted composer, Horneman is indeed a well-integrated and extraordinary individual as well. Like many great spirits, he possesses electrifying powers which, as is well known, both attract and repel. His brilliant foresight and capacity for invention, his energetic and effusive opposition to all forms of pettiness, require a large setting; in a smaller one, in addition to enthusiastic friends, these qualities will also create—bitter enemies. These enemies have often made things extremely unpleasant for him and really have contributed to stifling many an undertaking that he, with great enthusiasm and prospects of a good result, has begun. What a pity! Among such aborted undertakings I will mention the concert association *Euterpe*, which, as a result of his initiative, was established by several musicians in 1864 in order to make possible the performance of works by younger Nordic composers.[14] Later he established the "Saturday Soirees", a grand idea by which he intended to give ordinary people an opportunity to hear good music, and finally also "The Concert Association" ("Concertforeningen"), the purpose of which was to build pathways to the understanding of new music of all schools. That the last-named institution is still flourishing under the capable leadership of Mr. Otto Malling[15] is adequate proof of the viability of the idea. In the attempt to bring these fine ideas to realization, Horneman has had many opportunities to experience the narrow-minded cliquishness that has ravaged Copenhagen's artistic circles. Through these experiences he has gained the harmonious superiority that makes him richly

---

[10] Norwegian author Bjørnstjerne Bjørnson (1832–1910).

[11] German poet Heinrich Heine (1797–1856).

[12] Text by Danish author Poul Martin Møller (1797–1838).

[13] German poet Johann Ludwig Uhland (1787–1862).

[14] *Euterpe*—a parallel to the Leipzig association by the same name—was founded by Horneman, Grieg and their mutual friends and colleagues the Norwegian Rikard Nordraak (1842–66), and the Danes Louis Hornbeck (1840–1906) and Gottfred Matthison-Hansen (1832–1909). Their main aim was to advocate new music, both through discussions and concerts. The first public concert was given on March 18, 1865, the last on April 23, 1867. By 1867 Nordraak had passed away and Grieg had moved to Christiania.

[15] Danish composer and organist Otto Malling (1848–1915).

deserving of the fame that can now no longer be denied him and that he enjoys in full measure as founder and teacher at the music institute that bears his name. This institute has now worked for several years with a dual purpose: to train not only artists but the entire younger generation of those with an interest in music.[16]

Throughout Horneman's ideas one can find universal, genuinely philanthropic basic concepts. One will look in vain, on the other hand, for any trace of national-folkish ecstasy. It is worth noting that during the time when it was politically popular to be "super-super-Danish", he continued to be unmoved by this phenomenon, which inexplicably spread in all directions at that time. How often, verbally as well as in music, he has fought with the warmth of conviction for the universal against the parochial, for the cosmopolitan against national one-sidedness. In other words: How often he has shown the attentive observer that he is one of those who—without knowing it himself, I think—belongs to the future!

Since, as I have indicated, Horneman earlier had to work without the understanding that every true artist needs in order to thrive, it is a pleasant duty to be able to state that now, more and more, people are beginning to realize his significance as an artist. To this fact is tied the hope that the great expectations with which one looks forward to his further creative activity may not be in vain. I urge influential men in Denmark—through a state grant or some other form of public support—to give him the financial independence with the help of which his homeland as well as the entire musical world will learn what a power Denmark possesses in him.

---

[16] Horneman's private conservatory of music was established in 1880, as a protest against the traditional spirit of the Royal Danish Conservatory of Music, led by Niels W. Gade. Horneman's institution survived the death of its founder, remaining in operation until 1920.

Halfdan Kjerulf: A Eulogy (1868)

Except for Grieg himself, Halfdan Kjerulf (1815–68) was the leading composer of songs in Norway. Indeed, he may be said to have been the creator of the Norwegian art song. His compositions and his many activities in the music life of the Norwegian capital were extremely important. His arrangements of Norwegian folk music preceded Grieg's by nearly a decade, and Grieg undoubtedly got some ideas from them—although he explicitly denied it in a letter of April 25, 1881, to his biographer Aimar Grønvold (1846–1926): "I am not aware of any deeper influence by Kjerulf despite my warm admiration for many of his songs."[1]

Grieg's eulogy on his distinguished predecessor was published in the 1867–68 volume of the Danish journal *Illustreret Tidende*, Copenhagen.

The Norwegian newspapers carry the sad news that the composer Halfdan Kjerulf passed away on Tuesday, August 11, at Grefsen Spa near Christiania. For the past twenty-five years he suffered from a lung disease that long ago had been declared incurable but that, during all this time, not only allowed him to stay alive but even vouchsafed to him the most unimpaired creative power and youthful warmth and enthusiasm.

Kjerulf was born in 1815 in Christiania. He entered the university in 1835 and the following year took a position in the Ministry of Finance. But a growing urge to dedicate himself to art gave him no peace, so soon thereafter he gave up his position in the Ministry in order to become a musician. At first he studied for a time in Christiania with the outstanding German composer Carl Arnold,[2] working simultaneously as a music teacher and as conductor of the Norwegian Student Male Chorus. Finally in 1849, with the help of a royal grant, he went abroad. He went first to Copenhagen to meet Gade,[3] whose brilliant early works had enthused him. At that time, as Kjerulf himself has related, he totally lacked confidence in himself. He brought with him to Copenhagen several songs that he had composed, but they did not succeed in winning the approval of the Danish artists with whom he came in contact at that time, and he had still not dared to approach Gade. But one fine day he screwed up his courage, and look what happened! Gade recognized his talent, expressed his pleasure and encouraged him to press courageously forward. Now the die was cast. Full of hope and confidence he journeyed to Leipzig, where the young Romantic school created by Mendelssohn and Schumann[4] shone in all its beautiful springtime glory. He took into his soul the rich well of poetry that he encountered there, hid it and

---

[1] See Finn Benestad (ed.), *Edvard Grieg: Letters to Colleagues and Friends*, Columbus, Ohio 2000, p. 308.
[2] German pianist and composer Carl Arnold (1794–1873) came to Norway in 1848. He settled in Christiania, where he made an important contribution to Norwegian music.
[3] Danish composer Niels W. Gade (1817–90).
[4] German composers Felix Mendelssohn (1809–47) and Robert Schumann (1810–56).

Halfdan Kjerulf was Grieg's most important Norwegian predecessor.

preserved it well, for even in his most distinctively Norwegian works from later periods one notes the fragrance of Romanticism.

After having spent a year in Leipzig he returned again to his homeland, where ever since—except for summer trips abroad, which he took almost annually—he worked without interruption on behalf of music, and he persevered with determination and true love for his art amidst contemporaries who theretofore had had no inkling of his significance. It appears, however, that in the very recent past the recognition of his importance has begun to take root in Norway, public evidences of which he received in 1863 when he was awarded the medallion *pro literis et artibus*, and this year, when he finally was made a Knight of the Order of St. Olaf.

Kjerulf emerged at a time when Norwegians as a people were still living in their very earliest childhood. His expression of their emotional life at that time, therefore, had almost as a necessity to be naive. He had no predecessor to lend him support. There was nothing but folk ballads, the outward expressions of the most primitive spiritual life. These he took as his starting point, and he chose the art song as the vehicle for his creative activity. For this we owe him thanks, because only in this area was it given to him to capture the national color by which our music can achieve its natural and healthy development. The music of each nation proceeds in the course of time from the folk song through the small forms and then into the larger, richer, more complex forms. If Kjerulf had attempted large forms such as the sonata or the symphony, he would have been attempting a task unsuitable for him. His significance would have been doubtful because he, in accordance with the temper of the times, would not have succeeded in incorporating the national element. His strength lies in the fact that he clearly saw his task and did not desire to be what he was not. Kjerulf was one-sided, and precisely for that reason he was great.

Like so many other composers, Kjerulf has had the experience of seeing his least important works become the most popular ones. His compositions for men's chorus, however, constitute exceptions to this statement, especially his music to A. Munch's[5] poem "The Bridal Procession in Hardanger" ("Brudeferden i Hardanger"), a composition from his youth that has even found its way far beyond the borders of Scandinavia. It was this song that helped the men's chorus from Uppsala[6] to score its triumph at the competition in Paris last year. His songs for solo voice and piano will live as long as Nordic art is loved amongst us; nearly all of them have a surprising freshness and originality. His folk-like songs to texts from Bjørnson's[7] novellas vie for superiority with his settings of Welhaven's and Wergeland's[8] erotic poems. His settings of Danish and Swedish poems also rank high. Sweden was really the first country to recognize Kjerulf, and nearly all of his compositions have been published in Stockholm. His collected works perhaps total no more than twenty small albums—a circumstance that is understandable when one considers the state of his health and the fact that he was over twenty-five years old when he decided to devote himself seriously to music.

---

5 Norwegian poet Andreas Munch (1811–84).
6 Uppsala, Sweden, at that time had one of Scandinavia's most successful student glee clubs.
7 Norwegian author Bjørnstjerne Bjørnson (1832–1910).
8 Norwegian poets Johan Sebastian Welhaven (1807–73) and Henrik Wergeland (1808–45).

As previously stated, Kjerulf's essential significance consists in the fact that he knew how to strike the national chord, but it is characteristic of him that he nonetheless hated the musical "language controversy",[9] a weed that he unfortunately had to see beginning to shoot up around him. He saw that what was great in the national idea could be united with the universal and could have no future if it got lost in its own singularity. He was right up to date regarding the events of his time. He did not stand aloof but absorbed into his own individuality that which was great and worthy of recognition in the music of other countries. It is only by having this in mind that the representatives of Norwegian music can in truth be said to have understood him and made him their own.

---

[9] The prevailing language in educated circles in Norway at this time was *bokmål*, a form of Norwegian strongly influenced by the Danish language as a result of Norway's political and cultural subordination to Denmark for over 400 years prior to 1814, when Norway was ceded to Sweden. During the nineteenth century, as Norwegians began to aspire to independence in all spheres of their national life, a small but influential group of people led by Ivar Aasen (1813–96) began to agitate for a return to an indigenous Norwegian language, which was presumed to exist in the dialects spoken by the farmers and other uneducated people of rural Norway—people whose language had not been "corrupted" by direct exposure to Danish influences. Aasen, drawing on these dialects, created a language that later was called *nynorsk*, i.e., "new Norwegian," and the country soon found itself sharply divided over the issue of which language should prevail.

Kjerulf's Songs (1879)

Grieg was well aware that the principal significance of his great predecessor Halfdan Kjerulf (1815–68) was as a composer of songs, of which he wrote no less than 126 during a lifetime cut short by tuberculosis at age 53. Of these, 70 were published during Kjerulf's lifetime, the other 56 posthumously.[1]

Grieg's review of Kjerulf's songs was published in the Christiania newspaper *Aftenbladet* on February 1, 1879.

In the nearly one hundred songs by the Norwegian composer who is so much loved in Scandinavia—which songs are here gathered together for the first time—we encounter a fine, distinguished personality. A few of the songs have been sung in Germany by Norwegian artists, but the vast majority of them are hitherto completely unknown here. Unfortunately! For they possess true, genuine feeling, a singular freshness and simplicity, and sometimes originality of expression—qualities which, as we all know, do not grow on trees nowadays.

If Kjerulf's talent admittedly was strictly limited inasmuch as he almost without exception wrote only songs, he has understood all the better how to enclose a spiritual life within those narrow confines. If one immerses oneself in one of his most beautiful volumes of songs, one realizes that here one is dealing with a talent of rare concentration. There are artists whose works seem untouched by the outward conditions of their lives—and there are artists whose creations are so closely knitted to their life-history that they can be correctly appraised only when seen in connection thereto. Kjerulf belongs to the latter category. He dedicated himself to art late in life. Struggling with a consumptive lung disorder throughout his life, living in a place far removed from the musical world and at a time when his home country deprived him of nearly every artistic influence, wandering alone through life and withdrawn into himself, he sang his most beautiful melodies. Therefore many of his songs bear the stamp of renunciation, of resignation—merits which, to be sure, were dearly bought but which are nonetheless the very ones that give his creations an inexpressible charm.

Kjerulf was nothing less than a master workman. He worked slowly and exercised strong self-criticism before he published anything. That is also evident in many of the songs included in the second volume, first published after his death—and, in my opinion, in a disrespectful manner.

As far as I am aware, Kjerulf studied in Leipzig at the end of the 1840's,[2] and Schumann's rich springtime of song—which was then flourishing—had an unmistakable influence on his later output. But at the same time, he worked his

---

[1] Kjerulf's *Samlede Verker* (Collected Works) have recently been published in five volumes by Musikk-Huset A/S, Oslo, under the editorship of Nils Grinde. The songs comprise vols. 1 (1977) and 2 (1980).

[2] Kjerulf studied with Niels W. Gade in Copenhagen in 1849–50 and at the Leipzig Conservatory of Music in 1850–51.

way more and more into his own style as well, and above all he was the first person to emphasize the great significance of Norwegian folk melodies for our national music. He has carried this out in a noble and engaging way, and he must, therefore, be credited with fulfilling a mission in Scandinavian music history the scope of which must not be underestimated.

Luckily for Kjerulf, his creative work occurred at a time when the national movements found their first powerful expression in virtually all of the arts and sciences of the Norwegian people, who in 1814 had achieved their independence from Denmark.[3] In painting there were Gude and Tidemand,[4] in poetry Wergeland and Welhaven, in history the brilliant scholar P. A. Munch[5]—all of whom expressed, each in his own way, distinct national tendencies. Ole Bull's[6] violin evoked images of a highly varied mélange of national characters: Now it was melancholy folk ballads, then suddenly the unrestrained jollity of a *halling* or *springdans*.[7] It is no wonder that all of these phenomena made a deep impression on Kjerulf's personality.

In the revolution year of 1848,[8] when so many Norwegian artists returned home, an undreamt-of artistic life awoke in Christiania. This happy coming together of kindred spirits proved to be decisive for Kjerulf. Gude and Tidemand painted their famous "The Bridal Procession in Hardanger", for which Andreas Munch wrote his beautiful poem of the same name. Kjerulf then composed a piece for men's chorus to this text, and with this music he has won an eternal place in the hearts of the people of Scandinavia.[9]

These brief and patently rhapsodic notes must suffice as a cursory sketch of the background of Kjerulf's artistic character.

If we now turn to the melodies at hand, it is clear that the center of gravity in Kjerulf's talent lies in the elegiac-erotic sphere. In this sphere he is a master. Here he knows how to let the voice flow out quite wonderfully and to let the piano add color just as wonderfully. A bold, passionate element is not to be found in Kjerulf. One will seek in vain for this "Rejoicing to high heaven, grieved to death".[10] He never plucks a string of either jubilation or despair in such a way that it is in danger of breaking. One never sees him as transported into higher spheres.

---

[3] Norway had been subject to Denmark from 1380 to 1814 when, by the Treaty of Kiel ending the Napoleonic wars, Norway was ceded to Sweden. At the time when the present essay was written, Norway remained under the Swedish crown—a condition that continued until 1905, when Norway became fully independent.

[4] Norwegian painters Hans Gude (1825–1903) and Adolph Tidemand (1814–76).

[5] Norwegian historian Peter Andreas Munch (1810–63).

[6] Norwegian virtuoso violinist Ole Bull (1810–80).

[7] *Halling* and *springdans*: two types of indigenous Norwegian peasant-dance tunes.

[8] Grieg is referring to the spate of revolutions that engulfed much of continental Europe in 1848–49.

[9] On March 1, 1849, the national-romantic movement was given tremendous momentum in three evening programs in which the elite members of the Norwegian art world all participated. The climax was a *tableau vivant* in which Gude and Tidemand's painting was depicted by live performers as Kjerulf's choral composition was sung by a student chorus.

[10] Grieg quotes these lines in German: "Himmelhoch jauchzend, zum Tode betrübt". They are from Goethe's *Egmont* 3, 2 (1788), "Clärchen's Love Song."

The demonic is foreign to him. Yet, despite all this: What tones he coaxes from his lyre, what nobility permeates its sound! Leaving aside the above-mentioned posthumous songs, the remainder of the rich collection includes almost none that one would wish were not there.

Unfortunately, some of Kjerulf's most beautiful songs are not included—for example, the spirited "Up on the Mountain" ("Upp på fjellet") to a poem by Kr. Janson.[11] His best, most inspired melodies were written in the 1850's. One also finds many of his most popular creations emerging later, but the freshness and the happy grip on the folk tune gradually recede and unfortunately are often replaced by a rather bland salon tone.

Formally, and in his handling of the voice, he does indeed offer us precisely in his later works many things of interest, yet without succeeding in compensating us for the lack of what is most essential. But the collection as a whole is hereby recommended most warmly to all friends of genuine, noble song. It contains pearls of great price. Among the most beautiful, in my opinion, are the folk-like songs of op. 6: nos. 1, 2, 3, 4, 6.[12]

Next I would mention the following songs from the first volume: nos. 2, 3, 4, 6, 8, 9 (one of the most wonderful products of his genius), 11, 13, 14, 36, 37, 38 and 45. The last-named song exhibits a broader structure than one is accustomed to with Kjerulf. The first half, to be sure, presents nothing unusual, but that only makes the profoundly agitated conclusion all the more gripping. The last song in this volume, no. 46, is most unusual. The ballad tone is masterfully struck and an evocative aura of mystery hovers over the whole picture. The second half, a unison passage followed by a choral refrain, creates a beautiful effect.[13]

---

[11] Norwegian poet Kristofer Janson (1841–1917).

[12] The numbers in op. 6 mentioned by Grieg are the following. The original titles are given first, English translations in parentheses. Op. 6 is identical with nos. 15–20 in the first volume of the collection of songs as published by Abraham Hirsch, Stockholm:

No. 1: Vejviseren synger (The Guide Sings), text: Johan Sebastian Welhaven.
No. 2: Ved Sjøen den mørke (At the Dark Sea), text: Henrik Wergeland.
No. 3: Synnøves sang (Synnøve's Song), text: Bjørnstjerne Bjørnson, Norwegian poet (1832–1910).
No. 4: Ingrids Vise (Ingrid's Song), text: Bjørnson.
No. 6: Venevil (Little Venevil), text: Bjørnson.

[13] The numbers from the first volume of Kjerulf's songs:

No. 2: Længsel (Longing), text: Christian Winther, Danish author (1796–1876).
No. 3: Du frågar mig, min hjertans kär (You Ask Me, My Beloved), text: Emanuel Geibel, German author (1815–94).
No. 4: Det var da (It was then), text: Johan Ludvig Runeberg, Finnish author (1804–77).
No. 6: Lokkende Toner (Enticing Tones), text: Welhaven.
No. 8: Så ensam uti natten (So Lonesome in the Night), text from a Viking saga.
No. 9: Hvile i Skoven (Rest in the Forest), text: Welhaven.
No. 11: Spansk Romans (Spanish Romance), text from a Spanish songbook.
No. 13: Kärlekspredikan (A Sermon of Love), text: Friedrich Rückert, German author (1788–1866).
No. 14: I Skoven (In the Forest), text: Winther.
No. 36: Aftenstemning (Evening Mood), text: Bjørnson.
No. 37: Søvnen (The Sleep), text: Bjørnson.
No. 38: Dulgt Kjærlighed (Hidden Love), text: Bjørnson.
No. 45: Længsel (Longing), text: Theodor Kjerulf, Norwegian poet, Halfdan Kjerulf's brother (1825–88).

In the second volume, the first song—no. 47—is exceptionally charming by virtue of its simple melody. So also is no. 49 and especially no. 50, with its ethereal harmonies. No. 51 is wonderful—light and airy, but difficult to sing clearly. No. 55, too, has some beautiful passages. No. 60 is very poetic even though it is not noteworthy. No. 61 is certainly coquettish. And no. 66, "Land of the Elves", must also be singled out. All of the songs from 75 to 79 are noteworthy. No. 81, "The Whispering of the Elves", is typical, and finally no. 83, despite the simplicity of its structure, harbors true magic.[14]

All of the songs mentioned here are unusually melodious, and the accompaniments are most delicate and well adapted to the voice. But—although these songs present no major difficulties, they need nonetheless to be sung. Above all they demand a decisive *noblesse* suitable for this kind of music—indeed, a chastity of understanding—without which qualities Kjerulf's intentions will be lost. Hopefully the esteemed male concert singers will not miss the opportunity to enrich their repertoires with such significant and rewarding novelties. The time cannot be far off when Kjerulf's songs will also find a home in the German musical world and be acclaimed as creations of a truly beautiful soul.

Lastly, it can just be mentioned that the poet and experienced translator Edmund Lobedanz[15] has nearly always performed his difficult task successfully, and at all times with sensitivity and intelligence.

---

[14] The numbers from the second volume of Kjerulf's songs:

No. 47: Det var saa tyst (It was so still), text: Jeremiah (James) Joseph Callanan (1795–1829), Irish poet.

No. 49: Hyrdepigens Sang (The Song of the Shepherdess), text: Richard Monckton Milnes, English poet (1809–85).

No. 50: Serenade, text: Lord Byron, English author (1788–1824).

No. 51: Skovbækken (The Forest Brook), text: Robert Burns, Scottish poet (1759–96).

No. 55: Sjömannsflickan (The Seaman's Girl), text: Runeberg.

No. 60: Af Maanens Sølverglød (The Moon's Silvery Light), text: Geibel.

No. 61: Sangfugl hvorhen saa snar? (Songbird, where so soon?), text: Geibel.

No. 66: Alfeland (Land of the Elves), text: Welhaven.

No. 75: Buesnoren (The Bowstring), text: Welhaven.

No. 76: Syng, Syng! (Sing, Nightingale!), text: Theodor Kjerulf.

No. 77: Elveløbet (The River), text: Welhaven.

No. 78: Paa Fjeldet (On the Mountains), text: Welhaven.

No. 79: Romance af *Aly og Gulhundy* (Song from *Aly and Gulhundy*), text: Adam Oehlenschläger, Danish author (1779–1850).

No. 81: Af Alfernes Hvisken (The Whispering of the Elves), text: Welhaven.

No. 83: Nøkken (The River Sprite), text: Welhaven.

[15] Edmund Lobedanz (1820–82) was a Danish author of German parentage who also translated some of Grieg's song texts into German.

Wolfgang Amadeus Mozart (1896)

Grieg wrote two articles on Mozart. The first and longer of the two was written in response to a request of August 20, 1895, from *The Century Illustrated Monthly Magazine*.[1]

Grieg at first declined the invitation from *The Century* because of poor health, but a year later—August 8, 1896—he wrote again to Mr. Johnson telling him that he had finished the Mozart article and asking if he would still be interested. Johnson replied affirmatively, and on August 26 he wrote to Grieg that they were very pleased with the article and planned publication for 1897.[2] Grieg, at Johnson's request, submitted his article in German. The German manuscript was forwarded to American writer Henry T. Finck (1854–1926), who translated it into English. It was published in Finck's translation in the November 1897 issue of the magazine.[3]

After the Mozart essay had been published in *The Century*, it appeared in its original form in the Norwegian periodical *Samtiden* in 1898 (pp. 112–124), including five passages not to be found in the version printed in *The Century*. The present translation has been made from the Norwegian article as it appeared in *Samtiden*.

---

[1] *The Century* had previously published a lengthy article by Grieg on Robert Schumann (1810–56). See pp. 255–274. Robert U. Johnson (1853–1937), associate editor of *The Century*, was very complimentary regarding Grieg's earlier contribution: "The treatment of the Schumann article was exactly right. In this respect it was the most satisfactory paper in the series. We should like you to make a similar critique of Mozart, considering among other things how his music stands the wear and tear of the modern schools. As before, you will be good enough to remember that this is written for an untechnical audience, although our audience includes a large proportion of the amateur and professional musical people of America."

[2] See Grieg's letters to Mr. Johnson in Finn Benestad (ed.), *Edvard Grieg: Letters to Colleagues and Friends*. Columbus, Ohio, 2000, pp. 453–456.

[3] The editor had added an introduction written not by Finck but by another American music critic. It reads as follows: "Edvard Grieg, the author of the following article in *The Century's* series of articles on great musicians, is the foremost exponent of Scandinavian music. His life has been given to building up the artistic movement in Scandinavia, which has found expression in all forms of art, though perhaps most powerfully in letters. In artistic convictions and principles, and most powerfully in patriotic instinct, Grieg has necessarily found himself opposed to all the Wagnerian propaganda. The present review of Mozart is perhaps more sympathetic because Mozart, in awakening the spirit of German music, did what Grieg proposed to himself and accomplished for his own native land." Grieg was very unhappy with this introduction and sent corrections to *The Century* as well as to various editors in Europe and America. The statement that appeared in the Norwegian newspaper *Verdens Gang* of December 12, 1897, reads in English translation: "The editor has attached an introduction to my article in the November issue of *The Century* that contains two or three statements likely to create confusion in the minds of those who read the article and at the same time to place me in a false position in the music world. Therefore, I should like to get these statements corrected as quickly as possible. Firstly, I am not a representative of 'Scandinavian' but only of Norwegian music. The national characteristics of the three peoples—those, respectively, of the Norwegians, the Swedes and the Danes—are totally different and their music is equally different. Secondly, my artistic opinions and principles are by no means 'opposed to all the Wagnerian propaganda'. I have pointed out the Wagnerites' errors regarding Schumann and Mozart. But I myself make propaganda for Wagner wherever I can, though I am no adherent of the so-called 'Wagnerianism'. To tell the truth, I am not a devotee of any kind of 'ism'. I am neither more nor less than an admirer of Wagner—indeed, so great an admirer of him that there is hardly anyone who admires him more than I. Thirdly, it is not the case, as the editor of *The Century* assumes, that my review of Mozart is 'more sympathetic because Mozart, in awakening the spirit of German music, did what Grieg proposed to himself and accomplished for his own native land.' I must protest most vehemently against such a statement. My boundless admiration for Mozart goes far beyond any regard for nationality. Moreover, it is not correct to suggest that Mozart's principal merit consists in his having 'awakened the spirit of German music'. Before Mozart, Bach—and later, Beethoven and Wagner—did this to a much greater extent."

In a letter to Grieg of January 7, 1898, Johnson expressed regret regarding the introductory lines and enclosed a long letter from the anonymous author of the introduction. The latter, however, expressed no regret and retracted nothing.

An English writer asks, "What kind of face would Bach, Handel, Haydn and Mozart make if they heard a music-drama by Wagner?"[4] I shall not attempt to answer for the first three, but it is safe to say that Mozart, the universal genius whose soul was free of philistinism and one-sidedness, would not only be wide-eyed but would be as delighted as a child over all the new advances in drama and orchestra. It is in this light that Mozart must be viewed.

Speaking of Mozart is like speaking of a god. When Gretchen asks Faust, "Do you believe in God?" he answers, "Who dares name him, who confess him?"[5] It is in these profound words of Goethe that I would express my feelings for Mozart. Where he is greatest, he embraces all times. What does it matter if this or that generation is so blasé as to want to overlook him? Beauty is eternal, and the edict of fashion can obscure it only for a moment. So far as our day is concerned, it is good that Wagner has inscribed the name of Mozart on his shield. His belief in Mozart is indubitably evident from his writings,[6] and he has thereby taken a position in sharp opposition to those musicians of our time who are so advanced that they no longer care to hear Mozart's music and only grudgingly give it a place in their concert programs.[7] I hope that this arrogant ignorance has not taken root among [my] readers[8] and it is, therefore, my intention to speak to them on the assumption that they are favorably disposed toward the unattainable master.

My use of the word "unattainable" may grate on the ears of many readers. For what shall we say about Bach, Beethoven and Wagner? But in a certain sense, Mozart is the unattainable one even when he is compared with these heroes. In

---

[4] German composers Johann Sebastian Bach (1685–1750), George Frederick Handel (1685–1759), Joseph Haydn (1732–1809), and Richard Wagner (1813–83).

[5] From *Faust*, Part I, scene "In the Garden ("Im Garten"), by Johann Wolfgang von Goethe (1749–1832).

[6] Richard Wagner, *Sämtliche Schriften*, vol. 1, Leipzig (1871), in the chapter "Über das deutsche Musikwesen", pp. 160–161: "Finally we see, however, that it was a German who raised the Italian opera to the perfect ideal. In this way he extended and ennobled it to universality and gave it to his countrymen. This German, this greatest and most divine genius was Mozart." Translated from Hella Brock, *Edvard Grieg als Musikschriftsteller*, Altenmedingen 1999, p. 178, footnote 2.

[7] On November 18, 1896—during the period when Finck was translating the article—Grieg sent a letter to Johnson requesting some changes in his essay: "Instead of [what I have written] I wish to have the following: 'It is too bad that in his writings Wagner has not proclaimed the same unambiguous admiration for Mozart that he has expressed for such other great masters as Bach, Beethoven, Gluck (1714–87) and Weber (1786–1826). By this omission he has contributed in no small degree to the emergence in our day of a group of musicians for whom the most important thing is to appear modern, i.e. to adopt Wagner's views on everything. There is a possibility that Wagner has not exactly idolized Mozart. Consequently, there is no need for us to do it either! Had the Bayreuth master been able to foresee the consequences of his silence regarding Mozart he would certainly have disassociated himself most emphatically from these hyper-modern musicians who fancy themselves so modern that they can no longer stand Mozart's music." Grieg's letter to Johnson was forwarded to Finck, who advised Grieg to drop the changes. Grieg obviously listened to his advice, and the essay was printed in *The Century* and subsequently in Norwegian and German periodicals without the changes. In a letter of February 23, 1900, Grieg expressed his gratitude to Finck for having "prevented the appearance [in the essay] of an erroneous assertion on my part regarding Wagner."

[8] Grieg allowed the text to be varied slightly at this point to adapt it to different readerships. In the American version he wrote, "in the healthy musical youth of the free West". In the Norwegian version this was changed to "among *Samtiden's* readers."

Bach, Beethoven and Wagner we admire above all the depth and energy of the human spirit; in Mozart, the divine instinct. His loftiest inspirations seem untouched by human labor. Unlike the creations of the other masters mentioned, no trace of effort remains in the forms in which he cast his material. Mozart has the childlike, happy Aladdin[9] nature that overcomes all difficulties as if they were child's play. He creates like a god, effortlessly.

Let us dwell for a moment on the world of beauty that we call Mozart. His life extended from 1756 to 1791. What a short span of time! What an ocean of works! Had Mozart done nothing else in his whole life except write music, this large quantity would have been astonishing. But only when we consider how much time was taken up by concert tours do we begin to get a proper understanding of the unique rapidity with which he worked. Schubert,[10] who did not live even as long as Mozart, is his equal in this respect. But Schubert's life was quiet and secluded.

What above all excites our admiration for the child Mozart, in addition to his supreme talent, is his precocity. His mastery of the technique of composition is just as astonishing as his concert achievements on the piano. The phenomenon can be explained only by his upbringing. No other composer, perhaps—not even Mendelssohn[11]—received such training. We know that Mozart's father, who was an excellent musician himself, devoted his whole life and work above all to making a man of his son while at the same time guiding and developing his musical talent. When we see the young Mozart write in a letter, "Next to God comes papa,"[12] we understand how highly he regarded his father. In his moving filial love we find one of the pillars on which rests the purity of his art. Thus, his early mastery of technique and of the pure beauty of form he undoubtedly owes to the upbringing he received in his loving home.

His early and complete mastery of composition inevitably evokes an interesting comparison with Wagner. Both of these composers won immortality with their operas. Both threw themselves with all the enthusiasm of youth into this branch of art. Wagner's experience, which was acquired by early activity as a conductor, has its counterpart in the strict training that Mozart went through in his compositions, which he began producing already in his childhood. The result in both cases was clarity. Both of these musicians were from the beginning complete masters of the complex apparatus required to write an opera—an apparatus which most composers learn to control only after long and laborious effort, with

---

[9] Aladdin (Arabian *Ala ad-din*), the main character in one of the fairytales in *A Thousand and One Nights*.
[10] Austrian composer Franz Schubert (1797–1828).
[11] German composer Felix Mendelssohn (1809–47).
[12] Hella Brock, *op. cit.*, p. 179 footnote 5, states that this saying is not to be found in Mozart's letters. It was, however, quoted in a letter from trumpeter Andreas Schachtner in a letter to Mozart's sister Maria Anna—"Nannerl" (1757–1829). Schachtner writes that it was a favorite phrase with Mozart.

Wolfgang Amadeus Mozart. Posthumous oil portrait by Barbara Krafft.

hard struggles and big disappointments. Let us place side by side the two youthful masterworks, *The Abduction from the Seraglio* and *Tannhäuser*. There is no vacillation in either of them, but complete certainty regarding the aim as well as the choice of means. On the basis of this technical mastery, each artist's individuality develops with astonishing speed. The step from *Tannhäuser* to *Lohengrin* is just as big as the step from *The Abduction* to *Figaro*.[13]

Lohengrin and *Figaro*! The warm light of fully conscious personality shines from each note of these two masterworks. And when we look further at the creative activity of those two composers, what melancholy seizes us as we contemplate Mozart's fate! All of Wagner's most important works were still to be written—yes, also Mozart's two greatest works, it is true: *Don Giovanni* and *The Magic Flute*[14]; but after them his life was snuffed out just as his manhood was beginning. Mozart's death before he had completed his thirty-fifth year is perhaps the greatest loss the musical world has ever suffered. Of modern masters, the one who with respect to form most resembled Mozart—Mendelssohn—lived

---

[13] *The Abduction from the Seraglio* (1782) and *The Marriage of Figaro* (*Le Nozze di Figaro*, 1786), operas by Mozart; *Tannhäuser* (1845) and *Lohengrin* (1850), operas by Wagner.

[14] *Don Giovanni* (1787) and *The Magic Flute* (1791).

only a little longer; and it was fortunate for him that he died then, for he had already reached the zenith of his development. How different with Mozart! To his last hour his genius continued to develop. In *The Magic Flute* and the *Requiem*[15] we get a hint that new, hidden springs were about to gush forth. That Mozart learned to know and love Bach so late in his life must be viewed as an essential circumstance in connection with this fact. The deep fervor with which he allowed this man—about whom Beethoven said: "His name should not be *Bach* (brook) but *Ocean*"—to take root in his own personality we observe, among other things, in the lovely figured chorale[16] in the last act of *The Magic Flute*. As for Wagner, it was his polyphonic skill that secured him his later triumphs; and that same skill would have led Mozart to new triumphs had he been permitted to live longer. For it was this skill that, despite Italian influence, lay in the depth of his Germanic soul, and that Bach first helped him to release from the hidden depths of his own personality.

It has been said that unprincipled people took rapacious advantage of Mozart in the last years of his life and thus hastened his death. Schikaneder,[17] the author of the more than dubious libretto of *The Magic Flute*, did indeed contribute to giving the world this Mozart masterwork. But if, as has been said, he was one of those who dared to exploit Mozart for their own selfish ends and thus pull him down to their own level, then woe to him and his memory! In that case we can understand why he, when he heard of Mozart's death, went around like a man possessed and shouted, "His ghost pursues me everywhere—stands constantly before my eyes!" But even if he helped to break down Mozart's health and thus to shorten his life, he did not succeed in impairing the loftiness of his creative power, as *The Magic Flute* proves. Schikaneder is mere superficiality. In the hands of Mozart, even the superficial becomes symbolic, and a deep ethical spirit pervades the whole work.

When I hear people exclaim, "Yes, but what an abominable text!" I reply, "Yes—but don't you understand that the text has been recreated by the music, ennobled by it, and thereby elevated far above triviality?" If music did not have this power, many of its greatest masterworks would be utterly unpalatable. I can easily understand that an erudite man of letters who is incapable of hearing how the text is refined and vivified by the music, one who looks at it from a purely literary standpoint, might find it disagreeable to listen to *The Magic Flute*—yes, even to operas with much better texts. A great composer knows how to animate each detail of the poem, no matter how inane it may be; and he who attends an

---

[15] *Requiem* (1791) was unfinished from Mozart's hand.

[16] Norwegian: "figurerede Koral"; German: "figurierter Choral". The words denote a species of organ chorale in which a certain melodic figure is used consistently, in one or several of the contrapuntal parts, against the plain notes of the chorale.

[17] Austrian dramatist, theater director, actor, singer and composer Emanuel Schikaneder (1751–1812).

opera performance with basically literary interests runs the risk of missing the most inspired moments. For, strange as it may sound, such moments often soar the highest against a low literary background. There are excellent texts that absolutely require music. The following story is told regarding a great modern poet who heard Wagner's *Tristan and Isolde* for the first time. As is well known, there are scenes in this music-drama which, because of their long duration, must seem not only tiring but downright parodic to all for whom the text is not idealized by the music. The poet had gone to the theater with no prior bias, and for a time he also watched what transpired on stage with a serious and expectant countenance. But after awhile he could no longer sustain it, and despite the tragic situation a smile suddenly crept over his lips. The smile grew into laughter that in the end shook the bench so violently that the friend who was with him had to whisper in his ear, "My goodness, X . . . , we can leave if you wish." "Yes, we can!" groaned the poet, who had also begun to realize how painful the situation had become. And in the middle of the act the two men made their way to the door. I offer this story as food for thought, especially for those who listen to an opera like *The Magic Flute* first from a literary, and then from a musical, point of view. Such people will always say, "Yes, but look at the text!" We must advance so far, in our understanding of a drama consisting of words and music, that we comprehend that music at times supplements the words and *vice versa*. Otherwise works such as *The Magic Flute* will for many remain like the book with seven seals.[18]

When we compare Mozart and Wagner, the truth of the proverb "Extremes touch one another"[19] forces itself upon us. That these two masters represent the "extremes" is easily understood by any lover of music, but perhaps it will be necessary to show where they "touch one another". To be sure, Weber must be regarded as Wagner's immediate predecessor; but when Gluck is mentioned— and not unjustly—as the man on whose shoulders Wagner stands, neither must we forget how much Wagner owes to Mozart. For Mozart's greatness lies in the fact that his influence on the music-drama extends right down to our day. I think, for example, of the highly developed recitative, where Mozart more and more trod upon paths that it was left for Wagner, in his dialogue, to develop still further for the modern music-drama. A few recitatives of Donna Anna and Elvira in *Don Giovanni* set the pattern according to which our whole concept of the recitative has been fashioned. That Wagner also knew how to make direct use of Mozart

---

[18] An allusion to Revelation 5:1.

[19] This is a literal translation of the Norwegian "Yderlighederne berører hinanden" and of the German "Gegensätze berühren einander" used by Grieg, both of which appear to be derived from the French "Les extrêmes se touchent", a line coined by Jean de La Bruyère (1645–95) in *Caractères* (1687). Finck, in his translation of Grieg's article, uses a similar proverb, "Extremes meet", which comes from Louis Sébastien Mercier (1740–1814), *Tableaux de Paris* (1782), used in Thomas Hood (1799–1845), "The Doves and the Crows".

is evident, oddly enough, at one place in *Lohengrin* which, albeit with genuine Wagnerian coloring, in its conception has its musical counterpart in *Don Giovanni*. Compare, for example, Ortrud's lines in the second act of *Lohengrin*:

> *Strike them with death who profane your altars!*
> *And strengthen my soul to avenge your wrongs!!* [20]

with the conclusion of the first act of *Don Giovanni*, with the music to Donna Anna's words and the chorus: "Tremble, wretched evil-doer!"[21]

I mention this in passing to show that the Wagnerites would do best to speak softly when they talk about ignoring Mozart. This contempt would be too laughable to require being taken seriously were it not for the fact that so many of the best opera conductors are one-sided Wagnerites. How often in Germany have I not heard outstanding performances of Wagner's music-dramas under the leadership of the same conductors who rush carelessly through a Mozart opera in the most shameful manner! Indeed, in some places these operas are even left to second-rate conductors, while the principal conductor is reserved for Wagner. Under such circumstances, it is expecting too much to think that one should leave a Mozart performance with an impression that is even approximately commensurate with the opera's worth. It can drive one to despair to think that such a condition is tolerated—yes, even more, that it is approved. But it is also a satisfaction to be able to cite exceptions! As one of the most eminent of these I shall mention Arthur Nikisch.[22] For him, that which is great is great, whether the composer's name be Wagner or Mozart. His masterly interpretations of Wagner's *The Ring of the Nibelung*, *Tristan* and *The Mastersingers*[23] will live in memory among all those who were so fortunate as to live in Leipzig at the time when he conducted the opera there. But it is equally certain that they will remember his performance of *Don Giovanni*—his reverent interpretation and careful attention to detail, not least in the recitatives. On these occasions the auditorium echoed with the same jubilation that one hears at Wagner performances. May the time soon come when at least the masters who belong to history will be treated with equal justice by their only representatives, the musical directors in whose hands their fate lies! May these gentlemen be brought to a full understanding of their great responsibility!

---

[20] *Stärkt mich im Dienste eurer heilgen Sache,*
Vernichtet den abtrün'gen, schnöden Wahn!

[21] *Bebe, schwarzer Missethäter!*

[22] Hungarian-German conductor Arthur Nikisch (1855–1922) was appointed musical director of the Leipzig City Theater in 1878; in 1895 he became conductor of the Gewandhaus Orchestra in Leipzig and of the Berlin Philharmonic Orchestra, and in 1905/06 he took the position as opera director in Leipzig.

[23] The *Ring of the Nibelung* is a tetralogy consisting of four music-dramas: *The Rhinegold* (Das Rheingold, 1854); *The Valkyrie* (Die Valküre, 1856); *Siegfried* (1869) and *Twilight of the Gods* (Götterdämmerung, 1874). The complete first performance of the tetralogy took place in Bayreuth in the summer of 1876. Grieg wrote eight articles about these performances for the Norwegian newspaper *Bergenposten*. See pp. 290–318.

We find here the hidden principal reason for the fact that our generation acts as if it has outgrown Mozart. If a Wagner music-drama were presented in as slovenly a manner as Mozart's operas often are, we would see some strange things; and we will see such things when the inevitable reaction sets in. Then Wagner will get that which is Wagner's and Mozart that which is Mozart's. Just wait until a more objective and reverent period arrives following the propaganda of the Wagnerites!

All art that belongs to history must be viewed historically. All of our day's achievements in the areas of orchestration, harmony etc. had their counterparts in Mozart's time. He, too, was new—so new that his boldness aroused strong opposition among many musicians of the time. And Wagner will also one day be seen from the same distance and will be judged in the context of history. Then it will be seen how much it means to stand upright like Mozart in spite of changing times. It is not difficult to stand when one is surrounded by nothing but the supportive sentiments and the full recognition of the entire younger generation— a generation, moreover, that has been brought up to make proselytes for the master's cause, and that will not rest until his ideas have been forced upon all.

Mozart had no pupils and had to entrust his works to the fortuitous caprices of posterity. A new generation found new tasks in the field of the music-drama. Mozart was not only neglected; we have heard how his operas are performed in opera houses throughout Europe. The scandalous performance of *The Magic Flute* in Paris showed that Mozart did not have a single person to defend his cause and his ideals.[24] Mozart's operas had a fate similar to that of the magnificent Catholic buildings of the Middle Ages that were brutally plastered over by the Protestants after the Reformation. Posterity did everything it could to obscure their beauty. {But as people little by little scraped off the plaster and beheld with wonder the original treasure-trove of beauty it concealed, so also are Mozart's works beginning once again to be dimly perceived by the few who have begun the labor of justice—through beautiful performances worthy of his genius—to retrieve him from the dust of irreverence that, in the course of time, has attached itself to all the fine features of his noble countenance.}[25]

But, someone will ask, whence comes this lack of respect for Mozart among so many talented young musicians? This is the heart of the matter. Many of us, in our early youth, have loved—indeed, idolized—Mozart, but then we ate of the fruit of modern knowledge—a sin that, like the sin in the Garden of Eden, has driven us out of our Paradise. Some of us were lucky: We avoided a complete fall and found our way back. I openly admit that I, too, have undergone this

---

[24] Grieg is referring to a Paris performance of *The Magic Flute* in 1801, in which several sections were deleted and parts from other Mozart operas were inserted, for instance the "Champagne Aria" from *Don Giovanni*.

[25] Here and elsewhere, braces signify material that was omitted from the *Century* version of Grieg's article.

transformation: I loved Mozart, then I lost him for a time, but I rediscovered him and shall never lose him again. A modern musician can easily find the cause of these transformations; it lies in the relation of the young to drawing and colors. We commence our art education by learning the lines. Our teachers depict for us the great masters of the past, who in this respect have never been surpassed. We study them and learn to love them and imitate them. We still do not know modern art at this time; as far as possible it is kept away from us. But then we are allowed out for the first time—and look! The vivid, shining colors to which our time has given the place of honor call enchantingly to us from every page. We are intoxicated, enthralled. We forget our former ideals and surrender unconditionally to the seductions of the intoxicating colors. This is what happened to the preceding generation, and the newest of the new composers find their pleasure more than ever in drowning themselves in the sea of color, where no ideas or forms or lines can save them any more or prevent them from sinking deeper and deeper. "Color, color and more color" seems to be their motto. To be sure, if one looks carefully, one can still find a few lines here and there, though more often than not they are wretchedly drawn. But there are signs of an impending change. Already a small minority feels so strongly the need for clean lines that we can hope to see it lead before long to some result. I do not think that the art of the future, like a Rinaldo,[26] will flee from color as from an alluring siren that at the sound of the Crusaders' simple, chaste melody loses all her charm. No! The new art will first of all preach the gospel of the true joy of life. It will fuse colors and lines and it will show that it has its roots in the entire past and that it draws its nourishment from old as well as new masters.

{It is understandable and excusable that the youth are dazzled by the world of color that suddenly makes its appearance. But young people grow older, and when they have had their fill of nothing but color, employed to achieve modernity's most sophisticated effects, they will instinctively look back to find the masters of drawing, and out of the various periods will create an art in which colors and lines are equally apportioned. We bid this happy instinct welcome. It will also bring us a new generation of men capable of fusing the old and the new, fully equipped for the great task of being representatives for the masters of all times—and then a Mozartean era will return. A famous picture of Vautier[27] depicts a supplicant. In the anteroom of the home of a great man the most varied group of people is waiting for an audience. Among these is a man in simple garb

---

[26] The title role in George Frederick Handel's opera by that name (1711).

[27] Swiss-German painter Marc Louis Benjamin Vautier (1829–98). In the original version of the article Grieg had stated that the picture was by German painter Ludwig Knaus (1829–1910). In his letter to associate editor R. U. Johnson of November 18, 1896, he requested that the attribution be changed. He could have spared himself the effort, however, as the entire paragraph enclosed within braces was omitted from *The Century* version of the article. *Samtiden* included the paragraph but did not make the change, nor did it appear in the abbreviated German version of the article in *Die Zeit.*

who, upon being addressed, speaks these telling words, which are the motto of the picture: "I can wait." So it is with Mozart—even if in another sense he is the great man and not the supplicant. He can wait. He is modest. He does not ostentatiously demand to be given an audience. He will wait until his time comes—for he knows that it will come.}

What I have said to this point concerns above all Mozart's dramatic works, but it can with full justice be applied also to his orchestral works. In the complicated circumstances of our time it is natural to become a specialist. Thus we see Wagner concentrating exclusively on the music-drama. The older school was more comprehensive, and it is especially true of Mozart that his greatness as an opera composer must not delude us into overlooking other facets of his oeuvre. Here we have a new evidence of Mozart's universality. In church music, chamber music, in the concert hall—everywhere he is equally great. Fortunately, in the course of time Mozart has been less mishandled in the concert hall than in the theater, thanks primarily to outstanding virtuosos, many of whom were excellent musicians. Under the protection of these masters, many of Mozart's most beautiful piano concertos, sonatas, string quartets and quintets have managed to retain their place in the concert-goers' souls as revelations of the most sublime beauty. Indeed, even in the art song, where new times have produced new masters who opened new pathways for this genre—even here a little song such as "The Violet" can stand comparison with the songs of Schubert, Schumann, Franz and Brahms.[28]

Several composers in our time have attempted to subject Mozart to a modernization process in order to make him more palatable to a public whose taste buds have been destroyed by strong spices. A dangerous undertaking. Thus the Russian master Tchaikovsky[29], with admirable discretion and sensitivity, has collected a few of Mozart's more or less well-known piano and choral pieces into an orchestral suite in modern instrumental garb. The author of this article has himself tried, through the use of a second piano, to give some of Mozart's piano sonatas a sonority that appeals to modern ears; and in his own defense he wants to add that he did not change a single one of Mozart's notes, thus showing the master the reverence that we owe to him.[30] I do not mean to suggest that this was an act of necessity. Far from it. Assuming, however, that one does not do like Gounod, who transformed a Bach prelude into a modern, sentimental and trivial piece[31]—a process of which I thoroughly disapprove—but tries to preserve the

---

[28] German songwriter Robert Franz (1815–92); Johannes Brahms (1833–96).

[29] Peter Tchaikovsky (1840–93): *Suite no. 4 "Mozartiana"*, op. 61, which is an arrangement and orchestration of four Mozart pieces.

[30] In 1877, Grieg made arrangements for two pianos of four of Mozart's piano sonatas: *Mozart's Piano Sonatas with a Freely Composed Second Piano Part*, EG 113: F Major, KV 533 & 494; C Minor, KV 475 & 457; C Major, KV 545; G Major, KV 189 h = KV 283.

[31] Bach-Gounod: "Ave Maria,"—Gounod's melody on top of Bach's first prelude (C Major) from *The Well-tempered Clavier*, vol. I.

unity of style, then there certainly is no reason to protest because someone attempts a modernization in order to show his admiration for an old master.

Mozart's orchestral works show us that he has colors fresh enough to charm the ear both of our time and probably on into an indefinite future. We still have much to learn from Mozart's orchestration with regard to clarity and sonority. They who would study beauty of sound can open Mozart's scores wherever they wish and they will reap rich rewards. But this orchestral beauty of sound has the priceless quality of being dispensable: Creating a piano reduction of an orchestral score of Mozart does not thereby reduce it to nothing (as is the case, for example, with the scores of Berlioz[32] and his imitators); for Mozart's music is such that it can be deprived of its colors without losing its charm.

A glance at his three wonderful symphonies in E-flat Major, G Minor and C Major[33] (the last-named of which is called the "Jupiter" symphony because it seems perfect, as if created by a god), demonstrates this fully. They show us the master at the zenith of his powers. All three were written in the summer of 1788, i.e., three years before his death. It is difficult to say which of the three symphonies warrants the highest admiration. We note immediately the huge step from Haydn's to Mozart's handling of this, the most sublime of instrumental forms, and our thoughts turn automatically toward the young Beethoven, who, with no break worthy of mention, went on from the point where Mozart reached those lofty peaks which he alone had been chosen to ascend. In the opening measures of the E-flat Major symphony, just before the first *allegro*, we encounter harmonic progressions of unprecedented boldness. They are introduced in such a surprising way that they will always sound with a new freshness. The minuet in this symphony, arranged for piano, has traveled around the world on the concert programs of many virtuosos. In the G-Minor symphony, Mozart reveals himself to us in all his grace and depth and genuine emotion. It is worth noting what surprising effects he attains in this symphony with the help of chromatic progressions. With the exception of Bach, who here as everywhere is the foundation on which all modern music rests, no one has been as adept as Mozart in employing the chromatic scale to give musical expression to the sublimest of the sublime. We must go all the way to Wagner before we find chromaticism used for the expression of profound emotion. In Spohr,[34] who used it extensively, and who in so many respects followed Mozart, it has no deeper significance.

In the "Jupiter" symphony we are astounded above all by the playful ease with which the biggest problems of the art of composition are overcome. No one who is not initiated into the secrets of the art can have any idea of the astonishing

---

[32] French composer Hector Berlioz (1803–69).

[33] Symphonies no. 39–41, KV 543, 550 and 551.

[34] German composer Louis Spohr (1784–1859). As for Grieg's relation to Spohr and his music, see "My First Success", p. 81, and Grieg's letter to Henry T. Finck in Benestad (ed.), *op. cit.*, p. 229.

contrapuntal knowledge Mozart manifests in the humorous playfulness of the *finale*. And then this ocean of euphony! Mozart's feeling for euphony was in truth so absolute that it is impossible to find in the entire corpus of his works a single instance where euphony is sacrificed for other considerations. That is not true of Beethoven, who never hesitated to waive euphony in order to achieve a higher goal. With him began the new era, the motto of which can be expressed in the words: "Truth first, then beauty." And here we find Schumann as the first composer who followed in Beethoven's footsteps.

Of Mozart's chamber compositions we shall mention as especially admirable the *String Quintet in G Minor*[35] (notice the splendid chromaticism in the first theme), the *Piano Quintet in E-flat Major*, and the *Piano Quartet in G Minor*.[36] It is a curious fact that whenever Mozart composes something in G minor, he always surpasses himself. In the beautiful middle movement of the piano quintet he amused himself by introducing the motive from Zerlina's aria in *Don Giovanni* —"If you are very good, I will assist you"[37]—and how beautiful is this reverie! Of his string quartets, the so-called "six famous ones" are rightly admired. The introductory section of the C-major quartet also contains bold chromatic passages that even liberal musicians of his day could not swallow. The music historian Fétis[38] won unenviable notoriety for his foolhardy attempt to change this introduction, which he found "impossible": a typical critic who, like a wet dog, lies down on the very best places.

Of the piano concertos, the one in D minor is the most famous and the most beautiful. Parenthetically, I will recommend the use of Mozart's original version rather than the Hummel[39] edition, which is supplied with superfluous ornamentations and other arbitrary alterations. A typical illustration of Mozart's method of work can be adduced here. Not long ago I saw in Vienna the manuscript of the D-minor concerto.[40] In the *finale*, Mozart had for some reason or other been interrupted in his work. When he resumed, he did not continue from the point where he had previously stopped. He crossed out the excellent fragment and wrote a new *finale*—the one we all know! No laborious quest to find the lost thread! It appears as if Mozart preferred to complete a large form in one single great burst of effort. No wonder, therefore, that even the most practiced eye and ear cannot find any trace of splicing. We can only look wonderingly at this way of working, which only the few chosen ones are privileged to employ.

In his piano trios Mozart took a kind of siesta, so to speak. He has often given

---

[35] Grieg wrote *String Quartet in G Minor* but he obviously meant the *String Quintet [no. 3] in G Minor*, KV 516.

[36] *Piano Quintet in E-flat Major*, KV 452, and *Piano Quartet in G Minor*, KV 478.

[37] Grieg quotes this line from *Don Giovanni* in German: "Wenn du fein fromm bist, will ich dir helfen".

[38] French musicologist, critic, teacher and composer François-Joseph Fétis (1784–1871).

[39] Austrian pianist, composer, teacher and conductor Johann Nepomuk Hummel (1778–1837), who wrote cadenzas for seven of Mozart's piano concertos.

[40] Grieg is probably referring to the D-minor concerto from 1785, KV 466.

us some of his best work, on the other hand, in his sonatas for violin, and not least in those for piano. We stand in awe as we observe the huge step from Haydn's naiveté to Mozart's profundity. That he is not always equally profound should not surprise us. Quite the opposite. We read in Mozart's biography about his desperate situation that compelled him to compose for all and sundry, rarely out of inner impulse, and we understand what infinitely rich inner resources he must have had to draw upon when so many of these works, too, have the power to stand the test of time.

{The willingness with which Mozart welcomed every request for compositions also casts the most favorable light on his amiable character. His many piano variations and concert arias bear witness to this amiability, and even if they hardly have the vitality to interest audiences of our time they nonetheless characterize the master and cast a sidelight on Mozart the man. Thus, they were not written in vain. In the surroundings of his time these works certainly made their mark. What would we not give today to hear the master's own tones from the harpsichord during one of the "academies" (corresponds to our "concerts") that Mozart gave in Vienna. The site of these concerts still exists on the first floor of a building where the restaurant—not unknown to musicians—"Zum rothen Igel" ["The Red Hedgehog"] in our day attracts artists such as Brahms to its modest and unassuming rooms. Yes, had the phonograph been invented by that time, we could now have heard Mozart play. Then we would be spared all the dust that the musicologists have stirred up about Mozart's tempi, his dynamics, the style of his performance, etc. Much useless strife, much hate and enmity would have been avoided. The future, in that respect, will be better off than we are. It will be able to maintain both a visual and an aural picture of our time and its mission. Everything that is great will be transmitted to people via the wonders of science; the future will seem closer to happiness—until perhaps a great natural catastrophe sweeps it all away, and everything begins anew from the beginning. New times, new forms for the same yearnings, the same longings. The eternal circular motion. But now I am going astray.}

Before I conclude this essay, I want to dwell for a moment on Mozart's swan song, the work that, filled with the spirit of eternity, was conceived and born when the cold hand of death was already outstretched toward the master. Perhaps more than any of his other compositions, his *Requiem* shows us, even in its uncompleted form, what incalculable treasures he took with him to the grave. Which parts of this work are Mozart's and which are not is a question that now perhaps should be regarded as resolved. But in view of all the treasures contained in the *Requiem*, we nonetheless cannot refrain from expressing our surprise over the fact that the same master who could write a "Requiem aeternam", a "Rex tremendae", a "Recordare", a "Confutatis", a "Lacrymosa"—whose nobility is beyond description—that this same master could incorporate in the same work a number like

"Tuba mirum" with its worse than poor beginning, its absolutely desperate obligato trombone (or bassoon) and its unrelenting worldly pomp.[41] If this is really Mozart, only one explanation is possible: that he, for the sake of convenience, used a fragment that was composed at a much earlier period. It appears to be strongly influenced by the Italian school, {and I also well remember with what affection it was treated by an Italian ensemble at a performance in a Roman church. The solo part was even sung by *castrati*, which further robbed it of any shred of profundity. However: If one wishes to hear the choral movements of Mozart's *Requiem*, one should go to Italy. Never have I heard such vocal sonorities, such *pianissimos*, such mighty *crescendos*, such *fortissimos*. In the beautiful "Lacrymosa", where the whole mass of sound struggles upward in a great *crescendo*, at the end it was as if the arches of the church had to shatter. How many people have derived comfort and healing from these sounds! Ole Bull[42] asked his wife to play portions of Mozart's *Requiem* in his last moments. For us, Mozart's life comes to a beautiful, albeit melancholy, conclusion precisely through this *Requiem*. True, his body was allowed to be lowered into a poor, unidentified pauper's grave. But through his *Requiem* we follow him to higher spheres.}

Mozart stands for us as an incarnation of childlike *joie de vivre*, amiable good will and modesty. He was able to present his *Magic Flute* in Schikaneder's "theater shed" without compromising his artistic dignity. If he could look down to us, he would certainly say: "You modern masters, what is the purpose of all this commotion! Why do you want to dress in all this external dignity? It means nothing for your art; it only kills the original human feeling that is the real salt of art."

Although Mozart was not esteemed in accordance with his true worth during his lifetime, posterity, as is well known, has placed him in its pantheon as one of the greatest masters of all time. When I, in my discussion of him and his relation to our time, began by saying that he is still not respected as he deserves, I repeat that my remarks apply only to the class of modern musicians who both have the opportunity to perform his greatest works in a worthy manner in the theaters, and who nonetheless do not do so. Beethoven has been more fortunate. Belief in the trinity of Bach, Beethoven, Wagner has been elevated to an article of faith in the catechism of the new Romantic school. But it fails to acknowledge Mozart's merits, and it probably will be quite some time before the new Romanticism will decide to include Mozart in its primer. The blind one-sidedness of the young brood of new Romanticists reminds me of Hans Christian Andersen's[43] fairytale, *The Snow Queen*, where the story is told of a magic mirror

---

[41] In his unfinished *Requiem* score, Mozart only indicated the instrumentation of *Rex tremendae, Recordare, Confutatis* and *Tuba mirum*.

[42] Norwegian virtuoso violinist Ole Bull (1810–80).

[43] Famous Danish writer Hans Christian Andersen (1805–75), especially beloved for his children's stories.

that a band of demons carried through the air. They engaged in a lot of pranks as they flew, and in their overweening pride they dropped the mirror to the ground, where it broke into countless little pieces. One of the splinters flew into the eye of a nice little boy, and the result was that everything he saw—not only with his physical eye, but with the eye of his soul as well—was distorted. The beautiful seemed to be ugly, the large appeared small, and his common sense was destroyed by overripe knowledge, affectation and a hypercritical spirit. One could almost believe that many of our influential musicians have gotten a splinter from the magic mirror in their eyes that prevents them from seeing Mozart's beauty in its full glory. May what happened to the boy soon happen to them! By a lucky accident, the splinter was removed. The outward appearance of the precocious little monster disappeared, and the child entered his soul again.

{I conclude: Long live the art that, while scaling the loftiest heights and plumbing the deepest depths, nonetheless preserves—the child! Long live the incomparable master who taught us to love this child! Long live Mozart!}[44]

---

[44] Surprisingly, Grieg's verbal "coda" was omitted from the Century version of the article.

Mozart and His Significance
for Contemporary Music (1906)

Grieg's second article on Mozart was written upon invitation from the editor of *Neue Freie Presse* in Vienna in connection with the celebration on January 26, 1906, of the sesquicentennial of Mozart's birth. It is in considerable measure an abbreviation of the earlier article.[1] It exists in three versions: (I) Grieg's original German draft, preserved in Bergen Public Library; (II) the German version, "Mozart und seine Bedeutung für die musikalische Gegenwart", printed in *Neue Freie Presse* on January 21, 1906; and (III) a Norwegian version, "Mozart og hans Betydning for den musikalske Nutid", published in the Christiania newspaper *Verdens Gang*, also on January 21, 1906.[2] The English translation is based on the Norwegian version of the article as published in *Verdens Gang* (version III). Differences between this and the other two versions are indicated in the footnotes.

Mozart's greatness will shine forth in every era, as long as music exists.[3] If one generation or another should be so blasé as to[4] want to overlook him, what difference would it make? Beauty is eternal, and the laws of fashion can obscure it only for a short time. Mozart's significance for posterity can be judged only according to the light by which each succeeding generation is capable of discovering him.[5] Does our generation stand at the high level that is required to judge Mozart aright? Does our age have the discriminating view, the healthy naiveté, that are prerequisites to achieving a profound understanding of Mozart? Or better: Do the musical leaders of our time possess these qualities? Such questions must be said to be well suited for discussion, particularly at this time.

In the previous generation, it was above all Richard Wagner who dominated the scene. His admiration for Mozart is indubitably evident from his writings. In expressing himself as he did, he took a position in sharp opposition to those contemporary musicians who are so advanced that they can no longer stand to hear Mozart's music and only grudgingly grant it a place in their concert programs. But an era that harbors such an arrogant[6] imprudence can only be temporary and fortunately cannot seriously hurt the unattainable master.

My use of the word "unattainable" may perhaps jar on many ears. For what shall we then say about Bach, Beethoven and Wagner? But Mozart, compared to

---

[1] See Grieg's diary entries of January 14, 18 and 29, 1906.

[2] When Grieg undertook to write an article or letter in a foreign language, it was his practice to first write a Norwegian version. Then he would draft a translation to which he would make numerous revisions and corrections, and lastly he would make a fair copy of the revised draft. That is presumably what he did in the present case, but the original Norwegian draft is not extant.

[3] The phrase "as long as music exists" is missing in (II).

[4] The phrase "be so blasé as to" is missing in (II).

[5] This sentence is missing in (II).

[6] The word "arrogant" is missing in (II).

such heroes as Bach, Beethoven and Wagner, is the incomparably greatest. In Bach, Beethoven and Wagner we first of all admire the depth and energy of the human creative spirit, whereas in Mozart we admire the divine instinct. His loftiest inspirations seem untouched by human labor.[7] The ease with which the material is formed under his hands does not suggest victory through struggle as in the works of the other masters. Mozart is the childlike, happy Aladdin figure who overcomes all difficulties as if they were child's play.[8] He creates like a god, without pain.

Let us dwell for a moment on the world of beauty that we call Mozart.[9] He stayed for only 35 years on this globe! What would he have achieved if he had lived as long as Wagner? If we think of his astounding capacity for development, which was even increasingly evident in the last operas—*Figaro, Don Giovanni* and *The Magic Flute*—then we are gripped by sadness at Mozart's fate and at the treasures that were lost with him. That Mozart had to die in his early manhood is perhaps the greatest loss that the musical world has ever suffered. His development continued until his final hour.[10] In *The Magic Flute* and the *Requiem* we have a presentiment of new hidden sources that are about to break forth. Only near the end of his life did Mozart learn to know and love Bach. One of the compositions in which the deep sincerity with which he absorbed Bach is evident is the wonderful figured chorale in the last act of *The Magic Flute*. Wagner's later triumphs were indebted to such polyphonic mastery, and this mastery would have won new victories even for Mozart if the thread of his life had not been cut off so early. For it was the genuine feeling for polyphony that, despite the influences from the Italian school, lay at the bottom of Mozart's German nature—and it was only through Bach that he discovered it in the hidden depths of his own personality.

{When we compare Mozart with Wagner, the truth of the proverb "Extremes touch one another" lies near at hand. That these two masters represent the "extremes" is easily understood by every music lover, but it may be necessary to show where they "touch one another". To be sure, Gluck and Weber are regarded as Wagner's most important predecessors. However, we must not forget how much he owed to Mozart. For Mozart's greatness lies in the fact that his influence on the musical drama extends down to our own time. I think, for instance, of the recitatives in Mozart's later works, in which he trod on paths that Wagner was to develop further for the modern music-drama. Some of the recitatives by Donna Anna and Elvira in *Don Giovanni* create the patterns on which our understanding of the recitative is founded. That Wagner also understood how to pick up ideas from Mozart can, interestingly enough, be demonstrated by a passage in

---

[7] This sentence is missing in (II).

[8] The phrase "who overcomes all difficulties as if they were child's play" is missing in (II).

[9] This sentence is present only in (III).

[10] This sentence is present only in (III).

Lohengrin that has hitherto been ignored in this connection. It has a genuinely Wagnerian color, but it reveals a direct parallel [to a passage] in *Don Giovanni*.}[11] Just compare the music to Ortrud's words, "Strike them with death who profane your altars! And strengthen my soul to avenge your wrongs!" in the second act of *Lohengrin* and the music to the words of Donna Anna and the chorus, "Tremble, wretched evil-doer!" at the end of the first act of *Don Giovanni*.

I mention this to show that the Wagnerites[12] of our day ought to speak rather carefully about neglecting Mozart. Their behavior, ridiculous as it is, might seem to be of little significance. But if one considers the fact that so many of the best contemporary opera conductors are one-sided Wagnerites, then, unfortunately, this attitude towards Mozart has a very harmful impact. How frequently in Germany have I not heard Wagner's music-dramas presented in the most perfect performances by the same conductors who have rushed through a Mozart opera in a purely conventional way. Indeed, from time to time assistant conductors have been used for Mozart's works, while the principal conductor is reserved for Wagner. Under such circumstances, it is actually to demand too much that we should be expected to get a suitable impression from a performance of a Mozart opera that is only marginally commensurate with the worth of the opera itself. It is enough to drive one to despair that such things are tolerated, are even regarded as a matter of course.

People who like to look down on Mozart should not forget that he, too, was new at one time—yes, indeed, so modern that his audacity aroused strong opposition among many contemporary musicians. They should also realize that some day Wagner will be viewed at the same distance and judged historically. Then it will be seen how much it means to stand upright as Mozart did through the rocks and breakers of changing times. It is not difficult to stand when surrounded by a young and enthusiastic group of students who have been recruited specifically to make proselytes for the cause of their master—young people who will not rest until the master's ideas have been impressed upon the public consciousness.[13]

Mozart had no such group of students. He had to leave his works to the casual whims of posterity. He has not only been neglected. We also know, unfortunately, *how* his operas have been performed on the European stages. The scandalous first performance of *The Magic Flute* in Paris many years ago proved that the master,

---

[11] In (I), the text within the braces is abbreviated as follows: "As for Wagner's aforementioned veneration of Mozart, it is not strange that one can find a Mozartean influence on Wagner—and this influence should not be underestimated, even though Gluck and Weber must be regarded as his immediate predecessors. It was reserved for Wagner to develop further the extensive recitative in the modern music-drama, for which Mozart had broken new ground in his last operas. That Wagner did not escape direct allusions to Mozart is evident in a surprising way in a passage in *Lohengrin* which, although genuinely Wagnerian in color, in its conception has a counterpart in *Don Giovanni*."

[12] In (I) Grieg substitutes the word "neo-Romanticists" ("Neuromantiker") for the more pejorative "Wagnerianere" (Wagnerites).

[13] This paragraph is missing in (II).

Detail from a painting by Mozart's brother-in-law Joseph Lange. Constanze Mozart considered it an excellent likeness of her husband.

who had already been dead for a long time, had no one to champion his cause and his ideals.

The Mozart operas suffered the same fate as the magnificent Catholic buildings of the Middle Ages, which after the Reformation were brutally plastered over by the Protestants. Posterity did everything possible to obscure their beauty.[14] But just as one removes the successive layers of whitewash and discovers with astonishment the wealth of beauty that has lain hidden underneath, so also will the true spirit of Mozart's dramatic works be recognized by the few[15] who have devoted themselves—through beautiful, worthy performances—to the noble task of removing the layer of irreverent dust that through the years has covered and misrepresented the fine features of his noble face.[16]

What I have stated here applies mainly to Mozart's dramatic works. His orchestral works and his chamber music have fared much better. Fortunately, in the concert hall Mozart has, in the course of time, been subjected to much less distortion than the dramatic works. This has come about thanks in large part to good virtuosos, among whom there were even many brilliant musicians. Under

---

[14] (I) and (II) substitute "to rob them of their beauty".
[15] (I) and (II) substitute "unveiled by those people".
[16] (I) and (II) substitute "the works of the master".

the protection of these artists, a number of Mozart's most beautiful piano concertos, sonatas, string quartets and string quintets have been able to secure their place of honor as marvels of beauty in the consciousness of the concert public.

Ours is the age of colors, Mozart's was the age of lines. But Mozart's orchestral works provide abundant proof that he possessed colors that are vivid enough to captivate the unspoiled ear both in our time and, in all likelihood, into the indefinite future. With respect to clarity and sonority, we can still learn much from Mozart's instrumentation. Those who wish to study beauty of sound can open Mozart's scores wherever they wish, and they will reap rich rewards. His instrumentation, with the means available at that time, is exalted beyond all criticism. It is incomparable. Moreover, his music has the priceless characteristic of being able to get along without the flattering sonorities of the orchestra. Unlike many sensational orchestral works of recent years, an orchestral score of Mozart that is transferred to piano loses nothing in the process. In this respect, one could especially recommend to [adherents of] the newer German school that they take lessons from Mozart![17]

But our time can learn quite a lot, not only from Mozart the composer but also from Mozart the man. He stands before us as an incarnation[18] of childlike *joie de vivre*, amiable benevolence, and modesty. He could conduct *The Magic Flute* in Schikaneder's shed without compromising his artistic dignity. If he were able to look down upon us, he would certainly say: "You new masters, why gird yourselves in this external dignity? This can do nothing for your art. Quite the opposite: It only kills the true humanity, which for art, too, is the true salt."

The neo-Romanticists have endeavored to incorporate the trinity Bach, Beethoven, Wagner in their catechism. But not Mozart. Whether or not a long time will pass before they decide to include Mozart, who knows? If all signals are not delusive, the present extreme[19] Wagner cult will soon take on a normal character. Then Mozart—particularly on the stage[20]—will again beam in full glory, and his name, even among the progressive composers,[21] will conquer the place that is ready for him in the history of art.

The young crowd of talented and enthusiastic neo-Romanticists of our day—who, however, have wandered into a *cul-de-sac,* but who think they have a monopoly on the highest artistic ingenuity—remind me, in their blind one-sidedness, of the fairytale "The Snow-Queen" by the Danish author Hans Christian Andersen. The fairytale tells about a band of young demons who flew through the air with a magic mirror. They engaged in a lot of pranks as they flew,

---

[17] This paragraph is missing in (I) and (II).

[18] (I) and (II) substitute "a picture".

[19] The words "present extreme" are missing in (I) and (II).

[20] The words "particularly on the stage" are missing in (II).

[21] The words "his name, even among the progressive composers" are missing in (I) and (II).

and in their overweening pride they finally let the mirror fall to the ground, where it was smashed to bits—indeed, into millions of tiny pieces. One such tiny piece got into the eye of a good little boy, causing him to see everything distorted, not only with his physical eye but also with his spiritual eye. The beautiful seemed ugly, the big small, because precociousness, sophistry and hyper-criticism had destroyed his sound senses. One would think that many of the representatives of the young musicians who set the tone in our day have gotten such a demonic little splinter in their eyes, rendering them incapable of perceiving Mozart's beauty in all its glory. May what happened to the boy happen also to them: By a lucky accident, he was able to weep again—and suddenly he was freed from the splinter. The outward appearance of the precocious little monster disappeared, and the child entered his soul again.

I conclude: Long live the art that, while scaling the loftiest heights and plumbing the deepest depths, nonetheless preserves—the child! Long live the incomparable[22] master who taught us to love this child! Long live Mozart!

---

[22] (I) and (II) substitute "great".

Rikard Nordraak's Songs Op. 2 (1865)

Grieg frequently acknowledged his debt to his friend and colleague Rikard Nordraak (1842–66). In a letter of February 9, 1897, to Norwegian composer Iver Holter (1850–1941), he wrote: "Nordraak's importance for me is *not* exaggerated. It really is so: Through him and only through him was I truly awakened. (. . .) He was a dreamer, a visionary, but he lacked the inborn ability to bring his art to the same level as his vision. (. . .) I willingly admit that the influence of Nordraak was not exclusively musical. But that is precisely the thing for which I am most grateful to him: that he opened my eyes to the importance of that in music which is *not* music."[1]

Grieg wrote three articles about Nordraak. The earliest of the three, a review of Nordraak's *Songs* op. 2, was published in the Danish magazine *Flyveposten*, Copenhagen, on August 24, 1865. It is probably the first article Grieg wrote for publication and provides an early hint of the engaging and lively mode of expression that was to become characteristic of his writing. The review—signed "g."—was sent to Nordraak, who was then studying in Berlin, and Nordraak wrote back enthusiastically on September 2: "Thank you again and again for your good opinion of me! God grant that I may be worthy of it. And thanks because you have begun a revolution in the world of music criticism! It must continue, and we Norwegians— we who have felt the fresh, unpolluted mountain air—can discern more clearly than most the miserable, dishonest products of the spirit in the music of our time."[2]

Chr. E. Horneman's publishing company has recently released *Five Songs,* to Norwegian poems by Bjørnstjerne Bjørnson and Jonas Lie, music by *Rikard Nordraak*. Op. 2.[3] (Dedicated to Mrs. Magdalene Thoresen.)[4] It must be viewed as a most deplorable sign of the state of musical criticism here in this country[5] that not only have these songs not been made the subject of an extended discussion but they have hardly even been vouchsafed a review. The only newspaper that can compliment itself on having directed attention to them is *Illustreret Tidende*, although the reviewer has been as reserved and brief as possible.[6] And yet, what we see here is something that in many respects is new. There is something that awakens a hope for the future—not only for Norwegian music, but for all Scandinavian music—in these short works, which have sprung from a temperament that both feels and thinks deeply. They are imbued with a pure Nordic tone, free of the welter of meretricious inauthenticity that lately has threatened more and more to gain ground. Here there is no anxious fumbling; here there is a firm hand, as immediate and true as only genius can make it.

---

[1] See Finn Benestad (ed.), *Edvard Grieg: Letters to Colleagues and Friends,* Columbus, Ohio 2000, p. 417.

[2] Nordraak's letter is preserved in Bergen Public Library. The quoted portion is printed in Norwegian in Finn Benestad & Dag Schjelderup-Ebbe, *Edvard Grieg: Mennesket og kunstneren (Edvard Grieg: The Man and the Artist),* Oslo 1980, p. 81.

[3] Nordraak's op. 2 was written in 1861–62.

[4] Norwegian authors Bjørnstjerne Bjørnson (1832–1910) and Jonas Lie (1833–1908), and Danish-Norwegian author Magdalene Thoresen (1819–1903).

[5] Grieg's article was written in Denmark and intended for a Danish readership.

[6] Grieg is alluding to a short, unsigned review in *Illustreret Tidende,* Copenhagen, on June 4, 1865.

Rikard Nordraak

The very first song, "The Tone",[7] indeed arouses our full interest. Rarely have we heard the elegiac tone as free of all sentimentality as it is in this song. Here truth prevails—pure, unvarnished truth. Who does not feel it when, after having sung "there he had heard such a curious song,"[8] he drifts off in the mystical, dreamy, "strange" postlude? And yet the same postlude takes on quite a different and remarkable significance after the last stanza, which Bjørnson ends so aptly: "All of the other tones count for but little in comparison with this that you strive

---

[7] The original Norwegian titles of Nordraak's op. 2 are: 1. Tonen; 2. Træet; 3. Solvejge; 4. En underlig vise; 5. Killebukken. Nos. 1, 2, 4 and 5 have texts by Bjørnson, no. 3 by Jonas Lie. The titles are given in English translation in the main text.

[8] Norwegian original: "Der hadde han hørt slik en underlig sang."

for but never attain!"[9] This thought—"never attain"—Nordraak has captured and expressed most beautifully.

No. 2, "The Tree", leads us into a completely different world, a world full of childlikeness and spontaneity. Here the composer obviously has now and then credited the singer with more declamatory talent than one usually dares to assume, for if the performance indication "fervent" is not strictly observed—and it is difficult to do so because of the high tessitura of the melody—the mood easily becomes something very different from "lively". Quite the opposite: It becomes dry and trivial. The [parallel] fifths in the third verse will most likely provide occasion for many philistine remarks.

In No. 3, "Solvejge," all the Nordic seriousness and melancholy has found a beautiful expression. And even in his gentlest minor strains, Nordraak has a hidden power that is quite characteristic of him. His melancholy never becomes maudlin, his yearning never insincere; one sees throughout the intellectual vitality of a man who clearly is aware of his goal. If one were to criticize this song for anything, it would have to be for the somewhat incoherent postlude. Still, we defer here to the composer, who in just this interrupted way of thinking has thought to find, and has in fact found, a true expression for his lament.[10] The striking example of a couple of effective [parallel] fifths in the fifth measure, as well as the marvelous conclusion, must surely make amends for all kinds of criticism.

No. 4, "A Strange Song", undeniably fits the title exceptionally well, perhaps altogether too well, but the folk-song character is so masterfully rendered, the half-crazy mood that pervades the poem is captured so completely, that all criticism of apparent declamatory errors must cease—all the more inasmuch as the prevailing rhythm in Norwegian folk songs often makes the natural accent of the words bow to that of the music. The penultimate stanza, with its utterly tragicomic effect, must be emphasized: "While the sun was shining, I drowned; if you wrote the song, I did not."[11]

And now finally the last, lovely, naive song that in time will undoubtedly become a folk song: "The Young Billy-goat". Here the composer's forte indeed manifests itself as he strikes the right note with the opening chord. From the very first measures that prance out to meet us, so to speak, there is nothing artificial; everything seems natural, innocent and roguish.

It has been our wish through these lines to call the attention of the art-loving public to these small, poetic works. If we have succeeded in doing this, we are convinced that appreciation of the songs will not fail to materialize.

---

[9] Norwegian original: "Alle de andre dog litt [=lite] forslår mot denne du søker, men aldri når."

[10] In 1876, when Grieg included this song in his collection of *Norway's Melodies (Norges Melodier)*, he replaced Nordraak's postlude with one of his own invention.

[11] Norwegian original: "Mens solen skjein, så druknede jeg, —har du skrevet visen, så er det ikke mig."

Rikard Nordraak's Songs Op. 1 (1870?)

Grieg's second article about Rikard Nordraak (1842–66) was a short but rather effusive review of his late friend's *Six Songs* op. 1, four of which were to texts from Bjørnstjerne Bjørnson's stories of peasant life.[1] The review is undated but appears to have been written around 1870. It evidently was intended for a Danish publication but was never printed. The manuscript is preserved in Bergen Public Library.

A new edition of the most beautiful flowers in the sphere of the Norwegian folk song has just been published. To review them now might seem superfluous were it not for the fact that this album of songs has been unavailable to the public, especially the Danish public, ever since 1863 or since right after the composer's death.[2] The simple, unaffected integrity with which the poems are interpreted is so striking that one could believe that in poet and composer one has to do with one and the same personality. And that is in fact virtually the case, for Nordraak is to an astonishing degree a revelation in music of Bjørnson's genius. How this can be is explained by the fact that they are nothing less than first cousins.

If one were to single out one of the songs for special praise, it would have to be "Synnøve's Song"[3]—first because it is so infinitely beautiful in itself, but also because it is especially interesting to see how different Nordraak's setting of this poem is from that of Kjerulf.[4] The author of these lines remembers how Nordraak, fiery and reckless as he was, fumed about how Kjerulf could make something so anemic and pitiful out of Synnøve in this mood. An unbiased reader would also feel this and, what is most important of all, would see that Nordraak had a right to make such a judgment because his reading of the poem, though melancholy, is much more lighthearted—and more Norwegian.[5]

Everything in the album deserves to be known and admired and loved.

---

[1] Norwegian author Bjørnstjerne Bjørnson (1832–1910) was Nordraak's cousin. His *Stories from Peasant Life (Bondefortellinger)* contain a number of lyric poems that have been set to music by many Norwegian composers, including both Nordraak and Grieg.

[2] Nordraak's op. 1, *Six Songs*, was written 1860–61 and published for the first time in 1863.

[3] The poem is taken from Bjørnson's novella *Synnøve Solbakken* (1857).

[4] Norwegian composer Halfdan Kjerulf (1815–68), creator of the Norwegian art song.

[5] This assessment stands in sharp contrast to what Grieg wrote in 1879 about Kjerulf's songs, including "Synnøve's Song": "Among the most beautiful, in my opinion, are the folk-like songs of op. 6: nos. 1 [=Synnøve's Song], 2, 3, 4, 6." See Grieg's complete review of Kjerulf's songs on pp. 221–224.

Homage to Nordraak (1900)

Grieg's third article on Rikard Nordraak (1842–66), an encomium printed in the Christiania newspaper *Verdens Gang* on April 4, 1900, was written in connection with a concert that was to be held on April 28 of that year to raise money for a monument to Nordraak. A brilliant statue by Norwegian sculptor Gustav Vigeland (1869–1943) was completed in 1905, but was not unveiled until 1911. It stands to this day on Nordraak Square in Wergelandsveien, Oslo, not far from the Royal Palace.

Mr. Editor:

You ask me to give *Verdens Gang* a few words about Rikard Nordraak. Just a few words! And one of my dreams has been to write a whole book about him. I scarcely know, therefore, where to begin and where to end in order to accommodate your wish. And yet—I've got it! I will both begin and end by directing attention to a concert that will be given on Saturday the 28th to raise money for a monument to the brilliant composer. He died in 1866—at age 24.[1] Thus his compositions are exceedingly few in number. I am told, however, that even these few (the incidental music for *Maria Stuart in Scotland,*[2] a dozen songs, a couple of piano pieces and some songs for men's chorus), far from being the country's common treasure, are still known only to a very few. If this is true, then it is not very flattering to us, and it is high time that we do something about it. I am further informed that, while everyone who sings "Yes, we love this land, our country"[3] thinks of Bjørnson, the great mass of people still think of the melody as a song that just "invented itself". And it did, too, inasmuch as it came into being in a moment of inspiration. But let it be known by everyone in this country that the composer was Rikard Nordraak. And let it not only be known. Let it not be forgotten. A cause for which we will now strike a blow.

This national anthem is one of the most beautiful—above all, one of the most original—to be found in any country. Nordraak had no idea that it would become our national anthem. He was enthused by the poem, and, warm friend of the homeland that he was, one day, in the innocence of his heart, he wrote music for it in the form of a quartet for male voices. As we all know, for large gatherings the melody is a hard nut to crack, for it begins down on the ground floor and soars heavenward all the way up to the attic. Anyone who cannot scale those heights has to drop down again and continue on the ground floor. In other words: For its practical purpose, the range of the song[4] is an apparent impossibility. But

---

[1] Nordraak was born on June 12, 1842, and died on March 20, 1866, i.e. a few weeks before his 24th birthday.
[2] *Maria Stuart i Skottland*, a drama by Bjørnson (1864).
[3] The Norwegian national anthem, text by Bjørnson, music by Nordraak: "Ja, vi elsker dette landet" (1864).
[4] The song has a range of an octave plus a fourth.

nonetheless, it has triumphed brilliantly over all practical obstacles because it is so infinitely moving, because it matches exactly the sentiments of the poem.

Unfortunately, Nordraak did not live to see that it became a song loved by all. Perhaps we should not say "unfortunately", for more than one clear-sighted person is of the opinion that it was good for him that he died so young. People who knew him well—including a world-famous psychologist—have said that Rikard Nordraak had to die because he was not created to live life as intensely as he lived it. I, too, share this opinion. When I, as a friend and artist, consider him now—almost forty years after his death—I understand better than I did then both his greatness and his limitation. He could only depict moods of the moment. He is a remarkable example of the fact that a brilliantly gifted person can be devoid of the technical ability that is an indispensable condition for further development. He lacked a feeling for writing in the larger forms and for orchestration. The only technique he mastered was that required to write songs and pieces for male chorus. Luckily for us. For what he has left us in these areas is as perfect in form as it is new and fresh in its inventiveness. Hear how hard and wild he can sound in a minor key—and how gentle and graceful in a major key! Let anyone who has ears to hear take note of this—for it is unique. It is a manifestation of a great originality and of an intuitive feeling for the soul of our folk music—about which, as he himself said, he knew practically nothing, and in which he did not find time to immerse himself. This new mixture of soft and hard I recognize also in Bjørnson's poetry. But then, Nordraak was also Bjørnson's cousin.

On Saturday, in the large auditorium of the Masonic Lodge, we will perform most of the works Nordraak has left to us. A handful of fragrant spring blooms. Nordraak was a spring person who lived and died with a glowing faith in Norway's future. He communicates this faith to us right down to the present day through his nationally colored music. That is what we thank him for in his distant grave. It is this gratitude that we all want to unite in expressing.

Julius Röntgen (1907)

The German-born Dutch pianist, conductor and composer Julius Röntgen (1855–1922) was one of Grieg's closest friends. They met for the first time in April, 1875, at a concert in Leipzig where Swedish-born violinist and composer Amanda Maier (1853–94) played a violin sonata that she herself had composed, with Röntgen at the piano. Röntgen and Maier married in 1880.

In 1877 Röntgen moved to Holland to become a piano teacher at the "Maatschappij tot Bevordering der Toonkunst"[1] in Amsterdam. Grieg visited the Röntgen family for the first time in December, 1883, and the two men quickly developed a lasting friendship. Röntgen visited Norway on fourteen occasions during Grieg's lifetime, and through the years the two friends exchanged more than 400 letters. This correspondence has been published in the original German by Finn Benestad & Hanna de Vries Stavland in *Edvard Grieg und Julius Röntgen. Briefwechsel 1883–1907*, Amsterdam 1997. Grieg dedicated his *Lyric Pieces*, op. 54, to Röntgen.

Grieg's article on Röntgen, written in connection with the latter's visit to Norway in February–March 1907, was published on March 2, 1907, in the Christiania newspapers *Aftenposten* and *Verdens Gang*.

This outstanding German-Dutch composer, who will perform for the first time on a Norwegian concert podium this evening at the Music Association, enjoys the greatest esteem as a pianist and composer in European music centers. He is an artist of sterling quality who has earned well-deserved renown, especially by his renditions of Beethoven and Brahms. After he had played Brahms's *Piano Concerto in B-flat Major*, the composer exclaimed: "But you play just like a photograph of myself!"

Röntgen's specialty is chamber music, and in this genre it is again above all Brahms for whom he has fought with every ounce of his personality and with unfailing courage and energy—and he has triumphed. But he has also won new territory for many other modern composers.

Röntgen is no ordinary virtuoso. For him, all technique is only a means in the service of the idea. What is sensational about him is that he is chemically cleansed of all sensationalism. He sits down at the piano and starts in with the sole objective of performing his task. This he does with such verve that he carries the rest of us along with him. Unconcerned about everything around him, he cavorts with the tones in such a convincing interpretation that the listener is enchanted and comprehends its deeper meaning. He is a full-blooded Germanic spirit in whom the great, healthy pathos is inborn.

The same is true of him as a composer. He doesn't want to astonish you with his originality, but he is fresh, natural, and poetic, and he handles himself in all genres like a fish in water. Despite being strictly disciplined in the German-

---

[1] Association for the Promotion of Music, a music school that acquired conservatory status in 1884.

classical school, through steady development his free-spirited nature has succeeded in banishing any hint of scholasticism. I know of virtually no other musician who shares Röntgen's ability to discern that which is of lasting value in the various artistic trends of our time. This ability has also found expression in his own compositions. One quickly observes that he is not a party to the new German school.[2]

It is of particular interest to us Scandinavians to observe the warm appreciation for our musical heritage that is often reflected in his music. It should be stressed in this connection that Röntgen knows Norway as do few foreigners. He is an interested and perceptive observer of our literary, political and social life, and as a zealous mountain-climber he often ventures up to the mountain plateaus of West Norway in summertime.

Röntgen, who is of Dutch ancestry, was born and raised in Leipzig, but a national instinct later led him back to the land of his forefathers, where he has lived and worked for almost a generation. He is a son of the late concertmaster of the Gewandhaus Orchestra in Leipzig, Engelbert Röntgen.[3] His talent manifested itself already in childhood in a degree that was remarkable even by Leipzig standards, and his development progressed so spectacularly that he became what he doesn't care in the least about having been: a child prodigy. But his parents perceived the danger, and instead of public performances, he engaged in the most comprehensive studies. These studies laid the groundwork for the superb artistic culture that ennobles his entire being. In his parental home he associated with great art and great artists from childhood onward. This experience taught him respect and modesty—qualities that he has retained throughout his life. Once when someone made the mistake of confusing him with his renowned cousin, the discoverer of X-rays,[4] he quickly exclaimed, "No, no, not the famous one!"

Since his youth, when he settled in Amsterdam, he has for many years—as concert-giver, teacher and choral conductor—earned the deep appreciation of the music-lovers of that city. With the strong support of a number of music friends who are as genuine as they are generous, he has taken on the task of advocating the significance of chamber music. Under his leadership, Amsterdam has become a major center for this most intimate of all musical genres. Many are the composers, not least Scandinavian composers, whose works have become known and loved in Holland through his efforts.

As stated earlier, he has devoted a quite special interest to Norwegian music,

---

[2] Grieg presumably is alluding to program music such as that written by, for example, Franz Liszt (1811–86) and Richard Strauss (1864–1949).

[3] Engelbert Röntgen (1829–97).

[4] German physicist Wilhelm Konrad Röntgen (1845–1923), the scientist who discovered X-rays. X-rays are called "Röntgen rays" in the Germanic countries and throughout northern Europe.

Julius Röntgen

for which he has been the most indefatigable and enthusiastic spokesman both at home and on his many concert tours. These are great services that he has rendered and continues to render to Norway, services for which we all owe him our deepest thanks.

As is the artist, so also is the man Julius Röntgen. An incurable optimist. No hidden depths. He is straightforward, unpretentious, warm, benevolent. I almost wanted to say: There is no evil in him. His benign and harmonious being is so engaging that there probably is not a place where he has appeared where the hearts of the people have not been drawn to him. The same will happen in Christiania. Here, too, he will again feel that at one point the Röntgen rays of art triumph over those of science: Their scope within the human being is boundless!

To the happy owner of these unlimited Röntgen rays, the noble artist and warm friend of Norway, we shout a hearty "Welcome to our country!"

Robert Schumann (1893)

In March, 1893, Grieg received a letter (dated February 28) from Robert U. Johnson (1853–1937), associate editor of the American journal *The Century Monthly Illustrated Magazine*. Johnson wrote: "I doubt very much if you have any idea to what an extent your own compositions are performed in this country. Within the last five years they have become a part of the musical literature of America, and hardly a concert is considered complete that does not contain something of yours. (. . .) The *Century Magazine*, of which as you will see above I am the Associate Editor, is now engaged in publishing a series of papers on musical subjects. The list as arranged will include articles by Messrs. Massenet, Gounod, Saint-Saëns, Reyer, Paderewski, Dvořák and others. I send you herewith a copy of the magazine containing Saint-Saëns's article on Liszt. Mr. Reyer has written on Berlioz. Mr. Paderewski is to write on Chopin, and Dvořák on Schubert.[1] We should be very glad to know whether you would write for this series of papers an article of reminiscence and appreciation of Schumann, with whom, if we mistake not, you associated during the last years of the master's life in Leipzig. We should like to have this article present a graphic picture of Schumann, to give anecdotes and incidents connected with your friendship with him, and also to give your critical opinion of his value and characteristics as a composer."[2] The honorarium offered was one thousand francs.

Grieg replied from Menton on the French Riviera on April 4, 1893,[3] that Schumann had died two years before he himself came to Leipzig, but he gladly accepted the invitation and wrote the article during a stay at Grefsen Baths in Christiania. The article, written in Norwegian, was sent to New York on July 18, 1893. It was translated into English by Norwegian-American author Hjalmar Hjorth Boyesen (1848–95), professor of Germanic languages and literature at Columbia College, New York.

Upon receiving the translation, Mr. Johnson wrote to Grieg on August 14: "I hasten to tell you how entirely satisfactory it is to us, and how admirably it answers the purposes of this series. Certainly it could not be improved upon, and I have found it altogether admirable and charming. In its acute criticism and its careful judgments it is calculated to arouse, in this country, a new interest in Schumann, whose personality you have attractively presented."

Grieg's article was published in the January 1894 issue of *The Century Monthly llustrated Magazine*. It is presented here in a new English translation which was made directly from the Norwegian original as published in the Norwegian periodical *Nyt Tidsskrift*, 1894.

Some years ago, aboard a steamer on the coast of Norway, a young lady was sitting at the piano, singing. When she paused, a stranger stepped up to her and introduced himself as a lover of music. They began to converse and had not talked long when the stranger exclaimed, "You love Schumann? Then we are friends!"— and offered her his hand.

---

[1] Robert U. Johnson's list of composer-writers: Hector Berlioz (1803–1869), France; Frédéric Chopin (1810–49), Poland; Antonín Dvořák (1841–1904), Czechoslovakia; Charles Gounod (1818–93), France; Franz Liszt (1811–86), Hungary; Jules Massenet (1842–1912), France; Ignaz Paderewski (1860–1941), Poland; Ernest Reyer (1823–1909), France; Camille Saint-Saëns (1835–1921), France; Franz Schubert (1797–1828), Austria.

[2] The letters from Johnson to Grieg are preserved in Bergen Public Library.

[3] A draft of the letter is preserved in Bergen Public Library and is printed in its original English form in Finn Benestad (ed.), *Edvard Grieg: Letters to Colleagues and Friends*, Columbus, Ohio, 2000, p. 453.

This is characteristic, for it illustrates the intimate quality in Schumann's art. To meet in quiet comprehension of the master during a secret tête-à-tête at a piano—that is genuinely Schumannesque. To swear by his banner in clubs and debating societies or amid the glare of festal splendor—that is decidedly non-Schumannesque. Schumann has never ostentatiously summoned any crowd of adherents. He has been a comet without a tail, but, for all that, one of the most remarkable comets in the firmament of art. His adherents have always been the "loners". There is something of the character of the mimosa in them; and unfortunately, they know so well how to hide themselves and their admiration under the leaves of the "Blue Flower" of Romanticism[4] that it would seem a hopeless undertaking (in comparison with the Wagnerites,[5] for example) ever to gather them into a closed phalanx. Schumann has made his way without any propaganda other than that which lies in his works. His progress, therefore, has been slower but all the more secure. Without attempting to anticipate the future by artificial means, he lived and labored in accordance with his own basic motto: "Just become an ever greater artist; everything else will come to you of its own accord."[6]

That this principle was a sound one has been confirmed by the present generation, among whom Schumann's name is known and loved even to the remotest regions of the civilized world—indeed, up to the very Ultima Thule.[7] It cannot be denied, however, that the best years of his artistic life passed without his significance being understood, and when recognition at last began to come to him, Schumann's strength was broken. I received a vivid impression of this sad fact in 1883, when I paid a visit to his famous wife, Clara Schumann, in Frankfort on the Main. I thought to please her by telling her of her husband's popularity in so distant a region as my native country, Norway. But I was mistaken. Her countenance darkened and she murmured dejectedly, "Yes, *now!*"[8]

The influence that Schumann's art has exercised and continues to exercise in modern music cannot be overestimated. Along with Chopin and Liszt, to this day he dominates the whole literature of the piano, while the piano compositions of

---

[4] A blue flower was the central image in the visions of the main character in *Heinrich von Ofterdingen* (1802), a famous mythical romance by Friedrich von Hardenberg (1772–1801), who wrote under the pen name "Novalis". The blue flower became a widely recognized symbol of the Romantic movement.

[5] "Wagnerites" is used to translate Grieg's pejorative Norwegian term "Wagnerianere", meaning followers and slavish imitators of Richard Wagner (1813–87). The neutral Norwegian adjective "Wagnersk" is translated "Wagnerian".

[6] A quotation from Robert Schumann: "Musikalische Haus- und Lebensregeln", in *Neue Zeitschrift für Musik*, a special insert in no. 36, 1850: "Werde nur immer ein grösserer Künstler; alles andere fällt dir von selbst zu." Published, *inter alia*, in Richard Münnich (ed.), *Aus Robert Schumanns Briefen und Schriften*, Weimar 1956, p. 324. See Hella Brock, *Edvard Grieg als Musikschriftsteller*, Altenmedingen 1999, p. 133, footnote 1.

[7] Ultima Thule, the northernmost region of the earth; Grieg is here alluding to Norway.

[8] Grieg made an extensive concert tour in Germany in the autumn of 1883, and his visit to Clara Schumann most likely took place in connection with a chamber-music concert in Frankfort on the Main on December 14, when he played some of his own piano pieces and, with the concert master of the Frankfort orchestra, his first *Violin Sonata* op. 8.

his great contemporary, Mendelssohn,[9] which were once exalted at Schumann's expense, seem more and more to be vanishing from concert programs. Together with his predecessor, Franz Schubert, and more than anyone else of his generation—not even excluding Robert Franz[10]—he dominates the world of the art song, while here, too, Mendelssohn is relegated *ad acta*. What a strange trick of fate! But it is the old story of Nemesis. Mendelssohn, as it were, received too much admiration in advance, Schumann too little. Posterity had to even things out. But in its demand for justice it has, in my opinion, identified itself so completely with Schumann and his cause that Mendelssohn has been treated unfairly—indeed, he has been directly wronged. This statement applies, however, only to the genres mentioned earlier: piano music and the art song. In orchestral compositions, Mendelssohn still maintains his position, while Schumann has taken a place beside him as his equal. I say his equal, for surely no real significance can be given to the fact that among some of the youngest generation of musicians (primarily the Wagnerites) it has become fashionable to treat Schumann, as an orchestral composer, condescendingly. These inordinately conceited hotheads, who consider it their duty to level everything that in their opinion interferes with the free view from the alpine peaks of the master of Bayreuth, dare to shrug their shoulders at Schumann's orchestration, to deny his symphonic prowess, to attack his periodical structure and his ability in formal construction. They even have the gall to characterize his entire orchestral output as a failure, and to justify this accusation they advance the audacious theory that Schumann's orchestral works are nothing but orchestrated piano music. The fact that Schumann did not occupy himself with the formal piquancies of a Mendelssohn, or that he was not an orchestral virtuoso à la Wagner—this is turned upside down as they declare him totally devoid of any capacity for either formal structuring or orchestration. At the same time, they neglect to emphasize all the lofty merits that first and foremost make Schumann the world-conquering force he now in reality has become.

All of this seems almost too ridiculous, too stupid, to require refutation. Nevertheless, this snobbishness has become so prevalent of late that it has gained a certain authority—indeed, it has even been expressed in the most sensational terms in the press. It seems to me, therefore, that it would not be out of place to investigate it in some detail. For we know only too well what is the source of all this commotion. It will be remembered that one fine day in 1879 the *Bayreuther Blätter* carried an article entitled "On Schumann's Music".[11] The article was signed by Joseph Rubinstein,[12] but—this is an open secret—it was

---

[9] Felix Mendelssohn (1809–47).

[10] Renowned German composer of songs Robert Franz (1815–92).

[11] "Über die schumannsche Musik", in *Blätter. Monatshefte des Bayreuther Patronatsvereins*, August 1879, pp. 217–229. See Brock, *op. cit.*, p. 136, footnote 6.

[12] Pianist Joseph Rubinstein (1847–84), an ardent admirer of Wagner, played an important role in making Wagner's music accessible to a broader public by providing piano transcriptions of selected works.

unquestionably inspired by, and probably more than inspired by, none less than Richard Wagner himself. The general perception, certainly justified, was that the style and tone, as well as the ruthless audacity with which the writer hurled forth his taunts, were so genuinely Wagnerian that they point to the master of Bayreuth as the one who bears responsibility for its appearance—despite the fact that he attempted to disguise himself by using simpler sentence constructions than those which we recognize in his public writings. In this incredible article, everything under the sun is asserted to reduce Schumann's art to an absurdity. Not a single positive word is uttered. Indeed, the master's greatest qualities—his glowing imagination and his soaring lyricism—are dragged down into the dirt and depicted as the dullest banalities. His orchestral music, his piano compositions, his songs—all are treated with the same contempt. One does not know who should be the greater object of astonishment: the man who did not sign his name to this pamphlet, or the man who did. The latter is said to have been one of Wagner's Bayreuth piano lackeys who was so spineless as to allow himself to be used as a screen. About him there is nothing more to be said except that he will not even attain the fame of a Herostratos.[13] Wagner's relation to Schumann, on the other hand, becomes through this article so characteristic that it cannot well be overlooked.

It goes without saying that I will not deal here with Wagner the man, and in view of my deep admiration for Wagner the artist, henceforth I can only surmise that he was as one-sided as he was great. Regarding Schumann, the very opposite is true: He was anything but one-sided. He constitutes, in that respect, a remarkable counterpart to Liszt. The rare ability of both of these masters to acknowledge any great and new achievement in their surroundings stands in contrast, as beneficent as it is glaring, to the uncomprehending and illiberal attitude toward the greatest contemporary talents, which is so prominent a trait of Wagner—and, concerning Schumann, to some extent also of Mendelssohn.[14] If we but compare Wagner's harsh judgments of Schumann, Mendelssohn, Brahms[15]—to name only the most important examples—with Schumann's warm and sympathetic criticism of the great men of his day, as it is found on

---

[13] Herostratos was a slave in Ephesus, a city in ancient Asia Minor. In order to ensure that his name would not be forgotten, he set fire to the famous temple of Artemis in his native city. (According to legend, this act occurred on the same night in 356 B.C. on which Alexander the Great was born.) Herostratos was condemned to death, and the condemnation also stipulated that his name was never to be mentioned. He was beheaded, but his wish was fulfilled in that to this day the phrase "herostratic fame" is used to mean "unenviable notoriety".

[14] This is a very strange remark by Grieg. He cannot have been aware of Mendelssohn's many laudatory remarks about Schumann's music. See Brock, *op. cit.*, p.137, footnote 9, for further details.

[15] Wagner's harsh critique of Schumann is, *inter alia*, to be found in *Gesammelte Schriften*, vol. 8, pp. 255–256; of Mendelssohn in *Über das Judentum in der Musik*, in *Gesammelte Schriften*, vol. 5, p. 66ff, of Johannes Brahms (1833–97) in *Gesammelte Schriften*, vol, 8, pp. 321–322. Further details are given in Brock, *op. cit.*, p. 137, footnotes 9–12.

nearly every page of his collected writings, we will not without qualification agree with the poet's words, "All that is great is one-sided."[16] One of the most beautiful memorials to Schumann is the one that he himself has left through his openness to that which was significant in his surroundings. I need only mention his introduction to the musical world of such names as Berlioz, Chopin, Brahms, Gade[17] and others.

We find Schumann in his youth so busily occupied with clearing the way for others that we cannot but wonder how, at the same time, he found it possible to develop his own deep self as he did during the first great creative period of his life, which was devoted primarily to piano music. What a new and original spirit! What wealth, what depth, what poetry in these compositions! The *Fantasy in C Major*, with its daring flight, and its hidden undertone "for him who listens secretly",[18] as the motto declares; the *Sonata No. 1 in F-sharp Minor*, with its romantic infatuation and its burlesque abandon; *Kreisleriana, Carnaval,* the *Davidsbündlertänze,* the *Novelletten*[19]—to name but a few of his principal works: What a world of beauty and intense emotional life are hidden in these! And what a charming, euphonious world of sound—coaxed out of the very soul of the piano—for one who is able to interpret, for one who can and will listen! But the above-mentioned Bayreuth hireling cannot find enough cruel epithets for Schumann's piano music, which he finds to be written in a certain virtuoso style, only false and external. "The difficult passages in Schumann," he even says, "are effective only when—as is most commonly the case—they are played unclearly and indistinctly." A mean witticism! And this talk about the virtuoso style, the falseness, and the extravert character of Schumann's piano music! Can one imagine anything more unjust? Ought one not rather to emphasize much more his moderation in the use of virtuoso technique—compared, for example, with Liszt or Chopin? And to even accuse him of writing piano music ill suited for the piano—well, that is the same as denying his familiarity with the piano.

It is, however, a fact well known to every true pianist that Schumann could not have written a single one of his many piano compositions without being intimately familiar with the deepest secrets of that instrument. It is also well known that he was an outstanding pianist. One of the best friends of Schumann's youth—the late Ernst Ferdinand Wenzel,[20] formerly a teacher at the Leipzig

---

[16] Grieg uses the German words: *Alles Grosse ist einseitig.*

[17] Danish composer Niels Wilhelm Gade (1817–90).

[18] Grieg uses the German words: *für den, der heimlich lauscht.* They come from a poem by German author Friedrich von Schlegel (1772–1829). Schumann had used a verse from this poem as a motto for his *Fantasy in C Major,* op. 17: "Durch alle Töne tönet / in buntem Erdentraum / ein leiser Ton gezogen / für den, der heimlich lauscht." (Literally: "Through all tones sounds / in a colored earth-dream / a soft tone revealing itself / for him who listens secretly.")

[19] *Sonata no. 1 in F-sharp Minor,* op. 11; *Kreisleriana,* op. 16; *Carnaval,* op. 9; *Davisbündlertänze,* op. 6; *8 Novelletten,* op. 21.

[20] Ernst Ferdinand Wenzel (1808–80), one of Grieg's piano teachers in Leipzig.

Conservatory, with whom I often talked about Schumann—used to recall wistfully the many evenings in former days when he would sit at twilight in the corner of a sofa in Schumann's small room and listen to his magnificent playing.

This attempt to ascribe defects to the master in the very areas where he displays his greatest merits is such a clever tactic that one might justly accuse the author of familiarity with that "jurisprudence" that he flings into Schumann's face, reproaching him with having devoted altogether too much time to it at the expense of his music. However much energy and demonic ingenuity in the invention of grievances one must attribute to the writer, here—in the question of piano technique—he has become so zealous that he has even forgotten to cover his tracks. He wants to hurt Schumann, but he ends up hurting himself. He openly

Robert Schumann. Etching after a Danish photograph. Schumann's family regarded this as the most faithful and characteristic image of the illustrious composer whose music Grieg so greatly admired.

reveals how utterly devoid he is of any concept of piano technique. Liszt, whose judgment on everything relating to the piano Wagner otherwise respected, had, as is well known, a quite different opinion of Schumann's piano compositions, of which he always spoke with the warmest admiration—and for the recognition of which he was an enthusiastic and significant pioneer. Liszt spoke up on behalf of Schumann at a time when no one else ventured to do so. Wagner, on the other hand, tried to destroy his reputation long after his death, when his renown was as firmly established as that of Wagner himself. If this matter concerned only Wagner the man, I would rightly have excused myself from discussing it in an article on Schumann. But in my opinion, the issue has just as much to do with Wagner the artist. It is *possible* that Wagner the man didn't *want* to see Schumann's greatness, but it is quite *certain* that Wagner the artist *could* not see it. Be that as it may, his effort to dethrone Schumann has fortunately been a total failure for the simple reason that it was an impossible undertaking. Schumann stands where he stands, impregnable—as does Wagner.

So much for Schumann the piano composer. Turning now to his chamber music, here, too, we find some of his most beautiful inspirations. It has been asserted that he is at his best in the smaller forms. But the *Piano Quintet,* the *Piano Quartet,* the *Trio in D Minor,* both of the sonatas for violin, and the *String Quartets in A Major* and *A Minor* demonstrate that he also had a wealth of beauty at his command when writing in the larger forms.[21] It cannot be denied that in his blending of the timbres of piano and string instruments he never attained the heights reached by Mendelssohn and especially Schubert. It has also been alleged that he neglects absolute sonority, that he sometimes has the string instruments carrying the melody in something other than their most favorable range, etc. But these are trifles that an inspired interpretation and careful study can easily remedy. The most important element—the enchanting power, the illusion—is rarely lacking.

Strangely enough, one does encounter in Schumann some minor impracticalities of a sort which hundreds of lesser spirits easily avoid. In the *Piano Quartet,* for example, he has had the delightful idea of uniting the *andante* and the *finale* movements thematically. But the retuning in the cello of low B flat to C, which is a necessity at this point, excludes the immediate transition to the last movement, thereby spoiling the exquisite effect that has obviously been intended.

The three string quartets (op. 41) are conceived with as much originality as love. Schumann, to be sure, often ignores the traditional notion that a string quartet should be exclusively polyphonic in character. His quartets have,

---

[21] *Piano Quintet in E-flat Major,* op. 44; *Piano Quartet in E-flat Major,* op. 47; *Piano Trio no. 1 in D Minor,* op. 63; *Violin Sonata no. 1 in A Minor,* op. 105 and *no. 2 in D Minor,* op. 121; *String Quartets in A Minor* and *A major,* op. 41, nos. 1 and 3, respectively. *String Quartet in F Major* is op. 41 no 2.

therefore, been criticized both for their lack of conventional quartet style and for the fact that the instruments are not being used to their full advantage. But who, having heard, for example, the A-major quartet splendidly performed by a Brodsky[22] and his fellow artists, will ever forget the ocean of harmony that can be evoked from Schumann's string instruments when they are in the hands of superior artists?

It is reported by reliable contemporaries that these quartets did not find favor in Mendelssohn's eyes. It was during the time when both masters were in Leipzig that Schumann one day confided to Mendelssohn that he had suddenly been seized by a desire to write string quartets, but that he had already decided to take a long-planned trip to Italy and was, therefore, in a bad quandary. "Then just stay here and write the quartets," advised Mendelssohn—and that is what he did. Schumann followed Mendelssohn's advice, stayed in Leipzig and concentrated all of his energy upon completing the task that he had set for himself. But when Mendelssohn later saw the quartets he is reported to have said, "Now I wish that Schumann had gone to Italy instead."

We ought not to be surprised at this. Mendelssohn, in his compositions for string instruments, rarely if ever departed from the strict principles of polyphony as practiced by Haydn, Mozart, and the early Beethoven. Schumann was more rooted in the later Beethoven, who, like Schubert, was not afraid of employing a homophonic—yes, even a symphonic-orchestral—style in his string quartets. Herein one finds a proof—one of many—that although Mendelssohn and Schumann can indeed be said to represent the same period, they did so—and this is the main point—in different ways: Mendelssohn by closing a great artistic period, Classicism, Schumann by preparing and introducing us into a no less great one, Romanticism. Both masters meet, so to speak, upon the same threshold. And they certainly did not pass each other by in chilly silence. On the contrary, they exchanged many inspired words. It must even be said that it would have been better for Schumann if he had listened less to Mendelssohn's maxims and followed his own instead. Schumann's admiration for Mendelssohn certainly is beautiful, but there is in this beauty a certain weakness that is perhaps closely connected with Schumann's later tragic fate.[23]

A survey of Schumann's art reveals that, after emerging from his youth and early manhood, he was no longer able, as it were, to think his own thoughts with full consistency to the end. He was afraid of himself. It was as if he did not dare acknowledge the implications of his youthful enthusiasm. Thus it happened that he frequently sought shelter in the world of Mendelssohn's ideas. From the moment he did this he was past his prime, soul-sick, doomed to destruction—

---

[22] Grieg is alluding to his friend Russian violinist Adolf Brodsky (1851–1929).

[23] Schumann's last years were darkened by depression, and he died in a private asylum in 1856.

long before the visible symptoms of insanity set in. It is, therefore, a futile undertaking to try to find the real Schumann in his later works—as one may do in the case of Beethoven and Wagner. This is most evident when we consider his last choral compositions.

First and foremost, however, we fortunately have the satisfaction of being able to list as masterpieces of imperishable worth a series of orchestral compositions, and pre-eminently among these his four symphonies. Who has not let himself be carried away by the youthful freshness of the B-flat Major symphony! By the great sweep of the C-major symphony, with its wonderful *adagio* wherein the violins soar ethereally heavenward! By the E-flat Major symphony, with its mystic-medieval movement in E-flat Minor (Schumann is said to have imagined here a procession entering the Cologne Cathedral). And lastly, who has not marveled at the conception of the D-minor symphony, with the tragic mood of the introduction and its magnificent unity! Truly: The proud, victorious trumpet blasts with which the first symphony begins, bear witness to a noble self-esteem that is fully justified.[24]

By the way, there is an interesting tradition regarding this opening, namely that it was originally written a third lower, like this:

Trumpets and horns in B flat.

But during the first rehearsal it became evident that the old natural instruments —the only kind in use at that time—were not capable of producing the stopped tones A and B. The practical Mendelssohn promptly came up with the suggestion to place this motive a third higher, as we now have it. In this way it came to consist of nothing but "natural tones", which could be rendered with all the brilliance desired. Thus, if Schumann had written his work today, when the natural instruments have been supplanted by valve instruments, he would have retained the motive in the range in which it was first conceived and where, consistent with the opening of the *allegro*, it properly belongs. If I were to conduct the B-flat Major symphony today, I would not hesitate to change this passage and carry out Schumann's original intention.

It is the B-flat Major symphony that the author of the above-mentioned smear in the *Bayreuther Blätter* chooses as the target for his poisoned arrows. Through a long series of musical examples, he attempts to prove that this work,

---

[24] Schumann's four symphonies: no. 1 in B-flat Major, op. 38 ("Spring"); no. 2 in C Major, op. 61; no. 3 in E-flat Major, op. 97 ("Rhenish"); no. 4 in D Minor, op. 120.

allegedly like Schumann's other orchestral works, is made up of an almost uninterrupted succession of what he calls *cobbler's patches*.[25] By this expression he means "repetitions of musical phrases at related pitches, such as composition students are especially wont to employ in their first attempts." Now, however, in the year 1893, every musician who is not too philistine will maintain as an indisputable truth that the means whereby a musical effect is produced are of minor importance compared to the effect itself. And it is of absolutely no concern to us if a student, by "repetitions at related pitches", achieves only what the author calls "the deadliest monotony", when Schumann, by virtue of his singular application of these "cobbler's patches", woven together by the force of his genius, succeeds in enchanting and enthralling us. Schumann's "repetitions" always sustain the flight of his thought; and where he fails to equal his own best efforts, it is not the "repetitions" but lack of inspiration that is to blame. Moreover, these oft-assailed "repetitions" are to be found in the music of all the great masters from Bach to—Wagner himself. A repetition, sensitively employed, has the same aim in music as in spoken language: to produce a penetrating, stimulating effect. It will not do, therefore, to prejudge every "repetition at related pitches" as a "cobbler's patch".

Before leaving the B-flat Major symphony, I cannot deny myself the pleasure of recalling the performance of this work at the Gewandhaus in Leipzig immediately after the appearance of the ominous Bayreuth article. It was as if the atmosphere in the auditorium were charged with electricity. The work was listened to as never before with excitement and breathless silence, and after the last chord died away there erupted a storm of applause, intensive and long-lasting, such as has seldom occurred in the Gewandhaus after the performance of an orchestral work. It was indeed a unique ovation. It was musical Leipzig protesting as one man against a tendentious assault on a work and its master—whom the nation loves despite all far-fetched accusations of "cobbler's patches".

Schumann's famous piano concerto occupies a unique place in his production. Inspired from beginning to end, it stands unparalleled in music literature and astonishes us as much by its originality as by its noble disdaining of an "extravert, virtuoso style". It is beloved by all, played by many, played well by few, and comprehended in accordance with its basic ideas by still fewer—indeed, perhaps by just one person: his wife.[26]

---

[25] Grieg uses the German word *Schusterflecke*. The Italian word is *Rosalia*, taken from an old Italian popular song, "Rosalia, mia cara", and used to describe the identical repetition of a melody phrase a step higher. See *The New Grove Dictionary of Music and Musicians* (edited by Stanley Sadie), vol. 16, p. 192.

[26] Grieg heard Clara Schumann perform as soloist in Schumann's *Piano Concerto in A Minor*, op. 54, at a Gewandhaus concert in Leipzig on November 29, 1860. Nearly half a century later—on January 20, 1907—he wrote in his diary: "I came to Leipzig in 1858 and a few months after my arrival heard the bewitching Clara Schumann play the concerto, and each tempo was indelibly impressed on my soul. Youthful impressions such as that do not lie." See also p. 163.

Among Schumann's choral works, *Das Paradies und die Peri* stands out by virtue of its enchanting fantasy and its oriental coloring. The whole first part is one uninterrupted inspiration. Whether Schumann employs larger or smaller forms, everything here is equally brilliant. The broadly conceived chorus with which this part concludes is beyond all praise. Here Schumann is truly an architect in the grand style. The second part is equally dazzling. I shall just remind my readers of the passage where the plague is depicted. It is as if poisonous fumes lie concealed within these chords. The third part is also rich in beauty, but here it appears that the breadth of conception required to conclude so great a work is lacking. What a pity that the handling of the text in this part necessitates a division into small forms—which in my experience ends up by being a bit tiresome. Nevertheless, in performing the work in my homeland I have never been able to bring myself to omit a single measure, for every page is teeming with evidences of genius that we cannot leave out. All things considered, *Das Paradies und die Peri* must be characterized as the choral work in which Schumann reached his peak.[27]

From old residents of Leipzig I have heard the account of the first performance of this masterpiece, which took place at the Gewandhaus in 1843 with Schumann himself as conductor. The part of the Peri was sung by Mrs. Livia Frege,[28] who at that time was as renowned in Leipzig for her beauty and charm as for her glorious voice. Immediately after having put down the baton, Schumann, who was known to be a man of few words, rushed up to Mrs. Frege, gracelessly ripped one of the flowers out of her hair as he mumbled dryly, "I should like to have one of these." That was his way of thanking her.

Both Mendelssohn and Schumann admired Mrs. Frege. Some years ago I met both her (she was still a stately and beautiful old lady) and her husband, and I used the opportunity to query the latter regarding the personal relationship between Schumann and Mendelssohn. But the old gentleman reacted as if I had stabbed him. He abruptly terminated the conversation and walked away. There was no doubt that I had inadvertently touched upon a subject that he obviously found improper but into which, from the point of view of music history, it would have been of importance to gain an insight. Now, as both Mr. and Mrs. Frege— in whose hospitable home all the art-loving people of Leipzig used to gather— are gone, and virtually all the friends of Schumann's youth have also passed away, there is little hope of ever clearing up this interesting matter.

Much is whispered in secret about the attitude of Schumann and Mendelssohn toward each other. For the unbiased observer, however, one curious fact

---

[27] *Das Paradies und die Peri*, op. 50, to a text from *Lalla Rookh* by English author Thomas Moore (1779–1852). Grieg conducted the work for the first time at a concert in Christiania on April 5, 1874.

[28] German soprano Livia Frege (1818–91), married to Leipzig professor Waldemar Frege (1811–90). See Brock, *op. cit.*, p. 144, footnote 28.

stands out, namely that Schumann's writings contain numerous and striking evidences of his boundless admiration for Mendelssohn, whereas the latter, in his many letters, does not once mention Schumann or his art. This can hardly be a mere happenstance. Whether Mendelssohn really was silent, or whether the editor of his letters, out of regard for his memory, has chosen to omit all references to Schumann, is basically irrelevant. This much is certain: The silence speaks, and we—posterity—have a right to draw our inferences from this silence. And we come to the conclusion that we have here the key to a correct judgment as to the two masters' opinions of each other. It goes without saying that there can be no suspicion of petty envy on Mendelssohn's part. He was of too pure and noble a character for that, and moreover, his fame was too great and too well established in comparison with Schumann's. But his horizon was too limited for him to see Schumann for what he was. How understandable! His forte lay in clear deline-ation, in classical euphony, and where Schumann fell short of his requirements in this respect, it was not possible for him, honest as he was, to pretend to an unqualified recognition that he could not honestly grant.[29]

Another musical and warm-hearted family in whose home Schumann was a frequent guest during his residence in Leipzig was that of the Voigts. It was to the lady of the house, Henriette Voigt[30]—his close friend—that Schumann dedicated his beautiful G-minor piano sonata.[31] The silent Schumann loved this peaceful home. It is said that he was in the habit of daily entering the drawing-room unannounced, giving a friendly nod to the lady of the house, walking the length of the room and departing by another door without having uttered a single word. All he wanted was to see her!

But—back to the choral works. Besides *Das Paradies und die Peri*, his music to Byron's[32] *Manfred* must he counted among his most glorious compositions, notwithstanding the fact that it belongs to his last period. The overture is a tragic masterpiece from beginning to end. His music to Goethe's[33] *Faust* also contains many lofty passages, but as a whole it is uneven and cannot be termed a monu-mental work in the same sense as the ones previously mentioned.

If we now return to the last choral works—*Der Königssohn, Des Sängers Fluch, Vom Pagen und der Königstochter, Das Glück von Edenhall, Neujahrslied, Requiem*[34]—it is indeed easy for those who wish to destroy Schumann to find

---

[29] Grieg's description of the relationship is most likely somewhat exaggerated. Hella Brock (*op. cit.*, p. 145, footnote 29) quotes a letter from Mendelssohn in which he describes Schumann's second symphony as "an enrichment for the concert repertoire". Mendelssohn even conducted the first performance of this symphony at a concert in the Gewandhaus, Leipzig, on November 11, 1846.

[30] Henriette Voigt (1808–39).

[31] *Piano Sonata no. 2 in G Minor*, op. 22.

[32] English author Lord Byron (1778–1824). Schumann's incidental music for *Manfred* is op. 115.

[33] German author Johann Wolfgang von Goethe (1749–1833). Schumann's *Szenen aus Goethes Faust* for soloists, chorus and orchestra has no opus number.

[34] *Der Königssohn*, op. 116 (text: Ludwig Uhland, 1787–1862); *Des Sängers Fluch*, op. 139 (text: Richard Pohl,

points of attack. For these productions reveal, almost without exception, soaring will and failing skill. His self-criticism is lax, and most of these works are unclear in both color and outline.

Here we have convincing evidence that the master's strength was forever broken. It would be better to pay no attention to these and similar late works that reveal his decline. But as regards the derogatory judgment of Schumann, which has recently become the fashion in certain influential cliques, I may be permitted to ask: Why should not Schumann be judged by the best that he has done, as all other creative spirits rightly are? "Even the good Homer can sleep from time to time."[35] And I should think that one need not search long in Schumann's production to find its core. Although his later works include such glorious achievements as *Manfred*, the violin sonatas, the E-flat Major symphony, etc., one certainly can, if one wishes, ignore this entire period and judge Schumann by his opuses 1–50. I should think that among these one would find a sufficient wealth of priceless jewels to entitle Schumann to a seat among the immortals of music. If we were to judge Mozart by his concert arias, Beethoven by his *Prometheus*, *Christ on the Mount of Olives* and the *Triple Concerto* for piano, violin and cello, Mendelssohn by his *Antigone, Ruy Blas, Lobgesang* and the *Reformation Symphony,* Schubert by his dramatic works, Wagner by *Rienzi*—in short, if we were to hunt high and low to find the weak moments of great souls—then, in view of the imperfection of all that is human, we would always find material for this unrewarding work. But it is not in this way that the cause of justice is served. Fortunately, the rules governing the establishing of a reputation are the same in art as in life: The good is cherished, the mistakes are forgotten—especially when, as is the case with Schumann, the good weighs so heavily in the balance.

Schumann's two violin sonatas bring his chamber music to a beautiful conclusion. Notably the first (A Minor, op. 105), and in this the opening movement, especially, has always struck me as particularly significant. Every time I read or played it, I heard in these tones the master's portentous lament over the heavy fate that soon thereafter would become his lot. The violin's first wonderfully melodious motive is characterized by a gripping melancholy, and the surprising return of this motive in the last movement shows how much importance Schumann attached to it. It is the worm gnawing at his mind, which, in the midst of the passionate effort of imagination to exorcise it, lifts its head anew. Contrasting marvelously with all this inward soul struggle are the gentle, light, pleading—

1826–96, after Uhland); *Vom Pagen und der Königstochter,* op. 140 (text: Emanuel Geibel, 1815–84); *Das Glück von Edenhall,* op. 143 (text: Wilhelm Hasenclever, 1837–89, after Uhland); *Neujahrslied,* op. 144 (text: Friedrich Rückert, 1788–1866); *Requiem,* op. 148 (liturgical text). *Neujahrslied* and *Requiem* are for chorus and orchestra, all the other works for soloists, chorus and orchestra.

35 From Horace (65–8 B.C.) in *Ars poetica* 359. The saying is used today to excuse a blunder that has been committed.

yes, beseeching—melodies that suddenly emerge. Is it not as if we heard the cry, "May this cup be taken from me"?[36] But fate has decreed that the horrible reality shall come to pass. And the work ends in strong, noble resignation, without a sign of the muddiness and groping that, as stated earlier, characterize so much of Schumann's production from this period.

I spoke earlier about the slowness with which Schumann's popularity spread during his lifetime. This is all the more striking since he enjoyed so many outward advantages. He lived in the very center of the musical world. He occupied important positions, including that of teacher at the Leipzig Conservatory.[37] He was married to one of the most soulful and famous pianists of his day. With his Clara he even made concert tours, from which he brought home with him many evidences of his unpopularity. In 1843, for example, he accompanied his wife to Russia, where she was received with great enthusiasm in many of the country's largest cities, and where she also introduced her husband's works. It must be remembered that by 1843 Schumann had already written and published much of his most beautiful chamber music, piano pieces and songs—yes, even his B-flat Major symphony. Nevertheless, it is said that at a court soirée where Clara was the honored guest of the evening, one of the most prominent persons present addressed the composer as follows: "Well, Mr. Schumann, are you, too, musical?" To be sure—and what artist is there who cannot confirm it from his own experience?—the reigning princes and their train of attendants seem to have a unique ability to say stupid things when they have the misfortune of straying into the region of art. But what happened to Schumann here is indeed a prime example of the sort of thing that can be said by those representing the attitude, "We alone know!"

That Schumann, after such an experience, could dedicate his C-major symphony to a prince, albeit this time a really musical one—Oscar I of Norway and Sweden[38]—only shows, however, that he had not yet reached the point of emancipating himself from the naive belief of an earlier day that the king is the best guardian of art. Despite the abnormal relation of King Ludwig of Bavaria[39] to Richard Wagner, our age is fortunately in the process of abandoning this great misconception.

The chief impediment to Schumann's popularity was his total lack of the capacity for direct communication that is absolutely indispensable to the creation of a good conductor or a beloved teacher. But he does not seem to have been noticeably troubled about this lack. He was too much of a dreamer. There are

---

[36] Words spoken by Jesus in *Matthew* 26:39.

[37] The Leipzig Music Conservatory was established by Mendelssohn in April, 1843, and, at Mendelssohn's request, Schumann began working there in the same year as teacher of piano and composition.

[38] Oscar I (1799–1859), King of Sweden and Norway 1844–59.

[39] Ludwig II (1845–86), King of Bavaria 1864–86.

even indications that he was proud of his unpopularity. In a letter to his mother he once wrote, "I do not even wish to be understood by all."[40] On that score he need not have been concerned. He is too profound, too introspective, too subjective to be angling for the acclaim of the masses.

I cannot leave Schumann's larger works without pausing for a moment at the opera *Genoveva*,[41] a work that has been called his "child of sorrows"—and rightly so. It cost him much of his best power and gave him the biggest disappointments. So many pens have been set in motion, primarily against this composition (especially by Wagnerites) that it seems almost foolhardy to want to interject a word in its defense. Nevertheless, I must maintain as my deep-rooted conviction that Schumann's music cannot be summarily dismissed as undramatic. There are so many passages in this opera that furnish unambiguous proof that what Schumann lacked was not dramatic *talent* but dramatic *knowledge*. The most excellent dramatically inspired things stand unconnected side by side, often lacking only a few transitional measures to knit them together. On the other hand, there seem here and there to be too many transitional passages. The stage setting is not always used with sufficient practicality. One need think only of Wagner's unique skill in this area. But, as I have said, the dramatic flight is often enough present. I am convinced that the day will come when a production under committed and skilled leadership will yield at least a portion of that which Schumann, in certain passages, has intended and hinted at, but which he lacked sufficient technique to clearly express. Had Schumann in his youth spent a few years as musical director of a theater orchestra, perhaps we would also have had the experience of seeing him admired as a composer of dramatic music. The great public will not be content with a dramatic spirit if this spirit is not incorporated in a dramatic body. The public demands, so to speak, that the spirit be presented on a serving tray. And that is exactly what Schumann could not do—and perhaps had absolutely no wish to do, if this conclusion may be inferred from his own words: "German composers most often go aground in striving to please the public. But just let someone offer, for once, something individual, profound, German, and he will see if he does not achieve more."[42] No one will deny that Schumann's reasoning here is esthetically correct. But it is obvious that Schumann, constituted as he was, would nonetheless have acted more prudently by not ignoring the public's legitimate demand for clear dramatic characterization. To descend to the level of an

---

[40] The letter is dated August 9, 1832 and printed, *inter alia*, in Richard Münnich (ed.), *Aus R. Schumanns Briefen und Schriften*, Weimar 1956, p. 90. The German text is given in Brock, *op. cit.*, p. 151, footnote 37: "Ich möchte nicht einmal, dass mich alle Menschen verstünden."

[41] *Genoveva*, op. 81, Schumann's one finished opera. The composer compiled the libretto from texts selected by Robert Reinick (1805–52) from plays (also entitled *Genoveva*) by German authors Ludwig Tieck (1773–1853) and Friedrich Hebbel (1813–63).

[42] See *Neue Zeitschrift für Musik*, September 6, 1842. More details are given in Brock, *op. cit.*, p. 152, footnote 39.

ignorant public would have been an impossibility for him. On the other hand, by paying more attention to the objective requirements of the drama, and by being more attentive and realistic in his scenic stipulations, he would undoubtedly have achieved infinitely more.

I have deliberately chosen to consider last the portion of Schumann's art that more than any other shows him to us as what he really was: a poet. I refer to his songs. Not even the Bayreuth critic possessed by all the demons of hate is able to reduce him to a nonentity in this genre. In order to minimize even this expression of his genius, however, he resorts to far-fetched humor. I cite the following mouthful verbatim: "Since nowadays people do not find it ridiculous when, in our salons, a lady, holding a fan and a fragrant lace handkerchief between her gloved fingers, sings of her former lover as a 'lofty star of glory' who 'dares not know her, the lowly maiden'—or when a gentleman in swallow-tail coat assures us that in a dream he has seen the serpent that gnaws at the heart of a certain unknown but in any case 'wretched' person—then one certainly ought not, primarily, to be angry with the composer because, in his effort to create musical settings of such poems, which are very popular in the 'better circles', he has employed all the depths and heights of musical expression so as not to be outdone by the poet."[43]

What an abundance of genuine Wagnerian gall is concentrated in this tapeworm of a sentence! But—it goes too far. Schumann's songs emerge from this mud-bath as pure as they were before they were dipped into it. If there is anything that Schumann has created that has become, and has deserved to become, world literature, it is his songs. All civilized nations have made them their own. And there is probably in our own day no young person interested in music to whom they are not, in one way or another, interwoven with his most intimate ideals. Schumann is the *poet* in contrast to his greatest successor, Brahms, who is primarily a *musician*, even in his songs.

For Schumann, the poetic conception of the poem plays the leading role to such an extent that technically important musical considerations are subordinated—indeed, they are often disregarded. And yet, even those of his songs in which this occurs exert the same magic. I am thinking here of the great demand that Schumann makes upon the range of the voice. With Schumann, it is often no easy task to determine whether the song is intended for a soprano or an alto, for in one and the same song the melody moves from the lowest to the highest register. Several of his most wonderful songs begin in the low register and gradually rise to the very highest, and it is a rare singer who can handle both extremes.

---

[43] *Blätter. Monatshefte des Bayreuther Patronatsvereins.* August 1879, p. 227. The critic, Joseph Rubinstein, here quotes words from Schumann's song cycle *Frauenliebe und –Leben* to texts by Adalbert von Chamisso (1781–1838).

Schumann, to be sure, occasionally tries to obviate this difficulty by adding a melody of lower pitch, which he then indicates by smaller notes placed below the melody of his original conception. But how often he thereby reduces his most beautiful flights, his most inspired climaxes! I shall mention here just two examples: "Ich grolle nicht"[44] and "Stille Tränen"[45]—for which one will scarcely ever find a singer who can do equal justice to the beginning and the end. But an interpreter who has a voice capable of such a feat will produce all the greater an effect. In this connection, I remember hearing as a child (1858) the then 55-year-old Mrs. Schröder-Devrient[46] sing "Ich grolle nicht", and I shall never forget the shiver that ran down my spine at the last climax. The perfectly beautiful timbre of her voice was of course no longer present, but the power of the expression was so absolutely overwhelming that everyone was completely enthralled.

To be able to sing Schumann calls for a special ability that many otherwise excellent singers do not possess. One must be born with it. I have heard one and the same female singer render Schubert to perfection and Schumann downright badly. For with Schubert, most of what is to be done is explicitly indicated, whereas with Schumann one must know how to read between the lines, to take the smallest hints. A Schubert symphony, too, plays itself, so to speak. A symphony of Schumann has to be studied with a sensitive ear to uncover here and there what seems to be veiled in the master's intentions. Otherwise it won't work.

The wide vocal range required to sing Schumann's songs, mentioned earlier, refers primarily to the more broadly conceived ones. As a rule, the smaller and more intimate songs do not overtax a voice of ordinary range.

Schumann had a special talent in the area of the epic song and ballad. In this genre he has created unrivaled masterpieces. I shall mention by way of example Chamisso's "Die Löwenbraut"[47] and (from opus 45) Eichendorff's "Der Schatzgräber"[48] and Heine's "Abends am Strand".[49] In the last-named song, Schumann achieves a realistic effect of great intensity. How vividly he describes here the different peoples, from those who dwell on the banks of the Ganges to the "dirty Laplanders" who in an absolutely impressionistic manner "quack and scream"! Strangely enough, there are as yet not many who both feel and are able to render these songs. Thus, they are almost never heard in a concert hall. A ballad the popularity of which (according to E. F. Wenzel) vexed Schumann was Heine's

[44] "Ich grolle nicht", from Schumann's song cycle *Dichterliebe*, op. 48 no. 7; text by German poet Heinrich Heine (1797–1856).
[45] "Stille Tränen", from *Zwölf Gedichte*, op. 35 no. 10; text by German poet Justinus Kerner (1786–1862).
[46] German soprano Wilhelmina Schröder-Devrient (1804–60). The concert in question took place in Leipzig at a *Matinée Musicale* on March 6, 1859.
[47] "Die Löwenbraut", from *Drei Gesänge*, op. 31 no. 1; text by Chamisso.
[48] Der Schatzgräber, from *Romanzen und Balladen I*, op. 45 no. 1; text by Joseph Freiherr von Eichendorff (1788–1857).
[49] "Abends am Strand", from *Romanzen und Balladen I*, op. 45 no. 3.

"Die beiden Grenadiere" because he—perhaps rightly—regarded it as one of his weakest compositions.[50]

A collection that contains works of the very highest order, and that for some incomprehensible reason is almost unknown, is op. 98a: *Lieder und Gesänge aus Goethe's "Wilhelm Meister"*. Once in a while one may perhaps hear the magnificent, grandly conceived ballad, "Was hör' ich draussen vor dem Tor!".[51] But the most beautiful song in op. 98—"Kennst du das Land, wo die Citronen blühn"[52]—is never sung. It is a song with which I have seen a gifted interpreter of Schumann move an audience to tears.

It is rarely the happiest inspirations of a creative spirit that win the hearts of the many. In that respect, the musical intelligence of the so-called cultivated society leaves much to be desired. By the way, the other arts have not had much better luck. Everywhere it is cheap art that has a monopoly on the popular understanding.

One cannot say that Schumann was the first composer to allow the so-called accompaniment to his songs to play a prominent role. Before him, Schubert had let the piano depict the mood as no one before him had done. But what Schubert began, Schumann developed further; and woe to the singer who tries to render Schumann without paying close attention to what the piano is doing, even to the minutest shades of sound. I have no faith in a singer of Schumann's songs who fails to understand that the piano has just as great a claim upon interest and study as the vocal part. Indeed, I would even venture to assert that a person who cannot to a certain degree play Schumann cannot sing him either.

Furthermore, in his treatment of the piano Schumann was the first composer who, in a modern spirit, employed a relation between song and accompaniment that Wagner has later developed to a degree that best demonstrates the importance he attached to it. I refer to the carrying of the melody by the piano—or the orchestra—while the voice is engaged in a recitative. God forbid, however, that I should insinuate that Wagner consciously could have received an impulse from Schumann. A dyed-in-the-wool Wagnerite would, of course, regard even a cautious hint of such a possibility as evidence of an outrageous lack of reverence for the master of Bayreuth, an aspersion amounting almost to libel. It is, nonetheless, a fact that great contemporaries influence each other whether they want to or not. That is one of nature's eternal laws, to which we are all subject. Someone may ask: Where is the mutual influence of Rossini, Beethoven and Weber?[53] To that I will

---

[50] "Die beiden Grenadiere", from *Romanzen und Balladen II*, op. 49 no. 1.

[51] The first line of "Ballade des Harfners", op. 98a no. 2.

[52] Op. 98a no. 1.

[53] Italian composer Gioacchino Rossini (1792–1862), German composers Ludwig van Beethoven (1770–1827) and Carl Maria von Weber (1786–1826).

reply only that it is of a negative character—but it is still there. In the above-mentioned particular case, however—that of Schumann and Wagner—it is absolutely positive. It is true, however, that Schumann only hints at that out of which Wagner constructs a complete system. But it must be said that Schumann is here the forward-looking spirit, the one who planted the tree that later, in the music-drama, was to bear such glorious fruit.

The gradually increasing conservatism that, in the case of an artist, usually is a mark of personal decline, was never noticeable in Schumann. Even though in the end his creative power suffered shipwreck when his spirit was engulfed in the darkness of insanity, this in no way affected his philosophy of art, which remained fresh and youthful to the end. His enthusiasm for the young Brahms is a striking proof of that receptiveness to new trends, which he retained even during the decline of his short career. We gain hereby a beautiful glimpse of the purity of his character as it revealed itself even in his younger years in relation to Mendelssohn and others. And as Schumann was the first interpreter of true emotions in modern music who could exclaim with Beethoven, when the latter had completed his *Missa Solemnis,* "From the heart it has come, to the heart it shall go," so now, after poor judgment, pettiness, and envy have disappeared, all hearts, old and young, respond jubilantly to Schumann as a man, a pioneer, and an artist. This Schumannesque conception of art will again come into its own when that army of inflated braggarts who most unjustly call themselves "Wagnerians" and "Lisztians" will have lost its influence. I explicitly distinguish, however, between the true and genuine admirers of these two mighty masters and the howling horde who call themselves "–ians". These patent-holders of speculative profundity do not seem to know the most priceless jewel of art: *naiveté.* How, then, could they love Schumann's art, which possessed this rare gift in such rich measure? The interpretation of Schumann by many of the so-called Liszt performers is decisive here. In most cases these performers will, indeed, give you a genuine interpretation of Liszt, but their rendition of Schumann, on the other hand, is garbled beyond recognition. All attempts at artistic treatment and a well-rehearsed execution of details cannot replace the warm, deep sound that a true interpreter of Schumann must be able to produce. As different as Mendelssohn's orchestration is from that of Wagner, so different is Schumann's coloring from that of Liszt. To bring this coloring to life on the piano is so great a challenge for the performer that it lays claim to his whole personality. He must be able to orchestrate on the piano. Only then does he become a "Schumann-interpreter" in the sense in which one speaks, for example, of a "Chopin-interpreter"—that is to say, a performer who, to be sure, plays a good deal else as well but *can* play only Chopin to perfection. Wagner somewhere expresses the opinion that only those who are favorably disposed toward him can comprehend his intentions. This is no less true of Schumann, who, in his demands on the performer's comprehension, ventures to propound the postulate: "Perhaps only genius can completely understand genius."[54]

That these lines, in addition to giving some of my personal understanding of Schumann, are also concerned in a relatively large degree with Mendelssohn and Wagner, was implicit in the nature of the case. All these masters stand in a peculiar relation of reciprocity to each other. Each in his own way, as indicated above, has either sought the influence of the others or has purposely avoided such influence. Like mighty planets in the firmament, they have either attracted or repelled one another. Each owes the others much, either positively or negatively. As for Schumann, perhaps he did not achieve what his rare gifts entitled us to expect—because his need for external influences is intimately connected with that seed of an early breakdown that prevented him from consistently pursuing his goal. But whatever his imperfections may be, he nonetheless remains one of the foremost representatives of art, a genuine Germanic spirit to whom one dares to apply Heine's profound words concerning Luther[55]: "In him, all the virtues and all the faults of the Germans are united in the grandest way, so that he personally also represents the wonderful Germany."[56]

---

[54] Robert Schumann: "Musikalische Haus- und Lebensregeln"; see Brock, *op. cit.*, p. 158, footnote 44.

[55] German theologian and reformer Martin Luther (1483–1546).

[56] Heinrich Heine: *Deutschland. Zur Geschichte der Religion und Philosophie in Deutschland. Erstes Buch: Deutschland bis Luther*, Paris 1834. See Brock, *op. cit.*, p. 158, footnote 45.

Christian Sinding (1889)

In 1874 Grieg and his friend and colleague Johan Svendsen (1840–1911) were awarded annual public grants of 400 *spesidalers* each by the Norwegian Parliament (*Stortinget*)—the first Norwegian composers to be so honored. Their joint application for such grants is printed on p. 64. In 1889 Grieg, on his own initiative, wrote to the Parliament urging that a similar grant be awarded to his young colleague Christian Sinding (1856–1951), who was the leading Norwegian composer of his generation. His *Piano Quintet in E Minor*, op. 5 (1883–85), had made him known in the great concert halls of Europe, and he was acclaimed far and wide as an outstanding representative of Scandinavian music.

The Parliament rejected Grieg's proposal for an annual grant for Sinding at this time, but they did grant him a two-year stipend. In the years that followed, Sinding received a number of public grants, thanks not least to Grieg's persistent efforts on his behalf. He was finally awarded an annual grant in 1910.

Grieg's letter of recommendation was printed in Proceedings of the Norwegian Parliament (*Stortingsforhandlinger*) 1889, Part 5, Document no. 26.

I hereby take the liberty of requesting from the Parliament now in session an annual state grant in the amount of 1,600 crowns for the composer Christian Sinding. I shall briefly sketch the rationale for this application. It has long been known by experts in the field that Sinding is one of our leading talents, and in that respect I need only to add my admiration to that which has been expressed from so many quarters in recent years. The great attention that one of his works[1] has recently elicited in Leipzig, the city of music, provides a suitable occasion to direct the attention of the Parliament at just this time toward one of Norway's most gifted sons—especially in that support of this talent is amply called for by the circumstances. These are:

1. Sinding is totally without the means necessary to survival. For that reason an application for support was sent to the Parliament at an earlier date, but it was not considered because it was expected that Sinding would get the Houen grant. This expectation was in fact fulfilled, but after having received the Houen grant for some time he is now again without financial resources.[2]

---

[1] On January 19, 1889, Sinding's *Piano Quintet* op. 5 had been performed with great success in the Leipzig Gewandhaus by pianist Ferruccio Busoni (1866–1924) and the string quartet of Adolf Brodsky (1851–1929). Grieg had heard the quintet a year earlier at a party at Brodsky's home in Leipzig. Peter Tchaikovsky was also a guest at that party. Grieg wrote of the event in a letter to Frants Beyer (1851–1918) dated January 29, 1888: "Sinding's quintet is a large-scale work—at times too garish, even brutal (which Sinding considers a virtue!), but of great, rare power." (The letter is published in an English translation by William H. Halverson in Finn Benestad (ed.), *Edvard Grieg: Letters to Colleagues and Friends*, Columbus, Ohio 2000, p. 51.) The "garish" and "brutal" elements to which Grieg alludes presumably are the "forbidden" parallel fifths and octaves in the fourth movement concerning which Tchaikovsky, after reading through the quintet at the Brodsky party, is reported to have said, "I have allowed myself much, but something like this—never."

[2] In 1886 Norwegian businessman Anton Christian Houen (1823–94) had created an endowment of 200,000 crowns, the interest from which was to provide support for young Norwegian artists. Sinding received a

Christian Sinding

2. Sinding does not have the good fortune to be a conductor or performing artist in addition to his work as a composer. Thus he does not have
   the opportunity to earn fees that could contribute to his life work.[3]
3. Sinding's music is such that it may take many years before he achieves in
   Norway the broad general recognition that he deserves.
4. As a composer, Sinding has already completed a long period of fermen-
   tation. He has written many works both large and small—most of
   which, to be sure, still exist only in manuscript. Recently, however, he has
   succeeded in getting two of his most important compositions published,
   one by the famous C. F. Peters Music Publishing Company of Leipzig.[4]
   This is strong evidence of the growing respect with which he is coming
   to be regarded abroad.

All these conditions seem to indicate, therefore, that never has the case for
public support of a Norwegian artist been stronger than the present one. As I submit my application, I do so in the hope that through the Parliament's liberality
one of young Norway's most vital shoots will be preserved for the future. It is not
difficult to foresee that this future will bring honor to our homeland.

Houen grant of 1,500 crowns in 1886 to enable him to spend a year studying abroad, and the grant was
renewed in 1887. In 1888, however, his application for another renewal was turned down. (Mr. Houen subsequently established several large endowments in support of Norwegian art and culture, and the earnings from
these gifts have played an important role in Norwegian cultural life down to the present day.)

[3] Sinding was also trained as a violinist, but throughout his adult life he insisted that he wanted to devote
himself exclusively to composition.

[4] Prior to 1889 a number of Sinding's compositions had been published in Christiania and Copenhagen. The
first of his compositions to be published by C. F. Peters was *Suite for Violin and Piano* op. 10 (1888).

Frank van der Stucken (1883)

Grieg met the American-born composer and conductor Frank van der Stucken (1858–1929) for the first time in Leipzig in 1878. Van der Stucken reported the meeting to Grieg's American biographer Henry T. Finck (1854–1926): "One morning, after breakfast, I was sitting in my lonesome den in the Post-Strasse at work on a new song, when a rap at the door announced my first visitor; and presently a little gentleman, with flowing blonde locks, with friendly and bright blue eyes, walked towards me and introduced himself as the Norwegian composer Grieg who wanted to make the acquaintance of the young musician whose first compositions he had received and read with great interest."[1]

Van der Stucken was active as a conductor in both Europe and the United States. He was, among other things, the first conductor of the Cincinnati Symphony Orchestra (1895–1907) and served as an important link between the music centers of Europe and the emerging cultural life of America.

Grieg's review of van der Stucken's songs was published in 1883 in *Musikalisches Wochenblatt*, Leipzig.

FRANK VAN DER STUCKEN:
Jünglingslieder. Liederkranz (*Young Love*, a garland of Songs),
    published by Schlesinger, Berlin
Drei Lieder (*Three Songs*) for alto voice, op. 3
Blumen (*Flowers*), four songs for a deeper voice, op. 4
Neun Lieder (*Nine Songs*) for a medium voice, op. 5.
    Reviewed by EDVARD GRIEG.

The composer of the songs listed above—a young American who has lived for some years in Germany—must be greeted as a very promising talent. He grew up in Belgium and received his musical training from Peter Benoit.[2] As far as I know, except for some pieces for male chorus, these song albums are the only compositions that he has published. But it would be rash to conclude from this fact that van der Stucken is only a composer of songs. To the contrary, a quick look at these song albums shows clearly that the composer regards song-writing as a kind of transitional stage and that he is striving toward quite different goals.

This comment must not, however, be construed as a criticism of the songs in themselves. The Wagner[3]-inspired dramatic tendency evident in several beautiful newer songs—in contrast to the lyrical direction represented by Schumann[4] and others—shows very clearly that there are two kinds of song-composers to whom one can apply the predicate "good," and from what is said here you can

---

[1] Henry T. Finck, *Edvard Grieg*, New York 1906. Revised edition 1909.
[2] Belgian composer, conductor and teacher Peter L. L. Benoit (1834–1901).
[3] Richard Wagner (1813–87).
[4] Robert Schumann (1810–56).

easily guess to which category the songs being reviewed belong. What creates interest in them is, above all, power, passion, and boldness of expression—characteristics that hold rich promise for the young composer's future. Moreover, the five albums reveal such pronounced progress with regard to clarity of form and mastery of the technical means—yes, in general they show a great creative power combined with such a strongly accentuated urge toward broad pathos—that we certainly will not have to wait long until the composer will also make himself heard in larger—above all, dramatic—works.

Even the first book, entitled *Jünglingslieder* (*Young Love*)—written by a composer who himself had scarcely reached young manhood—contains many of the merits mentioned above, even if we here have to do with an excess of *Sturm und Drang*. One notices immediately the beautiful treatment of the language and the feeling for polyphony in the harmonic texture. These are qualities that, for one who proposes to write dramatic music, cannot be overestimated, and they come to the fore even more clearly in the succeeding albums. In this connection, the very first song—"Anbetung" ("Adoration")—provides a good indication of the composer's intentions. The fiery and fervent "Jugendliebe" ("Youth in Love") also deserves to be singled out. In the second and third albums (opp. 3 and 4) the voice leading becomes more interesting, the accompaniment less ponderous, the details more ingenious. In short: Evidence of a talent that knows what it is doing becomes more and more noticeable.

One can, of course, question the use of this and that [parallel] fifth, various crude chord progressions, etc. It is possible that the composer will hear more than

Frank van der Stucken

one critical remark about his naive rashness in this connection. But let no one overlook the significant qualities concealed behind the youthful exaggerations. Op. 4, in any case, includes one song—"Am Kreuzweg" ("At the Crossroads")— that deserves in every way to be hailed as a masterful song. One rarely encounters such integrity of expression, such depth of feeling and such an intense immersion in the mood of the poem. (In measure 13 the right thumb in the second chord must play F instead of the notated E flat.) No one will object to the fact that in measure 6 there is a chord that "götterdämmert,"[5] as this passage, strangely enough, does not really sound at all Wagnerian.

It is not uninteresting to note that the composer, as an enthusiastic devotee of Wagner—yes, as one who, with respect to boldness, from time to time is even "more royalist than the king himself"—is not for that reason one of the Wagner-imitators that one encounters so frequently in Germany. Even during the time that these songs came into being, one perceives a gradual emancipation from Wagner. As a result of this emancipation, the last two albums (op. 5) are the ones that will give the reader the most pleasure. The first of these contains some very successful pieces, such as no. 1, "Motto", and no. 5, "Wonne der Wehmut" ("Joy of Wistfulness"). In the second album we encounter—in "Muttertraum" ("Mother's Dream") and above all in "Am Feuerherd" ("By the Fireside")—dramatized songs of great vigor and distinctiveness. One could wish that the piano part, with its strongly passionate colors, had been orchestrated, for one has the feeling that what the composer is really striving for here is the rich, colorful palette of the modern orchestra.

All in all: The young composer *wants* something and *knows* something. He has high goals—and he will accomplish much. May a lucky star guide him in such a way that he can follow his natural bent and his intentions! That, after all, is the decisive point. A statistical record regarding the number of great talents who have suffered shipwreck on the reefs of life would certainly have been very unpleasant to behold.

---

[5] Grieg is alluding to similar chords in Richard Wagner's music-drama *Twilight of the Gods* (*Götterdämmerung*).

Johan Svendsen's Concert (1867)

The Norwegian composer and conductor Johan Svendsen (1842–1911) was second only to Grieg as the most important Norwegian composer of the nineteenth century. His orchestral works were played all over the world with great success. Svendsen was also an outstanding conductor who devoted more than a decade of his life to raising the standard of orchestral music in his homeland—beginning in 1872, when he became co-conductor with Grieg of the Music Association Orchestra in Christiania. In 1883 he was appointed musical director of the Royal Theater in Copenhagen, where he served with distinction until his retirement in 1908.[1]

Grieg and Svendsen first met in Leipzig in 1865 and initiated at that time a warm friendship that was to last throughout their lives.

Upon finishing four years of study at the Leipzig Conservatory in 1867, Svendsen gave a concert in his native Christiania. After attending a rehearsal for that concert on October 8, 1867, Grieg wrote to his Danish friend Gottfred Matthison-Hansen (1832–1909): "Today I attended a rehearsal for Johan Svendsen's concert and heard his symphony. That was really something! The most scintillating genius, boldest national flavor, and truly brilliant handling of the orchestra. Where he has gotten this from the gods only know, but I think it is from Berlioz,[2] about whom I unfortunately know too little to venture to affirm a strong influence here. But be that as it may, when I heard the symphony I was completely jolted. Everything had my fullest approval and forced itself upon me with irresistible power."[3]

Grieg continued his laudatory evaluation of Svendsen in a review entitled "Johan Svendsen's Concert" which was printed in the Christiania newspaper *Aftenbladet* on October 14, 1867.

Today Norwegian art has celebrated one of its great triumphs. For triumph it must be called when a musically unenlightened audience—an audience of only a few hundred people—is so carried away by that which is absolutely new and great that it forgets its archenemy, the symphony—"that artificial music", as it is called—and breaks out in enthusiastic applause. And anyone who attended the concert could easily see that it was not a *succès d'estime*.[4] The brilliant composer was regarded with real and immediate admiration. A fresh current of excitement coursed through the audience, which unfortunately was all too small. The excitement of the listeners in turn affected the performers, who deserve warm appreciation for the manner in which they executed their difficult task.

The concert opened with Svendsen's *Symphony in D Major*,[5] a work that provides insight into an individuality so great that it would be easier to write

---

[1] See Finn Benestad & Dag Schjelderup-Ebbe, *Johan Svendsen: The Man, The Maestro, The Music*, Peer Gynt Press, Columbus, Ohio 1995.

[2] French composer Hector Berlioz (1803–69), known not least for his brilliant orchestration.

[3] The letter is published in Finn Benestad (ed.), *Edvard Grieg: Letters to Colleagues and Friends*, Columbus, Ohio 2000, pp. 493–494.

[4] *succès d'estime*: recognition of a work primarily because of who wrote it rather than on the basis of its intrinsic merits.

[5] *Symphony No. 1* op. 4 (1865–67), composed during Svendsen's years of study in Leipzig.

Johan Svendsen

books about it rather than pages. What primarily strikes one as so refreshing in this symphony—unconsciously, of course, to a non-musician, but to a musician in such a way that throughout the symphony he maintains a sense of comforting calm—is the perfect balance between the musical ideas and the craftsmanship. Svendsen makes great demands on his audience. He takes the listeners with him into the enchanted land of fantastic humor and Romanticism—but he doesn't let any of them decide at their own discretion whether or not to go along: He forcibly abducts the audience, so to speak, simply by virtue of knowing how to hit the nail on the head in his employment of the technical means. In this way he takes his audience by storm, even in those places where his ideas are so lofty that it would appear impossible for the average listener to understand him.

Svendsen's orchestration is as perfect as any to be found. It is this successful transformation of ideas into sound that has enabled him to capture not only the imaginative listeners but even those who in this respect are completely unendowed. His orchestral writing invites comparison with that of Scandinavia's most eminent master of orchestration, Niels W. Gade,[6] and it is interesting to observe how, with respect to the handling of the instruments, Svendsen's principles go in the very opposite direction. Gade tries so far as possible to combine the various timbres so they blend into one big whole. Svendsen, on the other hand, deliberately separates the various groups of instruments, which mutually echo one another. The result is the generally mellow tone colors of Gade's music and the sharp contrasts in Svendsen's. That Svendsen uses a greater variety of resources results, of course, from the fact that he belongs to a newer age. The piquant *Scherzo* does not come across as a mere striving for effect, for the soft, murmuring *pizzicato* is consistent with the musical ideas.

The freshness and boldness with which the first movement begins immediately creates great expectations, and the listener is not disappointed. The second theme, to be sure, is distinctly Wagnerian, but the singular way in which Svendsen later develops it in conjunction with the principal theme banishes any thought of reminiscence. In the *Andante* he moves smoothly along in beautiful harmonic progressions, in the course of which the flutes' lamenting national tones are heard and then fall silent again. This movement, too, shows mastery in the thematic treatment, though it would certainly have produced a greater impression of unity if the movement had ended after the big climax with the ensuing high point instead of once again repeating the theme *piano*. The *Scherzo* is thoroughly national and contains the most inspired and delightful combinations. The composer demonstrates that gigantic powers slumber within him in the introduction to the *Finale*, where he proudly gives indications of the principal theme. There is grandeur in this rising tension, which, in combination with the canonic art that Svendsen reveals at this precise point, warrants the prediction of a great future for him.

Steenberg's "Minuet"[7] has obviously been treated with great affection. Svendsen's arrangement allows the full string orchestra to sing out the beautiful, melodic secondary theme and adds a sonorous, albeit somewhat lengthy, *finale*.

The *Andante with Variations*[8] for strings sounded somewhat colorless after the orchestral pieces. It was performed most excellently and contains some beautiful passages.

The same is true of the *Caprice*[9] for violin and orchestra, which, despite the

---

6 Danish composer and conductor Niels W. Gade (1817–90).
7 Norwegian farmer and fiddler Johannes Steenberg, who was active around 1800. Svendsen had made an orchestral arrangement of Steenberg's "Minuet" in 1866 (Work 204 in Svendsen's List of Compositions. See Benestad & Schjelderup-Ebbe, *op. cit.,* p. 396).
8 The second movement of Svendsen's *String Quintet* op. 5 (1867).
9 Work 122 in Svendsen's List of Compositions. Composed in 1863, before Svendsen commenced his studies at the Leipzig Conservatory.

talent to which it bears witness, nonetheless appears to be somewhat formless. It is scarcely necessary to add that it, too, is well orchestrated, though perhaps a bit lacking in contrast.

The concert concluded with vigor and force: Liszt[10] would surely have been delighted to hear his *Hungarian Rhapsody*[11] orchestrated so brilliantly. Here Svendsen has rightly pulled out all the stops. Piccolos and bass drum constitute the extremes, and between these Svendsen, with the most astonishing brilliance, has built a structure so fantastic that not even a Berlioz could have done it better.

The audience in the large auditorium of the Masonic Lodge yesterday consisted of approximately 400 people. Of these, about one out of three had purchased tickets. That an artist of Johan Svendsen's caliber, after such meager financial rewards, will pack his bags and leave as quickly as possible, is only to be expected. But it will be a shame if something is not done to keep him here among us. We have only a few national talents—enough, however, that through their mutual efforts a true artistic life might be established. We are convinced that Johan Svendsen would not have left us if the public's reception had not forced him to do so. It is a sad thought, but it must nonetheless be expressed, that if the public consistently goes on treating the best of our own people in this way, it will not be long before Norwegian music in our homeland will be nothing but an empty phrase, whereas abroad—especially in enlightened Germany—it will find the recognition it deserves.

Svendsen intends to leave as early as next week, probably for Leipzig.

---

[10] Hungarian composer Franz Liszt (1811–88).
[11] Liszt's *Hungarian Rhapsody no. 2*, which Svendsen had arranged for orchestra in 1866 (Work 206).

Giuseppe Verdi (1901)

Grieg was for a number of years in close contact with Olav Anton Thommessen (1851–1942), editor of one of Christiania's principal newspapers, *Verdens Gang*. After the death of Giuseppe Verdi (1813–1901) on January 27, 1901, Thommessen asked Grieg to provide an article for his paper about the late maestro. Grieg accepted the assignment, writing the article in Copenhagen on January 31, 1901. It was published in *Verdens Gang* on February 7, and since neither Grieg nor Thommessen had copyrighted it, reprints soon appeared in magazines all over Europe.

Verdens Gang requests that I write a few words about the late master. But when we read "Verdi is dead!" do not these few words speak in a way that no newspaper article can? And besides: Is Verdi's significance for me personally a matter of interest to your readers? And what else is there to say? Biographical notes? They can be found in any encyclopedia. Some superficial outlines of a snapshot of Verdi as seen through the eyes of a Scandinavian artist? But that requires an objectivity that I am not quite sure I possess. Still, I will make an attempt. And I have a special reason for doing so, for I am not blind to the significance of the fact that a Norwegian daily will devote space in its columns to a subject like this. In so doing, it performs such a beneficent and educational influence on the awareness of music in my homeland that it is the duty of every musician to contribute to this purpose as he is able.

Verdi's death marks the passing of the last of the great composers. If it were appropriate to compare artistic greatness, I would say that Verdi was greater than Bellini, Rossini and Donizetti.[1] Yes, I would even say that he, alongside Wagner,[2] was the greatest dramatist of the century. However, as you will know: great, greater, greatest do not exist in the realm of art. What is great is great. Period. What we all feel at Verdi's passing is this: How infinitely empty it seems at this moment with him gone! Where will we now find, among the younger generation in the world of music, the new, the distinctive, that which bears a strong stamp of individuality—first and foremost in the field of dramatic art? Where? In Germany? France? England? Russia? Scandinavia? Nowhere do we see it as yet. But there are some "faint touches," signs that it already lies in swaddling clothes. And if these signs are not misleading, before long the big copy-machines now in vogue aping Wagner and Verdi will soon be consigned to eternal oblivion. There is an expectation of individuality. That is why Verdi's death fills us with such a singular sadness.

---

[1] Italian opera composers Vincenzo Bellini (1801–31), Gioacchino Rossini (1792–1862), and Gaetano Donizetti (1797–1848).

[2] German opera composer Richard Wagner (1813–87).

When Gade[3] died here in Copenhagen eight years ago, a clergyman by his bier made the stupid statement that his place would be filled by another. It was reserved for a Protestant clergyman to give voice to such a colossal stupidity, one bearing witness to an unbelievably undeveloped concept of the significance of beauty. A Catholic priest could never have said such a thing, least of all an Italian one. For in Italy, all classes of people have, without exception, a strikingly direct rapport with their great men. They take a happy pride in them. I shall never forget the reverent awe with which common people in Rome utter the name of one or another of their country's great men.[4] It was this rapport, which Verdi knew how to establish with his countrymen, that dictated his relationship to his homeland. What he has meant to his country can be best understood when we read that in Milan, when Verdi's death was reported, the magistrate called a meeting in the middle of the night to discuss how the deceased should be honored; that in Rome, where all the schools have given the pupils a vacation until the funeral is over, the Senate held a meeting dedicated entirely to Verdi's memory.

I mention this because it shows Verdi as the national hero that people perceived him to be. He was a national artist in every respect. First and foremost. That is how he began. His great triumphs from his youth and his mature years, including the now less well-known operas *Nabucco* and *I Lombardi,* and a decade later the famous *Rigoletto, Il Trovatore* and *La Traviata,* all manifest a national standpoint.[5] But then the marvel occurred: As a fully mature man, Verdi mightily broadened his horizon and, while still retaining the national element in his art, became a cosmopolitan. Even in *La Traviata* he is in many respects walking—personal peculiarities aside—in the footsteps of his countrymen. He belonged to a school that in the musical center of our century—Germany—was scorned. At the Leipzig Conservatory in the 1850's and 1860's all they could spare for Verdi was a disdainful shrug of the shoulders and a haughty smile. The learned circles regarded this music as inferior because they rejected its national element. Neither Mendelssohn nor Schumann[6] was in a position to understand Verdi's music as a true expression of the emotional life of his people. It was Wagner who not only understood this, but who also honestly admitted how much he had learned from the Italians, especially Bellini.[7] Since then it has been widely

---

[3] Danish composer Niels W. Gade (1817–90). Grieg's memory was somewhat faulty here. Gade died on December 21, 1890.

[4] Grieg had visited Rome four times: 1865–66, 1869–70, 1884, and 1899.

[5] First performances: *Nabucco:* Milan 1842; *I Lombardi:* Milan 1843; *Rigoletto:* Venice 1851; *Il Trovatore:* Rome 1853; *La Traviata:* Venice 1853.

[6] German composers Felix Mendelssohn (1809–47) and Robert Schumann (1810–56).

[7] As far as is known, Wagner's writings contain no evaluation of Verdi, but much regarding Bellini. See the article "Bellini. Ein Wort zu seiner Zeit" (1837) in Richard Wagner, *Sämtliche Schriften und Dichtungen,* vol. XII, Leipzig 1911, 5th edition, pp. 19–21, referred to by Hella Brock in *Edvard Grieg als Musikschriftsteller,* Altenmedingen 1999, p. 232, footnote 8.

Giuseppe Verdi

acknowledged in Germany that one has to hear this period's Verdi in Italy in order to appreciate the truly national element in his music.

As far as I am aware, there is a pause in Verdi's dramatic production following *La Traviata*.[8] Then in 1871 comes *Aida*. What a colossal development! What enormously significant years in Verdi's inner life it presupposes! If I were asked to say what school this work belongs to, I would be at a loss for an answer. It stands on the shoulders of all the art of its day. Both France's and Germany's more recent masters have given him impulses. But no more than that either. *Aida* stands as a masterpiece wherein his own originality unites with a great and sympathetic view of the best of his contemporaries. Verdi the Italian and Verdi the European join hands. The language he speaks here is a world language, which one does not have to go to the composer's homeland to understand. That is why, with *Aida*, he triumphed in every respect. His melodies, his harmonies, his handling of orchestra and chorus—everything evokes the same admiration. And one thing more: the Egyptian coloring. This is achieved not merely by means of sophisti-

---

[8] Grieg's memory was faulty at this point. Verdi composed several famous operas between *La Traviata* and *Aida*: *I Vespri Siciliani* 1855; *Simon Boccanegra* 1857 (revised version 1881*)*; *Un Ballo in Maschera* 1859; *La Forza del Destino* 1862; *Don Carlos* 1867 (revised version 1884).

cated technique, but first and foremost through the power of imagination to visit the places depicted in the text. As one example among many, I will just mention the night scene on the Nile at the beginning of Act 3, where the harmonics of the cellos and double basses, the *pizzicato* of the violas, and the combined *tremolo* and *arpeggios* of the violins accompany a most exotic flute melody. One feels transported to the solitude of an African night, hearing the mysterious and indeterminate sounds of nature. Here imagination and technique unite to produce an effect that is moving in its superb characterization.[9]

After *Aida*, in 1887 comes *Otello*. A hiatus of sixteen full years. This work signifies another new period. Here Verdi stands on the highest peak that he was destined to reach in the course of his long life. The lengthy training in various musical styles was necessary in order to create the broad, lofty vision that characterizes this proud work.

Tchaikovsky, in his memoirs, expresses regret that Verdi did not reach this summit until so late in life. He thinks it could have happened while imagination still had the mobile adaptability of youth if Verdi had become acquainted with the contemporary dramatic masters of other countries somewhat earlier. Unfortunately, I do not have the book at hand, but I remember that Tchaikovsky developed this thought in very striking words.[10] I do not agree with him, however. One cannot simultaneously possess youth and the results of a long life. In order to create *Otello*, Verdi had to undergo the slow, uninterrupted transformation. Here the aging master evinces a capacity for further development, for deepening, for universality, that is absolutely astonishing. And it is clear that, in lieu of youth, he manifests a youthful spirit that is able to master the wildest passions of the unwieldy material. The old Verdi had everything at his fingertips. The music is infused with a Shakespearean sense of the demonic. And he does not shrink from taking on so hazardous a task as setting to music Iago's great monologue, with its somber, atheistic philosophy of life and death. And what a loftiness he attains in precisely this scene!

Among the many noteworthy features in the orchestration of this opera is the employment of all the resources of the orchestra to produce a *pianissimo*. But it is also a terrifying *pianissimo*. This effect is certainly new. I do not remember having encountered it in the works of any other master.

---

[9] It is interesting that Grieg himself, only a few years after the appearance of Verdi's *Aida*, in his incidental music to *Peer Gynt*, op. 23, hints at exotic musical coloring, for instance in "Arabian Dance" (no. 15).

[10] In 1872, Russian composer Peter Tchaikovsky (1840–93) had written an essay about Italian opera in the Russian newspaper *Russkije vedomosti* (no. 231), in which he described Verdi's position in words similar to those used by Grieg. A Russian edition of Tchaikovsky's reviews and critical articles, *P. I. Chaykovsky: muzïkal'noye feletonï i zametki*, was published by H. Laroche, Moscow 1898. A German translation of this book, *Musikalische Erinnerungen und Feuilletons*, was published in 1899. It presumably is the latter edition that Grieg is referring to. See *The New Grove Dictionary of Music & Musicians*, vol. 18, pp. 634–635, and Brock, *op. cit.*, p. 234, footnote 10.

It appears that *Aida* and *Otello* vie with one another for preeminence in Verdi's oeuvre. I mentioned the Egyptian coloring in *Aida*. But Verdi has demonstrated equal brilliance in striking a different tone in the prelude to the last act of *Otello*. This opera, which was excellently performed under the inspired leadership of Johan Svendsen[11] at the Royal Theater in Copenhagen, had a capable interpreter of the title role in Frederik Brun.[12] I attended often and enjoyed that magnificent work to the utmost. But when the prelude to the last act began, I always felt a pair of questioning eyes—those of musicians in the orchestra, or of some of the audience sitting nearby—resting on me. I wanted to know the reason for this, and I was told that people thought Verdi showed here an intimate acquaintance with contemporary Norwegian music. To what extent this may have been the case, I am not able to decide. On the basis of this prelude, however, I take it for granted that Verdi was familiar with Norwegian folk music. It is a moving, melancholy piece in which the master, in an admirable way, lets the woodwinds depict Desdemona's premonitions of death.[13]

If I were to enter on a more comprehensive characterization of the beauty of this work, it would take a long time. *Otello* will stand with *Aida* as a milestone not only in Verdi's oeuvre but also in the total dramatic production of our time.

Falstaff,[14] his last opera, is the new Verdi from beginning to end, but one notices that it is an old master who is proclaiming the new ideas. The imagination does not soar as it did before. Now and then there is something breathless about it. Nonetheless, *Falstaff* contains a real treasure trove of interesting details.

In discussing Verdi's art, one cannot neglect to mention his *Requiem* and his swan song: the four sacred pieces for choir and orchestra.[15] They represent Catholic culture at its highest level, and they are full of the most beautiful and profound inspirations that have ever captured the master. His excellent string quartet, too, demonstrates not only his versatility but also his fine sense of the intimate world of chamber music.[16]

---

[11] Norwegian composer and conductor Johan Svendsen (1840–1911), musical director of the Royal Theater Orchestra in Copenhagen 1883–1908.

[12] Danish opera singer Frederik Brun (1852–1919).

[13] Grieg is alluding to a striking melodic motive in the first measures of the prelude: from the octave via the seventh to the fifth. This motive, often called the "Grieg formula" or the "Grieg motive", is very characteristic of Norwegian folk music, and it permeates most of Grieg's oeuvre. See, for instance, the opening of his *Piano Concerto in A Minor*, op. 16, and the opening of his *String Quartet in G Minor*, op. 27.

[14] *Falstaff* was first performed in Milan in 1893.

[15] *Messa da Requiem* for four soloists, mixed choir and orchestra had its first performance in Milan in 1874. *Quattro pezzi sacri* were composed at different times: "Ave Maria" for unaccompanied four-part choir (1889); "Laudi alla Vergine Maria" for unaccompanied four-part women's choir (ca. 1890); "Te Deum" for double mixed choir and orchestra (1895–96); and "Stabat mater" for mixed choir and orchestra (1898). Verdi rated the four pieces highly and gave detailed instructions for their first performance in Paris in 1898. He wished to have the score of the "Te Deum" buried with him!

Interestingly, Grieg's last composition was also to be a sacred work: *Four Psalms* for baritone solo and mixed choir, op. 74, based on Norwegian folk melodies (1906).

[16] Verdi's *String Quartet in E Minor*, his only work in that genre, was written in 1873.

Strangely enough, both Verdi and Rossini concluded their long dramatic careers by writing church music. It would not surprise me if certain of our theological wise men would see in this the repentance of an anguished conscience over the abominable sin of having devoted their lives to dramatic art, for in the art of interpretation these theologians have indeed received the gift of nimbleness. What was it that was said at Trinity Church in Christiania at Laura Gundersen's funeral? *Schwamm darüber!*[17] Let us forget it. She didn't hear it, but it shows our level nonetheless. It proves that our mountains still shut out light and air.[18]

Unfortunately, I did not know Verdi personally. I called on him once in Paris without meeting him, and I received in return his calling card at my hotel. I treasure as if they were sacred relics this card and the envelope on which he has written my—unfortunately not his—name. That is all. How I wish I had met Verdi the man, who would have inspired the same admiration as Verdi the artist. The magnificent home for musicians that he managed to get finished just before his death speaks, in its own way, just as loudly about his greatness as do any of his musical works.[19]

I ask the readers of *Verdens Gang* to be content with these unpretentious lines as they spontaneously took shape under my pen.

---

[17] *Schwamm darüber:* literally, "Sponge over it". The meaning is "No more of this! Forget it!" Quotation from the operetta *The Beggar Student* (*Der Bettelstudent*, 1882) by Austrian composer Carl Millöcker (1842-99); libretto by German conductor, librettist and composer Richard Genée (1823-95) and German-Austrian author Friedrich Zell (Camillo Walzel, 1829-95) after *Les noces de Fernande* by French dramatist Victorien Sardou (1831-1908).

[18] Laura Gundersen (1832–98), long a leading actress at the Christiania Theater, had died on December 25, 1898, and was buried on December 31. Grieg was in Denmark at the time but had read a report published in the Christiania newspaper *Morgenbladet* on January 1, 1899, of a talk given at the funeral by Rev. Christopher Bruun (1839–1920), who was known as a stern moralist. Although Bruun spoke warmly of Ms. Gundersen, Grieg reacted negatively to the following passage in the printed version of Bruun's talk: "I want to relate what I have heard about a famous actress—not here in Norway, to be sure, but in a large foreign city. At the time she came to her country's largest theater, the acting profession there was held in such low regard that to be a young actress was more or less equivalent to being a young woman of doubtful virtue. After she had been queen of the stage for some time, things were different: No young women anywhere guarded their virtue more strictly than the young actresses—and she had brought this about by waging war on wicked traditions and wicked people. (...) The theater's influence for both good and evil is great, and every actor who furthers the evil spirit on the stage and among his contemporaries will be pursued by the accusing voices of a people who have been led astray—voices reminding him of the ruination of human happiness and of the social fiber. And if he doesn't want to listen to such voices in this world, he will hear them in another world."

[19] Characteristic of Verdi the man is the fact that he regarded the *Casa di Riposi per Musicisti*—a home for aged musicians, built in Milan at his expense—as his most important achievement.

Richard Wagner and The Ring of the Nibelung (1876)

In January 1876 Grieg received a letter from Dr. Max Abraham (1831–1900), Director of the C. F. Peters Musikverlag in Leipzig, telling him that the sale of his compositions had been so good that the publishing company wanted to reward him by giving him tickets for the performances of Richard Wagner's *Ring* cycle in Bayreuth. Grieg promptly accepted the generous offer and also obtained an assignment from the Bergen daily newspaper *Bergensposten* to cover the great event.

The result of these arrangements was a series of eight lengthy articles dispatched by Grieg from Bayreuth to *Bergensposten* in the course of ten days. All of them bear witness to his extraordinary ability to write meaningfully about music. His evaluations also provide interesting proof of his ability to enter into the Wagnerian world, toward which he felt both fascination and repugnance. In a letter to his Norwegian biographer Gerhard Schjelderup (1859–1933) of May 11, 1904, he wrote that as early as 1858—the first year of his studies in Leipzig—he had seen Wagner's *Tannhäuser* at the opera: "It moved me so much," he confided, "that I heard it fourteen times in a row."[1] What he did not like, however, was the imitators of Wagner—the "Wagnerites", whom he once described with unconcealed scorn as "these pompous, self-important, brutal clique-mongers, who aren't worth a tinker's damn."[2]

The translation that follows has been made from the original articles in *Bergensposten*, where they appeared serially from August 20 to September 3, 1876. They are here presented in their entirety for the first time in English translation.[3]

I

(August 6)

Mr. Editor!
Here I am, as promised, trying my hand in a genre in which I have not yet set foot in the arena: as a correspondent. But even if I get bloodied up a bit by the half-wild ones among us, so what? I am used to it. It is with a feeling of responsibility, but also of duty, that I attempt to give my countrymen an overview of the remarkable events occurring down here these days. If I succeed in contributing a little to the dissemination in Norway of the view that what is going on here is something great, something that should indeed captivate anyone who has a

---

[1] See Finn Benestad (ed.), *Edvard Grieg: Letters to Colleagues and Friends*, Columbus, Ohio, 2000, p. 608. Grieg's recollection regarding this matter 45 years after his stay in Leipzig may be somewhat inaccurate. According to Joachim Reisaus, *Grieg und das Leipziger Konservatorium*, Leipzig 1988, p. 142, *Tannhäuser* was performed no more than ten times at the Leipzig City Theater during the years 1858–62.

[2] Letter to Grieg's American biographer, Henry T. Finck (1854–1926), of July 17, 1900. See Benestad, *op. cit.*, p. 238.

[3] The first Norwegian reprint of the articles, though in an abbreviated form, was made in Øystein Gaukstad (ed.), *Edvard Grieg: Artikler og taler* (*Edvard Grieg: Articles and Speeches*), Oslo 1957, pp. 75–96. An English translation of this abbreviated version was given in Bjarne Kortsen (ed.), *Grieg the Writer*, Vol. I, pp. 48–63. The first German translation of the original articles was printed in Hella Brock, *Edvard Grieg als Musikschriftsteller*, Altenmedingen 1999, pp. 83–119.

Richard Wagner

feeling for our legends about gods and heroes and their transmittal into the modern consciousness via musical-dramatic performance, then I will consider my mission accomplished. While I shall try to express myself as clearly and explicitly as possible, if now and then I should stray into the territory of subjective sentiments I must ask the reader to charge this to the fact that I am a composer. I will give my dispatches the form of a diary. This, I think, is the way in which I can best manage my material.

The much-discussed event that has brought me here—the performance of Richard Wagner's musical-dramatic trilogy,[4] *The Ring of the Nibelung*—begins in eight days. I have been here since yesterday, however, to attend the dress rehearsals, which start today at 6 P.M. I have received a firm promise that I will be admitted to them, but from what I hear it is still highly questionable, as the King of Bavaria arrived last night (he always travels by night for purely romantic reasons) and wants to have the dress rehearsals all to himself. (He is anthropophobic, as a matter of fact.) It is said that he will not attend the performances. Unfortunately, it is altogether too likely that Wagner will have to accommodate

---

[4] Grieg regularly refers to *The Ring of the Nibelung* as a trilogy, treating *The Rhinegold* as a prologue to the three dramas comprising the trilogy.

The Festspielhaus in Bayreuth in 1876

his royal friend and patron, who has contributed so greatly to the impressive results that are now at hand.[5] Well, we shall see. I want to hear the dress rehearsal somehow or other. One doesn't come all the way from Norway just to stand outside.

I visited the Wagner theater (or, as it is called here, the *Festspielhaus*[6]) this forenoon. It is situated on a gently sloping hill a short distance outside the town. The view from the terrace is beautiful. The building's exterior, on the other hand, is rather unattractive. Outwardly it looks crude, primarily because of the big, steep-roofed, warehouse-like building in back that projects high above the façade and houses the stage itself and its complicated machinery. All the side wings can be hoisted up and down in their entirety, so they don't have to be rolled; that is why the building has to be so enormously high.

Entering the theater, however, one is totally won over, for here one gets an overwhelming impression of loftiness and noble simplicity. The idea for the layout of the interior was borrowed from the amphitheater of antiquity: no box seats, no balconies (except for the royal box way in the back). The seats are grouped in amphitheater style in ascending rows, and in the place occupied by the side-galleries in a modern theater are two rows of handsome Corinthian

---

[5] In 1864 King Ludwig II (1845–86) of Bavaria, a lifelong supporter of Wagner, had subsidized the composer's work on the *Ring* series with a grant of 30,000 *gulden*. See Brock, *op. cit.*, p. 85, footnote 2.

[6] The cornerstone of the *Festspielhaus* in Bayreuth was laid in 1872. The theater was dedicated with three consecutive performances of the complete *Ring* cycle, August 13–30, 1876.

pillars. Above these are frosted glass fixtures that illuminate the auditorium. Especially striking is the fact that the orchestra pit is so low that the musicians are completely hidden from the view of those in attendance. The conductor can survey the stage but cannot be seen by the audience. This idea—according to which the viewer relates directly to the action on stage without the illusion being disturbed by all the busy hands in the orchestra—is truly excellent. When you add to this the fact that the vocal parts have a better opportunity to be heard, the recited words can more easily be understood, and the orchestra, albeit somewhat damped, nonetheless sounds like a more harmoniously blended whole, there certainly can be no doubt that the future simply must adopt the principle, perhaps with improvements that time will bring. Would that these novel inventions might be employed in our new national theater in Christiania, which cannot be delayed for long.[7] May we in any case adopt the idea of the ancient amphitheater and, so far as the orchestra is concerned, arrange things in such a way that it can be raised and lowered as circumstances require. For all types of music do not, of

Grieg in the late 1870's

---

[7] The National Theater (*Nationaltheatret*) in Christiania was dedicated in September, 1899—twenty-three years after Grieg's article was written. It is a much more traditional structure than the *Festspielhaus*. The National Theater orchestra was established with 43 musicians under the capable leadership of Johan Halvorsen (1864–1935).

course, require the same degree of lowering of the orchestra. In the lighter genres, where a smaller orchestra is employed, one can, for the time being, follow tradition. Only in the presentation of exalted, serious subjects ought the lowering of the orchestra to be employed. We should be among the first to demonstrate that we understand these matters, for we have a musical future. To be sure, the present Christiania Theater must begin little by little to enlarge its orchestra instead of reducing it. Here the orchestra consists of 125 men. And what artists they are—all first-rate! One can say that with respect to sonority, each musician plays for two. Thus this orchestra is comparable to an ordinary one of at least 200 members. But then this theater is also one of the largest of our time. An orchestra of fifty members would suffice for our situation and would by no means be impossible to develop. But enough about that.

I will now dwell a bit on the material that Wagner has employed in his writing, not least because for us Norwegians it has a special power of attraction in that it is all based to a large extent on the *Volsung Saga* and the *Elder Edda*.[8] In addition to these sources he has made use of the German *Nibelungenlied*, and, with poetic license that approaches the limit of what is permissible, has woven his drama together from these themes. It must be reckoned to Wagner's great credit that he has limited himself primarily to Nordic sources, and above all that he has not, through the more recent *Nibelungen* epic poem, adopted Christian views and customs. Consequently, the myth stands before us in its original, pure greatness. How much of this original material Wagner has and has not employed is too complicated a subject for us to deal with here. On this matter, I must refer to the sources mentioned, which are readily available to all Norsemen. Wagner has used the Nordic names from the *Edda*, but he has given them a German form. He does not say Sigurd, but Siegfried; not Gunnar, but Günther; not Odin, but Wotan; not Loke, but Loge, etc. His verse form is also taken from the *Edda* in that he uses alliteration and assonance rather than rhyme.

The four music-dramas of which the trilogy consists have the following titles: 1) *The Rhinegold* (prologue), 2) *The Valkyrie*, 3) *Siegfried*, 4) *Twilight of the Gods*.

The Rhinegold

(First evening)

As the curtain rises, the poet-composer shows us nothing less than the bottom of the Rhine River, where, according to the legend, a great treasure— "The Rhinegold"—has been hidden. The treasure is guarded by the three

---

[8] The *Volsungs* were a legendary royal family descending from the Frankish King Volsung. The Volsungs play a role in Germanic heroic epics—in the *Nibelungenlied*, for example. Legends about the Volsungs came to Scandinavia during the sixth and seventh centuries. Toward the end of the thirteenth century the Icelandic *Volsungesaga* was written, based on the Eddic poetry. *The Elder Edda* is a collection of Old Norse myths and legends found in *Codex Regius*, an Icelandic parchment manuscript dating from 1270, preserved in The Royal Library, Copenhagen.

Rhinedaughters—Woglinde, Wellgunde and Flosshilde—who, amidst joking and laughter, swim back and forth from boulder to boulder. Alberich, the leader of the dwarfs, comes clambering up from Nibelheim. He speaks affectionate words as he tries to get hold of one of them, but they mock him. Then the sun comes up and shines upon the gold. A bewitching light pervades the deep. The Rhinedaughters tell of the gold's magic power: *He who can forge a ring from the Rhinegold will gain the whole world if he forsakes all love.* Then Alberich suddenly seizes the gold and disappears into the depths, cursing love. It is night. The Rhinedaughters vainly scurry after him, and from the sea is heard Alberich's mocking laughter.

Like the leader of the dwarfs, Wotan, the leader of the gods, desires to extend his power. Indeed, it is his highest wish. Wotan promises Fasolt and Fafner, the rulers of the giants, that they shall have the goddess Freia if they will build a castle for him. In the course of a single night, the castle is finished: When Wotan awakens, it stands gleaming before him! But now Freia dashes in, pursued by the giants, who demand their reward. The wily Loge has advised Wotan to enter into this arrangement. With Loge's help, Wotan hopes to be able to break the agreement. Loge now tells about Alberich, who has forsaken love to get the Rhinegold, and about the gold's magic power. Immediately, the giants grow envious. But Wotan, too, becomes greedy for the treasure. Both he and the giants are now willing to relinquish Freia in order to possess it. Then Freia is carried away as surety until Wotan, before evening comes, is to give them the gold. The gods suddenly grow old—for the poet takes the liberty of letting Freia be in possession of the apples of Ithunn, which give the gods eternal youth—and there is great sorrow in Valhalla. Then Wotan and Loge venture down to Nibelheim to win back the gold and the lost youth.

Alberich has forced his brother, the ingenious smith Mime, to forge him a helmet of gold. Mime senses the gold's secret power and does not want to give up the helmet, but Alberich seizes it from him, puts it on his head, mumbles some magic words, and suddenly becomes invisible. Then Wotan and Loge come, and they hear from Alberich about the marvelous helmet. Then Alberich shows himself again, and Wotan asks for what purpose he will use the treasure in Nibelheim. Alberich declares boastfully that with its help he will conquer the whole world. At last, Loge succeeds in getting him to tell the secret of the gold's hidden powers. Loge acts as if he doesn't believe it, whereupon Alberich transforms himself into a fearful dragon, then into a brazen hussy.

This is what the gods have been waiting for. In a flash, Wotan places his foot on the hussy's head; Loge tears the helmet off, and under Wotan's foot Alberich shrinks down to his real self. They bind him and bring him up to the world above the water. He can get free only by relinquishing both the helmet and the ring. When Alberich refuses, Wotan tears the ring from his finger. Freed from his bonds, Alberich curses the ring: It shall be the cause of an evil fate for anyone who owns it. Then he disappears into the depths. The giants return with Freia. Day dawns, and the gods recover their youth.

The gold lies ready. The giants pile it up around Freia. According to the agreement, only when she is fully covered will she be handed over to them. Fafner can still see Freia's hair, so Loge must put the helmet on the heap of gold. Fasolt, still able to see the goddess's eyes, demands the ring. Wotan angrily refuses, and now the outraged giants want to take Freia with them. Then Erda (in Norway: Vala) rises from the depths and admonishes Wotan to flee from the fateful ring. He asks: "Who are you?" She tells him who she is and adds:

> All that is shall end,
> a gloomy day
> is dawning for the gods!
> I counsel you to avoid the ring![9]

Deeply shaken, Wotan wants to know everything, but Erda has wished only to warn him. She sinks back into the deep, whereupon Wotan throws the ring onto the stack of treasure. Freia is freed and scampers jubilantly back to the gods. Now the giants begin to fight over the gold. Fasolt demands the ring and is killed by Fafner. Fafner then flees with the treasure. The gods become frightened by the curse that follows the ring. Wotan wants to find Erda to learn more about the gods' fate, but Fricka turns his thoughts in other directions as she shows him the magnificent castle on the other side of the Rhine. Donner (god of thunder) and Froh (god of light) conjure up a rainbow over the valley. Upon this, the gods march toward the castle that glows in the evening sun—the castle that, in accordance with Wotan's wish, shall be called Valhalla. From the depths of the Rhine is heard the Rhinedaughters' lament over the lost Rhinegold. The curtain falls.

The entire Prologue consists of just one act lasting about two and a half hours. About the text itself, I shall of course not express any final judgment, but it is noteworthy that the entire so-called prelude has been forced into a dramatic setting that is not suitable for it, for it is essentially epic in character, and in the past it has always been treated as such. In fact, these mermaids, giants, gods and goddesses do not evoke our feelings. One looks at them, one admires them on the stage, but where—as is the case here—they do not interact with human beings who can engage our human emotions, we get tired of them.

I will speak about the music tomorrow. Now off to the dress rehearsal.

---

[9] *Alles, was ist, endet, / ein düsterer Tag / dämmert den Göttern! / Dir rath ich, meide den Ring.* In the Norwegian articles, Grieg's citations from Wagner's librettos are always in the original German.

II

(August 7)

Mr. Editor!

Yesterday brought me face to face with the preeminent example of musical-dramatic art produced in this century. I now understand Liszt's[10] judgment regarding Wagner's masterpiece when he says: "It towers over the entire art of our time like Mont Blanc over the rest of the Alps."

The reports were correct: The king had wanted no audience in the theater, and no one—not even the closest friends of the author-composer—was allowed in [for the dress rehearsal].

However, I saw my chance to slip into the orchestra, which constitutes a world of its own down there in the depths. Here, among musicians whom I knew, I soon felt right at home and found a good place from which to view the stage. The performers assembled little by little, and the place swarmed like an anthill of people and instruments. The conductor, the brilliant Hans Richter,[11] took his place, and we were urged to silence with the whispered announcement, "The king is coming". Wagner's bellowing voice was heard shouting from the royal box — "Begin!"—and then something began to happen down there at the bottom of the Rhine in the famous prelude to *The Rhinegold*, which moves along on the E-flat Major chord for 136 measures. For the deep E flat, Wagner uses lower-tuned double basses, specially designed tubas, and a 32-foot organ pipe constructed for this specific purpose. From a naturalistic point of view, the effect is one of the most overpowering in the annals of music. One cannot imagine the ocean floor depicted in a more lifelike way than in this sea of sound that slowly rocks back and forth—green on green, one could call it. And as the curtain rises, what a ravishing picture, and what a sound of nature in the singing of the Rhinedaughters! And then, what a transition toward the demonic as Alberich enters the stage! Wagner introduces the contrasts in a way that is as new as it is brilliant. He achieves this by means of specific musical *motifs* through which he depicts the most important characters and elements in the text. The *motif* recurs constantly as a flexible symbol that reminds the listeners of what has already occurred and foreshadows what is to come. It fills in the gaps in the drama where the capacity of poetry to do so ceases.

Wagner organizes his *motifs* in accordance with his firm ethical idea, and, succeeding one another in many guises, they constitute in themselves the musical form. The Rhinedaughters have their own *motif*, Loge has his, Fafner his and so

---

[10] Hungarian composer Franz Liszt (1811–86).
[11] Austro-Hungarian conductor Hans Richter (1843–1916) remained one of the regular conductors at the Bayreuth festivals to the end of his life.

on for the ring, the renunciation of love, Valhalla, the Nibelungs (the smith *motif*), Erda, etc. Thus, where Fricka enters and shows Wotan the fortress, the Valhalla *motif* is heard. It is characteristic of Wagner that he depicts giants and dwarfs much more convincingly than he depicts gods. He lacks the elevated calm, the noble simplicity, with which Wotan must be drawn, but on the other hand he has a unique mastery of the mystical-demonic dimension required for the portrayal of the supernatural inhabitants of the mountains and the underworld. One of the most brilliant passages, both musically and scenically, occurs when Wotan and Loge descend to Nibelheim to reclaim the gold and their youth. They disappear through a cleft, from which arises a sulfurous mist that little by little engulfs the entire stage. With the stage enveloped in mist, the scene is changed as the orchestra paints a magnificent picture of their descent to the underworld. Suddenly, from the middle of the sulfurous mist, one hears a profusion of anvil and hammer blows in distinct rhythms (the smith *motif*), the mists begin to clear, and one sees Nibelheim and its busy inhabitants.

Wagner's rare ability to depict a scene such as this has the effect that one is carried along involuntarily, and one forgets that the material is less dramatic. But it turned out as I thought it would: The long dialogues of the gods cannot be made more interesting by the music. To me, and to many others, they became tiresome. But then the Rhinedaughters reappear and sing even more beautifully than they did the first time. One is captivated by the most enchanting nature symbolism. After that, the Valhalla *motif* is heard in all its splendor and the curtain falls.

I go home and say to myself that despite everything that one might criticize, despite the restlessness with which the gods are depicted, despite the many chromatic transitions, the ceaseless changes of harmony after which one is eventually afflicted by a nervous irritability and finally by complete lethargy, despite the abundance of filigree work and the total lack of resting places, despite the outer limit of beauty on which the whole thing stands—despite everything, this music-drama is the work of a giant the likes of whom is perhaps to be found in the history of art only in Michelangelo. Such originality, such unity of style, such brilliant orchestration, such mastery of the art of saying just what is presented here, is not to be found anywhere else in our day. The only thing missing here is spiritual impotence or downright drowsiness.

I hardly need to report that the production was superb. I will discuss it in some greater detail after the public performance. Today we hear that Wagner has convinced the king how important it is for him to hear how everything sounds in a full auditorium, and that the king has, therefore, permitted the distribution of free tickets. The rehearsal of *The Valkyrie* is this evening. I will give you a short summary of the plot.

The Valkyrie

(Second evening)

Wotan descends to Erda, whom he overpowers with the help of a love potion. She bears him nine daughters, who shall help him prevent the destruction of the gods. They are the valkyries. They will choose the battlefield and win the victory. They are armed for war and ride out to the field of battle. They lift the fallen heroes on their shields, bring them to Valhalla, and support the gods in their struggle against the enemy powers, who for the time being, solely because of a truce, are obliged to act peacefully toward the gods. Erda warns Wotan anew. The ring is now owned by Fafner, who, in the form of a dragon, guards the treasure. But to kill the dragon requires a hero who—not supported by the gods, but on his own initiative—slays it and takes possession of the ring. Taking the name Wälse, Wotan descends to the world of human beings and marries a beautiful woman. Their twin offspring are Siegmund and Sieglinde. Wotan and his son Siegmund set out together on a trip of adventure. In their absence, the mother is killed and the daughter kidnapped by Hunding. She sits brooding sadly on her wedding day. Then a one-eyed stranger comes in, plunges a sword into the trunk of an ash tree and says that he who can pull the sword out again shall be its owner. No one is able to do so.

Siegmund has roamed around, struggled alone against superior force, fled weaponless, and comes by night to Hunding's house (here begins the first act) without knowing whose house it is. Hunding has just gone out with the intention of killing Siegmund, who has slain some of his relatives. Sieglinde refreshes the famished stranger and confides to him that she does not love Hunding. Siegmund's sentiment changes to love. Hunding returns. He recognizes him and promises him protection until the next morning. He commands Sieglinde to go to the bedroom and follows her. Deeply agitated, Siegmund remains by the dying fire of the hearth. How shall he, weaponless as he is, be able to slay an enemy tomorrow? He falls into deep thoughts. Then the door opens softly and Sieglinde comes in. She has given Hunding a sleeping-potion. She shows Siegmund the sword as she tells about the one-eyed man. Then Siegmund's soul is enlightened and he embraces Sieglinde in the certainty that she is the bride who has been chosen for him. At the same moment the back door springs open. Outside it is a glorious spring night, the full moon shines in upon them, and with rapture they look into each other's eyes and see that they are both Wälse's children. With a mighty tug, Siegmund pulls the sword out of the ash tree, and the two siblings fall as lovers into each other's arms.

The following morning (here begins the second act) the fight with Hunding, whom Siegmund has twice insulted, is to take place. Wotan commands the valkyrie Brünnhilde to give the victory to the Volsung [Siegmund]. Brünnhilde was the daughter of Erda whom Wotan loved best. She wants to carry out his order, but the jealous Fricka comes in and demands that Siegmund shall fall because he has violated the marriage vow. Wotan is weak and changes the command: Siegmund shall fall. Against her wish, Brünnhilde must hurry to Hunding's castle to inform Siegmund of his impending death. Siegmund would prefer to kill both Sieglinde and himself rather than to be separated from her. Brünnhilde is overcome with admiration and decides to contradict Wotan's command and save the hero. Hunding's voice is heard. He comes out and they fight. Siegmund is at the very point of giving the death blow when Wotan stretches his spear out toward Siegmund in such a way that Siegmund's sword breaks to pieces. Siegmund is stabbed by Hunding. Sieglinde, who heard his last gasp, collapses with a shriek. Quickly Brünnhilde lifts the unconscious Sieglinde up onto her horse and disappears with her to escape Wotan's wrath. Wotan stands consumed by sorrow over Siegmund's death, and with only a contemptuous gesture lets Hunding fall dead upon the ground. Thereafter he hurries away to summon Brünnhilde to punish her.

The third act begins with Brünnhilde hurrying away to the Valkyrie rock, where all the other eight valkyries are waiting. She begs for protection for Sieglinde. In vain. At Brünnhilde's advice, Sieglinde flees into the forest where Fafner guards the treasure, and where Wotan does not come. She gives her the broken pieces of Siegmund's sword and tells her that in her flesh rests the world's greatest hero, the Volsung Siegfried. Wotan approaches in a thunderstorm. He expels Brünnhilde from the society of the gods and condemns her to lie in a deep sleep on the Valkyrie rock, at the mercy of any man who may waken her. Brünnhilde is frightened and begs for mercy, but to no avail. Finally Wotan accedes to her prayer that the mountain shall be surrounded by a wall of flame. His old love for her awakens as they part. He kisses her eyes until they close and covers her with a big shield. Only a hero will now venture to approach the flame-encircled mountain. This is the content of "The Valkyrie".

On the basis of my acquaintance with the work, I expect infinitely more than I did from *The Rhinegold*. Here there is more dramatic life and also lyrical passages of the greatest beauty. Siegmund and Sieglinde are characters with whom we become totally engaged emotionally. Wagner has been blamed for offending our moral sense by depicting here a romantic relationship between brother and sister. Unjustly, in my view. Thus it is told in the myth, and the literature presents it with ruthless greatness. One joins in rejoicing over the all- conquering love that in the myth encounters no obstacles. To the contrary! When the lovers realize that they are siblings, Wagner the poet brings the rejoicing to a climax. The music, too, reaches the apex of beauty at this point. And then the marvelous valkyrie character, Brünnhilde! And the magnificent scene with all the valkyries together! I have the highest expectations.

III

(August 12)

Mr. Editor!
As you will see from the date, I have had to allow some time to elapse since my last report. During this time, I have attended the dress rehearsals of the whole gigantic work, but I have not had a moment to spare in which to take up my pen. The place is so swarming with composers, authors, and painters from all over the world that one stumbles over them, so to speak, wherever one goes. The biggest names in Europe are all gathered here—yes, even from America there are many who have flocked here. In the long run, this profusion of artists would not be endurable. I am not staying in a hotel but in a private home, and I thought that in that way I would have some time to myself when I was in my quarters. But no, one meets celebrities in corridors and stairways. Next door to me is a famous opera composer, on the other side of the corridor a famous singer, on the floor below a famous court musical director, and in the room above mine a famous critic. Sitting here now, I can hear Wagnerian *motifs* being hummed, sung, yodeled and bellowed nearby. I go to the window and see both valkyries and Rhinedaughters, both giants and dwarfs, both gods and men strolling around and enjoying life in the shadowy alleys. I slam the window shut in order to have it quiet. I draw the blinds, but Erda's mighty alto voice penetrates the thick walls. It's no wonder that I sit here bewildered.

But now, back to the subject. As I said, I approached *The Valkyrie* with the highest expectations, and when I say that I was not disappointed, even this is an understatement.

The entire first act is so perfect that one could not wish a single measure to be different. It gets better and better as you go along. The prelude depicts in the most brilliant way a storm that is about to abate as the curtain rises. The growing interest with which Siegmund and Sieglinde regard each other is masterfully expressed—as is also Hunding's appearance, which is accompanied by a dark, piercing, very distinct *motif*. Not a word about the love scene. In all its fervor and purity and loftiness, it defies any attempt to describe it. And then the valkyrie scenes in the second and third acts! How one can hear them charging through the clouds on their wild horses in the mighty "Ride of the Valkyries"! Here is the Old Norse spirit—something that one generally seeks in vain in Wagner, as I shall discuss later. Brünnhilde's deep pain after Wotan has repudiated her is also gripping. She sings at the beginning almost without orchestra, but so innocently and fervently that one readily sympathizes with her as she, timidly and with restraint, begins:

> *Was it so shameful,*
> *what I did,*

that you had to punish it so disgracefully?
Was it so mean,
what I did to you,
that you had to give me such deep humiliation?[12]

And when the orchestra joins in—how fervent, how heart-rending! And at the end, when Wotan kisses her eyes until they close! More gripping music has never been written. Accompanied by completely new languorous, slow chromatic harmonies in contrary motion, ethereally orchestrated, she sinks, with eyes closed, back into his arms. Then follows the equally novel "Magic Fire" (*Feuer-zauber*), where Wotan conjures up the fire around her bed. Here Wagner unites three different *motifs* in the most imaginative way, and yet the real "magic" lies in the orchestral sonority itself. Here the Wagnerian orchestration celebrates its greatest triumph.

I will now turn to the plot in *Siegfried*.

Siegfried

(Third Evening)

Wotan, disguised as a wanderer, roams around the world and observes the occurrence of everything of which he has had a premonition. In the forest, where Fafner, in his cave, guards the treasure, the dying Sieglinde gives birth to Siegfried. He grows up under the care of the cunning Mime, who wants to rear him to become Fafner's slayer. But Siegfried hates the ugly dwarf and prefers to live by himself in the forest and learn on his own. He does not know that Mime possesses the pieces of his father's shattered sword, which Mime is not able to forge together into a whole sword until Siegfried himself joins in the task. He succeeds, and with the new sword, *Nothung*, he will slay the dragon. Mime brews a poison drink for the champion in order to be able to kill him as soon as the dragon has been slain. Siegfried performs the mighty deed without knowing anything about the booty he now owns. He had gotten a little of the dragon's blood on his finger and happens to touch his lips with it. Then he suddenly understands the birds' song. On their advice, he takes the ring and the helmet and kills the assassin Mime. Now he himself is master of the treasure. But what does he care about that? In the deep loneliness of the forest he is gripped by a longing for love, and joyfully he follows the bird, who has told him about Brünnhilde, to the flaming mountain.

Wotan is beset by doubts because of Erda's dark prophecies. He sees Siegfried approaching the mountain and wants to hold him back, but Siegfried

---

[12] *War es so schmählich, / was ich verbrach, / dass mein Verbrechen so schmählich du bestraf'st? / War es so niedrich, / was ich dir that, / dass du so tief mir schaff'st?*

crushes Wotan's spear with his sword. This event foreshadows the destruction of the gods, for the agreement with the giants was inscribed on the spear. Siegfried plunges triumphantly through the flames, but he doesn't know how to waken Brünnhilde. He kisses her long and passionately until she opens her eyes. Quietly and solemnly she rises. She praises the gods when she hears that it is Siegfried who has wakened her. She thinks wistfully of life in Valhalla; she still cannot accept the idea of belonging to a man. But love for her rescuer triumphs, and she happily falls into his arms. The curtain falls.

Except for the scenes in which Wotan appears, which, though grandiose from the epic point of view, are dramatically ineffective—yes, even the scene where Wotan conjures Erda up from the earth, which in all its loftiness nonetheless comes across static on the stage—the threads of the plot begin to come together more and more, and one is filled with premonitions about what is to come.

The music maintains the same level nearly all the way through. As the curtain rises, we hear the sword *motif.* Mime is sitting by his anvil and diligently pounding away on a sword intended for Siegfried. Here Wagner is in his element. The character is consistently maintained throughout, just as Mime, from a musical point of view, is one of the best limned figures. Siegfried's carefree spirit is depicted no less skillfully in the music. In the whole scene in which he is forging the sword, word and music go hand in hand in such a way that the one is unthinkable without the other. When he, in his joy over the result, splits Mime's anvil in two with a single blow from Nothung [the sword], the orchestra joins in the jubilation in rhythms that are strongly reminiscent of the scherzo in Beethoven's *Ninth Symphony*, although the passage is thoroughly Wagnerian in spirit.

The second act was another of these long dialogues of which it is difficult not to tire. What is unfortunate is that the situation doesn't have the interest that, independent of the words, can captivate the listener. These dialogues are a matter of principle for Wagner. He defends them passionately. And they really require a brilliant defender, as they cannot speak for themselves—not even from a musical point of view, for as Wagner, with a predilection that completely overrates the power of music, tries to characterize individual words in music, the result is formlessness. His dialogues, set to music, are even longer than the longest dialogues in the writings of Schiller or Goethe[13]—in which, however, one can understand every word. And then comes the real secret: One realizes that they are the products of reflection. For the inspiration here always stands many degrees below that of the scenes in which the fresh flow of action also gives wings to the music.

---

[13] Friedrich von Schiller (1750–1805), Johann Wolfgang von Goethe (1749–1832).

I must not forget to discuss the wonderful evocation of nature in the second act ("Forest-weaving"—"Das Waldweben"), where Siegfried, sitting alone in the forest, looks up toward the blue sky and thinks about how his father and mother may have looked. His attention is drawn more and more to the birdsong, and no wonder! The audience listens with him, for a lovelier evocation of a woodland with birdsong and a murmuring forest breeze has never been heard in music. Add to that a superb orchestration—and an outstanding performance! One can only wonder how much the invisible orchestra may contribute to the preservation of the illusion in such a moment. Later, when Siegfried comprehends the birdsong, the effect is further enhanced as the bird voices are heard not only in the orchestra but on stage as they (through children's voices sounding off stage) inform Siegfried from the treetops where he will find the treasure and Brünnhilde.

To depict the monster Fafner is a task that appears to lie beyond the realm of music. But what does Wagner do? Just a couple of slow, deep bass notes from the tubas and the organ pedal—tones with strong *crescendos* and *diminuendos*— and he has achieved the effect in its entirety. One literally shudders as the monster slowly waddles out of its cave accompanied by these sounds. And still more when it opens its jaws and lets out some terrible roars. For inside the dragon there are both a singer and a voice tube.

The beginning of the third act shows us Wotan conjuring Erda up from the bowels of the earth. The whole scene, as it stands, is in all essentials the Edda's *Vegtamskvida*.[14] The tone color is predominantly tragic, but the music cannot be said to reflect the tone of the saga. The entire concluding scene between Siegfried and Brünnhilde is full of beautiful passages, but considered as a whole it does not come up to the scene between Siegfried and Sieglinde in *The Valkyrie*. The final postlude, where the jubilation breaks out in trills, sounds most peculiar. The effect is achieved by simple means but is nonetheless novel and beautiful.

IV

(August 13)

Mr. Editor!
I come now to the last of the four music-dramas:

Twilight of the Gods

(Fourth evening)

As the curtain rises it is night. One sees the three Norns (Erda's daughters)

---

[14] *Vegtamskvida* is part of the *Elder Edda*.

winding the golden thread of fate. In muffled seriousness, they predict the destruction of Valhalla and of the gods. Recalling Alberich's curse on the ring, the thread is broken, their knowledge is ended, and they sink down to Mother Erda.

The next morning Siegfried, who has spent a day and a night with Brünnhilde, sets out to perform new heroic deeds. Brünnhilde has told him all about his ancestry and about the ring that he gives her as a farewell present. He leaves her on the mountain, protected by the flames, while he visits his relatives, the Gibichungs, on the Rhine. Because of her earthly love, Brünnhilde has lost the ability to see into the future. Thus she no longer knows of the ring's power but regards it simply as a pledge of faithfulness from Siegfried.

Siegfried comes to Gunther, the king of the Gibichungs, and his wise brother, Hagen, who is not a Gibichung but is nonetheless Gunther's brother. Their mother, Grimhilde, gave birth to him after once allowing herself to be charmed by Alberich's gold. Hagen now begins to plot Siegfried's defeat in order to regain the ring for his father, Alberich. Gunther's sister, the beautiful Gutrune, has begun to love Siegfried even before she sees him, after Hagen has told her in laudatory words about his fight with the dragon. Hagen mixes a magic potion for her which she, well aware of what she is doing, gives Siegfried by way of welcome. Siegfried drinks. Immediately he forgets Brünnhilde and insists that Gutrune become his wife. Gunther promises her to him, but demands in return that Siegfried shall get Brünnhilde for him. Her name no longer wakens any memories in Siegfried. He enters into a pact of blood-brotherhood with Gunther, and they set out together for the flaming mountain.

Brünnhilde sits on the mountain in the evening sun and, enraptured, contemplates the ring. Then a valkyrie, one of her sisters, comes down from Valhalla and commands her sternly to give the ring back to the Rhinedaughters. But Brünnhilde will not relinquish it. No sooner has the sister ridden away with a woeful cry than Siegfried arrives. He has plunged through the flames with the help of the helmet's magic power, but he is transformed into Gunther's body. Brünnhilde, who is no longer a valkyrie but just a weak woman, is helpless. He takes the ring, the symbol of marriage, and forces her to the bridal chamber, but he lays the sword Nothung between them and thus preserves fidelity to his blood-brother Gunther.

The night is over. In the hall by the Rhine, preparations are being made for a double wedding. Gunther and Brünnhilde arrive. Brünnhilde sees Siegfried and discovers with horror that he does not recognize her. She is on the verge of collapsing, and Siegfried supports her with the hand on which he is wearing the ring. Brünnhilde recognizes the ring, which she thinks Gunther has taken from her. She wants to know how it all hangs together. But Gunther remains silent. Siegfried says that he has not gotten the ring from any woman, but that it was his reward for killing Fafner. Hagen has been waiting for this moment. He now convinces Brünnhilde that Siegfried must have come into possession of the ring with the help of treachery. Brünnhilde sees through the deceit, shrieks aloud in her pain and vows revenge on Siegfried, whom she regards as guilty. She declares aloud that she is not married to Gunther but to Siegfried. Siegfried reminds her of Nothung, which separated them, but Brünnhilde does not understand this. She is thinking only of the first marriage, and accuses him of lying. Siegfried swears by Hagen's spear that he has been faithful. Brünnhilde swears that he has broken all of his vows and now is committing perjury anew.

Everyone is seized by the greatest consternation. Only Siegfried refuses to let his exhilaration be disturbed. He embraces Gutrune and goes off happily with her to the wedding feast. Brünnhilde, Gunther and Hagen remain and decide that Siegfried must die.

The men go hunting. Siegfried tries unsuccessfully to overtake a wild animal and, separated from the rest of the hunting party, finds himself in a lonely forest region by the Rhine. The three Rhinedaughters emerge from the water. They promise him a good catch and ask him in return for the ring on his finger. Siegfried will not give up the memento of his victory over the dragon. Then they make it clear to him that if he keeps the ring he will die. But now the heroic valor in him awakens. He will not relinquish the ring.

The rest of the hunting party catches up with him again. He tells them in the happiest of moods about the Rhinedaughters' prophecy and about the birds, whose language he understands. He asks for something to drink. Hagen secretly pours into the drinking-horn the juice of an herb that counteracts the effect of the drink of forgetfulness. Siegfried drinks and, after his memory has returned, relates how, with the help of a bird, he found the flaming mountain —and Brünnhilde. Gunther is astonished. Has his wife been Siegfried's wife? Two ravens fly over Siegfried's head. Hagen interrupts his narrative: "Can you also guess what these ravens whisper?" Siegfried jumps up and looks at the ravens. At that moment he is struck from behind by Hagen's spear. The dying man heaves his shield aloft to crush Hagen, but his strength fails him and he collapses with a bang. Hagen says calmly, "I avenged the perjury," whereupon he walks away. Siegfried's last words are a farewell to Brünnhilde.

The corpse is carried away in a solemn cortege of mourners. The cortege arrives at the castle of the Gibichungs, and the weeping Gutrune throws herself upon the corpse. Hagen, Siegfried's slayer, claims the ring. Gunther also lays claim to it. They fight. Gunther falls. Hagen approaches the corpse to take possession of the ring, but springs back in fear when the hand of the dead man raises itself threateningly.

Brünnhilde now realizes all the unhappiness she has caused by her wild thirst for revenge. Her love for Siegfried flames up again. Proudly she turns Gutrune away from the corpse as she makes a claim to be regarded as Siegfried's wife—she, and no one else! Siegfried is laid on the pyre, and Brünnhilde demands that she be allowed to share it with him. She takes the ring from Siegfried's hand, lights the fire, mounts her horse, and springs into the flames.

The Rhine overflows its banks, and swimming on its waves come the Rhinedaughters. Hagen rushes toward them with the cry, "Away from the ring!" But two of the Rhinedaughters encircle him with their arms and draw him with them down into the deep. The third one triumphantly holds up the ring, which she has found in the ashes of the collapsed pyre. In the sky, one sees in the background a red glow: a reflection of the fire that is consuming Valhalla.

Thus ends the fourth drama, which begins in the night after Siegfried and Brünnhilde's true marriage. It lasts for three full days and concludes in the fourth night.

The poet-composer had first called the work *Siegfried's Death* (*Siegfrieds Tod*) but later changed the title to the more significant *Twilight of the Gods* (*Götterdämmerung*). Our forefathers used the latter expression to symbolize the struggle between light and darkness which, because of the increasing power of evil, eventually had to culminate in the defeat of the gods—who were not guiltless themselves. Wagner has made this ancient Norse world-view the foundation for what he has written, and a noted German critic certainly is right when he says that in so doing the poet has given it a moral seriousness and loftiness that must captivate everyone who is receptive to that which is good and beautiful. For he allows not only Siegfried and all those responsible for his death to be destroyed, but also the gods, who were depicted as guilty from the beginning. Had the gods not taken possession of the gold but given it back to the Rhine, mankind would never have learned of its pernicious influence.

There is no doubt that *Twilight of the Gods* is the foremost, and dramatically the most effective, of the four dramas. Here the great tragic conflict toward which the other dramas are pointing actually occurs; here the fate of men and of gods is consummated; here, for the first time in the entire trilogy, Wagner includes the masses (men and women of the Gibichungs). He certainly knew what he was doing in saving these means for the ending. And how everything here happens thick and fast! And what a conclusion! Just as in the first drama the Rhinedaughters appeared as the guardians of the gold, so at the conclusion of the fourth they show up again to regain possession. Thus the poet compels us to take a retrospective glance, and we survey again the whole cycle, the high points of which impress themselves upon us with renewed power. All the misfortune the ring has created suddenly stands before us. This is a brilliant idea. Therefore, too, the title of the whole cycle, *The Ring of the Nibelung*, is the only proper one.

I hardly dare to single out for special emphasis any of the music from this last giant work. It offers such a world of greatness and beauty that one can almost choose any passage at random. When I hastily page through the music, I stop at the very beginning with the song of the Norns. The dark timbre of this piece is remarkable. The monotonous strains sound absolutely ominous in relation to the harmonies, so full of presentiment; the orchestra spins the thread of life every bit as well as the Norns, who basically only produce a background of intermediate voices. I once heard this scene performed in Berlin under Wagner's own leadership. There were no Norns at that performance; he let the orchestra play quite calmly by itself and hummed along with it. I mention this because it provides grist for my mill when I contend that the vocal parts in the whole work are not essentially related to the orchestra but function almost as appendices. The orchestra is exploited to the utmost. Why not also the singers? Is it perhaps because in that case the words could not be heard? To that I would reply that by and large they cannot be heard anyway—unless they are in the hands of unusually brilliant performers—if one has not made oneself carefully acquainted with the text beforehand. In any case, either the vocal part should have the same right as the orchestra to express the deepest emotions moving within a human breast or else it should not be there at all. But in the latter case we are dealing with a melodrama. A transitional style like this, an in-between something that is both song and non-song, has no future, no understanding at all—even though it is defended in a whole literature of pamphlets. It is the feeling of untenability in Wagner's theories about the handling of the voice that always puts a stop to the immediate enjoyment that a great work of art should be able to give. This, of course, has nothing to do with the great *ideal* value that is embodied in Wagner's music, and that I enthusiastically join in calling unique in the dramatic music of our time. What is most unfortunate, however, is that even the most lofty ideas are often made inaccessible because of the handling of the vocal parts. Beethoven's greatest strength, as we know, did not lie in the employment of the human voice, but he used it nonetheless to accomplish climaxes. I would not want to hear the *finale* of the Ninth Symphony without the human voices, but I must admit that the song of the Norns in the aforementioned concert sounded just as good *without* the Norns as it sounded *with* them in Bayreuth.

It is not a pleasant duty to pour as much "ice water in the blood"[15] as I now have done, but I had to express my conviction. How much more pleasant it is just

---

[15] Grieg is alluding to *Peer Gynt* by Henrik Ibsen (1828–1906). In Act 2, Scene 6, the Mountain King shouts to his followers, who are attacking Peer: "Ice water in your blood!" The premiere performance of *Peer Gynt* with Grieg's incidental music had taken place in Christiania just a few months previously—on February 24, 1876.

to emphasize and dwell on that which is perfect! And I have many opportunities to do that. I find one reason that *Twilight of the Gods* is so inspired in the fact that it is human beings with human feelings and passions who are depicted, and as previously mentioned, Wagner is much more successful here than in his representation of the gods. For the same reason, this drama engages our interest and sympathy from beginning to end. And how superbly the sinister Hagen is depicted in contrast to Siegfried, who is so full of life! And how sensitive and graceful Gutrune appears! But from the very moment when Hagen raises his horn calling the men together for the wedding preparations, the music takes on a breadth and power, and at the same time a structural rounding-off, rarely seen in Wagner's music. Here one also occasionally finds traces of the ancient Norse tone—something that one naturally cannot demand from Wagner. But that these are present shows how strong his inspiration has been. What one cannot finally hold against him, but must nonetheless regret, is that the Nordic folk music is foreign to him. I mean, of course, merely that one might wish that he had used it here where he depicts the Nordic past—a unique product of which is our heroic ballads. He may, of course, treat his Medieval German heroes as "primordial Germanic". But I think that if a Scandinavian of Wagner's talent were born, and if he treated the myth of Sigurd Fafnersbane, we would hear more echoes of the *Edda* in the music. It's a shame that Wagner is obviously unfamiliar with such works as Hartmann's *The Valkyrie* and *The Legend of Thrym*,[16] for these are brilliant examples of the Nordic spirit that a man with Wagner's view would have to find gripping.

Some of the loveliest and most charming tone color in the whole work is in the Rhinedaughters' last song to Siegfried as they plead with him to return the ring to them. Here harps and voices unite to create absolutely indescribable effects. But if I were to name what is greatest in *Twilight of the Gods*—indeed, the climax of the whole trilogy—I am drawn relentlessly to Siegfried's death, and I say: This is it! Here the appalling events that we have witnessed in the preceding moments are brought together in a funeral march to the somber beat of which Siegfried's funeral procession slowly begins to move. In fact, through this music the entire demonic-tragic dimension is being tamed. This funeral march is a monument to Siegfried's heroic life. And what a monument! Not since Beethoven's march in *Eroica* has anything been written that can be compared with this. And then Brünnhilde's song when she decides to die with Siegfried! It is this melody that a German critic calls "the melody of love's redemption" ("die Melodie der Liebeserlösung"), and it does indeed have a power to release, culminating at the end—after Brünnhilde has mounted the pyre just as the

---

[16] *Valkyrien*, op. 62 (1861) and *Thrymskviden*, op. 67 (1868), ballets by Danish composer Johan Peter Emilius Hartmann (1805–1900). Grieg regarded Hartmann as one of Denmark's leading composers.

flames envelop the old gods. Then this melody, accompanied by ethereal harp chords, soars heavenward as a symbol of the redeemed love returning to its eternal wellspring.

Thus my over-all impression of the whole work, as you can see, has been overwhelming. Perhaps at the public performance much will be modified, much will be elevated, but the essentials will remain the same. I have now dwelt on the content, but unfortunately—since the power of words is limited—I have been able to do no more than briefly hint at the beauty of the music. After the performance, when I shall give a concluding report, I will focus on the externals: the acting, the stage set, the audience, and anything else that has to do with the actual festivity.

V

(August 14)

Mr. Editor!

To be a correspondent when the thermometer shows 26 degrees Réaumur[17] in the shade is a difficult assignment, Mr. Editor. But presumably you think as I do: If one has said *a* one must say *b*. I shall, therefore, try my best to give a picture of the first public performance of *The Rhinegold*, which took place yesterday.

So: The day has begun, the town is decorated with flags, the weather is radiant, and the inhabitants no less so, for the German emperor[18] has arrived— to crown with his presence the first work of dramatic art since the days of the Greek tragedies, according to the most rabid Wagnerites. Others, who seem to be well informed amongst the center party, say that the emperor has come to humor Mrs. von Schleinitz,[19] Wagner's ardent supporter in Berlin. Be that as it may, the fact is that he really has come and that the commotion is great. The King of Bavaria, on the other hand, has cleared out—as people here who know him feared he would—despite the fact that it was he who invited the emperor. The performance, which was to start at 5 P.M., in accordance with the emperor's wish, was rescheduled for 7 P.M.—for which he deserves the thanks of all true lovers of art, for gathering in the theater at 5 P.M. would be tantamount to taking a Russian steam bath. It is 4 o'clock now, and already groups of people dressed to the hilt are walking down the dusty road to the Wagner Theater. Carriages and formal dress make it evident that the people here are from the highest circles. Youth and

---

[17] Réaumur is a system for measuring temperature in which 0° is the freezing point and 80° the boiling point of water. Thus 26° Réaumur = 33° Celsius = 91° Fahrenheit.

[18] Wilhelm I (1797–1888), German emperor from 1871, attended the performances of *The Rhinegold* and *The Valkyrie*.

[19] Marie von Schleinitz (1842–1912).

beauty are well represented, artists are counted in the thousands, excitement and happy anticipation can be read in the faces of all. People gather in groups on the terraces in front of the theater and in the large Wagner Restaurant, where spirits are refreshed and the theme of the day is discussed. But time flies, I elbow my way through the huge crowd of people—controlled by the military—that threatens to completely block the road. Finally, after many trials and tribulations, I am in my seat in the theater amongst a bejewelled audience that exceeds in elegance anything I have ever seen. There is a hush. Into the royal box strides one royal personage after another, each with his entourage. Lastly comes the stately old Emperor with his amiable, kind-looking countenance. He is met by a veritable storm of jubilation as he comes all the way to the front of the box, warmly greeting people in all directions. It becomes pitch dark, and immediately thereafter the performance begins. The very warm temperature and the over-packed auditorium make the orchestra sound more dampened than at the rehearsals, and perhaps contribute also to the result that here and there the pitch of the singers is almost imperceptibly higher than that of the orchestra. But the overall impression is beautiful.

Among the performers[20] must be mentioned, first of all, Vogl as Loge and Schlosser as Mime. One does not know which of these one should admire most. Loge is rewarded with a thundering ovation after one of his mile-long solos; otherwise there is total silence. Even Louise Jaide's splendid Erda does not get the clapping going. That is natural, say the radicals, because one is so preoccupied with the situation; but if I am going to judge on the basis of my own impression, I would say it is because the long, undramatic dialogues of the gods have exhausted the audience.

But then the curtain falls and there is an ovation that goes on and on. "Wagner! Wagner!" is shouted from every corner. But no Wagner is to be seen, despite the fact that the emperor is standing in his box waiting and clapping and waiting and clapping again. Why Wagner does not show his face is, of course, explained in various ways. The radicals say it is because he is furious about several botched stage effects. The conservative but petty right wing thinks, on the other hand, that in Munich he is accustomed to receiving acclaim in the royal box and considers it beneath his dignity to come onto the stage. I will leave it to the Germans to fight

---

[20] [The footnote that follows is Grieg's own. The dates given here and in footnotes 21 and 22 are taken from Brock, *op. cit.*]:

Since it might be of interest to the many Norwegians who are now beginning to get acquainted with German art and artists, I will list the performers: Wotan: Franz Betz [1835–1900] from Berlin; Donner: Eugen Gura [1842–1906] from Leipzig; Loge: Heinrich Vogl [1845–1903] from Munich; Fasolt: Albert Eilers [1830–96] from Coburg; Fafner: Franz v. Reichenberg [1855–1905] from Stettin; Alberich: Karl Hill [1831–93] from Stettin; Mime: Karl Schlosser [1835–1916] from Munich; Fricka: Friderike Grün [1836–1907] from Coburg; Freia: Marie Haupt [1849–?] from Cassel; Erda: Louise Jaide [1842–1914] from Darmstadt; Woglinde: Lilli Lehmann [1848–1929] from Berlin; Wellgunde: Marie Lehmann [1851–1931] from Cologne; Flosshilde: Minna Lammert [1852–?] from Berlin.

over who is right. (I say "fight over" because, unbelievable as it sounds, questions like this are regularly decided at the Wagner Restaurant not over but *with* beer tankards. The one who has been rendered unfit for battle by getting hit on the head with one of the well-known, massive *Töpfchen* has obviously lost.)

If Wagner was displeased with the staging, in any case, it is not without reason, for the fact is that it left much to be desired. As for occasional glitches—the back curtain being removed too soon, thereby revealing the whole back stage; the scene changes taking too long, as a result of which the orchestra had to play more slowly so as not to finish too early; and a rainbow that was supposed to appear on the right side showing up on the left—one could say that they were the sort of thing that could happen anywhere. But since both Wagner and his friends have year after year castigated the most meticulously prepared performances of his music-dramas at Germany's top theaters (including *The Rhinegold* and *The Valkyrie* in Munich) as true monstrosities, as a puppet show that absolutely destroys the master's intentions, and have pointed to Bayreuth as the place where the impossible would become a reality, I may be permitted to say: Here nothing is permitted to fail. But consider also much of that in which the performance does not fall short, where everything really does transpire in accordance with Wagner's intentions! How ineffective, often childish, it looks! When Alberich steals the Rhinegold and disappears with it, one is supposed to get the impression that it really is he who takes the gold, that he has it on his person, that one really should see its shining glow follow him into the depths. But none of this! A light is extinguished somewhere up above, and anyone unfamiliar with the plot would find it difficult to understand that this is the fateful moment when Alberich absconds with the stolen gold. It is not the master's intentions I mean to be attacking here, but merely the self-righteousness and arrogance pervading Wagner and his clique and surrounding them with an unhealthy stench of infallibility.

Apart from the fact that Valhalla looks more like a king's castle than an abode of the gods in the heavens, the stage settings are otherwise exceptionally effective. But I must admit that on the basis of the dress rehearsal, I had anticipated a greater overall impression from *The Rhinegold*. The fact is that since my report about this work, I have heard the dress rehearsals of the three works that follow, with their steady heightening of tension and the powerful conclusion. *The Rhinegold* certainly is a masterwork—but one should not have heard *Twilight of the Gods* beforehand. It is, to use a homespun analogy, like coming from the spectacular scenery of Filefjell and Lærdal to Bergen, with its seven very respectable mountains. Even the great becomes small when one comes from something still greater.

VI

(August 15)

Mr. Editor!

Today Wagner has had posters put up on the street corners asking the public not to give the performers curtain calls "so as not to bring them out of the artistic framework." In this connection, the tankards are flying once again, for the less benevolent people think that Wagner—who never has been truly willing to acknowledge Vogl's merits, and in annoyance over the triumph he has scored as Loge—has allowed himself to be misled into taking this step. Wagner must certainly have foreseen that curtain calls would occur, and he should rather have had this poster put up one day earlier if he did not want to be blamed for acting out of personal motives. I will again let the parties concerned fight it out to their hearts' content, and I hasten to relate that the performance of *The Valkyrie* last evening was masterful in every respect.[21] (The emperor was in attendance again, but for the last time, as he left town already last night.)

Niemann as Siegmund is one of the most complete all-around dramatic performers I have ever seen. He must be said to be past his peak as a singer. And if one cannot exactly accuse him of treating that which is delicate with delicacy (for example, the moonlight scene in Act 1), he pulls everybody along with his full, warm personality. Every movement is permeated with powerful inspiration—and it is quite an achievement to preserve the inspiration in the portrayal of a figure such as Siegmund. For here, as he often does, Wagner—presumably in order to achieve tragic breadth—has the orchestra play between question and answer, depicting whatever is vibrating in the soul at the moment. For the singer, filling out these pauses is a task that makes enormous demands in terms of mime that very, very few performers can manage successfully. Sometimes, too, there is such a time lapse between decision and action that the effect is almost as comical as that of some of the older operas—which Wagner and others so strongly criticize, and justly so—where one constantly hears "Away! Away!" but for an extended period of time, nobody moves an inch. Of such scenes I will mention the one where Siegmund springs up and grasps the sword in order to pull it out of the tree trunk. Here, with his hand on the hilt of the sword, yet looking away from the sword itself, he sings a long passage. The result is that anyone who cannot understand the words is tempted to think that he cannot get the sword out, or

---

21 [Grieg's own footnote]:

    The performers: Siegmund: Albert Niemann [1831–1917] from Berlin; Hunding: Albert Eilers [1830–96] from Coburg; Sieglinde: Josephine Scheffzky [1843–1912] from Munich; Brünnhilde: Amalia Materna [1845–1918] from Vienna; the other valkyries: Marie Haupt, Lilli Lehmann, Marie Lehmann, Louise Jaide, Antonie Amann from Dresden, Minna Lammert, Hedwig Reicher-Kindermann from Munich and Johanna Wagner from Berlin; Wotan and Fricka: the same as before.

that he has simply forgotten about it and is once again expatiating upon Sieglinde's loveliness.

Miss Scheffzky as Sieglinde handles her role very well, although she does not come close to Niemann in performance ability. Betz as Wotan does not live up to the expectations one has for this outstanding artist. But it also appears impossible to give the viewer the impression of a god in this figure. The part incorporates plenty of musical beauty, but dramatically it is ineffective. I got this impression even more strongly at the public performance than at the dress rehearsal. What kind of a fickle and weak-willed god is it anyway who every moment changes his commands depending on the whims of the jealous Fricka! In Act 3, he is supposed to appear in a thunderstorm, roused to anger by Brünnhilde's disobedience. The heightening of tension is brilliant, the anticipation is amplified to the utmost. One expects to see the angry god in the clouds, so masterfully has Wagner succeeded in stimulating the viewer's imagination— and then, from one of the wings, a man comes hurrying in to inform us that Wotan has suddenly been detained! What a letdown! And one feels even more of a letdown when, in the next instant, one observes that this man is indeed Wotan—the boring Wotan from the previous act, and not at all Wotan such as Wagner, in the immediately preceding scene, has so brilliantly heralded him.

Although Mrs. Materna as a valkyrie does not give us as much as she does later, in *Twilight of the Gods*—where, stripped of her divine qualities, she appears as a mortal woman—her performance here, too, is highly effective. Her vocal art culminates in the well-known "Ho jo to ho" (Act 2). Here she executes the most difficult intervals—yes, even trills—with playful lightness as she, bubbling with joy, leaps from rock to rock.

In Act 3, the ensemble of valkyries—some of the most inspired music Wagner has written—came across as brilliantly realistic. After this, human nature overcame upbringing: There was a real storm of applause. And no less after the conclusion. I think this work would make a powerful, immediate impression on any unbiased, reasonably receptive person. There is such an enormous power of nature, especially over all the valkyrie scenes, that I instinctively place them in the Jotunheimen region of Norway rather than in the Rhine area. I returned to my lodgings with the feeling of having seen one of the most elevated revelations of Wagner's genius.

VII

(August 17)

Mr. Editor!
Today a few words about *Siegfried*, the first Bayreuth public performance of

Richard Wagner.
Reproduction of a
photograph, by Elliot
& Fry of London.

which took place yesterday. Thus, it was postponed for one day because of the bass—Betz's (Wotan's)—indisposition. The one-day postponement was worth its weight in gold for us poor listeners. Between each performance of the trilogy, Wagner has directed that there shall be three "days of rest" ("Erholungstage"). But he could just as well have inserted an additional three days between each play in the series, so agitated and enervated does one feel after each of them. It is a unique experience to be forced into the theater like this four days in a row for pleasures of such a penetrating nature. The performance lasted from 4 P.M. until about 10:30 in the evening. To be sure, the intermissions lasted about one hour each, but this hour is entirely spent in physical activity: one must elbow and fight one's way through the crowd to get something to wet one's tongue—which is sorely needed if one is to have the strength to get through the next act.

Among the performers in *Siegfried*[22] it is again Schlosser as Mime who stands out. He plays the cunning dwarf with a striking characterization. One understands

---

[22] [Grieg's own footnote]: *The performers:* Siegfried: Georg Unger [1837–87] from Mannheim; the wanderer (Wotan), Betz; Mime, Alberich, Fafner, Erda and Brünnhilde: the same as before.

much of the text because he recites more than he sings, thereby taking a big step in the direction of melodrama. In addition there is not a second of silence that he does not fill with first-rate miming. Here one notes that poet, composer and performer are working together.

Mr. Unger's Siegfried is not outstanding, but he doesn't completely ruin anything. It is said that Wagner chose him only because of his strapping physique and that he later regretted having done so. Betz gives here a comely picture of Wotan flitting about the earth in the guise of a wanderer, but so also has the poet-composer done. That is what produces the pure, grandiose effect. The staging of the scene with the dragon certainly is unobjectionable, but it is a risky matter when the stage experiments have to play as prominent a role as they do here. In *Der Freischütz*[23] one can put up with seeing the Wolf Glen scene even if there are some glitches here and there. If the owl should lack a wing or another animal a foot, one feels nonetheless that this is a minor matter. In *Don Giovanni*[24] one does not ask what the furies look like. Nothing else depends on them. With Wagner, it is different. The dragon is of the very first importance. The viewer's anticipation has been awakened in advance and his attention repeatedly directed toward the monster that is soon to appear. The colossal dragon's body, like Fricka's rams, Wotan's ravens etc., were ordered from London, because everything was to be of top quality. And yet the dragon, for example, produces an almost comical impression just because the head, which had not yet arrived at the time of the dress rehearsal—to the advantage of the effect, I must say—absolutely must play a role. The eyes roll, the mouth spews venom—and moves in the conversation with Siegfried. Thus the illusion is destroyed. Fantastic creatures like Fafner in the form of a dragon should only be heard about; on stage they should be seen as little as possible.

In my earlier discussion of *The Rhinegold* I have already had occasion to call attention to the excellence of Erda. The staging of her conversation with Wotan was especially impressive. She emerges out of the depths in a beam of bluish light. She looks as if she is covered with hoarfrost. Her hair and robe appear almost luminous. Farther up, at the base of a rock, clad in a long cape and drooping hat, stands Wotan in a beam of yellow light. The effect of these contrasts is highly mystical.

The conclusion of each act was followed by loud and persistent applause—especially that of Act 2 with its "Forest-weaving", which again convinced me that here Wagner has outdone himself. Brünnhilde's awakening was gripping. Now it is the situation and the music that create the result, for it is hardly possible for the actors and actresses to fill out the long pauses with appropriate movements.

---

[23] *Der Freischütz*, opera by German composer Carl Maria von Weber (1786–1826).
[24] See Grieg's comments on *Don Giovanni* in his articles on Mozart, pp. 225–245, especially pp. 230–231.

Wagner is merciless to the audience, to some extent also to the orchestra, but in scenes like this, most of all to the actors and actresses. The length to which he drags this scene out is incredible. It is true, of course, that Siegfried and Brünnhilde are supposed to be absorbed in mutual gazing for awhile, but for the listener that sort of thing quickly grows old. Finally the gazing ends and the lovers sing the duet—which is so marvelous, especially near the end—in which Mrs. Materna conveys an enthusiasm that wins the hearts of all.

VIII

(August 18)

Mr. Editor!
Today Bayreuth has laid aside its festival garb. Many hundreds of visitors have left the town tonight, and the place has taken on a soothing stillness of which I shall take advantage to conclude my account of these memorable days. Yesterday's performance of *Twilight of the Gods* was profound and moving throughout. The tragic greatness of *Twilight of the Gods* makes it every bit as shocking as *The Valkyrie,* whose effect is due to its mighty power of nature. I can't think of anything in particular to add to my account of the dress rehearsal. The performance as a whole was excellent. Mrs. Materna's Brünnhilde, especially toward the end, rises above all criticism. Mr. Niering's[25] Hagen is sharply and darkly delineated, as is appropriate. Mr. Gura plays Günther with great power and depth of interpretation, especially in the last scenes. One rarely hears such perfectly blended singing as that of the Rhinedaughters. One could also hear in the audience that peculiar whispering that is a sign of the highest ecstasy. The effect achieved by Siegfried's funeral procession and the accompanying funeral march was indescribable. Absolutely overwhelming.

When the curtain fell after the last act, where the master displays all his creative powers at their maximum, the applause was so great that I thought the theater was going to collapse. The whole auditorium reverberated to the shout: "Wagner!" After one of those present had called for three cheers for the creator of the brilliant, huge masterwork—cheers that were echoed in thousand-voiced chorus by the entire audience—Wagner finally made an appearance in front of the curtain and spoke a few words of thanks for the ovation. Unfortunately, one could not make out what he said. I heard just this much, that he was moved by the applause of "his friends" and by the magnificent generosity of his fellow artists. He concluded with approximately these words: "We have now demonstrated that we *can* have an art. Now it is up to you (he pointed to the audience),

---

[25] Joseph Niering (1835–91).

to your will, whether in the future we *shall* have an art or not." His words once again evoked loud expressions of passion, and they certainly were not spoken without a measure of proud self-esteem. But I think it would be expecting too much of him to demand that he not feel a good deal of that.

Whatever criticism one might have of some of the details, one thing is certain: Wagner has created a masterpiece, a work full of bold originality and tragic sublimity. He has brought to life the mighty material—which is still almost totally unknown in Germany—in a new and inspired way, and by his brilliant musical-dramatic treatment he has engendered admiration where otherwise it would not have won any understanding. Much of that in the material which is most profound, which previously

Caricature of Richard Wagner

has been a closed book for many, will survive and will be popularized through the dramatic presentation. It is like when one gives pictures to children: The eye assists the thought. For a period like ours, with its marked tendency to create parties and people of limited integrity instead of whole personalities, it can also be a good medicine to absorb these broad, idealized heroes and heroines with their strong passions, their great, self-sacrificing actions and complete, warm personalities. Moreover, the ethical background that Wagner has given the material—very much in accord with recent philosophical trends—will perhaps become significant for the future of the work outside the field of art. Be that as it may, the result of the whole event is wide-ranging. Wagner has inaugurated a new and significant chapter in the history of art. The thousands who have experienced these days will tell the world that in Bayreuth German art has scored a triumph that is totally unique.

Part III

Miscellaneous Articles

Grieg was by no means an essayist in the sense of one who pens carefully crafted treatises on a variety of topics that happen to engage his interest. That he *could* have been a fine essayist is evident from the short article on "French and German Music" (1900), the delightful "Soria Moria Castle" (1901) in which he sings the praises of Voksenkollen Sanitarium, and his warm tribute to Bjørnstjerne Bjørnson entitled "With Bjørnson in Days Gone By" (1902). All of these, it will be noted, date from near the end of Grieg's life. It would seem that prior to that time the hectic pace of his life as a composer, conductor and pianist did not provide the leisure or the atmosphere of calm reflection required for such writing.

Throughout his life, however, Grieg was a formidable polemicist. He often lashed out in letters to the editors of various newspapers against groups or individuals who had incurred his wrath for one reason or another, or on behalf of issues that seemed important to him. Grieg was a man with a mission, and that mission was to raise the standard of musical life in his homeland to a level comparable with that on the European continent. Although he did not conceive of this mission in religious terms, it was nonetheless for him a kind of holy mission, and anyone who disagreed with him or opposed him was, therefore, in his opinion, a deserving target of his righteous indignation. Like many zealots, he tended to interpret personal affronts as attacks on his holy mission. Thus, a quarrel that may have looked to others (or may look to us as readers) like a petty private dispute always had for him a deeper significance. It is important to keep this in mind when reading some of his more outspoken tirades.

*Edvard and Nina Grieg, who often performed together as accompanist and
soloist, respectively.*

A Norwegian Music Academy (1866)

In 1866 Grieg settled in Christiania, where he earned his living primarily by giving piano lessons. He soon came in contact with the composer and music critic Otto Winter-Hjelm (1837–1931), who for two years had operated a private music school in the city. On September 14 and 16, 1866, Winter-Hjelm had written two extensive articles in the Christiania newspaper *Morgenbladet*, entitled "On Norwegian Music and Some Compositions by Edvard Grieg", in which he welcomed his talented younger colleague back to Norway. In these articles, Winter-Hjelm offered analyses of some of Grieg's compositions and suggested the possibility of establishing a music academy in Christiania.

The two colleagues soon agreed to expand Winter-Hjelm's music school by offering more advanced instruction for students who wished to become professional musicians or music teachers. On December 12, 1866, they published a joint article (dated December 10, 1866) on this topic in *Morgenbladet*.[1] It is impossible to determine what portions of the article were written by each, but since Grieg signed his name to it, it is included here in its entirety.

The Academy commenced operations in January, 1867. Within a short time, however, some subjects had to be removed from the curriculum because of an insufficient number of students. In autumn 1869, when Grieg went to Italy, the Academy closed. Thereafter, Winter-Hjelm continued operating his private music school for several years.

In autumn of 1864, when Winter-Hjelm started the local music school as an essentially elementary teaching institution based on the principle of cooperation, it was his intention that this should be the first step toward the establishment of a music institute of larger proportions similar to those that have long existed in the capitals of other countries. Just as the aforementioned music school immediately won much acclaim, which has continued right down to the present day, so also have the results of its activity not only even surpassed the expectations of the extraordinarily powerful method of instruction that the founder has employed from the beginning, but—according to what we hear—has, as a rule, pleased the pupils' parents and guardians as well. The arrangement whereby several pupils work together in a system alternating between verbal explanation and practical execution has produced results that one could hardly have expected under the traditional method, and it is, indeed, owing to this arrangement that the school boasts several pupils who have already achieved unusual musical maturity for their age.

The number of pupils has fluctuated between 35 and 50, and the school has had the good fortune to retain as its core clientele the very pupils who have demonstrated the greatest musical aptitude. Thus, of the piano pupils, seven have

---

[1] The first Norwegian reprint of the article, though somewhat abbreviated, was published in Øystein Gaukstad (ed.), *Edvard Grieg: Artikler og taler (Edvard Grieg: Articles and Speeches)*, Oslo 1957, pp. 222–226. An extract was printed in English in Finn Benestad and Dag Schjelderup-Ebbe, *Edvard Grieg: The Man and the Artist*, Lincoln, Nebraska 1988, p. 101.

received instruction in elementary harmony, and as many as eleven have participated in ensemble playing in which the violinist Bøhn[2] himself has joined the pupils in playing duets of Beethoven, Mozart, Haydn, Onslow, Kuhlau[3] and others.

These fortunate results in the elementary music school, together with the steadily growing desire to get a real academy in the capital, have encouraged the undersigned to unite our efforts even now in the establishment of such an academy, since the prospects of getting public funding for such an institution seem to be very dim.

The undersigned Winter-Hjelm, in a review of Edvard Grieg's compositions (*Morgenbladet* 1866, Nos. 254 and 256), has given a number of indications as to why such an academy must be said to have become a necessity. We refer those who wish to look more deeply into the matter to these articles.

The evident and steadily increasing growth of our music life, and the highly appropriate effort to put a Norwegian stamp on this area as well, make it ever more clear that we can no longer depend solely on foreign countries and their conservatories. The need for such an institution in our city is evident if one but considers the development in the future of a larger musical public—something that we think is more promising than people in general suppose, if only we work devotedly toward that goal. We entertain the hope that the amateur musicians who will be sent out from such an academy will become a healthy and powerful nucleus in this respect.

The unique growth that amateur students experience in an academy through association with teachers and fellow students will unquestionably have a refreshing effect on their musical sensibility, for here they will develop their ideas and become accustomed to seeing things elucidated from various angles—which is how one is freed from one-sided tendencies and narrow-mindedness in one's understanding. One is coaxed out of the isolation in which each student sits flailing in his own nest when the pupils grow up together and learn to know each other's personal qualities, both musically and otherwise. This experience will inspire courage and tolerance in each of them. And for those wishing to become teachers, how appropriate it is especially for them to have the opportunity to develop their minds through participation in a comprehensive exchange of ideas contemporaneous with their thorough professional training. Here we must call attention to the incentive in this direction that can be given to the academy's pupils through the frequent evening programs, where all of them come together and have an opportunity to hear good music, also to the insight they gain into music history through lectures for all the pupils.

---

[2] Norwegian violinist Gudbrand Bøhn (1839–1906), one of the leading musicians in Christiania.

[3] The composers mentioned: Ludwig van Beethoven (1770–1827), Wolfgang Amadeus Mozart (1756–91), Joseph Haydn (1732–1809), French composer Georges Onslow (1784–1853), and German-born Danish composer Friedrich Kuhlau (1786–1832).

Moreover, the current situation has other serious practical drawbacks. For those wanting to commit themselves totally to music, there unfortunately are, as we see each day, altogether too many hard fights to wage under the conditions currently prevailing here. It is extraordinarily costly to maintain oneself abroad for an adequate period of time, not only because the tuition at these conservatories is substantial (usually from 60–80 *spesidalers* regardless of the number of courses one takes), but even more because of the high cost of living in a foreign country, where one lacks the opportunity for gainful employment. The result is that relatively few (unless they are so fortunate as to get a public grant) are able to enjoy a comprehensive and truly fruitful training such as only an academy can give them.

Furthermore, there are many who in their early years demonstrate musical ability and a certain degree of talent in an as yet vague and undefined direction. Whether this interest in and inclination toward music is a strong shoot that can be expected to yield results in either performance or composition sufficient to decide whether the individual in question should devote himself or herself to art—this is something that can be decided with certainty only through rational, comprehensive guidance through a course of study including, among other things, simultaneous training in theory and practice, and through attentive observation of the ease and independence with which the young person is able to master one or the other of the branches of music. Here, of course, a faculty could at least observe with more eyes than can a single teacher—a fact that is obviously of great importance where it is a matter of finding the talent and identifying its distinctive nature and bent. And that talent, which perhaps feels repressed and discouraged, will then—with encouragement and sensible leadership—bear rich fruits.

The great importance of having a music academy in one's own country is, therefore, as clear as day. One gets the opportunity for the same training as that given in the foreign conservatory, yet it is not even necessary to immediately burn all one's other bridges. Thus, if one lacks the courage to continue, one has not wasted one's best years. We believe, therefore, that the present moment—during the strongly emerging development of the feeling and love for music that is taking place among us—is the right time for the establishment of a conservatory, and the support that the existing music school has won leads us to believe that the public will place the same confidence in its logical sequel, the academy.

The advantages of establishing an academy have been clearly stated at length elsewhere, so we will just take the liberty of citing a few statements by authorities on such matters. Thus, the prospectus for the Leipzig Conservatory—which, as is well known, was founded by Mendelssohn-Bartholdy[4]—states, "The

---

[4] The Leipzig Conservatory of Music was established by German composer Felix Mendelssohn (1809–47) in 1843. Grieg studied there 1858–62.

participation of several students in the same subjects and disciplines of study produces many good results: It arouses and vivifies the students' true musical feeling, it stimulates diligence and a competitive spirit, and it guards against one-sidedness in development and style preference—which it is of great importance for everyone to avoid during the conservatory years."

Similarly, the Berlin musician Gustav Engel has written a singular treatise on this subject from which we, because of limitations of space, can offer only a few quotations: "What characterizes the academy educational program is the comprehensive—or in any case the many-sided—training and the group instruction. A piano virtuoso who has no theoretical-musical training is almost inconceivable to us, and when singers often neglect this as well as piano-playing, they do themselves great harm; for with some theoretical knowledge, they can resolve difficulties that otherwise are often almost insurmountable for them, and without being able to play the piano they are at a disadvantage when it comes to learning the voice parts." Likewise he says "that it is all too common for amateurs to struggle to master mechanical difficulties that they could resolve much faster if they had some theoretical insight into the essence of the matter." He also expresses himself warmly regarding the necessity for the musical individual to acquire a suitable stock of theoretical knowledge, because the enjoyment of the musical compositions is thereby enhanced or even rendered possible. For many, especially men, often just scorn music "because in the long run their spirit cannot be satisfied by an activity that concerns only feeling without a clear conscious-ness" in that "insight into the laws and organism of music is lacking." In general, Mr. Engel asserts that group training in a comprehensive program evokes and strengthens self-awareness, confidence, and individuality.

We stated above that such an academy also is necessary to strengthen the struggle for national identity in our art that has also been awakened in music. Although we want the national element to be respected, we of course do not intend any kind of narrow isolation. Our desire is only that the music student shall also become acquainted with that which is our own, that which is closest to him and is perhaps best suited to have a fruitful effect on his imagination; consequently, when all that is great and mighty in the music of other lands is paraded before him, it will not overwhelm him to such an extent that his impression of our own music is erased—which, unfortunately, is often the case at present. If the student has his own ideas that need to be developed and made secure, this will occur much more easily than it would if, after having worked wholeheartedly with foreign music, he were to try to recover his own ideas—because the effort to do so would not be made on the basis of the sounds that hopefully were sung into his soul from infancy onward. Thus, in fact time is saved in the development process when one preserves the national impression in the student. He will learn to treasure what is beautiful and perfect in these melodies, and if he, thereafter, wants to imitate the great masters he will not imitate their fashions and distinctive characteristics but their greatness and their perfection in the development of his *own* ideas.

The importance of letting the student occupy himself with Norwegian music from childhood onward led the undersigned Winter-Hjelm to allow the more advanced students in the music school to play Norwegian folk melodies, primarily as set forth in Lindeman's work,[5] and the desire that was always present, without exception, with respect to these melodies, gave more and more impetus to the idea of arranging folk melodies specifically for instructional purposes and adapted to the various instructional levels. These arrangements by Winter-Hjelm are already far advanced and will, as soon as possible, be published and introduced in the academy.

The academy will include a *music school*, essentially in the same form as the present one, a *higher academy*, and a *college* for the training of teachers.

In addition to the subjects that the undersigned Winter-Hjelm and Grieg will teach, for the remaining subjects we have been fortunate to secure for the academy the services of the ablest artists. Thus, all violin instruction will be given by Gudbrand Bøhn, all cello instruction by Hans Nielsen. The teaching of singing will be handled by Henrik Meyer. The institute has also been fortunate to secure the services of Fredrik Lindholm.[6]

As in the past, the *music school* will continue to accept pupils from childhood ages and on. Instruction in this division will be given in piano (Winter-Hjelm, Christian Cappelen and Miss Kjølstad[7]), violin (Bøhn), cello (Nielsen)—and, when the pupils are ready for it, elementary harmony (Winter-Hjelm).

In the *higher academy* and in the *teachers' college*, instruction will be offered in:

I. Piano playing by Grieg and Winter-Hjelm. Fredrik Lindholm has promised to take over the instruction of the most advanced students.

II. Ensemble playing (piano with violin or cello, or with both instruments, as the case may be).

III. Violin instruction by Gudbrand Bøhn.

IV. Cello instruction by Hans Nielsen.

V. Individual voice training by Henrik Meyer.

VI. Choral singing.

VII. Harmony, by Grieg and Winter-Hjelm.

VIII. Composition and score reading by Grieg and Winter-Hjelm.

---

[5] Ludvig Mathias Lindeman (1812–87), *Ældre og nyere norske Fjeldmelodier* (*Older and Newer Norwegian Mountain Melodies*), a large collection of folk music published in installments 1853–67.

[6] Norwegian cellist Hans Nielsen (1840–74), Norwegian voice teacher Henrik Meyer (1835–1924), Swedish-Norwegian pianist and composer Fredrik Lindholm (1837–1901).

[7] Norwegian organist and composer Christian Cappelen (1845–1919). "Miss Kjølstad" has not been identified.

IX. Rudiments of music and methodology (theory of instruction), particularly for the teachers' training course, by Winter-Hjelm.

X. At suitable intervals, lectures will be given on the main trends and periods in the history of music.

In the *higher academy*, the instruction will be given from the point where it concludes in the *music school* and will proceed in the same sequence as in foreign conservatories.

Evening programs will be given on suitable occasions—programs to which, as a rule, only the academy's teachers and students will be admitted and where the more advanced students will get the opportunity to play for a larger audience. This is a practice contributing very much to arouse a competitive spirit, increase confidence, and develop individuality—which is why it is always employed in foreign conservatories.

Examinations will be given annually, and then there will be an opportunity for parents and guardians to attend a musical event at which the best students will perform. Moreover, upon leaving the conservatory, each student will receive a certificate indicating the level of study and the degree of competence reached in his/her specialty.

Recognizing the importance for students to *hear* a lot of good music at the same time that they themselves are working in this direction, the conservatory will, so far as it lies within its power, secure free admission for them to important musical performances.

The tuition in the *music school* has been set at 24 *spesidalers*[8] per year for each subject, *including* a class in elementary harmony. In the *higher academy* and in the *teachers' college* the tuition for each subject is 24 *spesidalers* (*without* a class in harmony), and for each subject *with* a class in harmony it is 30 *spesidalers*. If somebody wishes to take instruction simultaneously in three subjects plus a class in harmony, the tuition will not exceed 60 *spesidalers*. Instruction in ensemble playing, choral singing, rudiments of music, and methodology, as well as the lectures in music history are given without charge.

The pupils are committed for a half year, and payment is to be made monthly. In this connection, we take the liberty of adding that, while it is a virtual necessity for the students in the *teachers' college,* and for those who are preparing to become performing artists, to study harmony, we think it reasonable for others who wish to enjoy a rational and progressive course of study in the academy to also study harmony in addition to their primary area of concentration. The demands customarily placed on musical training nowadays make it highly undesirable to neglect the study of harmony.

---

[8] One *spesidaler* was equivalent to approximately one American dollar.

We have, however, also established tuition charges for each field without harmony class. In so doing, we have had in mind principally people from other parts of the country who come to Christiania to stay for half a year wishing to use the time to pursue intensive instruction in a single field.

Assuming that a sufficient number of students enroll, the academy will commence operations at the beginning of the new year. The location will be Storgaden No. 31.

Protest against Unfair Treatment in the Press (1876)

In a letter of July 17, 1900, to his American biographer Henry T. Finck,[1] Grieg spoke of his wife Nina in a very beautiful way: "I don't think I have any greater talent for writing songs than for writing any other kind of music. Why, then, have songs played such a prominent role in my oeuvre? Quite simply because I, like other mortals, once in my life (to quote Goethe[2]) had my moment of genius. And it was love that gave me this glory. I loved a girl with a wonderful voice and an equally wonderful gift as an interpreter. This woman became my wife and has been my companion through life down to the present day. I dare say that for me she has remained the only true interpreter of my songs."[3]

Nina and Edvard often gave concerts together, and she became a favorite among the artists and the musically literate public. Occasionally, however, she did not receive the respect she deserved. After a concert in Stockholm on December 7, 1876, Grieg felt compelled to send a strong protest to the editor of the Stockholm newspaper *Dagligt Allehanda*, which had carried a review that was not only unfavorable but, in his view, unacceptably disrespectful. His protest, dated Christiania December 20, 1876, and printed on December 23, 1876, is given below.

Mr. Editor!

Your distinguished newspaper recently carried a review of a concert given by my wife and me in Stockholm on December 7. I have never seen the likes in any respectable newspaper of the improper tone and aggressive personal attack contained in this review. By way of example I need only cite the following tirade: "As performers, both are really mere dilettantes, and they certainly don't claim to be anything else either." With your reviewer's permission, Mr. Editor: To the contrary, we claim the right to be called artists! Later it is even stated: "In Mr. as well as Mrs. Grieg's outward appearance in front of the audience, there is a certain affectation that obscures the expression of" etc.

It goes without saying that I never get involved in how the press discusses my art; indeed, I have always found unfriendly reviews—yes, even the sharpest condemnation of my art and of the ideals for which I am striving—both interesting and instructive. But when art—for what a true *artist* performs is *art*—is stamped as dilettantism, and when, in addition, artists' personal appearance on stage, i.e., their individual mannerisms in front of an audience, is made the object of malicious criticism, then they ought to avail themselves of the weapons that the press gives them and protest with contempt against such an unworthy concept of the reviewer's task. That the reviewer finds my and my wife's mannerisms affected is only a personal opinion, which in this respect is irrelevant to the public

---

[1] Grieg's letter to Henry T. Finck (1854–1926) is printed in English translation in Finn Benestad (ed.), *Edvard Grieg: Letters to Colleagues and Friends*, Columbus, Ohio 2000, pp. 225–239. The passage cited is on p. 236.

[2] German author Johann Wolfgang von Goethe (1749–1832).

[3] Nina Grieg, née Hagerup (1845–1935). Their marriage took place in Copenhagen on June 11, 1867.

and to art criticism. I will not comment on the lack of chivalry displayed in ridiculing a woman's personal appearance in the concert hall.

Inasmuch as I regret that you, Mr. Editor, have found it appropriate to print something that so blatantly exceeds the bounds of legitimate criticism, I request that you bring these lines to the attention of the Swedish public through publication in your distinguished newspaper.

One-sidedness (1880)

Grieg served as conductor of the Music Society Orchestra "Harmonien" in Bergen for two
seasons, 1880–81 and 1881–82. This orchestral society, the predecessor of the modern Bergen
Philharmonic Orchestra, dates back to 1765; thus it is one of the oldest such organizations in
the world. Grieg was often highly irritated by the lukewarm attitude of the Bergen newspapers to his work. That is the background for the following article, which was printed in *Bergens
Tidende* on November 22, 1880. It is here presented for the first time in English translation.

Mr. Editor!
There is one thing that our liberal newspapers tend to overlook, namely: anything
in the realm of culture that in one way or another, directly or indirectly, cannot
be used in the service of the "political business". We have, for example, something
called national music. It, too, often allows itself to be used advantageously as an
implement of "political business". (Excuse my weakness for this expression, Mr.
Editor, but I find it so trenchant that we should all be grateful to the county judge
who has provided the occasion for it.) That our music is not so one-sided—
indeed, that it, too, can serve politics—this is something that we have seen
recently in (among other things) *Bergensposten's* reviews of my most recent
concerts, about which reviews it must be stated as a matter "beyond all doubt"
that they had a strongly and politically tendentious background. I am not
criticizing this, just stating it as a fact.

But now comes our Music Society "Harmonien", which, by virtue of its
primarily cosmopolitan tendency, does not appear to lend itself to national-
political purposes. You cannot blame the many who join me in guessing that this
is the reason why the two concerts given by "Harmonien" during this season have
not enjoyed the honor of so much as a mention in your newspaper. (The concert given last Thursday was not mentioned in *Bergensposten* either.) This is not
as it should be. We have a right to demand from our liberal newspapers that they
do not leave it to the conservative camp around the country to report what is
going on in our city in the area of art. Or have *Adressen* and *Aftenbladet*[1] perhaps
gotten a monopoly on all critical talent in this society? Is Bergen really so small
that a brief review could not be presented by more than two people out of 40,000?
You can't get me to believe it. You may reply that a superficial review is worthless
and without educational value, but it is even more certain that completely
ignoring the concerts has a demoralizing and misleading effect. Be that as it may:
Shall we really declare ourselves bankrupt? Shall we prove the reactionaries right
when they say that it is only the conservative papers that represent "the enlightened segment of the country"?!

What we are trying to say, then, is that our liberal papers cannot decently
remain silent about such important elements in the development of our cultural
life as "Harmonien's" concerts without being rightly accused of—one-sidedness.

---

[1] Grieg is referring to the Bergen newspapers *Bergens Adressecontoirs Efterretninger* and *Bergens Aftenblad*.

Correction of an Interview (1889)

Grieg's music was exceptionally well received by music lovers in Germany, and people flocked to his concerts whenever he appeared—despite the fact that his works were often excoriated in the conservative press. Thus, he was understandably sensitive about anything that might occur to decrease his standing with the German public. On March 20, 1889, the *Pall Mall Gazette* in London had carried an interview that, upon reflection, Grieg felt might be misunderstood if it were reprinted in Germany. He demanded, therefore, that the *Pall Mall Gazette* print a correction. On April 12, he wrote to the Norwegian journalist Hans Lien Brækstad, who was at that time Norwegian vice-consul in London, requesting that Brækstad send a copy of the printed correction to the editor of the *Berliner Tageblatt*: "For the very thing I feared has happened. I have learned via letters received from Germany today that people in Berlin have attacked me because of the interview article."[1]

Grieg's correction, dated "The Cedars, Clapham Common, March 25, 1889", has been translated from the Norwegian version given in Øystein Gaukstad (ed.), *Edvard Grieg: Artikler og taler (Edvard Grieg: Articles and Speeches)*, Oslo 1957, pp. 116–117.

Dear Sir!

I would be much obliged to you if you would permit me to correct certain expressions that your interviewer has attributed to me in the article printed in your newspaper on March 20. I am afraid that my poor English has resulted in my being misunderstood when I spoke about my experiences in Germany.

Your interviewer thinks that I have said "that the Germans are so preoccupied with their own music that they could not appreciate what is good in the works of composers from other countries; that their patriotism makes them petty and envious; that foreigners do not have an easy time of it in Germany; that German music criticism often is mean-spirited in the extreme; that my experiences among the Germans have not been pleasant." What I wanted to say was that the great traditions of German music often make German musicians and critics one-sided in their judgment of the works of foreign composers, and I might wish to add here that I, for my part, am not surprised at this, for no other music has reached my heart like German music.

Regarding your interviewer's report that I am supposed to have said that the foreigner does not have an easy time of it in Germany, I am sorry to have to say that your interviewer is quite mistaken. My own experience in Germany—the way in which Norwegian music in general, and my own in particular, has been received—is proof that the very opposite is the case, and it would be more than ungrateful of me to forget this and all the acceptance that the German public as well as German musicians have shown to me—indeed, even more so since it is especially through Germany that my music has reached England.

---

[1] Grieg's letter to Hans Lien Brækstad (1845–1915) has been published in English translation in Finn Benestad (ed.), *Edvard Grieg: Letters to Colleagues and Friends*, Columbus, Ohio 2000, p. 150.

A Mushroom: A Christmas Letter to Dagbladet (1890)

As Grieg himself explains at the beginning of the article, "A Mushroom" was written in response to a request from the editor of the Christiania newspaper *Dagbladet* that he write something suitable for inclusion in the Christmas issue of the paper. It is the most cheerful vignette he ever wrote about his years in Christiania, which he usually described with bitterness and scorn. The article was published in *Dagbladet* on January 2, 1890.

Copenhagen, December 3, 1890

Mr. Editor!

You want "something" from me for your Christmas issue—an autobiographical note or something about Ole Bull,[1] for example. Well, that's easily said, but as for an autobiographical note, I have never kept a diary,[2] and to write about Ole Bull would be for me a dangerous undertaking. That has already been done by our best pens. In addition to that there is the fact that I, a Bergensian who knows Bull primarily from Bergen, would trespass on the territory of the Bergensians. Need I say more? Isn't Bergen so dimly regarded in Norway's capital at the present time that a good Christiania man gets a bellyache at the mere mention of Bergen? Why should I contribute to that? I gladly admit that just this circumstance is altogether too amusing to allow it to lie unused. Still, the Bergensians are not without humor. Thus a humorous treatment of the subject would by no means be unreasonable. But that is not for me.

Let me, therefore, immediately leave Bergen and the Bergensians by express train—I mean the express train of thought, a means of transportation that fortunately can be produced without a public subsidy. So here you have me in Tigerville,[3] where, despite a poor memory, recollections from my more than ten-year stay there spring up like mushrooms. Yes, just like "mushrooms". That is the picture. For their varieties are as different as the mushrooms. Some are inedible to the point of boredom. Others are rotten. Still others are poisonous, dangerous even to touch. But—there are also a few that can be of use. And of these few I have just found one—a genuine *champignon*—which, to be sure, is best enjoyed by musicians, but which I will nonetheless serve to you. We certainly have to train one another in versatility.

I wonder if some of your readers still remember the artistic conditions in Christiania in the winter of 1873–74, with the singularly pulsating musical life at that time? I cannot believe otherwise. It was the richest season I ever experienced

---

[1] Norwegian virtuoso violinist Ole Bull (1810–80).
[2] Grieg is mistaken about this, for he had in fact kept a diary in 1865–66. See pp. 3–57.
[3] "Tigerville" (*Tigerstaden*): a derisive name given to Christiania by Norwegian author Bjørnstjerne Bjørnson (1832–1910).

Johan Svendsen in the late 1870's

in Norway—thanks to Christiania's titan, my brilliant colleague Johan Svendsen,[4] whom I had the good fortune to persuade to alternate with me in conducting the Music Association Orchestra. We managed to present no less than eleven concerts, which gave a powerful boost to the appreciation for music—yes, in the end it even brought many respectable people who otherwise had little or no interest in art to entertain the thought that good music in a community just might be something more than a necessary evil.

In those days we held our orchestra rehearsals (I say this with all due respect) in Tivoli's Apollo salon—a facility, since renamed, which had a doubtful reputation by virtue of its *café chantant* evenings, which were dedicated to lesser gods.

---

[4] Norwegian composer and conductor Johan Svendsen (1840–1911), who was a native of Christiania.

Whether Apollo himself would have been content with the achievements of those evening programs I cannot say. But I can vouch for the forenoons, for then we had people such as Beethoven to air the place out after the evening's debaucheries. And then the Music Association Orchestra strove enthusiastically to reach the heights of great art.

There was one forenoon when it fell to my lot to rehearse Beethoven's *B-flat Major Symphony* [no. 4 op. 60]. I was just about to begin when I was informed that our excellent timpanist—his name was Theodor Løvstad—had to leave the rehearsal in a few minutes. I was unhappy, for the timpani plays an unusually important role at several places in this symphony. I had been looking forward especially to the famous *pianissimo* passage in the first movement, just before the statement of the principal theme. After reaching F-sharp Major in the development section, Beethoven—completely unexpectedly, and in a new and striking way—has the timpani play a soft tremolo on B flat while one thinks one is hearing A sharp: an enharmonic change of unparalleled effect whereby he also achieves a mysterious preparation for the immediately ensuing B-flat Major that marks the beginning of the great *crescendo.* And mind you: The timpani is heard here all by itself—all of the other instruments are silent during this strangely ominous timpani passage—and I wasn't going to enjoy it, for Løvstad had already disappeared. I was rehearsing the first movement, which moved relentlessly forward, and I dreaded the empty nothingness that would soon gape back at me. I come closer and closer to the place—there it is—and I turn resignedly toward the first violins, who pick up the dialogue at this point. But in the same moment —how on earth is it possible?—my ears detect a distant timpani roll, so marvelously performed that I was about to conclude that it was Apollo himself who had come to my aid. Quick as lightning, my glance—and that of many others— was directed toward the timpani. And what did we see? Johan Svendsen, intently watching the baton with eyes that radiated happiness, was playing the timpani! My joy was indescribable. Apollo, Beethoven, Svendsen—I could have embraced the whole world in that moment. And the gods only know where Svendsen came from, for no one had seen him before then. He must have slipped in through the back door at the last moment. And then this, that he had the fortunate ability to immediately size up the situation! *This* passage just had to be saved. And how it was saved! One thing is certain: If Svendsen had not become one of Europe's leading conductors and orchestral composers he would have become its foremost timpanist! And *such* a "timpanist" Norway can afford to give up. In truth: a rich country![5]

---

[5] Grieg is being facetious. He considered it inexcusable that Norway, which had such a dearth of first-rate musical talent, could not offer Svendsen a position that would make it possible for him to remain in Norway. From 1883 until his retirement in 1908 Svendsen served as musical director of the Royal Theater Orchestra in Copenhagen.

More than once in gatherings of artists I have related this little episode, including some in which Svendsen himself has been present. He laughed heartily along with the rest of us, but his laughter quickly turned into an almost wistful smile. This smile said clearly enough: "Yes, yes, that was indeed a wonderful time, in spite of everything!" And he was right. With glowing artistic ideals as our focus, we had a mutual interest in and affection for our tasks which created a vivid feeling of collegiality rather than a spirit of cliquishness. There were indeed those who stirred up the mud in an attempt to separate us, but they did not succeed. We stayed together anyway, instinctively. In this regard, the episode which I have just related illustrates in the most vivid way Svendsen's artistic personality.

This, then, was my "mushroom". However: In eastern Norway they use a different word for mushrooms.[6] Yet another Bergensian confusion. Sorry!

Yours truly,
EDVARD GRIEG

---

[6] I.e., *sopp* instead of *paddehatt.*

Misery at the Christiania Theater (1893)

Henrik Ibsen's *Peer Gynt* with Grieg's incidental music, op. 23, was staged three times in Christiania in Grieg's lifetime—in 1876, 1893, and 1902—but Grieg never heard his own music (twenty-six pieces in all) in its entirety. Neither did he have the pleasure of seeing it in print. The complete score was first published as volume 18 of *Edvard Grieg: Complete Works*, C. F. Peters, Frankfurt/London/New York, 1988.

Grieg's article deals with his irritation regarding a performance at the Christiania Theater at which his music was played by an orchestra in which two horns were lacking—an unforgivable affront, in his view.

The article was written at Grefsen spa on June 8, 1893, and printed in the Christiania newspaper *Verdens Gang* the following day.

Mr. Editor!

I see in the newspapers that yesterday the theater gave a benefit performance of *Peer Gynt* for Miss Parelius.[1] I have already told the stage director why I have not seen and do not wish to see the new production, and it happens that just now there is every reason to make the public aware of this "why". The reason is simply this, that the theater is deliberately destroying my music. It has summarily omitted two instruments from the orchestra (two horns), without which the whole thing not only loses all color and brilliance, but some passages become musically ugly—yes, meaningless.[2] And this is done, from what I hear, because those two miserable horns are not to be had in Norway's capital. But since such an excuse is patent nonsense, all that is left is the dirty fact that the theater does not want to pay for the two additional musicians. In 1876, when *Peer Gynt* was produced for the first time[3]—and when our musical resources were significantly more primitive than they are now—there was no thought of such an artistic aggravation. Of course the instruments lacking in the theater orchestra had to be found somehow—and they were. Now, seventeen years later, they are not to be had. But at the same time, in order to perform a *foreign* work (*Mefistofele*),[4] the theater can put forth enormous effort, even to the point of securing a female harpist from Germany!

I ask, therefore: How can such a course of action be defended? No doubt you will find an excuse, you honorable theater directors, but mark my words: You are acting unjustly, unartistically, and above all—unpatriotically. Without a vigilant artistic and national conscience, it is impossible to manage an art institution. I shout to you some words that I have seen posted on a private cabin up here on Grefsen Hill: "Caution! Beware of spring-gun!" In other words: Be careful not to tread too close to art. It could give you your deathblow.

---

[1] Norwegian actress Sofie Marie Parelius (1823–1902).
[2] [Grieg's footnote]: "For those who are not musically knowledgeable, just this: One could just as well omit two roles in a play. The one is as impermissible as the other."
[3] The premier performance of *Peer Gynt* took place at the Christiania Theater on February 24, 1876.
[4] The opera *Mefistofele* (1868) by Italian composer, librettist and poet Arrigo Boito (1842–1918).

The Norwegian Music Festival in Bergen (1898)

In 1897–98, Grieg was deeply involved in planning for a comprehensive Norwegian music festival to be launched in connection with a big fishing and industrial exposition in Bergen in the summer of 1898. He wanted to invite the Concertgebouw Orchestra of Amsterdam to come and show a Norwegian audience how a real orchestra was supposed to sound. Despite Grieg's known desire to engage the Dutch orchestra, however, the planning committee chose instead to invite the Music Association Orchestra from Christiania—whereupon Grieg angrily resigned from the committee. Realizing that the project could not succeed without him, the committee then disbanded and the festival was canceled. But local sentiment in favor of the festival was too strong to allow the idea to die. The very next day a new committee was appointed, and Grieg was given full authority to engage the Concertgebouw Orchestra.

Such was the troubled birth of the Bergen Music Festival, the first event of its kind to be held in Norway. It ran from June 26 to July 3, 1898, and it was enormously successful. Grieg wrote excitedly to Max Abraham (1831–1900) of the C. F. Peters Publishing Company in Leipzig: "Everything worked out! I have never heard better performances, not even at the Gewandhaus in Leipzig. Everyone is delighted, and everyone agrees that I was right. Now in both Bergen and Christiania people are saying, 'We must have a better orchestra!' That, for me, is the greatest triumph." [1]

Fierce attacks were launched against Grieg both before and after the music festival, and he felt obligated to defend himself. Three articles by Grieg relating to the festival are printed below. They are addressed, respectively, to Christiania Music Association conductor Iver Holter (1850–1941), to composer and music critic Otto Winter-Hjelm (1837–1931), and to the general public. The one addressed to Holter is dated Copenhagen, April 16, the one to Winter-Hjelm, Troldhaugen, July 26, 1898, and the one to the general public, Troldhaugen, September 6, 1898.

1. The Music Festival in Bergen

(Published in *Aftenposten* April 18, 1898)

Mr. Editor!

In the April 9 issue of *Aftenposten,* Mr. Iver Holter has published a free arrangement of excerpts from some telegrams exchanged between him and me regarding the hoped-for participation of his choir in the Bergen music festival. Mr. Holter intends by this maneuver to exonerate himself by making me the culprit. It is necessary, therefore, to publish not only the telegrams themselves in their context but everything that has transpired concerning this matter.

Therefore: As early as last fall, in the course of a verbal conference Mr. Holter indicated that he thought his choir could be counted on. Thus, Mr. Holter had

---

[1] Letter of July 6, 1898, printed in Finn Benestad & Hella Brock (eds.), *Edvard Grieg: Briefwechsel mit dem Musikverlag C. F. Peters 1863–1907,* Frankfort on the Main 1997, pp. 396–397.

*Program cover for 1898
Bergen Music Festival*

the whole winter to take up with his choir the question of their possible participation. The winter passed, and when, after many birth pangs, the music festival finally was confirmed, so much time had passed that the most important task, as everyone who knows about these things will understand, was to organize the big festival choir as quickly as possible. It was not on February 7, as Mr. Holter says, but on January 25 that I wrote to Mr. Holter from Leipzig asking him to inform me *as soon as possible*[2] if it was likely that his choir would participate. No answer. After waiting in vain until February 7, I sent him a telegram:

"*Can your choir be counted on and how many?*"

The answer was:

"*I assume so. Number later. Letter.*"

After waiting in vain for this letter until the 11th, I sent another telegram:

"*Must know by the evening of the 13th whether or not the choir will participate.*"

The answer:

---

[2] [Grieg's footnote]: All italics are mine.

"*The choir will participate if nothing unforeseen occurs.*"

Now I began to smell a rat. On the 13th, therefore, I sent another telegram in the final hope of getting a real answer:

"*Must have yes or no.*"

The answer came, and it was:

"*Drive slowly. The choir wants negotiations, not commands.*"

Now I was unfortunately no longer in doubt, and I immediately cabled as follows:

"*I am driving as the late date requires. We'll get along without your choir.*"

With that I broke off negotiations, as I had more important things to do than to reply by telegram to rude remarks. There was work to do. The next day, the 15th, a significantly milder telegram arrived from Mr. Holter. It read:

"Sorry, replied on behalf of the choir. *Nevertheless, the members must be asked.*"

But now the humbug became obvious, for in the letter promised on the 7th—which letter was not written until the 10th—Mr. Holter reported that he "*will have a rehearsal with the choir this evening and will present the matter to them then.*" So: *On the 10th he asks the choir, and on the 15th he sends a telegram stating that the choir must first be asked.*

These are the facts—and I think the interpretation of those facts is obvious.

Mr. Holter has had it in his power to create some difficulties for the music festival and for me. Well, since his level is such that he finds pleasure in employing this power, I can only regret it—but I cannot prevent it. Since, however, in the march of events I have been placed in charge of this festival, it is my duty to lead it forward to victory even if it happens without my letting my course of action and my tempo be decided by Mr. Holter. And hopefully it will be successful.

I could conclude here, but among my opponents in the matter of the music festival is a musician whom I will here take the opportunity to thank. That is Mr. Gustav Lange.[3] His article in *Aftenposten* expresses his standpoint in exactly the manner I would have expected from this noble artist. And this article brings me—while I have pen in hand, and in contrast to the many misleading statements in the press and the public—to state in a few words my concept of a Norwegian music festival. I understand thereby a festival whose task it is to present the best possible performances of Norwegian compositions. They will thereby be better understood and come closer to the hearts of the people. Whether accomplishing this purpose requires Norwegians, Germans, Japanese or Dutchmen is a matter of indifference to me. On this concept I will stand or fall.

All honor to the Christiania orchestra—which, incidentally, includes many

---

[3] Norwegian violinist and composer Gustav Fredrik Lange (1861–1939).

foreign members. It has never for a moment been my intention that this orchestra should not be used in the music festival, but I cannot see any crime in making use of the great artistic advantage that here, by a unique stroke of luck, presents itself. I cannot see how it would be a crime to accept the famous, splendid Amsterdam orchestra's offer, which is as unselfish as it is flattering to Norway and to Norwegian art. All of our Norwegian orchestras should be given an opportunity to come to Bergen during the music festival in order to convince themselves of the correctness of Schumann's words, "People also live behind the mountains".[4] For all of us who call ourselves Norwegian musicians have much to learn from the Amsterdam orchestra's superior performances. Every "disinterested" person who has not been made blind as a bat by chauvinism—whether he be an artist or not—will agree with me. And to all the others in Tigerville[5] who are now attacking me in anonymous letters and newspaper articles and who think, in so doing, that they have found a marvelous way to get rid of both me and the Bergensians once and for all—to them I can say with a respected author: "Stab, crush, scratch and tear!"[6]

I would be most grateful if the other leading Christiania newspapers would reprint these lines.

2. The Music Festival in Bergen
Reply to Mr. Otto Winter-Hjelm

(Published in *Verdens Gang*, August 2, 1898)

After every great undertaking that succeeds there is a postlude: the comedy put on by "the displeased". So also after the music festival in Bergen. I shall not, therefore, concern myself with the jabs and kicks, the yapping and biting, that have been directed at me in this connection *post festum* in the Christiania press. After all, it was inevitable. But when Mr. Otto Winter-Hjelm tries to give the Norwegian readers of *Aftenposten* the impression that I had an obligation to secure his permission to include one of his songs on the music-festival program, I cannot let the public remain in this delusion. I wish to inform the readers that throughout Europe it is considered an honor for a composer to be represented at a music festival, asked or unasked. On several occasions, my music has appeared on the program at German music festivals, and only after the fact have

---

[4] Grieg quotes these words in German: "Hinter den Bergen wohnen auch Leute"—thereby alluding (via a play on words) to the rivalry between Bergen and Christiania.

[5] "Tigerville" was a derogatory name given to Christiania by Norwegian author Bjørnstjerne Bjørnson (1832–1910) and often used by Grieg.

[6] Grieg's quotation in Norwegian: "Stik, rod, riv og slid!" This is slightly different from the line in the fifth part of the dramatic poem *Brand* (1865) by Norwegian author Henrik Ibsen (1828–1906): "Tal kun; skjær op, stik, riv og slid!"—"Speak out; cut up, stab, scratch and tear!"

I learned of it through the newspapers. It did not occur to me for that reason to heap jibes upon those responsible for these music festivals. To the contrary: I had nothing but feelings of gratitude toward them. A music festival is not, as Mr. Winter-Hjelm states, an exhibition. An exhibitor is the owner of that which he exhibits, but a composer—from the moment he has sold his work to a publisher —is no longer owner of it, and every concert in the whole world can include it on its program without asking his permission. Dramatic works constitute the only exception to this rule, and even these do so only under certain unique conditions. This has, legally as well as morally, long been the prevailing view everywhere with respect to both ordinary concerts and music festivals—not least for the simple reason that the composer, like the publisher, would be ill served if this were not the case. Moreover, if all composers had to be asked, every music festival—where the choice of individual pieces must necessarily be subordinated to concern for the whole—would become an impossible undertaking.

To return to the above-mentioned song, I can assure Mr. Winter-Hjelm that I not only had no intention to offend him but, on the contrary, wished to give him as much pleasure as possible commensurate with my artistic view of the festival's best interests. I have not expected any thanks for so doing—but, I confess, I expected even less to receive words of harsh criticism. I could not, in accordance with Mr. Winter-Hjelm's wish, "give him an opportunity to give his approval, and negotiate regarding what he wished to exhibit."(!) For Mr. Winter-Hjelm's significance as a Norwegian composer is not, in my opinion, such that I thought I should use the limited time available for an extensive composition from his hand. For this opinion—which I am hardly alone in holding—I am of course willing to carry the full responsibility. Therefore, I chose a song, and I chose this particular song because it appears to me to be one of the best compositions Mr. Winter-Hjelm has published and because it was excellently suited to the singer's voice and personality. I can still assure Mr. Winter-Hjelm that the song evoked extraordinary applause, and it was so beautifully performed by Mrs. Gmür-Harloff[7] that he would have enjoyed being in the audience.

Mr. Winter-Hjelm was invited to the festival, and it was a disappointment to me and others that he did not find it possible to accept the invitation. Moreover, if he had come he would have observed with great satisfaction that the festival did not exhibit a trace of all those ugly apparitions that he in his pessimism tries with such great virtuosity to conjure up for his readers. To the contrary: There was even—compared to what one might have expected in this land of discord— a surprisingly high degree of solidarity among the artists.

Mr. Winter-Hjelm dares to insinuate that "my interest at the festival did not exactly have to be that of Norwegian music".(!) Such an insinuation I can

---

[7] Norwegian soprano Amalie Gmür-Harloff (1864–1900).

confidently leave unchallenged. It is too contemptible. Moreover, anyone who knows me will understand how untrue it is.[8]

Above all: Why this bitter, hateful tone, Mr. Winter-Hjelm? It is not your own. I remember you from the good old days,[9] and I know that this tone is not rooted in your character. You should leave that sort of thing to those among your colleagues who have a natural talent for it. In you, fortunately, it is just something you have picked up, but to my great regret it demonstrates all the same that you, too, have been infected with the rancor that rages among the musicians in Christiania at the moment. Had these people been present at the music festival in Bergen, they would certainly have admitted its extraordinary cultural significance, directly and indirectly—a significance which, among impartial observers, is already a shining fact that one has to take into account, and to which, in the long run, even the people in Christiania cannot close their eyes.

With that, I have said all I have to say regarding Mr. Winter-Hjelm's relation to the music festival.

3. The Music Festival and What it Requires of Us
(Published in *Bergens Tidende,* September 8, 1898)

The music festival is over. The lassitude that follows every festive mood is gone. But what absolutely remains is a strong feeling of the significance of this festival for the development of our music life—a significance so far-reaching that no one is yet able to fathom it. We all know what the festival brought us: a presentation such as we in Norway have never before experienced of Norwegian music, which, through the superb rendition accorded it, was understood and appreciated by the public.

The music festival has taught us, therefore, that we possess a national music which, when excellently performed, is able to speak to *everyone*. This is the positive gain. But it has also taught us that we do not ourselves have the necessary resources to perform adequately either the national or the foreign music, and this is the negative gain, a result that lays upon us an obligation. This obligation is the realization that, since the music festival, forces itself upon all of us. But obviously, we ought not to stop with this realization. Quite the opposite. Now, as never before, is the moment to act—and it will not be easy to recreate such a moment in the future. The form of the action is very simple. We will create a fund to gather

---

[8] [Grieg's footnote]: In this connection I can report that, precisely in order to avoid misunderstanding by people of ill will, I recommended to the festival committee that they let me as a composer be unrepresented at the festival—a recommendation that, however, was decisively rejected.

[9] Grieg had cooperated with Otto Winter-Hjelm in 1866 on the establishment of a Music Academy in Christiania. See their joint article on this matter on pp. 321–327.

L to R standing: Ole Olsen, Thorvald Lammers, Christian Cappelen, Johan Halvorsen, Nina Grieg, Johan Svendsen, Christian Sinding. L to R seated: Amalie Gmür-Harloff, Agathe Backer Grøndahl, Grieg, Gerhard Schjelderup, Erika Lie Nissen, Iver Holter. On August 18, 1898, Grieg wrote to Dr. Max Abraham: "On the picture you will see wolves and sheep grazing together in brotherly fellowship just like on Noah's ark."

and maintain a good orchestra in Bergen. In order to reach this goal as soon as possible, I respectfully appeal to:

1) The municipality of Bergen, which is the natural guardian of such a fund.
2) The state liquor store.[10]
3) The savings bank.[11] The latter two institutions have, above all others, won a respected name because of their interest in socially beneficial projects.
4) The women and men whose generosity made the music festival possible. I appeal in particular to them, requesting that they commit the remainder of the music festival's guarantee fund to the purpose at hand.

---

[10] Norwegian: *Brændevinssamlaget.* In Norway, liquor is sold and distributed only through shops owned by the Norwegian state. Part of the surplus from this business is used to support cultural and social programs.
[11] Norwegian: *Sparebanken.*

5) Influential men in our community with artistic, national, and—not least—social interests, with a recommendation that they join together for the furtherance of the cause. An invitation to join a society dedicated to this purpose is being distributed at this time.

Thus, what the music festival requires of us is this: It shall not have been merely an occasion for the enjoyment of art; it shall be regarded as part of the education of our people. Whether or not this requirement will be fulfilled depends on us.

Let it be said, then, that Bergen not only has succeeded in making this music festival a reality. It has also possessed the vision to use the festival to take aim at something different from and greater than a festival—namely, the well-being of our cultural life.

To make a lasting contribution to our cultural life: Let that have been the real purpose of the music festival.

Opera Controversy in Christiania (1898)

The National Theater in the Norwegian capital was dedicated in September, 1899. The event was preceded by a big debate in the press about whether and to what extent opera should have a place at the new theater or whether the facility should be used exclusively for spoken drama. Bjørn Bjørnson (1859–1942), son of the famous author Bjørnstjerne Bjørnson (1832–1910), was appointed theater director. He proposed to include opera productions, as was the practice at other similar institutions including the Royal Theater in Copenhagen. As a matter of fact, he wanted an additional stage suitable for the performance of operettas. This view aroused strong opposition.

In the December 12, 1898 issue of the Christiania newspaper *Verdens Gang*, Grieg was asked to express his opinion on the matter. He did so in an article dated Copenhagen, December 19, 1898, and published in *Verdens Gang* on December 23. It is here presented for the first time in English translation.

When the National Theater opened its doors, it did so without a permanent opera ensemble despite the fact that the Theater could boast an excellent 43-member professional orchestra under the strong leadership of the newly appointed musical director, Johan Halvorsen (1864–1935). However, Bjørn Bjørnson, who was a strong opera enthusiast, presented *Carmen* by Georges Bizet (1838–75) and *Faust* by Charles Gounod (1818–93) during the first season, and both were exceptionally well received. In succeeding years, both operas and operettas were presented from time to time.

I have seen a wish expressed in *Verdens Gang* that I state my views regarding the opera controversy. Unfortunately, I have been able to follow only a portion of this debate and cannot, therefore, enter into its details. I can only indicate my basic view regarding the heart of the matter.

First of all, I must express my surprise that people in many circles in Christiania seem to regard spoken drama and opera as arch-enemies. This mistaken view is probably a fruit of the conditions that have prevailed in this city in recent years. In reality, the two art forms are the very best of friends; it is only by setting them up as competitors in one and the same theater that it might look on the surface as if they were enemies. There is not a city undergoing progress that cannot tell of the difficulties experienced during a transitional period in which spoken drama and opera must both be accommodated under one roof. No cultured society has yet for this reason excluded opera but has chosen the solution of giving it shelter along with spoken drama as long as it is impossible to create separate homes for each of the two art forms. Separate homes is what they are currently thinking of providing here in Copenhagen.[1] The same way of thinking is prevalent in cities that have grown to the point where they can afford it. I think that this also applies in Christiania's case, and I, therefore, give Mr. Bjørn Bjørnson's idea—two theaters under the same management—my warmest endorsement. This idea has often enough been successfully realized abroad.

---

[1] Copenhagen still has spoken drama and opera under the same roof: The Royal Theater. Oslo (formerly Christiania) got its first opera house in 1956 and is now making preparations for a new opera building to be opened ca. 2005.

As a musician, I naturally greet with the greatest pleasure the proposal for the reorganization of the orchestra, for it is my conviction that if such a step is not initiated we will wait indefinitely before the opportunity again presents itself. Meanwhile, we will continue to be spectators while Denmark and Sweden—yes, even Finland—race far beyond us.

It has been stated editorially in *Verdens Gang* that we ought not to have an opera house because in the area of opera we have no Holberg, Bjørnson and Ibsen.[2] This is to me an incomprehensible view concerning art. Do we not present on our stage plays by Shakespeare, Goethe, Molière etc.?[3] And does not opera, like spoken drama, make its great impact on a people by creating universal understanding through good performances of the masterworks of *all countries?* Shall we wait to establish a Norwegian opera house until we have a Norwegian Mozart or a Norwegian Wagner—geniuses that are born once in a century?

Moreover: We are not as poor as some people would make us believe. We have Norwegian operas of great worth that have never been performed. We have opera composers who are struggling just to make a paltry living abroad because we have no place for them here at home. I mention especially Gerhard Schjelderup in Dresden. The performance of his *East of the Sun and West of the Moon* would be a worthy undertaking for a Norwegian opera house.[4]

Mr. Bjørn Bjørnson replies to the above-mentioned editorial opinion in *Verdens Gang,* "If we want to have an opera, we will get it." To this I will only say that in my experience it is not in that way that progress occurs. No, no, no! He who has the vision, the ability and the energy must press forward, even if it be in the face of the cry: "Crucify him!" That is how everything new, everything with prospects for the future, comes into being. Thus has it always been, and thus will it continue to be.

Therefore, Mr. Bjørn Bjørnson: Press on! Your belief in the cause will be contagious. It seems to me that you are the very man to unite spoken drama and opera under one administration. You have dedicated your life to spoken drama. Thus, one need not fear that you would advance opera at the expense of spoken drama. Moreover, you have a mature musical sense. Therefore, the requisite conditions are present. I repeat: Press on! It would be very strange if, in the end, you did not find the support that your patriotic work for the furtherance of our dramatic art deserves—a work for which people ought to thank you instead of throwing suspicion on it.

---

[2] Norwegian playwright Ludvig Holberg (1684–1754) and Norwegian authors Bjørnstjerne Bjørnson (1832–1910) and Henrik Ibsen (1828–1906).

[3] English author William Shakespeare (1564–1616), German author Johann Wolfgang von Goethe (1749–1832), and French author Jean-Baptiste Molière (1622–73).

[4] Norwegian composer Gerhard Schjelderup (1859–1933), who composed many operas, spent most of his adult life in Germany because of the unfavorable climate for opera in his homeland. His opera *Austanfyre sol og vestanfyre måne—East of the Sun and West of the Moon* (1890) was based on a text by Norwegian author Kristofer Janson (1841–1917). It has never been performed in its entirety.

Musical Conditions in Bergen (1899)

Grieg was often depressed because of the low orchestral standard in his hometown of Bergen. He had made an all-out effort to improve it by conducting the distinguished old Music Society "Harmonien" (Musikselskabet "Harmonien")—an orchestra of professional and advanced amateur musicians—during the years 1880–82. In 1894, however, an organization calling itself the Music Association (Musikforeningen) was established exclusively for amateur musicians, and it soon found itself in competition with Harmonien. In March 1899, the Music Association applied to the city council for operating support, and another group called the Bergen Orchestra Association (Bergen Orkesterforening) sought support for a permanent city orchestra. The Music Association received a grant of 2,000 crowns, whereas a minority of the councilmen were willing, on certain conditions, to also commit funds to the Bergen Orchestra Association.

Grieg was furious over what he perceived as a decision to support amateurism in preference to professionalism. It was against this background that he wrote the following article, dated Troldhaugen, June 6, 1899 and entitled "Vore Musikforhold" ("Our Musical Conditions"). It was published in *Bergens Tidende* on June 7. He heatedly argued that the organizations had to cooperate but that amateurism had no place in true art. The article is here presented for the first time in English translation.

In 1901 the various organizations involved came to the realization that Grieg was right and joined together as The Music Association "Harmonien" (Musikforeningen "Harmonien"). Later, the original name—The Music Society "Harmonien" (Musikselskabet "Harmonien") —was restored.

The so-called Music Association, which was established in Bergen a few years ago with the goal of gathering our city's musical amateurs for regularly scheduled practice in orchestra-playing, deserved all the support it received at that time. Of course I, too, gave the idea my warmest endorsement and gladly signed my name to a public invitation to contribute to the realization of this beautiful aim.

This amateur association now functions as an arts organization that requests municipal support. I shall not here venture to criticize the filing of this request, but when such support is seriously recommended for approval by the Executive Committee of the City Council—in direct opposition to the report of the chief financial officer—even as it denies requests not only from Harmonien, our only musical arts organization that for many long years has fought for its existence, but also from the newly established Orchestra Association, whose aim it is to improve our orchestral conditions, then I consider it my compelling duty to sound a warning.

That artistic endeavors must step aside for amateurism is something that one often sees in smaller settings, but nowhere has anyone gone so far as to publicly support amateurism at the expense of true art. This outrage has been reserved for Bergen to manifest in the year 1899.

Obviously the Music Association understands that Bergen is not large enough to accommodate two competing concert institutions. And naturally the

Executive Committee also understands this. Nonetheless, these two institutions are in the most beautiful agreement that the society of amateurs, the Music Association, should be supported—in other words, that Harmonien should be destroyed. I do not understand how Harmonien has made itself deserving of such treatment, and I understand just as little how anyone can be blind to the fact that what is being proposed is a very dangerous step in the direction of lowering the artistic standard in this city.

Even if it lies in the nature of the case that Harmonien's orchestral achievements have not been of sterling quality, this Society nonetheless has the great advantage that it represents a venerable music tradition in our city, and above all, that for more than a generation it has stood on artistic ground as it has always sought to secure the largest possible number of professionals in the orchestra, the best possible conductors, and, so far as funds have allowed, our country's best talents in chamber-music and solo performances.[1]

I will not dwell here on all the factors that have worked together to produce a decision on the pending appropriation. I will just point out that the salaries proposed by the Orchestra Association for a projected permanent city orchestra are pegged as low as in all decency they could possibly be. Any further reduction, such as that considered by the Music Association, will result in a starvation wage that would exclude any possibility of having artistic performances of educational value.

"We can do it more cheaply!" seems to be the motto of the Music Association. To get this fact illuminated with dry numbers, I refer to Mayor Arctander's[2] report on the matter, which it would be most desirable to see published in the press as soon as possible. Each one can then judge for himself.

But now a question: Why in all the world can the amateur elements that demonstrate such a strong desire for musical involvement not attempt a collaboration with Harmonien, the Orchestra Association, and the theater instead of establishing a system that within a short time will completely destroy any music activity among us that is based on ideal standards?

There would be good use for the various institutions. Indeed, the professional musicians working in the Music Association are so capable that they would be warmly welcomed by the aforementioned institutions. If the Music Association represented an orchestra school whose more gifted pupils intended to prepare themselves to become artists, these could receive additional experience through participation in Harmonien's big concerts, in collaboration with the permanent city orchestra engaged for these concerts. In this way we would get real art, and

---

[1] The Music Society "Harmonien" was established in 1765 and thus is one of the oldest concert institutions in the world. It is the direct predecessor of the modern Bergen Philharmonic Orchestra.

[2] Bergen politician Sophus Arctander (1845–1924).

not amateurism and inferior art, in all quarters—which will without doubt become the case in the immediate future. For good orchestral music absolutely presupposes money—unfortunately! Regrettably, a majority of the Executive Committee appears to lack an understanding of this, and herein, in my opinion, lies the big misjudgment that has found expression in the motivation of the majority to appropriate funds for the Music Association.

Bergen's municipal leaders could at this moment, with a couple strokes of the pen, do the greatest service to art in our community that it will have an opportunity to do for a long time to come, namely: to demand as a condition of its support—not of the Music Association, but of the music activities of our city—agreement and cooperation among the Orchestra Association, Harmonien, the Music Association, and the theater. If this could happen, the present discord would become the beginning of a new and better era. If an annual appropriation were awarded to the Orchestra Association on the condition that it would take the initiative in arranging such cooperation, and would seek to create a situation in which all of the organizations would complement one another instead of competing, as they do now, then the knot would be untied, and the Music Association would have an opportunity to demonstrate that the core of the matter is the well-being of our music life, not merely special interests.

If I am not mistaken, the view of the majority is based on a faulty understanding of the nature of democracy as it finds expression in art. It appears as if what they want is: the lower class *contra* the upper class. But in art there is no lower class or upper class. Precisely herein lies, among other things, its educational potential. It appears to me that every democratic endeavor must seek to even out all class differences. Good art does that. To offer cheap art is to offer bad art—and with that, one does the opposite of educating the people. The big social secret of our time is not just equally good food and drink, but also equally good *mental* nourishment for all classes. With respect especially to art, the solution is this: Nothing is too high for ordinary people. To the contrary. Ordinary people hunger and thirst for the highest that can be imagined. Just find the funds for the highest *artistic achievement* and it will also become for the great mass of people the source of the highest *artistic enjoyment.* Everything else—people's *access* to the best art—is a practical problem that can easily be solved precisely because the yearning for such art is so enormously great. I can interject at this point that the distribution of free tickets to the less well-to-do classes appears to be superior to cheap tickets for everyone. In France the principle: *from each according to his ability* has been successful. Seats are available for from twenty francs down to one franc. In England the trend is in the same direction.

Before the Executive Committee made its fateful decision, an opinion was stirred up with such energy—an energy deserving of a better cause—that I perceive perfectly well the impossibility of getting it overthrown in the twinkling of an eye. Therefore, it is not my intention in these lines to try to put any pressure on the City Council, which will be meeting soon. The cause that I have advocated by means of my initiative to the Orchestra Association is of such great significance that it is understandable if it does not immediately gain general approval. Thus, like so many other good causes, it will perhaps fail to win approval for now—only to triumph later with all the greater splendor. I have written as I have, however, in order to lodge a definite protest against the efforts—being cultivated among us with such great success at this moment—to tailor art to fit the low community standards that happen to prevail at the moment. It is not in any way the role of art to go *down* to the people. No, a thousand times no! The people shall be raised *up* to art!

With that, I entrust this matter to the public discussion.

Response to an Inquiry Concerning Alfred Dreyfus (1899)

In 1894, Captain Alfred Dreyfus (1859–1935), a French army officer of Jewish descent, had been unjustly convicted of high treason and condemned to life imprisonment on Devil's Island. On June 3, 1899, Dreyfus's conviction was overturned and the case was referred to a new court martial in Rennes. Meanwhile, Dreyfus's supporters in France (the "Dreyfusards") sought to win public sympathy for the falsely accused man by soliciting statements from cultural leaders all over the world. In mid-June, 1899, Grieg received a letter from French musicologist Jules Combarieux (1859–1916) asking him to respond to a series of questions of principle highly relevant to the Dreyfus case. Grieg's reply, dated June 22, 1899, is given below.

The English translation has been made from the Norwegian draft of Grieg's response preserved in Bergen Public Library.[1]

Nothing is easier for sound reason and the modern sense of justice than to answer your questions:

1. Obviously: The problem, as the Dreyfus case makes evident in our day, is the eternal human one: Which power is stronger, the physical or the intellectual?
2. Obviously: There is no case in which a man should be convicted without having been informed regarding all the motives on which the accusation is based.
3. Obviously: Concern for the state can never have greater importance than the recognition of a person's innocence.
4. Obviously: The honor of a professional group cannot be tarnished as the result of an error committed by one of its members.
5. Obviously: There is no such thing as the honor of a professional group.
6. Obviously: A court that condemned a man and later acknowledged his innocence would only gain in authority and respect.
7. Obviously: A conflict may occur between a nation's intelligentsia and the raw power represented by the army—but such a conflict, fortunately, can be resolved.
8. Obviously: It is above all science and art that ideally represent the people of one nation to those of another.

EDVARD GRIEG

---

[1] See also Grieg's correspondence with Édouard Colonne (1838–1910) in Finn Benestad (ed.), *Edvard Grieg: Letters to Colleagues and Friends*, Columbus, Ohio 2000, pp. 199–202, and his account of his Paris concert of April 19, 1903, in a letter to Johan Halverson of April 23, 1903, *op. cit.*, pp. 351–353.

French and German Music (1900)

In September–October 1900, the Parisian newspaper *Le Figaro* invited the leading musicians in Europe to express their opinion regarding topics related to the development of music. Grieg responded positively to the invitation, apologizing that he—because of his lack of proficiency in the French language—had to write in Norwegian.

Grieg's article, preserved in Bergen Public Library, was published in a French translation in *Le Figaro* on October 4, 1900.

Mr. Editor:

You honor me in expressing the desire for a few musical words from my pen, and you are so kind as to leave to me the choice of a topic. Allow me, then, to use this opportunity to acknowledge the debt of gratitude that Scandinavian composers owe to French music. All countries certainly join with us in this expression of thanks, but we up here are in a special position. We are of north-Teutonic stock, and as such we have much of the Germanic people's propensity toward melancholy and brooding. However, we do not share their desire to express themselves broadly and verbosely. To the contrary. We have always loved brevity and succinctness, the clear and concise mode of expression—just as you can find it in our sagas, and as any traveler could observe even today in our social intercourse. These qualities are also what we aim for in our artistic endeavors.

Therefore, with all our boundless admiration for the profundity of German art, we are not enthused to the same extent about its modern form of expression, which we often find heavy and ponderous. Most Scandinavian musicians have studied in Germany. One would think, then, that this country's immortal masterpieces from its great classical period—works with clear lines and noble architecture—would certainly be a musical foundation that they would retain for life. But alas! That period belongs to the past. Young people pursue today's ideals —both the good and the bad in those ideals. It is entirely understandable, therefore, that they are intoxicated by the orgies of color of German neo-Romanticism and that they adopt its technical heaviness and indefinite lines—a ballast that later, when it is a matter of finding expression for individual and national characteristics, they have the greatest difficulty throwing overboard. Then it is the study of French art that helps them find themselves. Its light, unrestrained form, its transparent clarity, its euphony, its inborn capacity to use the means at hand become their salvation.

What I have said applies to the field of music, but it is a fact that the same French influence can be demonstrated in both our literature and our pictorial arts.

A famous composer—the late Danish master Gade[1]—to whom in my youth I presented a beginner's piece, stated his judgment about it in the following words, as apt as they are well-formed: "What good is it to have something that you want to say when you are not able to say it?" Here I am at the heart of the matter, for I think that the Scandinavian artist who has learned the secret of "being able to say what he wants to say"—he will not forget how much of this learning he owes to France. That is the source of his deep appreciation for French art and French artists.

---

[1] Danish composer Niels W. Gade (1817–90).

The Soria-Moria Castle (1901)

The exact origin of the fairy-tale name "Soria-Moria" is unknown. It denotes a castle where the hero of the fairy-tale at last finds the princess, whom he weds and with whom he lives happily ever after.

Grieg gave this name to the new Voksenkollen Sanitarium, which was situated on a hill on the outskirts of Christiania, not far from the famous Holmenkollen Ski Jump. The sanitarium was founded by Norwegian Dr. Ingebrigt Chr. L. Holm (1844–1918), the building being constructed in 1900. Grieg was very fond of the sanitarium, and during his last years he often sought refuge there in periods of illness. On February 13, 1901, he wrote to Norwegian author Jonas Lie (1833–1908): "We have spent three glorious months at the new Voksenkollen, a dream come true that the future will give the appreciation it deserves. This Dr. Holm is a good Norwegian in the *best* sense of the word."[1]

It was during this three-month stay at Voksenkollen that Grieg wrote the Soria-Moria article, printed in the Christiania newspaper *Verdens Gang* on January 12, 1901. It is here presented for the first time in English translation. The sanitarium was destroyed by fire in 1919 and was never rebuilt.

All of us of course remember the castle from Asbjørnsen.[2] We visited it in our childhood imagination, and as grown-ups, too. It has become a kind of symbol of something distant, unattainable.

Once upon a time I entered into a unique relationship with this castle. One day in the 1870's, a young poet whom I did not know strode into my sitting-room and announced, "I want to stay with you today!" Thereupon he pulled a manuscript out of his pocket—an opera text. It had to do with the Soria-Moria castle. On the title page I read, *"East of the Sun and West of the Moon", text by N. N., music by Edvard Grieg.* Even so audacious an assumption regarding the course of events, however, could not stimulate me to take hold of this text. Nor was I myself mature enough to perform the task.[3] In short: The Soria-Moria castle receded from me at the same time that it seemed to be so extremely close. Since then I have dreamt about this story, which more than any other Norwegian folk tale lends itself to a dramatic-musical treatment, but I never found anyone in Norway who could shape it in accordance with my concept. Little by little it disappeared from my fantasy-world.

Then last spring I heard that people in Christiania were beginning to speak with a certain puzzlement about the Soria-Moria castle—at Voksenkollen. I

---

[1] Grieg's letters to Jonas Lie are printed in English translation in Finn Benestad (ed.), *Edvard Grieg: Letters to Colleagues and Friends*, Columbus, Ohio 2000, pp. 471–478. The passage cited is on p. 478.

[2] Norwegian folklorist Peter Christen Asbjørnsen (1812–85), who collected and published a large number of Norwegian folk and fairy tales.

[3] The young Norwegian author was most likely Kristofer Janson (1841–1917). In 1890, Norwegian composer Gerhard Schjelderup (1859–1933) employed Janson's text in his opera carrying the same title. See also footnote 4 in Grieg's article "Opera Controversy in Christiania" on pp. 345–346.

listened. It seemed that my materials from the world of imagination had suddenly been plunked down in the real world. Someone else had found it. I got jealous, and I had to see the castle, for "Jealousy is a passion that anxiously strives for that which causes suffering."[4]

One fine day in May I drove up there, and what happened was what I had least expected: I was totally enchanted. The Christiania people were right: It really was a Soria-Moria castle! As it rises resplendent out of the dark spruce forest into the high, light air, with snow-covered mountains gleaming on the distant horizon, one's first impression is of a fairy palace. The king in the fairy-tale stands in the doorway and welcomes me, and he is every bit as good and kind as Asbjørnsen's fairy-tale king. He escorts me personally into the large foyer, which is in the style of an old Norwegian church; thereafter, to the dining room, then to the social room, then down the wide stairway to a veritable Vatican of rooms, every one a little fairy-tale, tastefully decorated to the point of sophistication with the greatest comforts of the day—and beyond that a certain something of which I don't even know the name but which immediately confirmed my decision: I will come back and live here.

This autumn I went up again and have now spent three months in these cheery heights without for a moment losing the fairy-tale feeling. Today, when

Voksenkollen in winter. Note the skiers in the foreground.

---

[4] A play on words, attributed to German theologian Friedrich Schleiermacher (1769–1834), which Grieg quotes in German: "Eifersucht ist eine Leidenschaft, die mit Eifer sucht, was Leiden schafft."

Some readers construed "The Soria-Moria Castle" as mere advertising, perhaps a quid quo pro *for free lodging. This cartoon appeared in the satirical Norwegian magazine* Vikingen *on January 26, 1901. The sign reads: "Soria-Moria Castle on Voksenkollen is the best and cheapest hotel anywhere in Norway."*

I came downtown and saw all the sleepy, dissatisfied townspeople, I thought: They must learn about the Soria-Moria castle! That it is something more than a clever, folkish name for a building. That it really is a fairy-tale castle concealing a rare treasure: a cure for everyone who has been sick and seeks to regain his or her lost equilibrium. The place is so infinitely large, outdoors as well as indoors, that each person can live as he or she wishes, among other people or in solitude. I have wandered around in this labyrinth of paths in the large forests without meeting anything other than black grouse and wood grouse. I have come home and gone up to my room without seeing a living soul. Not until the dinner-bell sounded was I snatched out of my solitude. And it is so cozy here, so pleasant. You are not in a hotel, but in a home. You are not a number; you are yourself—or, more correctly, whatever you yourself want to be.

I have visited several of the most famous foreign mountain hotels, including the ones at Semmering[5] that are often praised so highly, but none of these can bear comparison with Voksenkollen. I remember a prophetic statement made by Holger Drachmann[6] in the 1880's: "Norway's mountains will become Northern Europe's sanitarium." In Voksenkollen his idea has suddenly been realized in a nearly ideal form. Imitators will come, but—it takes more than venture capital to create something like this. Above all, you need a sterling personality. It takes people with a combination of many heterogenous talents that collectively I do not hesitate to call genius. One notices it here in all kinds of ways. I consider visionary people—such as the man whose spirit permeates this place—our country's pioneers and benefactors. His basic idea is the one Billroth[7] expressed

---

[5] Semmering, a popular resort area in the eastern Alps, not far from Vienna.
[6] Danish author Holger Drachmann (1846–1908).
[7] German surgeon and professor of medicine Theodor Billroth (1829–94).

thus: "If only one could help everyone!" In other words: He is a friend of humanity. Therefore, a good spirit hovers over this home: the spirit of empathy. Suffering humanity, harassed and exhausted from the excessive nervousness produced by competitive modern society, is called hither—and many will answer that call. Danes, Swedes, and Englishmen have already done so, and other nations will join in. Norwegians are still holding back, but of course they have an obligation to obey the slogan: "We're a-comin' even if not right away!"[8]

And they will come.

But: Come soon! You should not take Ivar Aasen too literally. Come to Soria-Moria castle—the sooner the better—whether you be old or young, and rediscover the fairy-tale dreams of your childhood! You will be richer and happier for having done so!

---

[8] A quotation from a poem by Norwegian author Ivar Aasen (1813–96), "Dei vil alltid klaga og kyta" ("They will always grumble and boast") from his play *Ervingen—The Heir* (1855).

With Bjørnson in Days Gone By (1902)

Bjørnstjerne Bjørnson (1832–1910) was one of the most influential figures in Norwegian culture in the nineteenth century, not only as a prolific and widely read author but also as a politician and public speaker. His influence on Grieg was substantial. In a letter of February 9, 1897, to his prominent colleague and close friend Iver Holter (1850–1941), Grieg wrote: "It is a sacred duty for me to call attention to the great influence that my association with Bjørnson from the autumn of 1866 to the spring of 1873 had on my art. He formed my personality in countless ways—that is to say, he contributed mightily to that process. He made me a democrat, both artistically and politically. He gave me the courage to follow my own natural bent. This time (the 1870's) was a wonderful time, with its surplus of courage and faith!"[1]

The stories that follow are typical of Grieg's ability to describe events in a vivid and amusing way. The article was prepared for *Bjørnstjerne Bjørnson. Festskrift*, Copenhagen 1902, published in connection with Bjørnson's seventieth birthday. Grieg wrote it at Troldhaugen in September, 1902.

It was Christmas Eve, 1868,[2] at the Bjørnsons in Christiania. They lived on Rosenkrantz Street at that time. As far as I can recall, my wife and I were the only guests. The [Bjørnson] children were very excited. An enormous Christmas tree shone brightly in the middle of the room. In came all the servants and Bjørnson began to speak, beautifully and warmly, as he is able to do. "Now you must play the hymn, Grieg," he said, and although I bridled a bit inwardly at being obliged to serve as organist, I of course obeyed without protesting. It was a Grundtvig[3] hymn with 32—thirty-two—stanzas. I resigned myself to my fate with stoic tranquility. At first I pressed on courageously, but the endless repetitions had a soporific effect. Little by little I became as languorous as a medium. When we finally had worked our way through all the stanzas, Bjørnson said, "Yes, isn't that a lovely hymn? Now I am going to read it for you!" And we got all 32 stanzas all over again. I was deeply impressed.

Among the Christmas gifts was a book to me from Bjørnson—his *Short Pieces*.[4] On the title page he had written, "Thank you for your short pieces! Here are some in return!" It happens that on that very day I had presented him with the first copy of my *Lyric Pieces*,[5] which had just been published. Among these is one with the title, "National Song". I played this for Bjørnson, who liked it so well that he wanted to write a text for it. I was happy, although afterwards I said

---

[1] Grieg's letters to Iver Holter are printed in English translation in Finn Benestad (ed.), *Edvard Grieg: Letters to Colleagues and Friends*, Columbus, Ohio 2000, pp. 406–427. The passage cited is on p. 419.

[2] Grieg is clearly mistaken about the date of this meeting with Bjørnson. See footnotes 5 and 7.

[3] Danish bishop, poet and hymn-writer Nikolai Frederik Severin Grundtvig (1783–1872).

[4] Norwegian: *Småstykker*

[5] *Lyric Pieces I*, op. 12, published for the first time in 1867 with the Norwegian title *Lyriske Småstykker*.

to myself, "He will never get beyond just wanting to. He has other things to think about." But the very next day, to my surprise, I met him brimming with enthusiasm over what he was writing: "It's going great! It will be a song for all the young people of Norway. But there is something at the beginning that I still haven't been able to get right. A specific expression. I feel that the melody requires it, and I won't give up until I get it. It will certainly come." Then we parted.

The next forenoon, as I sat in my attic studio on Øvre Vold Street giving a piano lesson to a young lady, I heard the doorbell ringing as if it were going to ring right off the door. Then there was a racket as of invading wild hordes and a roar, "Forward, forward! Hurrah! Now I've got it! Forward!" My pupil trembled like an aspen leaf. My wife, who was in the next room, was scared out of her wits. But when the door flew open and Bjørnson stood there, happy and glowing like the sun, everybody joined in the excitement. Then we heard the beautiful poem, which was nearly completed:

> *"Forward!" was our fathers' battle cry.*
> *"Forward!" We shall raise the banner high![6]*

The song was performed for the first time by the students in their parade in honor of Welhaven in 1868.[7]

The following year, Bjørnson's play *Sigurd Jorsalfar* was published.[8] It was going to be performed at the Christiania Theater on such short notice that I had no more than eight days to write and orchestrate the music.[9] But I had the flexibility of youth, and I managed it. The performance took place as planned, but without Bjørnson. Hartvig Lassen was director of Christiania Theater on the Bank Square at that time,[10] and there were misunderstandings as a result of which Bjørnson didn't set foot in the theater for a long time. Then came May 17, 1872.[11] The play was scheduled to be performed that day, and I persuaded Bjørnson to attend the performance. Good-natured as always, he agreed, and thus it came about that we sat together in the first row of the auditorium that evening.

---

[6] Norwegian text: "Fremad! Fremad!" Fædres høje Hærtag var. / "Fremad! Fremad!" Nordmænd også vi det tar!

[7] "National Song" (Norwegian: "Fædrelandssang") is op. 12 no. 8. After Grieg had received Bjørnson's text, he made an arrangement for men's chorus of the piano piece. It was performed by a student ensemble in a torchlight procession honoring Norwegian poet Johan Sebastian Welhaven (1807–73) on November 12, 1868, and published for the first time in 1869.

[8] Bjørnson's play was written in 1872 and had its first performance on April 10 of that year—with Grieg's incidental music. Sigurd Jorsalfar—Sigurd the Crusader (1090–1130)—was King of Norway from 1103 to 1130.

[9] Grieg actually sketched the music in the middle of March and informed the theater consultant that he needed two weeks to orchestrate it. His honorarium for all the incidental music to *Sigurd Jorsalfar* was just 35 *spesidalers*—equivalent to approximately 35 American dollars.

[10] Hartvig Lassen (1824–97) was dramatic consultant (not theater director) at the Christiania Theater in the early 1870's.

[11] May 17 is Norway's Constitution Day.

Edvard and Nina Grieg with their friends Bjørnstjerne and Karoline Bjørnson

Although it was usually said in those days that the Christiania Theater was a good place for those who desired solitude, such was really not the case on the 17th of May. The theater was packed from floor to ceiling. The curtain went up. I was on the verge of regretting that I had gotten Bjørnson to come, for at the beginning it was obvious that he was not enjoying himself. I understood why. On stage there was absolutely no trace of direction. One actor spoke his lines to the east, another to the west. Despite the fact that Bjørnson had come with the sincerest intention of being broad-minded and looking positively at the whole production, he was visibly nervous, and there were moments when soft, ominous grunts made it clear that the interior of the crater was not to be fooled with.

During the first intermission, Bjørnson stood up and walked out very, very fast. Over by one of the corner pillars stood our common acquaintance, Professor X, who, according to what he told me later, was not altogether pleased with the overall impression and thus was very unhappy to see Bjørnson charging directly towards him. He groped about for something to say to fit the occasion, but Bjørnson beat him to it: "This is really rough!" The professor stood there, not knowing what to say. He had expected anything else but not this. Unfortunately, I was not able to overhear the conversation. That it was quite short, however, was evident from the fact that immediately thereafter I saw Bjørnson walk away and talk with others who were standing around.

Then the conductor, Hennum,[12] gave the signal for the orchestra to begin, and Bjørnson returned to his seat. When the curtain went up, Mrs. Gundersen[13] had the opening lines. Her first monologue was moving. On the whole, from this point on the acting exhibited more momentum, both with respect to individual parts and in the ensemble as a whole. No further grunts of displeasure could be heard from Bjørnson. He sat there like a schoolboy in the classroom, calm and well-behaved. Little by little I even noted some friendly nods of approval. He grew more cheerful.

Now it was my turn to be nervous—indeed, almost to forget where I was. It isn't always pleasant for a composer to listen to the musical rendition from the stage. Hammer[14] certainly was a gifted actor. In the role of a skald, however, he was also supposed to be a singer. He did his best, but when he sang "The King's Song",[15] I had a strong feeling of displeasure that developed into such a torment that I wanted to slip away and hide. Instinctively I leaned forward more and more. Finally I was so far down in the seat that, bracing myself on my elbows, I could hold my hand in front of my face. I relate this to illustrate the degree to which Bjørnson now realized what the situation required of us, for suddenly he gave me a fairly hard jab and whispered, "Sit up!" I straightened up as though stung by a wasp and sat thereafter in irreproachable immobility in my seat until the very end.

But then the Constitution-day jubilation really broke out. The applause, which previously had been warm, now became tempestuous. There was one curtain call after another, and finally the audience shouted so loudly for Bjørnson and me that we had to go up on stage. Those who do not know what Christiania was like at the end of the 1860's and the beginning of the 1870's cannot understand what this meant to Bjørnson. When he used the phrase "Christian Friele and other ugly things" in writing about the editor of *Morgenbladet*,[16] there is no doubt that most of the bourgeoisie of that day both thought and said that Bjørnson, not Friele, was "the ugly one"—indeed, the epitome of everything that they regarded as "ugliness". He was for them nothing less than a revolutionary, a demagogue—yes, the very Antichrist. I know what I had to endure from my own generation in the Norwegian capital—those who thought they represented the city's high society—in order to be able to associate with those who shared their views.

But—back to the theater. We had ended up on stage, the curtain was lowered, and instantly everyone gathered on the stage realized what it meant that

---

[12] Johan Hennum (1836–94), musical director at the Christiania Theater 1866–94.

[13] Norwegian actress Laura Gundersen (1832–98).

[14] Norwegian actor Hjalmar Hammer (1846–96), who played the part of the skald Ivar Ingemundsen.

[15] Norwegian title: "Kongekvadet".

[16] The Christiania conservative newspaper *Morgenbladet*. Christian Friele (1857–93) was its editor from 1857 to 1893.

Bjørnson suddenly stood among them as if he had descended from heaven. Actors and actresses and supernumeraries flocked around him. It was his old group of faithful followers, who desired nothing more than to stand once again under his triumphant banner.[17] I shall not forget the admiration and devotion that beamed from every eye. There he stood, tall and imposing, open and cheerful, thanking them one and all. Then he was cheered most warmly.

Thereafter followed an episode the comical effect of which I shall never forget. I don't know who was funnier, Bjørnson or the actor Bucher,[18] the director of the play. They simply outdid each other, thanks to our above-mentioned friend, Professor X, who also had found his way up on stage and abruptly, without any preliminary comments, interjected these words: "Bjørnson, there is one thing I must call to your attention. You have one of Sigurd's vassals quote Gunnar Lidarende's words in Njål's saga: 'How beautiful is the hillside; never has it seemed to me more lovely!'[19] But Njål's saga had not yet been written at that time."[20] Tableau. Now the professor surely would win the battle. But if that is what he thought, he had failed to reckon with Bjørnson, who struck an imperious pose, stretched out his arm toward Bucher, and thundered in a stentorian tone, "Out, Bucher!" And the best part was that Bucher took this command so literally that he instantly bowed deeply to Bjørnson, turned around and, marching double-time with his funny little steps—one-two, one-two—disappeared between the wings. Then we all had a good laugh.[21]

I rode home with Bjørnson to his lodgings in Piperviken,[22] where we enjoyed some wonderful "old cheese"[23] in the big, cheery kitchen, which also served as a dining room. There, like happy children, we savored our triumph, which culminated when all the Bjørnson children came rushing in, with Bjørn[24] in the lead, shouting: "Just think, we were up in paradise[25] and saw father and Grieg come onto the stage."

Yes, that was quite a time! Thank you for it, Bjørnson!

---

[17] Bjørnson had been director of the Christiania Theater from 1865 to 1867.

[18] Norwegian actor and stage director Ole J. S. Bucher (1828–95).

[19] Norwegian: "Fager er lien, så den aldrig har tyktes mig så skjøn!"

[20] The events concerning Njål and his achievements took place around 1000, but they were not written down until the end of the thirteenth century. Thus, Sigurd Jorsalfar and his men could not have known anything about Njål and Gunnar from Lidarende. Notwithstanding the professor's learned observation, Bjørnson— exercising poetic licence—retained the lines of King Sigurd's vassal Sigurd Sigurdson. They occur at the end of scene 2 in the last act of the play.

[21] The Norwegian words used by Bjørnson were: "Stryk ut!" In Norwegian they have a double meaning, viz. 1) delete, cross out, cut out; 2) scram, get out of here!

[22] Piperviken was a poor area of Christiania near where the City Hall (*Rådhuset*) now stands.

[23] Norwegian: *gammelost*, a highly pungent, light brown cheese.

[24] Bjørn Bjørnson (1859–1942), who was to become director of the new National Theater in Christiania in 1899.

[25] "Paradise" was the children's name for the theater balcony.

Scandalous Reporting (1902)

On May 7, 1902, *Don Giovanni*[1] had been unsuccessfully staged at the National Theater in Christiania, and Grieg was asked to comment on the musical conditions at the theater in the course of an interview by the newspaper *Christiania Dagsavis*. The interview, "In Edvard Grieg's Home",[2] was published two days later. Only too late did Grieg realize that the interview could be misunderstood as offensive, particularly by Johan Halvorsen (1864–1935), musical director of the National Theater. To forestall inevitable criticism from his friends, Grieg sent a sharp protest—written aboard the steamship "Christiania" on May 10 en route to Bergen—but instead of sending it to *Christiania Dagsavis,* he sent it to *Verdens Gang,* where it was printed on May 13. Grieg also sent a disclaimer to Halvorsen, who responded warmheartedly: "Thank you for your beautiful and loving letter, which it was a joy to receive. The sun shines brightly both outside and inside, and I am still and will forever remain your old, devoted friend, Johan Halvorsen."[3]

Mr. Editor!

An interviewer in *Dagsavisen* has had the temerity to attribute to me statements that force me to defend myself.

I have not said, regarding the performance of *Peer Gynt,* that "in most cases it has cut out the very things that should have been retained." I mentioned just a few instances, and I added that with respect to cuts there can always be differences of opinion.

I have not said anything so utterly nonsensical as "that Ibsen has a pessimistic view of the Norwegian peasant character, Bjørnson an optimistic one, but neither of them was right"(!).

I have not said that "it certainly also destroys the illusion to see Solveig sitting and moving her lips although God and everybody else can see that she is not singing." To the contrary, I have recommended this procedure in order to get the song well sung. It is a procedure used successfully in many performances.

I have not said, regarding the performance of *Don Giovanni,* that "it was pure soup-cooking". I don't even know what this word is supposed to mean in this connection. I have said that the orchestra did an excellent job, one that did the greatest credit to both the orchestra and the conductor, but that some of what transpired on stage was amateurish—indeed, in Donna Anna's case it was even unacceptably poor by amateur standards. I said that in my early days in the 1860's, people here in Christiania were naive enough to believe that when you took

---

[1] The comic opera *Don Giovanni* (1787) by Wolfgang Amadeus Mozart (1756–91); libretto by Italian author Lorenzo da Ponte (1749–1838).

[2] Norwegian: "Hos Edvard Grieg".

[3] Halvorsen's letter is reproduced in Norwegian in Finn Benestad (ed.), *Edvard Grieg: Brev i utvalg 1862–1907,* vol. 1, Oslo 1998, p. 374, footnote 122.

someone from the so-called higher social strata and put them on a concert platform or on the stage, you thereby got art, even fine art. But, I said, we should now be done with such ideas. I said that the National Theater was not the place for that kind of art. And I think this cannot be said strongly enough.

I have not said "that the audience is so incapable" that it sits and claps but doesn't even know what it is clapping for. But I have said that through such amateurism the audience's good sense was misguided rather than guided. I have said that it is a sin and a shame that the excellent music of the orchestra should be spoiled by the impossible singing on the stage.

Dagsavisen quotes me as saying so infinitely much else that I have not said, but the things mentioned above are the most important. Still—one more! I have not said a single word of the following: "I am afraid of the intrusive and not especially representative reporters who camp on the doorsteps as they do here. One was here just recently. I didn't want to talk with him, so I let Nina (!) deal with him. She does much better with people like that than I do." What insolence! What crudity! The truth is that when I came home to the hotel I learned that there had been a reporter from *Intelligenssedlerne*[4] whom my wife unfortunately had allowed to come in.

Finally, a word about the reporter nuisance. The time has come to make a serious effort to turn against it. What do these people achieve? They earn a few crowns, of course. But in order to get hold of these crowns, they don't think twice about creating the greatest embarrassment for the rest of us, stamping both us and themselves as liars and bringing discredit upon the newspaper they represent. If such scandalous behavior cannot be completely eradicated, I then recommend that no reporter be allowed by an editor to write a word unless he solemnly has bound himself to submit his manuscript to the interviewee for his approval before it goes to press.

In the present case, the reporter represented himself as a correspondent for Danish newspapers. He did not mention a word to the effect that the interview was for *Dagsavisen*. Reason enough for me not to approach this newspaper but to request that you, Mr. Editor, kindly print the above clarification.

---

[4] *Norske Intelligentssedler*, Norway's oldest newspaper, issued its first number on May 25, 1763, in Christiania. In 1920 it was incorporated in *Verdens Gang.*

Word of Thanks to Danish Friends (1903)

Grieg always regarded Denmark as his second homeland, and he spent as much time there as he possibly could. He loved the Danish people and the Danish beech forests, and he understood very well that the artistic environment in Denmark was much better than that in Norway.

Grieg's love for Denmark was reciprocated by the Danish people, who regarded him as one of their own to such an extent that on one occasion a Danish journal went so far as to list him as a Danish composer. That was too much for the militantly patriotic Grieg, who fired off the following protest that was published in the Copenhagen newspaper *Politiken* on May 14, 1905: "When *Illustreret Tidende* (. . .) today lists me as a Danish artist, I must protest most energetically. I am Norwegian and cannot stand to see my nationality being misrepresented. My love for Denmark is great—but it is not *that* great."

His word of thanks to Danish friends after the celebration of his sixtieth birthday was written at Troldhaugen and published in the Copenhagen newspaper *Berlingske Tidende* on June 29, 1903. It is here presented for the first time in English translation.

The large, colorful painting by Danish landscape painter Godfred Christensen (1845–1928) to which Grieg refers now hangs behind the Steinway grand piano in the living-room at Troldhaugen.

As I walked into my living room on June 15, my sixtieth birthday, I was dazzled by the sight of Prof. Godfred Christensen's beautiful painting, "Forest View from the Vejle Region". But no presenter, no message, no letter, no address revealed from whom it had come. A strange fairytale-feeling came over me! It was the love of my youth—indeed, it was Denmark itself that in its most delicate poetry, its beech forests, had come to greet me! It was the magnificent gothic arcades, the soaring arches of the deciduous forests beneath which, in days of yore, my imagination so often took flight.

But who stood behind this wandering forest? Enemies, who came to strike me down like a "Macbeth"?[1] Impossible. For in Denmark I have no enemies. But finally—and this is why my thanks come so late—finally the riddle was solved with the delayed arrival of the salutation from Danish friends. A more beautiful expression of appreciative sentiment you could not have given me. It will always remind me of the brightest time in my life and of the country, so dear to me, in whose shelter I found a home in my youth for myself and my art.[2]

The press is the only avenue whereby I can reach all the givers. Therefore, I say through these lines, which I request be kindly reprinted in other Danish newspapers: Thank you, friends both male and female, both known and unknown—thank you sincerely for all the honor you have shown me.

---

[1] The title character in *Macbeth* (1606), tragedy by William Shakespeare (1564–1616).

[2] The "salutation" to which Grieg refers reads as follows: "Danish friends and admirers of your art send you a sincere greeting on the occasion of your 60th birthday. We ask you to accept the accompanying gift as an expression of our deep appreciation and a token of our gratitude for the compositions you have created in the many years during which we have had the pleasure of seeing you in our midst."

Protest Against an Unauthorized Performance of Peer Gynt (1903)

The financial arrangements for composers during Grieg's lifetime were not very favorable to the composer. There was no royalty system. The usual practice with respect to printed works was for the publisher to pay the composer a one-time honorarium. A young composer sometimes received nothing but the honor of being published by a well-known publishing company, and even when he received an honorarium for an authorized publication he had no protection against pirated editions of his works in other countries.[1]

Grieg had the good fortune to have developed a cordial relationship with the C. F. Peters Musikverlag in Leipzig early in his career. In 1889 he entered into a general contract with the firm whereby he received an annual retainer in addition to an honorarium for each new work. Peters, moreover, often voluntarily sent him an extra honorarium when a composition sold especially well.

The practice regarding public performances of musico-dramatic works was somewhat different in that the composer, like the playwright, received an honorarium for each production of a work. For the premiere production of *Peer Gynt* in Christiania in 1876, for example, Grieg and Ibsen each received honoraria of 200 *spesidalers*—approximately 200 American dollars. They received additional honoraria for subsequent productions of the play in Copenhagen (1886) and Christiania (1893 and 1902). Thus Grieg was furious when, in 1903, The National Stage (Den Nationale Scene) in Bergen launched a production of *Peer Gynt* without asking permission to use his music.

Grieg's account of the matter, written at Voksenkollen, Christiania, on November 30, 1903, was printed in *Bergens Aftenblad* on December 4.

Mr. Editor!

Since I assume that the telegrams exchanged between the Bergen National Stage and me yesterday, Sunday, will leak out among the public and there be reproduced in a manner that does not correspond with the truth, I wish to publish the telegrams in question.

As is well known, the copyright law forbids performance of dramatic works by our authors and composers unless prior permission has been given. Nonetheless, as of yesterday afternoon I had not been approached regarding permission to perform *Peer Gynt* with my music. I then sent the following telegram:

Mr. Theater Director Thomassen,[2] Bergen.
I forbid the use of my music at the performance of *Peer Gynt* at the Bergen National Stage since the theater has not found it in order to secure my permission.

EDVARD GRIEG

---

[1] The Bern Convention of 1886 was an attempt to address the latter problem, but it did little to protect Grieg during his lifetime. See Grieg's letter to Lyman Judson Gage of September, 1900, and his correspondence with Henrik Ibsen during the period December 25, 1898–January 16, 1899 in Finn Benestad (ed.), *Edvard Grieg: Letters to Colleagues and Friends*, Columbus, Ohio 2000, pp. 253 and 448–450, respectively.

[2] Norwegian actor and theater director Gustav Thomassen (1862–1929).

Shortly thereafter, the following two special-delivery telegrams arrived from Bergen:

> My sincerest apologies. I have acted contrary to your interests in good faith and without malicious intent. Do not let the theater and the public suffer because of my unintentional mistake.
>
> GUSTAV THOMASSEN

> The Bergen Theater Association hereby requests permission to use your music at the performance of *Peer Gynt*. If we have acted negligently, we deeply regret it. Such was not the intention of either the board or the theater director. The play is scheduled for this evening and all the tickets have been sold.
>
> JOACHIM GRIEG[3]
> Current President of the Bergen Theater Association

I then answered as follows:

> Joachim Grieg, Bergen.
> The negligence is well-nigh unbelievable, but out of regard for the Bergen public I waive my rights.
>
> EDVARD GRIEG

So much for the facts. I hope for the sake of the Theater Association that it has not also "in good faith and without malicious intent" neglected to get Henrik Ibsen's permission. It would not have escaped so easily in that case. But I will say this, that if Bergen had not been my home town, well . . .[4]

We condemn the Americans for robbing and stealing our literature and our music, but what we ourselves do is actually ten times worse. The Americans make unjust gains from the labor of foreigners. We Norwegians are slaughtering each other. What we are doing is engaging in civil warfare. It's genuinely Norwegian, what we are doing. Or, more correctly, it *was* genuinely Norwegian at one time, but it ought not to be so any more. We should no longer be proud of being able to raise a banner on which is written in capital letters: LONG LIVE BARBARISM!

---

[3] Bergen ship-owner and politician Joachim Grieg (1849–1932) was Edvard's second cousin.
[4] The elliptical dots are Grieg's.

The Copenhagen City Hall (1907)

In 1907, Grieg responded positively to a request from a Danish editor to write a few words about Copenhagen. However, the book in which his statement was published—*Dansk Portrætgalleri* (*Danish Portrait Gallery*), vol. 4, Copenhagen 1908, p. 199—did not appear until after his death. It is here presented for the first time in English translation.

It is wonderful to be able for once to express complete and unconditioned enthusiasm for a work of art, and that is my feeling regarding the new City Hall in Copenhagen. Rarely has Danish talent fascinated me as much as it has here. First, I admire the pure, noble lines of the structure as a whole. Then, looking more closely at the numerous outstanding and brilliant details, I become absolutely enthralled. It is indubitably true that the details express the most cherished fantasies of the Danish imagination, and they make such a positive impression here because they look as if they had grown right out of Danish nature and Danish ways of thinking.

Finally, looking once again at the impressive whole, I do not doubt that the generation of Danish people that can find so lofty an expression for its longing for beauty has a calling to perform great cultural deeds.

Grieg's Reflections on Some of His Own Piano Pieces

Although Grieg sometimes wrote eloquently about the works of other composers, he rarely characterized his own. One finds numerous references to his music in his letters and diaries, but little in the way of sustained accounts. Two letters are of particular interest in this connection, however. The first is the letter of December 14, 1875, to the conductor of the Christiania Theater orchestra, Johan Hennum (1836–94), in which Grieg writes in detail about the interpretation and performance of the *Peer Gynt* music, op. 23. The other is the letter of July 17, 1900, to his American biographer Henry T. Finck (1854–1926) in which he writes about his songs. Both of these lengthy letters are printed in their entirety in English translation in Finn Benestad (ed.), *Edvard Grieg: Letters to Colleagues and Friends*, Columbus, Ohio 2000.

Two instances in which Grieg discusses his piano music—also touching upon programmatic aspects—are given below. The first is his preface to *Pictures from Folk Life* op. 19, the second a preface to *Norwegian Peasant Dances (Slåtter)* op. 72. The latter includes his account of legends related to three of the folk dances.

Pictures from Folk Life, op. 19 (1872)

Grieg wrote very little program music in the strict sense of the word, although the titles of his compositions—especially of the *Lyric Pieces*—often hint at extra-musical images or events that he may or may not have had in mind when writing a particular piece. In one case, however —*Pictures from Folk Life* op. 19, written 1869–71—he himself explained in a printed preface what he was trying to depict in sound. The composition consists of three pieces: "In the Mountains", "Bridal Procession" and "From the Carnival".

The translation that follows is made from the Norwegian preface in the Horneman & Erslev first edition of 1872.

It should be noted that familiarity with the first two pieces is necessary to an understanding of the last. For in the third piece, "From the Carnival", in the midst of the milling crowd one gets a glimpse in the distance of a Norwegian wedding procession. The wedding procession is then replaced by giant figures that in a series of big "halling leaps"[1] (to motives from "In the Mountains"), clear the stage, as it were. Lastly comes the flying ride, which is indicated by the open fifth in A Major that occurs after the *Stretto*. At this point, the carnival turns into a scene of complete wildness. The whistling and yelling of the crowd, plus the snorting horses that in one unified motion pierce the air—everything blends together to create a picture of the most restrained wantonness.

In part, the ideas derive from the carnival season in Rome, but with no effort to depict it in detail. In part, also the memory of folk life in general has later given

---

[1] The *halling* is a somewhat acrobatic Norwegian solo dance (for men) in 2/4 time. The climax of the dance is the so-called *hallingkast*—the "halling leap". One of the folk dancers—usually a pretty girl wearing a national costume—stands on a stool holding a long pole six to nine feet from the ground. Towards the end of the halling, the male dancer makes a high wheeling leap, trying to kick the hat off the pole. A clever dancer always succeeds—if not the first time, then the second or third—while the fiddler continues playing.

the composer some vague ideas. In order to facilitate understanding of the work, the composer has found it relevant to explain these things.

Norwegian Peasant Dances (*Slåtter*) op. 72 (1903)

Norwegian Peasant Dances was Grieg's most advanced work. Here, in a quite remarkable way, he entered into the world of Hardanger-fiddle music and succeeded in adapting its uniqueness to the piano. He based the seventeen pieces on transcriptions made by Johan Halvorsen (1864–1935) of the tunes as played by the outstanding Hardanger-fiddle player Knut Dahle (1834–1921) from Telemark.[2] Dahle had learned the tunes from Torgeir Augundson (1801–72),[3] Håvard Gibøen (1809–73) and other well-known fiddlers. For further details see Grieg's letters to Dahle in Finn Benestad (ed.), *Edvard Grieg: Letters to Colleagues and Friends*, Columbus, Ohio 2000, pp. 203–206.

Grieg also included in the first edition some comments on three of the peasant dances: nos. 4, 8, and 17. In a letter of February 28, 1903, to the director of C. F. Peters, Henri Hinrichsen (1868–1942), he stated: "As in this connection the cultural-historical interest plays a prominent role, I consider the preface, as well as all notes and remarks, to be indispensable."[4] Grieg's comments are therefore also added after the preface.

The preface and the comments were printed in Norwegian as well as in English, French and German translations in the C. F. Peters first edition of the work in 1903. The present translation is made from Grieg's original Norwegian version.

These Norwegian *Slåtter* (*slått* is the Norwegian word for a peasant dance), which are here presented to the public for the first time in the original transcriptions for the Hardanger fiddle and in free arrangements for piano, have been written down as played by an old fiddler in Telemark. Anyone who has a feeling for these sounds will be entranced by their great originality, their juxtaposition of fine and delicate graceful beauty and bold power and untamed wildness, melodically and especially rhythmically. They bear the stamp of an imagination that is as audacious as it is bizarre—relics from a time when Norwegian peasant culture was isolated in remote mountain valleys from the outside world and precisely for that reason have preserved their authenticity.

---

[2] A Hardanger fiddle is a distinctively Norwegian instrument that differs from an ordinary violin in various ways. For instance, it has four sympathetic strings that sound softly when the instrument is played. A fiddle tune is nearly always played on two strings simultaneously: one with normal fingering, the other open.
  Because of their great artistic and musicological interest, Grieg insisted that Halvorsen's transcriptions of the original Hardanger-fiddle tunes be published simultaneously with his own piano arrangements.

[3] Augundson is affectionately known in Norway as "Myllarguten" ("The Miller's Boy"). He traveled widely as a fiddler from his early youth, learning peasant dances wherever he went, but he set his personal stamp on everything he played. At an early stage he met the internationally renowned Norwegian violin virtuoso Ole Bull (1810–80), and on Bull's initiative he gave—for a period of fifteen years beginning in 1849—a large number of concerts of folk music for an urban public in towns and cities all over Norway. In 1862 he also played in Copenhagen.

[4] The letter is printed in the original German in Finn Benestad & Hella Brock (eds.), *Edvard Grieg: Briefwechsel mit dem Musikverlag C. F. Peters 1863–1907*, Frankfort on the Main 1997, p. 495.

My task in transferring these pieces to the piano was to attempt—through what I might call "stylized harmony"—to raise these folk tunes to an artistic level.

It is in the nature of the case that the piano had to simply omit many of the small embellishments that are grounded in the character of the Hardanger fiddle and the peculiarities of bowing. On the other hand, the piano has the great advantage of being able to avoid an altogether too conspicuous monotony by means of dynamic and rhythmic variety as well as through new harmonizations of the repetitions. I have endeavored to draw clear, easily surveyable lines—indeed, to create a stable musical form.

The few places where I have found it artistically justified to develop the existing motives can be readily identified by comparing my arrangements with the original transcriptions made by Johan Halvorsen, which are being published simultaneously by the same publishing company, and which should be regarded as the source document.

Notwithstanding the fact that on the Hardanger fiddle the *slåtter* sound a minor third higher,[5] in order to obtain a fuller effect on the piano I have chosen to retain the keys in which the original versions were written down.

Grieg's Comment on op. 72 no. 4, "Halling from the Fairy Hill"

This halling is connected with the following legend: A man by the name of Brynjulf Olson had lost a bull. After searching for the animal in the mountains for several days, he got tired and fell asleep. He dreamt that he heard a wonderful, peculiar peasant dance. Behind a hill he saw a beautiful maiden, who called to him and said: "Yes, just like that you shall play on the fiddle, Brynjulf Olson, when you return home to wife and child, and—on the other side, where the mountains disappear—you shall find the bull."

Grieg's Comment on op. 72 no. 8, "Myllarguten's Bridal March"

According to a well-known fiddler from Telemark, this march was composed by Myllarguten when Kari broke off her engagement with him in order to marry someone else.

Grieg's Comment on op. 72 no. 16, "The Maidens from Kivledal. Springdans"[6]

In Seljord in Telemark there is a little valley called Kivledal. In ancient times there was a tiny church in this valley. One Sunday, when the community had assembled for mass, loud tones from the mountains suddenly reverberated

---

[5] Grieg is referring to the fact that the Hardanger fiddle is usually tuned a minor third higher than concert pitch.

[6] The *springdans*, also called *springar*, is a lively Norwegian folk dance in 3/4 time.

through the church. It was the three maidens from Kivledal, the last heathens in the valley, who—while watching their goats on the mountain-slopes—were blowing a *slått* on their ram's horns. The community rushed out of the church and listened enraptured to the enchanting tones. The priest followed and called to the maidens, bidding them to stop playing, but as they kept on blowing their horns, he raised his hands and anathematized them in the name of God and the Pope. The maidens from Kivledal and their herds were at once transformed into stones, and to this day you can see them standing high up on the mountain slope, the horns to their mouths and their herds around them.

This is the legend of the *slått* "The Maidens from Kivledal", as preserved by the farmers in the valley. They still play it on their fiddles.

The *slått* that follows is related to this same legend. There are in all three such tunes—one for each of the maidens—and only the fiddler who could play all three was considered great.

Part IV

Speeches and Impromptu Talks

Although Grieg was reputed to be an excellent public speaker, we do not know of a single original manuscript of a speech prepared by him in advance for delivery at some future date. The closest we come to this is his letter to the editor of the Christiania newspaper *Verdens Gang* printed on November 3, 1896, in which he wrote not what he had planned to say but what he remembers having actually said in an impromptu speech made at a banquet in Stockholm a few days earlier. One other speech—that given in honor of Norwegian author Bjørnstjerne Bjørnson (1832–1910) in celebration of his seventieth birthday on December 3, 1902—gives evidence of having been carefully prepared, as does also Grieg's brief tribute to Ole Bull given at the latter's funeral in August, 1880. In both cases, however, we are dependent on newspaper accounts for our text of the speeches.

With few exceptions, the speeches presented in these pages are derived from contemporary reports of impromptu remarks made in various situations in which Grieg felt obliged or inclined to speak a few words. Most are very short: The longest of them probably required no more than ten minutes for its delivery. As a speech-maker, Grieg was indisputably a miniaturist—but the best of his short speeches, like the best of his short piano pieces, are gems.

Eight of the speeches in this collection were given in honor of individuals who played roles of varying importance in Grieg's life. The other six are short talks on a variety of topics that engaged his interest. The order is chronological. Sources are given in the introductions to the respective items.

It is singularly appropriate that Grieg's last recorded talk, brief though it is, was an expression of homage to his beloved Norway.

Ole Bull monument in Bergen designed by Norwegian sculptor Stephan Sinding. Photo by Knud Knudsen.

At Ole Bull's Funeral (1880)

The world-famous violin virtuoso Ole Bull, who was born in Bergen in 1810, died on August 17, 1880. His funeral was on August 23. Grieg loved Bull's visionary view of the future of Norwegian music, and Bull's influence on his younger relative[1] had been substantial. In an interview in Berlin in 1907 Grieg stated: "It was Ole Bull who first aroused in me the resolve to compose characteristic Norse music. He recognized in me latent possibilities, and when I was fifteen years old, he sent me to Leipzig Conservatory where I studied composition and piano for four years—from 1858 to 1862. (...) Ole Bull was my good angel. He opened my eyes to the beauty and originality of the Norwegian music."[2]

Grieg's short tribute to Bull was printed in *Bergensposten* on August 25, 1880.

Because you brought honor to our country like none other, because you lifted our people up with you toward art's shining heights like none other, because you were a faithful, warm-hearted pioneer for our young national music—one who conquered the hearts of everyone—like none other, because you have planted a seed that will sprout and grow in the future, and for which coming generations will bless your name—with thousands upon thousands of thanks for all this, *in the name of Norwegian music* I lay this wreath on your casket. Peace be with you.

---

[1] Ole Bull and Edvard Grieg were distantly related through the marriage of Grieg's aunt, Johanne Margrethe Hagerup (1817–88), to Bull's brother, Jens Munthe Bull (1815–1905).

[2] Published in Arthur M. Abell's book *Talks with Great Composers*, Garmisch-Partenkirchen, 1964, pp. 203–204. See also Grieg's detailed report on his first meeting with Ole Bull in "My First Success", pp. 75–76.

To the Christiania Students (1889)

In autumn 1889 Grieg gave several concerts in Christiania that consolidated his reputation as Norway's foremost composer. Among other things, on October 19 he gave a first performance of the unfinished national opera *Olav Trygvason*, op. 50, to a text by Bjørnstjerne Bjørnson (1832–1910).[1] The University Student Association held a big meeting in Grieg's honor on October 23, at which the student leader proposed a toast to him. Grieg responded with a short speech addressed to the Norwegian youth.

Grieg's speech was published in the October 24 issue of the Christiania newspaper *Verdens Gang.*

I get both melancholy and happy upon seeing these young people and hearing this tribute. Melancholy, when I think back on the youth as they were when I worked here in Christiania: It was as if a rush of cold air was coming from them. Happy, when I see the youth as they are today. I see so many pleasant faces here this evening. I did not see them in the youth of yesteryear. There is also a welcome difference between the status of art then and now—although we are still only at the beginning. We must understand fully that art is a necessity of life. We must be brought up and must live in it. That is the message that I want the youth to take to heart—and I ask you to pass it on to the generation that will follow you.

---

[1] For further details concerning Grieg and Bjørnson's collaboration on the opera fragment, see Grieg's letters to Bjørnson in Finn Benestad (ed.), *Edvard Grieg: Letters to Colleagues and Friends,* Columbus, Ohio, 2000, pp. 112–125.

For Christiania (1889)

During their stay in Christiania in October 1889, Bjørnstjerne Bjørnson and Grieg were guests of honor at a banquet in the Grand Hotel. The keynote address was given by Bjørnson, who spoke powerfully of Grieg's work for their beloved homeland. Grieg, who had highly ambivalent feelings about the Norwegian capital, responded with some brief remarks about the city in which he had felt so lonely and mistreated early in his artistic career.

The translation of Grieg's talk that follows is made from a report in *Nordisk Musik-Tidende*, Christiania 1889, p. 165.

Christiania is for me a strange city, but now I think it is in process of becoming an absolutely wonderful city. At root, however, it is and always has been strange, for it both attracts and repels. There is something warm in its coldness and something cold in its warmth. Everyone in the country with abilities and gifts comes here. They give it a real try, and then they drift away again. It is as if this city will not let them go until they have received a blow—one such that they will never again be the same as they were before.[1] Either they must go abroad, or they get tuberculosis or some other affliction—one thing or another.

I hope that Christiania will some day become the kind of city where artists can live and thrive.[2]

---

[1] This statement is remarkably similar to the opening sentence of the novella *Sult* (*Hunger*) by Norwegian author Knut Hamsun (1859–1952), first published in 1890. It is not known whether Hamsun was present at the banquet where Grieg made these remarks.

[2] In his letters, Grieg often refers to Christiania as "Tigerville" ("Tigerstaden"), a derisive name coined by Bjørnstjerne Bjørnson.

On the Flag Controversy (1891)

On May 13, 1891, the University Student Association in Christiania decided that beginning on May 17—Norway's Constitution Day—the symbol signifying Norway's union with Sweden should be removed from the Norwegian flag and the "pure" flag flown atop the Association building. That autumn, however, the Association received a proposal to reinstate the union flag. Grieg was among the more than 800 people who attended a November 1 meeting of the Association where the issue was hotly debated.

Grieg spontaneously took the floor and asked those present to join in singing the Norwegian national anthem. According to the Christiania newspaper *Verdens Gang*, the anthem was sung "with an enthusiasm and warmth such as it perhaps has never before been sung by Norwegian young people."

Grieg's brief speech is taken from the report that appeared in *Verdens Gang* on November 2, 1891.

Ladies and gentlemen! I am neither a right-winger nor a left-winger regarding this question. I saw no need to lower the union flag this spring, but once we have done so and the three-colored flag is there—well, to tear this flag down again is a serious step. It seems to me to signify that Norwegians are trampling on old Norway. I think it is time to ask where our love really resides. Here, in this intellectual association, I dare to ask if we ought not to sing "Yes, we love this land, our country"?[1]

[The students sang the anthem with great gusto, whereupon Grieg concluded as follows]: Thank you, gentlemen! Forgive me for making the request. The whole thing took no more than half a minute and the song has warmed many hearts!

---

[1] "Ja, vi elsker dette landet", the Norwegian national anthem. The words are by Bjørnstjerne Bjørnson (1832–1910), the music by Rikard Nordraak (1842–66). Despite Grieg's plea, however, a majority of the students —429 for, 363 against—voted to reinstate the union flag. The incident initiated a continuing debate all over Norway concerning the flag issue, however, and the "pure" flag came into use in many places throughout the country long before the dissolution of the union with Sweden in 1905.

To Fridtjof Nansen and His Crew (1896)

The success of Norwegian polar explorer Fridtjof Nansen (1861–1930) in demonstrating that the ice of the polar sea drifted from Siberia toward Spitsbergen, and in designing a ship ("Fram") that could withstand the pressure of the ice during the polar winter, elicited an enormous outpouring of national pride and enthusiasm in Norway. During an expedition that lasted for over three years, and under inconceivably hazardous conditions, Nansen managed to reach the highest latitude (86° 14') reached by man until that time.

Nansen and his crew were greeted as heroes upon their return to Norway. In early September, when they arrived in Bergen, a public welcome was staged that reportedly drew a crowd of 30,000 people. Grieg was one of many speakers who expressed the nation's pride in the achievement of the intrepid explorers.

The following translation of Grieg's brief remarks was made from a report of the event in *Bergens Tidende* on September 3, 1896.

My Dear Fellow Norwegians!
At the center of the joy of this occasion stands the sacred feeling that inspires us all: love of our homeland.

There was once a foreigner who asked with astonishment about the reason for the enormous enthusiasm with which the entire Norwegian nation unites like one person in applauding the North Pole expedition, inasmuch as it is an undertaking the results of which can only be judged by those possessing appropriate scientific knowledge. "Well," was the answer—and it was a good answer, one that cannot be repeated too often—"it is because through this expedition we have a unique opportunity to show the world that there is a country, an autonomous and energetic country, called Norway."

This, for us, is the main point. No artifices can ever explain away the fact that the North Pole expedition was Norwegian, Norwegian, and only Norwegian, and we are proud to be children of the country that has produced Fridtjof Nansen and his men.

Therefore: Long live this land. Long live our mother country!

At a Banquet in Stockholm (1896)

In October and November of 1896, Grieg experienced in Stockholm what he described as "a singular success" and some "marvelous days," with four sold-out choir and orchestra concerts in the Royal Opera House. On October 31, after the third concert, a big banquet was held in Grieg's honor at Stockholm's Grand Hotel. Three hundred eminent guests were invited, including Prince Eugen[1] and Adolf Erik Nordenskiöld.[2] Grieg had the feeling that his trip to Sweden was a kind of patriotic mission at this time in the crisis between the sister countries. During the banquet he made a speech, concerning which he told Julius Röntgen: "I ventured to use that golden opportunity to touch upon the union question. I spoke as a Norwegian, you understand. We had just sung the Norwegian national anthem, and I managed to express myself so well—heaven knows how—that people came up to me afterwards to express joy and gratitude."[3]

The English translation has been made from Grieg's "letter to the editor" printed in the Christiania newspaper *Verdens Gang* on November 3, 1896. The newspaper gave it the title "Grieg har ordet"—"Grieg has the floor". He began with the following introduction: "People in Christiania have read Swedish newspaper reports of my talk at the banquet in Stockholm's Grand Hotel on Saturday, October 31. These reports are superficial, which is not so serious, but they are also misleading—and for that reason I think it appropriate that people in Norway should learn what I really said. The first part of the talk had to do with art. It included an acknowledgment of the profound debt of gratitude that I owed to all of those in the Swedish capital who had taken it upon themselves to become such excellent interpreters of my works. I will not recount this part of the talk here, since it is primarily of artistic interest. Thereafter, however, I continued as follows."

I have yet one more thing to say. After all the effusive manifestations of appreciation that I have encountered here, I could absolutely not bear the thought of trying to conceal anything from you. I admit that it was with fear and trembling that I, as a Norwegian, went to Sweden, since, as we know, all is not as it should be between us—thanks in large part to the press—and since it would be impossible for me to perform my music in surroundings where the mood was hostile to my homeland. I hasten to add, however, that my fear proved to be thoroughly groundless. Not only was I welcomed with open arms as an artist, a human being, and a Norwegian, but I also got an impression of the city, of the people, of your splendid language, of the contours of life as it is lived here—an impression such that I had to say to myself: This is noble, noble. Moreover, if everything does not

---

[1] Swedish Prince Eugen (1865–1947), son of King Oscar II (1829–1907), was a renowned painter.

[2] Swedish polar explorer Adolf Erik Nordenskiöld (1832–1901) completed the first successful navigation of the Northeast Passage.

[3] Dutch pianist, conductor and composer Julius Röntgen (1855–1932) was Grieg's closest foreign friend. Grieg's complete correspondence with Röntgen has been published in Finn Benestad & Hanna de Vries Stavland (eds.), *Edvard Grieg und Julius Röntgen: Briefwechsel 1883–1907*, Amsterdam 1997. The cited passage, which is from a letter of November 7, 1896, is on p. 174.

lie, if there is such a thing as sound logic, then I have the right to conclude that behind all this nobleness there also stands a noble people.

In this conviction I salute this nation and express the sincere wish that its future may be just as great and as glorious as its past. Not, however, in the way of military glory—for that such glory is obsolete is something that we modern people obviously agree on—but in the direction of free intellectual work. I raise my glass for the Sweden that understands that this work should be the only great goal for two nations that are equal *in every respect*—for the Sweden that loves the idea *that one nation's honor should be the other's joy*.[4] For this Sweden—and I know that all Norway joins me in this—I say with enthusiasm: Long may it live!

---

[4] [Grieg's footnote:] I articulated this in such a way that people had to understand that I was alluding to our representation in foreign countries.
[Editors' footnote:] Grieg is referring to the so-called "consular question", which was a major bone of contention between Norway and Sweden during the years 1892–1905. In 1892 the Norwegian Parliament (*Stortinget*) had passed a resolution establishing an independent consular service, which they thought Norway had a right to do. But the Swedish king had refused to approve the resolution on the grounds that Norway had no right to take such action without prior authorization from Sweden.

At a Concert for Laborers in Copenhagen (1899)

On December 10, 1899, Grieg participated in a concert given specifically for blue-collar workers in Copenhagen. On December 22 he wrote to his Dutch friend Julius Röntgen (1881–1951), "I tell you, during the performance one could have heard a pin drop. My old view was confirmed: *Here* is where one finds the *best* audiences! To hell with the blasé, bejewelled, so-called fashionable audiences, be they in the Gewandhaus in Leipzig or the Music Society in Copenhagen! No, the unspoiled people are capable of enthusiasm; the others, with rare exceptions, are not."

At the end of the concert somebody made a short speech to which Grieg responded with a few impromptu remarks addressed to the workers and their families. Grieg's remarks were reported in the Christiania newspaper *Verdens Gang* on December 14.

This evening represents for me the realization of the dream of my youth: that, as in ancient Greece, art shall reach out to all—precisely because its mission is to bring a message from heart to heart. I hope that this institution—the concert series for laborers—that strives to realize the goal of art, may flourish and be imitated in all the countries of the world. It is a hope expressed both for the people's sake and for art's sake. Long live art as the people's art!

To Bjørnstjerne Bjørnson on His Seventieth Birthday (1902)

On December 13, 1902, the University Student Association in Christiania held a festive event honoring Norwegian author Bjørnstjerne Bjørnson (1832–1910), who had celebrated his seventieth birthday on December 8. Nina and Edvard Grieg were present for the occasion, and after Bjørnson had thanked the students he focused his attention on Grieg: "I think everybody will agree on this, that among all the students Edvard Grieg is the finest! He, too, reads—but he does not lie down while reading. He doesn't sit, either. He stands on a conductor's podium, and then the whole world hears what he reads."

After accompanying Nina singing some of her husband's songs to texts by Bjørnson, Grieg went to the podium and spoke the words given below in honor of his friend. The speech was reported in the Christiania newspaper *Aftenposten* on December 14, 1902.

Bjørnstjerne Bjørnson

You all make both my wife and me quite embarrassed. We have not come here to receive toasts; we are here as adherents of Bjørnstjerne Bjørnson. When I now speak a word of thanks, I want to address myself to him. There is a thank-you that he should have received long ago, but he has not received it—namely, a thank-you from Norwegian composers. I shall extend it to him this evening, although I am well aware that there are people who think I am not the right man to do this. For there are indeed people who say that I am not a true Norwegian because I am just a native of West Norway, and as you know, people from Bergen are more or less foreigners. But if we are foreigners, then we certainly have a rather wide horizon—the same one, moreover, that all of you have.

Bjørnson has taught me and all the other Norwegian composers that art is something more than a merely regional phenomenon. He has taught us that we must go to the mountains, and look out over the whole beautiful Norway, and take it into our souls. He has taught us to long like Arnljot[1] for the ocean, and with him as our guide we have learned to see more distant coasts. Bjørnson has become the great cosmopolitan—and at the same time the great national—poet. We strive to follow in his footsteps.

He has taught me at least one thing more: There is something in every branch of art that lies beyond that art. Art that is sufficient unto itself may be excellent, but it does not achieve power over our minds. In Bjørnson's art, however, there is something beyond, something mysterious, something not written that points toward infinity.

You, Bjørnson, are like the king about whom you have written—the king who looked around and was entranced.[2] You have looked around and entranced us Norwegian composers. Therefore, we express to you our gratitude. And with that, we will shout nine "hurrahs" for Bjørnson with thanks from all Norwegian composers.

---

[1] A reference to Bjørnson's epic poem *Arnljot Gelline*. Grieg used a section of this poem in *Before a Southern Convent* op. 20, a composition for soprano, alto, women's chorus and orchestra.

[2] A reference to *Land-Sighting*, a poem about Norwegian King Olav Trygvason (968–1000), set by Grieg for baritone, male chorus and orchestra in op. 31.

To Bjørnstjerne Bjørnson at the Celebration of Grieg's Sixtieth Birthday (1903)

Bjørnstjerne Bjørnson (1832–1910), who was as renowned for his oratorical skills as for his poems, novels and plays, gave a strong speech in praise of the honoree on the occasion of the celebration of Grieg's sixtieth birthday on June 15, 1903. He said, among other things, that Norwegians often lacked the ability to set long-range goals. But Grieg, he continued, was one of those who had been able to take a longer view, and in so doing he had laid a foundation on which others could build yet further. Grieg's music, he stated, was as Norwegian as Norway's rugged landscape and had, like nothing else, brought Norway into homes throughout the world. "I truly believe," he concluded, "that if one will measure the stature of a great man, one must consider not only what he has done but also what he has *made it possible for others to do.*"

Grieg responded by expressing his great respect and affection for his friend and compatriot. The speech was reported in the Bergen newspaper *Bergens Tidende* on June 17, 1903.[1]

Ladies and gentlemen! Many strange things happen in this world. Man proposes, but—Bjørnson disposes.[2] To tell you the truth, I had imagined that the celebration of my sixtieth birthday would be something totally different from what it has become. I had been invited to England for these very days to participate in various concerts. Then the thought occurred to me: What if I, on the 15th of June, were a cosmopolitan giving a big concert in Albert Hall, which holds 10,000 people! That would have irritated our local chauvinists—and I am such an evil person that I enjoy nothing more than annoying the chauvinists, these mountain trolls whom I hate like the plague. No, they aren't even proper mountain trolls; they're just poor copies.

Well, I began to prepare for my trip to England. But suddenly the word went out in such a way that it was heard all over Norway—yes, and in Europe too: "I am coming to Bergen on the 15th of June." That made me change my tune. Such a beautiful, friendly thought by Bjørnson I could not resist. I got terribly busy. I wrote to east and west and got the whole England trip canceled.

This Bjørnsonian regimen is strange. There is something refreshing, goading, energizing, something downright uplifting about it. It has an effect on those who come under its sway similar to that which a voyage to America or a period of military service has on our farmers: It makes proper people out of them. Moreover, it is a rather strict regimen. It requires discipline. Not everyone can manage it. For my part, I must honestly admit that one fine day I broke from the ranks—yes, I simply ran away from it altogether and stayed away for a long, long

---

[1] See also Grieg's article "With Bjørnson in Days Gone By", pp. 358-362.
[2] Cf. St. Thomas à Kempis (1380–1471): "Man proposes, but God disposes." *Imitation of Christ*, Book I, Chapter 3.

Caricature of Bjørnstjerne Bjørnson by Swedish caricaturist Albert Engström

time.[3] But I was not happy. I longed and longed to return to the fold. Finally, I couldn't stand it any longer. I reported for duty again. That must be how it feels for a prisoner who has escaped—but who handles freedom so poorly that he commits a crime just in order to get back to the penitentiary again.

I have spent my happiest years in this Bjørnsonian institution. I have lived the most beautiful and festive hours of my life under Bjørnson's aegis. Where you were, Bjørnson, there was a festive atmosphere. It was either your books or your work for Norway or your personal presence that created the festive mood.

I remember one such festive occasion here in Bergen—and I think many of you will still remember it. It was a long time ago. It was in 1873. Ole Bull gave a concert in the beautiful facility called the armory to raise money for the Leiv Eiriksson[4] monument. He had invited Bjørnson—and Bjørnson came. Bull played, Bjørnson gave a talk about Leiv Eiriksson, and I conducted. Yes, I also accompanied Bull, and what was interesting for me was the fact that it was the only time in my life that I performed publicly with him.

After the concert, we were together in a private gathering—and then, Bjørnson, you gave a speech, and what a speech it was! You spoke, among other things, on behalf of Håkonshallen.[5] You wanted it to become a mausoleum

---

[3] During the mid-1870's, Grieg and Bjørnson had collaborated on what both had hoped would become a great national opera based on the exploits of legendary Norwegian King Olav Trygvason. Problems arose, however, leading in 1876 to an end to the collaboration as well as a rupture in their friendship that was to last for thirteen years. For further details, see Grieg's letters to Bjørnson in Finn Benestad (ed.), *Edvard Grieg: Letters to Colleagues and Friends*, Columbus, Ohio 2000, pp. 112–125.

[4] Leiv Eiriksson (ca. 975–ca. 1020), the discoverer of America. In 1964, October 9 was officially designated Leiv Eiriksson Day in the United States.

[5] *Håkonshallen—Håkon's Hall*—is a splendid structure erected by the Norwegian king Håkon Håkonsson (1204–63) in 1247–61 as part of the royal compound in Bergen, the political center of Norway at that time. The building had fallen into disrepair, and Grieg joined Bjørnson and other cultural leaders in a successful effort to have it restored. Today it is often used as a venue for concerts and other public events.

honoring Norway's cultural leaders, with Ole Bull standing in the most prominent place with a lowered bow. But then Ole Bull jumped up from his chair: "Why
with a *lowered* bow? No! I don't want to die. I want to live!"

I also remember that you named a series of Norwegian men one by one,
letting them step forward in our imagination in the surroundings that you
thought appropriate for each of them. Henrik Ibsen,[6] for example, you depicted
against the background of the ice church, surrounded by heavy, dark winter fog-
banks. Finally you came to me. I was not well known at that time, of course, but
you found the way to me nonetheless, and I remember now as if it were
yesterday that you said, "It is springtime. It is early in the morning. There is dew
on the grass. Your feet get quite wet." Later it occurred to me: Well, it's not the
worst thing to get wet feet; after all, there is such a thing as a water cure, isn't there?
But if it is true that one gets wet feet by coming close to me, how did it go with
those who came close to you? It was, after all, from you that all the wetness came.
You yourself were the waterfall—Norway's greatest waterfall, which boomed and
rumbled and splashed and foamed until the water surrounded you like an ocean.
It was just the spray and the roar of this gushing cascade that I—and the whole
circle of young people of which I was a part—loved, and that caused us to love
you. How the young spring sun shone upon this waterfall! For what you said is
true: It was spring then. Indeed, you yourself were the harbinger of spring.

And what a long and rich summer you gave us, as one shining literary work
after another sparkled in the sunshine. Now autumn is drawing near, but the birds
are still singing on the hillsides. Let their song continue! Remember Hamsun's[7]
words: "When you fall silent, there is a hush." No truer word was ever spoken. But
you will not fall silent yet. You will sing. And you will flog and be flogged, as you
yourself say. We cannot imagine you otherwise.

Yes, Bjørnson, as you sit here among us you are indeed the Norwegian who
is closest to our hearts. And why? Because you are always our wakeful conscience.
Because it is through you that we feel Norway's pulse.

And now, ladies and gentlemen, permit me to lead you in a "Hurrah!" for
Bjørnson.

---

[6] Norwegian author Henrik Ibsen (1828–1906). As for the *ice church*, Grieg is alluding to Ibsen's dramatic poem
   Brand (1865), in which the concept of the ice church plays a prominent role.
[7] Norwegian author Knut Hamsun (1859–1952).

In Memory of Ole Bull (1903)

At a banquet in Bergen celebrating Grieg's sixtieth birthday on June 15, 1903, one of the speakers, Johan Bøgh,[1] stated that Grieg was one of the people who had put red dots on the map of Norway, marking the location of famous places such as Troldhaugen. Grieg, in his response, picked up the thread, then concluded with a few words in memory of Ole Bull, who had meant so much to him in his youth.

Grieg's tribute was printed in *Bergensposten* on June 17, 1903.

I cannot agree with Johan Bøgh that there should be red marks identifying Troldhaugen and Aulestad,[2] but I will request in any case that if there are going to be such marks on the map of Norway, they should be placed at Aulestad and not at Troldhaugen. There was once a tourist book on Bergen and its environs that included a little "x" by Troldhaugen. The result was that everybody from America stormed in to such an extent that I had to go to the book dealer, Mr. Thorvald Beyer[3]—whom I have the honor of seeing here this evening—and ask him to cross out the "x". Therefore, I hope that Bøgh does not revive that prank. I suggest that we take the "x" away from Troldhaugen and place it by Valestrand and Lysøen.[4] There we really have, as Amalie Skram[5] says, "offspring".

It is a great pleasure for me to see Ole Bull's relatives here. His spirit certainly hovers over us in this room and, indeed, he also stands by the all too diminutive waterfall that is by no means commensurate with his fame.[6]

But this much is certain: I assume that the Bull family will not take it amiss if an "x" is placed at both Valestrand and Lysøen, and with their permission I ask that Ole Bull be remembered with gratitude for everything he has done for Norwegian art.

Long live the memory of Ole Bull!

---

[1] Norwegian art historian and museum director Johan Bøgh (1848–1933).

[2] Aulestad, near Lillehammer, was the home of Norwegian author Bjørnstjerne Bjørnson (1832–1910).

[3] Thorvald von Krogh Beyer (1858–1931), book dealer in Bergen. He was American deputy consul in Bergen 1900–13.

[4] Valestrand and Lysøen: two places in West Norway associated with the name of Ole Bull, who lived at Valestrand in his early years and who later built a villa on the island of Lysøen.

[5] Norwegian author Amalie Skram, nee Alver (1846–1905).

[6] Grieg is alluding to the Ole Bull monument in Bergen, which includes a small fountain. See p. 374.

To Johan Halvorsen (1903)

In 1899 Johan Halvorsen (1864–1935), to Grieg's great satisfaction, was appointed musical director of the new National Theater in Christiania, and in the years that followed he made an enormous contribution to the music life of the Norwegian capital. In 1903, he and his orchestra gave two concerts in Bergen in connection with the celebration of Grieg's sixtieth birthday. Grieg invited the whole orchestra to a breakfast at the Fløjen restaurant, which sits atop a mountain offering a spectacular view of Bergen and its surroundings. The weather cooperated and the breakfast took place as planned, with "beer, a shot of liquor and red wine".

Grieg's speech in honor of Halvorsen, which was given at the first orchestral concert, was reported in *Bergens Tidende* on June 17, 1903.

Now it is time for a toast. It is not as short as it is good. It is to Johan Halvorsen. At the time when he—bursting with all the possibilities that I knew he possessed—applied for the position of musical director at the new National Theater,[1] I was a pessimist. I did not think he would get it. I knew Christiania. But then

Johan Halvorsen

---

[1] The National Theater, a landmark in the heart of modern Oslo, was opened in September, 1899.

the happy thing occurred. I was absolutely wrong: He got it! The most unbelievable justice was done. We now have a situation that happens exceedingly seldom in Norway: The right man is in the right place, and he has really developed the Theater Orchestra. It is his achievement. He went out and gathered it, and he got the most outstanding musicians—for example, concertmaster Gustav Lange,[2] whom we have the honor of seeing with us here this evening. Halvorsen engaged many excellent musicians, and the orchestra got going and it progressed —and he grew too. As the orchestra grew, he grew along with it. He has this enormous ability to work like a horse, so he not only does all the work that would be enough for two musical directors, but he also composes music, each work better than the preceding one, and he creates the most beautiful melodramatic settings of our poets' works. Most recently, in [the incidental music for] *Kongen*,[3] he has produced a work of such quality that one only regrets that all of Europe was not present to hear it. One will marvel—if everything takes its natural course—at what he can become for Norway.

I want to ask all of you to thank him, first because he, despite an overabundance of work, came here to the celebration. We hope that he will continue to go forward on the straight road and that he may remain the Norwegian artist—artist first, and Norwegian artist subconsciously. The Norwegianness should not be conscious, not deliberate, for then it could turn into some kind of wrong-headed patriotism. He must continue to be a Norwegian artist such as he is in his flesh and blood, not a status seeker. But one doesn't have to say that to him: That's the way he is by nature.

Long live Johan Halvorsen!

---

[2] Norwegian violinist and composer Gustav Frederik Lange (1861–1939).

[3] Grieg is alluding to Johan Halvorsen's incidental music to the play *Kongen (The King)* by Norwegian author Bjørnstjerne Bjørnson (1832–1910), the first performance of which took place at the National Theater on September 11, 1902.

To Thorvald Lammers (1903)

The Norwegian baritone and choral conductor Thorvald Lammers (1841–92), regarded by Grieg as one of Europe's finest singers, came to Troldhaugen the morning of June 15—Grieg's sixtieth birthday—to present a valuable gift: a beautiful, two-tiered, sterling silver centerpiece, and a greeting signed by 230 men and women in Christiania. The greeting reads as follows: "To Edvard Grieg. On the occasion of your 60th birthday, friends in Christiania hereby join in presenting this gift as an expression of our deep respect. We ask you to accept it as a proof of the devotion and admiration we feel toward you and your art." Grieg then responded: "I don't really know what to say at this moment. When friends in Christiania do this, it must be because they have positive feelings toward me and because they remember the old days, when Svendsen[1] and I struggled together there to introduce Norwegian music. I will think of those days when I look at this lovely gift. The people of Christiania are like the Parisians: Sometimes they hate me, sometimes they love me. Currently, they must be in a period when they love me. And they who have given this gift, in any case, have had so much love that they have swallowed all hate!"[2]

Thorvald Lammers

---

[1] Norwegian composer and conductor Johan Svendsen (1840–1911), who in 1872 returned from abroad to Christiania, where he—together with Grieg—made a great contribution to the musical life of his native city. See also Grieg's article on Svendsen and the 1867 performance of his first symphony in Christiania, pp. 280–283.

[2] From the 1860's until near the end of his life, Grieg had a strained relationship with the Norwegian capital —"Tigerville", as he often called it, using Bjørnson's derogatory word to describe Christiania as an inhospitable and rough city. He settled there in 1866 and worked very hard for a decade to raise the musical standards in the Norwegian capital. In 1871 he established a permanent orchestra (*Musikforeningen*), which through the years evolved into the modern Oslo Philharmonic Orchestra. See also Grieg's speech for Christiania in 1889, p. 377.

Grieg's speech to Lammers was given at a banquet in Bergen on June 15, 1903, and was reported in *Bergens Tidende* on June 17.

Two endearing concepts[3] are represented at the table today: the Lammers and the Sars families.[4] They have found each other. They come from the Christiania that is just as endearing as they themselves—and, as I had occasion to say yesterday, Christiania can love just as strongly as it can hate. Therefore, one can understand that there are such people in Christiania as those I have taken the liberty of characterizing as "concepts".

Ladies and gentlemen! The Christiania that Lammers represents is not just Christiania. It is much more. In a quite singular way, it is Norway. When Lammers sings, and the word "Norway" occurs in the song, it is as if one were raising the colors. It really is good that Lammers has been in Christiania. I have known him for many years. He has held the banner high, and I want to express the wish that his inborn modesty will not prevent him from continuing to do so. We tend to get modest when our hair turns gray. May Lammers hold the banner high, and may he hold art—Norwegian art—high in Christiania.

Accept my sincerest thanks for coming here and letting yourself be used on this occasion. Thanks to you and your dear wife.

A toast to Lammers and his wife!

---

[3] Grieg here uses the term *begrep* (concept), which in Norwegian expresses great commendation when applied to individuals.

[4] Thorvald Lammers was married to Mally Sars (1860–1929), a member of a prominent family in Christiania.

To Julius Röntgen (1903)

The Dutch pianist, conductor and composer Julius Röntgen (1855–1932), who was Grieg's closest foreign friend, came to Bergen to pay homage to his famous colleague at the celebration of Grieg's sixtieth birthday on June 15, 1903. They had known each other since 1875, and they met again in December 1883 when Grieg came to Amsterdam at the end of a long concert tour in Germany and Holland. Through the years they had an extensive correspondence, of which nearly 400 letters have been preserved and published.[1]

Röntgen, himself a brilliant pianist and a very productive composer, was an ardent admirer, not only of Grieg's music but also of Norwegian culture and art in general and of Norwegian nature in particular. During Grieg's lifetime, Röntgen visited Norway no less than fourteen times, frequently joining Grieg and their mutual friend Frants Beyer (1851–1915) on long hikes in the mountains.[2]

After returning to Amsterdam from Bergen, Röntgen wrote to Grieg on July 10: "How are you after the festivities? Participating in them has been one of the *greatest* pleasures of my whole life."[3]

Grieg's speech in honor of Röntgen was made at a banquet in Bergen on Grieg's birthday and was reported in *Bergens Tidende* on June 17, 1903.

Ladies and gentlemen! It is a long voyage from Rotterdam to Bergen. I don't know how seasick Röntgen may have been, but by this time he surely has regained his strength. Perhaps you do not know his music as well as I do. He is an outstanding, talented composer. In addition to the love for everything great that permeates his music, there is something of that which the Dutch had many centuries ago when they fought against Spain: this "Hold the banner high!"[4] And his music makes it evident that he not only loves Norway's scenery but he loves the people as well. He loves us and he knows us to a tee. To talk with him about Norway is to put all of us to shame. He knows about every nuance of our emotional life.

He himself says, when there is talk about Röntgen: "I am not the famous one."[5] But I say: He is still more famous, deserves to be more famous, because the other Röntgen's waves stop at the bones, but his go right through.

I am quite sure that all of you sitting here have observed that he is second to none as a person who wins the hearts of people.

I want to propose a toast to him to thank him sincerely, both as his country's representative and for what he is as a human being.

---

[1] See Finn Benestad & Hanna de Vries Stavland (eds.), *Edvard Grieg und Julius Röntgen: Briefwechsel 1883–1907*, Amsterdam 1997.
[2] See also Grieg's article on Röntgen (1907), pp. 252–254.
[3] The letter is printed in Benestad & Stavland (eds.), *op. cit.*, p. 353.
[4] Grieg here uses the expression "hai hoch".
[5] Grieg uses the German words: "Das ist nicht der berühmte", i.e., not the German physicist Wilhelm Konrad Röntgen (1845–1923), the discoverer of x-rays.

Homage to Norway (1903)

The banquet at the Grand Hotel in Bergen celebrating Grieg's sixtieth birthday was attended by a representative group of men and women from Norway and abroad. The newspaper *Bergens Tidende*, which published a special Grieg edition a few days later, concluded that it had been a celebration "carried along by an atmosphere and enthusiasm completely worthy of the great master, who on this occasion was to receive the greetings and tribute of his native city and country."

Grieg's speech honoring his beloved Norway—given as a response to an address by Bjørnstjerne Bjørnson—was reported in *Bergens Tidende* on June 17, 1903.

Bjørnson has placed me on such a high pedestal that this evening my prospects really could look bleak if I had any talent in the direction of becoming a superman. But I don't. I am totally lacking in that area.

But wait! It can't be denied that recently in Paris I got a little presumptuous. It occurred when, after having conducted at the Colonne concert, I stepped outside to get into my carriage. It was surrounded by a double cordon of police —an impressive sight, and I must confess that there was something within me that said, "Are you such an important fellow?" I felt like some kind of a princely person or—a criminal. It is, after all, these two kinds of people who have the

Grieg viewing Bergen from Mt. Løvstakken

privilege of being escorted by the police. Who knows? Perhaps there is a distant relationship. Be that as it may—when the police were well out of sight, it was as if every speck of megalomania was blown away, and I was once again a quite ordinary human being.[1]

It is as such an ordinary human being that I stand here. Indeed, as a very small human being. I feel so deeply indebted to all of you, for what I have striven for down to the present day is nothing but what every good Norwegian tries to do: to add a small stone to the building called Norway. I have surely not been alone in doing this. All of you have probably helped me.

You are not aware of this, of course, but it is true all the same. For it is not just Bergensian art and Bergensian science from which I have drawn nourishment. Holberg, Welhaven and Ole Bull[2] have not been the only ones from whom I have learned. Not just an Armauer Hansen,[3] whose leprosy bacillus I have studied carefully. (Well, Armauer Hansen can't understand this—but that is because he is not sufficiently musical!) No, the entire Bergen milieu that surrounds me has constituted my material. Bergensian nature, Bergensian folk life, Bergensian achievements and initiatives of every kind have inspired me. When I read about the distant voyages of the ships of Christian Michelsen[4] and other great shipowners, it always cheered me up. And one needs good cheer in order to be creative. When I heard about Conrad Mohr's hog-raising,[5] I rejoiced in the depths of my soul. I should say parenthetically that the pig is my favorite animal. The odor from the Hanseatic wharf absolutely thrills me—yes, by George, I think there are both codfish and coalfish in my music. Unfortunately, there are no oysters, for I never see any such thing here in Norway. No doubt the Oldenburgians[6] ate them all up. It is said that you can still find a few at Lindås, but I do not have such intimate knowledge of this area as my friend Frants Beyer. That is where he is ahead of me, and that is what I begrudge him—that in his songs I sense the presence of fresh Lindås oysters. That must be why I am so fond of them.[7]

---

[1] Grieg had conducted the Colonne orchestra in Paris on April 19, 1903. The founder and director of the orchestra was Édouard Colonne (1838–1910). See Grieg's humorous account of this concert in his letter of April 23, 1903, to Johan Halvorsen in Finn Benestad (ed.), *Edvard Grieg: Letters to Colleagues and Friends*, Columbus, Ohio, 2000, pp. 351–352.

[2] Playwright Ludvig Holberg (1684–1754), poet Johan Sebastian Welhaven (1807–73) and virtuoso violinist Ole Bull (1810–80), all of whom were born in Bergen.

[3] Bergen physician Gerhard Armauer Hansen (1841–1912), whose research on leprosy demonstrated that the dreaded disease was bacterial in origin. Leprosy is often called "Hansen's disease".

[4] Bergen shipowner and prominent national political leader Christian Michelsen (1857–1925).

[5] In describing Mohr's enterprise, Grieg jokingly uses the Norwegian words *griseri* and *svineri*, both of which mean "piggish filth". Conrad Mohr (1849–1926) was a Norwegian merchant who also served as German consul in Bergen.

[6] German Count Christian of Oldenburg (1426–81) became King Christian I of Denmark and Norway in 1448. He was the founder of the Oldenburg dynasty.

[7] Bergen attorney Frants Beyer (1851–1918), Grieg's closest friend in Norway, was also an amateur composer.

Joking aside, however, I owe the whole city of Bergen and the people of Bergen my deepest gratitude. But not them alone. I must extend my gratitude to include the whole country—yes, the whole era in which we live.

But I will stop with our native country, that remarkably half-wild, ponderous, misguided homeland that we all love—perhaps most of all now, when it is like an injured bird. And the worst part is that we ourselves have caused the injury.

If pressed, I can understand that someone might destroy his country to prevent an enemy from ravaging it, but I cannot understand that people like us lay it waste out of nothing but sheer, unadulterated folly. There is only one word for this, and that word is: barbarism. Perhaps that is taking too dim a view of the situation, but I cannot feel otherwise. When I now ask you to raise your glass for Norway, it is with the wish that it might no longer be regarded as something especially desirable to behave like barbarians. Let us try to behave in such a way that we do not need to be chased out of this wonderful country by our own people but may stay at home and build further upon it. And with that: Long live Norway![8]

---

[8] Grieg is alluding to the fact that tensions were very high between Norway and Sweden at this time owing to Norway's demand for independence. There was talk of war on both sides of the border, and Grieg was deeply concerned that it might become a reality. The issue was resolved peacefully in 1905.

Chronology, Bibliography, Index

Edvard and Nina Grieg in Copenhagen in 1907.

Chronology of Grieg's Life and Works

The chronological survey gives a condensed account of Grieg's life and compositions and shows the point in the composer's career at which each of the diaries, articles and speeches printed in the present volume was written.

The dates of Grieg's travels are based primarily on statements in his letters about his travel plans. He may in some cases have altered his plans after the letters were written, so such dates should be treated with appropriate caution.

The dates of concerts are based on the concert programs preserved in the Grieg Archives, Bergen Public Library. The present list includes concerts in which Grieg participated as soloist, accompanist or conductor (or some combination thereof). Orchestral and chamber-music concerts are indicated, other concert arrangements only on special occasions. First performances are mentioned for Grieg's major works. In such cases names of performers are also given.

The list of compositions comprises works with opus numbers and works with EG numbers as assigned in vol. 20 of *Edvard Grieg: Complete Works* (Frankfurt/London/New York/ Leipzig 1977–95). Compositions are listed in the year in which they were completed, which is not always the same as the year of first publication. A more detailed list of works including titles in the original languages will be found in Finn Benestad (ed.): *Edvard Grieg: Letters to Colleagues and Friends,* Columbus, Ohio 2000, pp. 693–704.

G, in this chronology, denotes Edvard Grieg.

Year	Life	Compositions
1843	*Jun 15:* G is born in the family home at 152 Strandgaden (Strand Street) in Bergen. *Parents:* Judithe Gesine Grieg (1814–75) and Alexander Grieg (1806–75). *Siblings:* Maren (1837–1905), Ingeborg Benedicte (1838–1918), John (1840–1901), and Elisabeth Kimbell (1845–1905).	
1849–53	G attends grade school in Bergen and starts taking piano lessons from his mother.	
1853–58	G is enrolled in Tank's School in Bergen. Subjects: German, English, French, Norwegian, Religion, History, Geography, Arithmetic, Geometry, Natural History, Writing, Drawing, Singing, and Physical Education.	
1858	*Summer:* G visits an aunt in Larvik in eastern Norway. Later he meets for the first time the Norwegian violin virtuoso Ole Bull at the family summer house at Landås, a few miles south of Bergen. G plays some of his own compositions for Bull, and Bull is impressed. *Aug 31:* G is taken out of Tank's school to "become a musician". *Oct 6:* G is enrolled as a student at the Music Conservatory in Leipzig, an institution founded by Mendelssohn in 1843.	"Larvik Polka" (piano), EG 101. *Three Piano Pieces,* EG 102 (1858).

1859	G spends the summer at home, returns to Leipzig in the autumn.	*Nine Children's Pieces* (piano), EG 103 (1858–59). *23 Short Pieces for Piano*, EG 104 (1858–59). "Look to the Sea" (song), EG 121.
1860	*May:* G contracts a serious lung disease that requires him to interrupt his studies. He stays with his parents in Bergen through the summer, returns to Leipzig in the autumn. For the rest of his life only one lung is functioning.	*Three Piano Pieces*, EG 105. "Canon" (piano/organ), EG 179. "The Singing Congregation" (song), EG 122.
1861	*Aug 18: Concert in Karlskrona, Sweden.* This is G's first public concert, given en route from Bergen to Leipzig.	*Four Songs*, op. 2. "Fugue in F Minor" (string quartet), EG 114.
1862	*Apr 12: G's final examination concert in Gewandhaus, Leipzig.* (G plays three pieces from op. 1 for the first time.) After the concert he goes to Bergen, where he stays for a year with his family. *May 21: G's first public concert in Bergen.* (G performs three pieces from op. 1 and accompanies alto Wibecke Meyer in three songs from op. 2. His *String Quartet in D Minor* is performed for the first—and last—time by leading Bergen string players.) *Summer:* G goes with his parents and brother to London and Paris. In Paris he meets the Norwegian composer Halfdan Kjerulf. On *Jul 12* G applies for a scholarship from the Norwegian state; see pp. 58–59.	Various fugues for piano/organ from 1861–62, EG 184. *String Quartet in D Minor* (lost). "Dona nobis pacem" (mixed choir), EG 159. "In Retrospect" (mixed choir/piano, lost).
1863	G comes to Copenhagen in *Apr* and gets acquainted with his cousin Nina Hagerup (1845–1935), his future wife. He meets leading Danish composers Niels W. Gade and J. P. E. Hartmann and forms friendships with Benjamin Feddersen, Louis Hornbeck, Gottfred Matthison-Hansen, Julius Steenberg and August Winding. G's first meeting with Norwegian composer Rikard Nordraak takes place in Copenhagen. He starts working on *Symphony in C Minor*, EG 119.	*Four Piano Pieces*, op. 1 (1861–63). *Poetic Tone Pictures*, op. 3. *Four Songs for Male Chorus*, EG 160.
1864	G writes some music for the light opera *Courting on Helgoland* (libretto by Danish author Benjamin Feddersen), which is performed for the first time on *Jan 24*. He spends	*Six Songs*, op. 4 (1863–64). *Melodies of the Heart*, op. 5.

the spring in Copenhagen, the summer in Norway. *Symphony in C Minor* is finished *May 2.*

Jun 4: Concert in Copenhagen Tivoli (the three last movements of G's symphony are performed, conducted by H. C. Lumbye).

Summer: G visits Ole Bull at Valestrand near Bergen and meets several renowned Hardanger-fiddle players.

Sep 19: Concert in Bergen (chamber music).

G returns to Copenhagen in Oct, where he stays until Oct 1865. He has further significant contact with Nordraak. At *Christmas* G is secretly engaged to Nina Hagerup. Their parents reluctantly approve the engagement about six months later. G finishes *Melodies of the Heart.*

Symphony in C Minor, EG 119 (1863–64).
"Devoutest of Maidens" (song), EG 123.
"Clara's Song" from *Courting on Helgoland,* EG 124.
"Denmark" (mixed choir/piano), EG 161.
Album Leaves, op. 28 no. 1.

1865   G is one of the founders of the music society "Euterpe" in Copenhagen.

Mar 18: Euterpe concert (orchestra).

Apr 1: Euterpe concert (G conducts three movements of his symphony.)

Jul 31: G starts on a hike through the North Zealand countryside and begins to write a diary, the first part of which covers the period from Jul 31, 1865 to Aug 28, 1866; see pp. 3–15. G's first public article—a review of Nordraak's songs, op. 2—is published on *Aug 24* in the Danish magazine *Flyveposten;* see pp. 246–248.

G leaves Copenhagen for Berlin at the beginning of *Oct* to meet Nordraak and go with him to Italy. On *Nov 2* G leaves Nordraak, who lies seriously ill in Berlin, going to Leipzig to introduce his two sonatas, opp. 7 and 8. In Leipzig he meets his compatriot Johan Svendsen, then a student at the Conservatory, and they initiate a life-long friendship.

Mid-Nov: Concert in Leipzig (first performance of G's *Violin Sonata* op. 8, with Swedish violinist Anders Pettersson).

G arrives in Rome on *Dec 11* and stays there until *mid-Apr* 1866. On Christmas Eve he meets Henrik Ibsen for the first time.

Humoresques (piano), op. 6.
Piano Sonata in E Minor, op. 7.
Violin Sonata in F major, op. 8.
"Album Leaf", op. 12 no. 7.
"Agitato" (piano), EG 106.
"The Soldier" (song), EG 125.
"My Little Bird" (song), EG 126.
"I Love You, Dear" (song), EG 127.
"Tears" (song), EG 128.

1866   *Mar 24: Concert in Rome.*

Apr 6: G learns of Nordraak's death on Mar 20 and starts composing a Funeral March in memory of his friend. He leaves Rome on *Apr 19* and comes to Leipzig seven days later. On May 3 he goes to Berlin, where he visits Nordraak's grave the following day. He arrives in Copenhagen on *May 10.*

Jul 25: Charity concert in Copenhagen Tivoli (benefit for surviving victims of fire in Drammen, Norway).

Summer: G takes 15 organ lessons from cathedral organist Hans Matthison-Hansen in Roskilde, Denmark. He leaves Copenhagen for Bergen on Sep 5.

Funeral March for Rikard Nordraak (piano), EG 107.
Songs and Ballads, op. 9 (1863–66).
Four Songs, op. 10 (1864–66).
In Autumn. A Fantasy for piano four hands, op. 11. Revised and arranged for symphony orchestra in 1887 with

Oct 5: *Matinee concert in Bergen* (chamber music).
Oct 10: G settles in Christiania, which is to be his home city for approximately ten years.
Oct 15: *Concert in Christiania* (chamber music).
Dec 10: G co-authors an article about plans for a Norwegian Music Academy; see pp. 321–327.

the title *In Autumn. Concert Overture.*
"Intermezzo" (cello/piano), EG 115.
"Little Lad" (song), EG 129.
"Waltz", op. 12 no. 2.
"Waltz", op. 38 no. 7.

1867   *Jan 14:* The Music Academy begins operations. It would survive for only two years.
Feb 2: Concert in Christiania (Philharmonic Society Orchestra).
Mar 23: Concert in Christiania (Philharmonic Society Orchestra).
Apr 13: Concert in Christiania (Philharmonic Society Orchestra).
Jun 11: G marries Nina Hagerup in St. John's Church in Copenhagen. The newlyweds settle in Christiania in Øvre Voldgade 2. G earns his living as a piano teacher.
Oct 14: G reviews Johan Svendsen's Oct 13 concert in the Christiania newspaper *Aftenbladet*; see pp. 280–283.
Nov 16: Concert in Christiania (first performance of G's *Violin Sonata in G Major* op. 13, with Norwegian violinist Gudbrand Bøhn).
Dec 12: Concert in Christiania (a new orchestral subscription series organized by G).

Lyric Pieces I, op. 12.
Violin Sonata in G Major, op. 13.
"The Fair-haired Maid" I (song), EG 130.
Two Songs for Male Chorus, EG 162.

1868   *Feb 18: Concert in Christiania* (subscription concert).
Mar 17: Concert in Christiania (subscription concert).
Apr 4: Concert in Christiania (last subscription concert).
Apr 10: G's daughter Alexandra is born. In *Jun* G goes to Denmark with his family and takes lodging in Søllerød, a suburb a few miles north of Copenhagen. Here he composes his *Piano Concerto in A Minor* op. 16, the instrumentation of which is completed the following year. After the death of Norwegian composer Halfdan Kjerulf on Aug 11, 1868, G writes a eulogy that is published in *Illustreret Tidende* (no. 9), Copenhagen; see pp. 217–220. G returns to Christiania in *Sep.*

Cantata for the Unveiling of the W. F. K. Christie Monument (male chorus/wind instruments), EG 158.
Four Songs, op. 15 (1864–68).

1869   *Jan 10:* G sends an application to the Norwegian government for a scholarship, enclosing a recommendation from Franz Liszt; see pp. 59–61. G gets the scholarship.
Apr 3: G's *Piano Concerto in A Minor*, op. 16, is performed for the first time in Copenhagen by Norwegian pianist Edmund Neupert. G is not present.
Apr 13: Charity concert in Christiania (for the benefit of a monument for Halfdan Kjerulf).

Piano Concerto in A Minor, op. 16 (1868–69)
Two Symphonic Pieces, op. 14. These are arrangements for piano four hands of the second and third movements of *Symphony in C Minor*.

Apr 17: Concert in Christiania ("Farewell Concert").
Apr 27: Concert in Drammen.
May 13: Concert in Bergen.
May 21: G's daughter Alexandra dies in Bergen.
Sep 1: Concert in Bergen ("Farewell Concert").
G leaves Bergen and goes via Christiania to Copenhagen.
Oct 3: Concert in Copenhagen (chamber music).
Oct 9: Concert in Copenhagen (G conducts the *A-minor Concerto* with Edmund Neupert as soloist.)
G leaves Copenhagen *early Dec* and arrives in Rome on *Dec 23*, traveling via Berlin, Leipzig, Vienna, Venice and Florence. His second visit to Italy is to last for four months.

Nine Songs, op. 18 (1865–69).
Twenty-five Norwegian Folk Songs and Dances, op. 17.
"Norwegian Sailors' Song" (male chorus), EG 163.

1870   *Feb 17 and Apr 9:* G writes letters to his parents about his meetings with Franz Liszt in Rome; see Finn Benestad (ed.): *Edvard Grieg. Letters to Colleagues and Friends,* pp. 271–278. In a September report to the Ministry of Education G emphasizes the importance of his trip to Italy; see the present volume, pp. 62–63. G leaves Rome in *mid-Apr* and arrives in Copenhagen *Apr 20*. He stays in the Danish capital for two months. He spends *summer* with his family at Landås.
Aug 22: Concert in Bergen.
Sep 6: Concert in Larvik.
Sep 20: Concert in Christiania.
Nov 26: Concert in Christiania (Philharmonic Society Orchestra).
Dec 17: Concert in Christiania (Philharmonic Society Orchestra).
G starts collaboration with Norwegian author Bjørnstjerne Bjørnson.

"The Odalisque" (song), EG 131.
"The Miner" (song), EG 132.

1871   *Feb 11: Concert in Drammen.*
Mar 11: Concert in Christiania (Philharmonic Society Orchestra).
Apr 27: Concert in Christiania (Philharmonic Society Orchestra).
Sep 12: Concert in Bergen.
Sep 19: Concert in Bergen ("Popular Concert").
Oct 14: G, in cooperation with some leading figures in Christiania's cultural life, publishes an invitation to establish a "Music Association", the primary aim being to get a permanent symphony orchestra in the Norwegian capital. The invitation is well received, and G is appointed conductor of the orchestra.
Dec 2: Concert in Christiania (Music Association Orchestra).
Dec 16: Concert in Christiania (Music Association Orchestra).
In connection with the publication of *Pictures from Folk Life*,

Pictures from Folk Life, op. 19 (1869–71).
Before a Southern Convent, op. 20.
"The Princess" (song), EG 133.

op. 19, G writes a short preface explaining what he had in mind; see pp. 369–370.

1872   *Feb 22:* G is elected a member of the "Royal Music Academy" in Stockholm.
Feb 24: Concert in Christiania (Music Association Orchestra).
Apr 10: Bjørnson's drama *Sigurd the Crusader* with G's incidental music is performed for the first time at Christiania Theater.
Apr 18: G writes his first letter to Frants Beyer, who is to become his closest life-long friend.
May 4: Concert in Christiania (Music Association Orchestra).
May 17: Charity concert in Christiania (Bazaar at Akershus Fortress for the restoration of the Trondheim Cathedral, "Nidarosdomen"). G goes to Copenhagen in *Jun* and returns to Christiania in *Sep*. Johan Svendsen comes to Norway in *Oct* and joins G as co-conductor of the Music Association Orchestra.
Nov 30: Concert in Christiania (Music Association Orchestra; both G and Svendsen conduct).
Dec 7: Charity concert in Christiania (for families of shipwrecked Danish seamen).
Dec 15: Charity concert in Christiania (for Norwegian composer Gabriel Tischendorf).
Dec 21: Concert in Christiania (Music Association Orchestra).

Four Songs from B. Bjørnson's "Fisher Maiden", op. 21 (1870–72).
Incidental music to "Sigurd the Crusader", op. 22.
Land-sighting, op. 31.

1873   *Jan 4: Concert in Christiania* (Music Association Orchestra).
Jan 12: Concert in Stockholm.
Jan 14: Concert in Stockholm.
Apr 26: Concert in Christiania (Music Association Orchestra).
Apr 30: Concert in Christiania.
May 2: Concert in Drammen.
May 23: Concert in Arendal.
May 26: Concert in Kristiansand.
May 29: Concert in Stavanger.
Jun 11: Concert in Bergen.
Jun 15: Charity concert in Bergen (for the restoration of "Håkon's Hall").
Mid-Jun: G starts collaborating with Bjørnson on a national opera project, *Olav Trygvason.*
Aug 11: Concert in Bergen.
Dec 13: Concert in Christiania (Music Association Orchestra).
Dec 21: Concert in Christiania (Music Association Orchestra).

"The Old Mother", op. 33 no. 7.
Cantata for Karl Hals (tenor/women's choir/male chorus/piano), EG 164.
"At J. S. Welhaven's Grave" (male chorus), EG 165.
"Sighs" (song), EG 134.
"For L. M. Lindeman's Silver Wedding Anniversary" (song), EG 135.
"To Christian Tønsberg" (song), EG 136.
"The White and Red, Red Roses" (song), EG 137.
First three scenes of *Olav Trygvason,* op. 50, which were orchestrated in 1889.

1874   *Jan 23:* G receives a request from Henrik Ibsen to write incidental music for *Peer Gynt*. He responds affirmatively.
Jan 24: Concert in Christiania (Music Association Orchestra).
Jan 31: Concert in Christiania (Music Association Orchestra).
Feb: G and Svendsen send to the Norwegian Parliament (*Stortinget*) a joint application for annual grants. See p. 64.
Apr 5: Concert in Christiania (Music Association Orchestra).
Jun 2: G and Svendsen are each awarded an annual composer's grant of 1600 Norwegian kroner by the Norwegian Parliament (*Stortinget*).
Summer: G starts working on the *Peer Gynt* music. He goes to Copenhagen in Sep.
Dec 1: Concert in Copenhagen.

"The Fair-haired Maid" II (song), EG 138.
"Chorus for the Supporters of Freedom in Scandinavia" (male chorus), EG 166.
"At the Halfdan Kjerulf Statue" (tenor/male chorus), EG 167.
Album Leaves, op. 28 no. 2.

1875   G leaves Denmark for Leipzig at the beginning of *Jan*. He hears Wagner's *Tristan and Isolde* in Weimar on *May 15* and returns to Denmark five days later. He stays in Fredensborg in *Jul*, where he finishes the *Peer Gynt* score. He comes to Bergen in late *Aug* and stays there for approximately one year. Both of his parents pass away during the fall of 1875.

Norway's Melodies (piano), EG 108 (1874–75).
Incidental music for Ibsen's "Peer Gynt", op. 23 (1874–75).
"Morning Prayer at School" (song), EG 139.

1876   *Feb 24: Peer Gynt* is performed for the first time at Christiania Theater. G is not present.
Mar 28: Concert in Bergen.
Apr 17: Concert in Bergen.
Mid-Jul: G leaves Bergen. After a week in Copenhagen he goes to Bayreuth via Leipzig. He sends eight articles to the Bergen newspaper *Bergensposten* from the first performance of Richard Wagner's *The Ring of the Nibelung*; see pp. 290–318.
At the end of *Aug* G meets Ibsen in Gossensass. He is back in Christiania by the first part of *Sep*.
Dec 7: Concert in Stockholm.
Dec 8: Concert in Uppsala.
G protests against unfair treatment in the Swedish newspaper *Dagligt Allehanda*; see pp. 328–329.

Ballade, op. 24 (1875–76).
Six Songs, op. 25.
Five Songs, op. 26.
Album Leaves, op. 28 no. 3.

1877   *Mar 17: Concert in Christiania* (Music Association Orchestra).
G applies for a travel grant from the Norwegian government on Apr 18; see pp. 64–65.
Jun 2: Concert in Christiania.
G stays in Christiania until *mid-Jun*. Then he leaves the Norwegian capital for good and goes via Bergen to the Hardanger region of West Norway, where he will live for over a year, first at Ullensvang, then at Lofthus. He starts

"I Lay down so Late", op. 30 no. 1.
Mozart Piano Sonatas with a Freely Composed Second Piano Part, EG 113.
"Beside the Stream", op. 33 no. 5.

working on *String Quartet in G Minor*, op. 27, and *The Mountain Thrall*, op. 32, both of which are finished in 1878.
Oct 11: Concert in Bergen.
Oct. 19: Concert in Bergen ("Popular Concert").

1878 G corresponds with German violinist Robert Heckmann about the *G-minor String Quartet.* He leaves Lofthus in *Sep* to go to Germany for the premiere performance of the quartet.	*String Quartet in G Minor*, op. 27 (1877–78). *Album Leaves*, op. 28 (1864–78).
Oct 29: Concert in Cologne (first performance of the *String Quartet*, op. 27, by the Heckmann Quartet).	"Album Leaf" (piano), EG 109.
Oct 31: Concert in Bonn.	*Improvisations on Two Norwegian Folk Songs*,
Nov 30: Concert in Leipzig.	op. 29.
G stays in Leipzig until early *Apr* of the following year.	*Album for Male Voices*, op. 30 (1877–78). *The Mountain Thrall*, op. 32 (1877–78). "Andante con moto" (piano trio), EG 116.

1879 G meets Johannes Brahms for the first time on *Jan 1* and receives a treasured greeting in the form of a handwritten copy of the first four measures of the second movement of Brahms's *Violin Concerto* op. 77, dated Jan 3, 1879. In *Jan* G writes an article on the songs of Norwegian composer Halfdan Kjerulf; see pp. 221–224.
Mar 29: Concert in Leipzig (chamber music).
Apr 5: Concert in Copenhagen (orchestra; first performance of *The Mountain Thrall* op. 32, with Norwegian baritone Thorvald Lammers as soloist).
Apr 30: Concert in Copenhagen.
G goes back to Norway in *May* and stays for some months in Lofthus.
Oct 2: Concert in Bergen.
Oct 7: Concert in Bergen.
After the Bergen concerts G goes to Leipzig.
Oct 30: Concert in Leipzig.
G leaves for Copenhagen early *Dec.*

1880 G stays in Copenhagen until late *Feb* 1880.	*Twelve Songs to Poems by Vinje*, op. 33 (1873–80).
Feb 4: Concert in Copenhagen.	*Two Elegiac Melodies*,
Feb 11: Concert in Copenhagen.	op. 34.
G leaves Copenhagen to give four matinee concerts in Christiania, where he stays in *Mar* and *Apr.*	*Norwegian Dances*, op. 35.
Mar 7: Matinee concert in Christiania.	"On the Ruins of Hamar
Mar 21: Matinee concert in Christiania.	Cathedral" (song),
Apr 4: Matinee concert in Christiania.	EG 140.
Apr 18: Matinee concert in Christiania.	

G leaves Christiania after the concert series and goes via Bergen to Lofthus, where he remains until early *Sep*. He attends Ole Bull's funeral on *Aug 23*. See his tribute to Ole Bull on p. 375. G becomes musical director of the Music Society "Harmonien" in Bergen. In *Nov* he writes an article about the insufficient coverage of "Harmonien" in the Bergen press; see p. 330.

Sep 30: Concert in Bergen.

Oct 3: Concert in Bergen.

Oct 22: Concert in Bergen ("Harmonien" Orchestra*).*

Nov 18: Concert in Bergen ("Harmonien" Orchestra*).*

Dec 9: Concert in Bergen ("Harmonien" Orchestra*).*

"The Young Woman" (song), EG 141.
"The Forgotten Maid" (song), EG 142.

1881 *Jan 27: Concert in Bergen.*

Feb 1: Concert in Bergen ("Harmonien" Orchestra).

Feb 5: Charity concert in Bergen (for an Ole Bull monument).

Feb 15: Concert in Bergen.

Mar 8: Concert in Bergen.

Mar 31: Concert in Bergen ("Harmonien" Orchestra).

Apr 3: Concert in Bergen (repeat of Mar 31 concert).

Apr 11: Concert in Bergen (2nd repeat of Mar 31 concert).

In *Apr* G writes an article about Chr. F. Emil Horneman; see pp. 211–216. In *Jun* G spends several weeks at Karlsbad Spa, Germany, to treat a gastrointestinal disorder. He goes to Lofthus via Bergen in *Jul* and returns to Bergen in late *Aug*. He accepts an offer from "Harmonien" to serve as musical director for a second season.

Oct 4: Concert in Bergen.

Nov 1: Concert in Bergen ("Harmonien" Orchestra).

Nov 15: Concert in Bergen ("Harmonien" Orchestra).

Dec 1: Concert in Bergen *("Harmonien" Orchestra).*

Two Songs for Male Chorus, EG 169.

1882 *Jan 26: Concert in Bergen* ("Harmonien" Orchestra).

Feb 21: Concert in Bergen ("Harmonien" Orchestra).

Mar 30: Concert in Bergen ("Farewell" concert with "Harmonien" Orchestra).

Apr 3: Concert in Bergen (repeat of Mar 30 concert).

Apr 6: Concert in Bergen (2nd repeat of Mar 30 concert).

Apr 23: Concert in Stavanger.

Apr 24: Concert in Haugesund.

In *mid-May* G returns to Karlsbad Spa for further treatment. At the end of *Jun* he returns to Bergen via Christiania. King Oscar II appoints G "Knight of the Royal Norwegian Order of St. Olav" on *Jun 6*.

1883 *Feb 6: Concert in Bergen.*

Feb 11: Concert in Bergen.

G leaves Bergen early *Jul* and goes to Rudolstadt, Bayreuth, Leipzig and back to Rudolstadt, where he stays with his

Sonata for Cello and Piano in A Minor, op. 36.
Waltz Caprices, op. 37.
Lyric Pieces II, op. 38.

friend Frank van der Stucken for two months to study French and to prepare for an extensive concert tour in Germany and Holland. See Grieg's review of Van der Stucken's music on pp. 277–279.

Oct 16: Concert in Weimar.

Oct 22: Concert in Dresden.

Oct 27: Concert in Leipzig.

Nov 11: Concert in Meiningen.

Nov 12: Concert in Meiningen.

Nov 13: G is appointed "Knight of the Herzoglich Sächsischen Ernestinischen Hausorden".

Nov 27: Concert in Breslau.

Nov 29: Concert in Breslau.

Dec 4: Concert in Cologne.

Dec 8: Concert in Karlsruhe.

Dec 14: Concert in Frankfurt /M.

Dec 17: Concert in Arnhem, Holland.

Dec 19: Concert in the Hague.

Dec 20: Concert in Rotterdam.

Dec 21: Concert in Amsterdam.

G stays at Julius Röntgen's home, and they initiate a firm friendship that lasts for the rest of G's life. In *Dec* G is elected a corresponding member of the Music Academy of Leyden, Holland.

Fragments of a *Piano Concerto no. 2 in B Minor*, EG 120. "Greetings to the Singers" (male chorus), EG 170.

1884   *Jan 12: Concert in Amsterdam.*

After the concert G goes to Leipzig, where he meets his wife and Frants and Marie Beyer. On *Feb 1* they leave Leipzig on G's third trip to Italy, where G and his wife stay for about four months.

Mar 15: Concert in Rome.

G leaves Italy at the end of *May* and goes via Leipzig and Bergen to Lofthus, arriving on *Jun 17*. He stays in Lofthus until *Oct 31*. Then he settles in Bergen for six months. He attends the Holberg Jubilee and conducts his Holberg Cantata on *Dec 3* in Bergen. During the summer G buys a lot for a house a few miles south of Bergen, and the villa "Troldhaugen" is built during the winter.

Dec 7: Concert in Bergen.

Six Songs (Older and Newer), op. 39. *From Holberg's Time (Holberg Suite;* string orchestra), op. 40. *Holberg Cantata* (baritone/male chorus), EG 171. *Transcriptions of Original Songs* I (piano), op. 41. "Greeting", op. 48 no. 1. "One Day, O Heart of Mine", op. 48 no. 2.

1885   *Mar 12: Concert in Bergen.*

Mar 15: Concert in Bergen.

In *Mar* G writes a short article on the Norwegian composer Catharinus Elling for the Bergen press, and in *May* an article on the Danish composer J. P. E. Hartmann in connection with his 80th birthday; see pp. 203–204 and 205–208, respectively. In *Apr* G moves into "Troldhaugen", which is to be his home for the rest of his life, although mostly used during the summer half-year. G goes on a hike

Bergliot, op. 42 (orchestral arrangement). "Springdans", op. 47 no. 6. "Beneath the Christmas Tree" (song), EG 144.

in Jotunheimen with Beyer in *Aug* and leaves for Christiania beginning of *Oct.*

Oct 17: Concert in Christiania

Oct 21: Concert in Christiania.

Oct 24: Concert in Christiania.

Nov 3: Concert in Christiania (*Bergliot* is performed for the first time).

After the concert G leaves for Copenhagen where he stays for about six months.

Nov 14: Concert in Copenhagen.

Nov 23: Concert in Copenhagen.

Nov 27: Concert in Copenhagen.

Dec 10: Concert in Copenhagen.

Dec 18: Concert in Copenhagen.

1886   G assists at the rehearsals for the Danish premiere performance of *Peer Gynt* on *Jan 17* at the Dagmar Theater in Copenhagen.

Jan 30: Concert in Copenhagen.

In March G makes an extensive concert tour in Jutland, Denmark.

Mar 11: Concert in Ålborg.

Mar 13: Concert in Randers.

Mar 16: Concert in Århus.

Mar 18: Concert in Århus.

Mar 21: Concert in Horsens.

Mar 22: Concert in Vejle.

Mar 23: Concert in Ribe.

After the concert tour G spends a few days with relatives on the island of Fyn. He then returns to Copenhagen departing for Norway on *May 12.* He is back at Troldhaugen in *Jun*, but spends the summer at Lofthus. At the end of *Jul* he goes on a hike in Jotunheimen with Danish author Holger Drachmann. In *mid-Aug* he is back at Troldhaugen, where he writes an article about "The Composer's Hut"; see pp. 90–95. He stays at Troldhaugen until *Sep 1*, 1887, with the exception of a trip to Copenhagen in *Jun* 1887. At Troldhaugen he starts working on *Violin Sonata no. 3 in C Minor,* op. 45, which is finished the following year.

Lyric Pieces III, op. 43.
Reminiscences from Mountain and Fjord, op. 44.
"Christmas Snow", op. 49 no. 5.
"Ragnhild" (song), EG 181.

1887   G starts working on *Peer Gynt Suite No. 1,* op. 46. He leaves for Karlsbad Spa on *Sep 1* to start a new series of treatments for his gastrointestinal disorder. He stays in Karlsbad until end of *Oct.* He then goes to Leipzig, where he remains for approximately six months.

Dec 10: Concert in Leipzig (premiere performance of *Violin Sonata No. 3 in C Minor,* op. 45 with Russian violinist Adolf Brodsky). G is with Brahms and Tchaikovsky in Leipzig on *Dec 31.*

Violin Sonata No. 3 in C Minor, op. 45 (1886–87).
"Waltz-Impromptu", op. 47 no. 1.
"Album Leaf", op. 47 no. 2.

1888   G takes short trips from Leipzig to Berlin in *Jan* and *Feb*.
Feb 18: Concert in Leipzig.
G leaves Leipzig and arrives in London end of *Apr*.
May 3: Concert in London.
May 16: Concert in London.
G visits Ventnor on the Isle of Wight on *May 17–19* and returns to London on *May 20.* He leaves London ca. *May 24* and goes to Denmark, first visiting relatives on the island of Fyn for a few days, then going to Copenhagen to participate at the "First Nordic Music Festival" *Jun 3–10.*
Jun 4: Concert in Copenhagen.
Jun 7: Concert in Copenhagen (chamber music).
Jun 8: Concert in Copenhagen.
G goes to Norway after the Music Festival and reaches Troldhaugen *Jun 25*, where he spends the summer. In *mid-Aug* goes back to England to participate at a Music Festival in Birmingham.
Aug 29: Concert in Birmingham (first performance of the revised orchestral version of *In Autumn*, op. 11).
Aug 30: Concert in Birmingham.
In Birmingham G has first contact with the Unitarian movement. En route back to Troldhaugen G makes stops in London, Scheveningen and Copenhagen. He reaches Troldhaugen in *mid-Sep* and remains there for the rest of the year.

Peer Gynt Suite I, op. 46 (1887–88).
Lyric Pieces IV, op. 47 (1886–88).
In Autumn, op. 11, revised score finished.
Scenes from "Olav Trygvason", score finished 1888.

1889   *Jan 2:* G leaves Troldhaugen for Berlin.
Jan 21: Concert in Berlin (orchestra).
Jan 29: Concert in Berlin (orchestra).
G goes to Leipzig at the end of *Jan* and leaves on *Feb 16* to commence his third concert tour to England. On *Feb 26* he is appointed "Knight of the Royal Danish Dannebrog Order".
Feb 23: Concert in London (chamber music).
Feb 25: Concert in London (chamber music).
Feb 28: Concert in Manchester (Hallé orchestra).
Mar 9: Concert in London (chamber music).
Mar 14: Concert in London (Philharmonic Society Orchestra).
Mar 20: Concert in London (chamber music).
Mar 28: Concert in London (Philharmonic Society Orchestra).
Mar 30: Concert in London (chamber music).
G leaves London on *Apr 4* for Paris where he stays for a couple of weeks. Thereupon he goes via Leipzig and Copenhagen to Troldhaugen, arriving in *mid-May*. On *Jul 23* he starts on a mountain hike with Frederick Delius, Christian Sinding, and George Augener, returning to Troldhaugen on *Aug 10.* On *Aug 29* G signs a general contract (*Generalvertrag*) with C. F. Peters Musikverlag, dated

Six Songs, op. 48 (1884–89).
Six Songs, op. 49 (1886–89).
"Easter Song", EG 146.
"A Simple Song", EG 147.
"You Often Fix Your Gaze" (song), EG 148.

Aug 22, giving the Leipzig firm the world copyright on all his future compositions. On *Sep 14* he writes his so-called "Cosmopolitan Credo"; see pp. 96–97. He also sends a request to the Norwegian Parliament to give Norwegian composer Christian Sinding an annual grant, such as he and Johan Svendsen had been awarded in 1874; see pp. 275–276. G leaves Troldhaugen, arriving in Christiania on *Oct 4*.
Oct 9: Concert in Christiania.
Oct 19: Concert in Christiania (premiere performance of the opera fragment *Olav Trygvason*, op. 50).
Oct 26: Concert in Christiania (repeat of previous concert, plus first performances of "Tell Me Now, Did You See the Lad", op. 49 no. 1, and "Kind Greetings, Fair Ladies", op. 49 no. 3).
The Student Association hails G on *Oct 23*, and G makes a short speech to the students; see p. 376. G is honored by Christiania friends on *Oct 24* (see his tribute to Christiania on p. 377) and by the Artists' Association on *Oct 28*. Thereafter he goes to Copenhagen.
Nov 16: Concert in Copenhagen (orchestra).
Nov 20: Concert in Copenhagen (orchestra).
From Copenhagen G goes to Brussels.
Nov 30: Concert in Brussels (orchestra).
Dec 2: Concert in Brussels (orchestra).
Dec 8: Concert in Brussels (orcehstra).
From Brussels G goes to Paris, where he remains for nearly six weeks.
Dec 22: Concert in Paris (orchestra).
Dec 29: Concert in Paris

1890   *Jan 4: Concert in Paris* (chamber music).
Jan 26: G leaves Paris and goes to Stuttgart.
Feb 4: Concert in Stuttgart (orchestra).
From Stuttgart G goes to Leipzig. Here he meets Brahms again.
Feb 27: Concert in Leipzig (Gewandhaus Orchestra).
Mar 22: Concert in Leipzig (chamber music).
G leaves Leipzig end of *Mar*. En route to Troldhaugen he visits Berlin and Copenhagen. In *Aug* he hikes in Jotunheimen. Beginning of *Oct* he leaves Troldhaugen for Christiania.
Oct 18: Concert in Christiania (Music Association Orchestra).
Oct 26: Concert in Christiania (Music Association Orchestra).
Nov 2: Concert in Christiania (Music Association Orchestra).
G leaves Christiania and reaches Copenhagen on *Nov 11*, where he stays until *Apr 13*, 1891.
Dec 3: G sends a humorous story about Johan Svendsen to the Norwegian newspaper *Dagbladet*; see pp. 332–335.

Old Norwegian Melody with Variations, op. 50 (for two pianos).
Transcriptions of Original Songs II, op. 52.
Two Melodies for String Orchestra, op. 53.
"Last Spring" (song with orchestra), EG 177 no. 5.

1891 G leaves Copenhagen on *Apr 13* for Christiania, where he stays for about four weeks. He poses for portraits by two Norwegian painters: Eilif Peterssen and Erik Werenskiold. Leaving Christiania in *mid-May*, he reaches Troldhaugen on *May 18*. On *Jun 20* he is elected a corresponding member of the French "Académie des beaux-arts" in Paris. Julius Röntgen, Iver Holter and Frederick Delius visit Troldhaugen during the summer, and G goes hiking with them in the mountains. He meets the milkmaid Gjendine Slaalien on Skogadalsbøen, and she sings folk songs for him. G leaves Troldhaugen for Christiania on *Oct 2*.

Nov 1: Matinee concert in Christiania.

In the evening of the same day G participates at a meeting of the Student Association and makes a short speech; see p. 378.

Nov 14: Concert in Christiania (premiere performance of *Peer Gynt Suite No. 2*, op. 55).

Nov 21: Concert in Christiania (celebrating G's silver jubilee as a concert-giver in Christiania).

Nov 28: Concert in Christiania (an evening program of music by Christian Sinding).

G leaves Christiania on *Dec 11*, arriving at Troldhaugen *Dec 18*. He stays at Troldhaugen until *Sep 23, 1892*.

Lyric Pieces V, op. 54 (1889(?)–91).
"Gjendine's Lullaby", op. 66 no. 19.
"I Loved Him" (song), EG 153, from the unfinished oratorio *Peace*.
Unfinished *String Quartet No. 2 in F Major*, EG 117.

1892 *Jun 11:* G and Nina celebrate their silver wedding at Troldhaugen, for which occasion G writes "Wedding Day at Troldhaugen". On *Jul 3* he meets German Kaiser Wilhelm. G leaves Troldhaugen on *Sep 23* and reaches Christiania on *Oct 4*, where he stays until *Nov 19*.

Nov 5: Concert in Christiania (premiere performance of *Three Orchestral Pieces from "Sigurd the Crusader"* op. 56).

Nov 17: Concert in Christiania (chamber music).

G goes to Copenhagen on *Nov 19* and remains there for about two weeks.

Nov 24: Concert in Copenhagen.

G leaves Copenhagen on *Dec 7* and goes via Berlin to Leipzig. He spends Christmas in Berlin.

Peer Gynt Suite II, op. 55 (1890–92).
Three Orchestral Pieces from "Sigurd the Crusader", op. 56.
"Wedding Day at Troldhaugen", op. 65 no. 6.

1893 G stays in Leipzig until Mar 4.

Feb 7: Concert in Leipzig (orchestra).

Upon invitation from Max Abraham, director of C. F. Peters Musikverlag, G travels with Abraham and Sinding to Menton on the Riviera, and from there he goes to Bellagio and Meran. He comes to Christiania in the middle of *May*, and soon thereafter he is hospitalized at Grefsen Spa because of stomach troubles. During his stay at Grefsen he writes an article on Robert Schumann; see pp. 255–274. He leaves Grefsen on *Jun 25* and reaches Troldhaugen a few days later. In *Aug* G is appointed an honorary member of

Lyric Pieces VI, op. 57 (1890–93).
"Song of the Flag" (male chorus), EG 172.
"Election Song" (both song and male chorus), EG 147.
"Ave maris stella" (song), EG 150.

the Dutch "Maatschappij tot Bevordering der Toonkunst".
He returns to Christiania at the end of *Sep.*
Oct 5: Concert in Christiania (chamber music).
Oct 7: Concert in Christiania (Music Association Orchestra).
After the concert G goes to Copenhagen.
Oct 28: Concert in Copenhagen (orchestra).
Nov 29: Charity concert in Copenhagen (for surviving relatives of deceased Danish fishermen).
Nina Grieg is hospitalized for several weeks in Copenhagen because of severe nephralgia, and during that time G writes a number of songs that will be published in 1894: opps. 58, 59, 60. He also writes an article on the situation at Christiania Theater; see p. 336.

1894   *Jan 20: Concert in Copenhagen* (first performance of *Five Songs* op. 60).
Jan 21: Concert in Copenhagen (repeat of previous concert).
After the last concert G leaves for Leipzig.
Feb 1: Concert in Leipzig (Gewandhaus Orchestra).
G stays in Leipzig until beginning of *Mar.* He then goes to Munich and Geneva.
Mar 9: Concert in Munich (orchestra).
Mar 17: Concert in Geneva (orchestra).
After the concert G goes on a second trip to Menton, and thereafter to Paris, where he arrives on *Apr 10.*
Apr 22: Concert in Paris (Colonne Orchestra).
G stays in Paris until early *May.* He then goes to England to commence his fourth concert tour there. G is appointed Honorary Doctor of Fine Arts at Cambridge University on *May 10.*
May 24: Concert in London (Philharmonic Society Orchestra).
G returns to Grefsen Spa in Christiania on *May 26* to seek further help for his stomach problems. At the end of *Jun* he is back at Troldhaugen.
Oct 16: Concert in Bergen ("Harmonien" Orchestra).
Oct 18: Concert in Bergen (repeat of Oct 16 concert*).
Oct 20: Concert in Bergen (second repeat of Oct 16 concert).
Oct 21: Concert in Bergen ("Popular concert": third repeat of Oct 16 concert).
G leaves Troldhaugen on *Oct 27* and reaches Copenhagen on *Nov 1* to stay there for the winter.
Dec 11: Concert in Copenhagen (chamber music).

Five Songs, op. 58 (1893–94).
Six Elegiac Songs, op. 59 (1893–94).
Five Songs, op. 60 (1893–94).
Seven Children's Songs, op. 61.
"National Song", EG 151.

1895   *Jan 21:* King Oscar II appoints G "Commander of the Royal Norwegian Order of St. Olav". During spring and early summer G composes the song cycle *The Mountain Maid* (*Haugtussa*) op. 67.
Feb 28: Concert in Copenhagen (orchestra).
Apr 26: Concert in Copenhagen.

Lyric Pieces VII, op. 62.
Two Nordic Melodies (string orchestra) op. 63.
The Mountain Maid (*Haugtussa*), op. 67 (not published until 1898).

After the last concert G leaves for Troldhaugen, staying there until the end of *Sep*. Chr. F. Emil Horneman, Gottfred Matthison-Hansen and August Winding and their wives visit Troldhaugen as G's guests for two weeks in *Jul*. G and Frants Beyer take a mountain hike in Jotunheimen in *mid-Aug*. G visits Christiania in *Oct* en route to Leipzig.

Oct 12: Concert in Christiania (Music Association Orchestra; op. 63 is performed for the first time).

G arrives in Leipzig on *Oct 20* and stays there until *Apr 18*, 1896, with the exception of a short concert tour to Vienna in *Mar* 1896.

"Greetings from Christiania Singers" (male chorus), EG 173. *Six Songs with Orchestra*, EG 177 (1890–95). Orchestration of Edmund Neupert's piano piece "Resignation", EG 182. Piano arrangement of Johan Halvorsen's orchestral piece "Entry of the Boyars", EG 183.

1896   In *Jan* G receives the French "La légion d'honneur".
Mar 24: Concert in Vienna (orchestra*)*.
In Vienna G meets Brahms, Bruckner and Dvořák. G is back in Leipzig on *Mar 28*. He remains there until *Apr 18*, when he leaves for Copenhagen.
Apr 28: Concert in Copenhagen (Berlin Philharmonic Orchestra with Ferruccio Busoni as soloist in the *A-Minor Concerto*).
G returns to Troldhaugen, arriving on *May 13*. He celebrates his birthday on *Jun 15* at Lofthus. In *Jul* G, Beyer and Röntgen are guests at Børre Giertsen's mountain cottage "Trondsbu" at Lake Tinnhølen on the Hardanger Plateau. There G writes a long article on Mozart; see pp. 225–239. Most of *Nineteen Norwegian Folk Songs*, op. 66, is composed during this year. In *Sep* G salutes Fridtjof Nansen and his crew in a short address at their homecoming from the Polar regions; see p. 379.
In late *Oct* G leaves on a concert tour to Stockholm. After the third concert a banquet is given in his honor, at which G makes a short speech; see pp. 380–381.
Oct 24: Concert in Stockholm (orchestra).
Oct 29: Concert in Stockholm (orchestra).
Oct 31: Concert in Stockholm (orchestra).
Nov 1: Matinee concert in Stockholm (orchestra).
After the last concert G goes back to Christiania.
Nov 7: Concert in Christiania (Music Association Orchestra).
G leaves Christiania on *Nov 10* and travels via Copenhagen and Berlin on a concert tour to Vienna. He reaches Vienna on *Nov 15* and stays there for over six weeks.
Dec 16: Concert in Vienna (chamber music).
Dec 19: Concert in Vienna (orchestra).
Brahms attended the second concert and also a party after the concert. G spends the New Year weekend at Semmering.

Lyric Pieces VIII, op. 65. "The Blueberry" (song), EG 145. "Westerly Wind" (male chorus), EG 174. "Impromptu" (male chorus), EG 175.

1897   *Jan 2:* G attends a Brahms concert.
        Jan 6: Concert in Vienna (orchestra).
        G leaves Vienna, arriving in Leipzig on *Jan 11.* He is elected
        a member of "Akademie der Künste" in Berlin on *Jan 16.*
        From Leipzig he goes on a concert tour to Holland, where
        he is a guest at Röntgen's home. On *Mar 3* G is appointed
        "Officer of the Oranje-Nassau Order".
        Feb 13: Concert in Amsterdam (Concertgebouw Orchestra).
        Feb 16: Concert in Amsterdam (Chamber music).
        Feb 20: Concert in Amsterdam (Concertgebouw Orchestra).
        Mar 3: Concert in The Hague (orchestra). Grieg becomes
        honorary member of the music society "Diligentia".
        Mar 8: Concert in Amsterdam (chamber music).
        G leaves Amsterdam on *Mar 16* and goes via Berlin to
        Copenhagen, arriving on *Mar 18.* He stays there until *May 8.*
        En route to Troldhaugen he visits Christiania, Trondheim
        and Molde. He stays at Troldhaugen until *mid-Oct,* with the
        exception of a trip to Fossli in *Jul,* where he meets Röntgen.
        G goes to Denmark on *Oct 8.* He leaves Copenhagen on
        Oct 19 on his fifth concert tour to Great Britain. He travels
        via Hamburg, Cologne, Ostende, and Dover to London.
        Nov 20: Matinee concert in Liverpool (chamber music).
        Nov 22: Concert in London (chamber music).
        Nov 24: Concert in Manchester (chamber music).
        Nov 26: Concert in Birmingham (chamber music).
        Nov 30: Concert in Edinburgh (chamber music).
        Dec 4: Concert in London (chamber music).
        Dec 6: Concert at Windsor Castle for Queen Victoria
        (chamber music).
        Dec 9: Concert in Cheltenham (chamber music).
        Dec 11: Concert in Brighton (chamber music).
        Dec 13: Concert in London (chamber music).
        Dec 15: Concert in London (chamber music).
        G visits Brodsky in Manchester *Dec 17–20* and goes via Lon-
        don to spend Christmas at Röntgen's home in Amsterdam.

        Nineteen Norwegian Folk Songs, op. 66 (1891–97).

1898   *Early Jan:* Grieg leaves Amsterdam for Leipzig, remaining
        there for approximately three months. He is mainly
        occupied with preparations for the first Norwegian Music
        Festival that is to take place in Bergen *Jun 26–Jul 3.* G leaves
        Leipzig on *Apr 26* for Copenhagen, where he stays until
        May 18. En route to Troldhaugen he visits Halmstad (Swe-
        den) and Christiania. He reaches Bergen on *May 22.* He
        makes sketches for some of the piano pieces of opp. 68 and
        73. At the Bergen Music Festival, which is highly successful,
        G participates in four concerts.
        Jun 29: Concert in Bergen (Concertgebouw Orchestra).
        Jun 30: Concert in Bergen (repeat of Jun 29 concert).
        Jul 1: Concert in Bergen (Concertgebouw Orchestra).

        Symphonic Dances,
        op. 64 (symphony
        orchestra; 1896–98).
        The Mountain Maid
        (*Haugtussa*), op. 67, is
        published (1895–98).
        "Procession of Gnomes"
        (piano), EG 111.
        In the Whirl of the Dance
        (piano), EG 112.

Jul 2: Concert in Bergen (repeat of Jul 1 concert).

In connection with matters related to the Music Festival G writes several newspaper articles; see pp. 337–344. He leaves Troldhaugen on *Oct 12* for Copenhagen via Christiania. On the tour across the mountains he gets bronchitis and is confined to bed for several days in Odnes. He reaches Copenhagen on *Nov 3* and stays there for nearly four months. He spends Christmas at "Fuglsang", the estate of his friends Bodil and Rolf Viggo de Neergaard on the island of Lolland. He is back in Copenhagen on *Dec 30*. In *Dec* he writes an article about opera problems in Christiania; see pp. 345–346.

1899   *Feb 17: Concert in Copenhagen.*

G stays in Copenhagen until *Mar 7*, then travels via Berlin, Leipzig, Brenner, and Verona to Rome, arriving on *Mar 18*. *Apr 3: Concert in Rome* (Santa Cecilia Academy Orchestra). The Academia Santa Cecilia arranges a banquet in G's honor on *Apr 8*. G makes excursions to Naples, Sorrento and Amalfi. He meets Bjørnson in Rome and travels with him to Venice. He leaves Italy at the end of *Apr* and on his way home visits Milan, Lake Como and Lake Maggiore, St. Gotthard, Leipzig and Copenhagen. He arrives at Troldhaugen at the end of *May* and stays there for three months. In *Jun* he writes an article about the musical conditions in Bergen; see pp. 347–350. In *Jul* he takes a two-week hike in the mountains with Beyer and Röntgen. At the end of *Aug* he sets off for Christiania to participate in the inauguration of the new National Theater.

Sep 3: G conducts the incidental music for Bjørnson's play "Sigurd the Crusader" at a performance at the National Theater.

Sep 8: G begins a week-long visit with Bjørnson at his estate "Aulestad" near Lillehammer. There he writes a letter to French orchestral conductor Édouard Colonne in Paris concerning the so-called Dreyfus affair; see Finn Benestad (ed.): *Edvard Grieg: Letters to Colleagues and Friends*, Columbus, Ohio 2000, p. 199, and the present volume, p. 351. G is in Christiania again on *Sep 14* and leaves for Copenhagen on *Sep 17*. He takes a trip to Stockholm at the beginning of *Nov* to give concerts.

Nov 4: Concert in Stockholm (orchestra).

Nov 7: Concert in Stockholm (orchestra).

Nov 9: Concert in Stockholm (orchestra).

Nov 10: Concert in Stockholm (orchestra).

After the Stockholm concerts G returns to Copenhagen.

Nov 18: Concert in Copenhagen (orchestra).

Dec 10: Concert in Copenhagen (concert for laborers).

At the end of the *Dec 10* concert G makes a short speech to

Lyric Pieces IX, op. 68 (1898–99).

"Ave maris stella" (mixed choir), EG 151.

"At the Grave of a Young Wife" (mixed choir), op. 39 no. 5.

the audience as a response to some words of honor directed to him; see p. 382. G spends Christmas at "Fuglsang" on the island of Lolland.

1900   *Jan 9: Concert in Copenhagen* (chamber music).
       Jan 14: Concert in Copenhagen (chamber music).
       Jan 18: Charity concert in Copenhagen (arranged by Norwegian soprano Sigrid Schøller).
       G is back in Christiania *mid-Apr.*
       Apr 21: Concert in Christiania (National Theater Orchestra).
       Apr 22: Concert in Christiania (National Theater Orchestra).
       Apr 28: Concert in Christiania (benefit for a Nordraak monument).
       In connection with the *Apr 28* concert, G writes an homage to Rikard Nordraak in *Verdens Gang;* see pp. 250–251. After the concerts G goes to Troldhaugen. During the summer he takes a three-day hike in the mountains with Röntgen. On *Jul 17* he writes a long letter about his music to American author Henry Th. Finck; see Finn Benestad (ed.): *Edvard Grieg: Letters to Colleagues and Friends*, pp. 225–239. In *Sep* he writes an article about French and German music for the French press; see the present volume, pp. 352–353. G leaves Troldhaugen on *Sep 29* and reaches Christiania on *Oct 5.* On *Oct 15* he begins a long stay at Voksenkollen Sanitarium to relieve his problems with bronchitis and asthma. Here he writes an article about the institution; see pp. 354–357. He leaves Voksenkollen on *Jan 4, 1901* and takes lodging at Victoria Hotel in Christiania.

Five Songs, op. 69.
Five Songs, op. 60.
"To a Devil" (song), EG154.
"Yuletide Cradle Song" (song), EG 155.
"Gentlemen Rankers" (song), EG 156.

1901   On *Jan 14* G goes to Copenhagen, where he takes lodging at Hotel Phoenix. Here he writes an article on Giuseppe Verdi; see pp. 284–289.
       Mar 23: Concert in Copenhagen.
       Apr 24: Concert in Copenhagen (chamber music).
       G leaves Copenhagen on *May 4* and travels via Christiania to Troldhaugen, arriving on *May 8.* At the unveiling of the Ole Bull monument in Bergen on *May 8* G conducts a male chorus in a choral arrangement of his song "To Ole Bull". During the summer G spends two weeks at Maristuen and takes a trip to Lake Tyin. Röntgen and the Neergaards visit him at Troldhaugen.
       Oct 1: Concert in Bergen.
       Oct 5: Concert in Bergen (benefit for a Nordraak monument).

Lyric Pieces X, op. 71.
"The Mountaineer's Song", op. 73 no. 7.
"To Ole Bull" (both solo song and male chorus), EG 176.
"Inga Litamor" (baritone/male chorus), EG 168.
Seven Children's Songs, op. 61 (choir SSA).

1902   G leaves Bergen at the beginning of *Feb.* He travels via Christiania to Copenhagen. In *mid-Apr* he leaves Copenhagen for a concert tour to Warsaw.
       Apr 22: Concert in Warsaw (orchestra).
       G is back again in Copenhagen on *Apr 27.* A few days later

he returns to Troldhaugen via Christiania. On *May 10*, en route to Bergen on the steamship "Christiania", he writes a protest against an interview in *Christiania Dagsavis*; see pp. 363–364. He reaches Troldhaugen on *May 11*. Röntgen visits him a few days later. In *Jul* G takes a mountain trip to Fossheimseter and Løken in Vestre Slidre. In *Sep* he writes an article for a Bjørnson Festschrift; see pp. 358–362. G starts work on *Norwegian Peasant Dances (Slåtter)*, op. 72.

Oct 24: Concert in Bergen (chamber music).

Oct 26: Concert in Bergen (chamber music).

G leaves Troldhaugen at the beginning of *Nov* and reaches Christiania on *Nov 8*. Because of illness he has to spend a week at Voksenkollen Sanitarium.

Nov 23: Concert in Christiania.

Dec 5: Concert in Christiania.

Dec 16: Concert in Christiania (charity concert for unemployed people).

The Christiania students celebrate Bjørnson's 70th birthday in *Dec*, on which occasion G gives a short talk in honor of his friend; see pp. 383–384.

1903   G stays in Christiania until end of *Feb*. For the publication of op. 72, G writes a preface in which he gives some clues to the understanding of music for the Hardanger fiddle; see pp. 370–372. Because of Nina's ear problems, she and G move to Voksenkollen Sanitarium on *Jan 23*, remaining for four weeks. On *Feb 28* G begins a two-week visit to Copenhagen. He leaves Copenhagen on *Mar 17*, spending three days in Berlin en route to Prague.

Mar 25: Concert in Prague (orchestra).

From Prague G goes back to Berlin, where he stays until *Apr 9*. He then goes to Warsaw.

Apr 14: Concert in Warsaw (orchestra).

Apr 15: Concert in Warsaw (orchestra).

Immediately after the last concert G takes the train to Berlin and the following day to Paris.

Apr 19: Concert in Paris (Colonne Orchestra).

Apr 27: Concert in Paris (chamber music).

During the stay in Paris G makes some phonograph recordings. He leaves Paris on *May 5* and travels via Cologne, Leipzig, Berlin, Copenhagen and Christiania to Troldhaugen. On *Jun 15* there are several public events in connection with G's 60th birthday. G makes a number of speeches on this occasion—for Bjørnson, Ole Bull, Johan Halvorsen, Thorvald Lammers and Julius Röntgen; see pp. 385–393. At a banquet at the Grand Hotel in Bergen, G gives a short speech honoring Norway; see pp. 394–396. A short time afterwards he writes some words of thanks to Danish friends, published in the Danish press; see p. 365.

Norwegian Peasant Dances (Slåtter), op. 72 (1902–03).

Jun 15: Concert in Bergen (National Theater Orchestra from Christiania).

Jun 16: Concert in Bergen (National Theater Orchestra from Christiania).

During a mountain trip at the beginning of *Aug* G becomes ill and is hospitalized in Bergen for three days. Thereafter he goes to Framnes in Hardanger for a week's rest. On *Aug 17* he is back at Troldhaugen, where he stays until the beginning of *Sep.* After a stay in Bergen *Sep 5–18* he travels via Trondheim to Christiania, arriving on *Sep 21.* He takes lodging at Hotel Westminster, but also has to spend a few weeks—*Nov 28–Dec 21*—at Voksenkollen Sanitarium. There he completes two articles: "Protest against an Unauthorized Bergen Performance of *Peer Gynt*", and an autobiographical article, "My First Success"; see pp. 366–367 and 67–89, respectively. From Voksenkollen G goes via Eidsvoll to Bjørnson's estate "Aulestad", where he stays for approximately four weeks.

1904   G is back in Christiania on *Jan 18*, but is ill with a gastric inflammation requiring medical treatment. King Oscar II awards him the "Grand Cross of the Royal Norwegian Order of St. Olav" on *Jan 21.* G leaves for a concert tour in Sweden at the end of *Feb.*

Mar 2: Concert in Gothenburg (chamber music).

Mar 4: Concert in Gothenburg (chamber music).

Mar 7: Concert in Stockholm (chamber music).

Mar 10: Concert in Stockholm (chamber music).

Mar 12: Concert in Uppsala (chamber music).

Mar 14: Concert in Stockholm (chamber music).

Mar 18: Concert in Stockholm (orchestra).

Mar 20: Matinee concert in Stockholm (orchestra).

G returns to Christiania on *Mar 24.* In *May* he writes a eulogy on Antonín Dvořák; see pp. 199–202. At the end of *May* he goes home to Troldhaugen. In *Jul* he meets the German Kaiser Wilhelm II on two occasions. In *Sep* G hears *pianola* recordings for the first time. He leaves Troldhaugen on *Sep 11* for Christiania.

Oct 8: Concert in Christiania (National Theater Orchestra).

Oct 9: Concert in Christiania (National Theater Orchestra).

Oct 29: Concert in Christiania.

Nov 1: Concert in Christiania.

Dec 9: Charity concert in Christiania (purpose unknown).

G stays in Christiania until *Dec 29*, when he goes to Copenhagen via Gothenburg.

1905   G stays in Copenhagen until *May 24*, when he leaves for Christiania via Gothenburg. On *Jun 5* he sets out for Troldhaugen. He is on board a steamship from Christiania to

Old Norwegian Melody with Variations (symphony orchestra),

Bergen when he hears the news about the *Jun 7* action of the Norwegian Parliament declaring an end to Norway's union with Sweden. G stays at Troldhaugen until *Sep 20*, then returns to Christiania, where he takes lodging in Hotel Westminster. On *Nov 28* he starts writing a new diary, covering the time span from Nov 28, 1905 to Aug 31, 1907; see pp. 100–196. He meets the new Norwegian royal couple, King Haakon VII and Queen Maud, on several occasions. *Dec 6: Concert in Christiania* (Music Association Orchestra; first performance of *Lyric Suite* op. 54).

G is hospitalized during the Christmas week, but returns to Hotel Westminster on *Dec 30.*

op. 51 (1900–1905). *Lyric Suite* (symphony orchestra), op. 54 (the first four items of *Lyric Pieces*, op. 54). *Moods*, op. 73 (1898–05). "The Hunter" (song), EG 157.

1906   G stays in Christiania until *early Apr.* In *Jan* he writes a new article on Mozart for an Austrian journal; see pp. 240–245. On *Feb 5* he moves to Voksenkollen Sanitarium for two weeks owing to his poor health. He considers selling Troldhaugen and living permanently in Christiania. *Mar 21: Concert in Christiania.* *Mar 27: Concert in Christiania* (repeat of Mar 21 concert). *Mar 31: Concert in Christiania* (arranged by the Christiania students). *Apr 5:* G departs for a concert tour to Prague, Amsterdam and London, via Gothenburg, Berlin and Leipzig. On *Apr 11* he records six of his piano pieces at Ludwig Hupfeld's piano factory in Leipzig on the so-called "Phonola" electrical piano. He is very impressed by the quality. The next day he leaves for Prague. *Apr 16: Matinee concert in Prague* (orchestra). In the afternoon G leaves Prague and arrives in Leipzig in the evening. On *Apr 17* he records three piano pieces at Popper & Co. on the so-called Welte-Mignon piano. He leaves Leipzig on *Apr 20*, arriving in Amsterdam in the evening. *Apr 26: Concert in Amsterdam* (Concertgebouw Orchestra). *May 2: Concert in Amsterdam* (chamber music). During the stay in Amsterdam G takes excursions to Sandford, Voolendam and Brökkeln. He leaves Amsterdam on the morning of *May 10*, reaching London in the evening. Most of the time in London he stays with Edward Speyer, whose wife was an accomplished violinist. They perform together at some private receptions during his visit. On *May 15* G meets the Australian-born pianist Percy Grainger and six days later hears him play two of G's *Norwegian Peasant Dances (Slåtter)*, op. 72. *May 17: Matinee concert in London* (orchestra). In the evening G meets the Norwegian ambassador Fridtjof Nansen at a reception in the Norwegian club. It is the first celebration of the Norwegian Constitution Day after the

Four Psalms, op. 74.

liberation from Sweden. Three days later G attends a performance of *Tristan and Isolde*.

May 24: Concert in London (chamber music).

May 28: Concert in London (at an audience at Buckingham Palace with King Edward VII and Queen Alexandra. Nina sings a song and Edvard plays a piano piece for them).

On *May 29* G is appointed "Honorary Doctor of Fine Arts" at Oxford University. He leaves London on *May 31* and travels via Calais and Hamburg to Copenhagen arriving there on *Jun 2*. Here he has a reunion with Johan Svendsen, Bjørnson and a number of his old Danish friends. He leaves Copenhagen on the evening of *Jun 10* and arrives in Christiania the next day. On *Jun 12* he visits King Haakon VII and Queen Maud and conveys greetings from the British Royal Couple. G leaves Christiania on *Jun 16* arriving at Troldhaugen on *Jun 21*. On *Jul 6* G meets the German Kaiser Wilhelm II in Bergen. On *Jul 10–11* he takes a trip on the Voss Railway to Myrdal with Frants Beyer. Adolf Brodsky, with his wife and two young violin students, visits G at Troldhaugen *Aug 6–10*. On *Sep 15* G finishes three of the *Four Psalms*, op. 74, his last composition. He leaves Troldhaugen on *Sep 19* for Christiania, and three days later, on board the steamship "Alden" in Sognefjorden, he writes a eulogy on his Danish friend, composer Louis Hornbeck; see pp. 209–210.

Oct 18: Concert in Christiania.

1907   *Jan 12: Concert in Christiania* (Music Association Orchestra). On *Jan 21* G is guest at a dinner given by King Haakon at Bygdø Royal Estate. On *Feb 17* he writes an article about Julius Röntgen; see pp. 252–254. His Dutch friend arrives in Christiania a few days later to give concerts. On *Mar 5* G accompanies Röntgen to the Royal Palace, where King Haakon—on G's initiative—appoints Röntgen a "Knight of the Royal Norwegian Order of St. Olav". G leaves Christiania on *Mar 12*, arriving in Copenhagen the next day.

Mar 21: Concert in Copenhagen (orchestra).

Mar 26: Concert in Copenhagen (repeat of the previous concert).

G leaves Copenhagen on *Mar 28* for a concert tour in Germany. He arrives in Berlin the evening of *Mar 28* to have rehearsals with some of the soloists. He leaves Berlin on *Apr 1* for Munich.

Apr 7: Concert in Munich (Kaim Orchestra).

G leaves Munich the following day for Berlin. On *Apr 12* he visits Kaiser Wilhelm II in the afternoon.

Apr 12: Concert in Berlin (orchestra).

Apr 14: Concert in Berlin (matinee repeat of the previous concert).

G sees the opera *Salome* by German composer Richard Strauss on *Apr 15* and visits him two days later. He leaves Berlin on *Apr 17* for Leipzig, where he stays until *Apr 21*. He meets German composer Max Reger and the director of C. F. Peters Musikverlag, Henri Hinrichsen. On *Apr 21* he goes to Kiel.

Apr 26: Concert in Kiel (orchestra).

This proves to be G's final concert. He leaves Kiel on *Apr 27* and via Korsør arrives in Copenhagen the same evening. His health is very poor. On *May 2* he starts taking electric-light baths at Finsen's Institute in Copenhagen. He has six treatments, but they are of no help. He is hospitalized at Skodsborg Sanitarium near Copenhagen on *May 26*, staying there until *Jun 12*, when he boards the Norwegian steamship "Hellig Olav", accompanied by his Finnish friend Edvard Rudolf Neovius. They arrive in Christiania on *Jun 13* and leave four days later, arriving at Troldhaugen on *Jun 24*. Julius Röntgen visits him *Jul 22–26* and Percy Grainger *Jul 25–Aug 4*. G is hospitalized in Bergen on *Aug 27* but returns home on *Aug 31*. He still is planning to perform at a Music Festival in Leeds, England, *Oct 9–12*. G takes lodging at Hotel Norge in Bergen on *Sep 2*, the first step of his intended trip to Leeds. At his doctor's insistence, G is again hospitalized on *Sep 3*. He dies peacefully at the Bergen hospital on *Sep 4*.

The following year G's urn is placed in a crypt at Troldhaugen, a site that he himself had selected.

Bibliography

The list that follows is divided into seven sections: I. Original sources; II. Editions of Grieg's Writings and Speeches; III. Biographies; IV. Symposiums on Grieg and His Music; V. Books and Articles on Topics Related to Grieg and His Music; VI. Grieg's Complete Works; and VII. Other Bibliographies.

Part I, Original Sources, is subdivided into four sections corresponding to the four parts of the present volume, the items being listed in the order in which they appear in the book. Grieg's own titles, mostly in Norwegian, are given in parentheses. Dates of printings other than those listed here are given in the introductions to the respective articles. In Section D, the first seven speeches, which concern individuals, are arranged alphabetically, the rest chronologically.

In Parts II–V and in Part VII, the order of the items is alphabetical. English titles of books/articles written in a foreign language are given in parentheses.

I. Original Sources

A. Autobiographical Writings

1. *Diary of 1865–66* (Dagbøger). Original manuscript in Norwegian preserved in Bergen Public Library.
2. *My First Success* (Min første Succes). Original manuscript in Norwegian preserved in Bergen Public Library.
3. *The Composer's Hut in Hardanger* (Komposten). Published in *Norden. Illustreret Skandinavisk Revue*, Copenhagen 1886.
4. *A Cosmopolitan Credo* (Kosmopolitisk Trosbekjendelse). Published in *Musikbladet*, Copenhagen, October 8, 1889.
5. *Grant Applications and Related Documents.* Original applications in Norwegian preserved in the National Archive of Norway, Oslo.
6. *Bequest to Bergen Public Library* (Brev til Bestyrelsen for Bergens Offentlige Bibliotek, 12. November 1906). Original letter in Norwegian preserved in Bergen Public Library.
7. *Diary of 1905–07* (Dagbøger). Original manuscript in Norwegian preserved in Bergen Public Library.

B. Articles on Other Composers and Their Music

1. *Antonín Dvořák.* Published in *Verdens Gang*, Christiania, May 13, 1904.
2. *Catharinus Elling* (Lovende ung norsk Komponist). Published in *Bergens Tidende*, Bergen, March 14, 1885.
3. *Johan Peter Emilius Hartmann* (J. P. E. Hartmann). Published in *Musikbladet*, Copenhagen, May 14, 1885.
4. *Louis Hornbeck.* Published in *Politiken*, Copenhagen, September 9, 1906.
5. *Christian Frederik Emil Horneman.* Original manuscript in Norwegian preserved in Bergen Public Library.
6. *Halfdan Kjerulf: Eulogy.* Published in *Illustreret Tidende*, Copenhagen, 1867–68, pp. 404–406.
7. *Halfdan Kjerulf's Songs* (Halfdan Kjerulf. Lieder und Gesänge). Published in German in *Musikalisches Wochenblatt*, Leipzig, 1879, pp. 55–56, and in Norwegian in *Aftenbladet*, Christiania, on February 1, 1879.

8. *Wolfgang Amadeus Mozart* (Mozart). Published in Norwegian in *Samtiden*, Bergen, 1898, pp. 112–124, and in English translation in *The Century Illustrated Monthly Magazine*, New York/London, Vol. 55, no. 1, November 1897, pp. 140–146.

9. *Mozart and His Significance for Contemporary Music* (Mozart og hans Betydning for den musikalske Nutid). Manuscript draft in German preserved in Bergen Public Library. Published in German in *Neue Freie Presse*, Vienna, January 21, 1906, pp. 5–6, and in Norwegian in *Verdens Gang*, Christiania, January 21, 1906.

10. *Nordraak's Songs op. 2* (Review, under the heading Musik). Published in *Flyveposten*, Copenhagen, August 24, 1865.

11. *Nordraak's Songs op. 1* (Rikard Nordraak: Sange op. 1). Undated manuscript in Norwegian preserved in Bergen Public Library.

12. *Homage to Nordraak* (Rikard Nordraak). Published in *Verdens Gang*, Christiania, April 4, 1900.

13. *Julius Röntgen.* Published in *Aftenposten*, Christiania, and in *Verdens Gang*, Christiania, March 2, 1907.

14. *Robert Schumann.* Published in *Nyt Tidsskrift*, Christiania, 1893–94, pp. 217–239, and in English translation in *The Century Illustrated Monthly Magazine*, New York/London, Vol. 47, no. 3, January 1894, pp. 440–448.

15. *Christian Sinding.* Published in *Stortingsforhandlinger* (Proceedings of the Norwegian Parliament) 1889, Part 5, Document no. 26.

16. *Frank van der Stucken.* Published in German in *Musikalisches Wochenblatt*, Leipzig, 1883, p. 463.

17. *Johan Svendsen's Concert* (Johan Svendsens Concert). Published in *Aftenbladet*, Christiania, October 14, 1867.

18. *Giuseppe Verdi.* Published in *Verdens Gang*, Christiania, February 7, 1901.

19. *Richard Wagner and The Ring of the Nibelung* (Wagnerforestillingerne i Bayreuth). Eight articles published in *Bergensposten*, Bergen, from August 20 to September 3, 1876.

C. Miscellaneous Articles

1. *A Norwegian Music Academy* (Musik-Akademi under Ledelse af Otto Winter-Hjelm og Edvard Grieg). Co-authored by Grieg and Winter-Hjelm. Published in *Morgenbladet*, Christiania, December 12, 1866.

2. *Protest against Unfair Treatment in the Press.* Letter to the Editor, published in *Dagligt Allehanda*, Stockholm, December 23, 1876.

3. *One-sidedness* (Ensidighed). Published in *Bergens Tidende*, Bergen, November 22, 1880.

4. *Correction of an Interview* (Berigtigelse af Interview i *Pall Mall Gazette*). Published in English in *Pall Mall Gazette* on March 20, 1889; in Norwegian in *Musikbladet*, Copenhagen, 1889, p. 64.

5. *A Mushroom* (En Paddehat). Published in *Dagbladet*, Christiania, January 2, 1890.

6. *Misery at the Christiania Theater* (Usseldom ved Christiania Theater). Published in *Verdens Gang*, Christiania, June 9, 1893.

7. *The Norwegian Music Festival in Bergen* (Musikfesten i Bergen). Three articles published, respectively, in *Aftenposten*, Christiania, April 18, 1898; *Verdens Gang*, Christiania, August 2, 1898; *Bergens Tidende*, Bergen, September 8, 1898.

8. *Opera Controversy in Christiania* (Operastriden). Published in *Verdens Gang*, Christiania, December 23, 1898.

9. *Musical Conditions in Bergen* (Vore Musikforhold). Published in *Bergens Tidende*, Bergen, June 7, 1899.

10. *The Dreyfus Affair. Grieg's Response to an Inquiry Concerning Dreyfus.* Untitled manuscript, dated Bergen, June 22, 1899, preserved in Bergen Public Library.

11. *French and German Music* (Fransk og tysk Musik). Undated manuscript preserved in Bergen Public Library.

12. *The Soria-Moria Castle* (Soria-Moria-slottet). Published in *Verdens Gang*, Christiania, January 12, 1901.

13. *With Bjørnson in Days Gone By* (Med Bjørnson i gamle Dage). Published in *Bjørnstjerne Bjørnson. Festskrift.* Copenhagen 1902.

14. *Scandalous Reporting* (Usømmeligt Skriveri). Published in *Verdens Gang*, Christiania, May 13, 1902.

15. *Protest Against an Unauthorized Performance of "Peer Gynt" in Bergen* (Protest mod at *Peer Gynt* opføres i Bergen uden Tilladelse). Published in *Bergens Aftenblad,* December 4, 1903.

16. *Word of Thanks to Danish Friends* (Til danske Venner). Published in *Berlingske Tidende*, Copenhagen, June 29, 1903.

17. *The Copenhagen City Hall* (Rådhuset i København). Published in *Dansk Portrætgalleri* vol. 4, Copenhagen 1908, p. 199.

18. *Preface to "Pictures from Folk Life" op. 19* (Forord til *Folkelivsbilleder*). Published in the Horneman & Erslev first edition of the work, Copenhagen 1872.

19. *Preface to "Norwegian Peasant Dances" op. 72* (Forord til *Slåtter*). Published in Norwegian, French, German and English in the C. F. Peters first edition of the work in 1903.

D. Speeches

1. *At Ole Bull's Funeral* (Ved Ole Bulls Begravelse). Reported in *Bergensposten*, Bergen, August 25, 1880.

2. *To the Christiania Students.* Reported in *Verdens Gang*, Christiania, October 24, 1889.

3. *For Christiania.* Reported in *Nordisk Musik-Tidende*, Christiania 1889, p. 165.

4. *On the Flag Controversy.* Reported in *Verdens Gang*, Christiania, November 2, 1891.

5. *To Fridtjof Nansen and His Crew.* Reported in *Bergens Tidende*, Bergen, September 3, 1896.

6. *At a Banquet in Stockholm.* Published in *Verdens Gang*, Christiania, November 3, 1896.

7. *At a Concert for Laborers in Copenhagen.* Reported in *Verdens Gang*, Christiania, December 14, 1899.

8. *To Bjørnstjerne Bjørnson on His Seventieth Birthday* (Ved Studentersamfundets Fest i Anledning af Bjørnsons 70-årsdag). Reported in *Aftenposten*, Christiania, December 14, 1902.

9. *To Bjørnstjerne Bjørnson at the Celebration of Grieg's Sixtieth Birthday.* Reported in *Bergens Tidende*, Bergen, June 17, 1903.

10. *In Memory of Ole Bull* (Tale for Ole Bulls Minde). Reported in *Bergens Tidende*, Bergen, June 17, 1903.

11. *To Johan Halvorsen.* Reported in *Bergens Tidende*, Bergen, June 17, 1903.

12. *To Thorvald Lammers.* Reported in *Bergens Tidende*, Bergen, June 17, 1903.

13. *To Julius Röntgen.* Reported in *Bergens Tidende*, Bergen, June 17, 1903.

14. *Homage to Norway.* Reported in *Bergens Tidende*, Bergen, June 17, 1903.

II. Editions of Grieg's Writings and Speeches

Benestad, Finn & Bjarne Kortsen (eds.): *Edvard Grieg: Brev til Frants Beyer 1872–1907 (Edvard Grieg: Letters to Frants Beyer 1872–1907).* Oslo 1993.

Benestad, Finn & Hanna de Vries Stavland (eds.): *Edvard Grieg und Julius Röntgen. Briefwechsel 1883–1907 (Edvard Grieg and Julius Röntgen: Correspondence 1883–1907).* Amsterdam 1997.

Benestad, Finn & Hella Brock (eds.): *Edvard Grieg. Briefwechsel mit dem Musikverlag C. F. Peters 1863–1907 (Edvard Grieg: Correspondence with the C. F. Peters Music Publishing Company 1863–1907)*. Frankfurt /M 1997.

Benestad, Finn (ed.): *Edvard Grieg: Brev i utvalg 1862–1907 (Edvard Grieg: Selected Letters 1862–1907)*, 2 vols. Oslo 1998. (Approximately 1,600 Grieg letters in the original Norwegian or in Norwegian translations from other languages.)

Benestad, Finn (ed.): *Edvard Grieg: Dagbøker (Edvard Grieg: Diaries)*. Bergen 1993.

Benestad, Finn (ed.): *Edvard Grieg: Letters to Colleagues and Friends*. Columbus, Ohio 2000. (More than 500 letters in English translation by William H. Halverson.)

Brock, Hella: *Edvard Grieg als Musikschriftsteller (Edvard Grieg as a Writer on Music)*. Altenmedingen 1999. (Grieg's most important articles and a few letters.)

Carley, Lionel: *Grieg and Delius: A Chronicle of their Friendship in Letters*. London 1993.

Gaukstad, Øystein (ed.): *Edvard Grieg: Artikler og taler (Edvard Grieg: Articles and Speeches)*. Oslo 1956.

Huys, Bernhard & Eivind A. C. Eikenes (eds.): *Arthur de Greef – en venn av Edvard Grieg (Arthur de Greef – a Friend of Edvard Grieg)*. Stavanger 1994.

Kortsen, Bjarne (ed.): *Grieg the Writer*. Vol. I, *Essays and Articles*, Bergen 1972. Vol. II, *Letters to His Friend Frants Beyer*, Bergen 1973.

Röntgen, Julius (ed.): *Edvard Grieg*. The Hague 1930. (Selection of Grieg's German letters to Röntgen, with annotations by Röntgen in Dutch.)

Zschinsky-Troxler, Elsa von (ed.): *Edvard Grieg. Briefe an die Verleger der Edition Peters 1866–1907 (Edvard Grieg: Letters to the Publishers of Edition Peters 1866–1907)*. Leipzig 1932. (Selected letters.)

III. Biographies

Andersen, Rune J.: *Edvard Grieg, et kjempende menneske* (Edvard Grieg, a Fighter). Oslo 1993.

Asafiev, Boris: *Grieg*. Moscow 1948. (Augmented Norwegian edition of the Russian original by Asbjørn Ø. Eriksen. Oslo 1992. Eriksen has added a long and highly informative introduction in the Norwegian edition.)

Benestad, Finn & Dag Schjelderup-Ebbe: *Edvard Grieg: Mennesket og kunstneren*. Oslo 1980 (including Bibliography and List of Works with thematic incipits); revised edition 1990; Russian translation by Nicholai Mockov, Moscow 1986; English translation by William H. Halverson and Leland B. Sateren, *Edvard Grieg: The Man and the Artist*, Lincoln / Gloucester 1988; German translation by Tove and Holm Fleischer, *Edvard Grieg: Mensch und Künstler*, Leipzig 1993.

Brock, Hella: *Edvard Grieg*. Leipzig 1990; revised edition 1998.

Cherbuliez, Antoine-V.: *E. Grieg: Leben und Werk (Edvard Grieg: Life and Works)*. Zürich 1947.

Closson, Ernest: *Edvard Grieg et la musique scandinave (Edvard Grieg and the Scandinavian Music)*. Paris 1892.

Eikenes, Eivind A. C.: *Edvard Grieg fra dag til dag (Edvard Grieg from Day to Day)*. Stavanger 1993.

Fellerer, Karl Gustav: *Edvard Grieg*. Potsdam 1942.

Finck, Henry T.: *Grieg and His Music*. New York 1906; revised edition 1909.

Foerster, Josef B.: *Edvard Hagerup Grieg*. Praha 1890.

Horton, John: *Edvard Grieg*. London 1950.

Johansen, David Monrad: *Edvard Grieg*, Oslo 1934; English translation by Madge Robertson, Princeton / New York 1938.

Kálmán, Dobos, *Edvard Grieg – Élete és müvészete (Edvard Grieg—Life and Works)*. Budapest 1999.

Krellmann, Hanspeter, *Edvard Grieg* (Rowohlts Monographien). Reinbek bei Hamburg 1999.

Layton, Robert: *Grieg*. (The Illustrated Lives of the Great Composers). London 1998.

Levasjeva, Olga E.: *Edvard Grieg: Otsjerk sjisni i tvortsjeva (Edvard Grieg: Life and Works)*. Moscow 1962.

Monastier-Schroeder, Louis: *Edvard Grieg*. Lausanne 1897.

Schjelderup, Gerhard: *Edvard Grieg og hans Værker (Edvard Grieg and His Works)*. Copenhagen 1903.

Schjelderup, Gerhard & Walter Niemann: *Edvard Grieg: Biographie und Würdigung seiner Werke (Edvard Grieg: A Biography and an Assessment of His Works)*. Leipzig 1908.

Schlotel, Brian: *Grieg* (BBC Music Series). London 1986.

Stein, Richard H.: *Grieg: Eine Biographie* (Grieg: a Biography). Berlin & Leipzig 1921.

Törnblom, Folke H.: *Grieg*. Stockholm 1943.

Vestrhene, P. A. van: *Edvard Grieg*. Haarlem 1897.

IV. Symposiums on Grieg and His Music

Edvard Grieg. A Symposium (ed. Gerald Abraham). London 1948.

Edvard Grieg Today. A Symposium (Articles from a symposium held at St. Olaf College in Northfield, Minnesota, April 15–18, 1993; ed. William H. Halverson). Northfield, Minnesota 1994.

Studia musicologica norvegica 19, 1993: Edvard Grieg. Twenty-nine articles from the International Grieg Symposium in Bergen, 9–12 June 1993 (ed. Finn Benestad). Oslo 1993.

Musik & forskning 19, 1993–94 (Articles from a Grieg symposium in Copenhagen, November 12, 1993; ed. Jan Maegaard). Copenhagen 1994.

Grieg et Paris. Romantisme, symbolisme et modernisme franco-norvégien (Grieg and Paris. French-Norwegian Romanticism, Symbolism and Modernism). Articles from a symposium held at l'Université de Paris–Sorbonne, November 22–27, 1993 (eds. Harald Herresthal & Danièle Pistone). Caen 1996.

1. Deutscher Edvard-Grieg-Kongress 11.–12. Mai 1996 (First German Edvard Grieg Congress, May 11–12, 1996, ed. E. Kreft). Altenmedingen 1996.

2. Deutscher Edvard-Grieg-Kongress 5. bis 7. Juni 1998 (Second German Edvard Grieg Congress, June 5–7, 1996, ed. E. Kreft). Altenmedingen 1999.

V. Books and Articles on Topics Related to Grieg and His Music

Andersen, Rune J.: "Edvard Grieg and *Peer Gynt*", in *Studia musicologica norvegica* 19, 1993, pp. 221–228.

Bailie, Eleanor: *Grieg. The Pianist's Repertoire. A Graded Practical Guide*. London 1993.

Bailie, Eleanor: "Grieg's Piano Music: A Pedagogic Perspective from a British Point of View", in *Studia musicologica norvegica* 19, 1993, pp. 179–189.

Baumann, Jorid Nordal, Per Buer & Øyvind Norheim (eds.): *Det var dog en herlig tid, trods alt . . . —Edvard Grieg og Kristiania* (It Was a Wonderful Time, in spite of Everything . . . —Edvard Grieg and Christiania). Oslo 1993.

Benestad, Finn: "Et ukjent Grieg-brev om strykekvartetten i g-moll" (An Unknown Grieg Letter about the *String Quartet in G Minor*), in *Norsk musikktidsskrift*, vol. 10 no. 4, 1973, pp. 188–192.

Benestad, Finn: "Noen notater om Edvard Griegs ufullendte strykekvartett i F-dur" (Some notes on Edvard Grieg's unfinished *String Quartet in F Major*), in *Festskrift Gunnar Heerup*. Egtved 1973, pp. 255–263.

Benestad, Finn: "A Note on Edvard Grieg's 'Forbidden' Symphony", in *Analytica. Studies in the Description and Analysis of Music. Festskrift til Ingmar Bengtsson* (eds. Anders Lønn and Erik Kjellberg). Uppsala 1985, pp. 203–210.

Benestad, Finn & Dag Schjelderup-Ebbe: *Edvard Grieg. Chamber Music: Nationalism–Universality–Individuality*. Oslo 1993.

Benestad, Finn: "Grieg og den nasjonale tone" (Grieg and the National Tone), in *Musik & forskning* 19, 1993–94, pp. 23–40.

Benestad, Finn: "Edvard Grieg. A Norwegian Champion of National Liberation", in *Hemländsk hundraårig sång. 1800-talets musik och det nationella* (ed. Henrik Karlsson). Stockholm 1994, pp. 178–184.

Benestad, Finn: "Edvard Grieg og Bjørnstjerne Bjørnson. Et samarbeidsprosjekt om en norsk nasjonalopera—*Olav Trygvason*" (Edvard Grieg and Bjørnstjerne Bjørnson. Collaboration on a Norwegian National Opera), in *Nordisk Tidskrift för vetenskap, konst och industri*, vol 71, 1995, pp. 37–47.

Benestad, Finn: "Peer Gynt – The Fruits of Collaboration Between Two Cultural Giants—Henrik Ibsen and Edvard Grieg", in *European Review*, vol. 4 no. 2, April 1996, pp. 121–142.

Bergsagel, John: "Grieg and Denmark", in *Studia musicologica norvegica* 19, 1993, pp. 67–75.

Blok, Vladimir: "Grieg–Bartok; Grieg–Prokofiev: Aesthetic Parallels", in *Studia musicologica norvegica* 19, 1993, pp. 239–250.

Bøe, Finn: *Trekk av Edvard Griegs personlighet* (Traits in Edvard Grieg's Personality). Oslo 1949.

Brendt, Norbert: "Griegs Suite *Aus Holbergs Zeit* op. 40", in *1. Deutscher Edvard-Grieg- Kongress* 1996, pp. 49–64.

Brock, Hella: "Edvard Griegs Musik für Kinder" (Edvard Grieg's Music for Children), in *Studia musicologica norvegica* 16, 1990, pp. 21–29.

Brock, Hella: "Grieg und Deutschland" (Grieg and Germany), in *Studia musicologica norvegica* 19, 1993, pp. 97–102.

Brock, Hella: *Edvard Grieg im Musikunterricht – Betrachtungen unter interkulturellen und polyästhetischen Aspekten* (Edvard Grieg in Music Education—Considerations under Inter-cultural and Polyaesthetic Aspects). Altenmedingen 1995.

Brock, Hella: Edvard Grieg—ein Leitbild integrativer Musikpädagogik" (Edvard Grieg—a Model for Integrated Music Pedagogy), in *1. Deutscher Edvard-Grieg-Kongress* 1996, pp. 114–126.

Brock, Hella: "Edvard Grieg als Musikerzieher" (Edvard Grieg as Music Educator), in *Musikpädagogische Biographieforschung*, edited by R. D. Kraemer. Essen 1997, pp. 52–63.

Brock, Hella: ". . . kling aus ins Weite! Edvard Grieg und Felix Mendelssohn-Bartholdy" (. . . Let It Be Heard! Edvard Grieg and Felix Mendelssohn-Bartholdy), in *Studia musicologica norvegica* 25, 1999, pp. 59–69.

Cai, Camilla: "Edvard Grieg's Music in America: The Influence of Individuals, the Lutheran Church, Male Choruses, and Some American Reactions", in *2. Deutscher Edvard-Grieg-Kongress* 1998, pp. 155–168.

Cai, Camilla: "A Missed Opportunity for Grieg: Olaf Martin Oleson, the Emigrant", in *Studia musicologica norvegica* 25, 1999, pp. 226–235.

Carley, Lionel: "Grieg & Musical Life in England", in *Musik & forskning* 19, 1993–94, pp. 73–92.

Carley, Lionel: "The Last Visitor: Percy Grainger at Troldhaugen", in *Studia musicologica norvegica* 25, 1999, pp. 189–208.

Dahlström, Fabian: "Grieg und Finland", in *Studia musicologica norvegica* 19, 1993, pp. 77–85.

Denizeau, Gérard: "Grieg et la nature: du romantisme nordique aux affinités avec le symbolisme français" (Grieg and Nature: About Nordic Romanticism and Its Relationship to French Symbolism), in *Grieg et Paris. Romantisme, symbolisme et modernisme franco-norvégien*, pp. 85–97.

Dinslage, Patrick: "Edvard Griegs Jugendwerke im Spiegel seiner Leipziger Studienjahre" (Edvard Grieg's Youthful Works as a Mirror of His Years of Study in Leipzig), in *Svensk tidskrift för musikforskning*, Vol. 78, 1996, pp. 22–50.

Dinslage, Patrick: "Zu Edvard Griegs dritter Violinsonate opus 45 in c-Moll. Anmerkungen zur Harmonik und Form" (On Edvard Grieg's Third Violin Sonata op. 45 in C Minor—Notes on Harmony and Structure), in *Studia musicologica norvegica* 25, 1999, pp. 108–123.

Dorfmüller, Joachim: "Edvard Grieg und die Fuge" (Edvard Grieg and the Fugue), in *Studia musicologica norvegica* 25, 1999, pp. 144–156.

Dorfmüller, Joachim: "Die sakrale Musik Griegs" (Grieg's Sacred Music), in *2. Deutscher Edvard-Grieg-Kongress* 1998, pp. 118–129.

Edwards, Owain: "Music for the Saga of King Olav: Grieg op. 50 and Elgar op. 30", in *Studia musicologica norvegica* 25, 1999, pp. 168–188.

Ellingboe, Bradley: "A Practical Solution for Foreign Singers: A Phonetic Transcription of Grieg's Vocal Music", in *Studia musicologica norvegica* 19, 1993, pp. 147–153.

Eriksen, Asbjørn E.: "Griegs mest impresjonistiske romanse" (Grieg's most impressionistic Song), in *Norsk musikktidsskrift*, 1976, pp. 9–11.

Eriksen, Asbjørn Ø.: "Forholdet mellom harmonikk og tekst i noen Grieg-romanser" (The Relationship between Harmony and Text in a Number of Grieg Songs), in *Studia musicologica norvegica* 7, 1981, pp. 29–57.

Feldbek, Ole: "Griegs Danmark og Norge" (Grieg's Denmark and Norway), in *Musik & forskning* 19, 1993–94. Copenhagen 1994, pp. 11–22.

Findeisen, Peer: "Ethnofolkloristische Anmerkungen zu Griegs Klavierzyklus op. 66" (Ethno-folkloristic Notes to Grieg's Piano Cycle op. 66), in *1. Deutscher Edvard-Grieg-Kongress* 1996, pp. 135–151.

Findeisen, Peer: *Instrumentale Folklorestilisierung bei Edvard Grieg und bei Béla Bartók* (Instrumental Folklore Stylization in Edvard Grieg and Béla Bartók), in *Beiträge zur Europäischen Musikgeschichte* Bd. 2 (ed. E. Kreft). Frankfurt /M 1998.

Findeisen, Peer: "Naturmystik als Kern der Einheit von Ton und Wort in Griegs Liederzyklus *Haugtussa*, op. 67" (Nature Mysticism as the Nucleus of Unity between Tone and Word in Grieg's Song Cycle *Haugtussa*, op. 67), in *Studia musicologica norvegica* 25, 1999, pp. 124–143.

Findejsen, N. F.: *Edvard Grieg*. Moscow 1908.

Fischer, Kurt von: *Griegs Harmonik und die nordländische Folklore* (Grieg's Harmony and the Nordic Folklore). Bern/Leipzig 1938.

Flaten, Trine Kolderup: "Griegsamlingen i Bergen offentlige bibliotek" (The Grieg Collection in Bergen Public Library), in *Studia musicologica norvegica* 25, 1999, pp. 45–58.

Fog, Dan: "Chronologisierungsprobleme in der Grieg-Gesamt-Ausgabe" (Chronological Problems in the Grieg Complete Edition), in *Studia musicologica norvegica* 19, 1993, pp. 23–27.

Foster, Beryl: *The Songs of Edvard Grieg*. Aldershot 1990.

Foster, Beryl: "Grieg and the European Song Tradition", in *Studia musicologica norvegica* 19, 1993, pp. 127–135.

Foster, Beryl: "Interpreting a half-told tale—the Songs of Grieg and Schumann", in *2. Deutscher Edvard-Grieg-Kongress 5. bis 7. Juni 1998*. Altenmedingen 1998, pp. 169–179.

Foster, Beryl: *Edvard Grieg: The Choral Music*. Aldershot 1999.

Foster, Beryl: "Grieg and Delius – Settings of the same Norwegian texts", in *Studia musicologica norvegica* 25, 1999, pp. 209–219.

Grinde, Nils: "Griegs Vocal Arrangements of Folk Tunes", in *Studia musicologica norvegica* 19, 1993, pp. 29–34.

Grinde, Nils: "Griegs betydning for senere norsk musikk" (Grieg's Influence on Subsequent Norwegian Music), in *Musik & forskning* 19, 1993–94. Copenhagen 1994, pp. 63–72.

Halverson, William H.: "Nordic Wine in English Wineskins: The Challenge of Translating Grieg's Song Texts", in *Studia musicologica norvegica* 19, 1993, pp. 137–146

Halverson, William H.: "The Neglected Legacy", in *Edvard Grieg Today. A Symposium* (ed. William H. Halverson). Northfield, Minnesota 1994, pp. 69–75.

Halverson, William H.: "Grieg and MacDowell: A Tale of Two Edwards", in *Studia musicologica norvegica* 25, 1999, pp. 220–225.

Herresthal, Harald: "Edvard Grieg og Kristiania" (Edvard Grieg and Christiania), in Baumann, Jorid Nordal, Per Buer & Øyvind Norheim (eds.): *Det var dog en herlig tid, trods alt . . . —Edvard Grieg og Kristiania* (It Was a Wonderful Time, in spite of Everything . . . —Edvard Grieg and Christiania). Oslo 1993, pp. 7–57.

Herresthal, Harald & Ladislav Reznicek: *Rhapsodie norvégienne: Norsk musikk i Frankrike på Edvard Griegs tid* (Rhapsodie norvégienne: Norwegian Music in France at the Time of Edvard Grieg). Oslo 1994; French parallel edition: *Rhapsodie Norvégienne: Les musiciens norvégiens en France au temps de Grieg.* Caen 1994.

Herresthal, Harald,: *Edvard Grieg med venner og uvenner—tegnet og karikert (Edvard Grieg with Friends and Enemies, in Drawings and Caricatures).* Bergen 1997.

Herresthal, Harald: "Edvard Grieg – der Prophet, auf den alle warteten" (Edvard Grieg—the Prophet that Everybody Was Waiting for), in *2. Deutscher Edvard-Grieg- Kongress* 1998, pp. 68–77.

Herresthal, Harald & Ute Schwab: "Edvard Grieg und sein Verhältnis zu Carl Reinecke" (Edvard Grieg and His Relation to Carl Reinecke), in *Studia musicologica norvegica 25,* 1999, pp. 157–167.

Hurum, Hans Jørgen: *I Edvard Griegs verden* (In Edvard Grieg's World). Oslo 1959.

Hurum, Hans Jørgen: *Vennskap. Edvard Grieg og Frants Beyer i lys av glemte brev* (Friendship: Edvard Grieg and Frants Beyer in View of Forgotten Letters). Oslo 1989.

Kayser, Audun: *Edvard Grieg—in Words and Music.* Bergen 1993.

Kjeldsberg, Peter Andreas (ed.): *Your Grieg.* Bergen 1993.

Kjellberg, Erik: "Grieg and Sweden", in *Studia musicologica norvegica* 19, 1993, pp. 87–96.

Kleiberg, Ståle: "Grieg's *Slåtter,* op. 72: Change of Musical Style or New Concept of Nationality?", in *Journal of the Royal Musical Association,* Vol. 121, Part 1 1996, pp. 45–58.

Kortsen, Bjarne: *Zur Genesis von Edvard Griegs g-Moll Streichquartett Op. 27* (The Creational Process of Edvard Grieg's G-minor String Quartet op. 27). Berlin 1967.

Kreft, Ekkehard: "Grieg – Lyrismen und Parallelakkordik" (Grieg—Lyricisms and Parallel Chords), in *1. Deutscher Edvard-Grieg-Kongress* 1996, pp. 64–77.

Kreft, Ekkehard: "Griegs Bühnenmusik zu Peer Gynt op. 23 – lyrische und dramatische Komponenten" (Grieg's Incidental Music to Peer Gynt op. 23—Lyric and Dramatic Components), in *2. Deutscher Edvard-Grieg-Kongress* 1998, pp. 109–117.

Kreft, Ekkehard: "Grieg als Wegbereiter der Harmonik des 20. Jahrhunderts" (Grieg as a Pioneer in 20th Century Harmony), in *Studia musicologica norvegica* 25, 1999, pp. 229–238.

Kreft, Ekkehard: *Griegs Harmonik* (Grieg's Harmony). Frankfurt /M 2000.

Krummacher, Friedhelm: "Streichquartett als *Ehrensache* – Linie und Klang in Griegs Quartett op. 27" (String Quartet as a *Matter of Honor*—Line and Sound in Grieg's Quartet op. 27), in *Studia musicologica norvegica* 25, 1999, pp. 90–107.

Layton, Robert: "Grieg and England", in *Studia musicologica norvegica* 19, 1993, pp. 103–109.

Ledang, Ola Kai: "Individual Creation and National Identity: On Grieg's Piano Adaptations of *Hardingfele* Music", in *Studia musicologica norvegica* 19, 1993, pp. 39–44.

Lindenbaum, Walter: "Who the hell is Grieg? – Rockmusik in der Halle des Bergkönigs" (Who the hell is Grieg?—Rock Music in the Hall of the Mountain King), in *2. Deutscher Edvard-Grieg-Kongress* 1998, pp. 16–29.

Mangersnes, Magnar: "Volkston im Chorklang: Griegs *Vier Psalmen*, op. 74" (Folk Tune in Choir—Grieg's *Four Psalms, op. 74)*, in *Studia musicologica norvegica* 19, 1993, pp. 35–37.

Mönning, Annette: "Edvard Grieg als Anla malerischer Gestaltung im Kunstunterricht" (Edvard Grieg as an Opportunity for Creative Painting in Art Education), in *1. Deutscher Edvard- Grieg-Kongress* 1996, pp. 126–151.

Mokhov, Nicolai: "Grieg and Russia", in *Studia musicologica norvegica* 19, 1993, pp. 123–126.

Norheim, Øyvind: "Grieg som barnesangkomponist" (Grieg as Composer of Children's Songs), in *Studia musicologica norvegica* 25, 1999, pp. 24–33.

Oechsle, Siegfried: "Grieg und Gade", in *Musik & forskning* 19, 1993–94, pp. 41–62.

Oelmann, Klaus Henning: *Edvard Grieg als Streichquartettkomponist. Eine konzeptionelle und wirkungsgeschichtliche Studie* (Edvard Grieg as a Composer of String Quartets. A Study in Conception and History of Reception). Essen 1992.

Oelmann, Klaus Henning: *Edvard Grieg: Versuch einer Orientierung* (Edvard Grieg: An Attempt at Orientation). Egelsbach 1993.

Pistone, Danièle: "Grieg et la France", in *Studia musicologica norvegica* 19, 1993, pp. 111–116.

Reisaus, Joachim: *Grieg und das Leipziger Konservatorium. Untersuchungen zur Persönlichkeit des norwegischen Komponisten Edvard Grieg unter besonderer Berücksichtigung seiner Leipziger Studienjahre* (Grieg and the Leipzig Conservatory. Investigations Related to the Personality of the Norwegian Composer Edvard Grieg with Special Regard to His Years of Study in Leipzig). Leipzig 1988.

Rötter, Günther: "Die musikalische Form der Klavierwerke Edvard Griegs" (Musical Form in Edvard Grieg's Piano Compositions), in *2. Deutscher Edvard-Grieg-Kongress* 1998, pp. 49–67.

Schjelderup-Ebbe, Dag: *A Study of Grieg's Harmony with Special Reference to his Contributions to Musical Impressionism*. Oslo 1953.

Schjelderup-Ebbe, Dag: *Edvard Grieg 1858–1867; with Special Reference to the Evolution of his Harmonic Style*. Oslo/London 1964.

Schjelderup-Ebbe, Dag: "Béla Bartóks forhold til Edvard Grieg og Norge" (Béla Bartók's Relation to Edvard Grieg and Norway), in *Norsk Musikktidsskrift* no. 2, 1993, pp. 4–8.

Schjelderup-Ebbe, Dag: "Grieg og impresjonismen" (Grieg and Impressionism), in *Musik & forskning* 19, 1993–94, pp. 93–102.

Schjelderup-Ebbe, Dag: "Noen tanker om Edvard Griegs gjeld til Halfdan Kjerulf" (Some Thoughts about Edvard Grieg's Debt to Halfdan Kjerulf), in *Studia musicologica norvegica* 24, 1998 (ed. E. Nesheim), Oslo 1998, pp. 39–46.

Schjelderup-Ebbe, Dag: "Die Vinje-Lieder op. 33" (The Vinje Songs op. 33), in *2. Deutscher Edvard-Grieg-Kongress* 1998, pp. 78–87.

Schwab, Heinrich: "Die Präsenz beider Elemente – Zur kompositorischen Struktur von Griegs Klavierpoesie" (The Presence of Both Elements—On compositional Structure in Grieg's Piano Poetry), in *Studia musicologica norvegica* 19, 1993, pp. 155–170.

Schwab, Heinrich: "Griegs Klavierkonzert im Spiegel zeitgenössischer Kritik. Rezensionen, Wertungen und Konsequenzen" (Grieg's Piano Concerto Mirrored in the Contemporary Press. Reviews, Assessments and Consequences), in *2. Deutscher Edvard-Grieg-Kongress* 1998, pp. 30–48.

Schwab, Heinrich: "Zur Struktur der Kadenzen in Edvard Griegs Klavierkonzert op. 16" (On the Structure of the Cadenzas in Grieg's Piano Concerto op. 16), in *Studia musicologica norvegica* 25, 1999, pp. 71–89.

Skyllstad, Kjell: "Nordic Symphony: Grieg at the Crossroads", in *Studia musicologica norvegica* 19, 1993, pp. 213–219.

Stavland, Hanna de Vries: "Grieg und Holland", in *Studia musicologica norvegica* 19, 1993, pp. 117–121.

Stavland, Hanna de Vries: *Julius Röntgen og Edvard Grieg—et musikalsk vennskap* (Julius Röntgen and Edvard Grieg—a Musical Friendship). Bergen 1994.

Stavland, Hanna de Vries: *Musikkfesten i Bergen 26. Juni–3. Juli 1898* (The Music Festival in Bergen June 26–July 3 1898). Stavanger 1998.

Steen-Nøkleberg, Einar: *Med Grieg på podiet,* Oslo 1992; American edition: *Onstage with Grieg: Interpreting His Piano Music* (translated by William H. Halverson). Bloomington, Indiana 1997.

Storaas, Reidar: "Grieg, the Bergensian", in *Studia musicologica norvegica* 19, 1993. Oslo 1993, pp. 45–53.

Vollsnes, Arvid: "Grieg's Own Interpretations: Modern Use of Old Piano Recordings", in *Studia musicologica norvegica* 19, 1993, pp. 171–178.

Yang, Jing-Mao: "Untersuchung zu Griegs Nachlaß: *Andante con moto.* Triosatz für Klavier, Violine und Violoncello in c-Moll" (Investigation of Grieg's Heritage: Andante con moto for Piano, Violin and Cello in C Minor), in *1. Deutscher Edvard-Grieg- Kongress 1996,* pp. 103–113.

Yang, Jing-Mao: *Das "Grieg-Motiv". Zum Erkenntnis von Personalstil und musikalischem Denken Edvard Griegs* (The Grieg Motif. On the Recognition of Edvard Grieg's Personal Style and Philosophy of Music). Kassel 1998.

Yarrow, Anne: *An Analysis and Comparison of the Three Sonatas for Violin and Piano by Edvard Grieg (1843–1907).* Ann Arbor 1987.

Yarrow, Anne: "Grieg and the Violin Tradition: His Three Sonatas for Violin and Piano in Perspective", in *Studia musicologica norvegica* 19, 1993, pp. 191–202.

VI. Grieg's Complete Works

Edvard Grieg: Complete Works (20 volumes). C. F. Peters Musikverlag. Frankfurt /M, London, New York, Leipzig 1977–95. The contents of the respective volumes and their editors are as follows:

I. Instrumental Music

Solo Piano:

Vol. 1 Lyric Pieces I–X, ed. Dag Schjelderup-Ebbe.
Vol. 2 Other Original Compositions, ed. Dag Schjelderup-Ebbe.
Vol. 3 Arrangements of Norwegian Folk Music, ed. Dag Schjelderup-Ebbe.
Vol. 4 Arrangements of Own Works, ed. Dag Schjelderup-Ebbe.

Piano Four Hands:

Vol. 5 Original Compositions and Arrangements of Own Works, ed. Rune J. Andersen.
Vol. 6 Dramatic Music, ed. Nils Grinde.

Two Pianos:

Vol. 7 Original Compositions and Arrangements, ed. Arvid Vollsnes.

Chamber Music:

Vol. 8 Sonatas for Violin and Piano, Sonata for Cello and Piano, ed. Finn Benestad.
Vol. 9 String Quartets, Other Chamber Music, Arrangements of Own Works for Chamber Orchestra, ed. Finn Benestad.

Orchestra:

Vol. 10 Piano Concerto in A Minor, ed. Kjell Skyllstad.
Vol. 11 Original Compositions, ed. Finn Benestad and Gunnar Rugstad.
Vol. 12 Suites for Orchestra, ed. Finn Benestad and Dag Schjelderup-Ebbe.
Vol. 13 Arrangements of Own Works and Compositions Without Opus Numbers,
      ed. Gunnar Rugstad.

II. Vocal Music

Songs with Piano Accompaniment:

Vol. 14 Songs opp. 2–49, ed. Dan Fog and Nils Grinde.
Vol. 15 Songs opp. 58–70 and Songs Without Opus Numbers, ed. Dan Fog and
      Nils Grinde.

Vocal Compositions with Orchestra:

Vol. 16 Original Compositions and Arrangements of Own Works,
      ed. Hans Magne Græsvold.

Unaccompanied Choral Music:

Vol. 17 Original Compositions and Arrangements of Own Works, ed. Dan Fog.

III. Dramatic Music

Vol. 18 Peer Gynt, ed. Finn Benestad.
Vol. 19 Other Original Compositions, ed. Finn Benestad.

IV. Appendix

Vol. 20 Addenda and Corrigenda, ed. Rune J. Andersen, Finn Benestad and
      Klaus Henning Oelmann.

VII. Other Bibliographies

Several of the books listed above contain bibliographies of varying length and completeness. Two additional works (listed chronologically) are of special interest in this context:

Gaukstad, Øystein: "Edvard Grieg 1843–1943. En bibliografi" (Edvard Grieg 1843–1943: A Bibliography), in *Norsk Musikkgranskning. Årbok 1942*. Oslo 1943. A comprehensive list of works on Grieg and his music as of the date of publication.
Fog, Dan, Kirsti Grinde & Øyvind Norheim: *Edvard Grieg: Werkverzeichnis* (Edvard Grieg: List of Works). In preparation, planned for publication in 2001. This is expected to be an exhaustive compendium of books and articles on Grieg and his music, interviews with Grieg, a list of Grieg's own writings, and a complete list of Grieg's compositions, including thematic incipits.

General Index

This index includes names and topics in a single alphabetical list. Compositions by Grieg and other composers as well as major literary works will be found under the respective composers/authors, with longer works in italics, shorter ones in quotation marks. For cities, major geographical sites and institutions the respective countries in which they are located are given in parentheses. The names of newspapers and periodicals are italicized followed in each case by the place of publication in parentheses. Norwegian titles of relatively unknown literary works are given in parentheses. When a name occurs both in an introduction and in main text or in a footnote keyed to the text, only one page number is given.

Bold numbers indicate Grieg's principal writing(s) about the person or topic identified in that entry. Numbers followed by "i", "n" or "p" denote, respectively, the editors' introduction, a footnote, or a picture caption.

The Norwegian letter "æ" is alphabetized as "ae", "ø" and "ö" as "o", "å" and "ä" as "a", "ü" as "u".

The index covers pp. vii–x and 1–396.